PLANNING FOR TEACHING

CORRELATED FILMS

Five 16-mm sound motion pictures have been especially prepared for this book by the McGraw-Hill Text-Film Department.

Planning for Personal and Professional Growth

Shows four schoolteachers who have made certain adjustments and achieved success to various degrees in their teaching (19 min).

Effective Learning in the Elementary School

Shows a fifth-grade teacher and her class as they plan their daily work for the study of a unit on pioneer life (20 min).

Guiding the Growth of Children

Shows how a teacher may work to understand each child and to guide him in his growth and development (18 min).

Promoting Pupil Adjustment

Shows that a teacher must be alert and sensitive to student problems if classroom learning is to be effective and illustrates ways by which teachers can facilitate pupil adjustment (20 min).

Broader Concepts of Curriculum

Points out the great increase which is taking place in enrollments in secondary schools and some of the causes for this growth (21 min).

ii

McGRAW-HILL SERIES IN EDUCATION

Harold Benjamin, Consulting Editor-in-Chief

ARNO A. BELLACK Teachers College, Columbia
University
Consulting Editor, Curriculum and Methods in
Education

HAROLD BENJAMIN Emeritus Professor of
Education
George Peabody College for Teachers
Consulting Editor, Foundations in Education

HARLAN HAGMAN Wayne State University
Consulting Editor, Administration in Education

WALTER F. JOHNSON Michigan State University
Consulting Editor, Guidance, Counseling, and
Student Personnel in Education

FOUNDATIONS IN EDUCATION

Harold Benjamin, Consulting Editor

BROWN General Philosophy in Education

BRUBACHER A History of the Problems
of Education

BRUBACHER Modern Philosophies of Education

COOK AND COOK A Sociological Approach
to Education

COX AND MERCER Education in Democracy

DE YOUNG AND WYNN American Education

GOOD Dictionary of Education

MEYER An Educational History of the
Western World

RICHEY Planning for Teaching

THUT The Story of Education

THUT AND ADAMS Educational Patterns
in Contemporary Society

WIGGIN Education and Nationalism

WYNN Careers in Education

FOURTH EDITION

PLANNING
FOR
TEACHING

An Introduction to Education

ROBERT W. RICHEY

**Director of Summer Sessions for the University
and Professor of Education, Indiana University**

McGRAW-HILL BOOK COMPANY

NEW YORK, ST. LOUIS, SAN FRANCISCO, TORONTO, LONDON, SYDNEY

PLANNING FOR TEACHING

Library of Congress Catalog Card Number 67–20971

52337

1234567890 HDBP 7432106987

EDITOR'S FOREWORD

This book goes into its fourth edition with a distinction and a burden, both arising from the indisputable fact that it is now a classic in its field.

The book wears the distinction with the same jaunty and assured ease it displayed in 1952 when it first appeared in print and in 1958 and 1963 when its second and third editions were published. In each of those editions it was breaking away from many of the old-time trends in the pattern of texts for the first course in education. At the same time it was making a careful evaluation of all trends— the requisite feature of each revision. The author of no text in American education has ever done this kind of job better than has Robert W. Richey.

The burden of any book's existence as a classic grows heavier with each passing year and revision. Textbooks requiring a fourth edition are quite rare. They have proved their qualities by the lasting appreciation of their users. Sometimes this weights them in the direction of conservatism or even of that stodginess, which is worse than an out-of-print death.

Richey's text, in all its editions, has successfully avoided any of these conservative or stodgy trends. It comes to us, its many followers, in this fourth edition with the same kinds of fresh views, up-to-date aids, and new challenges to prospective teachers as those that marked its predecessors in this series of editions.

The present momentous and violent century is entering upon its final one-third, which may be even more violent than the first two-thirds; it will very probably be more momentous. Students planning to become teachers for this one-third of a century will need as never before an understanding of the profession's requirements, a grasp of its problems, an appreciation of its responsibilities, and a pride in its opportunities for local, national, and world leadership.

The fourth edition of Richey's *Planning for Teaching* will serve these recruits to the profession with the same dedication and verve that its predecessors gave to people who are now veteran teachers. How the new edition achieves this end with new and more comprehensive efforts can best be seen by reading this latest revision of the classic text.

Harold Benjamin

PREFACE

The first edition of this book developed from the questions and expressed concerns of over 4,000 students who were enrolled in an introductory education course at Indiana University. It represented the results of over four years' intensive experimentation with materials for the course. Each subsequent edition has undergone critical testing and appraisal from which many modifications and improvements in the book have come. It is a pleasure to express appreciation to the many students and colleagues at Indiana University and to other educators throughout the nation for their generous efforts and thoughtful suggestions. In terms of the present edition, I especially wish to thank the following people for excellent depth reviews of the third edition and/or their penetrating reviews of the manuscript for the fourth edition: Dr. George Ryden, Southwestern State College, Weatherford, Oklahoma; Dr. Robert Burton, University of Missouri; Dr. John Reisert, Indiana University; Dr. Paul Power, Western Kentucky University; Dr. Gilbert Nichols, Iowa Wesleyan College.

This edition represents a major revision of the book. Every effort, however, has been exerted to maintain the same clearly defined purposes as were used in the preceding three editions—to help a student in (1) gaining a valid and comprehensive understanding of what is involved in a teaching career, (2) acquiring a breadth of knowledge that usually is not formally included in general and educational psychology courses, in general and special methods courses, or in student teaching, (3) engaging in a variety of activities that will provide greater meaning or a rationale for subsequent professional course work to be taken, (4) seeing clearly the tasks which lie ahead in developing into an effective teacher, (5) gaining a reasoned dedication to the profession, and (6) planning with care and insight one's preparation for teaching, as well as his professional growth after entering the profession. Emphasis is placed upon self-analysis, self-direction, inquiry, and personal involvement in planning an effective and successful career in education.

In this revision, the last half of the first chapter is completely new, and is addressed to the challenge that educators face in the future. Chapters 2, 3, and 4 of the third edition have been condensed and combined to form Chapters 2 and 3. Chapter 6 has been retitled, and a new section on "Using Newer Instructional Materials and Procedures" has been added. Chapter 7 has been decidedly expanded to include a discussion of professional negotiations, sanctions, strikes, collective bargaining, professional autonomy, and political activity of teachers. Part III has been expanded to include a new chapter on "Legal Liabilities and Responsibilities of Teachers." Part VI of the third edition, "Nature of Our School System," has become Part IV of the new edition, and much information on recent federal assistance to education has been added. Chapter 14 has been reorganized and expanded, and a new section on "Some Current Contrasting Theories of Education" has been added. Chapter 17 on "Controversial Issues and Problems in Education" has been radically revised in view of the current educational situation.

The present arrangement of the chapters according to parts now provides for greater flexibility and a variety of approaches that may be made in an introductory course. For example, an instructor might prefer to give early consideration to Part V, "Our Educational Heritage," or to Part VI, "Broader Concepts of Education." One of the reviewers of the manuscript indicated that Chapter 17 of Part VI would be a good initial assignment for students in an introductory education course. These might be good reasons to consider Part III, "Economic and Legal Aspects of Teaching," before Part II, "Teachers and Their Work." With the possible exceptions of Chapter 1, Part I, and Chapter 18, the order in which the various parts of the book are considered is a matter for the instructor to decide. Resource Sections containing checklists, selected readings, audio-visual lists, and other relevant materials are located at the end of each part.

All of the content has been checked and, when necessary, has been rewritten (in some cases deleted) in terms of the increased sophistication level of college students today. All data have been brought as nearly up-to-date as possible in order to reflect recent changes, developments, and trends. Projections on such matters as school and college enrollments, demands for teachers' occupational needs, gross national products, teacher preparation, salaries, and school finance are presented. National and world populations are projected to the year A.D. 2000. Educational technology, such as television, teaching machines, electronic laboratories, data processing, and information retrieval systems, is discussed, and some implications for teacher preparation and schools of the future are included. A special effort has been made to include research findings on teachers and teaching. The "self concept," as it relates to teachers and teaching, has been treated more adequately. Efforts have been made to personalize the material to the fullest extent possible in order to assist students in identifying themselves with the content. Topics are approached from the point of view of encouraging students to explore them further and to expand their understandings of the teaching profession. Greater attention has been given to such topics as curricular innovations, flexible scheduling, nongraded schools, team teaching, new opportunities for educators, insurance plans and tax-sheltered annuities for teachers, federal assistance to education, the role of private and parochial schools in America, current concepts of education, international aspects of education, national assessment of education, vocational education, the relationship between religion and the public schools, the comparison of European and American schools, the "educational establishment," educating the culturally deprived, segregation, and some current criticisms of our schools. In Chapter 1, special attention has been given to the challenges which educators will face as a result of the rapid scientific, social, economic, and industrial changes that will probably take place in our society. Efforts have been made to help students become skilled observers of our culture, the teaching profession, pupil behavior, and teaching-learning situations. The needs of both elementary and secondary school teachers are taken into consideration, and greater emphasis is given to teaching especially on the junior college level.

The increased number of charts, graphs, and diagrams appearing in this edition are designed to assist students in visualizing important concepts and information. A number of the photographs have been changed in order to improve their effectiveness in communicating various concepts and understandings. A highly selective annotated list of 16-mm films, filmstrips, and recordings has been included at the ends of Chapters 1 and 18 and in the Resource Section for each part, with the hope that its use will assist the student in grasping the concepts and principles involved. Five 16-mm sound motion films have been especially prepared for this book by the Text-Film Department of the McGraw-Hill Book Company in order to demonstrate the ideas dealt with in certain chapters.

Changes have been made in the end-of-chapter materials. The "Questions for Your Consideration" frequently have been strengthened in order to stimulate thoughtful concern and discussion on basic ideas, concepts, and plans for teaching. The "Activities for You to Pursue" frequently have been improved. These activities, which emphasize the *doing*, encourage the student to work independently or in groups along lines of special interest, with stress placed upon the study of pupils, schools, teachers, communities, the profession, and the process of planning a career in teaching. The annotated lists of suggested readings at the ends of Chapters 1 and 18 and in the Resource Section for each part have been radically updated with the hope that the student will be encouraged to read beyond the confines of this book, to pursue special interests, and to acquaint himself with many other books and periodicals in the field of education. The glossary, located in the back of the book, has been revised considerably in order to help the student gain a better understanding of technical terms and specialized meanings attached to certain words in the profession.

The breadth of topics covered in this book is so great and the changes taking place in the field of education are so rapid that it is virtually impossible for an author to revise such a book without the assistance of authorities in various fields of education. The author is indebted to Dr. Donald N. Michael of the University of Michigan for the inspiration and much of the material in the last part of Chapter 1. Dr. David W. Beggs, III, of Indiana University revised the section on "Using Newer Instructional Techniques and Procedures" in Chapter 6. Dr. Maurice A. McGlasson of Indiana University revised Chapter 7. The late Dr. Lorin A. Burt of Indiana University prepared Chapter 10 and revised Chapter 17. Dr. Robert J. Garvue of Florida State University revised Chapters 11 and 12. Dr. Gordon E. Frazier of the Northwest Campus of Indiana University contributed to the revision of Chapter 14. The author is deeply grateful to these people for their excellent contributions and fine cooperation in revising the book.

Dr. Carolyn Guss and Mr. Robert Davis of the Audio-Visual Center of Indiana University helped update the lists of audio-visual materials. Miss Kathleen Dugdale of Indiana University critically read all of the manuscript and gave valuable suggestions. Mrs. Don David assisted in proofreading the manuscript.

Appreciation is extended to many publishers, and especially to the National Education Association, for their willingness to grant permission to use various materials. Mrs. Beatrice Clump Lee and Miss Virginia Stephenson of the research division, National Education Association, were most helpful in locating and in forwarding current relevant publications. Generous contributions were made from the photography files of the National Education Association.

In a more personal sense, I wish to express my deep gratitude to my wife Eloise for typing the manuscript, checking on many details, proofreading, criticizing copy, and making helpful suggestions. I also wish to recognize my son Bob who was a constant source of solid support and encouragement.

Robert W. Richey

TO THE STUDENT

Students in education today are vitally interested in being both successful and happy in life. One of the best ways for you to accomplish this is to engage in comprehensive planning during the initial stages of preparing for your lifework. An introductory course in education, therefore, should provide many opportunities for you to gain a thorough understanding of what is involved in a teaching career—to the extent that you see clearly the tasks ahead in developing into an effective teacher. An introductory education course should also test further the wisdom of your decision to become a teacher, so that you may be able to develop a reasoned dedication to the profession. It should help you plan with care and insight your preparation for teaching as well as your professional growth after entering the field. As a result of this type of course, subsequent studies and other professional activity should have greater meaning and purpose to you.

Planning for Teaching is designed to assist you in accomplishing these purposes of an introductory course in education. The book is divided into six integral parts. Each part is preceded by an overview designed to assist you in sensing clearly the relations of the chapters involved to the central purpose of the book. Part I attempts to increase your understanding of and skill in planning a career in teaching. The arrangement of the three chapters should assist you in grasping the logical sequence of some fundamental steps involved in career planning; i.e., you clarify the values and goals you desire in life, you study the teaching profession to see whether its potential values are consistent with your life values, you carefully examine the personal and professional requirements for success in the field, and you evaluate yourself in terms of these requirements and then develop detailed plans for meeting them. Emphasis is placed upon both individual and group aspects of planning. You also will examine certification requirements and explore the wide range of opportunities that a career in education provides, so that your interests and abilities may best be utilized and your success and happiness in the profession proportionately increased. The needs for both prospective elementary and secondary school teachers are taken into consideration.

Part II is concerned with such vital questions as: What relationships should teachers have with community members, pupils, parents, and other members of the profession? How does a teacher become increasingly effective in the classroom? What are some of the philosophical and psychological bases of modern educational practices? What are some of the newer instructional devices and procedures, and how can they be used effectively? What is the status of teaching as a profession, and how does it differ from other professions? What obligations and responsibilities will you have as a member of the teaching profession?

In Part III you consider such realistic matters as salary, sick leave, tenure, tax deductions, retirement, and other fringe benefits. Special attention is given to the legal liabilities and responsibilities of teachers. Part IV attempts to give you an initial understanding of the complex structure of school organization and of the ways schools are financed. The point is made that success and happiness in teaching are affected significantly by the adequacy with which you understand the different patterns of organization and work effectively toward the full realization of the school's function in our society.

In Part V, you explore some of the historical forces that have shaped our education system as well as theories of education. Part VI is designed to help you view the broad aspects of education and the professional challenge with which teachers today are faced. Special attention is given to the interrelationship of the school and the community and the resulting effect upon the role of the teacher. Some of the persistent problems and issues which you will face in teaching are pointed out. You are encouraged to plan ways in which you may aid in the solution of these problems and contribute effectively to the fuller realization of the school's function in a democratic society.

In Chapter 18 you are encouraged to assess some of the gains you have made in the course and to formulate further plans for moving effectively and happily into the teaching profession.

CONTENTS

13   Historical Development of Our Schools   425
14   The Development of Modern Concepts of Education   452
     Resource Section for PART V   479

PART VI   BROADER CONCEPTS OF EDUCATION

15   Community Educative Forces and Their Implications   489
16   Purposes of Education in American Democracy   521
17   Controversial Issues and Problems in Education   550
     Resource Section for PART VI   579

18   Your Plans and Your Future   597

     Glossary   613
     References   619
     Index   631

PLANNING FOR TEACHING

THE CHALLENGE
OF TEACHING

You are to be congratulated upon your interest in becoming a member of the teaching profession. It is the largest of all professions and is basic to all other professions. Assuming that you are well suited for such a career, you may look forward to an exciting and challenging life.

The importance of education to the welfare of our country is sensed by the general public more clearly today than ever before. Good teachers are vital to the progress as well as the safety of our nation. The increased importance that teachers and teaching have acquired in our society becomes apparent as you read various articles and books or listen to radio and television programs that are concerned with the welfare of our country. Books such as *Education, Manpower and Economic Growth: Strategies of Human Resource Development, Education as Power,* and *Education and the Public Good* are indicative of the concern for the quality of education in this country.

Never before have so many people in the various professions shared their talents in an attempt to provide the best quality of education possible for our young people. For example, educators are working with engineers to develop a variety of electronic instructional devices that may facilitate the learning process. Scientists and mathematicians are contributing technical assistance in developing programs in science and mathematics in keeping with the ever-increasing demands that result from our technological advancements. Architects are assisting educators in designing school plant facilities that will provide for greater flexibility of programs as well as for the use of a wide variety of instructional materials. Scholars in the various academic disciplines are assisting educators in developing programs that will more adequately meet the needs of youth as they face a demanding and rapidly changing world.

The successful orbiting of Sputnik 1 in 1957 perhaps did more than any other single recent event to focus the attention of the general public upon the need for good schools. This spectacular success of the Russians shook the American public out of its complacent, self-satisfied attitude with respect to its world position and system of education. Immediately following this event a clamor for better schools

1

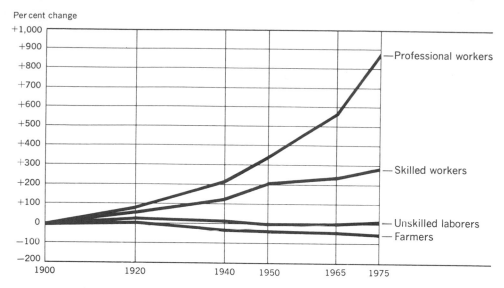

Per cent change

FIGURE 1–1.   The percentage of change in the number of workers since 1900. Major increases will occur in occupations requiring the most education and training. (*Source:* National Education Association.)[1]

arose. Subsequent advances, especially those made by the Russians, have tended to stimulate further research and experimentation concerning better ways of educating youth.

Importance of Education

In making a global study of the relationship of education, manpower, and economic growth, Harbison and Myers found that [123:1]:[2]

> Most nations today are development-minded. The less developed countries which have been poor and stagnant for centuries are in a state of revolt against poverty, disease, ignorance, and dominance by stronger nations, and they are no longer disposed to entrust their future exclusively to the forces of the market, the whim of nature, or the judgment of colonial rulers. The advanced countries likewise are committed to growth, and the more rapid and spectacular the better. Their aspirations, indeed, are no longer earthbound, but extend as well to the exploration of outer space and possibly even other planets. This almost universal quest for forward movement is in essence a revolution which has no precedent in history. It is fired by rising aspirations for economic, social, and political progress, and it is based upon the optimistic conviction that man, in this century of science, can move forward by leaps instead of steps.

Education is basic to the forward movement of nations throughout the world. At the center of these movements, therefore, stand the members of the teaching

---

[1] Figure credits may be found on page 36 and at the end of each Resource Section following each part or division of the book.
[2] References indicated by number are listed in an alphabetical reference section beginning on page 619.

The advent of the space age highlights the increasing importance of quality education in a demanding and rapidly changing world. *(Photograph from National Aeronautics and Space Administration.)*

profession. They are being challenged to meet the increasing educational needs of our own people and, at the same time, to help emerging nations in the creation and rapid improvement of their educational systems. Will the rapid technological, economic, and social development which these countries demand take place through totalitarian regimentation or under conditions of growing individual freedom and responsibility? This is a crucial educational as well as social, economic, and political question.

Education and the Dignity of Man

In our society we value highly the dignity and worth of the individual and are committed to the development of free, rational, and responsible citizens. We want each individual to achieve the promise that is in him. We want him to be worthy of a free society and capable of strengthening it.

The authors of the excellent pamphlet *The Pursuit of Excellence: Education and the Future of America* emphasize very effectively the deep concern of our society for the dignity and worth of the individual [205:1]:

> The greatness of a nation may be manifested in many ways—in its purposes, its courage, its moral responsibility, its cultural and scientific eminence, the tenor of its daily life. But ultimately the source of its greatness is in the individuals who constitute the living substance of the nation.
>
> A concern for the realization of individual potentialities is deeply rooted in our moral heritage, our political philosophy, and the texture of our daily customs. It is at the root of our efforts to eliminate poverty and slums at home and to combat

disease and disaster throughout the world. The enthusiasm with which Americans plunge into projects for human betterment has been considered by some critics to be foolishly optimistic. But though we may have gone to extremes in a naive belief that we could cure all of mankind's ills, we need not be ashamed of the impulse. It springs from our deepest values. We do not believe that men were meant to live in degradation and we are foes of the poverty and ignorance which produces that result. We deplore the destruction of human potentialities through disease, and we are prepared to fight such destruction wherever we meet it. We believe that man —by virtue of his humanity—should live in the light of reason, exercise moral responsibility, and be free to develop to the full the talents that are in him.

Our devotion to a free society can only be understood in terms of these values. It is the only form of society that puts at the very top of its agenda the opportunity of the individual to develop his potentialities. It is the declared enemy of every condition that stunts the intellect, moral and spiritual growth of the individual. No society has ever fully succeeded in living up to the stern ideals that a free people set themselves. But only a free society can even address itself to that demanding task.

The concept of the dignity and worth of the individual is not new. Mankind has been working toward its fuller realization for a long time. You will recall that the Declaration of Independence refers to "certain unalienable rights—Life, Liberty and the pursuit of Happiness." A similar statement is to be found in the French Declaration of the Rights of Man (1789). Free nations throughout the world have embodied the concept in such documents as the Atlantic Charter (1941), the Charter of the United Nations (1945), and the Universal Declaration of Human Rights (1948) adopted by the General Assembly of the United Nations. Reread

FIGURE 1–2.   Past and projected population of the world. Note that the population approximately doubled between 1760 and 1880 (120 years) and again between 1880 and 1960 (80 years). What new educational problems will arise if the population doubles between 1960 and the year 2000 (40 years)? *(Source: Saturday Review.)*

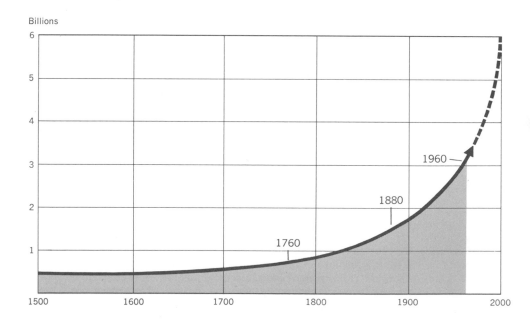

this Universal Declaration of Human Rights and note the strong emphasis placed upon the dignity of the individual.

Our free public school system reflects our deep desire that each student have the opportunity to develop the talents within him so that he may live a constructive and effective democratic life. No other country in the world provides opportunities of this kind that are equal to those provided in the United States.

Education and the Unification of Our Nation

It is difficult to appreciate fully the prodigious contribution made by the public schools during the past century in welding together people whose races, religions, national origins, and social and economic backgrounds are greatly diversified. You may have read the following inscription which is chiseled on the base of the Statue of Liberty:

> Give me your tired, your poor,
> Your huddled masses yearning to breathe free,
> The wretched refuse of your teeming shore,
> Send these, the homeless, tempest-tossed, to me:
> I lift my lamp beside the golden door.

The tremendous number of people from other countries who accepted this invitation presented a major challenge to American democracy as French points out [104:303–304]:

> That these huge numbers became Americanized and assimilated into the general population is a great tribute to them and to American institutions. Among these American institutions which made it possible to absorb so many people with diverse traditions and customs was the American public school. . . . (It) was largely the public school system which made the major contribution in this process both through educating the children of the immigrants and through Americanization and citizenship classes for the adults.

Through the processes of education and Americanization, many of those who came as immigrants rose from modest origins to positions of respect and dignity. Perhaps in no other place in the world have the doors of opportunity been open so wide. In discussing the contemporary challenge to American education, the Educational Policies Commission points out that [56:6–7]:

> Just as the purposes of the American school are unprecedented, so are its achievements. To it the American people owe the unity which has enabled them to master a continent and to forge from immigrant diversity a single people. It has helped to prevent the formation of rigid class barriers. It has fostered the diversification of talents, the ingenuity, and productivity which has brought this society to the highest level of economic prosperity ever known. On it are based many of the great American scientific and technological advances. And, perhaps most important of all, the spiritual stamina and fervor for freedom which have preserved individual liberty and guarded equality of opportunity through war and hardships have been derived from American Education. This majestic record has set the standard against which the rest of the world judges the value of universal education.

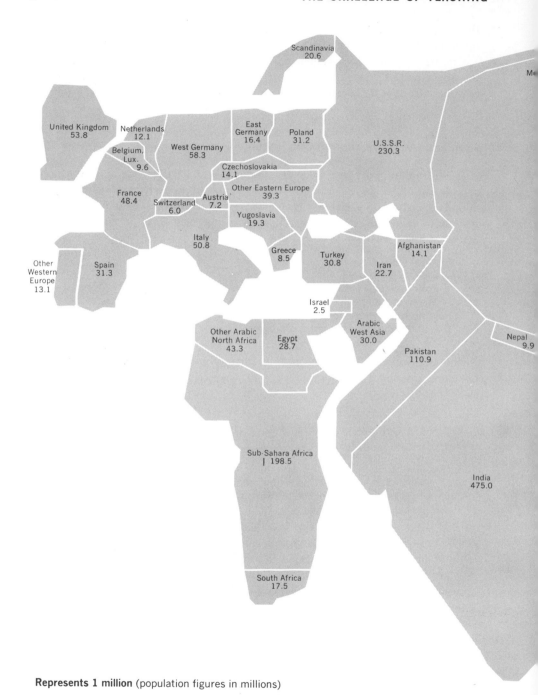

Represents 1 million (population figures in millions)

FIGURE 1–3. A map of the world with the size of each country proportionate to its approximate population. A major portion of the world's population is in underdeveloped countries, and approximately 85 per cent of the increase in world population between 1960 and the year 2000 will occur in these countries. (*Source:* Edwin O. Reischauer.)

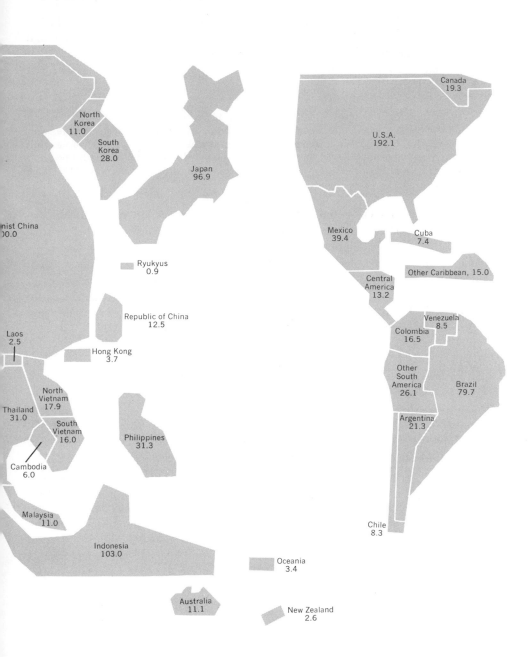

Frequent criticisms are made of our educational system. Much of this criticism is sincere and justified. Some of it is mixed with half-truths, misinformation, and ill-founded generalizations. There are those who would have us believe that European educational systems are far superior to our public school system. But let us recall that [7:4]:

> The educational system which is criticized today is the same one from which came the people who built the first atomic bomb, who flew the first airplane, who launched the first atomic submarine, who led the world in thermonuclear experiments, who developed mass industrial production of automobiles, bathtubs, and telephones. And, by the way, gave the world sulfa drugs, terramycin, and Salk vaccine.

In order to further ensure the welfare and growth of our nation through the development of each individual's capacities for effective democratic living, each state requires its children to attend school. These compulsory education laws place a moral obligation upon each child to develop his abilities to the fullest extent possible. As a future teacher, you will be responsible for devising programs of education that will enable American children to reach their highest potentials for democratic living. The future of our nation rests to a considerable measure upon the extent to which all teachers fulfill this basic responsibility [206:1].

Education and Democratic Responsibilities

You will recall that, throughout the history of our country, national leaders have emphasized that education is fundamental to the preservation of freedom and self-government. George Washington, in his Farewell Address of 1796, strongly encouraged the spread of knowledge: "Promote then, as an object of primary importance, institutions for the general diffusion of knowledge. In proportion as the structure of a government gives force to public opinion, it is essential that public opinion is enlightened." Thomas Jefferson warned that "if a nation expects to be ignorant and free in a state of civilization it expects what never was and never will be." He felt that "if the condition of man is to be progressively ameliorated . . . education is the chief instrument for effecting it." Abraham Lincoln stated that "upon the subject of education, not presuming to dictate any plan or system respecting it, I can only say that I view it as the most important subject which we as a people can be engaged in."

You may also recall statements made by recent Presidents regarding the fundamental role our schools play in the preservation and improvement of our way of life. Franklin D. Roosevelt, for example, stated that "our ultimate security, to a large extent, is based upon the individual's character, information, and attitude, and the responsibility rests squarely upon those who direct education in America." Dwight D. Eisenhower maintained that "because our schools help shape the mind and character of our youth, the strength or weakness of our educational system will go far to determine the strength or weakness of our national wisdom and our national morality tomorrow. That is why it is essential to our nation that we have good schools. And their quality depends upon all of us." In a message to Congress, delivered February 6, 1962, John F. Kennedy stated that:

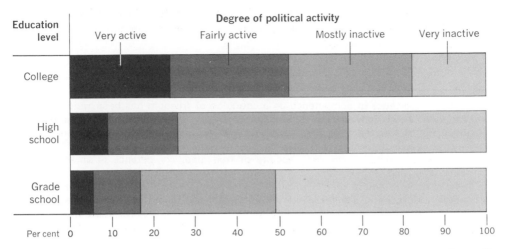

FIGURE 1–4. The relationship of education and political activity of American citizens, as indicated by a representative sample of 8,000 adults. What educational problems are related especially to the very inactive political groups of people? (*Source:* Chamber of Commerce of the United States.)

No task before our nation is more important than expanding and improving the educational opportunities of all our people . . . for education is both the foundation and the unifying force of our democratic way of life—it is the mainspring of our economic and social progress—it is the highest expression of achievement in our society ennobling and enriching human life. In short, it is at the same time the most profitable investment society can make and the richest reward it can confer.

In his State of the Union message to Congress in January, 1965, Lyndon B. Johnson stated that "Every child must have the best education the nation can provide."

Responsible citizens in all segments of American life express their faith in education in many ways. As will be indicated in a later chapter, they pay much money in the form of taxes to support free public schools and colleges. They donate both time and money for educational purposes. Over 650,000 people serve on local, state, and college boards [155:72]. Nearly 12 million people are members of the National Congress of Parents and Teachers. Mothers and fathers frequently make great sacrifices in order that their children may stay in school. The fact that citizens in all walks of life continue to expect the schools to accept more responsibility for the education of youth and adults reflects their persistent faith that both the individual and our American way of life can be improved through education. You as a future teacher will play a key role in this endeavor.

As we move into the future you will have the opportunity, as well as the obligation, to perpetuate and to strengthen our democratic way of life. Youth must gain a clear understanding of the values and traditions that have emerged from mankind's search for desirable ways of living. They must have an operational understanding of the democratic ideals and values that guide free people in acting responsibly, so that, ultimately, the welfare of society is seen as the combined welfare of all individuals. Factual knowledge alone does not ensure wise decision making since decisions are made largely in terms of the ideals and goals an individual cherishes. How can our schools do an even better job in meeting this basic need in a free world?

John W. Gardner, in his book titled *Excellence* [106:159–160], sounds a warning which all teachers should heed as they work with boys and girls:

> The importance of competence as a condition of freedom has been widely ignored (as some newly independent nations are finding to their sorrow). An amiable fondness for the graces of a free society is not enough. Keeping a free society free —and vital and strong—is no job for the half-educated and the slovenly. Free men must be competent men. In a society of free men, competence is an elementary duty. Men and women doing competently whatever job is theirs to do tone up the whole society. And a man who does a slovenly job—whether he is a janitor or a judge, a surgeon or a technician—lowers the tone of the society. So do the chiselers of high and low degree, the sleight-of-hand artists who always know how to gain an advantage without honest work. They are the regrettable burdens of a free society.

Individual competence, however, is not enough to ensure a strong, vibrant, creative, and productive society. Teachers must help boys and girls to value the dignity of work and the establishment of high standards of performance in all phases of life. Youth must learn to accept the responsibility for setting their own high standards of performance, for serving as their own hard disciplinarians, and for demanding quality performance upon the part of their fellowmen. They must feel that satisfaction at the level of mediocrity will result in the decay of the ideals that have made this country great. They must feel a sense of pride in and dedication to their work and to the basic ideals of our society.

Of course, pride and dedication are qualities that must be drawn from rather than taught to individuals. But you as a teacher can do much to stimulate and encourage the development of such qualities in girls and boys. Your feeling of pride and devotion to your work as a teacher may do much to inspire this type of reaction in youth as they later move into their various fields of work. You may also encourage pupils to take dedicated approaches to their various school responsibilities, to study the lives of others who reflect these qualities, to discover occupations that are best suited to their interests and abilities, and the like. Do everything possible to help boys and girls to thirst for knowledge rather than belittle its value, to desire constructive work rather than shirk responsibility, to appreciate rather than criticize the work of others, to admire rather than scorn the success of others, to be optimistic rather than pessimistic about their futures, to strive for the best rather than be satisfied with mediocrity, and to feel the thrill of success rather than the hopeless acceptance of failure.

Education and Equality of Opportunity

From your reading of such important documents as the Declaration of Independence and the Universal Declaration of Human Rights, you have noted the dominant belief which free nations have in the equality of men. Education is the medium through which this belief can best be recognized.

If we are to respect the dignity of man, however, we must provide the educational opportunities for each individual to develop his talents to the fullest. In

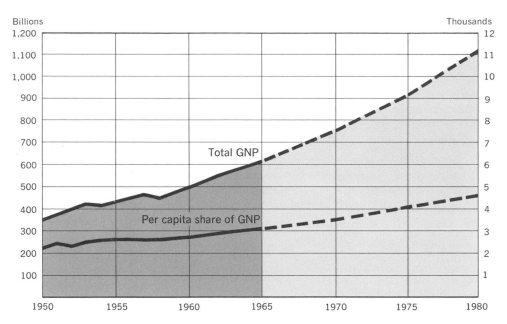

FIGURE 1–5.   Gross national product and per capita share of gross national prod-uct of the United States, 1950–1980. The United States has the manpower resources for a much higher standard of living. What role will the schools play in the realization of a higher standard of living? (*Source:* U.S. Department of Labor.)

other words, we are committed to the proposition that we must provide equal educational opportunities for all the children in our society. As members of the American Association of School Administrators point out [71:9], "The educational system is first of all society's instrument to discover talent and to develop that talent to a high peak of usefulness. No one can tell when or where a future genius is going to be born, and this is why our society casts a wide net for talent—why society needs mass education." This is a distinctive ideal of the American school system.

This proposition has a number of far-reaching implications for you as a teacher. How will you provide programs of education that meet the great diversification of abilities, interests, and needs of boys and girls? How will you work to remove such barriers as poverty, prejudice, and ignorance that interfere with equal edu-cational opportunities? How will you stimulate, encourage, and enhance the development of each individual's potentialities for effective democratic living?

Education and Economic Growth and Welfare

The economic growth of the United States is without parallel in the world. Although we compose only about 6 per cent of the world's population and occupy less than 7 per cent of the world's land area, we produce over 40 per cent and consume nearly one-third of the world's goods and services. We also consume one-third of the total energy produced in the world, and we own one-half of the

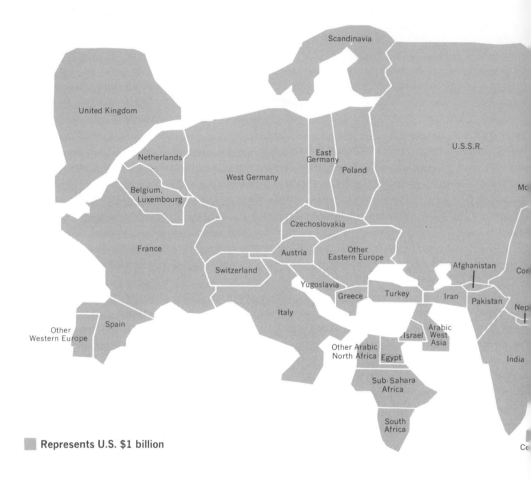

FIGURE 1–6. A map of the world with the size of each country proportionate to its gross national product. Contrast this map with Figure 1–3 on population. What conclusions can you draw regarding the standards of living as well as the educational opportunities in the various countries? *(Source:* Edwin O. Reischauer.)

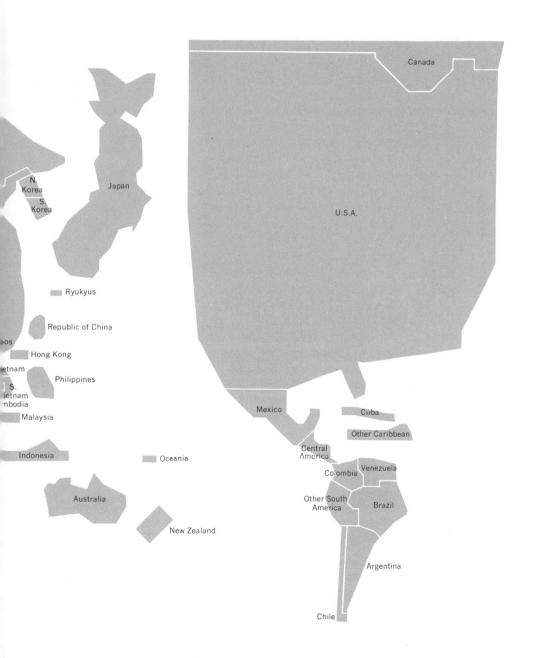

world's telephones, radios, and television sets [71:vi]. Our standards of living are the highest in the world.

In making their global analysis of education, manpower, and economic growth, Harbison and Myers found that [123:13]: "In an advanced economy the capacities of man are extensively developed; in a primitive country they are for the most part underdeveloped. If a country is unable to develop its human resources, it cannot develop much else, whether it be a modern political and social structure, a sense of national unity, or higher standards of material welfare."

From their analysis of human resources, Harbison and Myers [123:185] found that, throughout the world, "there is a high correlation and presumably some causal relation between enrollments in education (and hence investments in education) and a country's level of economic development as expressed by GNP per capita."

Harbison and Myers [123:185] found that "an initial investment in human resource development is necessary to get a country started on the road to self-sustained growth. Most of the underdeveloped countries, for example, would have had little or no modern development without expatriate high-level manpower." Perhaps this is the reason why our nation, in its program of aid to developing countries, is placing increasingly greater emphasis upon the development of human resources through education. Perhaps this is also the reason why increasingly greater amounts of federal money are being appropriated for preschool, elementary, secondary, higher, and adult education in the United States.

Walter W. Heller, a nationally recognized economist, interestingly points out how education plays an extremely important role in the growth and welfare of our economy, as well as in the security of our nation [129:9]:

> Policies designed primarily to stimulate economic growth often turn out to have a desirable dual purpose because the roots of economic growth lie deep in the economic and social strata. Education is a beautiful example. America has valued education for its own sake and has led the world in provision of free public education at all levels of society. Now it is apparent that education has improved the quality of the labor force, and that this investment in humans has been one of the major factors in the economic growth of the last half century. . . .
>
> The relationship between education and our military strength and national survival is equally direct. Higher and higher levels of education are required to supply a literate and well-trained source of military manpower in an age of electronic and nuclear weapons; to match and overcome the gains of the Soviet Union in missiles and space exploration; and, most important, to provide the understanding and wisdom required to outdo the Soviets in the competition for the minds of men. In this broad sense, education is a powerful weapon of great importance to our national defense. It spells the difference between being the world's first-rate and the world's second-rate power, scientifically and militarily.
>
> If we are to maintain world leadership, we must show that a free democratic society can solve its home problems—poverty, insecurity, unemployment, and inequalities of opportunity. Achievement of faster rates of economic progress and full use of our growing physical and human capacity is the surest way to demonstrate the resilience and vitality of our free economy.

Our economic welfare will be further strengthened through increased development of our human resources. In the future, more scientists, doctors, teachers, statesmen, engineers, and the like will be needed. Technological advancements

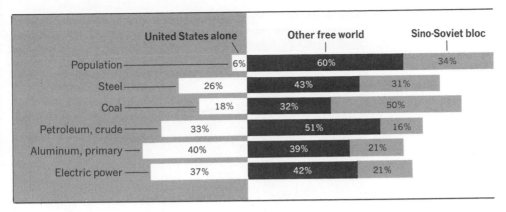

FIGURE 1–7. Where the balance of world resources lies. Our continued economic growth is dependent upon the wise use of our resources and upon trade with other parts of the free world. (*Source:* U.S. Bureau of Public Affairs.)

will require more highly skilled technicians. A strong and growing economy will require increasingly greater amounts of education for all.

Basically, the attitude and quality of teachers will affect the extent to which boys and girls make the effort to continue their educations and develop their abilities. Furthermore, greater efforts and amounts of money will need to be spent for education in an effort to reduce the number of educational failures. It is less expensive to educate people than to provide for the problems that may result from the lack of education. For example, "Each time we spend a dollar on education we spend $1.25 on crime and its prevention. To maintain a bed in a mental hospital costs $20,000 a year. To keep a youngster in the Youth Authority costs $8,000 a year. The public relief role averages $2,400 preventive maintenance" [147:469].

The strength of our future economy will also be affected by the extent to which future citizens make wise use of our natural resources—soil, minerals, forests, and water. As a teacher, you will have the opportunity to help youth understand how these resources have been abused and how they can conservatively use and develop them in the future so that quality of living may be enhanced.

In Figure 1-8 note that, in general, there is a direct relationship between the level of education and the economic advancement of individuals. The 1960 census showed that [71:2]:

Carpenters with an elementary education earned $4,800 a year, on the average, while carpenters who had completed high school earned $5,700. Electricians who had finished elementary school but *not* high school earned $6,100, while electricians who had graduated from high school received $6,600. For toolmakers, the figures are $6,700 and $7,300. The situation is the same for people who work in government. Local firemen who did not graduate from high school earned an average of $5,300, while those who held high school diplomas received $6,100.

Business and industry are demanding more and more education as a requirement for employment. The economic success of future citizens may be expected

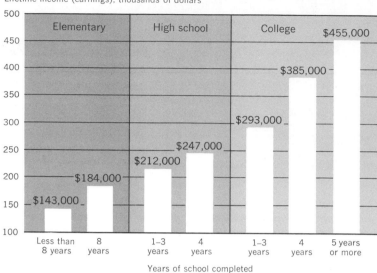

Lifetime income (earnings), thousands of dollars

FIGURE 1–8. Lifetime income (earnings) for males from age 18 to death, based on arithmetic means, according to the number of years of school completed. *(Source:* American Association of School Administrators.)

to require increasingly greater amounts of education. As a teacher, therefore, you will be helping others raise the level of their economic potentialities.

You will find a striking relationship between education and economic growth if you compare educational development, natural resources, and per capita income in various nations throughout the world [281:8]. Note in Table 1 that Denmark and Colombia present an interesting contrast. Colombia has abundant natural resources. Until recently, it had neglected education. Its per capita income in 1964 was the equivalent of $255. A century ago Denmark had a very low per capita income and its soil was not rich. It had few minerals and the growing season

TABLE 1   Relationship of Natural Resources, Education, and Income in Selected Countries

Nation	Natural resources	Educational development	Per capita income, 1964
Brazil	High	Low	$ 131
Colombia	High	Low	255
Denmark	Low	High	1,353
Mexico	High	Low	362
New Zealand	High	High	1,467
Switzerland	Low	High	1,783
United States	High	High	2,657

Source: What Everyone Should Know about Financing Our Schools, National Education Association, Washington, 1966, p. 8.

was short. But the people decided to place much emphasis upon developing good schools for their children. The per capita income in 1964, in contrast with Colombia's, was $1,353. Likewise, Brazil, very rich in natural resources but low in education, produced only $131 per capita. On the other hand, Switzerland, with limited resources but a well-developed educational program, ranked first in Europe in per capita income in 1964. Similar examples can be illustrated by many other countries. They show clearly that, regardless of natural resources, the development of educational potential increases per capita income.

The manifold ways in which good schools strengthen our society are well summarized in the excellent booklet *Education Is Good Business* [71:46–47]:

1. Well-documented evidence indicates that schools have made a magnificent contribution to our economic growth. More education means a more highly skilled work force; gains in worker efficiency achieved through education have accounted for 20 to 23 per cent of our growth in national product. Education is the base upon which the quality of research and development activities of American industry rests; the "advance of knowledge" achieved through research accounts for an additional 20 per cent of our prosperity.
2. Investments in education, accordingly, mean bigger markets for American businessmen. Rising markets give us strength in our economy.
3. Just as we want our economy to be generally strong, we want the many special benefits that education-based research helps to provide: freedom from disease, better communications, faster travel, clean water, and clear air in our growing cities.

FIGURE 1–9.   The relationship between unemployment and educational attainment in 1962. For every college graduate who was unemployed in 1962, seven persons with four or less years of education were unemployed. Dropping out of school before high school graduation has been termed "committing economic suicide." (*Source:* Chamber of Commerce of the United States.)

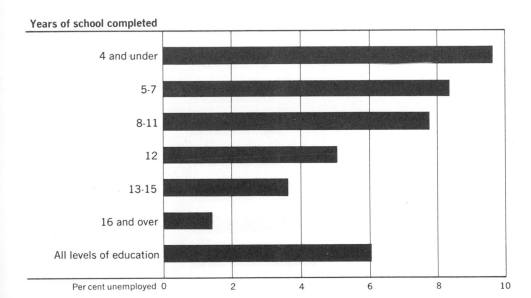

Years of school completed

4. We want a national government and an economic structure that can cope with chronic unemployment, a problem which appears to be characteristic of periods of rapid technological change. We believe that education, properly directed, is the chief means whereby people can find new kinds of jobs when the old kinds disappear. Labor, industry, and government must be sensitive to this fact.

5. For our whole system of government to function properly, we need strength and fiscal stability in our local governments. Good education is an important safeguard against economic stagnation and decay of local areas.

6. Of great importance are the benefits that education yields to the student as an individual. For the student, the zealous pursuit of education leads to higher income; the opportunity to choose among a variety of interesting and challenging kinds of work; a greater chance to participate in on-the-job training (in order to keep one's skills fresh and up-to-date); and, finally, job security.

7. By no means, however, are all the individual benefits of education in material form. Education promotes stability of family life, the improvement of educational opportunities for one's children through the early learning experiences that educated parents offer their boys and girls, and a vastly greater capacity to enjoy leisure. Furthermore, the attainment of full cultural maturity may be a central purpose of education.

8. Education is one of the chief ways by which we come to value human life in all its complexity. Through education, our children are led to develop a feeling of compassionate regard for their fellowmen—to be willing, on the one hand, to walk the extra mile to alleviate our neighbor's distress; and to be able, on the other, to share gracefully our friend's happiness in times of joy.

FIGURE 1–10.   The relationship between educational attainment and the mobility of males 25 years old and older. There is a direct relationship between an individual's level of educational attainment and his tendency to "pull up stakes" to seek more and better opportunities elsewhere. (*Source:* Chamber of Commerce of the United States.)

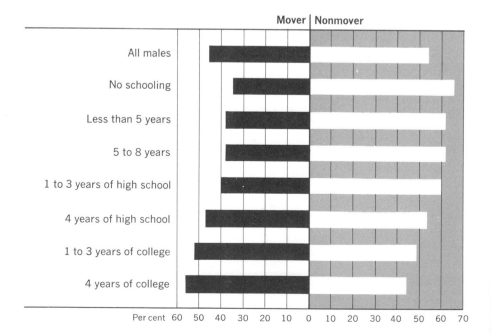

Democracy and Quality Teachers

In the history of our country we have never faced a period in which the demand for education has been greater. It seems obvious that, barring world catastrophe, the demands for educated intelligence will become increasingly greater.

In order to add strength to our nation and survive the strong threats to our way of life, increasing numbers of our most able young people must become teachers. Our future welfare rests so heavily upon the quality and quantity of education received by the young that only the best should teach. We, as a nation, can afford no less since our most important resources are the capacities, the energy, and the character of our people.

Alvin C. Eurich, in addressing the Chamber of Commerce of the United States, very effectively summarized the importance of education and the challenge with which we are faced [83].

America still means promise; it is still a land of opportunity. At this juncture of our history perhaps our greatest opportunity is in the education of our children. If we fail in this, we fail all succeeding generations. But there can be no bright future—as there never has been in any field—if we maintain the status quo. We cannot stand still. Every nation in the history of mankind has been defeated totally and miserably when it strove merely to protect what it had. New nations, including our own, have risen to the top through hardship and struggle, through ingenuity and the courage to create new patterns. Innovation has been basic to our economic well-being and growth. It is also basic to education, for creative imagination in education will determine our future and the future of our children.

Can you think of any better reason for being a teacher?

THE CHALLENGE OF THE FUTURE

If education is to play such a dominant role in the future, how will our schools and the work of teachers be affected? All of us are aware of the fact that we live in an era of unprecedented change and that the rate of this change will be greater in the future. This condition has profound educational implications. As the eminent anthropologist Margaret Mead points out, *"No one will live all of his life in the world into which he was born, and no one will die in the world in which he worked in his maturity"* [163:34].

As a teacher you will be concerned with helping future generations acquire the knowledge, skills, and attitudes they will need in order to live constructively in a world that will become increasingly different from the world of today. In order to fulfill your role adequately, you are faced with projecting the kind of world in which your pupils may be living and with modifying your role as a teacher in terms of your projections. At no other time in the history of mankind has so great a challenge been faced by teachers.

A number of scholars, according to Rice [218:8], are making careful studies of the changes that may take place, especially in such fields as science, military defense, space-age transportation, management, cybernation, social engineering, and biological engineering. For example, Donald N. Michael, in his challenging book

The Next Generation [165], indicates some changes that most likely will take place within the next 20 years and which will affect greatly the role of the school in society and the work of teachers. Much of the discussion that follows is adapted from two lectures he gave to prospective teachers in an introductory education course.[3]

A 20-year period, in the opinion of Dr. Michael, is a convenient span of time in terms of which teachers can project on probable changes since (1) the pace of change in politics, technology, society, and the world is so great that it is difficult to make useful predictions much beyond this period of time, (2) this is the period in which you as a teacher will assume major responsibilities as a citizen and as a mediator, moderator, and transmitter of the culture to the pupils you will teach, and (3) our next generation of young people will share, to a greater or lesser degree, the various value systems that exist in today's society. If we go much beyond 20 years, it is highly probable that the people who will be growing up and becoming adults will be emphasizing values that are importantly different from those we share.

The speculations that follow apply basically to the United States. What may happen in regard to the rest of the world is vague, extremely complex, and uncertain. It should be held in mind, however, that what happens to us in the next 20 years may be affected enormously by what happens in the rest of the world. Michael feels that "whether we live or die over these years may depend more upon what happens in the emerging nations, for example, than on what we do at home."

What, then, may happen during the next 20 years that has significance for you as a teacher and for those you will teach? Perhaps you already have considerable knowledge along such lines. *But frequently it is as important to be encouraged to think further upon matters with which we may be familiar as it is to be exposed to new ideas and information.*

1. *Our population will increase considerably and its composition will change significantly.* By 1975 there will be about 235 million people in the United States, and by 1980 the number will be about 250 million. In 1975 almost half of our population will be less than 25 years of age. By 1975 there will be at least 20 per cent more people who are over 65 years old than there are today. Improvements in medicine may increase the percentage of those over 65. This condition increases the polarization of our population. We face the increasing problem of meeting the pre-work force needs of the young and the needs of those who are retired or about to retire. Definite trends toward lowering the age of retirement will increase the percentage of our population who are in the post-work force. The needs of these two groups are quite different. What new educational demands will emerge from each of these groups of our population, and how will these demands differ? What new opportunities will be presented to teachers by the post-work force? How might the role of the school change?

2. *A much greater percentage of our population will be living in urban areas.* According to Michael, in 1980 approximately 80 per cent of our people will be living in urban areas. Most of these will be living in three major urban areas,

[3] Permission granted by Donald N. Michael.

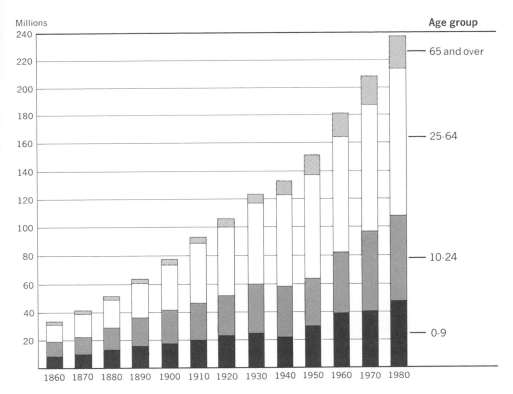

FIGURE 1–11.   Actual and projected growth and age distribution of the population of the United States, 1860–1980. Between 1960 and 1970 the elementary and secondary school age group will increase 14 per cent, and by 1980 it will have increased 25 per cent. As compared to the situation in 1860, the 65 and over age group will have increased phenomenally by 1980. What educational needs and problems will arise from these changes in the distribution of age groups? (*Source:* Chamber of Commerce of the United States.)

called megalopoli, which will consist of smaller cities that have become fused together. One such area will stretch from Maine to Virginia; another, from Minneapolis and Chicago to Buffalo; and a third, from San Francisco to San Diego. As a result, we shall have unprecedentedly large populations living in unprecedentedly large urban complexes. Rural life, as we have known it in the past, will be far removed from many boys and girls.

As the cities fuse together across state lines, the conventional forms of city and state government will be inadequate to meet the problems and potentials of the regional cities. During this time period, we will see interesting and, hopefully, not disastrous experiments in new forms of government for dealing with these regional cities. If you and your pupils are living in one of these regional cities as it develops, you will note that the geographic distinctions of communities fade away and that the perspectives and values held by the inhabitants change significantly.

How will these changes affect the lives and values of children, youth, parents, and adults with whom you will work? In what ways may the organization and

Half of all Americans in 3 supercities?

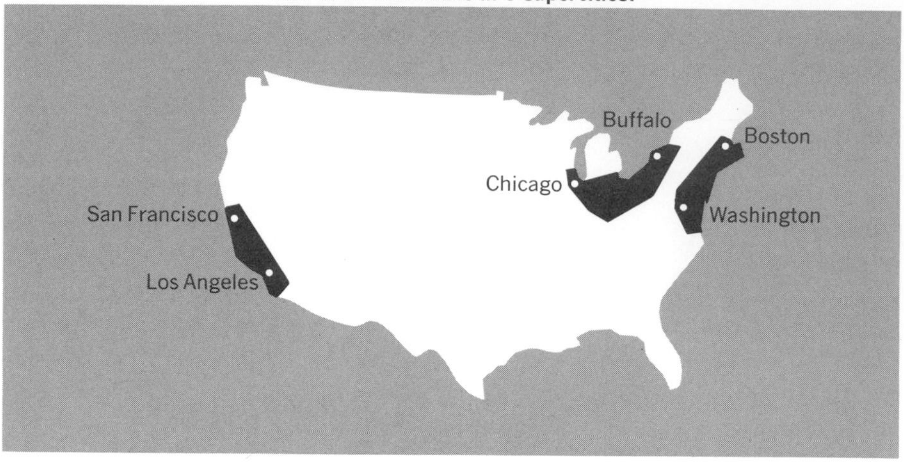

FIGURE 1–12. In 1965, approximately 43 per cent (83 million) of all Americans lived in the three "strip cities" outlined on the map. By 1985, one-half (125 million) of all Americans will be living in these three major metropolitan areas. What kinds of governmental, social, and educational problems will result from this change? (*Source: U.S. News & World Report.*)

financing of school systems be changed? What changes may need to be made in the certification patterns of teachers?

3. *The percentage of culturally deprived children may increase, especially in the central part of large metropolitan cities.* It has been estimated that, by 1975, 50 per cent of the children living in the central part of our large metropolitan cities may be considered to be culturally deprived. Unless rather drastic measures are taken to curtail the development of this condition, a very significant percentage of young people will never be able to develop fully their potential for effective democratic living. Benjamin Bloom, in his book *Stability and Change in Human Characteristics*, finds that the intellectual and emotional deprivation of many children begins early. His findings and conclusions are as follows [28:104–105]:

> The curve for the development of general scholastic achievement exhibits a relatively rapid early development followed by a rather steady rate of growth from ages nine to 18. . . . By age nine (grade 3) at least 50 per cent of the general achievement pattern at age 18 (grade 12) has been developed, whereas at least 75 per cent of the pattern has developed by about age 13 (grade 7).

What measures are being taken and what new measure should be taken in order to overcome the problems of cultural deprivation of people in our society? How can educators help in solving this problem? Since you may be working with some pupils who are culturally deprived, how will your role as a teacher be affected?

4. *It will be increasingly difficult for parents to guide their children wisely and well* [165:79–80]. A number of factors will affect the relationship between parents and children. For example, there may be more physical separation of parents and children. More mothers may find it necessary to work, either to satisfy career aspirations or to supplement the family budget. Greater emphasis undoubt-

edly will be given to preschool experiences which may lessen the contacts of parents with children under six years of age. Ease of transportation may cause children and youth to spend more time away from home in camping, using recreational facilities, traveling, and studying abroad.

With the trend toward urbanization and the formation of very large cities, parents and children may be less inclined to identify themselves with a community. Physical uprooting of families most likely will increase because of the need for parents to change jobs more often. Values may change and life-styles may become more complex. All these probable changes may result in teachers having to play an increasingly significant role in helping youth establish identity as well as values in terms of which they will direct their lives.

5. *Significant technological changes will take place as a result of more automation and the use of computers.* Automation might be defined as the replacement of human hands and senses by mechanical or electronic devices [166:7]. The term "automation," coined about 1947 [13:3], may be applied to machines that manufacture parts and pass them on to another machine for further processing without human intervention. It may also refer to the self-correcting mechanism by which machines keep track of their own experiences and correct their own deviations and mistakes [13:3]. Computers may be used to process symbols automatically and to control various kinds of automation.

Michael uses the term "cybernation" to refer to the use of computers in automation. He indicates that, through the use of a procedure known as numerical control, computers will replace many skilled workers who, in the past, have designed and fabricated complex components for such things as shipbuilding and automobile manufacturing. He points out that much of what is called design work, in such areas as architecture and engineering, is a fairly routine task of working through a series of alternatives. This type of design can now be done by computers. As a result, a person may try out different models of how an airplane might be designed, how a certain kind of an economic system might operate, how a particular national strategy might be construed, or how some type of educational program might function. In other words, a computer may be used to try out various ideas and refine them before they are actually put into operation.

It is easy to see that job opportunities, as well as the lives of many people, will be affected greatly by cybernation.

Many unskilled workers will lose out to machines, and some extension of the antipoverty program may be needed to provide them with the services they cannot afford. However, some unskilled jobs will remain and some new ones will be created. Automation will turn some jobs that now require skill into jobs that merely require watching a meter or a dial; other jobs which now require a high level of skill will be split into simpler ones that will be done in part by semiskilled workers and in part by machines.

Many skilled workers will be forced to retrain. Already, skilled machinists' jobs have begun to be abolished as computer-controlled machine tools take over their tasks. Gradually, many bank clerks, office workers, auditors, draftsmen, and middle-level managers and engineers will find their work being done by computers.

As time goes on, even the less highly skilled computer programers will find themselves displaced as libraries of preprogramed computer instructions are set up and as computers that do much of their own programing come into use [166:8–9].

The phenomenal expansion of technological knowledge and skills creates new demands in the education of youth as well as of adults. What are some of these demands, and how will they affect your work as an educator? *(Photograph from National Aeronautics and Space Administration.)*

Michael points out that the work of highly creative persons will not be threatened by cybernation. Rather, they will have more latitude for being creative. For example, creative people in such areas as economics, political science, and the behavioral sciences will be able to conceptualize about man and his environment in a much higher and different manner from that which is available without the assistance of the computer. Likewise, the demand for people in most of the professions will increase greatly, and the hours of work per week will tend to be longer than at present. It is highly likely that our educational system will not be able to prepare enough people for some of the professional occupations, as there seems to be no decided tendency toward larger numbers of young people desiring to enter these occupations.

The person who does a routine kind of physical or mental work, on the other hand, will be potentially subject to displacement. This means that, in the years ahead, we shall find many people being continually displaced from their jobs, having to learn new jobs, and having to live in a number of different locations and to learn new ways of life. It means that children will grow up recognizing the fact that many of them will have two or three careers which will involve seven or eight different jobs during their work years [273:11]. It means that they may spend a significant amount of their lives in school being retrained and reeducated. Obviously, the vocational education programs in our schools will need to undergo considerable reorientation. It also means that the demands upon teachers and vocational counselors will increase substantially.

6. *There will be a decided increase in management technology.* Management

technology, according to Michael, refers to a set of procedures, techniques, and approaches to organizing, on a national scale and over long periods of time, the manpower brawn and brains to accomplish major tasks. In other words, brain power may be organized administratively and procedurally in much the same way as we, in the past, have organized men to use their muscles. Management technology makes it possible to plan ahead and to undertake activities that may literally change our nation in terms of how our various resources and agencies are used.

Management technology started after World War II as a new approach to the development of our weapons system and has been applied to the space program. In the future, it most likely will be applied to city building and rebuilding, oceanography, education, and a number of other areas. This means that more and more people will be meshed in larger and larger administrative complexes. How will you, as a teacher, help boys and girls develop a sense of individuality, loyalty, dignity, and worth? What new skills, understandings, and attitudes will you help them develop?

7. *We probably shall experience a greater degree of social engineering.* By using the term "social engineering," Michael refers to the systematic application of social science to the organization, control, direction, and motivation of man and his institutions. The computer enables the social scientist to do two things he has never been able to do before. First, he can build enormously complex models about man in his institutions. In the past, his work was done using only simple models because he was unable to keep the many variables in mind and manipulate them. But the computer has the capacity to manipulate very large numbers of variables. This means that very complex and subtle models of how men behave in groups and organizations can be conceived of and simulated on computers. Second, by virtue of the computer, he can collect data about our society as it is now, check the computer models against them, and determine whether the models represent reality. In the past the social scientist was not able to do this type of verification, since it took a long time to collect the data and to process them. Because of the rapid processing of data, we now have the potential for developing far more sophisticated social sciences.

Dr. Michael indicates that we inevitably will have available, for good or for bad, many more opportunities to control or be controlled than we have had in the past. More funds will be available for research to evaluate and understand what is happening as growth takes place in federal programs dealing with such areas as education, poverty, counterinsurgency, and guerrilla warfare. It will be necessary to conduct this research in order that we will not flounder in our own complexity. This raises a basic problem of determining who is going to do the job of deciding what is to be controlled as well as that of controlling it. What are going to be the ethical bases for deciding what is to be controlled? Who is to be controlled and under what circumstances? This kind of power carries with it a potential for corruption, even for destroying our whole democratic system. Since education is bound to be affected to some extent, this profound ethical question will confront you as a future teacher.

8. *Major and dramatic advancements most likely will be made in biological engineering.* It is generally agreed that the developments in biological science

and their applications over the next two decades will be at least as spectacular as the development of atom smashers and the like in the field of physics. According to Michael, one development will be that of the increased ability to alter brain processes and personality characteristics. Agents, such as tranquilizers and experience-wideners, are only the beginning. There is evidence that memories can be enhanced or wiped out. Biologists probably will discover how to change characteristics that might be inherited. They may be able to predetermine the sex of a baby. They may be able to help old people revitalize their memories, skills, and abilities. We are going to have the increasing ability to manipulate emotional and cognitive characteristics of human beings.

This raises the question: Who has the right to make these changes? What are the implications of these advancements for dealing with behavior problems, psychological disorders, juvenile delinquency, potential school dropouts, crime, and the like? Will there be possibilities of motivating more young people to develop their capacities for democratic living to the fullest extent possible? What new educational needs and economic and social contributions may arise if it becomes possible to revitalize the memories and abilities of older people?

9. *More and more demands will be made for high-level social competence.* In the past our lives have been related basically to our local environments. In the future our lives will be affected more by our continental and world environments. So many things will be happening in so many places that the environment in which teachers and students live will become quite complex. The number of significant social interactions will become almost overwhelming.

Only recently have we begun to take seriously first-class citizenship for the Negro, as well as the recognition of the need to do something about poverty in our society. There are many other social requirements which we must set for ourselves. We are only beginning to recognize that we must be more humane and prepare sensible and meaningful lives for older people. There are questions regarding air pollution, traffic control, water pollution, and education. You will be able to think of many other social demands we should and probably will make upon ourselves as a society. All these interact with one another, and all these have assets and liabilities with regard to carrying out each of them. As a teacher, you will not be able to concentrate totally on the discipline you are teaching or on the community in which you are located. To be a good teacher you will have to transcend subject-matter disciplines as well as local attachments. These conditions will put a much greater burden upon you than teachers have had in the past, when life was less complex, less closely coupled, and less loaded with events of enormous implication.

10. *In terms of the way we shall be living (life-styles), there will be opportunities for greater diversity in the midst of conformity.* As you study life in various communities, you will note that the level of anonymity for the individual tends to increase as the population of a city increases. As our population and urban areas increase therefore, people will have greater freedom to experiment with the styles of living they desire. They will be developing and experimenting with different sets of values which will affect how they live, what they aspire to, how they want their children educated, what kind of educations they want for themselves, and where they want to live.

You currently see small but significant portions of people your age, both here and abroad, who are experimenting with different forms of political action as well as with styles of living. As a teacher, you will have the opportunity to work with a greater variety of life-styles. You also will be confronted with the more difficult task of helping youth as well as adults clarify their values in terms of which their behavior will be governed and to build more meaningful concepts of freedom and responsibility in a democratic society.

11. *Leisure will become an increasingly important part of the lives of many.* With the possible exception of some of the professionals who may be working from 60 to 70 hours per week [165:123], people will be working fewer hours per week as well as fewer years. Leisure, therefore, will become an increasingly important part of life. It will take on a legitimacy and a significance that our Protestant ethic-oriented society has not had in the past. Even though work will still be considered a moral obligation of the individual, leisure will be considered a more virtuous part of life. For some people, increased leisure time will present a wonderful opportunity in which they may grow—a time for fulfillment. For others it may be a period of boredom, frustration, and anxiety. If our children are to avoid the undesirable results of increased leisure time, they need to learn before they grow up how to find personal enrichment in their free time.

How to help both young and old learn to use leisure time for personal enrichment and fulfillment presents exciting and important opportunities for the teacher. How will your work as a teacher be affected? How might the role of the school in the community change? What changes may be made in the school's curriculum? Will cocurricular activities in the school take on added significance? What changes might take place in the use of the school's library, auditorium, playground, or fine arts and music departments? Will the use of the school's facilities tend to follow the 24 hours per day pattern of operation that more industries and businesses may adopt as a result of automation? What new requests for the services of teachers may be made by industries, businesses, recreation centers, and government agencies?

12. *There may be an increasing professionalization of the government and all activities having to do with the planning and administration of society.* Almost everyone will admit that, as our population increases, the task of governing ourselves will become more complex. We note the increasing role being played by the government in solving the complex and technical problems faced by our society. The solution of many of these problems calls for the services of people who are highly competent in governmental affairs. As a result, Michael feels that perhaps the greatest challenge for our society over the years ahead is going to be meeting the increasing professionalization of the government and of all other activities having to do with the planning and administration of our society. This condition raises the very important question of the role played by the citizen who is not part of the professional governmental processes by which our society will be conducted. It will become increasingly more difficult for laymen to find vital roles in the democratic process. How will teachers be able to face the critical challenge of helping pupils and adults identify themselves with and play significant citizenship roles in the direction of our nation and in other democratic processes?

13. *Both basic and applied knowledge will expand at a very rapid rate.* You

are familiar with the tremendous increase in the amount of scientific knowledge that is becoming available to mankind. This increase is understandable when we recognize the extent to which the computer has extended man's capabilities. Likewise, it has been estimated that more than 80 per cent of all the scientists who have lived since the dawn of history are living and working today [195:14].

In 1941, the total amount of money spent throughout the economy on research was less than $1 billion annually. By 1962, the amount was $15 billion per year. It is estimated that at least $25 billion will be spent for research in 1970 [13:7]. The National Aeronautics and Space Administration project, on which a great amount of government money is being spent, is designed primarily to expand man's knowledge. We may expect this trend in the expansion of knowledge to continue, not only in the area of science but also in all other areas. Since it is impossible for boys and girls to learn all that they will need to know, how will you attempt to help them become effective citizens, competent to deal with the problems they will face in life? What implications does this rapid increase in knowledge have for the in-service education of teachers?

14. *The educational attainment of our population will continue to rise.* Between 1965 and 1985 the percentage of men 25 years of age and over who have completed four years or more of college is expected to increase from 11.4 to 19.4 per cent, and the increase for women is expected to be from 6.4 to 9.7 per cent [202:1]. During this period of time the total number of high school graduates is expected to rise from about 47 million to 87 or 88 million among persons 25 years old and over. At the same time it is anticipated that there will be a sharp reduction in the percentage of persons 25 years old and over who have had less than five years of formal schooling. The expected increase in the median years of school completed by those 25 years old and over may also serve as an indicator

FIGURE 1–13. Years of school completed by those in the United States who are 25 or more years old. The educational attainment of adults will continue to rise. What effect will this condition have upon the educational needs of youth and of adults? (*Source:* U.S. Bureau of the Census.)

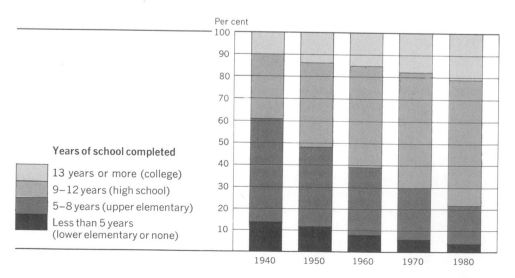

of improvement in educational attainment. Between 1960 and 1985 the median is expected to increase from 10.5 to 12.4 years of formal schooling [202:2]. What effect may this expected increase in educational attainment have on the pupils as well as on the parents and other adults with whom you will work? How will our economy and social structure be affected?

15. *There will be a growing demand in this country and elsewhere for fuller recognition of human dignity.* According to a committee concerned with education for freedom and world understanding [70:24–25], this demand will be in the form of "(a) self-determination and the end of all forms of colonialism, (b) equal rights and opportunities, without discrimination as to sex, race, caste, class, or religion, (c) accelerated economic development and expanding employment opportunities, (d) enlarged opportunities for education for both young and old and (e) wider creative participation in the arts and other cultural activities." How will you as a teacher help youth as well as adults work effectively toward the fuller recognition of human dignity? How will you as a citizen work toward the achievement of this worthy goal? What opportunities for working abroad will result from this demand, and what kinds of understandings, training, personalities, and aspirations will be needed by those who wish to engage in this type of work?

16. *There may be a definite increase in the number of women in the labor force.* Between 1964 and 1980, the labor force is expected to increase 24.4 million, reaching a total of 101.4 million [146:129]. Approximately 21 million, or 87 per cent, of this increase will be due to the growth in population, and the rest probably will be due to the increased number of adult women entering the labor force. An increasing number of employed women will be between the ages of 20 and 44 [146:130,137], and a majority of them may be part-time workers. In what ways may the educational needs and objectives of girls change? How may your work as a teacher be affected by this tendency for an increasing number of mothers to work at least part time in the labor force?

17. *Teachers will face increasingly greater challenges in the future.* In addition

FIGURE 1–14. Percentage of women in each age group who will be in the labor force in 1980. What modifications should be made in the public school education of girls? What obligations do public schools have to adult women? (*Source:* U.S. Bureau of Statistics.)

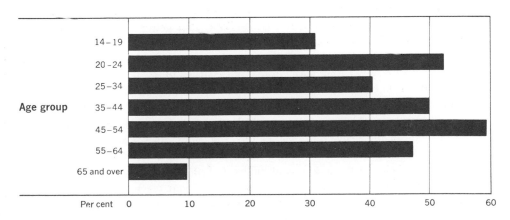

to those already mentioned, what are some of the other challenges which the future holds for teachers?

a. What is going to be the balance you create between being the agent for conserving the styles of the past and acting as the cutting edge for disrupting traditions and inventing new ones? It has always been a question whether the task of education is to prepare people to fit the society or to prepare them to change the society. In the past, we have been able to be rather casual about the problem because the nature of our society did not change very fast. But the future is going to change society fast and radically, and you are going to be confronted perpetually with the problem of determining your role as a conserver of the past and as an innovator so far as the future is concerned.

b. What will be an appropriate role model for you? In the future the status of the teacher in society will increase because the welfare of our society will be more and more dependent on education of all sorts and at all ages.

Education will be available almost on a cradle-to-grave basis. More children of all economic groups will attend nursery school and kindergarten. Post-high school education will be more widely available and, with increased recognition that a well-educated population is a national necessity, government subsidies for higher education will be more general.

Many different kinds of institutions will provide opportunities for lifelong education. Community colleges, vocational schools, centers for instruction in recreation activities, and institutions attached to industry, business, and government will cater to all individuals, regardless of age: Indeed, we will see more and more intermingling of age groups as education becomes a general condition of living rather than just early preparation for it [166:11–12].

As a result of these highly probable conditions, you as a teacher will play an exceedingly important role in the lives of your pupils as well as in those of many adults. To your pupils you will be an expression of adulthood and the opportunities which being an adult presents. Expressing the adult world through what you teach and relating it to society become a very interesting, difficult, and challenging task for the teacher.

c. How are you going to educate your pupils for wisdom? We shall need people who are more than skilled engineers, scientists, and technicians. We shall need people who are humanists, who have the intuition that is necessary to understand the human predicament, and who have the insight to do the things that the large society with its high aspirations sets for itself. It is going to take wise men and women, indeed, to act in such ways that save the individual from being lost sight of in the mass. In the past we have been able to bumble through and manage to get along with only a few wise people. No man could do very much good or evil to mankind. But this will not be the case in the future. To do good in the future will require more than technological skill. It will require wisdom. "Without wisdom, technical brilliance alone could lead to social or physical disaster and the destruction of the democratic way of life. Somehow, our schools and homes must educate for and practice wisdom, compassion, courage, tolerance of uncertainty, and appreciation of the unique and different" [166:14]. You as a teacher will play a vital role in developing wisdom in the pupils you teach and the adults with whom you work. It will be an enormous and exciting task.

SUMMARY

In the first part of this chapter you doubtless sensed the basic role that education has played in the growth and development of our nation. More than ever before in the history of mankind, progress in the welfare as well as in the security of our nation is, to a great extent, dependent upon how well our schools fulfill their role. Stated differently, the need for quality education has never been greater, and, in the years to come, the need will increase still more. This, therefore, constitutes one of the important reasons for becoming a teacher.

In the second part of the chapter, an attempt was made to indicate some of the technological and social changes that may take place as you move into teaching and to indicate the ways you can help those of the next generation acquire the knowledge, skills, and attitudes that will enable them to deal successfully with the increasing complexity of life. You face the challenge of discovering new ways of helping youth as well as adults gain the competencies they will need to cope adequately and effectively with the complexity of problems they will face and to preserve and refine the basic freedoms that characterize our way of life. Never in the history of mankind has the need for education been greater. Never have teachers faced so great a challenge.

QUESTIONS FOR YOUR CONSIDERATION

1. What features of the American school system have especially contributed to the phenomenal growth and success of America?
2. Have you ever experienced any school practices and procedures that showed a lack of respect for the dignity and worth of the individual? How will you attempt to avoid the use of such practices and procedures?
3. Are there any evidences that we are losing some of the ideals that have made this country great? If so, what are they, and how will you attempt to inculcate these ideals into the minds of your pupils?
4. Does the concept of equal educational opportunity mean that all pupils should receive the same kind and amount of education?
5. What basic differences in the aims of education exist between Russia and the United States? How does the work of teachers in these two countries differ?
6. John W. Gardner has stated that: "At this moment in history, free institutions are on trial." What evidences would support (or not support) such a statement?
7. In an age of advancing technology, upon what bases can you defend a program of general education as a part of your college education?
8. How can we justify spending so much effort and money in trying to educate all children, when future progress will depend so much upon the contributions of academically talented pupils?
9. How will technological changes that may take place during the next 20 years affect the function of the school and the role of the classroom teacher?
10. What changes may need to be made during the next 20 years in the nature of vocational education programs in public schools?

11. Lester Velie, in his book *New Careers in America's Classrooms*, states that the teacher has overcome his "shabby orphan of society" image and is now "the man of the hour." In what ways do you agree, as well as disagree, with this statement? How do you account for any changes that may have taken place in regard to the teacher's image?

12. Explain what is meant by the statement "Education should be viewed as an investment rather than as an expenditure."

13. If greater emphasis is placed upon helping youth "learn how to learn," how will the nature of the teacher's work change?

14. How will you attempt to educate youth for the effective use of leisure time?

15. How should the public school attempt to cope with the mounting problem of adult education?

ACTIVITIES FOR YOU TO PURSUE

1. List what you consider to be the major challenges that teaching holds for you. Discuss these challenges with some of your college teachers, or with other students who plan to teach, to see whether they agree with your challenges.

2. Read the entire book *The Next Generation* by Donald N. Michael and discuss its contents with your colleagues. Make a list of implications for education which emerge from his projections for the next 20 years.

3. Make a list of new opportunities that will open to teachers during the next 20 years as a result of technological and social changes that most likely will occur. Check your list with some of your colleagues and professors.

4. Confer with some leading executives in business and industry regarding their views on the importance of education to our economy. Ask them to indicate what educational responsibilities their businesses and industries may need to assume in the future.

5. Confer with employment agencies in your community regarding the changes in employment patterns they have noticed during the past few years. What changes do they anticipate so far as the future is concerned?

6. Visit one or more preschool projects especially designed for culturally deprived children. Observe the kinds of activities being provided for the children, and discuss with the teachers what they hope to accomplish.

7. Talk with one or more social workers and with those working in various welfare agencies regarding the importance of education. What solutions do they see for welfare problems? In their opinions, how will the lives of children whose parents are on welfare be affected?

8. Discuss with your colleagues the educational role, if any, that our federal government should take in alleviating the problems of people who are culturally deprived, who are unemployed, who have unequal educational opportunities, and who are living in the developing countries.

9. Write to your state department of education for any study that might have been made of educational attainment and per capita income by countries. Study the data to see if there is a correlation of these two factors.

10. Discuss with your colleagues the changes that most likely will take place in the United States within the next 10 to 20 years. Explore how elementary and secondary schools might need to change in order that they may function most effectively.

OTHER SOURCES OF IDEAS AND INFORMATION FOR CHAPTER 1

SUGGESTED READINGS

Adams, Don: "Education and the Wealth of Nations," *Phi Delta Kappan,* vol. 47, no. 4, pp. 169–174, December, 1965. Summarizes what we know and what we do not know regarding education as the key to the development of nations.

Barach, Arnold B.: *U.S.A. and Its Economic Future,* The Macmillan Company, New York, 1964. Presents the results of an extensive survey of the American economic system and projects where it is likely to stand in the future. Pages 63–70 deal especially with education.

Brickman, William W., and Stanley Lehrer (eds.): *Automation, Education and Human Values,* School and Society Books, New York, 1966. A series of readings on automation and its effect upon schools and human values.

Education: An Investment in People, Chamber of Commerce of the United States, Education Department, Washington, 1964. An excellent presentation of the value of education, our changing population, and the condition of our schools.

"Education and Automation: The Coming World of Work and Leisure," *National Association of Secondary-School Principals Bulletin,* vol. 48, no. 295, National Education Association, Washington, November, 1964. Discusses the educational problems arising from automation, cybernation, change, and technology, and relates these problems to vocational education, low ability groups, dropouts, guidance, and lifelong education.

Education and the Public Good, Harvard University Press, Cambridge, Mass., 1964. Contains an excellent statement on the challenge to education in a changing world by Walter P. Reuther.

Education in a Changing Society, National Education Association, Project on the Instructional Program of the Public Schools, Washington, 1963. An excellent discussion of the changes taking place in our society and their educational implications.

Education Is Good Business, American Association of School Administrators, Washington, 1966. Presents an excellent discussion of the economic and social values of education and the reasons why our nation has prospered.

Hanson, John W., and Cole S. Brembeck: *Education and the Development of Nations,* Holt, Rinehart and Winston, Inc., New York, 1966. A compilation of articles that focuses upon the vital role education plays in the development of nations.

Manpower Report of the President and a Report on Manpower Requirements, Resources, Utilization, and Training, U.S. Department of Labor, March, 1965. An extensive analysis of the status of manpower in the nation and its future needs. Contains many charts and graphs. Pages 97–140 relate most directly to manpower needs in education.

Michael, Donald N.: *The Next Generation,* Random House, Inc., New York, 1965. An excellent book on the prospects ahead for the youth of today and tomorrow.

Russell, James E.: *Change and Challenge in American Education,* Houghton Mifflin Company, Boston, 1965. Indicates changes that may need to be made in elementary, secondary, and higher education.

Thayer, V. T., and Martin Levit: *The Role of the School in American Society,* Dodd, Mead & Company, Inc., New York, 1966. The first three chapters are concerned with faith in education, acceptance of change, and the school as a supplementary institution.

"Tomorrow's Jobs: Where the Best Will Be," *Changing Times,* vol. 20, no. 2, pp. 7–11, February, 1966. Contains an excellent analysis of changes that will take place in job opportunities within the next two decades.

SUGGESTED FILMS, FILMSTRIPS, AND RECORDINGS

Films 16 (mm)

America: The Edge of Abundance (National Educational Television, 59 min). Explores the far-reaching economic and social consequences of the increasingly automated and computer-oriented society in the United States as viewed by British television. Traces America's growth from an agricultural base to a manufacturing society and focuses on automation. Shows the immense problems of retraining and suggests that leisure will become the new business. Concludes that United States values must be reexamined.

America's Crises: The Community (National Educational Television, 59 min). Evaluates the cultural, educational, religious, and physical aspects of America's cities and towns. Focuses on the small New England fishing community of Provincetown and compares it with San Jose, California, a booming Western community in the midst of accelerated growth. Discusses their similarities and differences, shows the effects of change, and suggests the problems that must be solved.

America's Crises: The Hard Way (National Educational Television, 59 min). Looks at the problem of poverty in the richest country in the world and emphasizes how today's poor are different from those of past generations. Focuses on slums, housing projects, public schools, and settlement houses in the St. Louis area.

America's Crises: The Individual (National Educational Television, 59 min). Examines the problem of the individual in a complex society by looking at various areas of American life in relation to man's needs for self-identification. Probes the effects of government planning in agriculture on individual initiative and community indentification.

America's Crises: The Parents (National Education Television, 59 min). Presents a documentary report on the changing problems of America's parents today and their attempts to find identity, meaning, and purpose in their lives. Features frank interviews with parents and children. Shows the effects of rural-urban-suburban social change and presents interviews with Benjamin Spock, Betty Friedan, and Paul Popenoe.

Assignment: Tomorrow (National Education Association, 32 min). Deals with the vital role of the schoolteacher in the life of our country. Stresses the importance of the teacher's work in the classroom, the place of teachers as citizens in the community, and their contributions as members of professional organizations.

Born Equal (Australian Instructional Films, 11 min). Uses specific examples to interpret the Declaration of Human Rights as it emerges from the United Nations Charter. Stresses the acceptance of individual responsibilities as well as rights and emphasizes the necessity of the nation's supporting the provisions of the declaration.

A Desk for Billie (National Education Association, 57 min). Presents portions from the life story of Billie Davis, "The Hobo Kid." Through dramatization and narration, shows how Billie's family, consisting of her parents, two brothers, and a sister, travels from place to place looking for a ready market to sell homemade baskets of flowers. Discloses Billie's quest for becoming like "real" people and attending church and school. Shows her achieving this upon graduation from high school.

Education Is Everybody's Business (Association Films Inc., 17 min). A look at higher education—past, present, and future. Shows the dramatic changes made since the turn of the century in America's economic and social life. Emphasizes the important role of higher education in providing the essential training, research, and specialized service needed in our expanding society. The problems that education will face in the coming decade are projected, and various solutions are given for these problems.

Education Is Good Business (State University of Iowa, 11 min, color). Emphasizes the direct relationship between a town's prosperity and the quality of its educational system by contrasting communities and quoting statistics from the U.S. Chamber of Commerce. Also compares income levels and educational standards of various countries.

Education: The Public Schools (National Educational Television, 29 min). Indicates the forces which have influenced the form of our public schools. Among those discussed are the great mobility of our population and the increased number of schoolchildren in the past two decades, new educational theories, increased government participation, building costs and new trends in architecture.

Learning for Life (National Education Association, 28 min, color). Gives overview of adult education as a new force in public schools through which people can learn to live for themselves and their communities. Explains the reasons for having adult education programs and shows how critically they are needed to meet the future challenges facing society. A brief historical treatment is given emphasizing the social changes in our country. The dividends of further education are highlighted by actual personal endorsements. Shows what such a program can offer the community, state, and nation.

Man and the Atom (National Educational Television, 59 min). Presents a report on the Atomic Energy Commission, its role, structure, and responsibilities. Highlights the revolutionary advances in medicine, science, and industry which have resulted from the development of atomic energy. Shows how the Atomic Energy Commission cooperates with private industry and scientific laboratories.

National Goals, No. 2 (New York University, 29 min). Presents a discussion of economic growth as a national goal. Reviews the causes and effects of inflation, unemployment, and rate of growth. Points out the effect of education in producing new employment patterns. Compares American and Soviet rates of expansion. Discusses problems of automation, standards of living, and individual initiative in our economic position.

Philosophies of Education: Education for National Survival (National Educational Television, 29 min). Emphasizes the fact that our national strength depends more on a high level of education achievement than any other factor. We must come to realize this, and we must be willing to spend a larger proportion of our national income on education. We must provide an educational challenge for our young people, and we must discover the best talent and see to it that this talent is developed to the highest possible degree.

The Population Problem: A Time for Decision (National Educational Television, 60 min). Analyzes United States population trends from colonial days to the present. Focuses particularly on the baby boom era, the increasing number of senior citizens, and the present and future problems to be faced in housing, rising crime, overcrowded schools, unemployment, and poverty.

Secure the Blessings (National Education Association, 25 min). Discusses the role of education in the United States as it prepares people to use the democratic method of solving problems. Shows five adults who are trying to solve their various problems in human relations objectively and says that it was in school that these individuals learned to make decisions.

Filmstrips

Challenge to American Education (New York Times, 57 fr.). Evaluates the educational process in the United States after the explosive effects of the Sputniks, compares United States and Soviet systems, and presents new vistas in shaping youth training and careers.

Directions for the Future (National Education Association, 115 fr., color). Presents backgrounds in such fields as technological development, urbanization, and population growth, which should be considered in planning instructional programs in the elementary school.

Education in a Democracy (Curriculum Films Inc., 26 fr., color). Presents the meaning of democratic education—its importance in maintaining an enlightened citizenry, its availability to all, and the opportunities it affords for an unhampered pursuit of knowledge.

Recordings

Education: The Foundation of Business (Educational Recording Service, 33⅓ rpm). Willis A. Sutton, former superintendent of schools of Atlanta, Georgia, and past president of the NEA, indicates how education affects the economic life of a community.

FIGURE CREDITS

FIGURE 1–1. (*Source:* "Schools and Scholarship in Demand," *NEA Research Bulletin,* vol. 37, no. 3, p. 76, National Education Association, Research Division, Washington, October, 1959.)

FIGURE 1–2. (*Source:* Harrison Brown and E. K. Fedorov, "Too Many People in the World?" *Saturday Review,* Feb. 17, 1962, p. 18.)

FIGURE 1–3. (*Source:* Courtesy of Honorable Edwin O. Reischauer, former American Ambassador to Japan.)

FIGURE 1–4. (*Source: Education: An Investment in People,* Chamber of Commerce of the United States, Education Department, Washington, 1955, p. 11. From Elmo Roper, *Political Activity of American Citizens.*)

FIGURE 1–5. (*Source: Manpower: Challenge of the 1960's,* U.S. Department of Labor, 1961, p. 3, and supplemental data provided by the U.S. Department of Labor.)

FIGURE 1–6. (*Source:* Courtesy of Honorable Edwin O. Reischauer, former American Ambassador to Japan.)

FIGURE 1–7. (*Source: An Act for International Development: A Program for the Decade of Development,* Department of State Publication, 7205, General Foreign Policy Series 169, Office of Public Services, Bureau of Public Affairs, 1961, p. 6.)

FIGURE 1–8. (*Source:* Data from *Education Is Good Business,* American Association of School Administrators, Washington, 1966, p. 1.)

FIGURE 1–9. (*Source: Education: An Investment in People,* Chamber of Commerce of the United States, Education Department, Washington, 1964, p. 20. Original data from U.S. Department of Labor.)

FIGURE 1–10. (*Source: Education: An Investment in People,* Chamber of Commerce of the United States, Education Department, Washington, 1964, p. 16. Original data from U.S. Bureau of the Census.)

FIGURE 1–11. (*Source: Education: An Investment in People,* Chamber of Commerce of the United States, Education Department, Washington, 1964, p. 27. Original data from U.S. Bureau of the Census.)

FIGURE 1–12. (*Source:* Reprinted from *U.S. News & World Report,* Washington. Copyright 1965 U.S. News & World Report, Inc., Nov. 15, 1965, p. 78.)

FIGURE 1–13. (*Source:* "Projections of Educational Attainment in the United States: 1960 to 1980," *Current Population Reports,* ser. P–20, no. 91, p. 2, U.S. Bureau of the Census, Jan. 12, 1959.)

FIGURE 1–14. (*Source:* Data from Sophia Cooper and Denis F. Johnson, *Labor Force Projections for 1970–1980,* Special Labor Force Report 49, U.S. Bureau of Labor Statistics, 1965, p. 134.)

ASPECTS OF PLANNING

Part I of this book is concerned with the nature and process of life planning in an increasingly complex and interdependent society, not only as this planning relates to you personally but also as it pertains to the lives of those whom you may teach. Even though emphasis is placed upon planning a career in teaching, it is to be recognized that this aspect of planning is only a phase of the total process of life planning.

As a background for planning your professional career, you noted in the preceding chapter the crucial importance of education in the preservation and progressive improvement of our American society. Since the teacher occupies a most strategic position in this process, the careful and comprehensive planning of a career in teaching is of utmost importance.

In Chapter 2 you will note basic steps and procedures that should help you in planning your career in the teaching profession. Competencies for teaching are identified, and suggestions are made for building up your strengths and overcoming any weaknesses you may have as you attempt to fulfill the many requirements for a happy and successful career. Chapter 3 is concerned with preservice programs of teacher education, with certification requirements for entering the profession, and with resources and procedures for continuing your professional growth after graduation. In Chapter 4 you will note the wide range of opportunities that a career in education provides.

The remaining parts and their respective chapters are designed to build added meaning into the content of Part I. As you proceed through the book, refer to Part I from time to time in order to maximize your effectiveness in formulating your plans.

2

PLANNING YOUR CAREER IN
THE TEACHING PROFESSION

The amount of success and happiness you experience in teaching will depend to a great extent upon how dedicated you are and how thoroughly you prepare for the job. Unfortunately, many students do not give careful consideration to their decisions to become teachers, or to the basic attributes required for successful teaching, or to the means by which they can develop into the most competent teachers possible, or to the specific types of positions for which they wish to prepare. Many prospective teachers likewise make decisions in terms of inadequate or erroneous information. Some decide to teach in secondary schools because, having been recently graduated, they are more familiar with this level. But if they investigate elementary teaching they often find themselves more interested in and more qualified to work with young children. Other students decide to teach high school largely because they feel that secondary teachers have more prestige than elementary teachers. Still others may find themselves majoring in English or social studies because they do not know of opportunities in other areas, such as speech or hearing therapy or library science, in which they might have been interested and well qualified.

Planning for teaching involves much more than being admitted to a program of teacher education, passing the required number of courses for certification, and securing a teaching position upon graduation. A career in education is a phase of life planning which involves fundamental values of life and which is integrally related to home life and citizenship. The completion of collegiate professional training is only an initial phase in the professional life of an educator and does not ensure professional success regardless of the quality of the courses completed. The full realization of values inherent in a teaching career depends largely upon the extent to which the individual attempts to realize those values.

The Nature of Career Planning

Planning is essentially a continuous life process in which action is directed by an individual's critically reasoned values and goals. It involves the constant weighing of these values and goals. The planner identifies courses of action, as well as possible alternative courses of action for reaching these goals, and selects those that seem most promising. He searches for all possible help, both in himself and in the environment, and selects those resources which seem to be most desirable. He uses these resources as he proceeds step by step toward his goal. He carefully appraises the progress he makes and prepares to meet difficulties which are likely to occur in the course of pursuing his planned objective. In brief, he has a clear idea of *what* he wants, *why* he wants it, and *how* he is to achieve it.

All plans obviously are tentative in nature. In fact, the very essence of planning is one of continuous change, modification, and adaptation. You can, therefore, expect many of the details of your master plan or blueprint to change as the years pass. But your master plan gives direction to your professional growth. The details enable you to expend energy efficiently and to gain greater realization of your goals in life.

SUGGESTED STEPS IN PLANNING YOUR CAREER IN EDUCATION

The broad outline of steps to be followed in planning your career in education is no different from that to be followed in planning for any career. Consequently, not all your efforts will be lost if, after thoroughly exploring teaching as a profession, you come to the thoughtful conclusion that this is not the lifework for which you are best suited. Your efforts will make it easier for you to plan in terms of another occupational objective.

The suggested steps in planning are not infallible, but they will at least allow you to marshal your resources in an orderly fashion and to avoid undue or worthless labor. At the same time, you may wish to deviate to some extent from the steps suggested as you work out the details of your procedure. What seems logical to one may not seem logical to another, and you should expect to revise and modify these steps as you see fit.

Importance of Values and Goals in Career Planning

An individual normally seeks to do the things that seem important to him. In other words, the things he values provide the foundation for his goals. It is important, therefore, that an individual's vocational goals be consistent with what he desires, strives for, and approves in life. For example, an outdoor career is advisable for the person who values nature above the man-made city environment; a financially fruitful lifework for the person who values most the things which money will buy.

Values are the intangible bases for behavior. They constitute the foundation for the things we cherish in life. They may be expressed in such terms as freedom, equality, individualism, dignity of man, self-respect, democracy, cooperativeness, service to mankind, the golden rule, prestige, trustworthiness, dependability, thrift, and open-mindedness. If a man values honor, for example, he establishes goals of conduct which allow expression of that value. His personal goals become manifestations of the ideals he holds to be important.

Values are acquired. They are cultural—learned through experience [235:71].

Man's behavior is governed by the values he has come to accept during the years of cumulative experiences that make up his lifetime. What he thinks, what he looks upon as "good," and what he does are controlled and restricted by the chains forged by his values: uplifting or debasing, humane or bestial—whatever his experience has made them.

Since the life experiences of no two individuals are the same, it is understandable that one man's values are not the same as another's in every detail. On the other hand, every society has certain values which characterize it, and the individuals who have grown up in that society tend to hold those values in common. In America, respect for the uniqueness and worth of the individual, freedom, equality, and shared responsibility for the common good are examples of common basic values.

Since the school is concerned with the developing, strengthening, and transmitting of values considered to be desirable in this society, it is important for you, as a future teacher, to have a clear and functional understanding of them.

Since each person develops his own values, some of his values will be more important to him than others. In fact, they will range from mild preferences to intense convictions. You can determine what an individual values most in life by observing the decisions or choices he makes. As you study others, you sense that many people never consciously examine their basic values or test the internal consistency of them. When you see this, you recognize that in planning your career you need first to think seriously about what seems to be of most importance to you in life. You then test these values for internal consistency. Since the teacher as a person is the most important single factor in the classroom, it is extremely important for him to have a clearly reasoned and consistent set of values which are in harmony with the tenets of a democratic society.

It will be relatively easy for you to identify a few of your outstanding values, such as service to mankind, and to use them as criteria for testing your career choice. It is more difficult to analyze all your values in great detail and to derive a whole pattern of criteria for testing teaching as a career. But if you construct this pattern as completely as you can, you will be much more certain of your decision.

Each occupation has its unique pattern of inherent values that may be pursued by an individual who engages in that occupation. If you discover that teaching fails to meet a significant number of the tests you have set up, you have your

FIGURE 2–1. Major steps involved in planning a career.

1	CLARIFICATION OF Values Goals Wants
2	ANALYSIS OF Career requirements
3	SELF-ANALYSIS Strengths Weaknesses
4	PLANS FOR CAREER College Intermediate Later life

warnings that conflict between your lifework and your personal values is likely and that hopes of achieving your real goals through this career are weak.

Thus far, emphasis has been placed upon the desirability of your thinking long and hard about the following questions:

1. What do I value in life?
2. Why are these my values?
3. Are these values desirable?
4. Are these values internally consistent?
5. What life goals emerge from my values?
6. Can I best realize my life goals through a career in education?

Influence of Requirements upon Planning for Teaching

Each career carries its own peculiar set of requirements for success. For example, a career in professional baseball requires physical fitness and skill. A career in the medical or the legal profession requires preparation in the things which make it a profession. A career in religion requires faith. A career as a winetaster requires a discriminating palate. We should not conclude, however, that physical fitness and skill are the only requirements for a career in professional baseball or that a discriminating palate is the sole requisite of winetasting.

Perhaps no career imposes more varied requirements on the successful worker than does teaching. Although general competency as a citizen seems to include most of the requirements for success in many careers, it is only the first requisite in teaching. Above and beyond this requirement lie the many aspects of special expertness demanded of the teacher. The basic concern at this point is to empha-size the need for you to make an analysis of the requirements which a career as a teacher imposes. Your analysis should include a stocktaking of your present qualifications. If the analysis of all your qualifications reveals certain deficiencies which you cannot or do not wish to remove, you again have warning of trouble ahead. Likewise, revelation of unusual strengths in this analysis should bear a strong implication for your future, and your plans in the field of education should involve use of these special strengths.

Your understanding of the competencies for teaching should be increased and broadened through the reading of a subsequent section of this chapter. Certifica-tion requirements prescribed by the respective states are discussed in Chapter 3. In Chapter 5 you will receive a rather clear indication of what will be required of you in order to perform adequately the many duties expected of teachers. Chap-ters 6, 14, 15, and 16 will also provide a rather comprehensive listing of unique skills, information, and artistry that a teacher needs in order to fulfill the broad functions of education in a democratic society.

Influence of Other Factors upon Planning for Teaching

Many other factors need to be taken into consideration in order to plan a career in education wisely. Various sections of this book are designed to help you in this regard. For example, you owe yourself a searching analysis of the various economic aspects that may be involved, such as salary, sick leave, retirement, and tenure

(Chapters 8 and 9). Furthermore, a career in education will give a wider range to your interests and abilities than will many other occupations. Should you be a nursery school or kindergarten teacher? Would you like teaching in the elementary school? Would you enjoy teaching in the junior high school? Would you be interested in high school teaching? Could you teach on the college level? Should you do specialized teaching, i.e., teaching the gifted, the physically handicapped, the mentally retarded, or the emotionally disturbed? For what advancement opportunities should you plan? Explore this vast range of opportunities so that your abilities and interests may best be utilized and your success and happiness in the profession may be proportionately increased (Chapter 4).

To plan your career competently, learn about the system in which you will be working—how the schools developed (Chapter 13), how they are organized (Chapter 11) and financed (Chapter 12), what changes may be expected during the time you will be associated actively with them, what crucial problems schools are faced with today (Chapter 17), and how and to what extent you may contribute to the solution of these problems. As you continue your reading and planning, you will discover other factors which should be investigated and evaluated.

Importance of Self-appraisal in Planning for Teaching

Cervantes advised, "Make it thy business to know thyself, which is the most difficult lesson in the world." His advice is certainly appropriate for anyone engaged in the process of planning a career. Understanding yourself is essential for understanding others. Two psychologists report the following about the relationship of self-understanding to the understanding of others [138:6]:

> What the teacher sees in the student, the way he feels about him, and what he derives from his dealings with him will be influenced not only by the kind of person the student is but also the kind of person the teacher is and by the kind of situation that is created when the two are together. To the extent that the student's behavior, as seen by the instructor, reflects the instructor's own perceptions and attitudes, he will be unable to understand the student unless he understands himself. Similarly, the way in which the instructor interprets or evaluates a student's attitudes or conduct will be influenced by his own values, likes, and dislikes. The greater this influence is, the more the instructor's perception of his student will be a reflection of himself rather than an objective, or unbiased, reaction. Therefore, it is essential for the instructor to take stock of his own involvement and, as far as possible, make allowance for it.

You may recall teachers who readily took offense to well-meant suggestions, teachers who were highly authoritarian in behavior and assumed that students were disobedient if they voiced any disagreements, and teachers who were defensive in their opinions and interpreted questions as forms of attack. Perhaps you will be able to recall other teachers and friends whose judgments reflected more the kinds of persons they were than of the persons being judged.

Jersild and Associates feel that understanding oneself and others involves more than an intellectual process [138:9]:

> One can master the facts, principles, and laws contained in a hundred books on

psychology and still understand neither oneself nor others. Self-understanding requires integrity rather than mere cleverness. It involves emotion. To know oneself, one must be able to feel as well as think. One must be able to recognize feelings, face them, and deal with them in constructive ways; and this is something quite different from reading or talking about them with detachment.

You may conclude, therefore, that how you view yourself—your self-image or self concept—will have an important bearing upon your success as a teacher. It is extremely important for you, as a prospective teacher, to study yourself frankly and honestly in an attempt to discover any weaknesses that might greatly handicap your future success and happiness. When these weaknesses have been identified, positive plans may be formulated in order to overcome them.

Importance of Removing Deficiencies and Capitalizing on Strengths

Career planning really becomes alive when you actively formulate steps for overcoming deficiencies and building up strengths. Your strengths are likely to persist and increase if you make intelligent use of them; your deficiencies may be due only to your present lack of preparation and experience. Therefore, extend your self-analysis to considering action which will make use of strengths and remedy weaknesses. Your academic preparation in subject fields, for example, is something which you may not yet have completed. Make a reasonably accurate estimate of both the time and the effort needed to eliminate this deficiency. In the same manner, estimate your success in removing other academic deficiencies and appraise your chances of capitalizing on your strengths.

As you continue to plan you may discover certain personal weaknesses which you are unable to remove through course work. Since teaching is so much a job of "human engineering," it is extremely important that you formulate plans for removing any deficiencies you may discover.

Further Suggested Procedures for Planning Your Career

In order to do a really effective job in planning for teaching, you will need to answer to your own satisfaction a number of questions and engage in certain activities. The following five major courses of action should help you in rounding out your plans in a concrete, workable manner.

Put your plans on paper. Many people have found that the act of writing out their plans is in itself of great help to them. The necessary labor involved in selecting and weaving in the various ideas causes planners to be more critical and objective. This procedure—often called "writing the planning paper"—has been used in colleges and universities for a number of years with considerable evidence of worthwhile results.

Many students experience difficulty in getting started in the writing of their plans. This is understandable in view of the fact that planning is, or at least should be, the most highly individual task that you will undertake. By virtue of differences in backgrounds, values absorbed, and goals desired, you differ from every other student. Unfortunately, our school system and our social setting are such that the average student has had little encouragement to come to grips with himself. Furthermore, most students seem to experience difficulty in putting down in black and white the things which they have always thought about.

There is no specific method of approach to prescribe for *all* students faced with the planning of a life career. Begin your planning in any manner which will bring the greatest benefit. Some students, for example, start by listing their strong points; others list their weaknesses, e.g., the things over which they worry. Some choose to list the major decisions with which they are or will be faced and to indicate the many aspects of their present and future life that may be affected by these decisions. Other students choose to study critically those previous experiences that have caused them to be the way they are today. In the latter approach, the student does not attempt to write an autobiography but rather attempts to isolate those aspects of his background that he believes have a bearing upon his problem of planning a lifework.

It would seem that you should first indicate all the things that you value in life, i.e., those things which are central to your beliefs and behavior. Directly or indirectly, values are involved in every decision you make, now and in the future; consequently, give thoughtful consideration to values. You may find it helpful to group them under major headings such as the following, which are merely suggestive. You may also use an objective instrument such as the Allport-Vernon Scale of Values to help clarify your beliefs further.

Intellectual values—such as scholarship, truth, knowledge, opportunities for self-expression, high standards of morals and ethics, clear and logical thinking

Physical and personal values—such as health and vitality, attractiveness, pleasing personality, and successful marriage and family life

Occupational values—such as service to mankind, intellectual stimulation, prestige, contacts with others, favorable working conditions, a reasonable degree of financial security, industriousness, self-sufficiency, opportunities for advancement, opportunities for creativeness, and opportunities for combining your occupation harmoniously with family life

Adjustment values—such as sense of personal worth, respect for human personality, tolerance, self-respect, independence, friendship, sense of humor, happiness, cooperativeness, and opportunities for choice and self-direction

Social values—such as social approval, stability, honesty, generosity, loyalty, kindness, fairness, justice, and impartiality

Aesthetic values—such as beauty, attractiveness of surroundings, and appreciation of cultural influences

Recreational values—such as ample time to devote to recreational activities, freedom to participate in a wide variety of activities, and stimulation to develop interests

In addition to listing these values, check to see whether they are consistent with each other, and analyze each critically to determine why you hold it, as well as whether it is desirable to continue to hold it. In order to gain an adequate understanding of the origin of these values, dip critically into your background. Early childhood experiences are much more important than one is inclined to suspect, so far as the formation of his values is concerned.

Any analysis of your values will automatically necessitate a consideration of goals. The balance sheet that you construct of your values and goals should assist you greatly in being objective and facile in the other aspects of your planning.

Talk to others about your background, values, and goals. You doubtless have discussed your life plans at length with your parents, your public school teachers, your school friends, and various older adults in your home community; and you will probably want to consult these people again, especially your parents, as you continue with your planning.

In view of the fact that college provides a superb opportunity for you to extend greatly your contacts, avail yourself of this resource for planning. In your beginning course in education you will contact many other students interested in the same career possibilities that you are. Both in and out of class you will have the opportunity to share your values, goals, and plans and to think them through critically. Participating in activities such as the Student National Education Association organization provides additional opportunities for engaging in intelligent, meaningful, and fruitful discussions. Seek out your college instructors as well as specialists in other fields, from whom you may receive valuable aid. In short, avail yourself of every possible opportunity to analyze and appraise your background, values, and goals. It is primarily through this process that your thinking is deepened and clarified, your horizons are extended, and your planning is directed. Furthermore, the act of engaging in these experiences should enable you to gain facility in helping the pupils whom you may teach to do likewise.

Some students experience difficulty in initiating the type of activities suggested above. If you are one of these, you may find it helpful to submit a list of your

FIGURE 2–2. Willingness of experienced teachers in 1965–1966 to teach again if given the chance to start over. Since only 9.1 per cent felt that they probably or certainly would not choose teaching, can it be concluded that teachers find a fairly high degree of satisfaction in their work? If the same question were submitted to those in other professions, what results would you anticipate? (*Source:* National Education Association.)

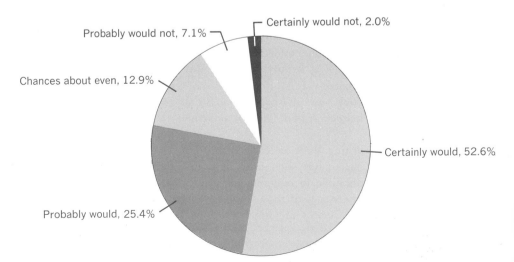

values and goals, or a self-rating, to someone for his opinion of it. Usually these activities produce fruitful discussions if they are approached in a sincere, honest, positive manner. Through this technique you extend the number of eyes through which you see yourself.

Appraise your general abilities as a prospective teacher. In order to use your time and energy most effectively in college as well as in later life, study how you compare now with what you want to be in the future. This kind of comparison gives direction to your efforts.

You will be able to appraise many of your abilities in terms of the requirements for success in teaching. For example, you can appraise your ability to master subject matter. Obviously, you must succeed academically in completing the college requirements. Your college academic record will bear some positive relation to success in teaching; i.e., the very poorly prepared teacher will probably not experience the success of one who has an excellent academic preparation. Colleges recognize this probability by requiring students to have specified minimum grade-point averages before they recommend a graduating student for teacher certification.

Perhaps one of the most effective ways of analyzing your abilities for teaching is to use various checklists or self-rating scales that have been prepared. One of these scales is located in the Resource Section for Part I of this book. As you check yourself on it, keep in mind that no rating of this kind should be considered final and that the rating represents only your present abilities. You should be able to do much to improve your ratings for teaching fitness through carefully planned future experiences.

After you have rated yourself, ask your adviser or some other competent person who knows you well to rate you on this same scale. Compare your ratings and discuss especially those ratings that differ greatly. Ask your adviser or friend to help formulate plans whereby you may remove the weaknesses and increase the strengths that you have for teaching.

Obtain objective data on your specific abilities. In using the preceding checklist you perhaps felt the need for objective data to support some of the relatively subjective judgments you made, especially if the appraisal of someone else differed appreciably from your own rating. You should be able to locate considerable objective data to help you appraise yourself and plan your future.

Data on your physical health may be obtained from your college health clinic or your family physician. Your speech department or clinic can give you objective data concerning your speech and hearing. A good personality test administered and interpreted by a clinician can supply emotional stability and personal adjustment data.

Practically every college and university today requires entering students to take a battery of tests. You may never have learned the results of these tests. For the purposes of planning a career, go to the proper agency in your school and ask for a copy of the results. Ordinarily the registrar's office, the guidance department, or some other agency administering the entrance tests will be glad to help you get these results. You are almost certain to find results on intelligence and English ability tests. Intelligence tests generally sample skill in the use of language symbols, nonlanguage abilities, apperceptive processes, spatial relationships, and logical and mathematical aspects of reasoning. The English tests usually cover at least three aspects of reading: vocabulary, speed of reading, and level of comprehension. If, for example, your English scores are appreciably lower than your intelligence test scores, you may conclude that you are not reading at your maximum capacity. In this case seek assistance and, if possible, plan to visit a reading clinic for consultation and advice.

More and more colleges are encouraging students to take some type of occupational-preference or interest test. Such tests attempt to indicate fields in which a particular person would be likely to experience happiness and success. Although the results of these tests are not conclusive, they do indicate data worthy of consideration.

Many students pursuing a specialized course in college tend to neglect their personal development along broad cultural lines. Educators generally agree that a teacher should have a well-rounded background in addition to the other requirements for teaching. Therefore, avail yourself of some kind of test that will indicate your achievement in each of the broad fields of knowledge. Plan to strengthen, either through course work or on your own, your understanding of areas in which you appear especially weak. Furthermore, gain evidence of the extent to which you are keeping abreast of the current happenings in each of these areas.

Teachers should be especially skilled in human relationships. Therefore, make good use of any instrument that may provide data for you in this regard. Your success in planning will be determined to a large degree by the extent to which you are able to draw logical conclusions from information at your disposal.

You may think of other kinds of test data that you will need in developing your plans. If your college does not provide the various tests for which you find a need, you can apply at the nearest testing agency. The cost is comparatively low, and the service usually includes a profile as well as an interpretation of the scores.

Remember that objective test data have limitations and these limitations are to be kept in mind at all times. In order to ensure profitable use of the information, a careful evaluation by a qualified person of the purpose and the results of each test is an essential part of any testing program. You may wish to develop a graphic picture of the information obtained in order to gain more value from it. Construct a profile chart or psychograph of all your test results. The psychograph would also help your adviser gain a better picture of you.

In the specific types of activities listed, you have by no means exhausted the possibilities through which you might approach your self-appraisal and overall problem of planning. You probably will discover additional activities which will be of equal or greater benefit to you in your planning.

Formulate your plans for the future. Planning for the future involves preparing for three rather clearly defined periods: the years in which you are still in college, the first five or ten years after graduation during which time you are becoming adjusted to your life's work, and your later life which extends into old age.

If you are a senior or graduate student, it is obvious that the amount of planning which you can do while still in college is fairly limited. You are faced more immediately with the need for detailed plans for the second period, the first five or ten years after graduation.

The material that follows is roughly divided into these three periods, and a few suggestions are given that may be of help to you.

Years in which you are in college. College is an unusual environment in which you are able to take advantage of many learning situations that may not present themselves in your local surroundings. For this reason your plans during the college years may differ significantly from other plans you may make.

If you feel, for example, that you need to improve your ability to work cooperatively and harmoniously with others, become an active member in some campus activities. You may be interested in opportunities to assume positions of leadership and responsibility; to develop certain traits such as sincerity, politeness, and understanding; to subscribe to professional magazines; and to participate in various discussion groups to develop the characteristics of a mature thinker. There are also many opportunities on campus and in the community that you can utilize to acquire a broad cultural education.

Other plans may include attempts to develop skills and insights for working with children. These include observing and participating in as many teaching situations as possible, taking part in camp and club activities with children, and acting as playground director or camp counselor during the summer.

Years immediately after college. You will want to consider the problem of finding a position where you are most likely to be successful. A number of changes may be necessary before you find the environment and the job in education where you want to spend the rest of your life. As you will note in the latter part of this chapter as well as in Chapter 3, certification requirements are increasing so rapidly that you should plan to get a master's degree in the relatively near future.

Give detailed consideration to plans for marriage, for locating and financing a home, for purchasing a car, for bringing up a family, and for securing the necessities of life. Since increasing numbers of married women are working, consider this possibility in your plans. Under such circumstances the lives of both the husband and the wife are affected—the wife, particularly, after the arrival of children. Such factors should be included in your planning.

Your social position in your community is another important aspect of your life. Consider becoming a member of civic and professional organizations as well as participating in other kinds of services within your community.

Prospective periods of summer employment provide many opportunities for systematic and constructive planning. Capitalize on the opportunities to promote continuous intellectual growth. Your recreational interests tend to change as you become older; hence, you will be less able to take part in activities that necessitate much physical energy. This should be considered in your planning for now and for later life.

Make plans whereby you can provide for your future financial security and for that of your dependents, through insurance, retirement benefits, etc. You cannot foretell when misfortune will come to your family.

Years in later life. There is much merit in looking far into the future and doing some "intelligent dreaming." Many people find added enjoyment, happiness, and security during their later years of life as a result of long-range planning.

It is largely during this later period that your family begins to leave home and seek employment elsewhere and that you often face much loneliness. A wide variety of cultural and recreational interests, a concern with civic and professional activities, a wise use of the increased time at your disposal, and an enlarged circle of friends can do much to promote wholesome adjustment at this time. It is important that you plan for this now.

If your plans are comprehensive and carefully constructed, you will derive much satisfaction from a job well done. In addition, your outline should serve as a useful guide in the future and should result in the elimination of much frustration which results from lack of foresight.

COMPETENCIES FOR TEACHING

As a prospective teacher you are very much concerned with the competencies essential to success in teaching. Having identified these competencies, you also are concerned with the ways in which you can become the most competent teacher possible.

In recalling the many teachers you have had, select those who stand out as having been especially good and analyze their characteristics carefully. As you study each of these teachers, write down the reason or reasons why you consider them outstanding. Have your friends engage in the same kind of activity. Compare and contrast your list with theirs.

In making this analysis you will probably note considerable difference in the personalities of the teachers. Some may have been quiet, gentle, and warm. Others may have been outgoing and aggressive. Whatever their differences, you may safely conclude that there is no *one* personality which teachers must have in order to assure success. Further study also may reveal that because of variations in situations, there is no *one* method of teaching that will ensure success. Each of your outstanding teachers probably had a distinct personality, as well as a distinct style of teaching.

The differences that you find in the characteristics of good teachers should not alarm you too much. Nor should you be discouraged if educators tell you frankly that they are not absolutely certain of the competencies that will ensure anyone's success in teaching. It is true that they know something about the abilities required, but they hesitate to say with complete conviction that a particular individual will be a very successful teacher and that another will be unsuccessful.

One reason why it is difficult to predict teaching success is that a teacher deals with the most complex thing in the world—the human being. A successful teacher must be able to affect people in such ways that desirable changes occur in behavior. He must be able to encourage the individual to think and to make intelligent decisions; he must guide his behavior with increasing effectiveness toward constructive, democratic ends. The complexity of the interaction of the teacher with his pupils is so great that superior teaching assumes the characteristics of an art which cannot be fully analyzed. Horace Mann, long ago, recognized this fact

What teacher competencies
will be required in order to
fully develop this child's abilities for living effectively and
constructively in our society?
*(Photograph by Carl Purcell,
National Education Association.)*

when he wrote in 1853, in his *First Annual Report*, the following: "Teaching is the most difficult of all arts and the profoundest of all sciences. In its absolute perfection it would involve a complete knowledge of the whole being to be taught, and of the precise manner in which every possible application would affect it."

In planning a career in education, examine searchingly the competencies which generally are conducive to success in teaching. As you examine each one, bear in mind that it is integrally related to all the others. The analysis you make should serve as a background from which you will be able to formulate specific and long-range plans for meeting these requirements to the highest degree possible. Obviously the thoroughness of the plans you make will be dependent upon the comprehensiveness and discernment with which you study these requirements.

Identifying the Competencies for Teaching

Hundreds of studies have been made of the personal and professional characteristics of teachers in an attempt to establish which traits are the most desirable for teachers to possess and which are definite handicaps. We shall examine the results of some of these studies. It may also be profitable for you to understand several techniques that have been used to collect the information. Study these results carefully, analyze yourself in terms of them, and then establish specific and detailed plans for meeting as many of these requirements as possible while you are in college. You will be unable to meet all of them, since some require a lifetime of experience, study, and effort.

Studying what teachers do. From an historical standpoint, especially, you should be familiar with the very exhaustive and comprehensive study conducted by Charters and Waples in 1929 [42:18] in an effort to determine desirable qualifications for teaching. They approached the problem by studying what teachers did. After tabulating the duties performed by teachers, they carefully studied the skills, abilities, and knowledges required in order to perform these duties successfully. They listed the following twenty-five traits needed by teachers: adaptability, attractive personal appearance, breadth of interest, carefulness, considerativeness, cooperation, dependability, enthusiasm, fluency, forcefulness, good judgment, health, honesty, industry, leadership, magnetism, neatness, open-mindedness, originality, progressiveness, promptness, refinement, scholarship, self-control, and thrift. The meaning of each of these traits was carefully defined by the authors.

In 1960, Ryans published the results of an extensive and rigorous scientific analysis of teacher characteristics. This study was sponsored by the American Council on Education [224:1–416]. As an initial step in the study, teacher supervisors, college teachers, school principals, teachers, student teachers, and students in education methods courses were asked to make analytical reports on teacher behavior in specific situations which might make a difference between success and failure in teaching. These reports served as a basis for the construction of a "critical incidence" blank upon which significant behavior relative to teaching might be recorded. The more than 500 critical incidents submitted by the participants in the study were reduced to the following list of generalized behaviors [224:82]:

Generalized Descriptions of Critical Behaviors of Teachers

Effective behaviors	Ineffective behaviors
1. Alert, appears enthusiastic.	1. Is apathetic, dull, appears bored.
2. Appears interested in pupils and classroom activities.	2. Appears uninterested in pupils and classroom activities.
3. Cheerful, optimistic.	3. Is depressed, pessimistic; appears unhappy.
4. Self-controlled, not easily upset.	4. Loses temper, is easily upset.
5. Likes fun, has a sense of humor.	5. Is overly serious, too occupied for humor.
6. Recognizes and admits own mistakes.	6. Is unaware of, or fails to admit, own mistakes.
7. Is fair, impartial, and objective in treatment of pupils.	7. Is unfair or partial in dealing with pupils.
8. Is patient.	8. Is impatient.
9. Shows understanding and sympathy in working with pupils.	9. Is short with pupils, uses sarcastic remarks, or in other ways shows lack of sympathy with pupils.
10. Is friendly and courteous in relations with pupils.	10. Is aloof and removed in relations with pupils.
11. Helps pupils with personal as well as educational problems.	11. Seems unaware of pupils' personal needs and problems.
12. Commends effort and gives praise for work well done.	12. Does not commend pupils, is disapproving, hypercritical.
13. Accepts pupils' efforts as sincere.	13. Is suspicious of pupil motives.
14. Anticipates reactions of others in social situations.	14. Does not anticipate reactions of others in social situations.

15. Encourages pupils to try to do their best.	15. Makes no effort to encourage pupils to try to do their best.
16. Classroom procedure is planned and well organized.	16. Procedure is without plan, disorganized.
17. Classroom procedure is flexible within over-all plan.	17. Shows extreme rigidity of procedure, inability to depart from plan.
18. Anticipates individual needs.	18. Fails to provide for individual differences and needs of pupils.
19. Stimulates pupils through interesting and original materials and techniques.	19. Uninteresting materials and teaching techniques used.
20. Conducts clear, practical demonstrations and explanations.	20. Demonstrations and explanations are not clear and are poorly conducted.
21. Is clear and thorough in giving directions.	21. Directions are incomplete, vague.
22. Encourages pupils to work through their own problems and evaluate their accomplishments.	22. Fails to give pupils opportunity to work out own problems or evaluate their own work.
23. Disciplines in quiet, dignified, and positive manner.	23. Reprimands at length, ridicules, resorts to cruel or meaningless forms of correction.
24. Gives help willingly.	24. Fails to give help or gives it grudgingly.
25. Foresees and attempts to resolve potential difficulties.	25. Is unable to foresee and resolve potential difficulties.

Admittedly some value or subjective judgments were involved in the formulation of these descriptive statements; the list does tend to objectify the types of behavior that make a difference in the success or failure of teachers.

Ryans points out that there is an increasing amount of evidence that certain characteristics may contribute to the model of the teacher. Data growing out of various research in which quite different approaches and criteria have been used suggest the following list of generalizations regarding the characteristics of outstanding teachers [224:366]:

> Superior intellectual abilities, above-average school achievement, good emotional adjustment, attitudes favorable to pupils, enjoyment of pupil relationships, generosity in the appraisal of the behavior and motives of other persons, strong interests in reading and literary matters, interest in music and painting, participation in social and community affairs, early experiences in caring for children and teaching (such as reading to children and taking a class for the teacher), history of teaching in family, family support of teaching as a vocation, and strong social service interests.

Questioning pupils. Another technique that has been used extensively is that of questioning pupils regarding the qualities of teachers they admire. It has been found that boys and girls who have spent considerable time with a teacher are able to pass rather valid judgments regarding his competence. Talk with some boys and girls after the first week of a school term and see how well they have the teacher "sized up."

Witty [288:386] analyzed approximately 12,000 letters on "The Teacher Who Has Helped Me Most" that were submitted by pupils from grades 2 to 12 all over the nation. The teacher traits mentioned most frequently by the pupils, in the order of their frequency, were the following: (1) cooperativeness, democratic attitude, (2) and (3) kindliness and consideration for the individual, patience, (4) wide variety of interests, (5) an attractive general appearance and pleasing manner, (6) fairness and impartiality, (7) sense of humor, (8) good disposition and consistent behavior, (9) interest in pupil's problems, (10) flexibility, (11) use of recognition and praise, (12) unusual proficiency in teaching a particular subject.

Witty summarized his findings by stating that "these boys and girls appear to be grateful to the school in proportion to the degree that it offers security, individual success, shared experience, and opportunities for personal and social adjustments. And these are precisely the factors which promote good learning."

Witty conducted three additional nationwide contests in an attempt to verify and expand the findings gained from the first contest. He found that the twelve traits mentioned previously were cited consistently, although their order varied from year to year [287:312].

Analyzing biographies of outstanding teachers. Another method of gaining understanding of competencies for teaching is to read carefully some of the many biographies as well as fiction books that have been written on outstanding teachers. You may remember, for instance, the heartwarming story of Hilton's *Goodbye, Mr. Chips.* You may find biographies to be especially helpful in gaining an understanding of the artistic qualities that characterize outstanding teaching as well as the human factors that have rich meaning in the lives of boys and girls. Discussion of these and other books may prove profitable. What seemed to be the life values of the teachers mentioned? What did they consider the job of the teacher to be? How were they able to stimulate the interest of boys and girls and to guide their growth toward desirable ends?

Educators' statements of competencies. Educators singly and in groups have developed lists of competencies for teaching, based upon their experiences as teachers and their observations of, and work with, other teachers. These lists often take the form of rating scales used in evaluating the work of teachers on the job and of students engaged in their student teaching. You may wish to see the scale on which your success in student teaching will be appraised and to study carefully the competencies involved. By having a clear understanding of these competencies you will be able to plan specific experiences that you should gain prior to your student teaching.

Combs [45:373] maintains that an effective teacher is "a unique human being who has learned to use his self effectively and efficiently for carrying out his own and society's purposes." In his opinion, teaching is a highly personal matter for which it is not possible to derive a common set of competencies [45:372]. Rather, he feels that teachers should be studied in terms of the kinds of beliefs, understandings, values, and concepts that make up the perceptual organization of good teachers. He points out that we have the following sources of information to draw upon for defining the probable dimensions of good teaching in perceptual terms [45:374]:

1. Perceptual psychology theory, especially that having to do with the nature of the self and fully functioning behavior

2. Research on the perceptions of good practitioners in other helping professions
3. The research already existing in our profession
4. The experiences accumulated by thousands of teachers engaged in day to day "action research" in the classroom

Drawing upon these four sources it would appear that a good teacher is characterized by typical perceptual organizations in six general areas:

A. His knowledge of his subject
B. His frame of reference for approaching his problems
C. His perceptions of others
D. His perceptions of self
E. His perceptions of the purpose and process of learning
F. His perceptions of appropriate methods

For each of the six major headings listed above, Combs [45:374–375, 377, 399] indicates a series of hypotheses concerning the teacher's characteristic perceptual organization. You may wish to refer to his book titled *The Professional Education of Teachers: A Perceptual View to Teacher Preparation* in which he develops his ideas at considerable length.

Some Implications for Your Planning

As you study various lists of competencies, you may be amazed at the number of requirements for teaching. The school of today requires far more of teachers than did the school of yesterday. This fact is understandable when you consider the expanding function of the school in American life. In earlier days the school in this country was limited primarily to teaching boys and girls the fundamental skills of reading, writing, and arithmetic. The home, the church, and the community provided most of the other learnings essential for effective citizenship. Life was relatively simple. Today, however, life is much more complex. This is due especially to the tremendous technological advancements that have been made. Great changes have also taken place in our social, economic, and political lives. The function of the school must change and expand in order to meet the needs of youth today and tomorrow. These changes give rise to new and broader requirements for teachers.

The teacher of today understands the cultural context in which all education takes place. He sees clearly the significance of industrialization, urbanization, corporativeness, economic planning, cultural lags, cultural fragmentation, the growth of a scientific attitude toward problems, and other outstanding characteristics of the contemporary American scene as they affect the lives of the people. He has the ability to understand modern problems in terms of historical conditions, to recognize the recurrent nature of many educational concerns, to use the resources of the past when faced with the problems of the present, and thus to discriminate between worthy traditional solutions and those solutions which are no longer pertinent. He understands the process whereby values are inculcated for the guidance of our conduct and judgments. He demonstrates, through his attitudes, skills, and habits, a basic understanding of democracy as a way of perpetuating the values of our culture, as a process by which each may develop his best self, as a method for solving problems, and as a process of disciplining himself for the betterment of our common lives. He possesses a critical understanding of the function of communities as agencies directing human growth and of the school as one agency by which society seeks to provide for its continued expansion as well as for the development of the individual. He sees the school as an institution which is charged with a major responsibility in determining the direction and character of this growth. He recognizes that the manner in which he goes about the teaching of boys and girls is determined by what he conceives to be the real function of education.

Educational research, during the past several years, has revealed new insights regarding human behavior and the learning process. The teacher of today needs an extensive understanding of the nature of individual development in all its various aspects so that he may recognize and anticipate the increasing needs of the student and provide the conditions which will promote his maximum growth. He is aware of the ways in which people are alike and of the ways in which they differ. He understands how the individual may become more like others and yet remain unique as he attains maturity. He comprehends thoroughly the nature of human learning, both in terms of the learner's habits, attitudes, skills, and abilities and in terms of his own role as an effective guide in the learning process. It is essential, furthermore, for him to possess expert skill in guiding the education of others toward desirable ends.

Some Teacher-competency Self-appraisal Forms

You may find some forms specifically designed for self-appraisal to be helpful to you. For your convenience, one of these forms, which is concerned with the teacher's personality, has been included in the Resource Section for Part I. Obtain other forms from your teacher-placement office to use in self-appraisal.

As you can detect from your study of competencies thus far, it is important for you to make a careful study of your personality in order to discover your strengths for teaching as well as any qualities that may handicap your success. Frequently, one undesirable personality trait may overshadow many desirable ones. Use other students, especially those preparing for teaching, as a basis for comparison in rating yourself on the various items in the teacher's personality checklist.

If, after you have finished rating yourself on the checklist, you find that you rank high on some items, do not assume that room for growth is impossible. Everyone can improve himself with respect to any item listed. For example, regardless of how beautiful a woman is, she usually seeks to improve her personal appearance. The schools would be fortunate, indeed, if teachers would attempt to improve themselves professionally to the same degree that women seek to enhance their personal appearance.

It is very important for you to cultivate a personality pattern that will exert a healthy and desirable effect upon your pupils. Remember that what you are as a person is by far the most potent subject matter that will be in your classroom. To paraphrase Emerson, "I cannot hear what you *say*, when what you are thunders so loud!" Furthermore, children are highly imitative, and it is through imitation especially that behavior patterns are established.

There has been some recent significant research completed on types of teacher personalities and their effects upon various groups of children [128:1–82]. Heil and his associates developed and applied what is called a "Manifold Interest Schedule" to over fifty public school teachers of grades 4, 5, and 6 and measured the progress of their children against the personality types of teachers identified by the schedule. It was found that children with a teacher having one type of personality made 50 per cent more academic progress than did children with a teacher having a decidedly different personality.

Another instrument called the "Children's Feeling Test," developed by Professor Heil and his associates, made it possible to identify four categories of children's personalities. One type of teacher appeared to have a deleterious effect upon children of the least well-adjusted category, whereas another type had a definitely beneficial effect upon such children.

As a result of this study, Heil and his associates concluded that the teacher's type of personality appears to have much effect on the progress of his pupils. Furthermore, it appears that the clear overriding factor in determining children's academic achievement is a positive and definite personality [128:66–68].

PERSONAL GROWTH TOWARD TEACHING

Much of your personal growth toward effective teaching is concerned with intangibles that are not learned in formal ways. In fact, you may get little direct help in this regard from all the formal courses you take in your preparation for teaching. You do have available in your college environment, however, many resources that you may use. The amount of growth you make will depend largely upon you. Of course, your professors, counselors, and close friends may be able to help you identify some of your strengths and weaknesses for teaching and to suggest appropriate resources.

Growth in Poise and Security

Teachers who are at ease in dress and manner and whose voice and speech are pleasing to others tend to be more effective in the classroom than those who are lacking in these qualities. Superintendents frequently remark that young people often lose the jobs they seek, almost before they speak a word, because of their untidy or inappropriate dress. Personnel managers in business and industry report a high incidence of people failing to be employed because of careless habits affecting personal appearance. Untidiness is related more to slovenly habits than to intellectual excellence.

New teachers are often tempted to wear out their leftover campus clothes during their first year of work. This may be desirable if your clothes are those that give you a sense of well-being and appropriateness. On the whole, however, campus fashions are not the most appropriate. You may need the aid of more mature dress to help you take your place as a person responsible for boys and girls. If you watch the purchases you make as you prepare for the professional responsibilities of student teaching, the transition to dressing for your first job will be easy.

The community you choose for your first teaching position will have certain customs in dress which you as a wise beginner will want to follow. Do not be unduly impressed by the more staid members of the group, but adopt the style which seems applicable to those of your age in your work. You have a right to be an individual, but you also have a responsibility to the group you have chosen to work with.

Good manners also are especially important for teachers. They smooth the way for pleasant relationships with others and provide examples for children to follow. To have good manners you must constantly think of yourself in the other person's place, and act accordingly. High on the list of professional courtesies are these:

1. Be considerate of students and of those with whom you work.
2. Make students feel at ease with you, and give them your complete attention.
3. Learn to be a good listener.
4. Avoid talking about yourself too much.
5. Keep confidential information to yourself.
6. Generally avoid controversial issues in professional discussions which may become bitter and personal.
7. Do your best to pour oil on troubled waters.
8. Never criticize your associates; such action creates problems and seldom solves a single one.

Although a pleasing appearance and genteel manners may help to create a good impression, your manner of speaking may utterly ruin that impression. How do you react when you hear someone speak with a distinctive accent or with mannerisms which make it difficult for you to understand?

Although most people have acceptable speech, almost everyone can improve his speech if he knows his own special needs. There is the true story of a young first-grade teacher who complained to her principal, "I can't underthand why

Teachers normally speak several thousands of words each day. How pleasant and attractive will they be? Is your speech a good index of the kind of person you are? Have you listened carefully to your voice and speech patterns? Is there any room for improvement? (*Photograph by Carl Purcell, National Education Association.*)

tho many of my children lithp." Children are great and often unconscious imitators. It is doubly important, then, for adults to perfect their speech—not only to improve themselves but also to serve as an adequate model for children.

As a prospective teacher you should make arrangements with a speech therapist for a voice and speech test. With the expert's help, you can make a careful study of the results. A trained worker will be able to help you with suggestions about pronunciation, tone quality, pitch, speed, and enunciation. There are prescribed remedial measures to assist you in each of these areas.

If professional help is not available, try making a voice tape. You will hear your voice approximately as others hear it. Certain problems may be obvious at once. How do you like your voice? Is your voice too high or too low to be pleasant? Are your words monotonous? Are there nervous pauses and repetitions? Do you speak too fast or too slowly to be distinctly understood? Do you hesitate on the pronunciation of words? Do you speak with expression appropriate to the speech? Are you sure of the correctness of your grammar? The checklist on voice and speech that appears in the Resource Section for Part I may help you appraise yourself systematically.

Making Decisions

A teacher is forced to make many decisions each day. These decisions have an effect upon the lives of his pupils, his colleagues, his parents, and other community members, as well as upon his personal and professional life.

During your college career you have many opportunities to improve your skill in decision making. It is a skill to which conscious effort should be directed. For example, how well do you use your time and energies toward personal and future professional fulfillment?

You cannot do everything. There are numerous pleasures to be had in life, but life may become so crowded with their pursuit that there is no energy left with which to do the more important things. A friend once remarked, "Saying that you are too busy is not an original excuse. It merely means that you are not adult enough to make wise choices."

Many decisions you make are simply a matter of picking the things which are of greatest interest and importance at the moment. Other decisions involve the making of value judgments, the careful selection of activities in the light of their real worth.

Value judgments and decision making are simplified for those whose ideals and standards point the direction that should be taken. For most people such standards spring from a belief in the goodness and power of God, a belief which they have verified in their experience with one another. Some young people have grown up firmly grounded in religious conviction, equipped to solve problems and to stand for the good. Their choices are made in the light of principles of worthy behavior.

Decisions are easier, too, for the person who has selected his specific goals. If you do not want to be carried hither and yon by every fancy, it is important to know where you are going and what kind of person you want to be.

Some students refuse to believe that there are basic laws for good that must be obeyed. Their decisions are made in the light of their own desires, and they are constantly puzzled by the need to make decisions. They rationalize their own undesirable behavior and excuse their own shortcomings. To be thus without resources to make wise decisions can be frightening in today's disturbed world.

Working with People

In most of the pursuits of life, people sooner or later must learn to work with others. Perhaps no other profession requires more skill in working with others than does teaching.

Perhaps the first prerequisite in learning to work effectively with others is to understand yourself. The more you know about yourself, the more you can know about others. Your fears, successes, and motives are probably shared by the vast majority of people.

Success in understanding and accepting others rests on your interest in them. Those who are interesting to you are seldom your enemies. Some young people show pseudo concern with others merely to reflect their own personalities. This is all too obvious to everyone. Real interest manifests itself in other ways—in sincere attempts to help, in recognition of merit, in willingness to listen, and in a desire to be with and to work with others.

The college campus should serve as your laboratory, in which you can study and gain greater skill in working with people—another important competence in successful teaching. Leadership experiences can be gained from participation in student government, sports, school publications, dramatics, musical activities, social and religious clubs, Student National Education Association activities, etc. School employment officials usually express much interest in the extent of participation in such activities since this tends to indicate competence in working effectively with others.

Participating in Group Work

Much of a teacher's life involves group work with colleagues, parents, and other community members. Likewise, the teacher is concerned with helping his pupils gain skill in effective group work. In order to be truly successful in his work, therefore, a teacher must have a high degree of skill in group work.

While you are in college you have many opportunities to work with others. Membership in clubs, fraternities or sororities, church and welfare organizations, sports groups, and professional societies offers a chance for you to strengthen your skills of cooperation that lead to habits of good group membership and leadership.

A good group member has several outstanding characteristics. First, he is a cooperating individual, freely contributing his ideas for group consideration and genuinely evaluating the ideas of others. He treats all suggestions put forth as worthy of attention. He does not monopolize the conversation. He tries to make his special experience count for as much as possible. He gives supporting data when he can. He thinks in terms of group purposes and plans, placing the collec-

Teaching requires a high degree of skill in working with others—colleagues, pupils, parents, and other community members. While you are in college are you taking advantage of the many opportunities afforded to develop this skill? (*Photograph by Joe Di Dio, National Education Association.*)

tive welfare above his personal gains and satisfactions. He tends to avoid "either-or" situations or arguments. He selects what seem to be the good ideas advanced by others and helps incorporate them into the general thinking. He thoroughly and promptly fulfills the responsibilities delegated to him. He does not become discouraged in the initial stages. He realizes that group discussion progresses slowly at first but is often productive in the long run. He trusts group thinking and action, realizing that each individual is superior to the rest in some respects and that the thinking of the collective body is usually clearer and more productive than that of a single member.

In order to increase your effectiveness as a group participant you may find it helpful to check yourself in regard to some questions titled "Am I a Good Group Participant?" which appear in the Resource Section for Part I.

One application of the principles of group participation can be a class discussion of some of the topics or problems found at the end of each chapter in this book. In order to get started, your instructor may temporarily assume leadership in helping your group select its subjects. After this initial step, he may wish to turn over his role to members of the group as quickly as possible so that they may gain leadership experience.

All members of the group should help decide how the group will attack the topic. Such projects as reading in the library, interviewing, bringing resource people to the classroom, writing reports, viewing films, having panel discussions, and the like may be involved. It may seem desirable for small groups to work on certain aspects of the problem and to report their findings to the entire group. The techniques of approaching problems are many, and you, as a prospective teacher, will want to become skilled in all of them.

Serving as a Group Leader

There is a significant difference between being a group participant and serving as discussion group leader. Since the latter more nearly approximates the role you will play as a teacher, gain as much leadership skill as possible while in college in your course work and cocurricular activities. As a group leader keep in mind the following:

1. Help the group define the problem clearly—its nature and scope or delimitations.
2. Encourage all participants to share their thinking, information, and experience.
3. Provide opportunity for all points of view to be expressed.
4. Keep the discussion directed to the problem.
5. Help group members to clarify their thinking and to summarize their progress.
6. Utilize all resources represented in the experience of group members.
7. Strive to develop a cohesive and productive group.
8. Avoid trying to save time by telling the group the right answer.

Keep in mind that the leader is not a group instructor; he is a guide trying to arrange conditions so that each member will do creative thinking. Group discussion is not a debating society. While disagreements are to be expected, the task of the group is to find more truth than each member brings to any group meeting. Help the group, therefore, to view the task as a cooperative quest in which thinking is creative rather than combative.

Using Time Most Effectively

Your development as a good teacher will be affected by the extent to which you become increasingly skilled in the wise use of your time. As Shakespeare advised, "Let every man be master of his time. . . ."

On an average, you have about eight hours each day which you spend in other ways than in going to classes, studying, sleeping, eating, and attending to personal grooming. The kinds of things you can do with this portion of time are numerous, and your opportunities for promoting your personal growth toward teaching are great.

As a college student you undoubtedly recognize the wisdom of planning your personal time, and you understand desirable procedures that may be used. For this reason the only points to be made are that the problem of using time effectively is ever present, that you need to check periodically to see whether or not you are using your time most profitably, that skill in the wise use of time may be gained as you work intelligently upon the problem and plan accordingly, that provision should be made for a well-balanced program of activities which takes into consideration all aspects of your personal growth, and that skill gained in the effective use of your time while in college will pay high dividends in your work as a teacher and as a citizen.

SUMMARY

As you think about yourself as a part of society, you recognize the role which planning plays in this increasingly complex and interdependent culture. You then begin to realize that an intelligent application of the process necessitates your becoming skilled not only in planning your own life, but also in helping those whom you teach to do likewise.

Several steps have been suggested for use in outlining the details of your plans for teaching. One of your first responsibilities is to determine the things in life that really seem important to you—your values. These values largely determine the things you seek to accomplish. You then look at a career in education to see whether it holds promise of fulfilling these needs. You must meet certain requirements to qualify for a teaching position. You face the responsibility of critically and comprehensively appraising yourself in terms of these requirements. You then develop detailed schemes for moving from where you are to where you want to go, keeping in mind that plans are always tentative, and that modifications are made as unforeseen factors develop.

Later, when you have acquired better understanding of the work of the teacher, the requirements for preparation, and the purposes of education, you will need to do some reevaluating of your thinking.

This chapter also has been concerned with competencies for teaching and with personal growth toward teaching. The results of several studies on teacher competencies have been presented so that you could compare them, note similarities, and evaluate yourself in terms of them.

Keep in mind that any statement of competencies for teaching must be considered as a whole. Specific competencies are listed for purposes of study and clarification.

No one can expect to meet all the competencies for teaching to the highest degree, either at the time of graduation or at the end of a lifetime teaching career. But with each year of experience, it is a teacher's professional obligation to move to a fuller realization of his potential. Weaknesses can be made strong, and strengths can be made stronger; hence there is always the horizon of greater fulfillment.

Your personal growth toward teaching is not to be achieved by merely following a recipe, even such a one as has been given in this chapter. Each individual is different in needs and abilities. Study yourself in the light of those qualities that seem characteristic of desirable professional people and then plan to acquire the ones you now appear to lack. The suggestions given here will point the way to many other possibilities. Call upon friends and teachers to assist you in your program of self-improvement. Explore the dozens of opportunities that your college campus offers.

Careful planning and conscientious execution of those plans will assist you in becoming a worthwhile citizen, a well-adjusted person, and an individual who understands himself; one who is poised and secure, and who knows how to work with others. Such a person can become important in his own right and can justify the investment of time and energy needed to help him take his place in his chosen profession. His values and ideals will be clearly recognized by all who know him. His personality will mark him as the kind of individual the modern world needs.

QUESTIONS FOR YOUR CONSIDERATION

1. Why is it more important for you to carefully plan your career in teaching than it would have been if you had started 30 years ago?
2. In your opinion, what values should a person have in life if he plans to teach?
3. "Values are acquired parts of an individual's life." What are some of the implications of this statement for the experiences you will plan for your pupils, and the personal influence you will attempt to exert upon your pupils?
4. In what ways do the values held in common by people in America differ from those that characterize people in an autocratic society?
5. In what ways might long-range planning have improved the lives of some of your friends?
6. Some people feel that group planning and work reduces everyone to the level of mediocrity. Is this necessarily true? If not, how can group work contribute to the development of the unique talents of an individual?
7. In addition to a thorough grounding in subject matter, what specific understandings, skills, and techniques are, in your opinion, essential to success in the teaching profession?
8. From your observations what are the most common weaknesses of beginning teachers? How can you avoid such weaknesses when you begin teaching?
9. How can you gain greater understanding of the emotional and social needs of children?
10. Do you feel that your image of yourself often is reflected in how others see you? Can you present any evidence to support this point, and what are its implications for your success as a future teacher?
11. In what ways does a teacher's personality affect the progress of his pupils? Can you recall incidents that support your point of view?
12. Does a school administrator or supervisor have the right to criticize a teacher for being untidy or inappropriately dressed? If so, why?
13. What instances can you recall in which poor manners upon the part of teachers had detrimental effects upon the learning of pupils?
14. What qualities of voice and speech in teachers are conducive to good discipline in the classroom?
15. How did you spend your time during the past week? Was your time distributed in such a manner that you would experience a maximum amount of growth toward teaching?

ACTIVITIES FOR YOU TO PURSUE

1. Make a list of the things you really value in life. After careful study, try to arrange them in descending order according to their importance to you.

Reflect upon your past experiences and try to determine why you attach importance to each of your values. Examine them carefully to see whether they are compatible with each other. Opposite this list indicate all the values you see in education as a career. Compare and contrast these two listings to determine the extent to which they seem compatible.

2. Question seriously some of your close friends regarding what they value most in life. In what ways do the values they hold differ from yours? How do you account for these differences? In what ways are their career plans being affected by their values?

3. Talk to some people who have been very successful in their careers. Question them regarding long-range plans they have followed in order to gain success. Study also the careers of some people who have not been very successful. What differences do you find in the career planning done by successful and unsuccessful people?

4. Talk with people who have retired. You will find some who are happy and well adjusted in their retirement and others who are not. Attempt to determine whether long-range planning, or the lack of it, accounts to some extent for the differences.

5. Assume that you as a teacher should be skilled in helping your pupils plan together in the effective solution of common problems. Consider some college activities in which you might engage for purposes of increasing your skill in this regard.

6. As suggested previously, collect as many objective data as possible on your special abilities for teaching. Study these data carefully, seeking help from your college instructors if needed; formulate plans for overcoming your weaknesses and building up your strengths.

7. Write a paper on "What I Value in Life," "What Life Means to Me," "My Philosophy of Life," or on a similar topic suggested in this chapter.

8. Interview informally a number of boys and girls about the qualities that they think teachers should have. Have them also indicate the qualities which they dislike the most in teachers. Check your findings against those of Witty.

9. Draw a line vertically through the center of a piece of paper. On the left-hand side, list the factors that characterize the teacher whom you most disliked while in school. On the right-hand side, list the factors that characterize the teacher you liked best. At the bottom of the page, list the characteristics of the teacher who was of most value to you. Compare and contrast the characteristics listed for all three in an effort to determine common elements. Check your results against the findings listed in this chapter.

10. Check yourself on the "Checklist of Important Factors in the Teacher's Personality" which appears in the Resource Section of Part I, and underline the qualities or traits in which you need to improve. Try to formulate some first steps to take in overcoming your weaknesses.

11. Consult your director of student teaching regarding competencies against which you will be evaluated in your student teaching. Secure copies of any forms that may be used, and study them carefully. Formulate specific plans for overcoming any weaknesses that may be revealed from a study of these forms.

12. Discuss with an experienced school superintendent the qualities he looks for when he is employing teachers. Also ask him to list the main weaknesses of beginning teachers.

13. Ask several of your close friends to use the checklists presented in this chapter to appraise your appearance and your speech. Compare their ratings of you with your own. Consider ways to work on the problems revealed by their comments.

14. Consult with the counseling services on your college campus to locate the various agencies which may be of service to you in your program of self-improvement.

15. Explore your college catalog in an effort to find those courses that may be taken to broaden your interests or help overcome a personality problem. Consider taking courses in mental hygiene, philosophy and ethics, science fields that are new to you, arts and crafts, camp counseling, folk dancing, sports, speech improvement, writing, or dramatics. There are sure to be many helpful possibilities.

16. In your future group activities carefully appraise the extent to which you fulfill the characteristics of a good group member. Formulate ways to strengthen any characteristics in which you find yourself to be weak.

17. Keep an accurate record of how you spend your time during a fairly normal week of school. At the end of the week analyze the distribution of your time to see whether you are making the best use of it. You may wish to discuss the results with your friends and instructors and to plan ways of gaining more value from the free time you have available.

3

TEACHER EDUCATION, CERTIFICATION, AND FUTURE PROFESSIONAL GROWTH

If you have the aptitudes and feel that you have a good chance of acquiring the professional skills and attitudes required for teaching, what more do you need to do in order to become a member of the profession?

You have to be licensed to teach, just as you have to be licensed to practice medicine, dentistry, or law. In other words, the state, territorial, or other educational authority must attest to your competence before you are permitted to practice your profession.

How do you get this license, credential, or certificate? You get it by undergoing various teacher education screening procedures which your college or university may have and by completing successfully a prescribed curriculum as discussed in the following pages. You also will need to engage in various professional activities and complete certain requirements after you have been certified.

PROGRAMS FOR TEACHER EDUCATION

Since more people are engaged in teaching than in any other profession in the world, it is to be expected that institutions of higher education are engaged in the preparation of more students for teaching than for any other profession. Of more than 2,000 institutions of higher education in the United States, approximately 1,300 are specifically approved by state departments of education for the preparation of teachers. Of these institutions, 1,198 are accredited by regional associations, 449 of which were accredited by the National Council for Accreditation of Teacher Education in 1967. The list of approved teacher education institutions in 1967 included 146 public and 153 private universities, 207 public and 601 private general or liberal arts colleges, 9 public and 11 private teachers colleges, 19 technical schools, 39 junior colleges, and 13 unclassified schools [252].

It is significant to note the steady change taking place in the institutions preparing teachers. Between 1951 and 1967, 139 teachers colleges and normal schools became state colleges or universities. This is a continuation of a trend away from single-purpose teacher education institutions. Many interpretations have been given to these shifts, especially the shift from teachers colleges to state colleges. Armstrong and Stinnett feel that the real explanation appears to hinge upon two factors [12:23]:

1. The trend toward professionalization of teaching which has resulted in the adoption in most states of college degrees and the completion of prescribed curricula for beginning teachers (which practice obtains in all recognized professions), and thus in the growing acceptance of teacher education as an integral part of higher education and as an accepted professional discipline.
2. In recent years, the pressures of increased enrollments have forced state legislatures to consider two alternatives: (a) to authorize the building of new colleges, or (b) to utilize existing ones by converting single-purpose teachers colleges into general or multiple-purpose colleges. Choice of the latter alternative as being more economical and feasible obviously helps to explain the widespread conversions described above.

Another significant trend is the decline in the number of junior colleges approved for teacher education, . . . from 181 in 1957 . . . to 50 in 1964, a total decline of 131 in the seven-year period. . . . This may be attributed to establishing the degree as the minimum requirement for teacher certification in all but six states. This trend to drop junior colleges as approved institutions, in terms of offering full programs for regular certification, will doubtless continue.

Importance of Teacher Education

The growing importance of teacher education is reflected in the trends indicated above. In general, universities have shown little or no interest in the preparation of teachers until the last few decades.

That recognition of the crucial importance of teacher education has been particularly slow in universities is due in part to the feeling that "anyone who knew his subject would be able to teach it." Strange as it may seem, there are some professors on college campuses, especially those in subject-matter areas, who voice this same feeling and express grave doubts about the value of professional education courses. In fact, they may vociferously condemn such courses, and the student preparing to teach often is either confused or inclined to develop negative attitudes toward the importance of professional education courses. Often the violence of the controversy over the relative importance of subject-matter courses to professional courses is directly proportional to the lack of understanding of the field being condemned.

FIGURE 3–1. Teacher education constitutes a major responsibility in higher education. Over 39 per cent of all recent bachelor's degree graduates of colleges and universities are prepared to teach. (*Source:* National Education Association.)

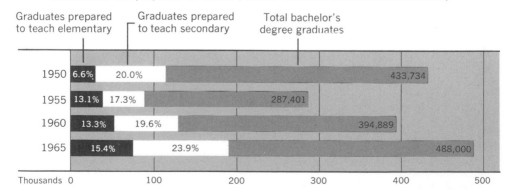

Some critics point to the fact that, on the college level and in private schools, one finds good teachers who have not taken any courses in education. The fallacy of this argument lies in the fact that these teachers are excellent in spite of their deficiencies. One may ask the question, "How much better might they have been?"

The fallacy of the belief that an effective teacher needs only a thorough knowledge of subject matter may be illustrated in various ways. As Chandler [41:5] points out, a passenger who has traveled extensively by air may feel that his experience qualifies him to pilot a plane. He may know much about aerodynamics, theory of flight, engines, flight patterns, regulations, schedules, etc. But if he should attempt to take charge of a flight, without having gone through the necessary long and intensive program of training, he immediately would discover the difference between being a pilot and flying as a passenger. Chandler feels that "the difference between lay teaching and professional teaching is comparable to the contrast between the recommendations of home remedies given by a layman for the sick and injured and the professional medical prescription and advice given by a doctor" [41:5].

There are other reasons why some prospective teachers may feel that a thorough knowledge of subject matter is about the only requirement for successful teaching. Unfortunately most of these students have attended schools in which attention has been given to little more than the sheer mastery of assigned subject matter. Furthermore, there is an element of security to be found by some students in assuming that the function of the teacher is to teach subject matter per se. These students, more than any others, have need for professional education courses.

Educational researchists, such as Smith at the University of Illinois and Turner and Fattu at Indiana University, have been conducting some sophisticated research that sheds light upon the controversy. Turner and Fattu, for example, have been working upon the assumption that any profession, to be worthy of the name, possesses an extensive and growing body of systematic, organized, and abstract knowledge which can be mastered only over an extended period of time by individuals who are selected for their aptitude and perform an essential public service better than any other group can perform such service. As a case in point, medical men ultimately justify their claim to professional status by being best able to solve problems within their domain because they are more competent than any other group in medical diagnosis and treatment. Similarly, teachers should be more competent than any other group in solving problems within their domain. Their research [276:1–29] clearly indicates that (1) teachers who have had a methods course perform better than those who have had none; (2) bachelor's degree graduates from teacher education programs perform significantly better than graduates in other areas including liberal arts; (3) teachers who have had teaching experience perform significantly better than those without such experiences; (4) teachers with one year of experience perform significantly better than those with no experience; (5) teachers with three to five years experience perform significantly better than those with one year of experience; and (6) teachers in large school districts where in-service teacher education is supported perform significantly better than those in small districts. This research should support you if you become involved in a discussion of the issue regarding the value of professional education.

General Pattern of Teacher Education

It is perfectly understandable, in the light of American education's brief and rapid development, that considerable variation exists in the specific nature of programs to be found in teacher education institutions today. Even if it were desired, no standardized pattern of preparation is to be found. There are, however, some characteristics that are common to most teacher education programs for the elementary and secondary levels. These programs may be studied in terms of three major areas: general education, subject-matter specialization, and professional education. In general, approximately one-half of your college work will fall in the area of general education if you plan to teach on the secondary school level, and definitely more than one-half will fall in that area if you plan to become an elementary school teacher. If you plan to become a secondary teacher, approximately one-third of your work will involve subject-matter specialization, and not more than one-sixth will be in professional education. As an elementary teacher, approximately one-eighth of your work may involve specialization and one-fourth will be classified as professional education. Since elementary teachers generally teach all the subjects offered in the elementary school, they need to take more courses in each of the major subject fields, which leaves less opportunity for specialization. Likewise, they must be concerned with methodology for all subject fields rather than with one or more subject areas of specialization, as is required for secondary school teachers.

There has been considerable controversy, especially during recent years, over the proportionate distribution of general and specialized course work and of professional education course work. Some of the critics seem to feel that a four-year teacher education program consists almost entirely of methodology or professional education. They bitterly condemn the "educationist" for most of the weaknesses in the American school system upon the grounds that almost all of a prospective teacher's education involves "learning how to teach." The facts of the case are these: approximately three-fourths of a prospective elementary teacher's preparation for teaching and approximately five-sixths of a prospective secondary school teacher's preparation involve study in the various subject areas. It would not seem excessive to devote from one-sixth to one-fourth of a student's time in college to a consideration of what education is for, of what young children and adolescents are like, and of how effective learning can best be promoted, as well as to gain some experience under expert guidance. Educators, in their feverish efforts to keep the amount of professional education to a minimum, realize that anything short of this proportionate amount does violence to any program designed to produce effective teachers. Those in other professions (medicine, dentistry, law, engineering, business administration) insist upon devoting a significantly higher percentage of their respective preparatory programs to professional education.

You should view general education, specialization in one or more teaching fields, and professional education as interrelated parts of a total program. The committee of the National Commission on Teacher Education and Professional Standards which prepared the report *New Horizons for the Teaching Profession* feels that [177:59]:

General education, specialization in a teaching field, and professional education

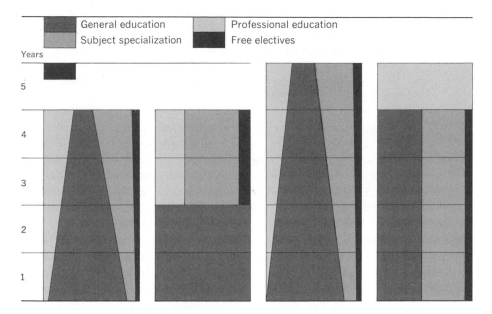

FIGURE 3–2. Four prevailing program patterns of teacher education in the United States. What are the advantages and disadvantages of each pattern?

can and should make an important contribution to helping the student to develop intellectual curiosity, a positive attitude toward learning, and a disposition to examine, inquire, and analyze; to build skills of logical analysis and of reasoned and orderly consideration of ideas; to gain understanding of and competence in using the different forms of reasoning employed in various fields; and to deepen respect for all areas of knowledge.

Further, a student should have opportunity in all parts of his program to become acquainted with resources for continuing inquiry and to build facility in their use. No part of a teacher education program is complete if it fails to give direct attention to helping the student derive principles and generalizations and to examine his actions on the basis of them. Important skills basic to effective interpersonal relationships must be a deliberate focus, not in one aspect of a program but throughout the total of planned experiences of every student.

Any discussion of the parts should be viewed in terms of the above desired outcomes of the total program.

General education. General education refers to the broad fields of knowledge, such as the humanities, the life and physical sciences, and the social and behavioral sciences, that are designed to help you solve personal problems and those of the society in which you live. General education is focused upon the needs and responsibilities which men have in common. It is designed to help you become a more alert, cultivated, and responsible individual and citizen [150:39]. According to the report *New Horizons for the Teaching Profession,* a program of general education should help the individual [adapted, 150:39–40]:

1. To develop understanding and the ability to use major ideas and principles of

the various divisions of knowledge as they bear on the range of common human concerns. The achievement of this goal involves developing intellectual curiosity; becoming acquainted with resources for continuing inquiry and study in a field, and learning how to use them; gaining an appreciation and respect for all areas of knowledge; acquiring experience with synthesizing and integrative properties of knowledge.

2. To cultivate those skills and habits of thought which constitute intellectual competence; for example, the ability to think logically and clearly, to gather relevant data, to draw conclusions from established facts. The student should gain an understanding of and competence in using the different forms of reasoning employed in the various fields. Becoming a disciplined and independent thinker calls for having a disposition to examine, inquire, and analyze; being willing to admit one's convictions and being able to defend them; acting on principle and daring to be different in supporting convictions.

3. To develop skills of communication and effective interaction with others. Each individual needs sufficient command of communication skills (lingual, numerical, and graphic) to be able to express his ideas clearly and to understand and intelligently utilize the rapidly developing mass media. He also needs to possess the skills that relate to a wholesome quality of interaction with others—the skills basic to effective interpersonal relationships.

4. To help the individual to examine intellectually his value system. The student may have essential knowledge, the skills of intellectual workmanship, and intellectual curiosity. Yet these rational processes may be of little worth unless they are tempered by moral responsibility and guided by values which derive from and fit into a reasoned view of existence.

5. To help the individual gain perspective regarding the relation of an area of specialization to all other fields.

Members of the teaching profession as persons need the same general education important for all thoughtful people. For the educator as a professional, however, general education has unusual urgency. *The teacher stands before his pupils in a special way, as a symbol and example of the educated person in the best sense of that term.* If he is a rounded and informed person, with a lively curiosity in many fields, he will stimulate students to join him in these interests. Further, his broad educational background will make him sensitive to pupil interests. Then, too, the teacher's central and critical role in the twentieth century, that of helping learners to intellectualize their experiences, gain new insights and develop the motivation to continue to learn and the ability to cope with the unknown, requires a new dimension in his own general educational.

As you analyze the program which your institution requires of students preparing to teach, you doubtless will find certain courses required in oral and written communication, literature and the arts, social sciences, and life and physical sciences which constitute the program of general education. By virtue of your public school experience, you already have gained considerable understanding and skill in each of these areas, although you may feel that you are weak in one or more of these areas. Regardless of what the situation may be, analyze your background critically in each of these broad areas. Your performance on standardized tests or inventories as well as your understanding of current affairs should assist in making an analysis of your present status.

The college campus may offer many opportunities for you to expand your cultural background, such as concerts, lectures, plays, and art exhibits. There also is the library with a wealth of books, periodicals, magazines, and newspapers from which you may gain breadth of understanding of the past as well as the present. During the time that you are in college you will want to establish the habits that will enable you to be a well-rounded, cultured person who is sensitive to the events in the world and to the enriching opportunities in life. There is much that you can do before graduation to develop the rich general background which you owe to yourself and to the pupils you will teach.

Subject-matter specialization. An elementary teacher is responsible for teaching virtually all subject fields. Although some schools do have special teachers in such areas as art, music, and physical education, it is common practice for the elementary teacher to assume responsibility for these special subjects. As a result, he needs a thorough grounding in more areas of learning than does the secondary teacher. The elementary teacher must develop enough depth of understanding in each of these areas to guide children into increasingly rich and challenging learning experiences. There is a trend, however, to require an area of subject-matter concentration of students preparing to be elementary teachers.

A secondary teacher is certified in one or more subject areas. He is responsible for bringing to his pupils a large store of knowledge in the courses he teaches. For this reason he takes a greater amount of advanced work in one or more subject areas than does the elementary teacher.

In advanced academic courses, you are likely to find students who are preparing for many occupations other than teaching. You may discover that these courses have been designed to meet the needs of all the students rather than of prospective teachers only. The student who plans to do nuclear research will have a somewhat different approach to the content of a physics course than you will. He will be concerned with the knowledge and skills that the course has to offer in terms of research in nuclear physics. But you, as a teacher, will be concerned with the implications of the course for guiding the intellectual growth of boys and girls.

Most secondary teachers begin teaching in small schools where it usually is necessary to teach in at least two subject fields. Only larger schools have sufficient classes in English, for example, to occupy a teacher's full time. For this reason, it is highly desirable to be certified in more than one subject, unless you wish to become a special teacher in such fields as fine arts, music, vocational home economics, or agriculture. You may be able, by very careful planning, to complete the certification requirements for a third or a fourth subject area. For example, some of your course work may be used to meet general education requirements, and some of the work needed for your major or minor may be applicable toward the requirements of a third or fourth certification area. Often only a small amount of additional work is needed to increase your number of areas. Effort spent in exploring such possibilities may prove very profitable, especially in securing the first teaching position.

The information contained in Chapter 4 should help you in making an intelligent and firm decision with regard to your field or fields of specialization. You also may wish to consult the education placement office to determine the probable future supply and demand for teachers having the same specializations in which you are interested.

As soon as you have decided upon the combination of subjects desired, you are ready to plan the course work. Institutions vary considerably in regard to the amount required for majors and minors. Also, within an institution the work demanded for a major or minor varies according to subject areas. Study carefully the respective requirements established by your teacher education institution and plan accordingly. If you anticipate teaching in another state, consult the specific state requirements for certification in the subject areas you elect in order that you may meet these requirements, if possible, upon graduation.

Professional education. During the past two or three decades rapid strides have been made in the professional education of teachers. This progress has been fostered especially by far-reaching research in the field of psychology. Techniques similar to those of the social psychologist, sociologist, and anthropologist have assisted educators in expanding the areas of investigation to include the more intangible aspects of education. Hundreds of studies have been made on such problems as the learning process, individual differences in pupils, methods of evaluating pupil progress, curriculum organization, child growth and development, utilization of community resources and audio-visual materials. Educational philosophers have provided clarification of the function of the school in society. The cooperative efforts of public school and teacher education personnel have helped to clarify the professional needs of the teacher. All these factors, and many others, have aided in establishing the professional education of teachers as a unique and scientific function.

The various statements of competencies listed in Chapter 2 indicate many qualities required of a successful teacher. It is this body of specialized knowledge, skills, and techniques that distinguishes teaching as a profession. Professional education courses are designed to assist students in developing the essential requirements for membership in the profession.

Teacher education institutions differ considerably in the specific ways in which they attempt to develop the professional competencies of teachers. This variation results from such factors as differences in state certification requirements, continued experimentation in the preparation of teachers, and rapid developments in teacher education. Any student who anticipates transferring to another institution during the time of his preparation for teaching should exercise great care in selecting his courses. Difference in requirements are so great among institutions that credits awarded at one college may not meet the specific demands of another. Whenever a transfer is anticipated, a student should check on the acceptability of the course work to be taken prior to the transfer. Careful planning along these lines often saves disappointment and delays in accepting desired teaching positions.

In spite of variations in the details of professional programs for teachers, there is a fairly common pattern in evidence. The programs generally can be divided into the following major areas, although the emphasis on each varies among institutions as well as within institutions according to the area or level of specialization:

1. Introduction to education
2. General and educational psychology
3. Human development
4. General methods
5. Special methods
6. Student teaching

From your reading, you doubtless have sensed the general content of each of these areas. Much of the remaining portion of this book will help you in seeing more clearly the rationale of these areas. The values, insights, understandings, and skills you gain in the sequence of professional courses required for certification will be affected greatly by the extent to which you recognize the crucial needs for each.

FIGURE 3–3. How a national cross section of experienced teachers felt about the extent to which their undergraduate teacher education programs had prepared them for actual teaching. (*Source:* National Education Association.)

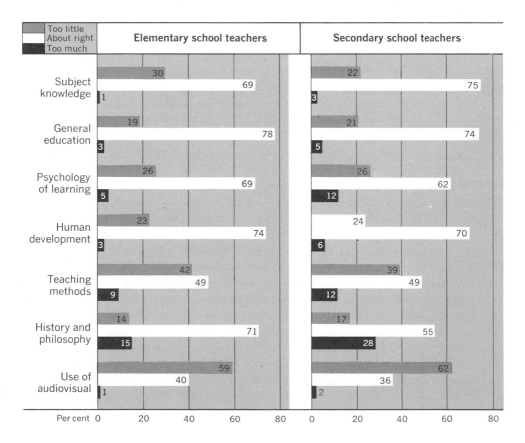

Students in elementary education generally are required to take more professional course work, mostly in special methods, than are students in secondary education. As indicated previously, elementary teachers are usually responsible for the child's education in all areas of knowledge, while secondary teachers specialize in one or more areas. Furthermore, elementary teachers tend to be more concerned with a child's total development, which requires many and deep professional understandings, whereas secondary teachers are more concerned with the teaching of their areas of specialization.

The professional preparation of elementary and secondary teachers is often similar in the initial stages. Differentiation designed for specialization normally occurs when prospective teachers take special methods courses and student teaching.

Institutions differ considerably with respect to the length of time during which a student will take his professional education. Some institutions will concentrate the program into the last year of college work. It is more common, however, to reserve professional education courses for the last two years of a four-year program. Currently there is a trend to spread a prospective teacher's professional learning throughout his entire college career. This trend is based upon the assumption that for a rich development of professional insights and techniques an extended period of time is required. Creative teaching does not consist of a "bag of tricks" and "cookbook recipes." Nor is it a "hot-house" product. Only time can provide the experiences from which prospective teachers may gain deep insights into human beings, the nature of the learning process, and creative ways of guiding boys and girls into expanding areas of effective living.

The authors of *New Horizons for the Teaching Profession* feel that not all professional education should be postponed to the fourth year of teacher preparation for the following reasons [150:65]: "(1) there is need for ideas about teaching to mature and to be tested before the student undertakes responsibility for the trusteeship of the teacher, and (2) when the student has selected teaching as his profession, the motivation that comes from exploring what is involved in teaching enhances rather than detracts from the values gained from work in general education."

Another reason why many prospective teachers fail to gain maximum benefit from professional education courses results partly from their limited experience in a leadership capacity and from their limited understanding of children and adults. When you, as a teacher-to-be, are responsible for guiding experiences of boys and girls, the experiences have greater meaning.

A number of institutions are requiring students to observe many teaching-learning situations, beginning with their first year of college. Case studies of children and participation in classroom situations are part of other professional education courses and are studied prior to a period of supervised student teaching.

There is much that you can do to gain a greater understanding of the behavior, interests, abilities, individual differences, and general characteristics of boys and girls. Many students participate in such valuable activities as teaching Sunday school classes, serving as camp counselors, working in youth centers, or settlement houses, serving as life guards or playground supervisors, or doing some baby sitting. Your college courses will have much greater meaning when you can relate

Education courses are of much greater value to students who have had many and varied contacts with boys and girls in a teaching-learning situation since these students bring to their courses greater understanding of the behavior, interests, abilities, individual differences, and general characteristics of boys and girls. *(Photograph by Carl Purcell, National Education Association.)*

the concepts and principles discussed to the rich and varied experiences which you have with boys and girls.

These are only a few of the many kinds of profitable experiences through which you may gain greater competence as a teacher. You owe yourself and your pupils the finest background possible for building the professional learnings, skills, and techniques of successful teaching.

Five-year Programs in Teacher Education

In considering educational growth and change, Sam M. Lambert, director of the research division of the National Education Association, maintains that the bachelor's degree in the relatively near future will be "outmoded as a basic requirement for teaching because it is becoming more difficult for a person to learn enough in four years to teach all the knowledge that should be acquired by today's children and youth" [77:47]. The President's Commission on National Goals advocated that by 1970 every state should require one year beyond the bachelor's degree as a requirement for secondary school teaching.

In view of this decided trend, a few teacher education institutions already have experimented with programs of five consecutive years of preparation for teaching. In studying five-year programs, Henry Harap of the Division of Higher Education in the U.S. Office of Education found that there is no predominant curriculum pattern [122:19]. In spite of considerable difference in the sequence of courses in general education, the curriculum falls into one of the following patterns:

1. Two years of general education followed by a three-year program of professional education, including subject-matter specialization
2. General education, subject-matter specialization, and professional education integrated in each year of the program
3. A year of professional education added to a four-year liberal arts program
4. Two years of subject matter and general education plus three years of subject matter and professional education

Although this is a trend in teacher education with which you should be familiar, no mass shift away from the four-year bachelor's degree program followed by a master's degree program is probable within the next decade. Harap indicates that advocates of the five-year program are not optimistic about its adoption for the following reasons [122:21]:

It is clear that the four-year sequence will remain as the dominant pattern of training for teaching for many years to come. Arguments for the four-year liberal arts–professional education sequence are powerful; it is unhurried and proceeds as a planned, step-by-step sequence; it permits the college graduate to begin contributing to society sooner; a four-year program, followed by several years of experience in teaching, is an assurance of more profitable graduate study both in the individual's teaching field and in education; the financial investment of the fifth year is an unreasonable expectation for great numbers of prospective teachers, particularly women whose teaching careers may be short; not all prospective teachers are able to profit from graduate study.

CERTIFICATION OF EDUCATORS

You may know a few older teachers who do not have a bachelor's degree; in fact, some have very little college credit. You may wonder why they are permitted to teach, while you are required to take so much more college work. A brief historical sketch of teacher certification may help you understand this situation and may indicate the tremendous amount of progress that has been made in the professionalization of teaching.

Progress in Certification of Teachers

Not many years ago, about the only qualification required for becoming a teacher was willingness to "keep school." Local employing officials usually considered "a bit of larnin'" desirable but not always essential. Samuel R. Hall, in his *Lectures on School Keeping* published in 1829, quoted a writer who was criticizing the low standards for teachers at that time [210:495–496].

Every stripling who has passed four years within the walls of a college, every dissatisfied clerk who has not ability enough to manage the trifling concerns of a retail shop, every young farmer who obtains in the winter a short vacation from the toils of the summer—in short, every person who is conscious of his imbecility in other business, esteems himself fully competent to train the ignorance and weakness of infancy into all the virtue and power and wisdom of maturer years—to form a creature, the frailest and feeblest that heaven has made, into the intelligent and fearless sovereign of the whole animated creation, the interpreter and adorer, and almost the representative of divinity.

Prior to the turn of the century a typical elementary teacher had less than the equivalent of a high school education. In those early days a few ambitious and professionally serious individuals attended what were commonly called normal schools to prepare themselves for teaching. These normal schools existed for the express purpose of serving the personal interests and needs of prospective teachers. They served essentially the same function as do the business schools today. In spite of their services, it is reported that as late as World War I approximately half of the 600,000 teachers in the country had no more than four years of education beyond the eighth grade [251:57].

In earlier days the common method of ascertaining a person's fitness for teaching was an examination. This examination frequently amounted to an interview in which the candidate was asked a few questions by the employing official, who often was very poorly qualified to judge the answers he received. Later, prospective candidates were given a written examination that was usually constructed, administered, and scored by the local school board, superintendent, or county superintendent. Far too often these examinations were most inadequate and amounted to little more than mere formalities.

Eventually a number of objections were raised, primarily by teachers, to the system of certifying teachers through local examinations. In the first place the examinations were not standardized for more than a small area of the state, and therefore the successful candidate was qualified to teach only in the district in which he took the examination. Furthermore, there often was little evidence that merit, as revealed by the examination results, constituted the basis upon which appointments were made.

Improvements in the examination system of certifying teachers were made by granting to some state agency, such as the state department of public instruction, the authority to supervise and coordinate certification procedures. As a result of this change, the responsibility for constructing and scoring examinations for teacher certification became a state function. Certificates for teaching thus became valid throughout the state.

It is important to note that local communities and school officials usually were very reluctant to release to the state the authority for certifying teachers. Many communities felt that they were losing certain rights and the ability to reserve teaching positions for local talent. This factor accounts largely for the slow progress that has been made in teacher certification.

Since 1922, certification requirements for beginning teachers definitely have been raised. Increasing emphasis has been placed upon college preparation for teaching, and less emphasis upon examinations as a means of certification. Two-year normal schools have given way to four-year teachers colleges. State departments of instruction have established certain standards of training for the various institutions engaged in the preparation of teachers. The state department normally accepts for certification the graduates recommended by the teacher education institutions within its domain. This procedure gives control over teacher education to the state and standardizes the minimum certification requirements.

Progress in teacher certification has resulted in a number of benefits. It has contributed much to the establishment of teaching as a profession. Pupils today are protected from incompetent teachers who gained the right to teach through unethical means. Qualified teachers are protected from competition with unqualified teachers. Teachers are encouraged to improve their competence for teaching. Since the control for teacher certification is vested in the state, it is possible to have a continuous inventory of teachers and their qualifications.

Types of Teacher Certificates

In earlier days it was the practice to grant "blanket" certificates to teachers whereby they were permitted to teach virtually all subjects in all grades. One of the positive trends in certification has been the differentiation of licenses granted for specialized grade levels and/or subject areas of instruction. Today a definite distinction is common between the certificates granted to elementary and secondary school teachers. The laws in some states even make distinctions between the

State teacher certification laws are designed to ensure competence on the part of teachers, thereby protecting and promoting the educational welfare of youth. They also protect the competent teacher from competition with unqualified teachers. (*Photograph from the Indiana State Teachers Association.*)

grade levels of elementary schools, such as lower, intermediate, and upper elementary.

Secondary school certificates usually are granted on the basis of the subject area or areas which the student has studied. Forty-seven states in 1967 issued endorsed certificates, that is, certificates on which is endorsed the one or more teaching fields or subjects in which the holder meets the specified requirements of the state [252]. There is a trend to grant licenses in *major fields of knowledge* rather than in specific subject areas. For instance, a teacher may be licensed to teach social studies and science rather than only history and chemistry. In time this major-area trend will decrease the odd combination of subjects that many beginning teachers often are asked to teach.

Upon meeting your state and college certification requirements, you normally will be recommended by your college to members of the state education department for the type of certificate for which you have prepared. Most states grant to beginning teachers some form of provisional license which specifies a limited period of validity. After this time has expired it may be renewed, provided certain conditions have been met, or it may be exchanged for a higher type of certificate. Many states grant some form of permanent certificate, usually upon evidence of a specified number of years of successful teaching and additional professional work. A permanent certificate, normally different from a life certificate, remains valid only so long as the holder teaches continuously or is not out of teaching beyond a specified number of years.

There is a trend away from the granting of life certificates to teachers. Many educators feel that standards change too rapidly and long-term certificates tend to stifle professional growth. They feel that the state should maintain some control over the training qualifications of its teachers. So much progress in teacher education is being made that a high standard today may easily become a low one within a decade. Unless some control is retained, the injurious effects of life certificates will exist long after the practice has been abolished—until the last holder of a life certificate has retired.

Some certificates expire through nonuse. Policies for renewal vary from state to state. The candidate is generally required to take some additional college work to reinstate the license.

The laws governing certification in the various states usually specify the conditions under which it may be revoked. If it can be proved that a teacher is immoral, incompetent, intemperate, or guilty of unprofessional conduct, he stands a chance of losing his certificate.

Present Status of Certification Standards

All the states and territories now have laws governing the certification of teachers in their respective areas. These laws in general indicate that certification is based on an applicant's having completed an approved program of teacher education, including student teaching or its equivalent, in an accredited college or university. It is not possible to describe accurately the more detailed provisions governing certification without discussing the laws of each state separately. Since certification is a state function, each state has developed its own certification requirements, resulting in considerable differences among the states in regard to the amount of training required and the types of certificates granted.

Each year Robert C. Woellner and M. Aurilla Wood publish a booklet titled *Requirement for Certification of Teachers, Counselors, Librarians, Administrators for Elementary Schools, Secondary Schools, Junior Colleges* that lists the certification requirements in each state. Every three years the National Education Association publishes a report, titled *A Manual on Certification Requirements for School Personnel in the United States,* which details trends and specific data concerning certification qualifications and contains the addresses of the chief state certifying officers. The state department of education, in the state in which you wish to teach, will also send you, without charge, information about local requirements.

You will find these reports helpful in planning your work, especially if you are attending college outside your home state or are considering the possibilities of teaching in various other geographic areas. You can save time and disappointment if, early in your training, you consult the specific certification requirements for the states in which you plan to teach.

A *general* idea of minimum certification requirements in states and territories in 1967 may be gained from Table 2. But if you plan to teach in a state other than the one in which you are taking your college work, do not depend upon a listing such as Table 2, since the requirements may have been raised. For example, Wis-

TABLE 2   **Minimum Requirements for Lowest Regular Teaching Certificates by States and Territories***

	Elementary school			High school		
State	Degree or no. of semester hours required	Professional education required, semester hours	Directed teaching required, semester hours	Degree or no. of semester hours required	Professional education required, semester hours	Directed teaching required, semester hours
Alabama	B	27	6	B	21	6
Alaska	B	24	C	B	18	C
Arizona	B	24	6	5	22	6
Arkansas	B	18	6	B	18	6
California	5	20	180 CH	5	15	120 CH
Colorado	B	AC	AC	B	AC	AC
Connecticut	B	30	6	B	18	6
Delaware	B	30	6	B	18	6
District	B	24	6	5	18	6
Florida	B	20	6	B	20	6
Georgia	B	18	6	B	18	6
Hawaii	B	18	AC	B	18	AC

* AC means approved curriculum; B means bachelor's degree of specified preparation; 5 means bachelor's degree plus a fifth year of appropriate preparation, not necessarily completion of master's degree; C means a course; CH means clock hours.

Source: T. M. Stinnett, *A Manual on Certification Requirements for School Personnel in the United States,* National Education Association, National Commission on Teacher Education and Professional Standards, Washington, 1967. (Data supplied by publisher in advance, from an incomplete survey.)

TABLE 2 *(continued)*

State	Elementary school			High school		
	Degree or no. of semester hours required	Professional education required, semester hours	Directed teaching required, semester hours	Degree or no. of semester hours required	Professional education required, semester hours	Directed teaching required, semester hours
Idaho	B	20	6	B	20	6
Illinois	B	16	5	B	16	5
Indiana	B	27	8	B	18	6
Iowa	B	20	5	B	20	5
Kansas	B	24	5	B	20	5
Kentucky	B	24	8	B	17	8
Louisiana	B	24	4	B	18	4
Maine	B	30	8	B	18	6
Maryland	B	26	8	B	18	6
Massachusetts	B	18	2	B	12	2
Michigan	B	20	5	B	20	5
Minnesota	B	30	6	B	18	4
Mississippi	B	36	6	B	18	6
Missouri	B	20	5	B	20	5
Montana	B	AC	AC	B	16	AC
Nebraska	60	8	3	B	AC	AC
Nevada	B	18	4	B	18	4
New Hampshire	B	30	6	B	18	6
New Jersey	B	36	6	B	24	6
New Mexico	B	24	6	B	18	6
New York	B	24	8	B	18	6
North Carolina	B	24	6	B	18	6
North Dakota	64	16	3	B	16	3
Ohio	B	28	6	B	17	6
Oklahoma	B	21	6	B	21	6
Oregon	B	20	4	B	24	6
Pennsylvania	B	36	6	B	18	6
Puerto Rico	68	53	6	B	29	5
Rhode Island	B	30	6	B	18	6
South Carolina	B	21	6	B	18	6
South Dakota	60	15	3	B	20	6
Tennessee	B	24	4	B	24	4
Texas	B	18	6	B	18	6
Utah	B	26	8	B	21	8
Vermont	B	18	6	B	18	6
Virginia	B	18	6	B	15	4–6
Washington	B	AC	AC	B	AC	AC
West Virginia	B	20	6	B	20	6
Wisconsin	64	26	8	B	18	5
Wyoming	B	23	C	B	20	C

consin is to require a bachelor's degree in 1972 for an elementary teacher's certi-
cate. Also the total hours required in professional education may include certain
specific courses, such as philosophy of education or tests and measurements. Even
the general categories vary considerably in the semester hours demanded. In 1967
the range of semester hours of necessary professional education courses ran from
8 to 53 (Puerto Rico), with a median of 24 for elementary and 18 for secondary
teachers. Semester hours in student teaching ranged from 2 to 8, with a median
of 6 for both elementary and secondary teachers. In the past, these differences
have made it difficult for teachers to move freely from one state to another.

Most states have requirements for teacher certification in addition to those
indicated in Table 2. In 1967, for instance [252], 32 states and territories required
that applicants be citizens of the United States, 25 required the signing of an oath
of allegiance or loyalty to the United States and to the state, 11 required as a
prerequisite evidence of having been hired to teach, and 42 required a recommendation from the college in which the student did his work or from the employing official if he was already an experienced teacher. General health certificates
were required in 21 states and territories, and chest x-rays were required in 15.
Although 12 states specified special courses, only 6 actually required special
courses which could usually be secured only in an institution in that state. Eighteen states specified no minimum age; two specified age 17; twenty-eight indicated
age 18; three required age 19; and one state specified age 20 [252]. In addition
to these requirements, several states require the successful passing of the National
Teacher Examination. Specific state requirements may be found in the manual
by Stinnett, indicated above. Your college library or placement office will probably
have a copy of this publication.

Limited Certificates

You may meet teachers who hold only emergency, substandard, or temporary
permits, which are issued to persons who do not meet the prescribed course requirements. The term "limited certificates" is used nationally to refer to these
certificates or permits.

The issuance of these certificates has created a serious problem since World
War II. In 1946, one in seven employed teachers was on an emergency certificate
[12:23]. In 1967, however, the ratio had dropped to approximately 1 in 20. Approximately 70 per cent of the emergency certificates involved elementary
teachers.

Several things should be remembered, though, with respect to this group. First,
many of the group are actually close to meeting all requirements for certification
and are good teachers. Second, the number of teachers required to care for the
mounting throngs of boys and girls has exceeded the number of available qualified
teachers. Third, relatively low salaries have prevented many desirable teachers
from remaining in the profession. Fourth, while some of these people should be
weeded out, many should be encouraged to stay because of the significant contributions they can make and are making. Ways and means should be provided
whereby those in the latter group can bolster their training, gain their professional
certificates, and continue their teaching.

Trends in the Certification Standards for Elementary Teachers

Table 2 indicates that an amazing amount of progress has been made in raising the certification standards for elementary teachers. As of January, 1967, a total of 47 states, including the District of Columbia, were enforcing the minimum requirement of the bachelor's degree for the lowest regular certificate for beginning elementary school teachers [252]. The remaining 4 states and Puerto Rico were requiring that prospective elementary school teachers have at least two years of college work. Three of these states (South Dakota, September 1, 1968; North Dakota, July 1, 1969; and Wisconsin, July 1, 1972) specified future dates when the bachelor's degree would become a requirement. In 1951, by way of contrast, only 17 states required the bachelor's degree; 3 required at least three years; 17, two years; 9, one year; and 2 states, less than one year.

A number of factors have contributed to the radical rise in certification requirements. Undoubtedly, the rapid adoption of the single-salary schedule has played a significant role in the increase in these requirements. Also there has been a growing understanding of the significance of elementary education in our society. The thinking of educators, as reflected in the following statement written in the 1940s by a prominent authority in the field of school administration, doubtless helped others to see the wisdom of raising the certification standards for elementary school teachers [210:498–499]:

School officials and the general public are coming to realize more and more that teachers of the lower grades need as much preparation as teachers of the upper grades; in fact, they are gradually coming to realize that there are valid reasons for requiring an even larger amount of preparation for teachers of the lower grades. They are coming to realize that the pupils in the lower grades need much more personal guidance from their teachers than the pupils in the upper grades. The pupils in the lower grades must acquire the tools of learning, and those tools cannot be acquired without the tutelage of a teacher. In the upper grades, on the other hand, pupils already possess an acquaintance with the tools of learning and in consequence are able to work somewhat independently. Those older pupils learn much through their own initiative, and they often learn in spite of poor teaching.

It may be properly contended, therefore, that the elementary school, and especially the first part of the elementary school, is of greatest importance among the school levels because it lays the foundation for the pupil's educational career and for life. It should have "prior rating" so far as the resources of the public are concerned; it is democracy's school *par excellence*. In those early years the pupils acquire the tools of knowledge and form habits and ideals which will remain with them throughout life. Unless the proper foundation is laid in the lower grades, the best superstructure for future educational accomplishment cannot be erected. Moreover, because they must start early to earn their living, or because secondary schools are not readily available to them, many pupils are unable to secure more formal education than that provided by the elementary school, and this is another potent reason for making the elementary school as thorough and as practical as possible. When these facts have become generally known by school officials and by the public, teachers in the lower grades will be required to have as much education as (if not more education than) teachers in the upper grades. And let not the teachers of the secondary schools and colleges forget the same facts, because where importance and difficulty of work are concerned they must humbly bow before the teachers of elementary schools.

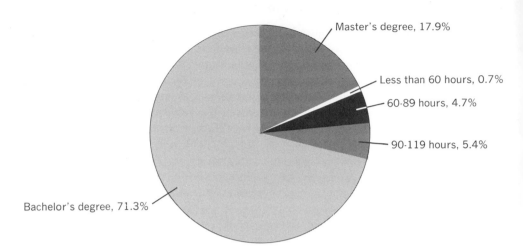

FIGURE 3–4. Preparation of elementary school teachers in 1965–1966. In recent years, dramatic improvement has been made in the preparation of elementary school teachers. Why can further improvements be anticipated? *(Source:* National Education Association.)

It is not uncommon to find people expressing concern over the rising standards for elementary teachers. They feel that this trend will tend to increase the shortage. There is considerable evidence, however, to indicate that the supply of elementary teachers will generally *increase* as standards are raised. This increasing supply-standards ratio is paralleled in other professions, e.g., law and medicine. The reasons are largely that higher standards are usually accompanied by higher salaries; both standards and salary operate to enhance the prestige of a profession. When all three factors—standards, salary, and prestige—are strengthened, the supply of potential candidates attracted to the field increases.

In regard to the preschool level, 18 states in 1967 required public nursery school teachers and 42 states required public kindergarten teachers to hold certificates [252]. Normally, then, all states maintaining nursery and kindergarten schools at public expense require certification.

Trends in the Certification Standards for Secondary Teachers

For a number of years a bachelor's degree from a recognized college has been the standard requirement for high school teaching. In 1967 all states were enforcing the requirement of at least the bachelor's degree for beginning high school teachers.

Arizona, California, and the District of Columbia require, with few exceptions, five years of college work for beginning high school teachers. Eighteen states in 1967 required for high school teachers the completion of the fifth year of training by the end of a specified number of years of teaching. Many educators feel that in the relatively near future five years of college training will become a common standard for the preparation of secondary teachers. A number of teacher education

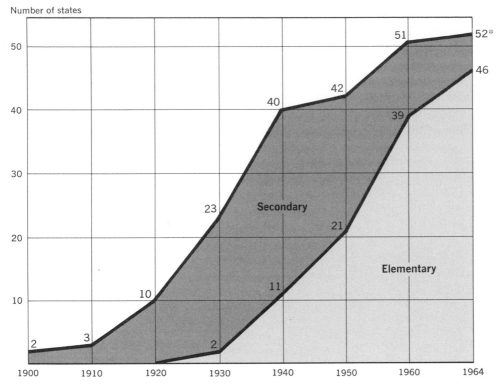

Number of states

FIGURE 3–5.   Dramatic progress has been made in the number of states enforcing the degree requirements for the lowest regular teaching certificate in elementary and in secondary schools. What changes do you anticipate in the future? (*Source: National Education Association.*)

institutions already include a fifth year of training as a regular part of the program. An increasing number of geographic areas provide higher salaries for beginning teachers who have had five years of preparation.

Certification Standards Prescribed by School Systems

Certification laws embody the minimum requirements established by a particular state for teachers. However, each school system within the state is free to establish requirements that exceed these minimums to whatever degree it desires. This means that you may be able to meet the state certification standards without being able to teach in a particular system. Therefore, try to familiarize yourself with the requirements of the specific school systems in which you may desire to teach.

The practice in school systems of requiring standards higher than the state minimums tends to raise the educational level of teachers. Unfortunately the practice is limited primarily to those school systems which have economic advantages over others. Most rural areas are able to demand only the state requirements. The school systems of larger cities especially may also require an applicant for a position to take a series of tests. These tests may cover language expression, reasoning ability, general culture, and professional information. A number of school systems require applicants to take the National Teacher Examination. This test is given each year in approximately 400 centers throughout the United States. Information about the test may be secured by writing to National Teacher Examinations, Educational Testing Service, Princeton, New Jersey.

Certification of Teachers in Private Schools

Only 17 states, by either law or regulation, require teachers in private or parochial schools, at some school level or under certain conditions, to hold certificates [252]. Fourteen of these states require elementary school teachers in private schools to hold certificates. Twelve states require high school teachers in private schools to hold certificates. The predominant practice in privately supported and controlled schools is to require certification only in the case that the school seeks accreditation by the state or to issue certificates upon the voluntary requests of teachers in the private schools. Twenty-five states in 1967 followed these practices at one or more school levels [252].

A number of conflicting principles are involved when one considers whether or not private and church-related school teachers should meet certification requirements. Church-related schools pose the problem of separation between church and state. Should the state impose *its* definition of competence upon such a school, or does the church-related school have a right to insist upon its concept of competence? Private schools have fought for their freedom of decision in the selection of teachers in order to maintain the excellence of their institutional programs. They feel that any attempt to curtail this freedom would violate the principle of free enterprise and would handicap the development of outstandingly good educational programs. On the other hand, the state, in fulfilling its educational responsibility, has an obligation to protect all boys and girls from persons of substandard qualifications. The authors of *New Horizons for the Teaching Profession*, in viewing the problem, express the following point of view [150:153]:

> Once the license represents a valid standard of competence, and once the granting of licenses is based on demonstrated competence there remains no valid argument against its application to both public and private schools—church-related, independent, and proprietary. Indeed it then becomes the moral obligation of the state to apply the standard throughout its jurisdiction.

In the years ahead the question of certification of teachers in private and church-related schools may develop into an interesting issue. As a member of the profession you will want to give further thought to it.

Trends in Certification Standards of Administrators, Supervisors, and Other School Personnel

An increasing number of states are requiring school personnel such as administrators, principals, supervisors, speech and hearing therapists, audio-visual directors, librarians, psychologists, and guidance officers to hold special certificates appropriate to their respective positions. These certificates usually require some successful teaching experience in addition to college course work applicable to the specific position.

As you may see from Table 3, in 1967 a master's degree or more was required for an elementary school principal certificate in 85 per cent of the states and territories; for a secondary school principal certificate in 90 per cent; and for a superintendent of schools certificate in 94 per cent of the states and territories [12:7]. In 1955 the certification requirement of five or more years of training was specified in 19 states for elementary school principals, in 30 states for secondary principals, and in 36 states for superintendents of schools. Compare these numbers with those in Table 3 and you will note the strong trend, during this twelve-year period of time, toward increasing the requirements for administrative certificates.

States are moving toward the six-year requirement for administrative certificates. In 1967, 20 states already required that much training for superintendents of schools. Undoubtedly other states will follow, especially since, beginning in 1964, the American Association of School Administrators has required its new members to have six or more years of appropriate training.

Some states require that in order to qualify for a principal's or supervisor's position, a candidate must hold a valid teacher's certificate for the level he wishes to administrate. For example, a state may specify that a person must hold an elementary teacher's certificate and complete the prescribed graduate work to be eligible for an elementary principal's or supervisor's certificate. Requirements such

TABLE 3 Summary of Minimum Preparation Required by States for Administrative Certificates, 1967

Number of college years of preparation or degrees required	Number of states requiring		
	Elementary school principal	Secondary school principal	Superintendent of schools
7 years or doctor's degree	0	0	1
6 years plus, but less than doctor's degree	0	0	1
6 years	3	3	18
Master's degree plus, but less than 6 years	7	7	3
Master's degree	34	37	26
Bachelor's degree plus, but less than 5 years	3	2	1
Bachelor's degree	4	2	0
Less than bachelor's degree	0	0	0
No certificate issued.	1	1	2
Total	52	52	52

Source: T. M. Stinnett, A Manual on Certification Requirements for School Personnel in the United States, National Education Association, National Commission on Teacher Education and Professional Standards, Washington, 1967. (Data supplied in advance of publication and subject to change.)

as these indicate healthy trends in the certification of administrators and supervisors. Unfortunately there still are far too many elementary principals who receive appointments solely on their merits as high school athletic coaches or teachers, and who know little about the administration and organization of a good elementary school.

Trends in the certification of other school personnel, such as supervisors, counselors, psychologists, speech and hearing therapists, and guidance directors, are not so pronounced as are those for school administrators. It is inevitable that the requirements for certifying such school personnel will be raised even more. Many educators visualize a sixth year of training as necessary for the competence to perform such technical tasks.

Trends in the Certification Standards for College Teachers

In 1967, there were ten states that required teachers in public-supported junior colleges to hold certificates [252]. In general, these were states in which the junior colleges were a part of the public-supported system and were usually maintained by the local school districts as an extension of secondary education. Three states required teachers in the state teachers colleges or state colleges which formerly were teachers colleges to hold certificates.

Normally each institution of higher learning establishes its own requirements for teachers, but the requirements may vary, within any one institution, according to subject field. In order to secure a full-time appointment on the college level, a person normally must have at least a master's degree, with a doctor's degree being preferred. Successful public school teaching experience is almost a universal requirement for teaching professional education courses.

A number of questions have been raised regarding the desirability of developing some form of licensure for those teaching in college and graduate school. The report *New Horizons for the Teaching Profession,* prepared by a committee of the National Commission on Teacher Education and Professional Standards of the National Education Association, indicates several differences bearing on the question that are worthy of note [150:153–154]:

> The freedom of the student at these levels to choose his school and to choose whether to go to school at all has bearing only insofar as the protection of the individual is concerned; it has no bearing on the state's obligation to the rest of the society.
>
> A second, more important difference is that college and graduate students should be expected to study on their own initiative, to depend relatively little on the teacher to show them how to learn what he has to offer. Yet adults still learn more rapidly and more thoroughly from a wise and skillful teacher. And as added knowledge and techniques have to be mastered by modern specialists, the efficiency with which they learn has become vitally important for their lives and the lives entrusted to them. It may be necessary to waive the requirement of teaching qualifications for various temporary functions as lecturer, consultant, clinical demonstrator, and so on, in order to get a person with other qualifications essential for the position. Such positions, however, are the exception, and they are used to best advantage in an institution whose policy-making staff has the full range of qualifications.
>
> Third, the candidates for full-time college and university positions can usually be chosen from a world-wide roster of experts. But this is no reason to condone the

choice of a person who is below standard in any qualification requisite for the responsibility offered to him.

Fourth, the choice of personnel can be made in first-rate colleges and universities by expert judges since they are the source of the best available judgment in their fields of specialization. Yet the expertness that can be counted on is limited to one field. It does not necessarily encompass all the essential elements of competence as a teacher.

Fifth, college and university departments have a responsibility, which is far less marked in the schools, to advance human knowledge beyond what may be believed or appreciated in the surrounding society. The institution of higher education needs all the freedom necessary for this peculiar and sometimes unpopular service. But the necessary freedom does not include the freedom for inept and unskilled teaching.

Consequently, an increasing number of college and university teachers and administrators are of the opinion that somehow a minimum level of professional teaching competence should be assured throughout higher education.

In view of these differences the committee makes the following recommendation [150:155]:

The qualifications essential for college and university teaching may not be subject to as general agreement as are those for high school teaching, or for university teaching in other countries where a candidate may be judged largely on his delivery of a lecture in his field. Before a standard can be adopted which will win assent, the elements of it will have to be hammered out by groups of specialists who have the respect of university teachers and administrators. A basic recommendation, therefore, is that such groups be brought together to define and propose the qualifications which they believe ought to be required. Only on the basis of such a proposal can there be useful talk of a license requirement in higher education.

Influence of Professional Organizations on Certification Standards

Significant progress in the raising of standards has, as in other professions, come primarily from the efforts of members rather than from the general public. Teachers are probably in the best position to judge the standards essential for accomplishing their function. Unfortunately, in some communities selfish motives and an unwillingness to pay for teachers with high qualifications have retarded greatly the improvement of certification standards.

The National Education Association has been outstanding in its efforts to raise the certification standards for teachers. Since the turn of the century it has advocated five years of college training for high school teachers. It now stresses the importance of all public school teachers having at least five years of college preparation. Since 1946, the major efforts of the NEA in certification have been channeled through the National Commission on Teacher Education and Professional Standards.

Mention should be made of the influence of certain accrediting agencies, such as the North Central Association of Colleges and Secondary Schools. In order to become a member, which is a high honor, a secondary school must meet many relatively high standards established by the association. The association checks annually upon its members to make certain that these standards are being maintained.

Influence of Teacher Education Institutions upon Certification Standards

Mention has been made of the positive effect that teacher education institutions have had upon the improvement of certification standards. Provisions for college training in each state have almost invariably exceeded the minimum certification requirements. For instance, today it is possible to secure a doctor's degree in elementary education in institutions where the state certification requirement for elementary teachers is two college years or less.

Teacher education institutions have been concerned with more than an increase in the number of years of training for teachers. Intensive efforts are being made continuously to improve the *quality* of training. It should always be borne in mind that the quality of teachers produced is far more important in the lives of children than is the number of years of teacher education prescribed for certification.

Reciprocity in Teacher Certification

Differences in the certification requirements of the individual states have handicapped the free movement of teachers throughout the United States. For example, a teacher certified to teach in New York might not meet the specific requirement for teaching in Texas. A number of factors have accentuated this problem: rapid transportation and communication; fluctuation in teacher supply and demand; and differences in salaries, tenure, retirement benefits, etc. Thus reciprocity in teacher certification has become a national problem.

Such organizations as the Council of Co-operation in Teacher Education of the American Council on Education, the National Commission on Teacher Education and Professional Standards of the National Education Association, the Association for Student Teaching, and the American Association of Colleges for Teacher Education have been quite concerned with this problem and have brought together a variety of groups who have had a logical concern for its solution. Particularly noteworthy in searching for a solution to the problem has been the National Association of State Directors of Teacher Education and Certification. Members of the association long ago agreed with leaders in the profession that the growing migration of teachers ought to be encouraged. They agreed upon the following advantages of the free movement of teachers [30:14]:

1. It tends to bring about balance between teacher supply and demand; which is essential not only to teacher welfare and prestige, but to improved educational opportunities for children.
2. It promotes national unity.
3. It tends to destroy provincialism and the inbreeding of ideas and practices in local school systems.
4. It provides a means whereby states having low standards of preparation may raise those standards to a desirable minimum.
5. It promotes teacher growth in service.

The members of the association also agreed that the following points should form the basis upon which progress in the reciprocity of teacher certification could take place [30:14]:

1. The certification of teachers is a function of the state and should never be delegated to other agencies.
2. Certification laws should grant broad general authority and not include detail which prevents flexibility in administration.
3. The baccalaureate degree should be the minimum level of preparation at which reciprocity becomes operative.
4. Only those who are graduates of teacher-education institutions approved by state departments of education and accredited by regional or national accrediting agencies should be accepted for certification by another state.
5. The definition of a good teacher should be the same throughout the nation.
6. The initial certificate should be issued only upon the recommendation of the head of the department of education of the teacher-preparing institution.

Regional reciprocity compacts have been established, with varying degrees of success, between states, especially in New England. In 1964, a total of seventeen states reported that they were members of reciprocity compacts [12:16]. Reisert [212:373] indicates that:

This procedure may entail either institutional approval or certificate exchange. In the case of institutional approval, certain teacher education graduates of these approved schools then receive reciprocity rights in all states of the compact. States recognizing certificate exchange grant reciprocity to any certificate holder from another compact state regardless of institutional approval.

These compacts, however, seem to be giving way to reciprocity agreements made possible through accreditation by the National Council for Accreditation of Teacher Education.

The National Association of State Directors of Teacher Education and Certification adopted a recommendation in 1958 that National Council for Accreditation of Teacher Education (NCATE) accreditation should be made the basis of reciprocity among the states. In other words, graduation from an institution accredited by NCATE should be sufficient basis for reciprocity in teacher certification. The regulation adopted by the state of Georgia appears to be typical [12:17]:

Graduates of out-of-state colleges are granted certification reciprocity in Georgia on the recommendation of an authorized college official confirming that the applicant has completed a program approved by the National Council for Accreditation of Teacher Education. The program must approximate the minimum standards outline.

Since 1958, considerable progress has been made in the use of NCATE accreditation as a basis for facilitating the certification of graduates from out-of-state institutions. For example, in 1966 some use of NCATE accreditation was reported by twenty-eight states—Alabama, Arizona, Colorado, Delaware, Florida, Georgia, Illinois, Indiana, Iowa, Kentucky, Maine, Maryland, Mississippi, Missouri, Nebraska, North Carolina, North Dakota, Oklahoma, Oregon, Pennsylvania, Rhode Island, South Dakota, Tennessee, Texas, Utah, Vermont, Washington, and West Virginia. In commenting upon the reciprocity of teacher certification existing between these twenty-eight states, Reisert [212:372–373] points out that:

In most states this reciprocity covers only the major field of study at the basic or probationary teaching level. A few states recognize reciprocity at the school ser-

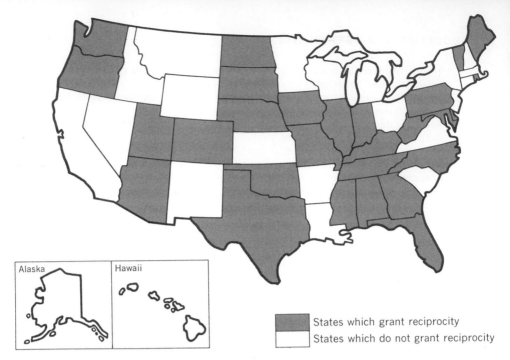

FIGURE 3–6. States which grant some measure of reciprocity privileges in the certification of teachers to graduates of institutions accredited by the National Council for Accreditation of Teacher Education, August, 1966. How many more states have since been added to the list? (*Source:* National Council for Accreditation of Teacher Education.)

vices and administrative levels and some recognize the minor preparation as well as the major preparation for endorsement reciprocity. One state, Oklahoma, recognizes NCATE reciprocity only from institutions in the other twenty-seven states utilizing this basis for reciprocity. Most states require graduation of the applicant subsequent to NCATE approval of the institution, while others operate on the principle, "once accredited, open to all." Institutions accredited by NCATE are listed in the council's *Annual List.*

It appears that NCATE accreditation will be the chief basis of reciprocity and that future graduates of institutions holding such accreditation (449 in 1967, which graduate approximately 80 per cent of all students prepared to teach) will not experience as much difficulty in moving from one state to another as have teachers in the past. Graduates of non-NCATE-accredited institutions are expected to meet the specific regulations of the states in which they seek certification, as has been the case in the past.

Some Criticisms of Teacher Education and Certification Practices

Since the quality of instruction received by pupils in our public schools is directly related to the quality of the teachers, it is to be expected that teacher education and certification practices are subject to considerable criticism. Two books in particular, one by Koerner on *The Miseducation of American Teachers* [144] and the other by Conant on *The Education of American Teachers* [51], were published in 1963 and were especially critical of teacher education and certification practices. Conant, for example, severely condemns specificity in state certification requirements. He feels that, for certification purposes, the state should require only a baccalaureate degree from a legitimate college or university, evidence of having performed as a student teacher under the direction of college and public school personnel in whom the state department has confidence, and a statement from the college or university indicating that the institution as a whole considers the person adequately prepared to teach in a designated field and grade level.

In reacting to Conant's position, Reisert [211:5] points out that not all preparing institutions offer quality programs, not all school boards are ethical, not all supervising teachers are master teachers, not all state departments are staffed and financed to supervise student teaching, not all college faculty members are interested in teacher education, and not all concerned parties are in agreement with the best approach. He cautions that, until such conditions exist, "we would be in a dangerous position to accept the Conant recommendations" [211:5].

Conant also condemns the use of NCATE accreditation as a basis of reciprocity. He feels that NCATE has become "a quasi-legal body with tremendous national power" [51:69]. In reacting to this point of view, Armstrong and Stinnett [12:17] point out that states generally use NCATE accreditation to expedite reciprocity, not to exclude graduates of other institutions from certification. Also, most states in the past years have used regional accrediting to expedite reciprocity in the same manner [12:17].

The Conant book is based upon a two-year study which Dr. Conant and his staff made of seventy-seven colleges and of state offices which grant certificates to teachers in the sixteen most populated states. It contains twenty-seven recommendations for the improvement of teacher education and certification. You may wish to study and discuss these recommendations with your colleagues.

Some Recommendations on Certification

Previous mention has been made to the publication *New Horizons for the Teaching Profession*, prepared by a committee of the National Commission on Teacher Education and Professional Standards. The committee expressed the feeling that certification of professional personnel will be effective [150:240]:

1. When the state maintains its authority to administer the issuance of licenses to teachers, but delegates to the profession responsibility for determining standards to be employed in licensure.
2. When the only purpose of legal licensure is to provide visible evidence that the candidate is competent as a beginning teacher.
3. When other purposes, now too frequently applied to licensure, are achieved:
   a. By accreditation of institutions and programs ensuring that candidates have been carefully selected and well prepared and are competent as beginning teachers.
   b. By institutional accountability for their recommendations of candidates for licensure.
   c. By wisdom of school and college officials in assignment of functions to personnel.

    d. By professional conduct by individuals in assuming only those assignments for which they are prepared and competent.
4. When the state issues only one license, the initial entrance license for teachers, based:
    a. Upon completion of an NCATE-accredited program of preparation.
    b. Upon recommendation by the preparing institution on the basis of demonstrated competency as a beginning teacher.
    c. Upon recommendation of teaching competence by the appropriate organization of teachers.
5. When specialized licenses beyond the basic one are developed and administered by the profession itself through its various associations of specialists.

You and your colleagues may wish to explore the implications of these statements for the future. Perhaps you should read the publications to gain further understanding of the position taken by the committee. Undoubtedly, further changes in certification requirements will be made, and these changes may affect you and your future plans.

FUTURE PROFESSIONAL GROWTH

The general public expects members of any profession to continue their educational and technical growth after entering their respective professions. For example, a medical doctor, even though he was graduated 30 years ago, is expected to have an understanding of recent research in the field of medicine and to utilize the findings of that research. Further, it is expected that each year of his practice will contribute to his expertness in diagnosis and treatment. In a similar fashion, teachers have a moral obligation to the general public and to their students to be aware of the rapid progress being made in the field of education. Each additional year of teaching should result in increased expertness in guiding the educational growth of children; otherwise, the policy of providing salary increases for each additional year of experience is an unwise practice.

Teachers must be well acquainted with recent research findings in regard to effective learning procedures, child growth and development, and newer techniques in teaching. Our understanding of the field of human relations is growing rapidly. The great expansion of knowledge which we are experiencing outdates much of the information gained a decade or more ago. Rapid changes are being made in community life and in social, economic, and political thinking which have far-reaching educational ramifications. If teachers are to fulfill their professional obligations, they must constantly be students of the world as it is today and as it may be tomorrow.

Educators recognize that the fundamental purpose of preservice professional education is to provide the prospective teacher with the knowledge, skills, techniques, and attitudes necessary for initial service. Perhaps one of the most important attitudes to develop during this period of time is the desire to learn and to improve.

It is an unfortunate commentary that many teachers do not maintain the spirit of the learner; they degenerate into teaching automatons. Many of them permit themselves to fall into a rut where they remain throughout their professional lives. In fact, many of them fall into the rut and proceed to dig the rut deeper; they regress rather than egress. Whereas education is potentially one of the most inspiring and intellectualizing professions, many employees neglect the opportunity to learn which is ever present; they forget that they are dealing with the most stimulating and precious, yet baffling, materials in the world, namely, the minds of pupils. School employees must constantly battle that most frequently found and devastating disease of all institutions, "institutional paralysis"; although the disease "creeps" and is painless, it will eventually kill its victim if it is not eliminated [210:536].

In formulating your plans for a career in education, make detailed provisions for your in-service growth. Actually anything that will promote your competence as a teacher may be classified as in-service growth. If you are familiar with the current developments in fields outside of education as well as within it, your effectiveness in the classroom and community should be increased. For practical purposes, formulate your plans so that they will be in harmony with the three major areas of your undergraduate preparation: general education, subject-matter specialization, and professional education.

Obviously, many of the things you will want to do will be highly individual and dependent upon your own needs, desires, and initiative. You may find that no definitely organized sources of assistance exist for meeting your particular needs. On the other hand, there are in-service educational needs common to all teachers for which sources of assistance generally are provided. Among these are supervision of teaching, reading, teacher education, conferences and workshops, and professional organizations.

Supervision

Almost all schools provide for some form of supervision. In small schools the principal or superintendent usually assumes, along with his administrative duties, the responsibilities of staff supervision. An increasing number of large school systems have established special personnel who devote full time to the supervision of instruction. A few school systems have designated one or more supervisors to work primarily with beginning teachers in getting them off to a good start, whereas other supervisors work with the more experienced teachers in helping them to improve their teaching.

Theoretically, supervision is concerned with the improvement of teaching. Modern concepts picture the supervisor as a well-educated, tactful, sympathetic, and constructive person who seeks to help each teacher realize his full capacity for educating boys and girls. The teacher looks upon the supervisor as a coworker from whom guidance and valuable assistance may be gained.

Study carefully the kind of supervision provided in any school system in which you may plan to teach. Although increasing numbers of schools provide the constructive, cooperative help indicated above, there still remain some systems in which supervisors consider their main responsibility to be that of *inspection* rather than guidance. Begin teaching in a school system in which you will receive a maximum amount of friendly, constructive assistance in the solution of problems that inevitably will arise.

Your principal or supervisor can help you with problems, especially those you may have when you begin teaching. *(Photograph by Carl Purcell, National Education Association.)*

Many teacher education institutions realize that follow-up assistance, for beginning teachers especially, is an important part of their programs. Obviously, a teacher's education is not completed upon receiving a diploma. A few institutions have extended their services by having staff members visit graduates on the job several times during the first year of teaching to help in every way possible. Some institutions invite recent graduates to return to the campus for one or more days to receive help on problems that have been encountered. Almost all institutions encourage their graduates to write or return to the campus for professional assistance.

A very large number of institutions automatically secure reports from employing officials on their graduates during the first year of teaching. These reports help an institution to locate graduates urgently in need of assistance, to evaluate the effectiveness of its teacher education program, and to secure data that may be used in recommending people for better positions.

Teachers' Meetings

You will be attending various kinds of teachers' meetings which may be of some help to you in your professional growth. Most of these meetings will involve the teachers in your school building, but some of them may involve all of the teachers in the school system.

Too frequently in the past teachers' meetings have been administration-dominated and have been run in a dictatorial fashion. They have been used too frequently as a "clearinghouse" for administrative detail and for the consideration of "housekeeping" problems. As a result, many teachers have felt that they received little or no professional help from these meetings and dreaded having to attend them.

Today teachers are taking more active roles in teachers' meetings. These meetings are planned in terms of purposes and are conducted in a spirit of helpfulness.

Teachers participate in establishing the purposes of the meetings and in conducting them. A variety of problems experienced by the teachers may be discussed. School policies may be reviewed, formulated, and adopted. Improvement or formulation of new curricular programs, research projects, grading practices and policies, school community relationships and projects, and a host of other activities may constitute the concerns of teachers in these meetings. Here you have the opportunity to become an important member of a team and to gain professional assistance from your colleagues.

Conferences and Workshops

Many teacher education institutions and public school systems provide educational conferences of one or more days' duration to aid the in-service growth of teachers. Conferences that are limited to one day usually consist of meetings in which outstanding educators discuss educational problems with the teachers and administrators. Often these conferences are designed to provide inspiration and to encourage professional growth.

For the past 25 years the workshop idea has experienced phenomenal growth. Basically, an educational workshop consists of a group of educators working cooperatively and intensively for several days on problems of concern to the group.

Workshops have the following common characteristics:

1. Working sessions are planned around the interests and problems identified by the participants. As examples, the members of the group may wish to improve their techniques of appraising the progress of pupils or the methods of teaching arithmetic. The problems selected by the group are delimited to such scope that successful progress can be made during the time available.
2. The organization of the workshop is flexible in order that group work may proceed in solving problems. There is no fixed program with lectures. Consultants are available for participation in group work and for individual conferences.
3. Although much of the work is done through small groups, general meetings serve such purposes as planning work sessions, sharing experiences, learning about new developments of interest to the entire group, or gaining specific assistance relating to the problems selected for study.
4. Various resources are available to facilitate progress in solving problems. The most significant resources are the members of the workshop group—participants and consultants.

Increasing numbers of teacher education institutions are providing workshop opportunities, on the campus or in the field, for which college credit is given. Many school systems sponsor workshops in which various members work on major educational problems, such as discipline, science instruction, or reporting to parents.

The intellectual stimulation gained from participation in a well-conducted workshop is bound to add much to a teacher's professional growth. Furthermore, when the collective intelligence of a group of educators is focused upon problems of common concern, fundamental improvements in educational practice will take place.

Workshops provide teachers excellent opportunities to improve their professional insights and skills. These teachers are attending a summer workshop on elementary school science so that they may be more effective when they return to their classrooms in the fall. *(Photograph from the News Bureau, Indiana University.)*

Professional Organizations

You will be concerned with at least three types of professional organizations—your local, state, and national teacher associations—and the effect of each upon your future professional growth. Since each of these associations will be discussed at length in a later chapter, the primary concern at this point is to see them as an integral part of an in-service educational program.

The amount of growth that you will gain through professional organizations will depend largely upon your initiative, your ability to work effectively with others, your desire to be an active member of the various organizations, and the adequacy of your plans for this type of growth. In addition to the many other values that may accrue, active participation should give you deep satisfaction and stimulation.

Additional College and University Work

Almost all the larger teacher education institutions and universities provide extensive summer sessions. In view of the fact that teachers normally constitute a large enrollment, the summer programs are designed specially to meet the needs of this group of students. Some prospective teachers use the summer session as a means of gaining additional credits or of speeding up their preparations for teaching. Experienced teachers often use the summer period for bringing their qualifications up to standard, working for advanced degrees, and/or extending their professional or subject-matter background, independent of degree credit.

Summer session programs usually attempt to serve the needs of these groups of students. The summer sessions generally are staffed by regular faculty members, but some large institutions attempt to secure the services of one or more outstanding educators also. This practice enables teachers to study with various educational leaders of the nation.

Some teachers combine summer school study with other types of experiences. For example, you can attend a college or university located near an ocean or high in the mountains where the weather is pleasant or in some section of the country with which you are not well acquainted. A number of colleges are granting credit during summer sessions for conducted tours to other countries. In fact, a special department of the National Education Association assists teacher education institutions in planning and conducting these tours. In this manner the entire world becomes the classroom from which the teacher may learn.

Extension courses and correspondence courses often are available to teachers during the regular school year. Statistics indicate that many teachers avail themselves of these opportunities to extend their professional and/or subject-matter backgrounds. Extension courses are offered on Saturdays or during the week by institutions in specified centers, usually where the interests and needs of a relatively large number of teachers may be met. In planning for teaching, take into consideration these educational opportunities, keeping in mind, however, the possible strain upon your time and energy. It would be exceedingly unwise for you to sacrifice your effectiveness in the classroom for what might be purely personal gains.

Give serious consideration to additional college work as you plan for your future professional growth. As noted previously, the fifth year of training is fast

FIGURE 3–7. Trend in the preparation of the typical public school teacher. Why must this trend continue? (*Source:* National Education Association.)

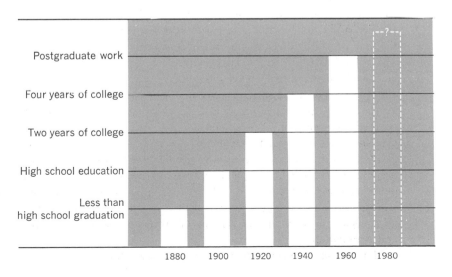

becoming the rule rather than the exception. The growth of knowledge in all fields is so great that you cannot stand still—either you drop back or you move ahead in your competence in teaching. Professional courses almost invariably prove much more interesting, meaningful, and helpful to a teacher after he has had some experience. Additional work should broaden your understanding of and deepen your insights into educational problems and should make your work a fascinating challenge to you. Furthermore, the better positions generally come to those who are best prepared for them. Salary schedules and standards in different school systems place increasingly higher demands upon the preparation of school employees. It is important that you plan not only to meet these demands but to go beyond them.

Reading

The printed word never ceases to be a source of intellectual stimulation and growth, regardless of a person's occupation. Perhaps more printed material is available in the field of education than in any other profession. The material is so great that, regardless of how avid a reader you may be, it would be virtually impossible to find time to read all of the current material published. Hence, you will be faced with the problems of becoming familiar with the different kinds of material available, establishing some criteria of selection, and planning a reading program that will enable you to experience the optimum amount of growth.

During your preparation for teaching, become acquainted with outstanding educational literature which may prove helpful to you later. Start developing your professional library long before you begin teaching.

Many professional books are published each year. In the *NEA Journal* a list of the best books in each of the major fields of education is published yearly. Almost all professional periodicals contain notices of new books being released. Often reviews are included. Since it is impossible to read all the books being published, you will find book reviews especially helpful in extending the scope of your literary contacts and in selecting materials for careful study.

Educational periodicals constitute the "newspaper of the teaching profession." They report the latest happenings of the school world, the controversial issues that are being debated, the latest theories that are being passionately advocated, and the most recent findings of educational research.

The majority of educational periodicals are published by national, state, and local professional organizations, although a few of them are undertaken by private enterprises. There are so many that it is not possible to discuss them adequately in the space available here. Virtually every significant aspect of education is covered by some kind of periodical. The articles appearing in periodicals are classified and catalogued in *The Education Index*, which is valuable in locating current literature pertaining to any significant educational problem. During your preparation for teaching, spend some time browsing through as many different periodicals as possible in order to become acquainted with the problems considered and the value of each periodical to you. Any wide-awake teacher knows where to go to secure assistance in the solution of problems and to gain professional insights and stimulation.

Membership in your national and state education associations entitles you to receive their respective monthly periodicals, the contents of which are of general interest to all educators. Subscribe to some periodical that is directed to your specific area of interest and/or specialization. The extent of your subscription to professional periodicals beyond this point is a matter that only you will be able to determine. You owe to yourself the number of subscriptions that will enable you to experience maximum professional growth. In some schools, teachers plan and share their personal subscriptions so as to avoid duplications and gain extensive coverage of periodical literature. Many schools provide in the budget for limited subscriptions to periodicals and for purchase of professional books for the in-service growth of teachers.

Do not limit your plans for reading to professional literature only. You owe to your pupils and to yourself as a citizen a good understanding of local, state, national, and international current affairs. Be familiar with some of the best books that are being published. Your reading should be so planned that your general education and your knowledge in your areas of academic specialization continue to expand as long as you live.

Other Sources of Growth

When well planned, your participation in community affairs can add much to your effectiveness as a citizen, your understanding of the needs of children and the community forces that play upon them, and your ability to develop harmonious working relationships between the school and the home. The teacher who fails to avail himself of the stimulation and growth that may come from active community participation is usually destined to become a cloistered, uninteresting person whose effectiveness in the classroom is limited.

It should be relatively easy for you to enter into the life of the community. Generally, the services of teachers are sought eagerly. It is important to remember, however, that your first obligation is to the boys and girls you teach and that the community activities in which you engage must be planned in terms of the welfare of these children.

Travel provides a never-ending source of intellectual stimulation and enrichment for the teacher. It is limited primarily by one's financial means. The average teacher should be able to plan for at least one extensive trip within the United States each summer and for one or more trips abroad during his professional career. In addition to the personal and professional growth acquired, many teachers collect photographs, take movies, gather specimens and other items during their travels in order to enrich the classroom experiences of their pupils.

In recent years the practice of public school teachers' exchanging positions, usually for one year, has received considerable attention. Much may be said for this plan, as it increases teachers' understandings of other areas and adds to their professional growth, especially when the exchange takes place on an international level.

It has been recognized for many years that teachers may profit from observing the work of others. A number of school systems are establishing policies that provide opportunities during the regular school year for teachers to visit outstanding schools and to observe other teaching methods. This practice permits comparing

An increasing number of teachers are furthering their professional competence through travel. Joye Tobin of North Kansas City in Missouri has been able to enrich her teaching back home as a result of her Teacher Corps experiences in Africa. *(Photograph from the National Education Association.)*

and contrasting to gain new ideas and insights that improve professional competencies.

SUMMARY

By far the larger proportion of prospective teachers now receive their preparation in institutions of college rank. Virtually all teacher education institutions have been greatly concerned with improving the quality of teaching as well as with increasing the amount of preparation for the profession.

Although considerable variation exists in the programs provided by different institutions, the preparation of teachers can be considered in terms of the following three major aspects: general education, subject-matter specialization, and professional education. Educational programs for elementary teachers tend to provide for more general and professional education, whereas secondary teachers tend to specialize in one or more subject areas and to take correspondingly less general and professional education. Professional education courses embody the specialized professional knowledge, skills, and techniques essential for successful teaching.

During the past 50 years the certification requirements for teaching have increased steadily. With higher certification requirements, teaching has become more widely recognized as a profession. The function of certifying teachers has been centralized in the state department of education.

The completion of approved teacher education programs, rather than the results of teacher examinations, now forms the basis for certification. Licenses have been differentiated according to the nature of the teacher's preparation. Life licenses have been gradually abolished. The level of preparation has been raised for all types of certificates. Specialized courses in education have been required in the preparatory programs of teachers.

These advancements have come primarily through the efforts of those within the profession. Teacher education institutions, accrediting agencies, such as the National Council for the Accreditation of Teacher Education, and the National Education Association have provided outstanding leadership. Present-day graduates, especially those trained for the elementary level, generally enter the profession much better prepared than teachers already in service. Since this condition provides added incentive for experienced teachers to gain additional training, the average level of preparation possessed by all teachers is higher than it used to be. A positive relationship seems to exist between the increase in the requirements for teaching and the supply of those entering the profession.

Preservice preparation constitutes only the minimum amount required for entering the profession. As long as you remain in teaching, you have a moral obligation to yourself and your students to continue to improve your professional competence. Several sources of in-service growth have been noted to help you formulate long-range plans. You doubtless will find many other sources that will enable you to meet your specific needs. Basically, the extent of your growth will depend on your desire to fulfill adequately your function as an educator and on your concern with raising the level of the teaching profession.

QUESTIONS FOR YOUR CONSIDERATION

1. In your opinion, what percentage of time spent in a four-year teacher education program should be devoted to general education, to specialized subject matter, and to professional education? What are the reasons for this distribution?

2. What leadership experiences with boys and girls have been of most value to you as a prospective teacher? Why? What other types of experiences should you have before you begin teaching?

3. What are the advantages and disadvantages of a teacher's taking graduate work without having had some full-time teaching experience?

4. What is the procedure for securing a teacher's certificate in the state in which you plan to teach?

5. Why are provisional certificates usually granted to beginning teachers?

6. Upon what grounds should a teacher's certificate be revoked?

7. Do you feel that a teacher should be required to sign an oath of allegiance or loyalty to the United States? What are your reasons?

8. Should the requirements for elementary teachers be as high as, or higher than, the requirements for secondary teachers? Why?

9. For what reasons should states require elementary and secondary school principals and superintendents to have six or more years of college work for certification?

10. What are the advantages and disadvantages of using the results of the National Teacher Examination in the screening of teacher applicants?

11. What are the advantages and disadvantages of granting life certificates to teachers?

12. How would you solve the problem of reciprocity in teacher certification?

13. What is your position with respect to requiring private and church-related school teachers to be certified? What are the reasons for your position?

14. Recall one or more teachers who, in your opinion, have ceased to grow professionally. What are the causes? In what ways have their pupils suffered?

15. Many school systems require teachers periodically to earn credit through additional college course work, travel, or research. What merits, if any, do you see in such requirements?

ACTIVITIES FOR YOU TO PURSUE

1. An increased number of educators feel that there are many common elements in the preparation of elementary and secondary teachers. Discuss with your colleagues the proposition that competency for teaching is the same, regardless of level. At what point, if any, should the preparation of elementary and secondary teachers be differentiated?

2. Some colleges and universities have developed programs in which all professional work for teachers is concentrated in the fifth year of college. Discuss with your colleagues the advantages and disadvantages of such a plan.

3. Investigate the possibilities of working with a group of children or young people in your community. Explore opportunities in scouting groups, community centers, recreation programs, church schools, and the like.

4. Examine a recent copy of Armstrong and Stinnett's *A Manual on Certification Requirements for School Personnel in the United States*. Note the specific requirements for teaching in the state in which you have some interest. Have any changes taken place?

5. Compare the requirements for teaching prescribed by the following: your state, the institution in which you are preparing for teaching, a rural school system, and a very large school system, all of which are within the same state.

6. Examine a copy of *The Education Index* and become thoroughly familiar with its potential value to you. In order to gain skill in its use, list a number of current articles that deal with some educational problem in which you are interested.

7. Browse through as many professional periodicals as possible in your college library. Note on a sheet of paper for each periodical you examine such things as the following: name of the periodical, publisher, editor, frequency of publi-

cation, cost per year, summary of the kinds of problems considered, and potential value to you. You may wish to keep these sheets in a folder for future reference, especially when you plan your professional subscriptions and when you meet various educational problems.

8. Investigate the types of in-service growth provided for teachers in school systems in which you may be interested in locating.

9. Make a list of some things you would like to do after you begin teaching to make your job more interesting and effective.

4

OPPORTUNITIES IN EDUCATION

You will probably find a good position more readily and enjoy greater success and happiness in your teaching if you review your plans in terms of the many opportunities in education. To do this, you will want to know what opportunities exist at the various levels and in all subject areas. There are greater demands at some levels and in some subject areas than in others. Furthermore, the law of supply and demand has some effect upon the salaries of teachers. Teachers prepared in specialties where the demand exceeds the supply tend to receive higher salaries than do those prepared in oversupplied specialties.

Obviously, you should not choose to teach a particular level or subject area solely because it holds the best promise of immediate employment. It would be exceedingly unwise to prepare for elementary teaching, for which there is great demand, if you are more skilled in working with older pupils and certain that you will be happier with them. A sound, intelligent decision in regard to age level and subject areas certainly will increase your chances of success and satisfaction in a career in education.

As you read this chapter and other materials on opportunities in education and as you observe in school situations, ask yourself such questions as the following: With what age level can I work most successfully? What academic areas interest me most? Do I prefer to work with individuals rather than groups? Have I explored all the different kinds of work of teachers? Would college teaching interest me? What type of work do I eventually want to do?

Your first position probably will entail classroom teaching. Most educators, regardless of the type of work in which they now are engaged, have taught in a public school classroom for a period of time. In considering your opportunities in the field of education, you will be concerned initially with securing a teaching position in the area and on the level of most interest to you.

General Factors Affecting Supply and Demand of Teachers

Broadly conceived, the demand for teachers consists of the total number of teaching positions to be filled in a given year. Demand is created through such factors as death, retirement, disability, dismissal, resignation, and the creation of new positions. Supply is created through the completion of certification requirements and the seeking of teaching positions. Some prospective teachers complete the requirements for certification but decide not to teach. Other teachers, who have left their positions for a different type of work, wish to return to the profession. Conditions vary from one part of the country to another.

It is estimated that the annual turnover of public school teachers throughout the United States is approximately 14 per cent of the total number of teachers

[282:17]. Six per cent move to other jobs and eight per cent leave the profession. Of the number who leave the profession each year, about one-third leave for marriage and family reasons, one-sixth retire because of age or disability, one-sixth (largely men) enter other types of employment, and one-third leave for miscellaneous reasons including not being reemployed. Approximately one-fourth of the positions vacated by those leaving the profession will be filled by teachers reentering active employment [265:28–29], thereby resulting in a net loss of approximately 8 per cent.

Some officials are often unable to fill all their vacancies with qualified teachers. As indicated in Chapter 3, these positions frequently are filled with teachers who hold limited (emergency) certificates and who are not properly trained for their positions. Positions held by these emergency teachers actually constitute a demand for qualified teachers.

A number of people feel that one method of meeting the demand for teachers represented by those holding limited certificates is to lower certification standards. They likewise feel that raising certification standards will result in an increase in the number of limited certificates issued. Neither of these feelings is substantiated by facts. In general, the greatest shortages of qualified teachers occur in rural schools, in elementary schools, and in states having the lowest certification standards and lowest salaries. Most states which issue a relatively small percentage of limited certificates not only have high standards but also pay above-average salaries and maintain good teacher retirement systems.

Another factor which affects demand is the number of pupils assigned to a teacher. For example, if 100 rather than 25 pupils were assigned to each teacher, only one-fourth as many teachers would be needed.

Educators generally recommend no more than twenty-five pupils per teacher.

FIGURE 4–1. Past and projected increase of population in the United States by decades from 1900 to 2000. (*Source:* U.S. Bureau of the Census.)

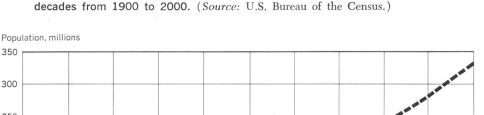

Population, millions

However, some research reveals that, so far as academic achievement in subject matter is concerned, the results obtained in a large class may be just as good as those in a small one. On the other hand, modern education assumes that the teacher contributes to the total growth of the child: emotional, social, and physical growth as well as to his knowledge of subject matter. "The educational process must be consciously designed to help the student (*a*) gain meaningful understandings, (*b*) develop desirable study habits, (*c*) speak effectively and listen critically, (*d*) build high ideals, and (*e*) gain respect and concern for others. In short, education today faces a growing responsibility for the development of habits and attitudes conducive to good adult citizenship in a local, national and worldwide society" [263:20]. In order to accomplish these aims adequately, the number of pupils per teacher, especially on the elementary level, must be lowered.

There are great variations throughout the United States in the pupil-teacher ratio. Generally it is lower (and therefore better) in secondary schools than in elementary schools, lower in areas where the population is sparse, and lower in areas where many one-room schools are found.

There has been a definite trend toward the reduction of the number of pupils assigned to a teacher. The pupil-teacher ratio in 1929–1930 was 30.1; in 1939–1940 it was 29.1; in 1949–1950 it was 27.5; in 1965–1966 it was 24.6 [207]. If the very desirable downward trend continues, a sizable number of new teachers will be needed.

The number of children born each year obviously has its effect on the number of teachers needed. During the late 1920s and throughout the 1930s the birthrate in the continental United States decreased. Following World War II the birthrate increased, as indicated in Figure 4–2, but has been decreasing during the past few years. Table 4 indicates what may be expected in kindergarten, elementary and secondary school, and college enrollments during the next few years.

FIGURE 4–2.   Births and deaths in the United States, 1930–1964. The number of births has risen more rapidly than the number of deaths, a fact which has changed the age composition of our population. (*Source:* U.S. Bureau of the Census.)

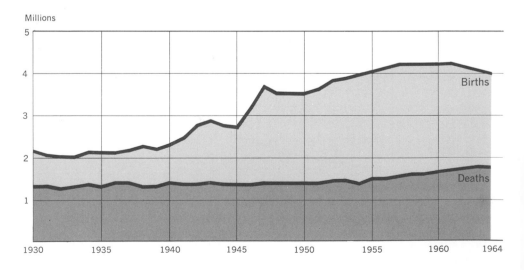

TABLE 4   Projections of Elementary, Secondary, and Higher Education Enrollments in
Public and Nonpublic Schools, 1970 to 1985

School year	Elementary schools and kindergarten	Secondary schools	Institutions of higher education	Total
1970–1971	36,409,000	14,961,000	7,105,000	58,475,000
1975–1976	35,821,000	16,264,000	9,120,000	61,204,000
1980–1981	39,791,000	15,679,000	10,866,000	66,336,000
1985–1986	46,586,000	16,999,000	11,575,000	75,159,000

Source: Statistical Abstract of the United States, U.S. Bureau of the Census, 1966, p. 11.

The demand for teachers also is affected by the number of pupils who remain
in school. For example, the phenomenal increase in the percentage of 14- to 17-
year-olds attending secondary school has created a great demand for teachers
during the past half century. The further increase in pupils attending secondary
schools will make demands for additional secondary teachers. Also, as public
school opportunities are extended upward to include junior college and extended
downward to include kindergarten and nursery school, appreciable demands will
be made for teachers qualified to teach on these levels.

Economic conditions affect the demands for teachers. In times of depression,
fewer high-salaried positions occur outside the profession to attract teachers, more

FIGURE 4–3.   Life expectancy in the United States. What educational, social, and
vocational problems arise from the increasing number of people who are 65 years
and older? (*Source:* U.S. Bureau of the Census.)

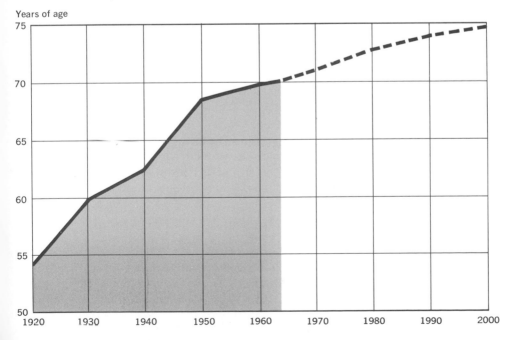

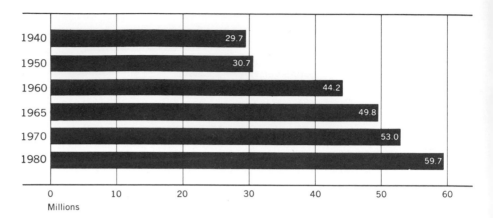

FIGURE 4–4.   Change in the population of the United States, 5–17 years of age, between 1940 and 1980. What are the implications of this change for opportunities in teaching as well as for education in general? (*Source:* National Education Association.)

married women continue to teach, and vacancies in school systems frequently are absorbed by the remaining staffs. In times of prosperity, more teachers leave the profession to accept higher-paying positions, a greater number of married women discontinue teaching, vacancies are filled by new teachers, and new positions are often created.

As the nature of the school program changes, the demand for teachers also changes. Certainly the percentage of Latin and Greek teachers is less today than it was at the time of the Latin grammar school. In recent years new demands have been made for instruction and services. If the school is to continue to meet the needs of boys and girls, these new demands must be met.

The attitude of society in general toward the existing proportion of men and women within the profession has an effect upon opportunities. Although teaching in the United States has been predominantly a woman's field, especially on the elementary level, the profession presents great opportunities for both sexes. Young men, who ultimately wish to become school principals, will do well to consider the possibilities of entering the field of elementary education where more men are especially desired.

Federal assistance to education tends to increase the demand for teachers. As a result of federal legislation during the mid-sixties, new opportunities exist for teachers at the preschool, elementary, and college levels as well as in adult education. For example, the number of guidance counselors in public schools almost trebled during the seven years following passage of the National Defense Education Act. In 1966, it was estimated that 300 experienced teachers and 1,200 beginning teachers were needed in the Teacher Corps [265:35].

As indicated in Chapter 1, the educational needs of adults will become increasingly greater as a result of technological and social progress. Subsequent sections of this book will emphasize some of the exciting and challenging demands that will be made of teachers at all levels and in all areas of learning.

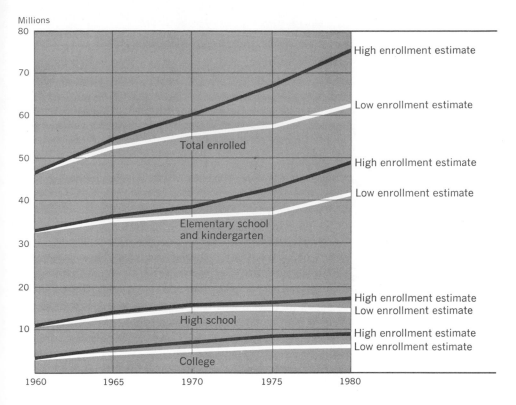

FIGURE 4–5. Between 1960 and 1980 enrollments in our schools, from kindergarten to the college level, may increase 61.3 per cent. In 1980 it is possible that one-half of our population will be of school age or approaching school age (under 5) compared to 45 per cent in 1960. How will schools and colleges as well as job opportunities be affected by these increases? (*Source:* Chamber of Commerce of the United States.)

Sources of Teacher Supply

It is extremely difficult to determine accurately the total number of certified teachers who are actively seeking teaching positions. For example, some teachers who have not taught for a number of years may desire to return to the profession. There is no precise way of ascertaining how many teachers for any given year will fall into this category. Furthermore, some students who have completed the requirements for teaching may never seek a teaching position or may postpone accepting a teaching position for several years.

Each year, approximately one in five of the elementary teacher graduates and three in ten of the secondary teacher graduates are not available for teaching positions. More secondary teacher graduates who major in physical education (women's), mathematics, library science, speech, music, foreign language, English, and industrial arts enter teaching than those who major in agriculture, journalism, commerce, and social studies. As might be expected, nonteaching occupations draw heavily on teachers who major in such areas as business education, chemistry,

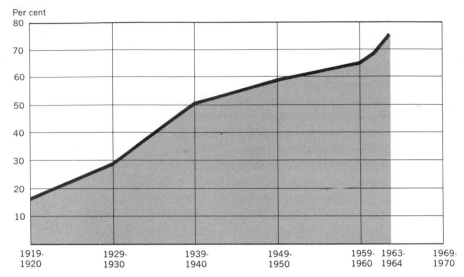

Per cent

FIGURE 4–6. The percentage of 17-year-olds who graduate from public and non-public schools has increased greatly since 1920. What factors have fostered this increase? (*Source:* National Education Association.)

agriculture, and physics. Approximately 6 per cent of the secondary teacher graduates continue formal study immediately following graduation, and 4 per cent become homemakers. A number of men enter military service upon graduation.

Another factor makes it difficult to determine the supply of teachers. An appreciable number of well-educated people, especially women holding bachelor's degrees and who have not taken teacher education as a part of their undergraduate work, are deciding later to take professional course work to meet certification requirements. A number of teacher education institutions have developed special fifth-year programs which have academic and professional respectability in order to prepare these people for teaching.

In the light of the variables indicated above, perhaps the most dependable rough indication of the supply of teachers is the number of college students completing standard certification requirements. The research division of the National Education Association sponsors studies that provide estimates of the number who, at the end of each school year (including summer sessions), qualify for standard teaching certificates. Table 5 is an example of the kinds of information which this annual research provides. From this table you can gain a fairly accurate picture of the supply and demand for teachers on various levels and in various subject areas, the relative number of beginning teachers who were assigned to teach full-time in their major areas, and the combination of major and minor subject areas to which beginning teachers were most frequently assigned. In studying the various combinations of subject areas for 1965–1966, for example, note that English major assignments were combined most frequently with social studies, foreign language, or speech minor assignments.

The results of these studies are published annually by the research division of

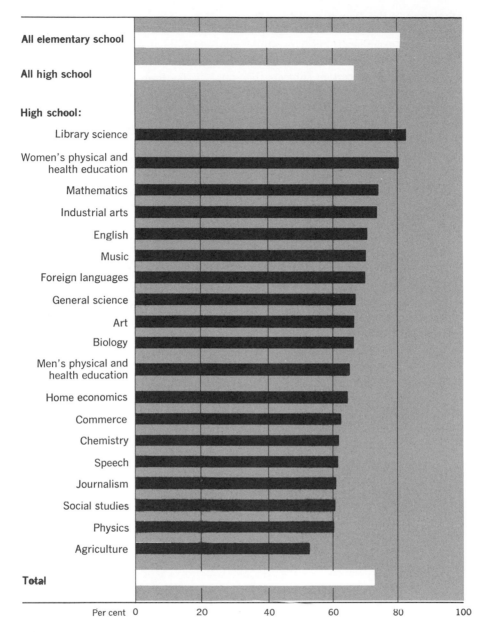

FIGURE 4–7. Percentage of certified graduates of 1965 who entered teaching service. (*Source:* National Education Association.)

the National Education Association. Since some changes occur from year to year in the supply and demand for teachers, consult the most recent reports available to note any trends that may be taking place. Also, check with your college placement officer to see whether these national data are typical of the supply-and-demand conditions in the local area which interests you.

Imbalance in the Demand and the Supply of Teachers

If you examine Table 5 carefully you will note that in some subject areas the number of qualified secondary teacher graduates exceeds the demand. On the other hand, in certain subjects the supply is far from adequate. Such data would seem to indicate that college students intending to become high school teachers choose their major fields without a thorough knowledge of the number of opportunities and the amount of competition in the various high school teaching fields.

The greatest imbalance, however, is to be found in the proportionately small number of elementary teachers who are being prepared. The ratio of elementary teachers to secondary teachers is 9½ to 7, but the ratio of new prospective candidates at the two levels is scarcely 6 to 9 [264:12]. The supply is almost exactly in reverse ratio to that of the number now employed at the two levels.

The excessive imbalance of teachers in the various fields and levels of teaching constitutes a serious problem in the minds of many educators. As a future professional educator you will be affected by this imbalance. How should the problem be solved? Do you feel that no planned attempt should be made to maintain a reasonable balance between the supply and demand of teachers? Do you maintain that it is undemocratic to limit, as does the medical profession, the number permitted to prepare for the profession? Do you maintain that the problem eventually will solve itself? Do you believe that, when the imbalance becomes too great, increased numbers of intelligent students preparing for secondary teaching will foresee the lack of job opportunities and therefore will not plan to teach?

Or do you feel that a definite plan should be developed to solve the problem of excessive imbalance in supply and demand? Is there no justification, so far as society is concerned, for allowing everyone to prepare for teaching who wishes to do so? Do you feel that both students and society will profit far more by guiding

FIGURE 4–8.   Secondary school enrollments have grown much faster than elementary school enrollments. Elementary school enrollments are expected to increase only 8 per cent between 1966 and 1975, but high school enrollments should rise about 30 per cent. (*Source:* Chamber of Commerce of the United States.)

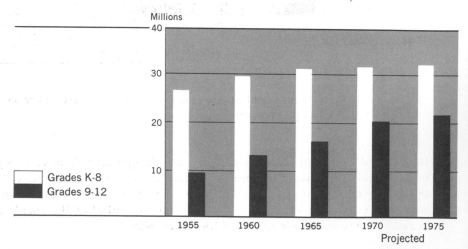

TABLE 5 Assignments of New Teachers Employed in 29 States, 1965–1966, and New Teachers Produced in 1964–1965

Major subject assignment	Minor subject assignments																				Total new teachers employed	Total new supply
	Agriculture	Art	Commerce	English	Foreign language	Home economics	Industrial arts	Journalism	Library science	Mathematics	Music	Physical education, men	Physical education, women	General science	Biology	Chemistry	Physics	Social studies	Speech	Other		
Agriculture	371	9		2	1		24			4		2	7	27	9	5		3	2	2	459	798
Art	1	833		40	8	3	11	8		6	4	4	7	8	1			21	6	12	967	1,776
Commerce	3		2,093	110	11	11	2			51	2	39	21	6	5	1		104		36	2,508	4,033
English	1	22	58	5,663	469	26	2	97	65	56	41	27	27	45	10	1		751	298	179	7,838	8,213
Foreign language	1		6	310	1,391	6	1	4	1	17	6	2	4	2		1	2	94	10	32	1,896	2,372
Home economics		12	7	50	4	1,525			9	8	3		39	75	18	6		39	3	23	1,823	3,146
Industrial arts	4	6	3	3	3	2	1,127	2		30		43		13	1			32		76	1,345	1,589
Journalism			2	27	1	1		20	1	1								2	3	5	63	68
Library science	3	1	2	50	4	1			442	1			2	1	1			11	2	5	526	320
Mathematics	1	5	32	59	25	3	13	1	5	3,898	9	78	20	338	35	59	146	94	6	41	4,868	3,945
Music	3	4	4	38	3	1			1	7	1,497	6	3	1	1			30	10	14	1,628	3,038
Physical education, men		4	11	15	2	0	18	1	1	36	2	1,075	7	91	39	13	3	204	1	54	1,563	4,599
Physical education, women		3	8	30	3	5			3	18	2	7	1,266	42	21		1	100	5	36	1,563	1,957
General science	10	3	2	25	13	18	8		1	223	3	92	25	2,185	201	72	49	66	2	34	3,033	1,309
Biology	2		5	12	1	6	3		1	35	1	40	15	189	431	118	39	20		27	945	2,317
Chemistry	1		1	3	1	1				46	1	1	2	83	58	157	103	3		20	481	513
Physics				1			2			54		3		40	23	59	58	6		19	265	146
Social studies	3	13	57	303	58	15	10	7	11	83	20	277	62	77	27	1	3	3,369	28	112	4,536	8,910
Speech				113	5	1		7	1	1	4	1	2	1				19	158	61	373	1,537
Other	1		26	126	22	5	11	4	11	10	5	21	9	21	19	18	19	66	41	2,456	2,880	1,081
High school total																					39,560	51,667
Elementary school total																					40,395	30,596

Source: Adapted from *Teacher Supply and Demand in Public Schools, 1966,* Research Report 1966–R16, National Education Association, Research Division, Washington, October, 1966, p. 36.

the less promising students into other occupations in which the probabilities of employment are much greater? Thus, many would avoid the possible bitterness of not being able to secure teaching positions and of having wasted the opportunity to prepare for something else.

A few institutions, especially in the eastern part of the United States, have attempted to limit the teacher supply by accepting only a certain number of candidates. Too often the quota plan does not give adequate attention to quality or probable fitness for teaching. Other institutions have made some attempts to control the number of graduates by raising scholastic requirements. The National Council for Accreditation of Teacher Education insists that approved colleges and universities admit to their teacher education programs only those students who have an overall grade average above that required for graduation. NCATE-accredited schools prepare approximately 80 per cent of the annual supply of new teachers.

As you move into your teaching career, you will have the opportunity to be concerned with the problem of imbalance in the demand and supply of teachers. Through the efforts of educators and public school personnel, some solution probably will emerge whereby employment opportunities will be decreased for the unfit and increased for those who hold the greatest promise for guiding our youth.

Too often, factors other than fitness operate in the selection of teachers for positions. The intelligent, promising individual who should prepare for teaching may foresee that appointments are not always based upon merit and may abandon the idea of teaching. Consequently, the quality of those preparing for the profession is lowered.

In planning your career in education you have the basic responsibility of securing and taking into consideration all possible available data regarding supply and demand, especially in those areas and/or levels in which you are particularly interested. Personnel in almost all teacher education institutions today have these data available. They will be able to advise you not only in terms of the national picture but also in terms of the conditions that exist in your specific locale. Since conditions do change from time to time, it is important that you maintain close contact throughout your preparation for teaching with the teacher-employment office which your institution probably maintains.

Analysis of Opportunities in Elementary and Secondary Schools

If the school system is to meet its responsibilities to society, the demand for thoroughly competent teachers must be met through (1) replacement of those who quit teaching, (2) accommodation of the increased enrollment, (3) reduction of oversized classes and elimination of half-day sessions, (4) provision for instructional and educational services not now generally available, and (5) replacement of unqualified persons now serving as teachers [264:30]. What, briefly, does each of these demands mean, so far as your opportunities for teaching are concerned?

You can estimate an annual net loss (departures minus returnees) of 8.5 per cent of the public school teachers due to retirement, disability, dismissal, or death. For example, in 1967 approximately 165,000 teachers were needed to replace those leaving the profession for the above reasons. Approximately 50,000 addi-

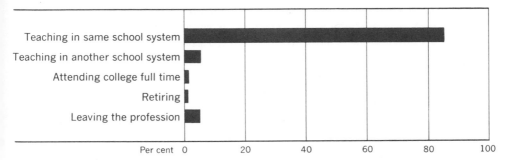

FIGURE 4–9. What teachers employed full time in 1965–1966 planned to do in 1966–1967. The teachers who expected to leave the profession were planning to work in a nonteaching occupation (1.5 per cent), become homemakers and/or rear children (2.9 per cent), enter military service, or be unemployed. (*Source:* National Education Association.)

tional teachers were needed to provide for the increase in school enrollment. The number of births per year foretells the approximate size of the school population in the years to come. The increasingly greater proportion of pupils remaining in the secondary schools will increase the demand for teachers unless the pupil-teacher ratio is increased.

In addition to these two very realistic needs, others have not been met and are likely to continue [264:30]. For example, approximately 30,000 teachers are needed to relieve overcrowded classrooms and to eliminate part-time sessions. The greatest problem, in regard to overcrowdedness, exists in the elementary schools, where both experience and mature judgment indicate that the effectiveness of the teacher falls rapidly as the 1-to-25 pupil-teacher ratio is exceeded. At the lower grade levels particularly, the immaturity of the child is such that personal attention should not be denied him. Also, an appreciable number of elementary and secondary pupils still attend half-day or triple sessions [131:3]. Unfortunately, elementary school children are less able than secondary school pupils to compen-

FIGURE 4–10. Pupils attending public elementary and secondary schools for less than a full or normal school day, according to regions, in the fall of 1964. (*Source:* U.S. Office of Education.)

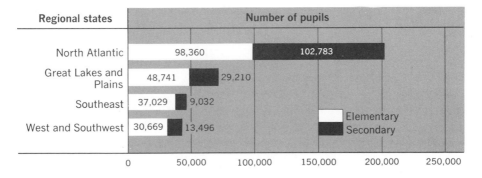

sate effectively for the loss of individual attention and assistance which results from such part-time emergency measures. It is easy to see that any relief from these educational inequalities will demand the services of a sizable share of the graduates who annually meet elementary and secondary teacher certification requirements.

As mentioned earlier, new demands for instruction and services are being made. Much attention is being given to such instructional fields as mathematics, chemistry, and physics. More foreign language is being advocated for elementary and secondary school children. Increasingly greater demands will be made for counseling and guidance services, library services, vocational education programs, work experiences, health education, recreation and safety programs, audio-visual materials, speech and hearing therapy, remedial reading, specialized instruction for the mentally retarded and for the physically handicapped, specialized instruction for the gifted, and instruction in subjects not now being offered in many of the smaller schools. A conservative estimate would indicate that 20,000 more teachers are needed if this additional instruction and services is to be provided.

Few people would argue the fact that some teachers are not adequately pre-

FIGURE 4–11.   A general working estimate of the number of children per thousand who are sufficiently handicapped to warrant special services. (*Source:* U.S. Office of Education.)

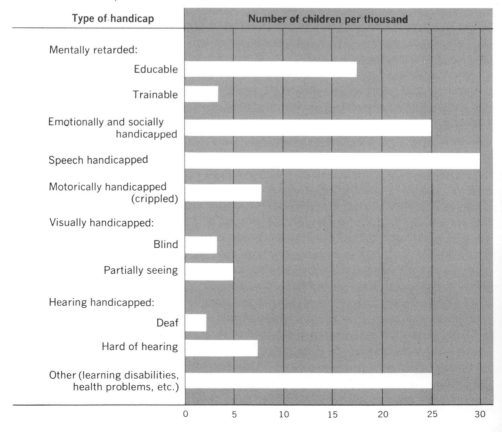

pared. There is no single answer, however, to the question "When is a person so completely inadequate that his removal from the classroom is justified?" Estimates of the number of teachers that fall in this category range from 10,000 to over 80,000 teachers [281:16]. On the other hand, it is gratifying to note that, when measured by the number of hours of college credit, much improvement in the preparation of teachers has taken place. For example, between 1948–1949 and 1965–1966 the percentage of elementary teachers having completed less than 60 semester hours of credit decreased from 16.9 to 0.7 per cent, and the percentage having 120 or more hours increased from 49.1 to 89.2 per cent [265:52].

From the above analysis, you may conclude that approximately 275,000 new teachers are needed each September [264:30]. If 150,000 (75 per cent) of the supply of qualified graduates of 1966 had actually taught, the net estimated shortage of teachers would have been 125,000 teachers.

In terms of the preceding information, you may conclude that the future looks bright for students who wish to prepare for teaching. As has been true in the past, the demand for elementary teachers will be especially great. With careful attention being given to the supply and demand for teachers in the various subject areas, you may look forward with much confidence to teaching in the secondary school area.

Subject Combinations for Teaching in the Secondary Schools

Many secondary teachers begin their teaching careers in small school systems, since city school systems usually prefer that their new appointees have a few years of successful teaching experience. Therefore keep in mind, as you plan your preparation for teaching, that you may need to teach in two or more subject areas. Even in large school systems many teachers teach in more than one subject area, as you may note from Table 5. Teachers in special areas such as agriculture, commercial subjects, fine arts, home economics, industrial arts, and music are more likely than other secondary teachers to teach in one subject area only.

The ease with which you obtain your initial appointment will depend to some degree on the extent to which the subject combination you select is in demand. A combination that is seldom in demand, such as foreign languages and physical education, is little better than a single subject, while foreign languages with English is demanded more frequently.

Fortunately the combination of subjects tends to follow definite patterns. Unrelated combinations, such as fine arts, agriculture, physics, and English, asked by employing officials in the past, are disappearing. Small secondary schools are revising programs of study so that various courses are offered in alternate years. Many small schools are reducing the number of highly specialized subjects that are offered. Furthermore, the trend toward school consolidation, which increases the enrollment and the size of the faculty of each school, means that teachers may be assigned more nearly according to their preparation.

Many studies have been made of the combination of subjects taught by secondary teachers. Your college teacher-placement officer probably makes an annual study of the subject combinations requested by employing officials. Although almost every possible combination may be found, there are certain ones that occur more often than others. You may gain some idea of desirable combinations of subject areas by studying Table 5. You will note considerable demand for such combinations as commerce and social science and/or English; English and social science, foreign languages, or speech; mathematics and general science, social science, or English; music and English; and men's physical education and social science.

The demand for various subject combinations fluctuates from year to year and varies in different sections of the United States. For example, in some states the secondary school candidates are heavily concentrated in certain fields, while in other states they are more widely distributed. Considerable variation in the demand for subject areas may exist between school districts. Your local teacher-placement officer may be of great help in selecting the combination of subjects that seems most desirable for you and most consistent with your abilities and interests.

Opportunities for Teaching on the College Level

You may plan to teach on the college level. A number of individuals value the opportunities that college teaching provides for writing, conducting research, and engaging in other scholarly pursuits. Some value highly the prestige that college instructors have, compared with that of public school teachers. Whatever the reasons may be, they may definitely affect your plans.

In some college departments, especially in the subject-matter areas, a few highly selected graduates are encouraged to work immediately for higher degrees. The students usually are granted assistantships that entail some teaching, supervision of laboratories, or the like, while they continue their studies. The assistantships pay a relatively small amount of money but provide fee exemptions for college work taken by the student. Others may receive scholarships or continue their educations at their own expense. You may wish to investigate possibilities along these lines.

A large percentage of college teachers began their teaching careers in public schools. They pursued graduate work during their summer vacations or returned for full-time study to complete their degrees. Usually they have found their public school experiences to be of great value in their college teaching. A number of years of successful elementary or secondary teaching experience is a prerequisite for securing a position in which you teach education courses.

Opportunities for college teaching will be affected by the extent to which college enrollments increase. For a number of years the percentage of the group of college students 18 to 21 years old has increased approximately 1 per cent a year. Recently this percentage has increased to 1½ per cent. If this trend continues, college enrollments may increase from approximately 5,000,000 students in 1965 to over 11,575,000 in 1985. In viewing these mounting numbers, Maul [266:11] calls attention to the following pertinent questions:

1. Will junior colleges continue to be the most rapidly growing division of higher education?
2. Will the universities concentrate to a greater extent upon graduate instruction?

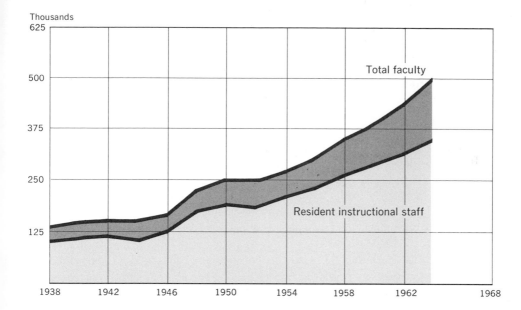

FIGURE 4–12.   Large faculty increases will be necessary to educate the influx of children born since World War II and the increasing proportion who will be seeking a college education. (*Source:* U.S. Department of Health, Education, and Welfare.)

3. Will the nonpublic institutions push their admission requirements higher, with the intent of holding enrollments at approximately the present figure?
4. Will the public universities restrict classes of entering freshmen to the top percentiles of high-school graduating classes?
5. Can the small nonpublic colleges survive in the competition for really competent teachers?
6. Will there be, in fact, an open college door for all who seek admission in the years ahead?

In addition to the number of students that may be involved, another variable to be considered is the load of each teacher. It has been estimated that the nation-wide student-teacher ratio in all higher-education institutions is approximately 14 to 1, although the range is great from institution to institution [266:11]. Efforts are being made to extend the utilization of faculty members. As Maul points out, efforts are being made to [266:11]:

1. Thrust greater responsibility upon the individual student for his own learning.
2. Eliminate nonessential and overlapping courses, and stem the tendency toward fragmentation of subject matter into highly specialized courses.
3. Experiment further with variations in class size.
4. Make joint use of teachers by two or more institutions.
5. Use mechanical and electronic devices, including television.
6. Use nonprofessional personnel to perform nonprofessional tasks.
7. Re-evaluate the committee system as a part of administrative procedure.
8. Improve the general climate and over-all working conditions on the campus.
9. Clarify further the role of the college teacher as a citizen in the community.

Another factor that will increase the demand for college teachers is the tendency for colleges and universities to extend their research function. During the
past few years, there has been an extraordinary increase in funds available for
research. For example, federal expenditure for research and development has increased tremendously since 1940, as will be indicated in Chapter 12. It is highly
likely that this trend will continue.

In studying the demand for college teachers, the research division of the National Education Association assumes that withdrawal from classroom service for
all reasons will continue at about 6 per cent a year. In view of past demands and
probable developments, it is anticipated that at least 31,000 new college teachers
will be needed each year at least until 1975.

The shortage of well-qualified teachers to meet the increasing college enrollments is reflected in the decrease of formal preparation possessed by the newly
employed teachers. For example, 31.4 per cent of the new teachers employed
in 1953–1954 held doctor's degrees as compared with only 27.2 per cent employed
in 1964–1965. During this same period of time (1953–1954 to 1964–1965) the
percentage of newly employed faculty holding the master's degree increased from
32.2 to 39.3 per cent. In 1964–1965, 12½ per cent of newly employed faculty
had less than a master's degree [266:13]. In junior colleges, approximately half
of the newly employed faculty in 1964–1965 held the master's degree, 6 to 7
per cent had the doctorate, 20 per cent had completed at least one year of graduate work beyond the master's degree, and approximately 20 per cent had not yet
attained the master's degree [266:42]. Approximately 30 per cent of all new
junior college teachers were high school teachers one year earlier.

The chief source of college and university teachers is the graduate school. The
number of doctoral degrees granted per year is continuing to rise. For example,
the number increased from 9,360 in 1958–1959 to 17,500 in 1965–1966. It is
anticipated that 35,800 will be granted in 1974–1975. Of those receiving doctoral

FIGURE 4–13.   Trends in the academic preparation of new university and college
teachers. (*Source:* National Education Association.)

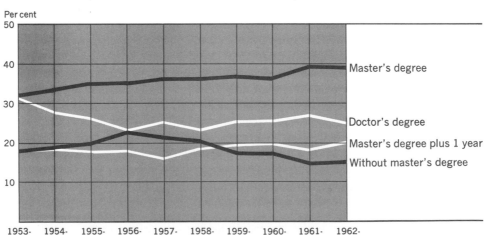

degrees who are available for positions, only about 45 per cent enter college teaching [266:53].

From the above information you may conclude that the opportunities for teaching on the college level are excellent. If you are interested, however, plan to become as well qualified as possible. In general, the better opportunities are directly related to the amount of college work you have taken.

Opportunities in Other Areas of Education

Unfortunately most people limit their concept of the opportunities in the field of education mainly to teaching in the public or private school classroom. It is true that over 80 per cent of those engaged in public school work are regular classroom teachers. On the other hand, there are specialized kinds of instruction and services to be rendered, such as counseling and guidance; research analysis; teaching speech and hearing therapy and remedial reading; teaching the mentally retarded, physically handicapped, partially seeing, hard-of-hearing, emotionally disturbed, the gifted and the culturally disadvantaged; serving as librarian; and teaching driver education and distributive education courses. Attention already has been called to the large number of superintendents, principals, supervisors, and others involved in administrative services.

It would be exceedingly interesting to analyze all the different kinds of work demanding the services of educators and to note the number involved in each. Unfortunately these data are not available. The following listing of the more common educational opportunities may be of interest to you. In no sense is the list complete.

I. Preschools—nursery and kindergarten
   A. Teacher
   B. Supervisor
   C. Consultant in child growth and development
   D. Research worker in child growth and development
   E. Director of a private nursery or kindergarten
II. Elementary schools
   A. Teacher for separate grades or combined grades
   B. Teacher of special subjects such as art, music, or physical education
   C. Teacher of a subject such as arithmetic or geography in a departmentalized school
   D. Teacher of physically handicapped, partially seeing, or hard-of-hearing children
   E. Teacher of exceptional children—talented, mentally retarded, or emotionally disturbed
   F. Critic teacher in a laboratory or experimental school
   G. General or special subject supervisor
   H. Assistant principal
   I. Principal
   J. Librarian
   K. Speech correctionist and/or hearing therapist

      L. Visiting teacher

      M. Child psychologist or counselor

      N. School nurse

      O. Curriculum consultant

      P. Guidance counselor

III. Secondary schools

      A. Teacher of subjects such as English, foreign language, social studies, or music

      B. Teaching of special subjects such as art, home economics, industrial arts and trades, music, physical education, driver education, speech and hearing therapy

      C. Critic teacher in a laboratory or experimental school

      D. Department head of a subject area

      E. Assistant principal

      F. Principal

      G. Supervisor of a subject area

      H. Curriculum consultant

      I. Athletic coach

      J. Guidance counselor

      K. Librarian

      L. Visiting teacher

IV. Administrative and special services

      A. Superintendent

         1. Full-time

         2. Part-time

      B. Assistant superintendent—usually assigned a specific phase of work such as finance, personnel, or instruction

      C. Business manager (supplies, purchasing, etc.)

      D. School secretary

      E. Research director

      F. Attendance officer

      G. Director of audio-visual materials

      H. Director of public relations

      I. School psychologist

      J. School psychometrist

      K. Vocational counselor and placement officer

      L. School statistician

      M. Clerical assistant

      N. Cafeteria manager

      O. Dietitian

      P. School physician or dentist

      Q. School nurse or health officer

      R. Adult education director

 V. Junior colleges

      A. Teacher of different fields (English, mathematics, science, etc.)

      B. Personnel director

      C. President or dean

      D. Registrar

      E. Business manager

      F. Health service officer

  VI. Teachers colleges

      A. Teacher of

         1. Subject such as English, science, etc.

         2. Subject in education

      B. Critic teacher in demonstration schools

      C. Head of department

      D. Head of demonstration or laboratory school

      E. Dean of instruction

      F. School psychologist and director of guidance

      G. Dean of men

      H. Dean of women

      I. Business manager

      J. Registrar

      K. Health service personnel

      L. Alumni secretary

      M. Director of public relations

      N. Director of placement service

      O. President

 VII. University positions

      A. Teacher of any subject field included in a large university

      B. Assistant to deans

      C. Dean of a separate college such as liberal arts, education, engineering, agriculture, law, medicine, fine arts, pharmacy, social service, dentistry

      D. Dean of instruction

      E. President

      F. Dean of men

      G. Dean of women

      H. Registrar

      I. Director of guidance

      J. Business manager

      K. Research worker

      L. Director of research

      M. Secretary and/or accountant

      N. Field worker for recruiting students

      O. Field worker for carrying services of university to the people

      P. Placement director

      Q. Health service personnel

VIII. Professional organizations like National Education Association; other national and state educational associations

      A. Director

      B. Executive secretary

      C. Research worker

    D. Field worker

    E. Writer

  IX. State departments of education

    A. State superintendent of instruction

    B. Deputy

    C. Special field worker

    D. Curriculum specialist

  X. Educational directors or consultants for noneducational agencies

    A. Publisher of newspapers, magazines, films

    B. Manufacturing firms—job training, recreation, testing, etc.

    C. Religious associations

    D. Chambers of commerce

    E. Aviation companies

    F. Service agencies, such as state tuberculosis association

  XI. Municipal, private, religious, and civic agencies

    A. City recreation director

    B. Boy and girl camps—director, instructor

    C. Director of youth organization

      1. Boy and girl scouts

      2. 4-H club

      3. YMCA and YWCA

    D. Teacher in a hospital

    E. Teacher in a church or Bible school

  XII. Federal agencies

    A. U.S. Office of Education

      1. International education (Teacher Exchange)

      2. Teacher Corps

    B. Department of Defense

      1. Dependent schools overseas

      2. Military service

    C. Department of Interior—Bureau of Indian Affairs

    D. Department of State (Peace Corps)

    E. UNESCO

  XIII. Foreign countries

    A. Teacher

    B. Conductor of tours

    C. Consultant

    D. Research worker

    E. Defense Department appointments, military government

It should be pointed out that many of the different kinds of educational work listed above do not exist in the small schools where you may begin your professional career. Small schools do not have the extensive programs and diversified types of work to be found in large schools. Furthermore, successful teaching experience normally is required for many of the positions not involving classroom teaching.

Do not overlook the educational opportunities that are continuing to develop in

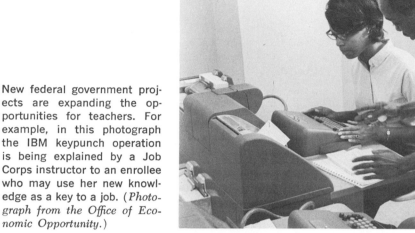

New federal government projects are expanding the opportunities for teachers. For example, in this photograph the IBM keypunch operation is being explained by a Job Corps instructor to an enrollee who may use her new knowledge as a key to a job. (*Photograph from the Office of Economic Opportunity.*)

the business world. Industries and businesses all over the country need educational directors, would be glad to employ them if they were available, and would give them opportunities to make very significant contributions to education in general. The field of educational radio and television is expanding rapidly. Textbook publishers and educational supply firms frequently employ teachers for sales or editorial positions.

The AFL-CIO, the International Ladies Garment Workers' Union, some cooperative associations, and the like already have educational directors. There are dozens of national organizations that would have educational directors now if they knew where to find them. Also, as will be discussed later, the whole field of adult education is barely getting started in this country. There is room for thousands of new jobs in that field for men and women with sound general training, creative imagination, and drive.

For the more adventurous person, the opportunities to work in even the most remote areas of the world continue to increase. For example, over 1,000 new teachers are needed each year in the American Dependent Schools Overseas [265:35]. The Peace Corps offers many opportunities to teach in a number of underdeveloped countries. You may wish to check upon the requirements and opportunities for working in schools in outlying states and areas of the United States and in schools and programs sponsored by the United States government, such as the American Dependent Schools Overseas, Teacher Exchange, Information Services, and Agency for International Development.

Preparation in the teaching profession certainly presents many different opportunities, and you can engage in the type of activity of special interest to you. If you are willing to prepare yourself well for a particular type of work, the chances of reaching your goal are good.

Barbara J. Wylie, of Ypsilanti, Michigan, joined the Peace Corps and was assigned as an English teacher in Katmandu, Nepal. As an outside project, she started a school for children of untouchable servants in her neighborhood. Normally these children would have received little or no schooling. Being a member of the Peace Corps provides an opportunity to render service while getting travel and teaching experience. (*Photograph by Paul Conklon, Peace Corps.*)

SUMMARY

The teaching profession is, by a wide margin, the largest of all the professions. Although women predominate on the elementary school level, the number of men is increasing gradually. Increases in salary and continued improvements in teaching conditions may result in larger numbers of men being attracted to teaching in the public schools.

Many factors affect the supply and demand for teachers. In periods of economic depression the supply tends to become greater than in times of economic prosperity. Birthrates, pupil-teacher ratios, and turnover and expansion or contraction of educational services rendered by the school affect significantly the demand for teachers.

The elementary schools are faced with an alarming shortage of teachers. The demands for personnel to handle new enrollments, replace teachers who annually withdraw from the profession, reduce the teacher-pupil ratio, and replace inadequately prepared teachers will far exceed the supply of teachers. This means that the educational welfare of many children will suffer.

As the need for secondary school teachers continues to mount, the imbalance in the demand and supply of teachers in the various subject areas will become more crucial. If you plan to teach on the secondary school level, pay careful attention to the imbalance that exists in the subject areas and note any changes that may be occurring in the demand and supply of teachers.

The large majority of positions in the profession involve classroom teaching, for which there is demand in all areas and on all levels, provided the candidate is highly capable and well prepared. In addition to teaching, the profession provides many other opportunities for meeting individual interests and abilities. Explore these opportunities and possibly consider some of them in your long-range plans.

QUESTIONS FOR YOUR CONSIDERATION

1. Many educators feel that more men should be attracted into public school teaching, especially into the elementary schools. Do you agree or disagree? What are your reasons?

2. Some individuals feel that the supply of elementary teachers would increase if the certification requirements were lowered. How could you defend (or deny) this opinion?

3. For what reasons can you expect the number of 14- to 17-year-olds attending secondary schools to increase significantly?

4. How might the percentage of certified graduates accepting teaching positions be increased?

5. What major and minor teaching combinations are in greatest demand? Least demand?

6. What suggestions can you make for solving the problem of excessive imbalance of teachers in the various fields and levels of teaching?

7. What sacrifices are made by pupils when they are forced to attend half-day sessions?

8. What preparation is necessary to teach on the college level? What financial assistance is being offered in an attempt to encourage students to prepare for college teaching?

9. What advantages and disadvantages do you see in teaching on the college level?

10. What solutions can you suggest for solving the increasing shortage of teachers on the college level?

11. If you had to change your subject area or level of teaching, what would you choose? Why?

12. What are some of the opportunities that exist in adult education?

13. In your opinion, what are the frontier opportunities for teachers in industry, business, and overseas programs?

ACTIVITIES FOR YOU TO PURSUE

1. Plan a number of visits to more than one school, during which you observe various elementary and secondary school classes. Attempt to make, or further verify, an original decision regarding the subject areas and/or the level you may wish to teach.

2. Plan some leadership experiences with children of different age levels to make, or further verify, an original decision regarding elementary or secondary teacher preparation. Experience as a camp counselor, playground

supervisor, boy or girl scout director, and the like should prove very valuable to you.

3. Consult your local superintendent to see if you might serve as an assistant in a school between the time public schools open in the fall and the time your college courses begin. Attempt to gain broad experience both in the classroom and around the school. Study these experiences in terms of your fitness for teaching, the level on which you should teach, and learning significant for future courses in education.

4. Question a number of teachers whom you respect, especially those teaching on the elementary level, regarding the advantages and disadvantages of preparing for teaching in the subject areas and/or levels which they represent.

5. Consult your local school administrator about the causes of teacher turnover.

6. Consult the adviser and the teacher-placement official in your college concerning the probable supply and demand for teachers when you expect to graduate. Secure from educational literature as much data on this problem as possible.

7. If you do not plan to teach in the locale where you are attending school, secure data on teacher supply and demand for the area in which you expect to begin your work.

8. Examine the organizational setup of a large city school system to discover the different kinds of positions involved. Talk with those individuals who hold positions that may interest you. Discuss such matters as qualifications, duties, advantages, and disadvantages of the work.

9. Discuss with your college adviser any occupational plans other than teaching that you may have in the field of education. Consider specific implications that these plans may have in your preparation for teaching.

RESOURCE SECTION FOR PART I

A SELF-RATING SCALE FOR DETERMINING
FITNESS FOR TEACHING

CHECKLIST OF IMPORTANT FACTORS
IN THE TEACHER'S PERSONALITY

CHECKLIST FOR VOICE AND SPEECH

AM I A GOOD GROUP PARTICIPANT?

SUGGESTED READINGS

SUGGESTED FILMS, FILMSTRIPS,
AND RECORDINGS

FIGURE CREDITS

A SELF-RATING SCALE FOR DETERMINING FITNESS FOR TEACHING

	Never	Sel-dom	Some-times	Often	Al-ways

I. Leadership ability
1. Have you served as leader in student groups; i.e., have you held an office, taken part in programs, or led discussions?
2. Do your fellow students respect your opinions?
3. Do they regard you as a leader?
4. Do your fellow students ask you for help and advice?
5. Do you sense how others feel, i.e., whether they approve certain proposals, or like or dislike certain persons?
6. Do you try to make others happy by listening to what they say, and by being courteous, friendly, and helpful?
7. Do you succeed in getting others to follow your suggestions without creating friction or ill will?

II. Health and physical fitness
1. Do you have good health?
2. Do you have lots of vitality? Can you stand to do hard physical tasks or nerve-racking work?
3. Can you engage in activities which others in your group customarily do?
4. Do you give others the impression that you are physically fit, well groomed and attractive in personal appearance?
5. Do you keep cheerful and even-tempered even when tired or ill?

III. Good scholarship
1. Have you maintained a better-than-average academic record?
2. Are you interested in the subjects you have taken or are taking?
3. Do you enjoy studying and find it easy to concentrate when you do study?
4. Do you express your ideas well before a class or public group?

Source: E. E. Samuelson and others, *You'd Like Teaching*, Craftsman Press, Seattle, Wash., 1946, pp. 31–35. Materials prepared and published, and permission for use granted, by Central Washington College of Education.

A SELF-RATING SCALE FOR DETERMINING FITNESS FOR TEACHING (continued)

	Never	Sel-dom	Some-times	Often	Al-ways
5. Is it easy for you to explain things so that others understand and can follow your directions?					

IV. Intellectual traits and abilities
1. Are school subjects easy for you?
2. Do you spend time finding out more about a topic discussed in class or covered in an assignment?
3. Do you read books or magazine articles on current topics?
4. Do you like to work out ideas on your own?
5. Do you suggest new ideas or plans which can be carried out by groups?

V. Emotional stability
1. Are you an even-tempered, cheerful, happy sort of person?
2. Can you "take it" without getting angry or upset?
3. Do you keep from worrying and feeling depressed?
4. Are you naturally patient with and tolerant of others?
5. Are you objectively critical of yourself?
6. Do you see the humorous side of everyday happenings even when you yourself are involved?

VI. Social aspirations
1. Are you interested in the problems other people meet and do you want to help them solve them?
2. Are you interested in finding ways by which you can help improve human living?
3. Do you like people—especially children?
4. Do you set high social standards for yourself and seek to reach and maintain these standards?
5. Do you cooperate readily with other people in socially desirable activities?
6. Are you willing to make sacrifices and endure inconveniences to reach a goal you consider worthy?

CHECKLIST OF IMPORTANT FACTORS IN THE TEACHER'S PERSONALITY

Directions: Consider each of the ten divisions in this list separately. Read each statement under the major headings carefully and underline any of the qualities or traits which obviously are missing in the personality being rated. Before you proceed to the next division, look back over any of the statements you may have underlined; then place a check mark in the column that expressed your general opinion of the person with respect to the particular aspect of personality being considered.

Suggested standard for traits or qualities	Below average	Fair	Good	Excellent

1. *Emotional stability and mental health.* Is free from fears, remorse, humiliations, and worries about trivial things; can make a realistic inventory of his mental resources; is not supersensitive to criticism; is resourceful in self-entertainment; is not easily irritated; is free from excessive shyness, temper tantrums, and daydreams; meets unexpected situations well; adapts readily to changing situations; exercises self-control; is free from complexes of inferiority and superiority; has control over moods, with no sudden shifts in extremes from ups to downs; can take disappointments in life in full stride.

2. *Personal appearance.* Is dressed appropriately for the occasion; is alert and well poised; is well groomed; gives appearance of being self-possessed; exercises good taste in selection of clothes; gives impression of being refined and cultured; chooses color combinations well; keeps clothes pressed and clean.

3. *Health and vitality.* Shows evidence of a "driving force"; is physically and mentally alert; is enthusiastic and cheerful; looks healthy; is dynamic; is wide awake to the potential possibilities in every situation; has a happy expression; has reserve energy.

4. *Honesty, character, and integrity.* Shows a good sense of values; can be expected to do the right thing under all conditions; is trustworthy and loyal; admits mistakes; keeps his word; is fair and just in his dealings with others; fulfills obligations; is intellectually honest, maintains high standards of conduct.

5. *Adaptability.* Accepts gracefully and understands quickly suggestions from others; accepts responsibility for making a positive contribution to a situation; is willing to inconvenience self in helping others; is challenged by new situations; is sympathetic and patient in shar-

Source: Howard T. Batchelder, Maurice McGlasson, and Raleigh Schorling, *Student Teaching in Secondary Schools,* McGraw-Hill Book Company, New York, 1964, pp. 9–12.

CHECKLIST OF IMPORTANT FACTORS IN THE TEACHER'S PERSONALITY (cont'd)

Suggested standard for traits or qualities	Below average	Fair	Good	Excellent

ing and understanding the thoughts and difficulties of others; says what must be said with
diplomacy and minimum offense; responds
readily to necessary routine.

6. *Cooperation.* Can work with others for attainment of a common goal; volunteers services
when they are needed; fits in where most
needed; welcomes suggestions and tries to improve; places welfare of the group before self;
is willing to share in the "extra" tasks; is a
constructive worker on a committee.

7. *Voice and speech.* Shows refinement and evidence of cultural background; speaks clearly
and distinctly with proper degree of inflection;
has well-modulated tone, controlled, and
adapted to the size of the group; has an accepted and natural accent; attracts favorable
attention; is easy to understand; pronounces
words correctly; is free from distracting and
irritating mannerisms or defects of speech.

8. *Leadership.* Commands respect; is self-confi-
dent; shows ability in planning, organization,
and execution; can persuade others to a proper
course of action; can act in emergencies with
decision; uses good judgment; inspires others
to do their best; shows mastery of a situation;
exercises initiative and originality; has the
ability to put into words the thinking of a
group; possesses courage to support sound
convictions.

9. *Resourcefulness.* Has suggestions for meeting
a difficulty; is discerning and quick in selection
of the most promising solution; can "see
around a corner"; has an abundance of reserve
energy upon which to draw; knows when to
take action; suggests power of mental strength,
and vigor.

10. *Sociability.* Knows the rules of etiquette sufficiently to avoid embarrassing, offending, or
irritating others; is unselfishly interested in
others; is a stimulating conversationalist with
a wide range of interests; has a sympathetic
point of view; puts others at ease; seeks association with others; is tolerant of the opinions
of others and of community life; wins and
holds friends; is a good listener; knows when
to be playful and when to be serious; creates
a comfortable and pleasant atmosphere; sees
the humorous element in situations; is a good
sport.

A CHECKLIST FOR VOICE AND SPEECH*

There are two ways in which this checklist may be useful: (1) you may wish to ask some trained person to evaluate your teaching voice; or (2) the results may prove helpful when two or three student teachers rate each other, and later compare notes.

Speech factors	Needs attention	Satisfactory or superior

Quality of voice: Is his voice
1. Too high pitched?
2. Nasal?
3. Strained?
4. Breathy?
5. Varied in pitch?
6. Clear and distinct?
7. Rich and colorful?
8. Adapted to the size of the listening group?
9. Well controlled and modulated?
10. Resonant?

Unpleasant speech mannerisms: Does he speak
1. Too fast?
2. In a drawling manner?
3. Lispingly?
4. Gruffly?
5. Too slowly?
6. In an uncertain, halting, or stumbling manner?
7. With an affected accent?

General speech: Does he
1. Pronounce words correctly?
2. Enunciate carefully?
3. Use slang inappropriately or excessively?
4. Keep calm, free from anger and excitement?
5. Employ concepts adapted to his audience?
6. Adapt voice to the occasion?
7. Use proper inflection?
8. Show evidence of an adequate vocabulary?

* Only two columns at the right are employed in order to emphasize the items to which the teacher should give remedial attention.
Source: Howard T. Batchelder, Maurice McGlasson, and Raleigh Schorling, *Student Teaching in Secondary Schools,* McGraw-Hill Book Company, New York, 1964, p. 15.

AM I A GOOD GROUP PARTICIPANT?

1. Do I propose new ideas, activities, and procedures? Or do I just sit and listen?
2. Do I ask questions? Or am I shy about admitting that I do not understand?
3. Do I share my knowledge when it will prove helpful to the problem at hand? Or do I keep it to myself?
4. Do I speak up if I feel strongly about something? Or am I shy about giving an opinion?
5. Do I try to bring together our ideas and activities? Or do I concentrate only on details under immediate discussion?

6. Do I understand the goals of the group and try to direct the discussion toward them? Or do I get off the track easily?
7. Do I ever question the practicality or the "logic" of a project, and do I evaluate afterwards? Or do I always accept unquestioningly the things we do?
8. Do I help to arrange chairs, serve refreshments, and even clean up when the session is over? Or do I prefer to be waited on?
9. Do I encourage my fellow group members to do well? Or am I indifferent to their efforts and achievements?
10. Do I prod the group to undertake worthy projects? Or am I happy with mediocre projects?
11. Am I a mediator and a peacemaker? Or do I allow ill feeling to develop?
12. Am I willing to compromise (except where basic issues such as truth and justice are involved)? Or do I remain inflexible?
13. Do I encourage others to participate and to give everyone else a fair chance to speak? Or do I sit by while some people hog the floor, and do I sometimes dominate it myself?

Source: "Am I a Good Group Participant?" *NEA Journal,* vol. 45, p. 168, National Education Association, Washington, March, 1956.

SUGGESTED READINGS

The number in parentheses following each suggestion denotes the chapter for which it is best suited.

Armstrong, W. Earl, and T. M. Stinnett: *A Manual on Certification Requirements for School Personnel in the United States,* National Education Association, National Commission on Teacher and Professional Standards, Washington. Revised triennially. Contains an excellent listing of certification requirements for school personnel and indicates trends in certification. (3)
Borrowman, Merle L. (ed.): *Teacher Education in America,* Teachers College Press, Columbia University, New York, 1965. A documentary history of teacher education. (3)
Brembeck, Cole S.: *The Discovery of Teaching,* Prentice-Hall, Inc., Englewood Cliffs, N.J., 1962. Chapter 1 presents the answers of 100 student teachers to the following questions: "What do you find most rewarding in teaching?" "Does teaching differ from what you expected?" Chapter 3 is concerned with the suggestions of 100 student teachers to prospective teachers. (2, 3)
Calvert, Robert, Jr., and John E. Steele: *Planning Your Career,* McGraw-Hill Book Company, New York, 1963. Designed to help college students plan their careers. (2)
"Can We Measure Good Teaching Objectively?" *NEA Journal,* vol. 53, no. 1, pp. 34–36, 73, National Education Association, Washington, January, 1964. Two opposing positions are presented regarding the measurement of good teaching. (2)
Combs, Arthur W.: *The Professional Education of Teachers,* Allyn and Bacon, Inc., Boston, 1965. Discusses characteristics of good teachers and ways of achieving these characteristics. (2, 3)
"The Editor's Bookshelf," *Saturday Review,* May 18, 1963, pp. 77–79. Reviews James Koerner's book *The Miseducation of Teachers* and points out weaknesses in his criticisms and recommendations. (3)
"Education and Poverty," *Saturday Review,* May 15, 1965, pp. 68–72, 85–89. A series of articles describing the work of the Job Corps and other projects. (4)
Erikson, Marion, J.: *The Mentally Retarded Child in the Classroom,* The Macmillan Company, New York, 1965. Discusses the nature of the work in educating the mentally retarded child. (4)
"The Famous Twenty-seven," *Phi Delta Kappan,* vol. 45, no. 9, pp. 440–442, June, 1964. Lists the twenty-seven recommendations Conant made in his book *The Education of American Teachers.* (3)
Fine, Benjamin: *Opportunities in Teaching Careers,* University Publishing and Distrib-

uting Corporation, New York, 1964. A detailed treatment of the many opportunities for careers in the field of education. (4)

Fisher, Margaret B., and Jeanne L. Noble: *College Education as Personal Development,* Prentice-Hall, Inc., Englewood Cliffs, N.J., 1960. An excellent book for college students on personal development. (2)

Innovation in Teacher Education, Northwestern University Press, Evanston, Ill., 1965. Discusses the relationship between colleges of education and colleges of arts and sciences, as well as the relationships between universities and state departments of education. (3)

Jersild, Arthur T.: *When Teachers Face Themselves,* Teachers College Press, Columbia University, New York, 1955. A study of the emotional strains and stresses of teachers. (2)

Kinney, Lucien B.: *Certification in Education,* Prentice-Hall, Inc., Englewood Cliffs, N.J., 1964. Summarizes the current status of certification in the field of education. (3)

Lindsey, Margaret (ed.): *New Horizons for the Teaching Profession,* National Education Association, National Commission on Teacher Education and Professional Standards, Washington, 1961. Chapter 4 deals with the preparation of professional personnel. Chapter 6 indicates recommendations regarding the certification of teachers. (3)

Milestones in Teacher Education and Professional Standards, National Education Association, National Commission on Teacher Education and Professional Standards, Washington, 1966. An excellent booklet, containing a number of tables and graphs indicating the progress that has been made in teacher education and professional standards. (2–4)

Mitchell, James V., Jr.: "Personality Characteristics Associated with Motives for Entering Teaching," *Phi Delta Kappan,* vol. 46, no. 10, pp. 529–532, June, 1965. Presents the questionnaire results concerning personality characteristics of prospective teachers. (2)

"The Nature and Characteristics of Adult Education in the United States," *Facts and Figures on Adult Education,* vol. 1, no. 1, National Education Association, Division of Adult Education Services, Washington, April, 1963. Discusses the nature and characteristics of adult education in the United States and indicates the large task that lies ahead. (4)

Reisert, John E.: "Migrating Educator? What about Your Teaching Credentials?" *Phi Delta Kappan,* vol. 47, no. 7, pp. 372–374, March, 1966. Gives some excellent suggestions for improving the reciprocity of teacher certification. (3)

Ryans, David G.: *Characteristics of Teachers: Their Description, Comparison and Appraisal,* American Council on Education, Washington, 1961. Presents the findings of extensive research on the characteristics of good and poor teachers. (2)

Six Areas of Teacher Competence, California Teachers Association, Commission on Teacher Education, Burlingame, Calif., 1964. Analyzes six teacher roles and indicates the competencies teachers should have in order to fulfill these roles. (2)

Skinner, B. F.: "Why Teachers Fail," *Saturday Review,* Oct. 16, 1965, pp. 80–81, 98–102. An eminent psychologist indicates some of the reasons for teacher failure. (2)

Stinnett, T. M., and Albert J. Huggett: *Professional Problems of Teachers,* The Macmillan Company, New York, 1963. Chapter 18 is concerned with the professional education of teachers and Chapter 19 involves problems concerned with the certification of teachers. Chapter 20 is concernd with the professional accreditation of teacher education. Chapter 6 discusses opportunities for advancement in teaching. (3, 4)

Stoffel, Frederick E.: "Teaching in Overseas Schools," *NEA Journal,* vol. 53, no. 5, pp. 8–9, National Education Association, Washington, May, 1964. Describes teaching in dependent schools overseas. (4)

Stretch, Bonnie Barrett: "Classroom Learning Is Not Enough," *Saturday Review,* June 19, 1965, pp. 62–63, 73. Describes how college students are gaining valuable experiences working voluntarily with culturally deprived children and adults. (3)

Teacher Supply and Demand in Public Schools, Research Report, National Education Association, Research Division, Washington. Latest issue. An excellent yearly publication indicating the supply and demand of public school teachers. (4)

"Values and American Education," *The National Elementary Principal,* vol. 42, no. 2, pp. 6–63, National Education Association, Department of Elementary School Principals, Washington, November, 1962. A series of articles devoted to values as they affect education and the work of educators. (2)

Wahlquist, John T.: "A New Horizon: College Teaching," *Phi Delta Kappan,* vol. 47, no. 8, pp. 437–441, April, 1966. Indicates the vast opportunities for college teaching. (4)

Weiser, John C., and James E. Hayes: "Democratic Attitudes of Teachers and Prospective Teachers," *Phi Delta Kappan,* vol. 47, no. 9, pp. 476–481, May, 1966. Presents the results of a study suggesting that teachers as well as their students may have an inadequate or distorted understanding of the meaning of democracy and the Bill of Rights. (2)

Wiggins, Sam P.: *Battlefields in Teacher Education,* George Peabody College for Teachers, Nashville, Tenn., 1964. Discusses some of the controversial issues in teacher education. (3)

Woellner, Robert C., and M. Aurilla Wood: *Requirements for Certification of Teachers, Counselors, Librarians, Administrators for Elementary Schools, Secondary Schools, Junior Colleges,* University of Chicago Press, Chicago. Revised annually. Presents the certification requirements by states for various school personnel. (3)

Wrenn, C. Gilbert: *The Counselor in a Changing World,* American Personnel and Guidance Association, Washington, 1962. Indicates the pressing need for guidance counselors in schools today. (4)

SUGGESTED FILMS, FILMSTRIPS, AND RECORDINGS

The number in parentheses following each suggestion denotes the chapter for which it is best suited.

Films (16 mm)

America's Crises: The Teacher Gap (National Educational Television, 60 min). Focuses on teachers and school administrators in Newton, Massachusetts, where the problems of quality and quantity are being solved, and in Bay City, Michigan, where they are not. Presents details of how the Newton schools are operated and shows results in terms of lack of dropouts and numbers of students who go beyond high school. (4)

And Gladly Teach (National Education Association, 28 min, color). Discusses teachers and "the company they keep." Points out the satisfactions of and opportunities in teaching. (2)

Appointment with Youth (McGraw-Hill, 27 min). Presents a high school teacher recalling college days and early experiences as a teacher as he seeks answers to the question "Is teaching a good profession?" Concludes that teaching gives deep personal satisfaction resulting from doing a good job and that it is a good profession which needs good teachers. (2)

Choosing Your Occupation (Coronet Films, 10 min). Outlines the services that are presently available for helping one choose an occupation; describes various tests to determine one's interests, abilities, and personality patterns; and suggests information which one needs concerning his chosen occupation. (2)

Developing Leadership (Coronet Films, 11 min, color). Describes how to become a leader and a group member. Shows how the changing pattern of leadership in a democratic group occurs and suggests leadership qualities which individuals should possess. (2)

Emotional Health (McGraw-Hill, 21 min). Shows interviews of a college student with a physician and then with a psychiatrist who uncovers his fears and helps him become emotionally adjusted. Uses occasional flashbacks to the boy's childhood. (2)

Golden Age (McGraw-Hill, 27 min). Reviews problems faced during the retirement age through the experiences of three men. Each man has a different approach to the retirement years. (2)

Guiding the Growth of Children (McGraw-Hill, 17 min). Shows how a teacher may work to understand each child and to guide him in his growth and development. Deals with seven problem cases and suggests possible ways of handling them. Shows a variety of techniques that a teacher may use but insists that underlying each technique is the teacher's genuine desire to help plus his sympathetic, patient understanding. (2)

Helping Teachers to Understand Children, Part I (United World Films, 21 min). Points out the need for teachers to understand children and illustrates a variety of ways through which a knowledge of child behavior can be gained and interpreted. Presents a case study of one child and suggests the use of school records, interviews with teachers, the child's writing and artwork, home environment, and anecdotal records as sources of information. (2)

How to Conduct a Discussion (Encyclopaedia Britannica Films, 24 min). Presents the results of a survey of about fifty adult groups to find common elements of a good group discussion. Illustrates the qualities of good leadership by showing various groups in action and exemplifies eleven important elements of effective group discussions. Uses narration and synchronized sound to portray the different groups and summarize the important points. (2)

Introduction to Student Teaching (Indiana University, 19 min). Dramatizes the experiences of three beginning student teachers. Suggests getting well acquainted with the school, its personnel, and its policies; becoming accustomed to handling routine classroom matters; becoming familiar with a wide variety of instructional materials, their preparation, and their use; learning as much as possible about the pupils. (3)

Maintaining Classroom Discipline (McGraw-Hill, 15 min). Contrasts situations in which first poor and then good discipline result from the teacher's varied approaches. Emphasizes the importance of stimulation of interest, the teacher's personality, and the handling of minor incidents. (2)

Not by Chance (National Education Association, 28½ min, color). Traces the general education and the special preparation of a truly professional teacher. (3)

Our Teacher, Mary Dean (Firth Films, 22 min, color). Depicts the satisfactions a teacher finds in her work and in her life outside the school. (2)

Philosophies of Education: Education for Psychological Maturity. (National Educational Television, 29 min). Quotes from Dr. Jersild's book *When Teachers Face Themselves*, such as "Education should help children and adults to know themselves and to develop healthy attitudes of self-acceptance," set the tone for this program. Proposes that efforts to promote self-understanding should be incorporated into the nation's total educational program. (2)

Planning for Personal and Professional Growth (McGraw-Hill, 17 min). Shows four schoolteachers who have made certain adjustments and achieved success in their teaching to various degrees. A middle-aged woman found teaching dull with many frustrations; she was not aware of her problems and could not adjust satisfactorily. A science teacher made long-range plans for his growth through graduate study but found that he had to reevaluate his ambitious plans. A foreign language teacher had conflicts between family life and teaching, but by relating her teaching to life she made a desirable adjustment. An elderly woman was enthusiastic about teaching, loved children, and found teaching a rich, rewarding experience. (2, 3)

Preparation of Teachers (United World, 20 min). Uses the experiences of two prospective teachers during their training periods to show that teaching is not just the business of getting information across but includes sharing children's excitement and experiences. Emphasizes the fact that a teacher must have a well-rounded background in order to help children to become useful and responsible citizens. (3)

Teachers for Tomorrow (University of Wisconsin, 22 min). Shows how prospective teachers are chosen and trained at the University of Wisconsin. Pictures many phases of the student teacher's work with pupils, supervisory teachers, faculty members, and teaching materials. Shows the need for more teachers and presents the values of teaching as a career. (3)

Teaching (Carl F. Mahnke Production, 10 min). Begins by discussing attractive features of teaching such as contact with young people, long summer vacations, relative economic security through tenure laws and contracts, pensions, and stimuli to continual self-improvement. Outlines personal and professional qualifications. Concludes with suggestions on getting into the field and a discussion of the responsibilities and opportunities of teaching. (2)

Tips for Teachers (Jam Handy Organization, 18 min). Explains the importance of personality, preparation, and presentation in good teaching. Uses classroom situations to show that a teacher must also use showmanship, salesmanship, and dramatic ability to help speed up the learning process. (2)

What Greater Gift (National Education Association, 28 min, color). Presents the teacher as a professional person and shows something of the nature of teaching. Stresses that today's teacher needs professional preparation to acquire the understanding and skills essential to good teaching. (3)

What Is a Good Observer? (Indiana University, 30 min). Considers the differences between a good and a bad observer. Points out that the use of conclusions based on observations of similarities alone results in a limitation of our awareness of the world, while the use of conclusions grounded on observations that consider differences also is a mark of the mature mind. Available for nontelevision use only. (2)

What Is a Teacher? (University of Texas, 59 min). Defines the concept of a teacher by showing her performing in various instructional situations from the first through the sixth grade. Emphasis is placed on the teacher's role in the development of good mental health and intellectual growth. (2)

Who Will Teach Your Child? (National Film Board of Canada, 25 min). Discusses the problem of maintaining high-quality teaching staffs in the public schools. Compares the work of good and poor teachers and suggests ways to attract the best young people to the teaching profession. (2)

The Workshop Process (University of California at Los Angeles, 12 min). Follows the step-by-step procedure involved in the organization, operation, and evaluation of a teacher's workshop developed under the guidance of the superintendent of the Montebello School District in California. (3)

Filmstrips

Informal Pointers for Teachers (Jam Handy Organization). A series of filmstrips averaging 55 frames or 22 minutes each (1. *The Teacher;* 2. *Some Principles of Teaching;* 3. *I Want to Learn;* 4. *The Lesson Plan;* 5. *Make Your Chalk Talk*) that present basic attributes and qualifications for a good teacher. Illustrates fundamental techniques and methods. (2)

Let's Take a Look at Teaching (Wayne University, 50 fr.). Gives an overview of the teaching profession and what it has to offer in terms of salary, tenure, working conditions, opportunities for travel, and individual interests. Pictures a typical school day showing the varied demands on the teacher and her responsibilities. (2)

Planned Life (Visual Education Consultants, 27 fr.). Contains suggestions on how to plan one's life to achieve happiness and well-being and how to contribute one's share to a democratic society. (2)

Preparing to Teach (American Council on Education, 56 fr.). Shows how students are preparing for the teaching profession in a representative teacher education institution in the United States. Includes academic and cocurricular activities, student-faculty relations, and student-community relations. (3)

Tagline for Success (Bristol-Myers, 25 fr., color). Stresses importance of training, attitude, and grooming in getting and holding a job. (2)

The Teacher (Jam Handy Organization, 56 fr.). Illustrates effective pedagogic attitudes, conduct, appearance, and methods to be used by the teacher to avoid alienating or distracting the attention of the class. (2)

The Teacher (McGraw-Hill, 33 fr., color). Shows a young boy who moves to a new community finding his adjustment a happy one because of the interest and help given him by his new teacher. (2)

Teaching as a Career (National Film Board of Canada, 47 fr.). Examines the pros and cons of teaching as a career with special reference to educational requirements, personal aptitudes, specialized training, remuneration, and opportunities for advancement. (2)

Your Future in the World of Work: Selecting Your Life Work and Preparing for It (Society of Visual Education, 49 fr.). Indicates the importance of aptitudes, interests, and personality factors in the selection of your lifework. (2)

Recordings

Characteristics of a Good Teacher (Recording, Educational Recording Service, 33⅓ rpm). Professor A. S. Barr, department of education, the University of Wisconsin, discusses the personal qualities and characteristics of a good teacher. (2)

Critical Issues in Education: How Should America's Teachers Be Educated? (National Tape Recording Project, 40 min). Professor Arthur Bestor, Jr., and Professor Karl W. Bigelow present opposing points of view, each being allowed 20 minutes to make his presentation. (3)

A Forward Look for the Teaching Profession (Educational Recording Service, 33⅓ rpm). W. S. Elsbree, professor of education, Teachers College, Columbia University, presents a challenge to anyone planning to teach. (2)

Teachers Are People Too (National Tape Recording Project, 15 min). Presents teachers as sincere, cooperative, hardworking individuals. (2)

FIGURE CREDITS

FIGURE 2–2. (*Source: The American Public-school Teacher: 1965–66 Preliminary Report*, National Education Association, Research Division, Washington, p. 16.)

FIGURE 3–1. (*Source: Milestones in Teacher Education and Professional Standards*, National Education Association, National Commission on Teacher Education and Professional Standards, Washington, 1966, p. 6.)

FIGURE 3–3. (*Source: "On Teacher Preparation," NEA Journal*, vol. 52, no. 9, p. 34, National Education Association, Washington, December, 1963.)

FIGURE 3–4. (*Source: Teacher Supply and Demand in Public Schools, 1966*, Research Report 1966–R16, National Education Association, Research Division, Washington, October, 1966, p. 52.)

FIGURE 3–5. (*Source: Milestones in Teacher Education and Professional Standards*, National Education Association, National Commission on Teacher Education and Professional Standards, Washington, 1966, p. 21.)

FIGURE 3–6. (*Source:* National Council for Accreditation of Teacher Education.)

FIGURE 3–7. (*Source:* Adapted from *Public Education and the Future of America*, National Education Association, Research Division, Washington, 1955, p. 63.)

FIGURE 4–1. (*Source:* Data adapted from *Statistical Abstract of the United States*, U.S. Bureau of the Census, 1966, p. 4.)

FIGURE 4–2. (*Source: Statistical Abstract of the United States*, U.S. Bureau of the Census, 1966, pp. 48, 56.)

FIGURE 4–3. (*Source:* Data adapted from *Statistical Abstract of the United States*, U.S. Bureau of the Census, 1966, p. 52; and from "Projections of the Population of the

United States, by Age and Sex," *Population Estimates: Current Population Reports,* ser. P–25, no. 286, U.S. Bureau of the Census, July, 1964.)

FIGURE 4–4. *(Source: What Everyone Should Know about Financing Our Schools,* National Education Association, Washington, 1966, p. 21.)

FIGURE 4–5. *(Source: Education: An Investment in People,* Chamber of Commerce of the United States, Education Department, Washington, 1964, p. 31. Original data from U.S. Bureau of the Census.)

FIGURE 4–6. *(Source: Ranking of the States, 1966,* Research Report, 1966–R1, National Education Association, Research Division, Washington, January, 1966, p. 28.)

FIGURE 4–7. *(Source:* Data from *Teacher Supply and Demand in Public Schools, 1965,* Research Report 1965–R10, National Education Association, Research Division, Washington, June, 1965, pp. 24–25.)

FIGURE 4–8. *(Source:* "Our Greatest Asset: Better Educated Americans," *Washington Report, Economics of Change,* no. 4, Chamber of Commerce of the United States, Washington, 1966, p. 1.)

FIGURE 4–9. *(Source: The American Public-school Teacher: 1965–66 Preliminary Report,* National Education Association, Research Division, Washington, 1966, p. 16.)

FIGURE 4–10. *(Source:* Data from *Fall 1964 Statistics of Public Schools,* U.S. Office of Education, 1965, p. 13.)

FIGURE 4–11. *(Source:* Data adapted from Samuel Kirk, "Educating the Handicapped," *Contemporary Issues in American Education,* U.S. Office of Education, 1965, p. 89.)

FIGURE 4–12. *(Source: Trends,* Part I, *National Trends,* U.S. Department of Health, Education, and Welfare, 1965, p. 56.)

FIGURE 4–13. *(Source:* "Need for College Teachers Grows," *NEA Research Bulletin,* vol. 41, no. 4, p. 110, National Education Association, Research Division, Washington, December, 1963.)

TEACHERS AND THEIR WORK

The value of your formal preparation for teaching will be enhanced by the extent to which you see clearly the duties and demands that will be made upon you as a professional worker. Chapter 5 discusses the wide variety of responsibilities with which you most likely will be confronted in the classroom, outside of the classroom, and in the school community. Chapter 6 contains suggestions and procedures for you to use in gaining proficiency in further understanding pupils and in effectively guiding their educational growth. Undoubtedly, you will be called upon to use some of the newer instructional techniques and procedures as you work with boys and girls. In Chapter 7 you are confronted with some of the obligations and responsibilities which you will assume as a member of the teaching profession.

5

SCHOOL AND COMMUNITY RESPONSIBILITIES OF TEACHERS

What will be expected of you as a teacher? What will you have to do in school? What particular competencies will you need in order to perform effectively? To what extent will you be able to find interest and challenge in your duties? What will the community demand of you when you become a teacher? The answers to these questions tend to set the pattern for your professional work and, to some extent, for your future personal life.

CLASSROOM RESPONSIBILITIES OF TEACHERS

It is unlikely that anyone could describe with certainty the precise duties or responsibilities expected of *you* when you report for your first teaching position. Conditions in public schools differ considerably throughout the United States. There are great gaps between what an elementary teacher does in a one-room rural school and what a senior English literature teacher does in a large metropolitan high school. Teachers' lives vary in significant ways. At the same time there are many elements that are common to their work. These elements should be examined in some detail.

Number of Classes Taught

The number of classes you will be expected to teach varies for several reasons. Elementary teachers generally stay with their particular groups for the greater part of the school day, including the lunch period in many schools. In some school systems, elementary music, art, physical education, special reading, and speech are taught by highly specialized people who usually move from grade to grade in a single school or in several schools in a district. In addition, many school systems have attempted to provide some time during the school day for elementary teachers to use for planning, attending conferences, or relaxing from the tensions of the classroom.

In the secondary school, teachers generally meet several different classes in one day; the variety of subjects taught by each teacher is usually greater in small schools than in large ones. The number of courses offered in secondary schools has increased considerably over the years. In their attempts to provide for the needs and interests of their increasing enrollments, secondary schools have added many, many subjects. In fact, curriculum workers have viewed with much alarm the tendency to change the secondary school program merely by adding courses. The trend they prefer to encourage is toward reducing these numbers. Curriculum workers have suggested removing courses which are outmoded or inappropriate, combining several closely related courses into one new course, and reorganizing the common learning experiences of pupils in a given school around areas of living which draw upon many subjects and resources.

In attempting to assure reasonable teaching loads in member schools, the North Central Association of Colleges and Secondary Schools has recommended as one of its school accrediting policies that each teacher be assigned at least one conference and preparation period daily [193:14]. In schools operating on a six- or seven-period day, this would mean that a teacher should be assigned not more than five classes and/or study halls. In schools using eight or more periods, a teacher should be assigned not more than six classes and/or study halls.

Of course, the number of classes is only one aspect of a teacher's load. Other factors to be considered include the subject being taught, class size, length of period, administrative or supervisory duties, assignments in extraclass activities, counseling duties, and length of school day. In addition, recent innovations in teaching, such as television and other electronic aids, flexible scheduling, ungraded classrooms, team teaching, and the use of programmed material with or without machines, tend to make the "number of classes taught" a less and less accurate description of a teacher's day. Figure 5–1, therefore, gives only approximate distributions of time for elementary and secondary school teachers.

Size of Classes

The quality of your work in different teaching assignments will be influenced somewhat by the number of pupils in your classes. As indicated in the preceding chapter, there is no absolute agreement upon the optimum class size for a learning situation. The size is relative to the purposes that are to be accomplished. For instance, it might be possible to handle large numbers effectively in certain courses such as physical education and, occasionally, music classes; on the other hand, it would be desirable to have smaller groups studying foreign languages, laboratory sciences, or remedial reading.

The whole problem of class size is coming in for close attention and careful research. The many factors which affect the optimum size of a learning group complicate this work a great deal. Experimental studies have suggested the distribution of a student's time to be as follows: 40 per cent in large group instruction, 20 per cent in small group discussion, and 40 per cent in individual study [275]. Experimental use of team teaching, ungraded classrooms, flexible scheduling, programmed learning, educational television, and possibly media not yet discovered or employed undoubtedly will shed new insights and affect considerably the size of class groups you will have.

Planning Your Lessons

Good lesson planning is essential to good teaching. Likewise, good preplanning on the part of the teacher provides the basis for the most effective pupil-teacher planning within the classroom activities.

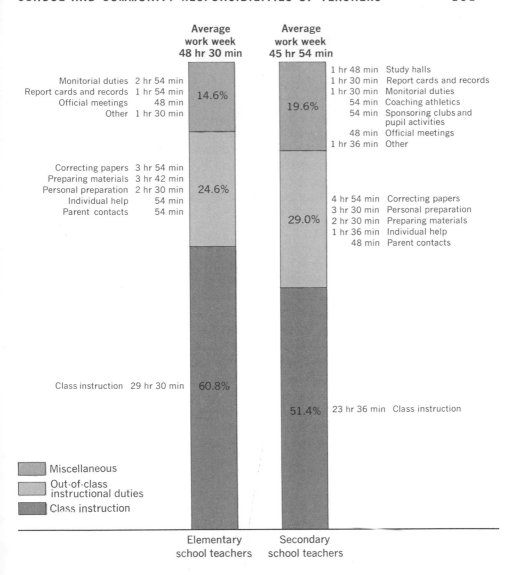

FIGURE 5–1. How elementary and secondary school teachers divide an average work week. (*Source:* National Education Association.)

In your student teaching and in your first year of teaching, especially, you will need to devote a greater amount of time to the planning of your classroom activities than will be necessary after you have gained a few years of experience. Beginning teachers frequently fail to devote adequate time to the planning of classroom activities, since they observe older and much more experienced teachers preparing relatively brief and general written plans. They may overlook the fact that, as a result of these years of experience, older teachers are able to visualize plans in much detail and that they have developed great skill in guiding pupils toward the desired objectives.

Advance planning and careful organization are essential for realizing the daily objectives the teacher has in mind. As a beginning teacher, you will want to pay special attention to the preparation of your daily lesson plans. (*From the film* Not by Chance *by the National Education Association.*)

Your lesson plans should (1) consist of flexible arrangements, procedures, or methods of action for achieving educational objectives which you consider to be desirable; (2) be records of your thinking about desirable school experiences for your pupils; (3) include a description of the specific learning experiences in which they will participate during the time included in the plan; (4) be both long range and short range in nature; (5) give you a sense of security—of knowing where you are going and why—as well as a basis for appraising how well you and your pupils have succeeded. Your written comments concerning the strengths and weaknesses of the plans after they have been used provide a basis for your future growth as a teacher.

Your general plans frequently will involve considerably more than the subject matter you are going to teach. You may need to prepare charts or graphs; secure photographs, maps, films, or records; prepare demonstrations, tests, or reading assignments; arrange for equipment such as projectors and tape recorders; survey library and community resources; study educational telecast schedules. A field trip may be desirable, in which case you may need to obtain permission from your school principal, make arrangements with the places to be visited, secure transportation, prepare the pupils for the trip, and help them appraise the experience. Many things may be involved and should be planned in order that you may provide your pupils with rich learning experiences.

There may be occasions when you resent the amount of time required to plan activities for your pupils. You may be tempted to feel that the teacher who regularly leaves the school building empty-handed shortly after the pupils have been dismissed is, after all, the wise one. But there is no substitute for the satisfaction of knowing precisely what you want your pupils to achieve, of being able to guide creatively the activities of pupils toward clearly perceived goals, of feeling that your work for the day has been well done. The relationship of good planning and good teaching is amazingly close.

Guiding Each Class Group

In guiding your class groups, your chief work as a teacher will be that of helping youngsters learn how to learn. This will mean helping them define their most pressing needs and interests and problems; helping them understand themselves better; and helping them understand their families, their friends, their whole community. Out of this will emerge certain specific objectives the youngsters will consider important to achieve. Your function will then be to help them formulate and appraise their objectives in terms of their value to the learners and to the community. It will be necessary to plan ways and means of arriving at those objectives which the youngsters feel are important to them. You should see that the learning experiences grow out of the everyday lives of the learners and that they utilize wisely the available resources—especially people—in the entire school community.

In order to keep learning from becoming sterile, pupils must be able to relate the facts they have discovered to their everyday lives. This requires numerous deliberate applications and the development of generalizations which make sense to the learners—which they can use to gain better control over their future behavior. Research seems to indicate that on tests of academic achievement requiring analysis, synthesis, evaluation, and application of knowledge, the more informal group processes described here obtain better results than more formal lectures and recitations [242:20]. These are important considerations, so far as your responsibilities relating to the guidance of learning are concerned. They apply, no matter what grade or subject you teach.

The modern classroom teacher, using standardized test results, careful observations, and records of past performances, gains insight into each student's level of ability. The teacher places those of somewhat similar abilities together for certain learning experiences. However, these groupings are flexible, and as students grow in their abilities, they move from one group to another. Through careful observation, teachers are often able to select groups with similar interests. Group interests may be used to solve mutual problems or to act as a motivating force for further learning. Grouping is only one of many teaching techniques which the modern teacher uses to individualize instruction. Ungraded classrooms and flexible scheduling enable teachers to group pupils in terms of their individual needs, interests, and abilities.

Fostering Self-discipline

The more conventional concept of discipline centers around order in the classroom, techniques of maintaining that order, and means of punishment. The modern concept is based on certain principles which have grown out of the findings of science and the viewpoints of such educators as Dewey and Kilpatrick. Sheviakov and Redl [238:9–16] listed some democratic principles which guide discipline practices in a modern conception of education:

1. Teachers use positive ways of guidance which communicate this belief in the value of each personality, rather than negative ways which undermine self-confidence and self-esteem.
2. Teachers consider each incident when discipline or order has broken down in

relation to the particular persons involved, their needs and their life histories.
3. Our schools provide a climate in which mutual respect and trust are possible.
4. Teachers build understanding and communication between individuals and groups.
5. Teachers help children to understand the reasons for standards and rules and to foresee the consequences of their own behavior.
6. Schools provide for children's growth in self-government through which they share increasingly in planning their own activities.
7. Teachers study children's behavior scientifically, searching for causes and formulating hunches and hypotheses about how changes may be made.
8. Teachers help young people to understand the reasons for their own and others' behavior and to develop more effective ways of meeting common conflicts.

These principles suggest self-discipline, the internalized behavior that Kilpatrick talked about—control from within rather than control from without. The teacher assumes vastly different duties in carrying out this modern concept of discipline. Instead of assuming the authoritarian, dictatorial role, the teacher takes the part of guide and director of the learning experiences which will provide opportunities to develop self-discipline. Planning with the students and evaluating these plans becomes an important teaching technique. Children help to build their own rules and regulations within which they will operate. Prevention of behavior problems is given keen consideration by both teachers and students. Teachers help children to channel their energies and initiative into socially acceptable behavior.

Pupils learn the democratic way of life by living it. Since self-discipline is a cornerstone of the democratic way of life, the learning experiences which the school provides must foster law and order from within each individual.

Handling Paper Work

There are several kinds of paper work which classroom teachers need to consider. Some of it is clerical and may seem incidental to the real work of teaching, but some of it is highly professional and very important in the teaching-learning process.

It will be necessary to keep a daily attendance record. You may be asked to do this on official state forms which are used in calculating state money allotments to individual school districts. In the secondary school, you may be asked to keep class records of every absence during the day.

Classroom teachers frequently file excuses for absence along with other notes, statements, or records of conferences and observations concerning their pupils. When various materials of this sort are organized so that there is a separate folder for each pupil, the teacher has a cumulative record system. In this folder you can keep significant writings and products of the youngsters themselves as well as grades and testing results of all sorts. Reports of home visits, medical histories, health examinations, home and family conditions, scores on standardized tests and rating scales, scholastic achievements, personality traits, participation in extra-class activities, interest inventories, educational and vocational objectives, work experiences, nonschool activities, and any other information which may be useful in helping you and other teachers understand the individual pupils—all of these should become a part of the cumulative records. Your responsibility for recording the information will vary from school to school, depending upon the provisions for clerks, secretaries, or other clerical help.

It is important that you keep accurate written records of any money for which you have collection responsibility. This is good business practice, and it serves as a protection to you as a teacher if any question should ever arise.

Another kind of paper work to which teachers must attend grows out of the planning and conducting of daily activities. Written reports of pupils need to be read and appraised. Drill work needs to be checked. Specific written assignments need to be read, corrections noted, comments given, and sometimes grades recorded. The amount of time required for these duties varies according to subject areas and grade levels. It is important that you schedule such work so that it does not take time unnecessarily from more important phases of your teaching and does not overtax your energy.

Taking Attendance

Actually, taking attendance is one of the minor clerical tasks for which the teacher is responsible. The way in which the job is done is of some importance. Calling the roll aloud has the advantage of helping fix names and faces for teacher and pupils alike, but it is very time-consuming. For you as a teacher, an ideal situation would be to know the group so well personally that anybody's absence could be detected instantly and recorded without disturbing the learning activity. On the other hand, here is an opportunity to promote pupil growth in the assumption of responsibility by delegating to various youngsters, in turn and under supervision, the recording of attendance.

Evaluating Pupil Progress

Throughout each learning experience, teachers and pupils must take stock of their progress to see whether the goals are being approached or whether the objectives need revising. They must appraise their procedures and decide whether they are the best that can be used and whether they are being used well. They must take inventory of their available resources to see whether their selection and use have been adequate and wise. These aspects of evaluation may require written reports, committee minutes, anecdotes, checklists, questionnaires, rating scales, personal documents such as diaries, projective techniques, and different kinds of tests. Some of the tests will be formal and standardized, whereas others will be informal teacher-constructed instruments, both essay and objective. In either case, the administering, scoring, and interpreting of the tests will be among your important functions. Where you decide to build the evaluative instrument yourself, whether you use an inquiry form or test, a great deal of help can be gained from your colleagues. Such sources of help should be sought out deliberately. Certainly, the use of a test should not mark the end of learning concerning any phase of school experience. These learnings should be used time and again in future experiences.

Reporting to Parents

The teacher is expected to keep parents informed about the progress of his pupils. If you do this systematically and regularly, it can prove to be one of the most fruitful avenues for bringing together the public and the schools. This should involve reviewing and summarizing the information you have about each of your youngsters, going over his activities and anecdotal records, looking into his cumulative record, observing testing results of various sorts, and, finally, making an appraisal of each. This should be done in terms of his growth and development toward those desirable purposes which together you have formulated and striven to achieve. It is difficult, at best, to grade pupils. Sometimes it is a heartrending process for parents, teachers, and pupils alike.

Most of the conventional systems of grading and reporting to parents have serious limitations. Many of them fail to inform adequately, and a few actually misinform parents. Parents, prospective employers, college officials, even the students and the teachers are frequently confused and misled by A-B-C grade reports. Where numerical percentages are used, the situation is even worse. Ability grouping further complicates the picture. Does an A in an accelerated group mean the same as an A in a slow-learning section?

The most common methods of reporting to parents are report cards, parent conferences, and letters to parents. The usual parts of a report card include letter grades, attendance and tardiness records, and a checklist section on personal characteristics [222:27–28]. In a few schools, usually on the elementary level, grades as we know them have been eliminated. However, even in most schools which have abandoned or supplemented the traditional report card, grades remain a part of the total evaluation of pupil progress. In view of the current emphasis on preparation for college and on college entrance requirements, it is probable that such grades will continue to be an important phase of pupil appraisal on the secondary level.

Parent-teacher conferences have gained in frequency, particularly at the elementary level and to some extent at the junior high school level. Research indicates that a preference exists at the elementary school level for reporting through a combination of cards and parent conferences [215:25]. It is obvious that parent-teacher conferences are more easily arranged in an elementary school than in a secondary school. In an elementary school such a plan involves perhaps twenty-five to thirty-five conferences with parents. In a secondary school such a plan involves conferences with 100 to 200 parents for each report period. The latter plan is practically impossible, and other patterns have been suggested, such as parent conferences with the homeroom teacher or designated counselors. At any rate the problem is a major one at the secondary level.

Some schools have experimented with letters to parents. However, such letters are time-consuming and frequently become almost as formalized as report cards.

In the final analysis, by far the most common type of reporting is that of the report card, with many schools combining it with parent-teacher conferences and a few using letters to parents. In most schools these reports are made either four times a year or more than five times a year [215:25]. In reporting to parents, new procedures and new instruments are urgently needed. Perhaps this is an area in which you can make a major contribution to your profession.

Caring for Your Classroom

You will be responsible for the condition of at least one classroom, although you may not carry on all of your work in one room. Your chief responsibility will be to see to it that your classroom is healthy, comfortable, and efficient for promoting the desired growth and learning of the pupils. This calls for a sense of function and balance in the manipulation and arrangement of furniture and equipment of many kinds. It involves artistic talent and ingenuity as well as certain elementary abilities, at least in working with construction tools and materials.

Strive to keep your room cheerful, tidy, and conducive to good work. No one can teach effectively in a classroom which is dark or cold or poorly ventilated. Alert teachers check quickly to see whether pupil-attention problems rest with the youngsters or with the room itself, and, if with the latter, they correct conditions as soon as possible.

Teachers and pupils working together can provide pleasant learning conditions in almost any classroom through colorful bulletin-board exhibits, interesting displays, growing plants, various types of room decorations, and orderly procedures of neatness and care of property. Even where lighting and ventilation are not satisfactory, careful study of the situation by the teacher, pupils, administrators, and custodians will usually result in suggestions for improvement under any classroom condition.

Seats and desks or tables and chairs need to be adapted to the pupils using them. The modern trend is toward rooms having several sizes of furniture or adjustable pieces to meet the individual needs of each pupil.

Our early schools developed furniture similar to that which characterized the colonial homes, sometimes modified by demands for economy. The result provided little or no comfort for pupils. Though American homes have undergone radical changes since colonial days, school furnishings have not kept pace. For our living quarters we normally have roomy, comfortable, upholstered chairs; tables

In addition to being of much help to you, pupils can gain valuable learning experiences by assuming a variety of responsibilities in caring for the classroom. (*Photograph by Carl Purcell, National Education Association.*)

of every level, size, and description; shelves, cupboards, and so forth to meet the different needs of all the members of the family. Sometimes home furniture is built in to provide more functional use of space. Light colors are popular because they are more cheerful and provide better lighting. Hard plastics are used for covering floors, table tops, and work spaces; soft plastics cover chairs, seats, and other surfaces. Foam rubber is used for padding the seats and backs of modern living-room chairs. New materials, new designs, new sizes, new shapes appear everywhere in the furnishings of the modern home.

Many schools today have equipped their libraries with comfortable chairs, sofas, and excellent lighting, so that youngsters can see and read in comfort. In some schools the floors of libraries, classrooms, and conference rooms are being carpeted in order to lessen the noise factor and to provide an environment that is more conducive to learning in comfort. Many offices of administrators and supervisors contain the latest and most functional and comfortable furnishings in their schools. But we have yet to meet the same needs for our pupils. It will be costly. It will take time and effort to help people understand the practical wisdom of such changes. Eventually, our schools will be as comfortable and efficient as our homes, our theaters, or our business offices. To the extent that you as a beginning teacher understand the problem and work toward its solution, you can hasten that day.

The seating arrangement of the youngsters in your room needs careful attention. What you can do will be affected considerably by the type of room and furniture you have, by the kind of learning experiences you plan and the way they are approached, and by the needs of the pupils themselves. Flexible seating may make it possible for three or four committees to work on separate problems at the same time in the same room. The organization of other groups for different purposes may require rearrangement of the furniture. Some activities may require that the entire space in a room be cleared of furniture; others, that the seats be arranged in a broad semicircle for discussion purposes.

There is much variety possible in the seating arrangements of pupils aside from the requirements of various learning activities. Some teachers seat their pupils on the first day of class and require that these same seats be retained for the entire semester. Often this is done alphabetically. Frequently the small children are seated in the front and the tall children are seated in the back of the room. Usually special allowance is made for pupils with sight or hearing deficiencies. Permanent seats permit the drawing up of a chart which will help you learn the names of your pupils. That is an important factor. Alphabetical seating will facilitate the collecting and distributing of papers and supplies, the taking of attendance, and the keeping of records in a book or file. On the other hand, if permanent seating is maintained for the entire semester, it has all the disadvantages of fixed seats; it blocks flexibility and variety in learning activities. Only rarely should it be necessary for you to insist that certain pupils sit in certain places. People like to group themselves in different ways for different purposes; they like to be near friends; they like informal and flexible arrangements. And pupils are people.

Ordering Learning Materials

Every teacher has some part to play in the selection, ordering, and handling of learning materials. Sometimes this means little more than the right to choose between two different state-adopted texts. However, some teachers have a great amount of freedom and responsibility in this regard. Some teachers go without certain kinds of materials needed for good classroom instruction because they do not know what to ask for, or they do not bother to ask for them. Know what you want and why you want certain materials. Your principal wants you to do a good job of teaching and will help you secure them.

If you did have unlimited choice in ordering learning materials, what factors would you consider? With respect to text and reference books alone, you would need to be familiar with the most recent and most important ones in your field. You would need to read many books as well as summaries and reviews. Your school's professional library for teachers should be useful to you. Professional journals and the book-review section of newspapers such as the *New York Times* could also prove helpful. Publishing companies will be glad to place you on their mailing lists, should you so request, and will keep you informed about new materials in your field.

Many learning materials can be procured at little or no cost by paying attention to the "yours for the asking" and similar columns in professional periodicals. Also available at a nominal cost are extensive listings of free and inexpensive materials. Regardless of your teaching field or level, be well informed concerning periodicals, newspapers, maps, pictures, charts, models, motion pictures, filmstrips, slides, records, tape recordings, and the like. If you intend to teach such secondary school areas as shop, art, music, home economics, or physical education, your responsibilities may include selecting, ordering, and handling a variety of materials peculiar to those areas. You will be expected to be sufficiently familiar with types of equipment, brands, qualities, prices, and the like to make purchases that are economical. You will also need to know how to use and care for the equipment and materials so that they may render best returns for their cost to the community. The criteria you establish to help you make decisions of selection and use of materials warrant careful study.

Being Responsible for Audio-visual Materials

The modern emphasis on the development of the intellectual, physical, emotional, and social growth of the individual pupil implies more than the use of just subject-matter textbooks. Today's program uses a multiplicity of teaching materials in order to assist the student in learning as much as is humanly possible in the relatively short period of time he is in school. At the same time, the student has the urgent need to gain skill in problem solving and to assume the attitude of a learner as he faces life.

Through research, scientists have found that learning is facilitated when materials of instruction appeal to more than one of the senses. Therefore, today's school uses films, filmstrips, records, tape recordings, and educational television, along with the library and reference books, pictures, maps, charts, globes, and bulletin boards. A wide variety of art materials provides opportunities for self-expression, creativeness, and development of skills. Materials from the natural environment provide learning experiences in science, and tangible aids in mathematics help to make the specialized area of numbers and symbols a more meaningful language. Radio and television keep the students in constant touch with

Photography is a popular hobby, and through it many teachers have found a means of preparing effective instructional materials. (*Photograph by Carl Purcell, National Education Association.*)

living history. Only the initiative and imagination of the school administrators, teachers, parents, and students limit the number of valuable teaching materials which can be used in the modern education program.

Utilizing Planning or Conference Periods

Many forward-looking schools provide a planning or conference period for each teacher, during which the teacher is unassigned in the daily school schedule. The practice is much more prevalent in secondary than in elementary schools. You will find such a period to be of great value to you in your many school duties. It provides an opportunity for you to hold scheduled conferences with pupils or parents, plan your work for the next few days, preview audio-visual materials, browse through various professional magazines and books, or observe your colleagues in different classes throughout the school. Such observation has been encouraged more and more by both teachers and administrators as being an important technique in the improvement of teaching.

In addition to these uses of your planning period, you will always find it most helpful in handling the paper work connected with your classes. Finally, there may be times when the period, or part of it, is needed to provide a time for relaxation from the tension of academic duties. A planning or conference period will prove especially helpful to you as a beginning teacher.

RESPONSIBILITIES WITHIN THE SCHOOL

In addition to your classroom duties, you will have many other opportunities and responsibilities within the school. Some of these responsibilities, such as homerooms, study halls, and cocurricular activities, are more highly organized in the secondary school than in the elementary school, but the principles involved in working with boys and girls remain the same .

Sponsoring Homerooms

It is difficult even to guess what will be expected of you as a homeroom teacher in a secondary school. Your duties here will depend largely upon policies and practices that exist in the school in which you teach. In some schools there are no homerooms; in others, the period appears on the schedule, but the purposes of the homeroom are poorly conceived or are misinterpreted by the school personnel. Its main purpose, in far too many instances, is to provide only for taking attendance, reading announcements from the principal's office, and conducting other items of school business. In the great majority of schools where the homeroom exists as an administrative device, it is held the first period in the school day and sometimes the first in the afternoon for periods of 5 to 15 minutes. In many other schools a longer daily homeroom period of 20 to 40 minutes is provided, which, on certain days, also serves as an activity period when clubs and other cocurricular activities meet. Too often this longer homeroom period becomes merely a study period because teachers and pupils have not planned for purposeful homeroom activities.

Rightly conceived, the homeroom can be one of the most important parts of any school. It is designed for youngsters, not for teachers or administrators. It is meant to be the youngsters' home at school. It should be a place where pupils and teachers grow to know and understand one another. Pupil guidance should take place within an atmosphere of informality and friendliness. In fact, guidance is the chief function of the homeroom. Since student and teacher come together regularly here and have no special subject to which they must devote their time, opportunities for guidance in the homeroom are exceptionally good. Plans should develop, under the teacher's leadership, to consider personal-social problems that are important to the pupils. These might best be handled on a discussion basis, through group guidance procedures, and sometimes by personal counseling.

As a homeroom teacher, your responsibilities will include studying your pupils carefully, so that you may know each one intimately and be able to counsel wisely. For this reason you will need to exhaust every resource to gain information. Tests will provide certain data, visits to homes will provide more, and conferences or conversations with various people will add still other information. Learn all you can about your pupils. Seek information from parents, other teachers, and, with discretion, from others who know your pupils well. Hold many conferences or conversations with the youngsters themselves. Observe them often and carefully, and keep objective anecdotal records of what you observe.

Much of the information which has already been gained in this way may be found in the cumulative pupil records, if the school uses this system. Where such records are available, study them carefully and use them judiciously.

As a result of a national study of the American high school, Conant has emphasized a slightly different function for the homeroom—its role as a social and governmental unit in the school. To promote its purpose in these phases of the school program, it has been suggested that the homeroom group remain together throughout the high school years and that the group be composed of a cross section of student abilities and vocational interests. The homeroom would then serve as the basis for representation on the student council [50:74].

Supervising Pupils outside the Classroom

Besides the management of their own rooms, teachers cooperate in the management of certain other aspects of the school as a whole. Hall duty, for instance, may become one of your responsibilities. In some schools this is merely a matter of being on the scene. The school may not be particularly crowded, or traffic may be handled by a designated student traffic squad—often under the supervision of the student council—or it may be that somewhere the youngsters already have learned how to conduct themselves when they leave the adult supervision of classrooms. In other schools the job is quite different. You may be the chief, possibly the only, traffic officer. You may have to keep traffic flowing in proper channels in order to prevent certain youngsters from being hurt and others from disregarding all the school's rules. You may have to inspect passes of all pupils who are in the halls during class periods to see that they are out of their rooms for legitimate reasons. You may even have to patrol the upper corridors and to inspect dark corners to see that a few adventurous youngsters have not paired off for obviously nonacademic purposes of their own.

In similar fashion, teachers often are required to supervise the cafeteria and the school bus. In the lunchroom you can help youngsters learn more about foods, table manners, desirable social customs, and the like. Certainly, the lunchroom is replete with opportunities for valuable learning. Traveling by school bus provides comparable valuable opportunities. It has been said by some that more significant learning takes place in these informal situations than in the typical classroom. At least it is clear that when young people reach the informal atmosphere of the bus, especially if the driver really enjoys youngsters, they are likely to behave as naturally as they know how. Here is one test of the learning which has taken place at home and in the school. Some youngsters who are tense and backward in the typical formal classroom frequently blossom out on the school bus, lose their fears, assert themselves vigorously, and even assume positions of leadership in the traveling group. If you should have opportunities to supervise children under such circumstances, you will find the task richly rewarding in terms of the new knowledge and understanding you gain. Bus duty may be related to athletic trips, class-project excursions, traveling dramatics groups, senior-class annual trips, and the like. Whether by volunteer system or by administrative appointment, teacher duties of this nature are usually proportioned among the staff group so that no undue burden falls upon anyone.

Classroom teachers are also called upon for incidental help with various other school activities. You may be asked to assume responsibility for taking tickets at basketball games or dramatic events. Or you may have to assume general charge of the auditorium during a public forum. You may need to be on hand when the physical education group or the home economics department puts on its annual demonstration. You may be asked to chaperon parties, picnics, and other social affairs. A total school program is a cooperative undertaking. Other teachers will need to help you in your school activities. Taken in the right spirit, such "duties" can be as relaxing and enjoyable for teachers as they are for pupils. Consider these opportunities seriously and make the most of them.

Sponsoring Cocurricular Activities

Most secondary and many elementary teachers have some responsibilities for the cocurricular program. In the past, many things youngsters wanted and needed from school simply did not appear in the academic curriculum. As a result, these things were gradually brought into the school by the pupils rather timidly and cautiously. At first they were ignored by the faculty, then violently opposed, and eventually accepted. Now they are firmly established. Many educators feel that they should be part of the recognized school program and handled on school time. This is the story of the school band, the dramatics society, the science club, the school paper, the student council, the assembly program, the camera club, the discussion group, the yearbook, the social club, and many other activities not usually associated with the formal curriculum of the school. It is unfortunate that the conduct of these so-called cocurricular activities is seriously handicapped by lack of adequate time in the regular school day and by lack of adequate financial support. Yet both the youngsters and the teacher-sponsors seem to balance this with high enthusiasm and seriousness of purpose in the pursuit of these activities.

As a professional teacher, consider very carefully the desirable characteristics of the cocurricular activities—the informal atmosphere, the large element of pupil planning and management, the flexibility, the pupil-centered purposes and standards, and the friendly relationships between teacher and group. To what extent does this part of the school program suggest improvements that might well be attempted in the regular curriculum?

In spite of the fact that attendance is voluntary, that meetings are held after school hours, that students often have to lend financial aid to the activities, and that no credit is granted for participation, cocurricular activities retain unusual popularity among students. There must be real and significant values in these activities which are pursued and supported so vigorously. You will experience a new relationship with youngsters and reap rich rewards for yourself by offering your leadership in the cocurricular program of your school. You might be the freshman-class sponsor or the senior-class sponsor, for example. Your duties in this connection would vary from one class to another and from one school to another. In larger schools, the more mature teachers usually gain these responsibilities; in smaller schools, even new teachers are likely to be assigned this role. Sponsorship of upper classes in the secondary school is usually far more complicated than that of the beginning classes. The upper-class sponsor exerts leadership and supervision over such affairs as the class play, the yearbook (seniors usually), school government, class organization, dances, and all other affairs which are peculiar to the separate grade groups in school. Such activities weld strong student friendships and loyalties and build high morale in the school. You will be fortunate if the

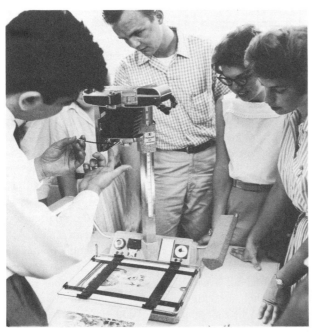

The teacher is called upon to assume responsibilities in connection with cocurricular activities such as those shown here. In what kinds of cocurricular activities will you be able to participate, and what could you expect to gain through such participation? (*Photograph at top from National Education Association. Bottom photograph by Carl Purcell, National Education Association.*)

opportunity to sponsor a class group comes your way early in your teaching career.

Meeting Certain Professional Responsibilities

Classroom teachers have still other duties of a miscellaneous nature which call for careful attention. You will have many letters and professional inquiries which must be answered. You may be asked to review books or to fill out checklists and questionnaires—often from college people or state officials who are conducting serious research. Then too, you must keep alert in your own field; and one way is to plan a regular time for the reading of professional books, journals, and other materials. Many teachers spend time and effort in educational experiments of their own or in original writings. All these things, and more, are part of the job. They take time, but they are rewarding in terms of professional growth and development. It is necessary to plan and experiment in order to gain efficiency in discharging these miscellaneous duties, but there are various sources of help. Usually some of the more experienced teachers in your school will be glad to discuss these matters with you. You will probably gain useful information about acceptable ways of doing things, about official forms and procedures that should not be neglected, about systematizing and routinizing and possibly delegating various jobs for which you are responsible in school.

Working with Administrators, Supervisors, Fellow Teachers, and Other School Personnel

When you start teaching you probably will find yourself working with several "team members." It is this skill in human relationships, the ability to work well with others, that quite often determines your success and happiness in teaching.

You will have an administrative superior, a superintendent who is directly responsible to the board of education and to the people of the community for providing a good education for the pupils. While the superintendent is responsible for the activities that take place in all the classrooms, he usually does not oversee the detailed work of each teacher. Much of his time may be involved in such matters as budgets, employment of teachers, housing facilities, and public relations. He expects the teacher to have considerable freedom in fulfilling his classroom responsibilities and to abide by the accepted policies of the school system in regard to such matters as curriculum organization, teaching procedures, standard report forms, and professional behavior. He depends upon principals and supervisors to ensure the effectiveness of classroom instruction.

The principal is responsible to the superintendent for all the learning activities that take place in his school building. He works more intimately with the teachers, pupils, and community members within his school district than does the superintendent. Principals are assuming increasing amounts of responsibility for the improvement of classroom instruction. Larger school systems usually employ supervisors whose major responsibility is the improvement of classroom instruction. It is to your principal and to your supervisor that you should look for assistance on the problems you encounter and for guidance in regard to any wide deviation from existing practices that you may wish to initiate. Look upon these people as your friends who are anxious to help you succeed to the fullest extent possible.

In larger school buildings you may need to work cooperatively with department heads, various kinds of special teachers, many others who are teaching the same grade or subject, health and social workers, business staff members, and custodians, all of whom play important roles in achieving a common goal—the education of boys and girls.

One of the ways in which you will most frequently work with other teachers is in teachers' meetings. The nature of teachers' meetings varies greatly in school systems. Some are democratic, and others are not; some are very interesting, constructive, and helpful, and others are not. Regardless of the nature of these meetings, however, you should attempt to participate in them.

You may also be asked to serve on various committees. Some of these committee assignments may involve rather immediate, short-term problems; others, such as curricular improvements, methods of reporting to parents, or evaluation procedures, may be of a long-term nature. As a beginning teacher, welcome the opportunity to serve on these committees, since they will enable you to become better acquainted with other staff members, to become accepted as a coworker, to assist in the solution of common problems, and gradually to assume a position of leadership.

As you approach your first teaching position, discover what the chief aims and purposes of your school are, what the general philosophy of the school is, and what the general patterns of instruction seem to be. It will be largely up to you to get acquainted with the various members of the school community and to learn their major interests, needs, and desires. You will be expected to pitch in and help further the school's program toward the goals they consider important.

Unfortunately, in many schools you, as a beginning teacher, may feel imposed upon rather heavily. Some schools expect the beginning teacher to carry the heaviest class load, the most difficult pupils, the least desirable teaching areas or cocurricular activities, or to work in the least attractive classroom space. Such schools operate largely on a seniority basis. Such practices represent gross inadequacies in administration and supervision. Modern trends are distinctly *away* from this.

Keep in mind that newcomers do not ordinarily turn things topsy-turvy and survive. You will meet a number of people in your work whose ideas toward certain educational matters are very different from yours. They, too, have studied carefully and thought seriously. They may be just as sincere as you are. You will want to proceed cautiously. Control the beginner's zeal which tempts many new teachers to feel that their answers are the only answers, their ways the only ways. Often the same goal can be reached by different paths. Sometimes a path that looks straight and clear at the start becomes devious and confused later on. If you are right on some matter and you know that you are, move slowly and without arousing undue antagonism. Not until you are rather well accepted as a person and as a coworker can you expect to play a very significant role in such matters as developing the school philosophy, changing the curriculum, or resolving basic issues. One of the best ways to gain that acceptance is by being diligent and helpful as you work with all your colleagues in school.

Appraising the Quality of Your Teaching

Every teacher should feel an obligation to review systematically the quality of his teaching. Through frequent self-analysis and appraisals a teacher gains insights with regard to ways in which his teaching may be improved.

In a very practical and informative booklet titled *Are You a Good Teacher?* Alexander [5] has prepared a list of twenty indicators of the quality of teaching. Review the list, which is located in the Resource Section for Part II, as a means of gaining further insight into your role as a teacher. When you begin teaching, check yourself periodically against this list.

FIGURE 5–2.   The results of a study of the number of times teachers were observed in their classroom work for five minutes or more, as reported by teachers, during the first half of the school year 1962–1963. (*Source:* National Education Association.)

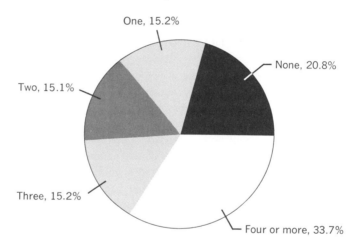

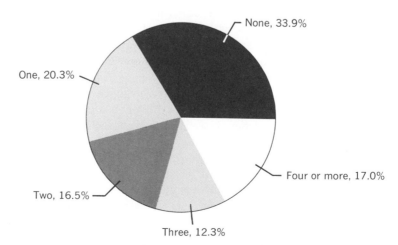

Undoubtedly the quality of your teaching will be appraised by your superior. This appraisal may follow very formal procedures, or it may be more casual. According to a study made by the research division of the National Education Association [164:12–18], written ratings or evaluations are required in three-fourths of the schools for teachers not on tenure and in two-thirds for teachers who are on tenure. The principal is nearly always responsible for evaluating teachers, although he may share this responsibility with another official, such as a supervisor. As you may expect, beginning teachers are evaluated more often during the year than are experienced teachers. Usually an appraisal is made as a result of observing the teacher teaching in the classroom. Other methods of determining a teacher's success (or lack of success) may include "gathering impressions of the teacher from seeing him [the teacher] outside the classroom, gathering impressions from pupils, study of pupil achievement records and office records on each teacher, and noting what parents and other teachers say about the teacher being evaluated" [164:13]. When you begin your teaching, you should not hesitate to ask for help and guidance in order to ensure greater success and happiness in your teaching.

COMMUNITY EXPECTATIONS OF TEACHERS

In planning a teaching career, you naturally are curious about the roles teachers play in the community. In the act of teaching, you will be expected by the community to show interest in your pupils, to be able to work effectively with them, and to know your subject matter well. Furthermore, when you enter a community as a teacher, you will be expected to show certain attitudes, understandings, and behavior patterns which members of the community have come to associate with teachers. Your work will be considered a public service, paid for at public expense and influenced very decidedly by what the public wants. You will also be considered a leader in the business of helping people grow and learn, of helping whole communities became better places in which to live.

Community Participation

Among the important areas of teacher community participation are religion, clubs, and politics. Religion is an important element in the lives of most people, and since teachers are expected to set good examples for the young, most communities expect them to be active in church affairs. A national survey indicated that teachers were meeting that expectation. Among teachers, 87.2 per cent indicated that they were members of a church or synagogue [8:27]. Almost two-thirds of these were active members and workers. Although comparisons were not made using the entire adult population, it seems clear that teachers are above the national average in this regard.

The types of organizations (other than churches) in which teachers most frequently are active members include lodges and related social groups; fraternities, sororities, and alumni groups; health and social-welfare groups; cultural and recreational groups, such as drama, bowling, and hobby clubs; men's and women's business and professional, service, and civic-social clubs; and religious-social youth-

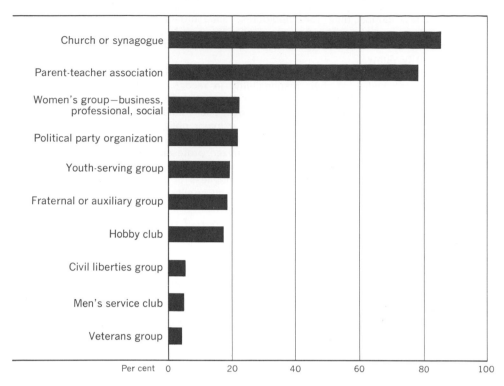

FIGURE 5–3. The percentage of teachers in 1965–1966 indicating membership in certain civic and community organizations. (*Source:* National Education Association.)

building groups. The frequency with which teachers participate in these organizations varies greatly from community to community. You may be certain that you will have many opportunities to assume a very active role in community organizations if you desire this kind of activity during your leisure time.

Traditionally the community political activity of teachers has been less extensive than their participation in the activities of churches and other organizations. However, teachers seem to be setting an example, at least in the act of voting. In the 1964 national election almost 90 per cent of all teachers voted. This percentage is decidedly higher than that for the nation. However, in 1961 only 2 per cent of all teachers had ever been candidates for elective public offices [8:33]. Perhaps the political activity of teachers is increasing. An opinion poll conducted in 1965 revealed that 66 per cent of the nation's classroom teachers thought they should work actively on their own time as members of political parties in nationwide elections; only 23 per cent felt this way in 1956 [261:64]. In the platform adopted by the National Education Association in 1965, the following recommendation was made:

It is recommended that every educational system in written personnel policies guarantee to all its teachers full equality with other citizens in the exercise of their political rights and responsibilities, including such rights as voting, discussing political issues, campaigning for candidates, and running for and serving in public office. Provisions should be made to enable teachers to serve in public office without personal loss and without curtailment of annual increments or tenure, retirement, or seniority rights.

A prerequisite to high quality in education is acceptance by the community and by governing bodies of their responsibility in recognizing the political and professional status and rights of teachers. The Association [NEA] stands ready to support any teacher whose status or rights have been unfairly menaced or restricted. Such support the association regards as a major obligation of professional organizations.

Many of the objectives which the organized profession has set for improvement of education can be achieved only with the active support of its members in influencing public decisions. Therefore, the willingness of the teacher to assert himself fully as a citizen is vital to the pursuit of high quality in education. [175:56–57].

A November, 1965, issue of the *NEA Journal* presents evidence of teachers' political influence in the state of Washington as reflected in the actions taken by the last session of the state legislature [120:49].

The legislature increased state school appropriations by $75 million, or 17 per cent, and guaranteed teachers an 11 per cent salary increase; it enacted a law requiring local school boards to negotiate with recognized teacher organizations; it made accumulated sick leave and placement on the salary schedule transferable from one district to another; it raised teacher retirement benefits by as much as 50 per cent.

In addition, the lawmakers appropriated funds to increase the number of community colleges in the state, adopted a new method for distributing state school funds, and revised the tax structure in line with recommendations made or approved by the Washington Education Association. They also established a guaranteed duty-free lunch period for all teachers and made available to them a tax-sheltered annuity program.

What is expected of you as a teacher will depend in part upon the community where you happen to be located. In small schools, teachers usually have personal relationships with a relatively large percentage of the total school population. Teachers in small communities come in contact with and are known and appraised by large percentages of the people. Because of the intimacy of these relationships and because of certain folkways of people in small communities in the United States, teachers in such places must anticipate somewhat less liberal attitudes than those they would find in large cities. The situation may be quite different where population centers are dense, where your school may be one of a dozen or two in the large city, where your school may be located in one section and your home in another part of the city. In such a situation, it would be possible for you to work many months without being intimately known by more than a handful of people in your school and another handful in the neighborhood where you live. At the same time, keep in mind that, regardless of its size, location, or essential nature, every community will have certain expectations of its teachers.

Personal Conduct

One of the most challenging aspects of the teaching profession is that most communities expect teachers to be laudable examples of personal-social living. This is further recognition of the significant influence teachers wield in the lives of their pupils. Most parents insist that this influence be of a desirable nature. You should recall again that there is wide variation in expectations of teachers from one community to another.

Parents often expect teachers to be better examples for children than parents themselves choose to be. In some communities teachers are expected not to smoke or drink alcoholic beverages in public places. Few communities frown upon such activities when practiced in moderation in private homes and parties. The teacher in many communities enjoys as much freedom in personal matters as any other professional person.

If you were to call upon a lawyer or a medical doctor for business reasons, either would be likely to appear before you carefully groomed and would display behavior considered appropriate to his profession. The same is expected of teachers. The teaching profession carries with it certain obligations with respect to behavior. Yet there is no need to be straitlaced about these matters either. For a new teacher in the community, it is best to discover exactly what the expectations are and to heed them carefully. After you are somewhat more experienced, better established in many groups, and well known as a capable teacher and respectable person, you can expect more freedom in matters of this sort. At the same time, remember that attitudes toward the personal behavior of teachers are continuing to change for the better. As a teacher, you could further this improvement by conducting yourself in a highly professional and respectable manner.

If you exercise good judgment it is unlikely that you will feel that your personal life is seriously restricted. In a nationwide study involving nearly 6,000 teachers [250:32–33], almost two-thirds of the teachers reported that their personal lives were not restricted in any way, and almost one-third indicated that their lives were restricted but not seriously. Only 2.1 per cent reported serious restrictions on their personal lives. As you might expect, the young teachers in small school systems felt that they had to exercise more caution than teachers in large cities. Single men seemed to feel a greater amount of restriction than did any other group of beginning teachers. Nearly 46 per cent of the single men reported that their behavior was somewhat restricted but not seriously, and 3.4 per cent reported serious restriction. Unmarried women did not feel quite so free of restrictions as did married women. A slightly higher percentage of teachers in secondary grades than in the elementary grades reported restrictions on their personal lives.

Public Relations

The classroom teacher, either purposefully or incidentally, helps shape public attitudes toward the school. In fact, the classroom teacher functions as the primary agent in the establishment of public relations—whether they be good or bad. As Frasier points out [102:10]:

> Good teaching is the best public relations for a school. The teacher's reputation in a community is determined largely by the children and their parents. If the teacher is doing a good job, the children are happy and bring home a positive attitude toward the teacher and the school to their parents, who transmit this feel-

ing to their friends. When a citizen says, "We have a fine school system," he usually means that he is pleased with the type of teaching his children or his neighbor's children are receiving. But if the pupils come from school unhappy and reflect a negative attitude, parents soon form the generalization that the schools in their community are not very good. Thus upon the classroom teacher rests most of the responsibility for good community relationships. No amount of planned public relations programs can affect a poor teacher, nor will the parent of a child who is pleased with his teacher be susceptible to unfair criticism of the school.

As you move about in the community, as you fulfill your citizenship responsibilities, as you work with others in various types of community agencies and activities you will be painting an image of your school as well as of the teaching profession in the minds of those with whom you come in contact. Attempt to reflect the feeling that you are proud of your profession; you are ethical, dependable, and considerate of others; you enjoy working with others; and you feel you are a part of the community [102:20–21].

The school today needs the understanding and positive support of the public more than ever before. Many teachers engage in a variety of activities in an attempt to promote lay interest and participation in schools. Too many, however, are not doing as much as they should.

The research division of the National Education Association has constructed a checklist for teachers so that they may appraise themselves on how well they are accomplishing their public relations function. Review this checklist, which is located in the Resource Section for Part II, as a means of gaining further insight with respect to ways in which you may promote effective school-public relationships.

FIGURE 5–4. The percentage of teachers who use various public relations techniques and who consider these techniques to be effective. Are there other techniques that should be used? (*Source:* National Education Association.)

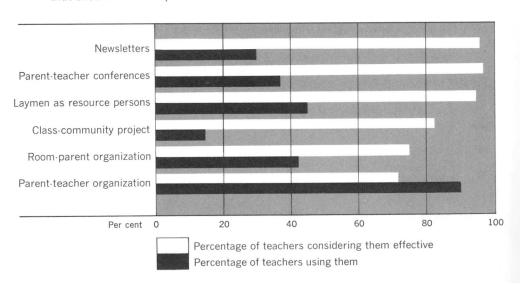

SUMMARY

Very few aspects of the teacher's work are purely mechanical. While the classroom and other responsibilities within the school that have been described may seem somewhat tedious at times, they are part of the mainstream of teaching and learning. Frequently they set the stage so that effective learning can take place. Often they present opportunities for rich learning experiences for pupils and teachers alike. In every case they require technical and professional know-how for their best management, as well as a sincere interest in and knowledge of youngsters—how they grow and develop, how they live and learn.

As you reflect upon the community expectations that have been presented in this chapter, remember that they exist for good reasons. They have changed somewhat through the years and will continue to change. By your own attitudes and behavior you may accelerate the change in desirable channels. Teaching is an intimate social work. It is a powerful molding force. It is small wonder that those who hire you for such work should scrutinize you carefully and set certain standards which they feel must be upheld. Such concern should be interpreted as a tribute and a challenge—a tribute to the significant role of teachers and a challenge to lead the community and all its people to a higher level of living. When you understand your school and your role in that school, when you understand your community and your role in that community, then you can be most effective in interpreting the school to the community—a responsibility of all teachers.

QUESTIONS FOR YOUR CONSIDERATION

1. It has been said that a teacher should know his subject matter, his pupils, himself, and how to organize these into learning situations. Do you agree? Do you feel that there is any priority among these items?
2. Do you believe that teachers are forced to spend too much time on routine details? What suggestions can you make for relieving the situation?
3. In your opinion how should the progress of pupils be evaluated?
4. How should the progress of pupils be reported to parents?
5. How can cocurricular activities help pupils develop greater interest in the curricular activities of the school?
6. Some parents feel that too many cocurricular activities are being sponsored by schools today. How do you account for this feeling? What is your opinion?
7. In what ways does the work of a teacher in a large school differ from the work of a teacher in a small school?
8. It is frequently pointed out that most teachers who lose their jobs do so not because of lack of knowledge in their teaching fields but because of lack of ability in working with others. What are some of the personal qualities involved in working successfully with others?
9. Many prospective teachers feel that there may be many restrictions on their personal lives. Do you feel this way? Why?
10. Parents often expect teachers to be better examples for children than parents

themselves choose to be. Do they have any right to make such demands of teachers?

11. How important is the teacher as a public relations agent? When does he serve as such an agent?

ACTIVITIES FOR YOU TO PURSUE

1. Spend as much time as you can for two or three days in succession observing the same teacher and class in school. Make a careful record of the duties the teacher performs. Try to identify those responsibilities which are most important. Examine those selected to determine whether they are of the mechanical or the leadership and human relations type.

2. Compare the daily schedule of classes of a small high school with that of a large high school. What differences do you observe in the number and variety of offerings? Consider both the regular curriculum and the cocurricular activities. How do the educational opportunities for pupils in the two schools compare in terms of available offerings? Which areas of teaching and learning appeal to you most? Why?

3. Become acquainted with a social or religious organization which serves children or youth in your community. Make several observations of the group at work. What relationships do you observe between the youngsters and the adult leaders of the group? Between the adult leaders and the parents of the youngsters? What similarities do you find between this situation and teaching in the public schools?

4. Organize student panel discussions in which you explore such topics as: What kinds of homerooms fulfill their function in a modern secondary school? What are some modern trends in reporting to parents?

5. Study the student handbook of a junior or senior high school. What opinions do you form concerning the school as a result of this study? What questions do you have?

6. Visit a number of modern classrooms and note improvements in the construction of school plants and equipment. Discuss with your colleagues how these improvements may help the teacher in meeting the educational needs of pupils today.

7. Through the use of the checklist in the Resource Section for Part II, appraise one or more of your former teachers to see how well each fulfilled his public relations function.

6

BECOMING EFFECTIVE
IN THE CLASSROOM

When a teacher first meets his class at the beginning of the school year, he begins the cycle that makes up the main portion of his responsibilities—the task of guiding the growth of his pupils. Here before him is the class waiting for—for what? As the person immediately responsible for the direction in which these young people will grow during the coming year, the teacher will have already asked himself that question, "For what?" And immediately the next question arises— "How?" Whether the pupils are first graders or high school seniors these same questions are to be answered. *What* are the goals and how are these particular pupils to be helped to attain these goals?

Perhaps the latter question presents greater concern for you at this stage of your preparation for teaching. The question would not appear to be so troublesome if you were to deal with only one pupil. But you will be responsible for a number of pupils, each quite different physically, psychologically, and socially. As a teacher, you will be concerned with each pupil and his total growth. Although it would be a dull world indeed if all persons were the same, the fact that individuals within one classroom can vary to a high degree poses problems for you. Some variations among pupils, however, will not be so great as to interfere with learning progress, while others must be dealt with individually.

GAINING PROFICIENCY IN TEACHING

The well-known axiom "Start where the pupil is" sums up the point that you deal with the pupil at his present stage of educational, social, and psychological development and plan for him and with him the program that will best help him to attain the goals expected of him. If you wish to be a good teacher, this task will challenge you to the limit throughout your entire professional career. It involves depth of understanding in regard to the behavior and needs of pupils, the nature of the learning process, the selection and guidance of the learning experiences, and understanding of and skill in human relationships. Your success as a beginning teacher, to a considerable degree, will depend upon the amount of understanding and skill you have regarding these matters. The rest of this chapter will give you a preview of principles and practices which will be spelled out in greater detail in professional education courses required in most teacher preparation programs.

In what ways do these children seem to be different? In what ways do they seem to be alike? How should the school attempt to meet their differences as well as their likenesses? (*Photograph from the National Education Association.*)

Understanding Pupil Behavior

Many beginning teachers fail to recognize the cues from a pupil's behavior that signal "Attention needed." If Mary fails to do any of the subtraction problems correctly because she subtracts the smaller digit from the larger regardless of position, it is obvious at this stage that she does not understand the process of subtraction. But what earlier signals did she give that indicated she was not understanding the process and, as a result, must now unlearn and then relearn? The experienced teacher might recognize that as soon as Dick begins to tap his pencil, learning for him has ceased and that his attention is now directed to more playful pursuits. But in Bob's case, pencil tapping signals only that he releasing some youthful energy while attending fully to the task at hand.

How can you become expert at understanding individual behavior? It is a process that one continues to learn throughout a lifetime. An infant soon learns the meaning of many of his mother's actions. A college student already has learned to interpret the meanings of many kinds of behavior. One familiar example is that of the student's wanting a raise in allowance. He observes his parents' behavior very closely for signs of a propitious moment to bring up the subject and, once having opened up the matter, seeks further signs to learn how well things are going. This same procedure should underlie your approach to understanding pupil behavior. Be a close observer.

The professional training that you receive includes course work and opportunities to gain skill in effective observation. Basic courses in educational psychology, child development, and adolescent development serve to provide the general principles underlying human behavior. Early practice in applying these principles will enhance later performance when you are actually responsible for guiding pupils toward educational goals.

Through many observations of boys and girls and discussion about their behavior, you will be able to gain greater depth of understanding of behavior, build confidence, and achieve competence as a teacher. Your immediate goal is to develop a sensitivity to significant cues. This means you must be sensitive to cues in general and be able to discriminate which are the significant cues for the purpose.

Unless observation is systematic, little useful information will be obtained. You cannot observe the total environment at one time. In a classroom context, the total environment includes not only the pupils but also the teacher, the materials, and the physical structure. Without an underlying system, you will tend to observe whatever attracts your attention strongly enough. With guides for observation formulated in advance, you can observe for specific purposes. While the experienced teacher will be able to keep several purposes in mind, you will probably gain more initially from your observation by attempting to answer only one question, say, "What was the general response of the class to the kinds of materials used during the observation period?"

To find answers to the question, observe in terms of the actual behavior of pupils. If the conclusion was made that the group responded well to the instructional materials selected by the teacher, the evidence for that conclusion would be in terms of actual behavior. What did the group do? Were there enthusiastic comments such as "Good! I like this book!" Were there eager anticipations of receiving the material, such as clearing a space to accommodate the books? Were the boys and girls alert in their facial and body expressions? On the other hand, did some pupils grumble and slump back in their chairs as if to say "That old thing again?"

While the questions to be answered during an observation might well be posed in general purposes and in abstract terms, the answers can only be made in terms of observed behavior. In answering the question, "How is day-to-day instruction being adapted to individual differences?" for example, you might observe the teacher's behavior in terms of group management. If you are observing an arithmetic lesson, are small groups made so that the wide differences within the whole group are lessened in order to meet the common needs represented by the smaller groups? After the teacher gets the small groups started, are there one or two individuals needing special help? Does the teacher find time to help these individuals? Are instructional materials selected from various levels of difficulty, or must all pupils, regardless of present achievement level, use the same materials?

Perhaps there is a pupil who needs guidance and help because social or psychological factors are interfering with his achieving educational goals. For example, a boy may aggressively be seeking attention. He also may be interfering with the

learning of other class members. Does the teacher use means that will permit him
to receive attention for doing constructive instead of disruptive work?

Remember one caution in drawing conclusions from observations: one instance
is not a sufficient basis on which to make general statements. Observations must
be made many times to discover the patterns of behavior which constitute the
reliable signals or cues on which a teacher operates.

Opportunities for informal observation are constantly at hand. All kinds of
situations may be used to observe the behavior of boys and girls. You may observe
them on the street, on a playground, at church, or at a basketball game. These
situations provide excellent sources for you to use in gaining skill in observing
behavior. In other words, observe the people you want to understand under all
conditions available to you. Classroom observation is more formal. On the other
hand, it provides the context in which the teacher works. An alertness to the influence on classroom behavior of factors coming from outside the school room,
however, should enable you to have a better understanding of behavior observed
in the classroom.

In learning to be a close observer, select only a few individuals and watch them
in terms of only one general question. With a little practice, you can include more
individuals as well as more questions. As a help toward systematic observation,
a guide sheet is presented below. For each of the first six questions included on

Learn to identify the psychological and social needs of pupils rapidly. These needs
are as important as their intellectual needs and affect academic progress greatly.
(*Photograph from the* Planning for Teaching *series of motion pictures.*)

this sheet, space is provided for you to record relevant observed behavior and to answer the question.

Guide Sheet for Observing Classroom Teaching

1. What are some of the positive techniques used in working with pupils?

   _____

   _____

   _____

2. How is day-to-day instruction being adapted to individual differences?

   _____

   _____

   _____

3. What are some evidences that the teacher is alert to physical, social, and psychological needs of individual pupils?

   _____

   _____

   _____

4. What are some evidences of pupil-teacher planning?

   _____

   _____

   _____

5. What are some evidences of a rich educational environment?

   _____

   _____

   _____

6. What is the place of the teacher in the group?

   _____

   _____

   _____

7. What questions from your observation do you wish to discuss with your college teacher?

   _____

   _____

   _____

As a teacher, you will have many opportunities to observe youth. Be alert to them in the cafeteria, on the playground, and at club meetings. Plan your class-work so that you may sometimes be on the sidelines watching as your groups work. Find occasions outside the school—at church, in the park, on the street—to see boys and girls as they really are. The efficient teacher records his observations for further study. He devises a simple scheme for collecting and organizing his information about individuals or groups. He then teaches himself to be objective in using his plan. Although the observations which you make now will be somewhat different from those you will make of your pupils when you begin to teach, recording the things you observe as you come in contact with youngsters will help you to become expert in gathering data and will afford practice in finding meaning in your observations.

Understanding the Needs of Pupils

From experiences in learning to know boys and girls, teachers grow in their understanding of what is required for growth and happy living. There is no real substitute for this insight and skill.

The needs of youth are of several kinds. Perhaps the first that must be satisfied is that which relates to good physical condition and health. All individuals need adequate food and clothing, freedom to be active, a place and time for rest, and immunity from disease. The physical organism demands all these things. If these persistent needs are not met, individuals sometimes react in undesirable ways.

Every morning about eleven o'clock John became a trouble spot in the fifth grade. He began to disturb his neighbors, to push and shove, to whine and fuss. Something was sure to go wrong in a short time; John seemed to be always in the center of it. This deviation from his normal behavior sent his teacher exploring. It did not take long for her to discover that John left his farm home quite early each morning on the school bus, having had his breakfast half an hour before. By eleven it was time for food again, and the rebellious John began acting up. A midmorning lunch for John solved the problem. Some teachers would have said that John was just a troublemaker.

Another example, directly related to schoolwork, is the case of a child who has trouble in reading because of a specific visual defect. You will be amazed at the number of experienced teachers who frequently fail to detect visual defects in children. While most children have normal vision, there are special cases, and the observant teacher is alert to possible physical factors which might interfere with progress. Does the child habitually squint his eyes? Does he hold his book at an unusual angle? Does he always turn his head slightly when listening? Is it because one ear is defective and he is adjusting for that defect? Early observance of physical needs of pupils can permit early treatment and adjustment.

Mental and psychological needs are as important as physical ones. All individuals experience them—the need to feel secure in the affection of someone, the need to be a part of the group, and the need to be a creative member of society. The understanding teacher keeps these needs always in mind. He demonstrates constantly that he likes boys and girls. He finds a way for each pupil to do something well every day. He explores with them many opportunities to be creative. He plans to help each pupil find a place in the group and each group widen its circle of friendships. He knows how important it is to be one of the team.

Meeting the mental or psychological needs of pupils will help them satisfy their social needs, too. But social needs require special skills and techniques which boys and girls have to learn. They need to know how to do things, how to express themselves clearly, how to meet situations with poise, and how to win acceptance from others in the group.

As a teacher you may meet an adolescent girl like Lydia, who was trying to

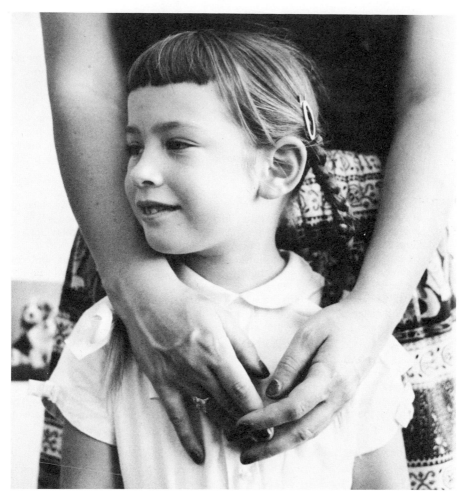

All individuals need to feel secure in the affection of someone. How will you attempt to meet this need in your classroom? (*Photograph by Carl Purcell, National Education Association.*)

find a place for herself in her group. An alert teacher recorded her observations of Lydia's struggle to learn the techniques that would satisfy her need to belong [101:44–45].

October

During the next several weeks Lydia came in frequently crying and saying: "I don't like it here. The girls don't like me." Each time I persuaded her to try it again and to try to get better acquainted with some of the teachers who might help her.

November

Lydia came to me several times complaining that the girls in her home economics class didn't like her. She even asked that I call some of them to my office to talk to them about it. I tried to bolster her self-confidence by helping her to see that the girls who worried her weren't too successful themselves and might be only trying to tease her. . . .

January

Two weeks later Lydia again complained. "The girls in home economics class don't like me. They sit and talk about me. I'd like to drop the course. Could I transfer to Girls' Technical High?"

End of January

Shortly after this Lydia turned in an excellent notebook in her home economics class and received the best grade in the class. This seemed to give her the confidence she needed. She told me about it and said maybe she really did know as much as the other girls in the class. She never again complained of their not liking her.

November

Lydia came in after morning club period (she belongs to "white-collar girls"—anyone may join until the quota is filled). She had on a white blouse and checked skirt and looked very neat. She smiled pleasantly and asked, "Miss Jones, may I come in and talk to you during the sixth period today?"

I had to tell her that I was attending a conference this afternoon, but could see her tomorrow if it were something that could wait. "Oh, tomorrow will be all right," she replied rather airily. She carried a white crepe paper bow and holding it up, said, "We white-collar girls have to wear one of these today." I said, "Oh, you are a white-collar girl. I imagine you enjoy that." She answered, "I was in study hall last year and I didn't want that again."

December

One day Lydia stopped in my office for a needle and thread to sew up a small rip in her skirt. She said, "Miss Jones, do you notice how much I've gained since last year?" I answered, "Well, your face looks fuller and it is becoming to you." She answered, "Oh, I feel better than I did last year. I laugh a lot now. You know some of the girls I thought didn't like me in home economics class are my best friends now."

The teacher must discover the individual differences which exist within his group. He must identify Dick who, although very brilliant, is too young socially for his class. He must uncover Patricia's talent for art and put it to work to help her make a place for herself among her companions. He must appreciate the fact that Carol should begin her new work in arithmetic where she left off last year and that she may not be ready to begin the assigned work of her grade. He must recognize that, even though David and Bill seem to be of about equal maturity and ability, the wide differences in their backgrounds and out-of-school experiences mean that the school day must be planned differently for each of them.

You are probably saying, "Do you mean that when I teach school I'll be expected to make a special plan for each of the forty pupils I'm likely to have? That's impossible!" Of course, you are right. It is not the purpose of the school to teach its pupils one at a time. As a resourceful teacher you will find many occasions when it will be highly desirable for the whole group to share an experience and to learn from one another. Small collective enterprises will help your boys and girls who have similar needs and who are of similar ability to work profitably together. Still other groups will bring together pupils who have common interests but who may be at different levels of maturity. Sometimes boys and girls from several grades will cooperate on worthwhile activities. In all this interchange, individual differences will come into play, and youth will have opportunities to satisfy their physical, intellectual, and social needs.

FIGURE 6–1. The school is confronted with the task of meeting a wide variety of individual differences. What are the major groups of differences suggested in this illustration? How will you attempt to meet the great diversification of needs of pupils? (*Source:* National Education Association, National Association of Secondary-School Principals, and the Educational Policies Commission.)

Understanding How Learning Takes Place

The word "learning" is commonplace in our language, but like the word "think," it is difficult to define precisely. As you proceed in your preparation for teaching you will devote much study to its precise meaning and implication for your work.

Young children, especially, reveal some of their characteristics, thoughts, and feelings through their creative activities. (*Photograph from the Audio-visual Center, Indiana University.*)

A teacher observes performance rather than learning and infers from it that certain learnings have taken place. Learning involves some change or modification in the behavior of a pupil. For example, suppose that a pupil has written a theme containing the sentence "They, was also going to make the trip." Two errors in performance were made—the comma and number of the verb. When these errors have been called to the attention of the pupil and explained, future performances will be checked to discover whether or not these particular behaviors have been modified. If commas are no longer misplaced and plural subjects are accompanied by plural verbs, then it is inferred that this bit of learning has taken place.

As you observe boys and girls you become more and more aware of the fact that there are times when learning becomes especially meaningful to pupils. There probably is one best time to teach everything, if teachers could only know that time. There are no magic or scientific formulas yet available for determining these exact moments when pupils should be taught. Your preparation for teaching will help you in determining when teaching will become most significant. Certain conditions, however, can be cultivated or arranged which foster effective learning. From their many contacts with boys and girls teachers know that pupils learn when they are motivated by their own needs and challenged to put forth their best efforts. They know that pupils learn best when learning is closely related to and grows out of past and present experiences. They know that pupils who have opportunities to plan their activities and to select their materials under the guidance of a wise and resourceful teacher are learning far more than those who must follow the direction of a classroom autocrat. Good teachers help boys and girls to experience in a great variety of ways, to use what they are learning, to evaluate the success of their plans, and to see real progress toward a goal.

This garden project of an elementary school in Battle Creek, Michigan, enables the pupils to relate specific principles to practical life situations. What other types of projects would encourage this kind of learning? (*Photograph from the National Education Association.*)

Selecting and Guiding Learning Experiences

Choosing the learning experiences which pupils should have may seem to you to be a big job for a young teacher. There are so many things boys and girls may do, so many choices to make. How does a teacher know in what directions to guide his pupils?

Modern teachers have many aids, one of the most important of which lies in the needs and interests of pupils. The knowledge of these needs, as you already know, comes from constant observation and careful study. Each activity leads the way to the next, pointing to new experiences which particular individuals need. Today's teachers, by their awareness of the community in which they live and by their understanding of the influences which affect young people, are able to help youth make wise choices. An appreciation of the demands of democratic living enlarges even more the teacher's vision of the kinds of goals for which youth should be reaching.

Leaders in education are pretty well agreed upon the kinds of experiences boys and girls need in order to participate fully in living today and in the future. These experiences include developing efficiency in the basic communication and mathematics skills, learning techniques of group planning and problem solving, making and taking responsibility for decisions, developing a knowledge of themselves and of other people that will contribute to better group living, and developing a knowledge and understanding of the environment in which all these activities take place. To these must be added participation in community activities, efforts to promote critical thinking, evaluation of experiences, building a wide range of interests that will contribute to the making of a well-balanced individual, and the development of personal and social values. (See Chapter 16.)

These are the kinds of experiences that teach the cooperation that is so increasingly necessary in today's world; they help each individual reach his highest potentialities. Do you find it difficult to see the traditional teacher as an educative force in such surroundings? Where is the teacher who merely assigns pages in a textbook, listens to the recitation of what has been read, gives a grade, makes the next assignment, and begins the cycle all over again?

The modern teacher is not only a good group leader but also a most resourceful one. He knows how to do things and where to find information. Pupils call upon him for technical aid in many situations. He is a sympathetic adult who does not berate them for not knowing. When group planning becomes bogged down, he is the one who can pull it out of the mire.

The teacher facilitates the experiences of his pupils. He senses the direction of their thinking and planning and can smooth the way to success. He helps them just enough, but not too much. He saves them from failures they cannot understand. He promotes good group relationships by foreseeing personality clashes and by helping them to accept each other. Oiling the machinery is an important job for the teacher.

The teacher helps boys and girls to evaluate their group work and aids each pupil in judging his own efforts in the light of his needs and ability. In a relaxed, friendly atmosphere youth learn to face their mistakes and shortcomings frankly and make plans for improvement. Failing to reach the goal the first time merely motivates a second and better try. Pupils individually and as groups ask and seek answers to such questions as these: "Did we accomplish what we set out to do?" "What part of our work did we do well?" "Why did some of our efforts fail?" "What shall we do differently next time?" "Were all group members participating?" "Did I do my part?" "How did I feel about my part of the job?" "What new things were learned?" "How can these new ideas be used?" "What new problems came up that need to be solved?" Surely these are more important than to ask "What grade did I get?"

The teacher is concerned that each individual, whether he be working alone or in a group situation, has maximum opportunity to develop his interests and abilities. He recognizes that the strength of a democratic society is dependent upon the full development of each individual's talents. Within a group situation the development of these talents provides not only for individual self-realization but also for the enrichment of the entire group. For example, as the teacher helps a pupil develop his special abilities in science, the pupil moves toward self-realization, assumes roles of leadership within the group, and enriches the lives of others through his contributions to the group. His life, in turn, is enriched through the sharing of unique interests and abilities possessed by other members of his group.

How will you select the activities in which your pupils engage? Experiences are not of equal educative value, and pupils can engage in only as many experiences as time will allow. You therefore need some yardstick of values against which you can make selections. This yardstick consists of the values which a democratic society prizes and covets. The following statement of principles should aid you in making these choices [adapted, 110:25–27]:

1. *The experience must begin and grow out of the needs of the pupils as they see them and as society sees them.* Such needs tend to be needs which the pupils themselves recognize or can be made aware of. They may be needs for knowledge, skill, expression, the satisfaction of an interest—any one or a pattern of needs.

2. *The experience must be managed by all of the learners concerned—pupils, teachers, parents, and others—through cooperative, democratic interaction.* Experiences in the modern school frequently draw in many people who do not give full time to the school. Parents contribute in many ways, as do many civic authorities, merchants, and others.

3. *The experience must take on meaning and unity as the pupils' purposes become clearer and their work moves through one stage after another toward completion.* At times pupils may purpose to do things which have relatively little meaning to them because of their meager experience, but as work progresses new understandings are added, horizons are pushed out, and the whole matter assumes new and lasting values.

4. *The experience must aid each pupil in improving his purposes and increasing his power to make intelligent choices.* Pupils' original choices may be trivial and of slight value because of their lack of experience and insight. As their work progresses, guided by a skillful and understanding teacher, the inherent values and meanings become apparent to the pupils and they purpose more and more wisely as their knowledge and insight grow. One of the major goals of all education is that of guiding the individual into ever higher and finer purposing, ever better and more worthy choices.

5. *The experience must aid each pupil to integrate past experience with present experience, making all available for future use.* Often, in the traditional school, learning has been of little permanent value because each skill or item of content was learned as a separate entity; the pupil failed to utilize past experience to solve present problems. As a result he saw little or no application of present learning to his own out-of-school experience, and the life value of the learning was negligible.

6. *The experience must increase the number and variety of interests which each pupil consciously shares with others.* One of the school's major tasks is that of opening up new and untried avenues of experience. A democratic society is one in which the genius of one individual can be utilized to enrich the entire mass and in which the level attained by the society as a whole is the aggregate of the levels attained by the interacting individuals within the society. Therefore it follows logically that the pupils need many leadership opportunities in cooperative interaction and sharing of experiences. When these shared experiences widen horizons and increase the number and variety of interests, their service is twofold.

7. *The experience must help each youngster build new meanings and refine old ones.* Real learning is forever a matter of adding new meanings and modify-

ing old ones. If the addition and modification refine, enrich, and enlarge the total fund of meanings which the pupil possesses, they add substantially to the working material which the pupil draws upon to understand and interpret other experiences.

8. *The experience must offer opportunity for each pupil to use an ever-increasing variety of resources for learning.* Resources for learning in life outside the school include people, firsthand and vicarious experiences, books, magazines, television, radio, movies, and many other avenues. The more resources a youngster learns to use under the guidance of the school the more readily and independently he will learn in his life outside of the school.

9. *The experience must help each pupil to use a variety of learning activities which are suited to the resources he is using for learning.* Pupils need to do wide reading and intensive reading, to work alone and in groups, to learn many skills and develop many abilities, and to use those skills and abilities in many ways.

10. *The experience must aid each pupil to reconstruct his past experience creatively as the new learning situation develops.* Again, it is a matter of helping pupils to draw upon their past experience to understand their present experience and in so doing to enlarge and enrich the total concept.

11. *The experience must challenge the thinking and call forth the effort of the youngster to bring it to a satisfactory conclusion.* Any really valuable experience is broad enough in the scope of its possibilities to provide worthwhile experience for the slowest learner and still challenge the more able learner and cause him to exert himself willingly to solve the necessary problems and carry on the work. Youth enjoy work which calls for effort and energy when they feel a need for it and understand its values.

12. *The work must end with a satisfying emotional tone for each pupil.* To work hard and intensively and to reach one's goal is highly satisfying to youngsters as well as adults, and that satisfaction provides a solid foundation for future work.

Are you wondering how you can prepare to be the kind of teacher described here? Take every opportunity to build a wide background of information and experience for yourself. Choose your college electives with a view to broadening your contacts with several areas of learning. Explore the community in which you live; try to identify the aspects of community living which will make worthwhile experiences for boys and girls. Build personal interests and hobbies in the areas which will contribute to your work with pupils. Read widely. Your college library is a resource you may never be able to duplicate later. If you are working with young people, utilize some of your ideas in guiding their experiences; try to be the kind of leader now that you want to be later as a teacher.

Planning with Pupils

Out of experiences with youth grows the curriculum of the modern school. From the circumstances of daily living at school and in the community come the plans which teachers and pupils make for the learning ahead. This planning is essential if pupils are to follow their own purposes and engage in learning that is meaningful to them. The teacher must help them clarify their aims and set up their goals. "What are we trying to find out?" "Why do we need this information?" "What are the resources for finding out?" "How will we know when we have found what we are seeking?" These and other questions will be answered cooperatively by pupils and teacher.

Learning the skills of problem solving is an integral part of planning with pupils. The teacher acts as an adult resource person who, because of his experience and wider knowledge, can advise and guide pupils through the steps needed to solve a problem. Teacher-pupil planning means that pupils and teachers actually plan together. It means that they identify the problems that are pertinent to them and the questions that they need to answer. The teacher as a group leader contributes his ideas and questions. Together they apply scientific methods to the solving of problems and critical thinking to the answering of the questions. They go about this work systematically, with the teacher helping the group direct its efforts profitably. They plan how and where to locate necessary information. They exchange opinions and ideas and try to locate all the resources within the group. They organize themselves for effective work and evaluate the progress they make. The teacher encourages the reticent, helps leaders to permit others to lead sometimes, and guides those who find it difficult to assume responsibility. Pupils and teachers work through their problems to a satisfying conclusion.

Does the concept of teacher-pupil planning, as indicated above, seem difficult for you? Would it not be easier just to tell your pupils what to do as perhaps you were told when you were in school? As you explore the kinds of responsibilities which citizens of the world face today, you can see that planning is important. Locating problems that need to be solved and knowing how to go about solving them are essential skills in democracy.

During your college days you may have opportunities to participate in group planning experiences. These will be invaluable to you later, if you take time to observe how people work together, how leadership emerges, how resources are utilized, and how conclusions are reached. If you are working with young people's groups, encourage them to do their own planning, and help them appreciate the fact that this is in itself a vital experience.

Building Relationships with Pupils and Parents

As you look forward to teaching, you may be most concerned about getting along with people. Managing a classroom of active pupils may seem one of the biggest challenges a teacher faces. You are no doubt remembering some of the experiences your own teachers had with students. As you prepare for teaching, your training experiences will help you to meet this challenge. Just now, while you are making plans for the future, it may be well to explore how good relationships with others are built.

Boys and girls who are interested in following their own purposes, who are working at their own level of ability, and who see the why of what they are doing have little desire to exhibit resistive behavior. An important study of teachers and their relationships to pupils has developed some revealing phrases to describe

Building good relationships with pupils is important for success in teaching. How well are you able to relate to pupils? (*Photograph by Marie Fraser.*)

effective and noneffective teachers. Here are some of the most telling items [adapted, 20:33–35]:

Effective teachers	Noneffective teachers
Have the ability to remain self-controlled in the midst of conflicting demands.	Display an inadequacy to classroom demands, easily disturbed.
Are habitually quiet, poised, and courteous in relationships with children.	Are demanding, imposing, impatient in relations with children.
Are constructive and encouraging in comments and manner.	Resort to threats and punishments, sarcastic, cross.
Are enthusiastic about pupils and teaching.	Are harassed, disturbed, unsure, with no interest or enthusiasm.
Possess sufficient self-restraint to allow children to work through their own problems.	Impose directions and requirements upon pupils, oblivious of pupil initiative and resourcefulness.
Are ingenious in utilizing opportunities for teaching.	Are unaware of opportunities for vitalizing classroom teaching.
Are careful in planning with pupils and in guiding them to successful completion of undertakings.	Expect children to know what to do and are seemingly satisfied if they keep busy.
Are skillful in directing pupils to evaluate their own work.	Fail to help pupils set up standards of their own.
Are interested in pupils as persons.	Are interested only in each child's academic progress.

As you go about visiting classrooms to observe teachers and pupils, try to identify the characteristics of the teacher who has established wholesome relationships with children. What do you think the teacher in the following situation is building for?

"If you don't finish your arithmetic, you'll have to stay in at recess. I've warned you for the last time."
"It doesn't make any difference how you did it last year. You're in the eighth grade now, and I'm the teacher."
"I can't imagine what your mother's thinking of, to let you read such things."
"The children in this group are the most trying I've ever had. Honestly, I think I'll shut the door and never come back."
"Don't you know any better? Only stupid folks have to be told as many times as I've told you."
"If you'd put as much effort on your lessons as you do on those model planes, you'd be better off."

Be on the alert for teachers of another kind. What are they saying to their pupils?

"If your idea works out well, there's no reason why we shouldn't try it together."
"Do you feel that this is the best you can do now? What do we do next to help you improve?"
"We all make mistakes, you know. It would be a pretty dull world if everyone were perfect."
"Let's skip the spelling until tomorrow. Then you'll have time to finish planning for the assembly."
"School wouldn't be much fun without the pupils. Every day is different, new, and exciting."

Building fine relationships with pupils is easiest when teachers and parents are well acquainted. The teacher, of course, cannot know his boys and girls completely nor guide their learning experiences adequately unless he himself looks beyond the classroom to the home. How are such relationships established?

When you meet a parent you will be able to sense that foremost in his mind is the question "How is my child getting along in school?" He expects you to say something about the youngster. Remember that children are the most precious possessions of parents. This concern represents a point of departure for your conversation with a parent.

It is important for you to evidence a sincere and genuine interest in the welfare of the youngster. It also is important to recognize that the parent is more intimately acquainted with him than you, that he has known the child from birth. Through the cooperative sharing of concern for the youngster you can develop a team approach that is in the best interest of the child and out of which may grow respect and understanding for you as a teacher.

In preparation for the day when you will be meeting the parents of your pupils, take every opportunity now to know the people of your community. Learn about their interests and problems. Practice the techniques of meeting adults with courtesy and thoughtfulness. Try to be skillful in the handling of controversial topics in the groups with which you meet. Learn to put yourself in the other person's place. Building good relationships with school patrons requires the same kind of skill that puts you at ease in any adult group. This skill plus your genuine interest in each pupil's welfare will see you safely through.

Creating a Wholesome School Environment

Because people are so much the products of their environments and because their reactions are greatly influenced by the setting in which they work and play, an attractive school home is essential. How does the modern school create its setting?

Teachers and pupils work together to build the physical surroundings. They plan cooperatively ways in which they can make the room a pleasant place to work. They take responsibility for keeping the bulletin boards up-to-date. They share the duties of keeping the classroom in working order. Because pupils have a part in making the room a comfortable place in which to study and carry out activities, they come to feel that it is truly their own. They are happy to be there and proud to show it to visitors. "My room at school" becomes a real part of living.

Many of you will someday walk into classrooms that you will say are hopeless. But you will be surprised to see what an energetic teacher and enthusiastic youngsters can do as a result of their imagination and perseverance. The fun of the doing will pay dividends in helping pupils to share a common task and to learn to work together for the good of the group. A happy school environment is not necessarily found in the newest and most costly school building; it may be found in the drab, barren room which boys and girls inherited and fixed up all by themselves.

Desirable relationships among teachers, parents, and youth grow best in environments that are suited to the activities of the modern school. How difficult it is to put new ideas to work in surroundings that were made for a different kind of education! Today's schools are "doing" schools; there must be places for pupils to do things. Today's schools are interested in individual children; there must be good light, suitable furniture, and proper heat and ventilation. Today's schools spill their activities out over the entire community; neighborhoods both close and far away contribute their part to the school's environment. Today's schools build for cooperation and social competency; there must be room to work and play with others.

A happy school environment, of course, goes far beyond matters of physical setting. The tone of the principal on the phone, the way the pupils greet their visitors, the look on the teacher's face when plans are unexpectedly changed are all evidences that suggest the atmosphere of the school. Even a short visit will reinforce these first hints and will indicate the measure of happiness that adults and pupils experience in working together in satisfying ways.

Was your school like the modern school described here? Find an opportunity to visit the schools in your own community. Can you feel the atmosphere of the school almost from the moment you step through the door? What evidences do you see of conscious efforts to create a real school home for young people?

USING NEWER INSTRUCTIONAL TECHNIQUES AND PROCEDURES

Changes are being called for and are taking place at all levels of the educational enterprise. Nurtured by widespread concern for instructional improvement and supported by the infusion of financial support from the federal government, a search has been going on for means to make the nation's schools even better. Reforms are taking place in both content and methods used in elementary and secondary schools.

The trigger for the accelerated rate of new educational programs and practices was the Russian launching of Sputnik 1 in October, 1957. Brickell [31:17], in his study of instructional innovations in New York State, found the rate of adoption of new programs and practices "more than doubled within 15 months" after the Russians' metal moon appeared to give Russia a lead in the space race. In addition, with the passage of the National Defense Education Act in 1958, the federal government assumed a new role of partnership in school improvement. The partnership was strengthened with the subsequent expansion of the provisions of the National Defense Education Act and the passage of the monumental Elementary and Secondary School Act of 1965. The latter provided a broader base of fiscal support for the introduction of innovative programs designed to improve education.

Convincing evidence has mounted to indicate that an educational revolution has begun. Throughout the country elementary and secondary school educators are formulating fresh, new approaches to teaching. Education has become a field in which innovation and experimentation are prized. Change, in an attempt to effect improvement, is in the air. The quest for new methods and programs has put education at the cutting edge of human development. The frontiersmen in this age do not seek new lands but explore new uses of education as a means of human development.

Since the late 1950s, programs designed especially for gifted pupils have cropped up, guidance services have been expanded dramatically, and emphasis has been placed on reforms in mathematics, science, modern foreign languages, and the social sciences. Educators have been trying innovative methods and formulating fresh programs to compensate for the educational deficiencies of children from socially and economically deprived backgrounds. Special consideration has been given to finding ways to improve the educational opportunity of the Negro. Prekindergarten educational opportunities, summer programs, and work-study projects are not uncommon today. More education and better instruction are thought to be imperative for contemporary and future living. And educators are at the front of the social force improving man's opportunities to develop his interests and abilities.

In 1959, the National Academy of Sciences held an important meeting at Woods Hole, Massachusetts. The conference director, Jerome Bruner [33], kindled a flame for curriculum reform in a book, *The Process of Education*, which reported the views of those attending the meeting. Bruner called for new methods of viewing content and argued convincingly for emphasis on developing understanding, as opposed to only acquiring facts, in teaching. Since 1959, curriculum reform has been going on in all the subject disciplines. Academicians have joined teachers in finding improved ways of organizing content with an emphasis on developing critical-thinking skills. What was taught a decade ago may not be taught next year. National curriculum projects in most all the disciplines have sought to organize knowledge in a sequential order and to give attention to nurturing the student's desire to learn.

As new programs have been developed, many teachers have taken additional college work or participated in workshops designed to prepare them to work in these new programs. The federal government, through the National Science Foundation and the National Defense Education Act, has sponsored summer and year-long institutes for teachers in order to help prepare them for curricular improvements. Philanthropic foundations also have pumped vast sums of money into projects for the reeducation of teachers. With the contemporary interest in school improvement and the production of new knowledge, the modern teacher is faced with the constant problem of keeping abreast of emerging trends and new developments in the disciplines.

In 1959, the National Education Association authorized the inauguration of the NEA Project on Instructional Programs of the Public Schools. By 1963, a three-volume report of the project had been prepared. This NEA project wove together proposals related to content and methods of organization. Not only were recommendations made concerning what should be taught, but recommendations were set forth calling for a change in the teacher's methods of instruction and in the school's organization. Further, a series of recommendations were made for educators to consider as the plan for instruction in the years ahead. This NEA report gave attention to both expanding societal objectives for education and suggested means to achieve them. Emphasis was put on suggesting means to individualize instruction.

While the development of improved curricular programs has been underway, attention also has been given to fresh approaches in organization for instruction. J. Lloyd Trump [275] called for team teaching, flexible scheduling, and an improved utilization of the schools' professional and material resources. Working as director of the Commission on the Experimental Study of the Utilization of the Staff in the Secondary School, Dr. Trump stimulated studies in 100 schools of the proposals later advanced in his book *Guide to Better Schools: Focus on Change* [274]. The outcome of the Trump studies was that ways were sought to further professionalize teaching and to develop means to individualize instruction. Efforts were made to take advantage of newer techniques and instructional devices that have resulted from our advancing technology.

Although much of the experimentation in instruction is being done by individual teaching, increased strength is provided if more than one teacher is involved in working on program improvement. Work that is shared appears lighter and obstacles may be overcome with several teachers working on a problem. The modern teacher no longer has to work in the isolation of a single classroom but may work with other teachers in planning and providing instruction. The contemporary teacher is engaged in the continuous process of evaluation and in searching for improved methods. Education has become a developing field, seeking original solutions to the complex problems associated with individual development.

Teacher Aides

Teacher aides are among the various techniques used in order to increase the effectiveness of the school. By employing housewives or other nonprofessional personnel to handle noneducational tasks (collecting lunch money, keeping records, and preparing equipment), the school frees the teacher to do what he was trained to do: teach. When the teacher has help for nonteaching chores and can devote his attention and time to instruction, results are most satisfying. The use of teacher aides, launched in Bay City, Michigan, in 1952, has been tried and proved effective in communities throughout Michigan and in Colorado, Connecticut, Iowa, Minnesota, Massachusetts, and Utah. This plan has also been tried in Chicago, Detroit, and New York. At the Ben Davis Junior High School in suburban Indianapolis aides supervise students as they work on independent study projects. In the Ridgewood High School, Norridge, Illinois, aides specialize in such tasks as preparing visual materials, type bibliographies and course materials, and assist students in locating and using materials.

Volunteer parent aides are used by the Fountain Valley Schools in California to help prepare instructional materials. (*Photograph from the National Education Association.*)

Team Teaching

An interesting outgrowth of the teacher-aide plan is team teaching. Just as the team approach has been used in clinics and in business organizations, a team-teaching situation permits teachers to do what they can do best. Instructional teams are organized to take advantage of the individual talents and special training of the teachers. Pupils gain a much broader experience from the team than is possible from teachers working alone with small groups. Eurich [84:21–22] points out that, apart from pupil gain, the team approach has suggested a new career pattern in public education that should encourage outstanding teachers to stay in the profession. By becoming team leaders they usually can qualify for higher salaries. In the past about the only future for teachers seeking advancement was to move out of the classroom and into administration or supervision.

Beggs [22:29–37] points out that there is an infinite variety of applications of the team concept. However, the advantages cited for teaming are generally agreed upon. Team teaching allows one teacher to profit from the judgment and advice of his colleague(s) since all the team members work with the same pupils toward commonly designated objectives. Team teaching provides the opportunity for each member of the team to contribute his particular strengths to the team's instruction. Team teaching makes it possible for teachers to vary the size of the group, depending on the instructional purpose. Teaming is intended to narrow the range of the teacher's preparation for daily class meetings. Thus, it is assumed the teacher's preparation can be sharper and more effective.

Teaming has been introduced widely in elementary, junior high, and senior high schools. The schools in Lexington, Massachusetts, were early adopters of the team approach at the elementary school level. Teaming is used in secondary schools, usually within a single content area. That is, teachers of English, for example, form one team and teachers of social studies form another team. Easton Area High School, Pennsylvania, uses teaming in most content areas.

Flexible Scheduling

Unlike team teaching, flexible scheduling is more widely associated with secondary schools. The flexible scheduling concept dictates that the frequency, duration, and instructional group size be varied depending on the particular requirements of the content. Some classes meet fewer than five times a week. And some of the time pupils are in classes of 7 to 15 pupils; at other times they are in classes of 40 to 150 or more. In addition, pupils in flexible-schedule schools spend part of their day working individually.

In a flexible schedule, the size of each class is determined by the instructional purpose. When the teacher wants to present content, test, or use audio-visual aids, large groups are mandated. When the teacher wants pupils to discuss, verify, question, or react, small groups are scheduled. The large classes usually last no more than 40 minutes, but the small-group classes are likely to last 90 minutes. Some laboratory sessions last for several hours.

Flexible scheduling encourages the use of team teaching. In some schools teachers work mostly with large groups, and in others teachers work almost en-

Period	Monday	Tuesday	Wednesday	Thursday	Friday
8.30 1	English	English	English	English	English
2	Mathematics	Mathematics	Mathematics	Mathematics	Mathematics
3	Science	Science	Science	Science	Science
4	Study hall	Study hall	Study hall	Study hall	Study hall
	Lunch	Lunch	Lunch	Lunch	Lunch
5	Social studies	Social studies	Social studies	Social studies	Social studies
6	Music	Music	Music	Music	Music
3.30 7	Physical education	Physical education	Physical education	Physical education	Physical education

FIGURE 6–2. A traditional secondary school schedule.

tirely with small groups. This allows teachers to specialize in those aspects of instruction they can do best.

Figures 6–2 and 6–3 show a typical pupil's program in a traditional and in a flexible school. In the flexible organization, the cycle is normally a week in length. In other words, the schedule does not repeat itself for five days. In the traditionally scheduled school, the cycle is the day. Each day's activities are the same as each other day's program.

Flexible scheduling has two prime objectives. First, it is intended to provide the organizational means for teachers to individualize instruction. Pupils can meet with teachers during independent study time. Also, pupils can work for blocks of time on their own or with other pupils on particular problems or projects.

FIGURE 6–3. A flexible secondary school schedule.

Module	Monday	Tuesday	Wednesday	Thursday	Friday
8.30 1	Mathematics	Music	Mathematics	Mathematics	Mathematics
2	Mathematics	English	English	Mathematics	Music
3	English	English	English	English	Music
4	Social studies	Independent study	Physical education	Independent study	Physical education
5	Social studies	Independent study	Physical education	Independent study	Physical education
6	Social studies	Independent study	Science	Independent study	Science
7	Social studies	Lunch	Lunch	Lunch	Lunch
8	Lunch	Science	Health	Lunch	Independent study
9	Science	Science	Independent study	Science	Independent study
10	Typing	Independent study	Independent study	Science	Independent study
11	Typing	Independent study	Independent study	Science	Independent study
12	Independent study	Independent study	Independent study	Music	Independent study
13	Independent study	Social studies	Independent study	Music	Typing
14	Independent study	Mathematics	Independent study	Music	Typing
3.30 15	Independent study	Mathematics	Social studies	Social Studies	English

Pupils can be excused from content presentations when these are not contributing to their intellectual growth. In this type of scheduling, pupils can become active in discussing, verifying, and working at task-oriented projects and activities. Second, flexible scheduling allows the teacher to use both human and time resources to the advantage of pupils. If one teacher likes to and can present content better than another teacher, then the teacher with this competency can work with more pupils in this way than the traditional schedule allows. If the teacher works best in small groups, then he can spend his time working with pupils in this way.

People learn from activity—from working, discussing, constructing, and experimenting. The flexible schedule provides the opportunity for pupils to be far more active in the learning process than does a traditionally scheduled school. Teachers in the flexible-scheduled school conserve time by giving content presentations once, to a large group of pupils, rather than repeating the presentation to smaller groups. The teacher's time, conserved by taking out the repetition, is used to buy the opportunity for teachers to work with individuals and with small pupil-centered groups.

Flexible schedules are often developed with the use of computers. Schedule determination is just one of the uses of the computer in modern education. Test score analyses, population studies, and other applications of computer technology are being used to provide educators with data with which more intelligent decisions can be made about pupils and the school's program.

Nongraded Schools

The nongraded school concept is being employed more often at the elementary than at the secondary level. The nongraded school has a basic organization of content which is analyzed in sequence so that a pupil may move through the curriculum at his own rate, gaining both breadth and depth on an individual basis. Pupils move from one consideration to another as they master the subject, as opposed to being locked into artificial grade-level units. The nongraded organization seeks to provide for the differences among learners. Each pupil in a nongraded school is in a class of his own.

In the elementary school the reading program is usually the first and easiest area to nongrade. However, some schools have nongraded all the content areas. Goodlad and Anderson [111:44–60] have advocated and watched the nongraded concept spread in elementary schools. They maintain that the nongraded concept offers one of the best means of individualizing instruction.

On the secondary school level Dr. B. Frank Brown, principal of the Melbourne (Florida) High School, has been a pioneer in developing a nongraded high school program. Brown [32:69–98] has called for the use of new curricula and fresh teaching methods in the nongraded secondary school. Pupils in the Melbourne High School are not bound by curriculum guides in texts, but they are able to go into a subject with as much breadth or depth as they are able to handle. Teachers work individually with pupils to chart a course of study. Heavy emphasis is put on independent study, where pupils work on their own or with a few others.

Schools using the nongraded organization necessarily must have a wealth of instructional materials, far more than is usually found in the typical school. At

Melbourne High School, for instance, the library is larger than the gymnasium. Modern libraries not only store data in books, but also provide resource information on electronic tapes, filmstrips, records, and film. Pupils are free to use these information sources as they use books. Machines, where necessary, are on hand for student use.

Teaching Machines

The classroom teacher has often devised special practice materials for pupils or has selected appropriate exercises from available workbooks for pupils needing additional work. This is not new, nor is recognition of the fact that pupils need to know the immediate results of their work in order to make corrections and proceed effectively. Textbooks and workbooks with answers in the backs of the books are not new either. Having such material already prepared in a systematic way, based on principles coming from the experimental laboratories and available to the pupil to use independently, is new in the sense that machine-type instruction has now been put to wide use. Allowing students to proceed at their own pace for drill work or even original instruction from programmed material frees the teacher to do what he can do best in person: guide the educational growth of pupils.

The teaching machine is a mechanical device used to help the pupil learn. The machine, however, is of less value than the program the machine contains. The learning program, housed in the teaching machine, divides organized information into small parts or frames. A user of a learning program goes from one to another related but more advanced piece of information. Immediately the pupil knows whether he has mastered the information being studied because the learning program gives feedback on what was previously learned.

The promise of programmed learning through the use of teaching machines is greater for the future than is its current ability to help teachers. Too few programs

This photograph shows a simplified type of teaching machine. What advantages do teaching machines have, and what are their limitations? What is the teacher's special responsibility in using teaching machines? (*Photograph from the National Education Association.*)

of substance have been developed, to date, to have a real impact on instruction. However, there are some excellent programs in use in some content areas. Programmed learning, for example, is used effectively at the John Marshall High School in Portland, Oregon, in a course in electricity. The body of knowledge in this course is taught largely through the learning program.

Data Processing

Data processing, well established in the business world, has begun to be applied to education. In addition to the use of data processing in school business offices and for class scheduling, data processing is being used as an instructional tool. Some schools have established telephone line connections with service bureau computers. These hookups are used by pupils, for example, as they study mathematics. Also, the computer is used to store and to retrieve a vast fund of information. Vocational training programs also are giving attention to the use of computers in preparing technicians. The applications of data processing in education are growing at a fantastic rate. These developments are being made by teachers as they seek improved ways to teach the principles of computer technology to pupils. At the Deerfield High School (Illinois), for example, students in advanced mathematics courses study through the use of a computer made in the school.

Educational Television

The use of television for regular instruction has expanded more rapidly perhaps than any other of the newer techniques. Its use is viewed with mixed feelings, ranging from disdain to great enthusiasm. Actually, television, like films, books, and radios, is a communication medium and not a teacher. As an instructional device, its worth depends on the quality of the teacher who is planning and presenting the material and on the planning and coordination of the classroom teacher who is viewing the lesson with his pupils.

Continental Classroom has been an outstanding example of direct teaching full year courses to individuals by television. Outstanding instructors, including Nobel Prize winners, have taught physics, chemistry, mathematics, and government to millions. During the American government course, for example, political leaders appeared for interviews or lectured along with the regular instructor. Such facilities are not available to the individual school without the use of television.

An example of coordinating television instruction with the usual classroom has been the airborne TV courses starting in 1961 in the Middle West. An airplane circling over northern Indiana broadcast TV courses to elementary, secondary, and college students in an area including parts of Illinois, Indiana, Kentucky, Michigan, Ohio, and Wisconsin, reaching a potential audience of 5 million pupils in 13,000 grade schools, high schools, and colleges. Use of this medium has brought to pupils in small, understaffed schools topflight teachers heretofore unavailable to them. Through coordination of plans, the classroom teacher prepared his class for the lessons and was present for discussion on an individual basis. The airplane was used because of transmission techniques available at the time. As the transmission of television signals improve, the airplane may be replaced by a space satellite. The focus is on television as a medium for instruction because of the greater facilities it offers.

Closed-circuit television is spreading in use throughout the country. Transmitting stations are set up in a single school or within a school system. Presentations, then, can be used at the time the teacher selects. Also, the school system can develop its own programs and store them on tapes for use as requested.

Electronic Laboratories

Electronic laboratories are to be found in most secondary schools and many elementary schools. The electronic laboratory is a system which allows pupils to hear taped presentations and frequently calls pupils to respond while the tape deck records the response. Even though electronic laboratories are used most frequently in foreign language instruction, they are employed in reading, speech, shorthand, and other areas as well.

The electronic laboratory allows the pupil to go through the content at his own pace. It also provides the opportunity for him to play back, sometimes over and over, what he has heard previously. This repetition reinforces what has been learned and allows the pupil to have the content etched in his memory. As with programmed instruction and television, the electronic laboratory is only as good as the content of the programs housed within it. The teacher makes these either useful or useless instructional tools. With careful development and precise utilization, the electronic laboratory can serve as a patient helper for the pupil in learning.

Other Technological Aids

Other technological aids, such as the overhead projector and the 8-mm projector, are available to help the teacher in communicating with pupils. Visual aids provide an appeal to another sense, sight, as the teacher communicates with pupils. Still other aids are on the drawing boards and in pilot stage use. For example, at the William Hall High School in West Hartford, Connecticut, an information retrieval system is being developed. A pupil can sit in a booth, dial for a particular program, and receive a closed-circuit television picture and hear the accompanying sound through earphones. This suggests another attempt at harnessing technology to support the teacher's efforts.

Much of the time now spent by the classroom teacher in presenting material to groups could be spent on individual tutoring. Pupils could learn independently more of the time if content were properly presented through technological aids. Imaginative uses of such devices free the classroom teacher to help students discuss and pursue ideas encountered in the material—and this can be the essence of teaching.

The point cannot be made too strongly that these innovations in teaching and learning aids are not gimmicks to provide miracle cures nor to replace rigorous learning and teaching with synthetic substitutes—they are a means to the end of better education. During your preparation for teaching you will want to become thoroughly familiar with these newer techniques, to know their limitations, and to gain skill in using them effectively.

A student in the public schools of West Hartford, Connecticut, is using the Dial-access System. The student first dials the program desired, according to the number listed in a card file. He then views and listens to the content presentation. This type of technology may be used for the presentation of any programmed material for enrichment, reinforcement, or for make-up purposes, by means of which the student is able to study at his own rate and level of sophistication. (*Photograph by Robert L. Nay, West Hartford, Connecticut.*)

Tomorrow's Schools

Changes in the schools of the future are certain to take place. The current emphasis on research, interest in innovative programs, and the development of new practices will make the schools significantly different, even from the most modern of today. Although an accurate picture of tomorrow's schools cannot be seen in detail, some obvious trends are in evidence.

The school of the future will be characterized by its focus on the individual. Group teaching methods, known for so long to us all, will tend to give way to individualized teaching. Teachers will work more with pupils on a one-to-one basis. Thus, new methods of personalized instruction will be used. The teacher will become more sensitive to variations among learners. And the teacher's role will change. In the school of the future the teacher will tend to become a diagnostician and prescriber, instead of a group teacher. Noncertified aides, flexible schedules, and independent study will result in the self-contained classroom becoming less self-contained.

School facilities also will be vastly different. More space in schools will be fashioned into laboratories and individual work stations. Less space will be used

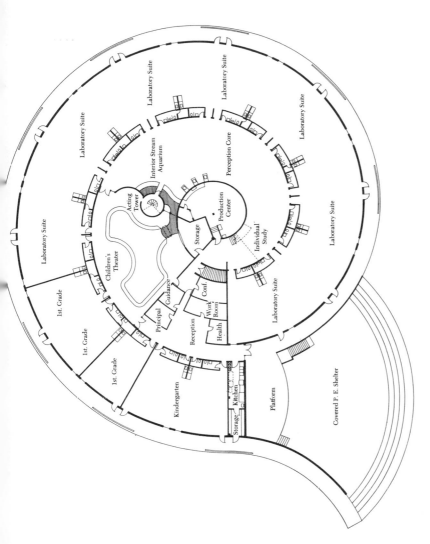

FIGURE 6–4. The Valley Winds Elementary School in suburban St. Louis is an example of the innovations being made in the designing of school buildings. The school building is shaped like a snail's shell with classrooms radiating from a central core. It is air-conditioned, is carpeted throughout, and has giant-sized classrooms to accommodate the ungraded curriculum. (*Source: Shaver and Company, Architects, Salina, Kansas.*)

for classrooms as pupils spend increased time working on their own and meeting with small groups of pupils. Large lecture rooms will be outfitted for presentation by teachers. In these areas the appeals will be made to the pupil's sense of sight, as well as to his sense of hearing.

The largest area in the school will be the instructional materials' center. Here all the advances of technology will be harnessed for aiding pupils. For example, dial-access systems, whereby pupils can retrieve information through a screen and earphone set, will be housed in the instructional materials' center. Rich storehouses of books and booklets will be available in every school, and study carrels, small stations giving privacy on three sides, will be used by pupils as they accumulate understandings and develop skills. The school year is likely to be longer than it is presently. Pupils will do more of their work in school, and schools will renew their emphases on curriculum activities and clubs. Developing leadership and fellowship traits will tend to be a major concern of service and vocational clubs. Group processes will not be foreign to pupils at any level of the educational system.

Course content will be drastically changed. Emphasis will be on nurturing skills of inquiry and organizing principles. The content taught in the schools will be varied to accommodate the range of abilities of youth in the schools. Unlike today a given group of children of the same age will be characterized by a difference in the breadth and depth of what they study. National curriculum projects most likely will continue to expand and provide sets of materials for pupils of diverse abilities and interests.

Public education undoubtedly will be extended past the twelfth year, into post-high school vocational and junior or regional college programs. Programs for children below kindergarten age will be common.

Conditions of teaching will change substantially. In addition to increases in compensation and in insurance and retirement benefits, teachers will have more and better tools with which to work. Accompanying these improvements will be a demand for continuing in-service education. The teacher of the future will be a more highly trained and skilled professional than today's teacher.

The constant for the future will be change. The continuing quest will be for improvement. Added resources for education, society's demand for fully educated people, and a developing profession will be the means for shaping the new schools of the future.

SUMMARY

Study boys and girls, not only in the classroom, but in their out-of-school activities. Become acquainted with them in their homes, if possible. Try to find out how each works and plays, how he reacts to various situations and people, and in what ways he is different from other youngsters.

Every pupil has physical, psychological, and social needs. Physically, he must have sufficient food and clothing; he must have an opportunity to be active; and he must have proper rest. Psychologically, he needs to be loved, to feel he is a part of the group, and to have confidence in himself as a creative member of society. Socially, he needs to know how to do things, how to express himself clearly, how to meet situations with poise, and how to win acceptance from others in the group. Help each pupil fulfill these needs. Discover in what way he is different from the others, and then plan his play and work accordingly.

It is difficult for a young teacher to know how to choose the learning experiences which pupils should have. To do this he must have a rich background of experience himself—experience that has taught him cooperation and helped him develop fully. The teacher must therefore read widely, have broad contacts, and build up personal interests and experiences that help him understand and promote desirable characteristics in his pupils. He must encourage pupils to cooperate with him in building a wholesome school environment, and above all, he must become a good group leader who plans with pupils and helps them clarify their aims, establish desirable goals, and devise effective ways of reaching these goals.

Various types of instructional materials are becoming available to teachers. In order to meet educational challenges of the future, gain skill in the effective use of such equipment and techniques. They will never replace the teacher. Their effective use depends on the creative imagination and ingenuity of the teacher in providing rich learning experiences for his pupils.

QUESTIONS FOR YOUR CONSIDERATION

1. Why is a knowledge of psychology so important for teachers?
2. What are some of the psychological and emotional needs of pupils and how can a teacher best meet these needs?
3. What are some of the social needs of pupils and what can the school do in order to meet these needs?
4. To what extent are schools helping boys and girls develop good human relationships? What are some of the effective means that are being used?
5. Account for the fact that many pupils lose interest in school and drop out before graduating. How has the school failed to fulfill its function in regard to these pupils?
6. What criteria will you use in selecting activities or learning experiences in which your pupils will engage?
7. What are some of the campus activities in which you can gain further skill in group participation and leadership?
8. Why should Skinner feel that "the present educational process is one which methods of imparting knowledge have changed scarcely at all"?
9. How does the use of such instructional devices as teaching machines and television affect the role of the teacher? What new skills will be required of you? How may these devices affect organization for classroom instruction?

ACTIVITIES FOR YOU TO PURSUE

1. Observe closely some of the boys and girls with whom you come in contact during the week. What can you find out about their interests, their needs, and their abilities?

2. Accompany a youngster you know well to a special event—a movie, football game, or church. Study his reactions to the various happenings. How does he identify himself with the things he sees? What does he talk about after the event? Does the presence of you as an adult seem to make a difference? Compare your knowledge of this child with descriptions which you may find in your reading.

3. Keep an anecdotal record of the successive activities and the conversation of a child whom you are able to observe unnoticed for a period of an hour or two. Try to be as objective as possible.

4. Visit an elementary classroom where children draw and paint freely. Study their artwork. Is there splash and verve or just timid daubs here and there? What differences can you see among children just from observing what they put on paper? Ask them to tell you the story of what they have painted.

5. Study the group process at work in the next group in which you participate. Who is the leader? What qualities does he exhibit? Is he a democratic or an autocratic leader? How does he motivate the group to work?

6. Visit an unattractive classroom in your community. Plan ways in which you could create a good learning environment there.

7. Work in a leadership capacity either in school or out with a group of boys and girls. Help them initiate plans for an activity, encourage them to carry out their plans, and lead them to evaluate their experiences. Analyze carefully your own part in the planning process.

8. Visit often in a classroom where the teacher seems to function in the manner described in this chapter. Note how teacher-pupil planning takes place and how the basic needs of the pupils are being met.

9. Observe classroom situations in which team teaching, teaching machines, and television are being used very effectively. List the specific abilities you will need in order to use these devices effectively.

7

THE TEACHING PROFESSION:

Its Status, Organizations,
Publications, and
Code of Ethics

What constitutes a profession? To what extent is teaching a profession? In what ways does it differ from other occupations? What is the importance of the Code of Ethics of the Education Profession? What different organizations exist in the teaching profession? In what ways may these organizations benefit you? Through what organizations can you contribute most to the profession?

It is only as individual teachers and groups of teachers give serious consideration to questions such as these that the teaching profession can continue to advance and to assume its deserved role among the great professions.

TEACHING AS A PROFESSION

When you become a teacher you become a member of a profession with responsibilities for improving the status of that chosen profession. As a professional person you may find it difficult at times to differentiate among your professional services in teaching, your personal life, and your work in the activities of the profession itself. Perhaps this sense of dedication is one of the distinguishing characteristics of a professional person. At any rate, in this chapter you are asked to think carefully about your role in the profession and its organizations.

Characteristics of a Profession

How would you define a profession? Many scholars and many scholarly groups have given careful thought to formulating an answer to this question. The professions have studied themselves in attempts to enlighten their own members and the public concerning the characteristics and role of a profession. Although these various statements have differed in many details, there seems to be consensus concerning some of the major practices descriptive of a profession.

A profession requires that its members:

1. Commit themselves to the ideal of service to mankind rather than to personal gain.
2. Undergo relatively long periods of professional preparation to learn the con-

cepts and principles of the specialized knowledge which earns the profession its high status.

3. Meet established qualifications for admission and keep up-to-date through in-service growth.
4. Establish and adhere to a code of ethics regarding membership, conduct, and practice.
5. Demand a high order of intellectual activity.
6. Form organizations to improve the standards of the profession, the services of the profession, self-discipline in the profession, and the economic well-being of its members.
7. Provide opportunities for advancement, specialization, and independence.
8. Regard the profession as a life career and consider membership in the profession as permanent.

Certainly there are differences among the requirements and characteristics of manual labor, skilled labor, the subprofessions, and the professions. However, in many cases it is not a simple task to differentiate between the subprofessions and the professions. The professions of medicine, law, and the ministry have long been recognized. But what of the additional groups that have sought recognition as professions—nurses, teachers, engineers, journalists, and many others? Although it is obvious that at present teaching is considered a profession, it is only fair to point out that this status is challenged by many persons.

Status of Teaching as a Profession

Teaching is actually one of the oldest professions. It is true that the requirements for entrance into the teaching profession have not always been as high as those for some other professions. It is also true that in the profession of teaching there are some members who have not lived up to desirable levels of conduct and service. Furthermore, many persons have used teaching as a stepping-stone to other professions. Finally, there are major differences between teaching and the other professions. However, these aspects of teaching and teachers do not deny to teaching its status as a profession.

In what ways does teaching differ from other professions? These differences lie in the control, support, size, and the ratio of the sexes [132:66–70]. The legal control of education belongs to the public, not to the profession itself. Thus, the members of the teaching profession must work constantly to inform the public and must participate extensively in public concerns. Public school teachers are paid from tax money, which presents certain limitations and problems not inherent in other professions.

The need for large numbers of teachers affects the policies of recruitment and selectivity within the profession, and the fact that women outnumber men in the teaching profession differentiates it sharply from law, medicine, and the ministry. Nevertheless, these differences should not prevent teaching from being accorded professional status.

Because of these differences between teaching and other professions, it has been said that teaching can never achieve professional autonomy; i.e., it can never become a self-managing profession. To achieve a high degree of autonomy, the members of the profession need to be clearly and firmly in charge of those aspects which are characterized as professional concerns. As Stinnett [253:12] points out, the profession should be responsible:

for determining the standards and seeing to their enforcement, for selection and admission to teacher education programs, for guidance, screening, and retention during preparation, for accreditation of teacher education institutions, for licensure and revocation of licensure, for professional growth, for working conditions, for protecting its members against unjust and capricious treatment, and for disciplining its members for unethical and unprofessional conduct.

In other words, professional autonomy means control by the profession of those standards on which it guarantees the competence of each member admitted to practice and permitted to continue in practice.

In recent years notable progress has been made in a number of states in achieving autonomy in the teaching profession [57:46–47]. Perhaps the most outstanding thrust has been made through the work of the National Commission on Teacher Education and Professional Standards. This very important commission will be discussed later in this chapter.

What are the conditions and characteristics which support teaching as a profession? Among them are the following:

1. Most teachers are working for the sake of giving service to mankind rather than for great personal gain. Naturally there are some people employed in our schools, as is true of any other profession, who work against the progress of the profession. However, the actions of a few should not be allowed to detract unduly from the ideals of service held by the profession.
2. Teachers are required by law to complete certain requirements for certification and entrance into the profession, and these requirements are constantly being strengthened.
3. Teaching requires careful skills and understandings.
4. Teachers have professional publications to help them keep up-to-date.
5. Teachers attend summer school, extension classes, workshops, conventions, and institutes and engage in a wide variety of other in-service activities.
6. Teaching is well regarded as a life career.
7. Teachers have their standards and ethics operating through the National Education Association and through state and local education associations. Teachers' rights are defended by these organizations, with the National Education Association as a body of ultimate appeal.

The great majority of public school teachers regard teaching as a profession. In a nationwide teacher opinion poll, for example, over 80 per cent of the teachers indicated that they regarded teaching as a professional occupation [283:44]. As the importance of education in our society and the level of preparation and status of teachers continue to increase, undoubtedly even greater numbers of teachers will view themselves as members of a profession.

Prestige of Teachers

Occupations differ in regard to the respect or prestige generally assigned to them by members of a community. There is considerable evidence that the prestige of teachers is increasing. For example, George Gallup, director of the American Institute of Public Opinion, found that the prestige of the teaching profession definitely had increased. In a nationwide survey, which was identical to one conducted in 1953, a representative sample of adults was handed a card listing a number of major professions and was then asked: "Suppose a young man came to you and asked your opinion about taking up a profession. Assume that he was qualified to enter any of these professions, which one would you first recommend to him?" The following list shows the difference in the public's rating of occupations:

	1953	1962
1. Doctor	29%	23%
2. Engineer—builder	20	18
3. Professor—teacher	5	12
4. Clergyman	7	8
5. Government career	3	7
6. Lawyer	6	6
7. Business executive	7	5
8. Dentist	6	4
9. Banker	2	2
Other	7	4
None, don't know	8	11

Gallup found that twice as many women as men—16 per cent to 8 per cent—selected teaching as the one they would recommend. He concluded that evidently women give less weight to financial considerations than do men.

The trend of future thinking on the prestige of careers, in the opinion of Gallup, is probably revealed best by the youngest group interviewed—persons in the 21–29 age group. Teaching came second among the choices of people in this age group. Their recommendations were as follows:

1. Doctor	26%
2. Professor—teacher	18
3. Engineer—builder	17
4. Lawyer	8
5. Government career	7
6. Dentist	5
7. Clergy	4
8. Business executive	3
9. Banker	2
Other	4
None, don't know	6

Perhaps a number of factors have contributed to this increased prestige of teachers. As previously indicated, the complexity of our technological and social world has placed an increasingly higher premium upon the need for education, and teachers are the chief instruments for obtaining this education. Research studies indicate that members of professions requiring extended and rigorous preparation tend to have greater prestige than those of whom little training is required. As stated previously, the number of years required to become a teacher has increased significantly. There is considerable evidence to support the fact that the holding power of a profession increases as the standards for entrance increase. Also, teachers are assuming an increasing role as political citizens in the life of the community, state, and nation [254:282–290]. You may feel certain that the amount of respect and prestige accorded teachers will continue to rise as professional standards, salaries, quality of members in the profession, and importance of education in everyone's life continue to rise.

Number in the Profession

In 1966–1967 there were over 1,800,000 public school teachers, over 230,000 private school teachers [155:75], approximately 14,000 superintendents, over 105,000 principals and supervisors, and over 75,000 librarians, guidance personnel, consultants, researchers, and other specialists in elementary and secondary schools [82:7, 12]. Another half-million faculty members were employed in colleges and universities [155:75]. In addition there were many thousands employed as staff members in professional organizations, in government offices of education, and in private agencies with educational programs.

As indicated in Chapter 4, the number in the profession will continue to increase for several reasons. The tremendously increased number of people 5 to 17 years of age between 1950 and 1960 will move into the adult group and will then be having children. There is a growing tendency to include kindergartens, nursery schools, and junior colleges in our free public school systems, and this will increase enrollment. Also, increasing numbers of boys and girls are continuing their high school studies rather than dropping out of school. New demands for comprehensively trained personnel are being heard in many fields of instruction, and those for educational services are equally urgent. There are needs for trained counselors, specialists in remedial reading and speech, and instructors of the handicapped and the culturally disadvantaged, as well as for teachers in other areas not commonly present in our school systems. Further demands are being made

FIGURE 7–1. Distribution of elementary and secondary public school teachers according to the highest degrees held in 1965. How will this distribution change by 1980? (*Source:* National Education Association.)

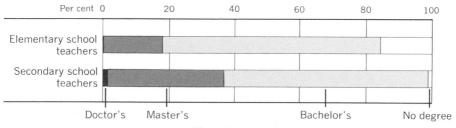

Highest degrees held by teachers

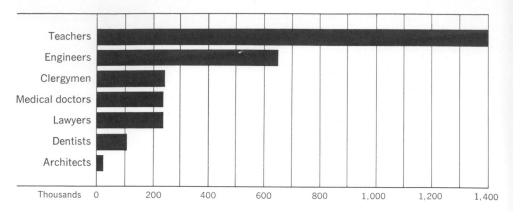

FIGURE 7–2. Approximate number of persons in the United States engaged in selected professional occupations according to the census of 1960. The number of public school teachers only approximately equaled the number of persons in six other major professions. (*Source:* U.S. Bureau of the Census.)

in the field of adult education, since the educational need of adults will continue to increase. Thus, the services of the school will extend in many different directions, and the size of the profession will continue to grow.

Distribution of Men and Women

Unlike European countries, where teaching has been considered a man's work, the United States has far more women than men teaching in its public schools. From 1880 to 1920 the percentage of men teachers in our public schools decreased from 43 to 14 per cent. In the 20 years that followed, the percentage of men rose to 23, but during World War II it declined to 15 per cent of the total. Since then there has been a steady increase; in 1966, it had reached 31.7 per cent of all

FIGURE 7–3. The age distribution of teachers by sex, February, 1965. How do you account for the differences in the distribution of men and women? What changes in these distributions may take place by 1980? (*Source:* National Education Association.)

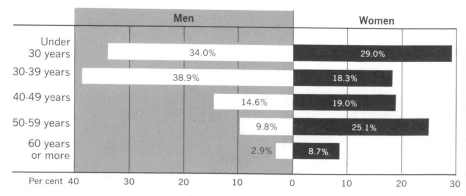

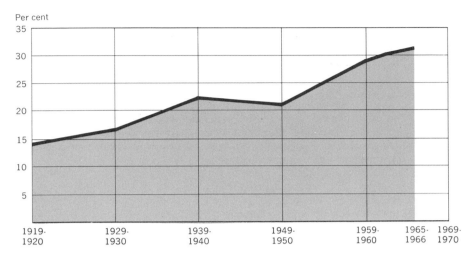

FIGURE 7–4. The percentage of men teachers in public schools has increased significantly since 1920. (*Source:* National Education Association.)

public school teachers [207:22]. More than 80 per cent of the men, however, teach in secondary schools. In the elementary schools, only approximately 12 per cent of the teachers are men. On the college and university level approximately four-fifths of the instructional staff consist of men [229:8].

Considerable effort is being made to attract more men into public school teaching, especially into the elementary schools. A majority of teachers definitely feels that more men are needed in classroom teaching [283:45]. The adoption of single-salary schedules has provided added incentive for men to consider teaching on the lower level, where the opportunities are great. Higher salaries for all public school teachers should encourage more men to enter the profession on all levels. As will be discussed more fully in a later chapter, it has been advocated that teachers with dependents should be given extra compensation. It is maintained that such a plan would attract more men to the teaching profession.

PROFESSIONAL ORGANIZATIONS AND PUBLICATIONS

Many years and the efforts of countless people have been involved in the development of the teaching profession in America. During this time the profession has developed a system of purposes, refined its procedures, set standards relating to training, and reduced to a definite code certain important elements in the behavior of its members.

One of the important conditions of professionalism is membership in various organizations. By sharing ideas and experiences with others through these organizations, teachers can improve the general level of their performance and exert their collective influence in bringing about more desirable conditions for work. A great portion of the improvements in education has resulted from the work of these organizations. In this world of special-interest groups, there is a very real need for teacher organizations.

In considering the services and characteristics of professional organizations, the Educational Policies Commission of the National Education Association, itself a professional organization, has suggested that they should aim to do the following [200:27–54]:

1. Encourage members to cherish education's distinctive knowledge and insight
2. Aid in disseminating information and understanding throughout the profession
3. Promote research, support research, encourage research by members, and foster the application of research findings
4. Help improve teacher education
5. Safeguard teachers' basic freedoms
6. Meet members' personal needs
7. Improve teaching loads and school environment
8. Seek adequate salary provisions
9. Promote professional ethics
10. Inform the public
11. Take positions on issues affecting education
12. Cooperate in counseling the public
13. Influence public policy
14. Cooperate with interested lay groups

Since the organizations for teachers are considerable in number and vary in scope of membership, purpose, and procedure, a few of the more important ones should be discussed.

Local Education Association

Local associations provide opportunities for teachers to consider matters that are of concern to the immediate community and teacher group. Through the association, teachers are able to participate in the formulation of local school policies, to keep the community informed regarding educational matters, and to influence the policies of their state and national associations. Outside of large cities, local units are frequently formed on a countywide basis. Local groups usually are represented in their respective state associations and participate in the election of state association officials.

Local teacher organizations differ considerably in form. Generally they include all the school personnel within a school system. The number as well as the nature of the meetings held each year varies. Frequently, the organizations are very strong in nature, and the members are vitally concerned with problems common to the group. Various subgroups may be working on such problems as reporting to parents, textbook selection, curriculum reorganization, and evaluation. Participation in these groups usually provides an excellent opportunity for a teacher to be professionally stimulated and to work constructively with his colleagues.

State Education Association

Educational workers are also organized at the state level. Membership of a state group is larger than that of the local groups. Dues are required. A journal is published, usually monthly, to keep teachers in the state informed on problems, trends, and events in education. Meetings of the total membership are arranged usually once or twice a year. Public schools may be dismissed for about two days, so that public school educators may attend the state convention. The state educational meetings generally are held in the capital city or in selected regional cities. Participation of many teachers and administrators is required in order to make these conventions successful and to carry on the activities of the association throughout the year. The typical state education association has a headquarters building and a competent central office staff, a comprehensive organizational plan, and a constitution and bylaws. Often significant experimentation and research are centered there, and the results are communicated to the entire professional body. State teacher associations frequently know of important job opportunities within the state, and some provide placement services. Some state associations also provide for members a program of term life insurance at rates lower than normally available to an individual.

Most state organizations provide legal protection for individual teacher members against unfair or unjust practices which may arise in local situations. Few individual teachers would be able to wield much influence or stand the expense involved if such a problem should need to be carried far in the courts. It is comforting for teachers to know that there is an organization ready and able to fight for their cause.

Since the central legal responsibility for education rests with the separate states in America, the state organization usually recommends minimum standards for teacher certification, school facilities, instructional programs, and the like. Some of the most significant laws relating to education in several states are created and promoted by the state education associations. The securing of favorable legislation and the improving of conditions in the schools are primary functions of state education associations. They warrant your enthusiastic support.

National Education Association

Medical men have the American Medical Association to represent them. Lawyers have the American Bar Association. Teachers have the National Education Association of the United States, usually referred to as the NEA, which is the oldest teacher organization in the United States. It began in 1857 when forty-three educational leaders from twelve states and the District of Columbia met in Philadelphia to establish the National Teachers Association for the purpose of elevating the character and advancing the interests of the teaching profession and promoting the cause of popular education. From 1870 to 1906 the organization was known as the National Educational Association, and the present name was adopted when the association was chartered by the Congress of the United States.

The association grew slowly at first. After World War I, teachers sought a more active role in the national organization. This was achieved through a reorganization of the association, whose control was then vested in a representative assembly made up of elected delegates from state and local teacher organizations that held membership in the NEA. At about the same time, a building in Washington, D.C., was secured to house the national headquarters. The NEA has grown in membership and influence to such a point that it approaches the status of being the official spokesman of the public school people of America. Well over half of the public school teachers in the United States belongs to the NEA. In 1967, the association was made up of more than 1 million members, and through affiliation of the local, state, and territorial associations, the NEA probably represented more than 1,600,000 teachers.

A change in the membership qualifications provided that after August 31, 1964, eligibility for new members in the NEA would require an earned bachelor's, or higher, degree or a regular vocational or technical certificate [175:15]. If a person is not able to meet one of these qualifications, he may become an associate member without having the privilege of voting for delegates or of holding office in the organization.

The annual dues for membership is only $10, payment of which permits you to attend the annual meeting, to receive the *NEA Journal* and the *NEA Reporter,* to call upon various divisions for assistance and services, and to participate in a term life insurance program at a substantial saving on premiums. Life membership is available for a cash payment of $225 or $25 per year for 10 consecutive years. In addition to the benefits described above, life membership also includes a subscription to the *NEA Research Bulletin* and a copy of the *Proceedings* of each annual meeting.

The services performed by the NEA are of tremendous variety and scope, but in order to gain some understanding of the total program and activities these services can be listed under the following broad categories: professional growth, public relations, defense of the teaching profession, research, professional standards, teacher welfare, federal relations, curriculum and instructional development, international education, selective teacher recruitment, and publications.

In its continuous efforts to elevate the standards of the teaching profession, the NEA provides services to local associations as well as to individual teachers. These services include various publications, consultative services, conferences, a clearinghouse for ideas, and special materials to local committee chairmen. An example of one such service is that of the research division of the NEA. This division renders a real service to teachers, associations, and government officials by collecting and publishing nationwide data on such problems as teacher load, salaries, tenure, certification, retirement, finance, legislation, welfare, and status. These data have been of much help to teachers and teacher associations in appraising the status of local conditions in comparison with the status in the United States as a whole.

As may be noted in the organizational diagram, Figure 7–5, there are now thirty-three different departments and associations within the NEA. Each one serves a particular level or other special concern of its members. As a responsible member of a significant profession, you will want to join the parent body and promote the work of improving education in America. You also should consider joining one or more of those departments or member associations which meet your special needs and interests.

As you will note on the diagram, the NEA has twenty-five committees and commissions. Of the commissions, perhaps the Educational Policies Commission, established in 1935, has gained the greatest amount of prominence. The commission considers issues facing the teaching profession and proposes policy for the

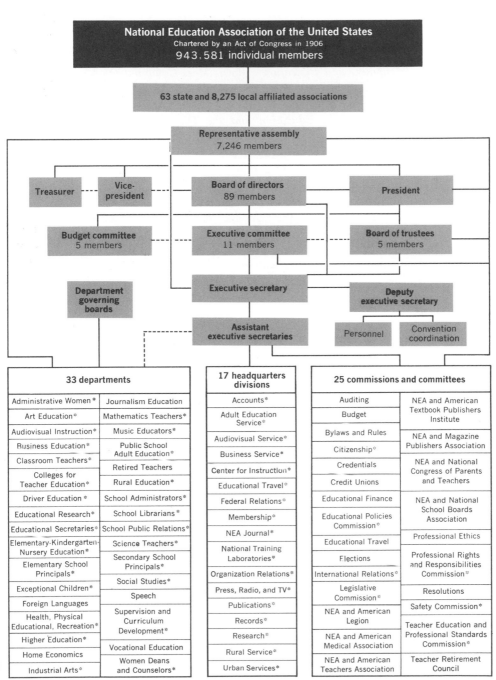

FIGURE 7–5. Organization chart of the National Education Association in 1966. (*Source:* National Education Association.)

conduct of education in this country and in its international relationships. Its publications have made major contributions to thinking on educational problems. Among these are the following: *The Unique Functions of Education in American Democracy* (1937), *The Education of Free Men in American Democracy* (1941), *Education for All American Children* (1948), *Moral and Spiritual Values in the Public Schools* (1951), *Education for All American Youth: A Further Look* (1952), *Manpower and Education* (1956), *Mass Communication and Education* (1958), *National Policy and the Financing of the Public Schools* (1959), *Contemporary Issues in Elementary Education* (1960), *The Central Purpose of American Education* (1961), *Education and the Disadvantaged American* (1962), *Social Responsibility in a Free Society* (1963), *Universal Opportunity for Education beyond the High School* (1964), *The Public Interest in How Teachers Organize* (1964), *Educational Responsibilities of the Federal Government* (1964), *The Unique Role of the Superintendent of Schools* (1965), and *American Education and the Search for Equal Opportunity* (1965).

Established more recently, the National Commission on Teacher Education and Professional Standards has become increasingly more important since its creation in 1946. More familiarly known as the TEPS Commission, this group has evolved into a nationwide organization with parallel state commissions. As its name implies, the commission is concerned with the recruitment, selection, preparation, and certification of teachers, and with the standards of the schools which prepare teachers.

The commission publishes *The Journal of Teacher Education* (four issues per year) and the *TEPS Newsletter* (three issues per year). Other publications include *Milestones in Teacher Education and Professional Standards* (1966) and *A Manual on Certification Requirements for School Personnel in the United States.*

Student Professional Associations

Probably many of you now belong to the Student National Education Association, and probably many of you belonged to the Future Teachers of America while you were in high school. From 1937 to 1957 the name "Future Teachers of America" referred to both the high school and college groups. Since that time the high school organization has been known as the FTA and the college organization as the Student NEA. Student NEA is designed for college students preparing to teach, and FTA clubs are for high school students exploring teaching as a career. Both organizations are sponsored and assisted in their work by the National Commission on Teacher Education and Professional Standards. In 1965 there were 250,000 high school students in over 6,400 FTA clubs and 118,500 college students in 970 campus chapters of the Student NEA [175:108–109].

Any student who is enrolled in a teacher education program in a properly accredited college or university may become a student member of the NEA, provided he joins through a chartered chapter [255:7]. Joining the Student NEA carries with it junior membership in the NEA and in the state education association in the state in which your college or university is located. Members also receive the *NEA Journal* and the journal of the state education association. In addition, student members are eligible to participate in the life insurance program of the NEA. Membership also includes $50,000 in liability protection while the member is doing his student teaching.

The Student NEA provides its members with opportunities in the following areas [255:8]:

(1) Personal and professional growth; (2) development of leadership skills; (3) understanding of the history, ethics, and programs at state and national levels; and (4) participation in professional activities at local, state, and national levels.

As an organization, the Student NEA should deepen the interest of capable students in teaching as a career; encourage the careful selection and guidance of persons admitted to teacher education programs; and, through higher standards of preparation and the dissemination of information, contribute to a reasonable balance in teacher supply and demand.

The Student National Education Association chapter on your campus offers you many opportunities to participate in professional activities and to begin to assume the responsibilities of your chosen profession. A record of your membership and participation can be an important part of your placement credentials.

Perhaps some of you may become the faculty sponsors or advisers to the FTA in the high school in which you begin your teaching. If so, you will have an op-

You may gain valuable experiences from your membership in the Student National Education Association. Here students and faculty members are viewing an exhibit on professional opportunities and requirements in education. (*Photograph from the Audio-visual Center, Indiana University.*)

portunity to encourage the finest boys and girls in school to enter the teaching profession. And in this capacity you will have close association with the local, state, and national professional units, and have an opportunity to become a leader in your profession.

The official purposes of the FTA are as follows [175:108]:

FTA seeks to enable its members (a) to study and to identify the qualities, traits, and aptitudes which are basic or related to successful teaching; (b) to acquire an understanding of the history and development of our public schools and their purposes and objectives and an appreciation of the contributions they have made to our democratic society; (c) to secure accurate information on vocational oportunities in education and the special competencies required, to aid in self-evaluation; and (d) to participate in prevocational activities.

FTA seeks to enable the profession: (a) to develop selective recruitment programs to identify capable candidates for teaching and to motivate them to choose appropriate fields of preparation; (b) to offer potential teachers appropriate experiences to help them develop readiness for college programs of teacher education; and (c) to achieve and maintain a balanced supply of qualified teachers.

American Federation of Teachers

Another organization with which you should be acquainted is the American Federation of Teachers, an affiliate of the American Federation of Labor–Congress of Industrial Organizations, with its national office in Chicago. The AFT originated in 1916 and, until the merger of the AFL and the CIO in 1955, was affiliated with the AFL. After considerable difficulty in getting started, it has experienced an appreciable increase in membership in the past 15 years, especially in some of our biggest cities.

In 1966 the total membership exceeded 117,000 in 625 local organizations. The official journal of the AFT is *The American Teacher*. The chief objective of the federation is to improve the educational situation for the nation as a whole, with special emphasis on securing money for schools, better pay and working conditions for teachers, and an improved and more democratic education for all youngsters. More specifically, the AFT has promoted integration within the schools, supporting the idea of equal educational opportunities for all. It has opposed any form of a merit-rating salary plan as educationally unsound. Although affiliated with the AFL-CIO, the AFT is a legal entity in its own right. It need not join the AFL-CIO in any specific action.

The question is frequently asked why the AFT insists on affiliation with the AFL-CIO. Answers include the support received from other organized labor groups, the opportunity for teacher influence on labor policy and action, and the social reform goals of the AFL-CIO [233:298–300]. On the other hand, there are many persons who consider it unwise for teachers to join forces with labor. They insist that there is a distinct difference between the public service rendered by teachers and the work-for-pay rendered by labor. They feel that it produces needless division of the ranks. There is a broad, national professional organization in the NEA. If teachers lend their full support to that body—in time, energy, and money—they may achieve such solidarity and influence in this organization as medical doctors or lawyers enjoy in theirs.

International Educational Organizations

As the nations of the world grow closer together, educators find that they have many common interests. In the first place it is the desire of the free world to have peace and security. The best way to ensure this peace and security is through the development of international understanding, which is a crucial task confronting teachers throughout the world. In the second place, because of the increasing relatedness of nations today, the welfare of the teachers in any nation becomes the concern of teachers in all other nations. For these reasons efforts have been made to develop an organization for the educators of all nations.

The World Confederation of Organizations of the Teaching Profession was established in 1952 as a result of a merger of various international organizations, including the World Organization of the Teaching Profession which originally had been founded in 1946 at the invitation of the National Education Association. The confederation seeks:

to foster a conception of education directed toward the promotion of international understanding and good will, with a view to safeguarding peace and freedom and respect for human dignity; to improve teaching methods, educational organization, and the academic and professional training of teachers so as to equip them better to serve the interests of youth; to defend the rights and the material and moral interests of the teaching profession; to promote closer relationships between teachers in the different countries [175:338].

There are more than eighty national member associations in the WCOTP in addition to constituent federations and international members. Representatives of these member associations meet annually to consider such themes as the following: education in a technical age, conditions of work for quality teaching, increasing international understanding through teaching about the United Nations, and equal opportunity through education [175:337].

WCOTP activities include leadership training seminars, research studies, and an extensive multilingual information program. In addition to its permanent committees for Asia, Africa, and the Americas, the WCOTP maintains committees in such fields as adult education, rural education, education for handicapped children, educational journalism, and technical and vocational education [38:24–25].

Although not all nations belong to the WCOTP, progress is being made in bringing about common understanding, in resolving prejudices, and in opening up the channels of communication by means of which teachers throughout the world become better informed about educational needs, interests, and problems. The WCOTP holds great potentialities for improving the status of the teaching profession internationally and, by greater universal educational opportunities, for promoting world understanding and peace.

UNESCO (United Nations Educational, Scientific, and Cultural Organization) was created in 1945 by the United Nations. According to the constitution of UNESCO, its purpose is "to contribute to peace and security by promoting collaboration among the nations through education, science, and culture in order to further universal respect for justice, for the rule of law and for the human rights and fundamental freedoms which are affirmed for the peoples of the world, without distinction of race, sex, language or religion, by the charter of the United Nations." Each year, delegates from countries that belong to the United Nations convene in order to share their ideas, to pool their thinking, and to develop plans for bringing about mutual understanding among the peoples of the world.

Within the framework of these purposes, UNESCO has engaged in many different types of activities. Those most closely related to education have included the organizing of educational missions to assist underdeveloped countries, the dissemination of educational materials, the holding of international conferences and seminars, the planning of programs of fundamental education to combat illiteracy, the promotion of international understanding, and the carrying on of research in world educational problems.

In essence, the United Nations Educational, Scientific, and Cultural Organization attempts to further world peace by encouraging free interchange of ideas and of cultural and scientific achievements; by removing social, religious, and racial tensions; and by improving and expanding education.

Other Education Associations

The *Education Directory*, issued regularly each year by the U.S. Office of Education, lists many national, regional, and state educational associations in addition to the few that have already been discussed. A good share of these are designed to meet the needs of various specialized groups of educators. Some of them are departments of the NEA, but many others are not.

If you teach in an elementary school, you may wish to become a member of an association such as the Association for Childhood Education International (ACEI), which is concerned with the education of children from 2 to 12 years of age. Most elementary teachers are interested in becoming members of the Department of Elementary–Kindergarten–Nursery Education of the NEA. Each subject area in high school has its own national association, such as the National Council for the Social Studies, the National Council of the Teachers of English, and the National Council of the Teachers of Mathematics. The *NEA Handbook* contains essential information about each of the NEA departments, such as historical background, activities, names of national officers, and the amount of regular and student dues.

Looking further into the future, some of you may wish to become a curriculum supervisor or consultant. In that case you will certainly want to be affiliated with the national association in your subject area and perhaps with the Association for Supervision and Curriculum Development (ASCD). Some of you may become principals or superintendents. If so, in addition to the associations already mentioned, you will want to become a member of the Department of Elementary School Principals (DESP); the National Association of Secondary-School Principals (NASSP); or the American Association of School Administrators (AASA).

As some of you advance in graduate work, as your interests become more highly developed, or as you move into college or university teaching, you may wish to become a member of a more specialized group, such as the National Society for the Study of Education, the John Dewey Society, the American Educational Research Association, or the American Association of University Professors.

The associations mentioned in this section are only a few of those in the field of education. The important point is that, regardless of your position and interest, there is a professional association composed of other persons with like positions and interests with which you can affiliate. Furthermore, it is the journals and yearbooks of these associations that provide much of the professional literature in education.

Honorary Educational Associations

While you are in college you may want to work toward such professional and honorary groups as Pi Lambda Theta (for women) and Phi Delta Kappa (for men), or Kappa Delta Pi (for both men and women).

Pi Lambda Theta is open to undergraduate and graduate women students and women faculty members who meet the necessary qualifications. General qualifications include evidence of high professional standards, qualities of leadership, and ability to live and work with others. In addition, there are more specific requirements for both student and faculty eligibility for membership. The specific purposes are to:

recognize women of superior scholastic achievement and high potential for professional leadership; foster creativity and academic excellence at all educational levels; support, extend, and interpret the function of education in a democracy; demonstrate the power of competence in the body of knowledge unique to the profession; stimulate, conduct, and utilize research; accept responsibility for evaluation and improvement of the profession of teaching; contribute to the solution of educational, social, and cultural problems of national and international concern; and promote professional fellowship and cooperation as a means of positive action [203:i].

Membership in Phi Delta Kappa is by chapter invitation to male graduate or undergraduate students who have completed at least 90 semester hours toward the baccalaureate degree, who give promise of success in a professional career in education, and who will contribute to the purposes of Phi Delta Kappa. Additional requirements include 15 semester hours of courses in education, scholarship acceptable for admission to candidacy for a graduate degree, and commitment to a life career in educational service.

The chief purpose of Phi Delta Kappa shall be to promote free public education as an essential to the development and maintenance of a democracy, through the continuing interpretation of the ideals of research, service and leadership. It shall be the purpose of Phi Delta Kappa to translate these ideals into a program of action appropriate to the needs of public education [137:n.p.].

Membership dues in the organization includes a subscription to the *Phi Delta Kappan*, which is published monthly, October through June of each year. This journal carries many articles, reviews, and features of special interest to educators.

Kappa Delta Pi is open to both men and women and is composed of outstanding junior and senior undergraduates, graduate students, and faculty members. In addition to the functions commonly performed by honorary educational organizations, Kappa Delta Pi has contributed to the general cause of education by issuing several significant publications. These publications include *The Educational Forum, The Kappa Delta Pi Lecture Series,* and the *Kappa Delta Pi Research Publications.*

These honorary educational associations exert positive influences upon the profession. You doubtless will feel highly rewarded if you should gain membership in any one of them and join forces toward a worthy cause.

Parent-Teacher Association

An opportunity for parents and teachers to work together effectively on both local and national levels is provided through the Parent-Teacher Association. Teachers are usually expected to take an active part in this association in those communities where it is established. All official local PTA groups are members of their state congress and of the National Congress of Parents and Teachers. The objects of this group of nearly 12 million members are as follows [184:i]:

> To promote the welfare of children and youth in home, school, church, and community.
> To raise the standards of home life.
> To secure adequate laws for the care and protection of children and youth.
> To bring into closer relation the home and the school, that parents and teachers may cooperate intelligently in the training of the child.
> To develop between educators and the general public such united efforts as will secure for every child the highest advantages in physical, mental, social, and spiritual education.

In most communities the PTA takes its work seriously, studies its problems realistically, and wields tremendous power in shaping trends toward better schooling. Unfortunately, some teachers feel that PTA work requires too much of their time. Some administrators feel that it provides another unnecessary opportunity for people to meddle in school affairs.

In most PTA groups, mothers far exceed fathers in number. Many PTAs fail to reach those parents in the community when response would be most advantageous to themselves, to their children, and to the improvement of the instructional program in school. These are typical problems which, through planning, hard work, and cooperation on the part of parents and school people, have been largely solved in individual communities.

You will have noticed in the organizational diagram, Figure 7–5, that the National Education Association recognizes the value of the PTA through a joint committee called the NEA and National Congress of Parents and Teachers. *The PTA Magazine* has won the School Bell Award of the National School Public Relations Association for distinguished service in the interpretation of education.

A parent-teacher association is the most natural group imaginable where important common concerns exist, because both parties usually have the best interests of the children at heart. You will be fortunate to work in a community where the PTA is a live and going concern. If this is not the case, you will be faced with the challenge of helping to make it so.

Code of Ethics for the Teaching Profession

Besides joining and working earnestly to promote the purposes of various professional organizations, every teacher is expected to conduct himself and manage his work affairs in such ways as are approved by the profession at large. Should you tutor your own pupils for pay? Should you leave a position suddenly in the middle of a semester? Is it legitimate to make political speeches favoring your party in classrooms? If your father is superintendent of schools back home, should you accept a position under his administration? The acceptable modes of behavior along these lines, and many others, are well established in a professional code of ethics. Medical doctors have such a code, lawyers have one, and teachers also have one. These codes are not legal enactments. Sometimes they are not even written down. Nevertheless, they are definite and well understood by the great body of the profession. It behooves you as a prospective teacher to become well acquainted with the code of the teaching group.

The NEA has spent a great amount of time and effort in developing and revising the Code of Ethics of the Education Profession. It is designed to be acceptable to all workers in education in all parts of the nation. The first national code of ethics for teachers was adopted by the NEA in 1929 and revised in 1941, 1952, and 1963. The most recent revision is presented here for your study [175:66–68]:

PREAMBLE

We, professional educators of the United States of America, affirm our belief in the worth and dignity of man. We recognize the supreme importance of the pursuit of truth, the encouragement of scholarship, and the promotion of democratic citizenship. We regard as essential to these goals the protection of freedom to learn and to teach and the guarantee of equal educational opportunity for all. We affirm and accept our responsibility to practice our profession according to the highest ethical standards.

We acknowledge the magnitude of the profession we have chosen, and engage ourselves, individually and collectively, to judge our colleagues and to be judged by them in accordance with the applicable provisions of this Code.

PRINCIPLE I

Commitment to the Student

We measure success by the progress of each student toward achievement of his maximum potential. We therefore work to stimulate the spirit of inquiry, the acquisition of knowledge and understanding, and the thoughtful formulation of worthy goals. We recognize the importance of cooperative relationships with other community institutions, especially the home.

In fulfilling our obligations to the student, we—

1. Deal justly and considerately with each student.
2. Encourage the student to study varying points of view and respect his right to form his own judgment.
3. Withhold confidential information about a student or his home unless we deem that its release serves professional purposes, benefits the student, or is required by law.
4. Make discreet use of available information about the student.
5. Conduct conferences with or concerning students in an appropriate place and manner.
6. Refrain from commenting unprofessionally about a student or his home.

7. Avoid exploiting our professional relationship with any student.
8. Tutor only in accordance with officially approved policies.
9. Inform appropriate individuals and agencies of the student's educational needs and assist in providing an understanding of his educational experiences.
10. Seek constantly to improve learning facilities and opportunities.

PRINCIPLE II

Commitment to the Community

We believe that patriotism in its highest form requires dedication to the principles of our democratic heritage. We share with all other citizens the responsibility for the development of sound public policy. As educators, we are particularly accountable for participating in the development of educational programs and policies and for interpreting them to the public.

In fulfilling our obligations to the community, we—

1. Share the responsibility for improving the educational opportunities for all.
2. Recognize that each educational institution may have a person authorized to interpret its official policies.
3. Acknowledge the right and responsibility of the public to participate in the formulation of educational policy.
4. Evaluate through approriate professional procedures conditions within a district or institution of learning, make known serious deficiencies, and take any action deemed necessary and proper.
5. Use educational facilities for intended purposes consistent with applicable policy, law, and regulation.
6. Assume full political and citizenship responsibilities, but refrain from exploiting the institutional privileges of our professional positions to promote political candidates or partisan activities.
7. Protect the educational program against undesirable infringement.

PRINCIPLE III

Commitment to the Profession

We believe that the quality of the services of the education profession directly influences the future of the nation and its citizens. We therefore exert every effort to raise educational standards, to improve our service, to promote a climate in which the exercise of professional judgment is encouraged, and to achieve conditions which attract persons worthy of the trust to careers in education. Aware of the value of united effort, we contribute actively to the support, planning, and programs of our professional organizations:

In fulfilling our obligations to the profession, we—

1. Recognize that a profession must accept responsibility for the conduct of its members and understand that our own conduct may be regarded as representative.
2. Participate and conduct ourselves in a responsible manner in the development and implementation of policies affecting education.
3. Cooperate in the selective recruitment of prospective teachers and in the orientation of student teachers, interns, and those colleagues new to their positions.
4. Accord just and equitable treatment to all members of the profession in the exercise of their professional rights and responsibilities, and support them when unjustly accused or mistreated.
5. Refrain from assigning professional duties to nonprofessional personnel when such assignment is not in the best interest of the student.
6. Provide, upon request, a statement of specific reason for administrative recom-

mendations that lead to the denial of increments, significant changes in employment, or termination of employment.

7. Refrain from exerting undue influences based on the authority of our positions in the determination of professional decisions by colleagues.
8. Keep the trust under which confidential information is exchanged.
9. Make appropriate use of time granted for professional purposes.
10. Interpret and use the writings of others and the findings of educational research with intellectual honesty.
11. Maintain our integrity when dissenting by basing our public criticism of education on valid assumptions as established by careful evaluation of facts or hypotheses.
12. Represent honestly our professional qualifications and identify ourselves only with reputable educational institutions.
13. Respond accurately to requests for evaluations of colleagues seeking professional positions.
14. Provide applicants seeking information about a position with an honest description of the assignment, the conditions of work, and related matters.

PRINCIPLE IV

Commitment to Professional Employment Practices

We regard the employment agreement as a solemn pledge to be executed both in spirit and in fact in a manner consistent with the highest ideals of professional service. Sound professional personnel relationships with governing boards are built upon personal integrity, dignity, and mutual respect.

In fulfilling our obligations to professional employment practices, we—

1. Apply for or offer a position on the basis of professional and legal qualifications.
2. Apply for a specific position only when it is known to be vacant and refrain from such practices as underbidding or commenting adversely about other candidates.
3. Fill no vacancy except where the terms, conditions, policies, and practices permit the exercise of our professional judgment and skill, and where a climate conducive to professional service exists.
4. Adhere to the conditions of a contract or to the terms of an appointment until either has been terminated legally or by mutual consent.
5. Give prompt notice of any change in availability of service, in status of applications, or in change of position.
6. Conduct professional business through the recognized educational and professional channels.
7. Accept no gratuities or gifts of significance that might influence our judgment in the exercise of our professional duties.
8. Engage in no outside employment that will impair the effectiveness of our professional service and permit no commercial exploitation of our professional position.

Rights, Responsibilities, and Enforcement of the Code

Most states and local school systems have adopted the NEA code or, in some cases, have established their own codes of ethics. The Professional Ethics Committee of the NEA is responsible for the development and interpretation of the code and provides materials and assistance to the ethics committees of state and local associations in their activities and studies.

Enforcement of the code of ethics is the responsibility of the National Commission on Professional Rights and Responsibilities of the NEA. It is also concerned with the defense of teachers and schools against unjust attack, development of professional personnel policies, tenure legislation, civil and human rights of the teaching profession, information regarding persons and groups criticizing and opposing education, and unethical conduct of members of the teaching profession [175:101–102]. The commission may hold hearings on alleged violations and make recommendations for disciplinary action to the NEA Executive Committee. Many state and local associations have established their own commissions or committees on professional rights and responsibilities.

Appraising Your Professional Ethics

As the individual member of the profession seeks to find himself and his own role within the code, he becomes a living, vital force in his day-by-day actions. Every teacher should ask himself periodically the question "How professional am I?" He may find the self-appraisal form titled "How Professional Am I?" which is located in the Resource Section for Part II of this book, to be helpful. Even though you are not actually teaching, you should find a number of the questions to be appropriate as you prepare for teaching. For example, do you speak proudly of the importance of education to society?

Not only will you be expected to live up to a professional code of ethics, but you will also be expected to promote the best interests of the profession on every possible occasion. If you are serious about your vocation, this will be the natural thing to do. Teachers should be well informed about their schools, their pupils, and their patrons. They should be enthusiastic about their work and should talk and look and act as if they are. It does not seem sensible for a teacher to speak poorly of his profession and to complain about conditions without working to improve what needs to be improved or without seeking what for him might be a happier situation in another line of work. If you want to be worthy of your profession, you will never lose an opportunity to tell its merits, its deep satisfactions, its real purposes. You will defend it against malicious gossip and distorted statements of all sorts. Yet you will not be blind to its shortcomings or to the whole range of its inadequacies. These, too, you should discuss constructively and professionally with your fellow workers and lay people so that a better understanding of problems may be achieved. Often it is because the heart of a problem goes unrecognized by a community that no action, or possibly the wrong action, is taken. Positive attitudes and wholesome public relations lead not only to better understanding of the significance of teachers and schools but to a realistic appraisal of the local educational situation, to mutual esteem and cooperation between school and lay people, and to improved conditions for living and learning. These things are worth planning for, working for, and so conducting our professional lives that they may soon come to pass.

Achieving Professional Goals

Teachers and the teaching profession have come far in achieving better salaries and salary schedules, better working conditions, greater professional recognition, and greater prestige and status—both locally and nationally. These accomplishments have been achieved largely through the efforts of many, many dedicated teachers working through organized groups on the local, state, and national levels.

In recent years a spirit of greater militancy has seemed apparent in the efforts of teachers, including those representing the NEA as well as those representing the American Federation of Teachers of the AFL-CIO. In achieving professional goals, the terms "professional negotiation" and "professional sanctions" have come into common use within the teaching profession, just as the terms "collective bargaining" and "strike" have been associated with labor for many years and are still associated with the AFT.

Under the leadership of the NEA, there has been increasing emphasis in local and state associations on the development and use of professional negotiation, which refers to "a set of procedures to provide an orderly method for teachers associations and school boards through professional channels to negotiate on matters of common concern, to reach mutually satisfactory agreement on these matters, and to establish educational channels for mediation and appeal in the event of impasse" [199:15]. In this type of negotiation, the teachers' association is recognized as the organization representative of the members of the teaching staff. A professional negotiation agreement may include sections on recognition, procedure, resolving disagreement, salaries, teaching conditions, teacher assignments, transfers, promotions, summer school, protection of teachers, leave pay, leaves of absence, procedure for grievances, and procedure for ethics [198:3].

It has been pointed out by representatives of the AFT that professional negotiations correspond quite closely to the collective bargaining procedures used by the AFT. In turn, the NEA claims the following strengths for professional negotiations: procedures are not subject to labor precedent; all members of the profession may participate; professional channels are used; fragmentation of classroom teachers into several groups is prevented (secondary, English, etc.); and appeal procedures through educational channels are used [44:4–7].

In many communities, teachers have been asked to decide by vote which group —the teachers association or the union—shall represent them before the school board. The AFT has had its greatest comparative success in the large cities where unionism has long been powerful, although there are many exceptions even here. In some cities, for example, New York and Detroit, representatives of both groups have been recognized as bargaining agents. The NEA has continued to show its great national strength in small cities, rural areas, and in entire states, for example, Utah, Oklahoma, and Washington. The first statewide professional negotiation law was passed in the state of Washington in 1965 [179:3].

These developments are also influencing the professional role of the school superintendent and the school principal. The AFT position has tended to exclude administrators, regarding them as part of "management" and thus representative of the "adversary" at the bargaining table. The NEA position has tended to admit administrators as a part of the total professional group, although there are many exceptions to this policy. National groups of administrators have developed and are developing statements of position in regard to their role in negotiation. For example, the National Association of Secondary-School Principals:

emphasizes that discussions and decisions on purely professional problems cannot be considered in the atmosphere characteristic of the bargaining table. It proposes instead that such considerations take place in an atmosphere of colleagues working together as a professional team. It welcomes the establishment of formal councils made up of representatives chosen by teachers, principals, and supervisors. . . . Such councils can evoke a partnership rather than an adversary relationship. They can encourage the search for solutions rather than victories [80:11–12].

In developing action policies related to professional negotiations, the NEA has placed increased emphasis upon professional sanctions:

As used by professional education associations, sanctions mean censure, suspension, or expulsion of a member; severance of relationship with an affiliated association or other agency; imposing of a deterrent against a board of education or other agency controlling the welfare of the schools; bringing into play forces that will enable the community to help the board or agency to realize its responsibility; or the application of one or more steps in the withholding of services [199:15].

Here again it has been pointed out by representatives of the AFT that the "professional holiday" and the "protest day" of the teachers' associations are essentially strikes. In turn, the NEA points out basic professional differences between its sanctions used by public employees in the public interest and the threat of strike as prescribed by labor.

The achievement of professional goals and the question concerning agencies and procedures through which to achieve those goals represent a complex problem [78:12–21]. Although there are proponents of extreme points of view, there are also those who attempt to bring about agreement, even to the extent of proposing a merger of the NEA and the AFT. It seems, however, that the fundamental question is whether teachers shall remain independent as a professional group using professional procedures and shall remain responsible to all people rather than to a particular segment of our population. It has been suggested by a representative of the school boards' association that, if we are to continue our state system of education operated at the local level, "teachers must accept a responsibility within the community, make themselves heard, and be a positive force for the multiple aspects of public education" [139:38].

This is a time of critical decisions for teachers and the teaching profession. Decisions made in the next few years will determine the course of American education and the role of teaching as a profession for many years to come. Through the help of teachers like yourself the profession of teaching can be further strengthened as it strives to accomplish the tasks of education and as it attempts to exemplify to an even greater extent the characteristics of a profession.

SUMMARY

The advancement of teaching as a profession depends in great degree upon the professional organizations and their membership. It is probable that as an individual you can contribute most to your profession and your own welfare through professional organizations. Within the field of education there are professional organizations based on geography—local, state, regional, and national in scope. There are organizations based on types of duties—teaching, counseling, administration. There are organizations based on level of teaching—elementary, secondary, higher. There are organizations based on subject-matter specialties. And there are organizations that are comprehensive in nature and include all of these types. Choose your organizations carefully.

Teachers need to support one another and to work together cooperatively for the good of their schools and their pupils. Joining forces in professional organizations of various sorts, studying their purposes and procedures, and playing a responsible part in those groups is one way of accomplishing the necessary cooperation. This you will want to do at the local, state, and national levels. Your activities in these organizations and in all other professional affairs, whether in the school or not, should always conform to the rules and regulations set down in the Code of Ethics of the Education Profession. This is your professional responsibility to your pupils, to your fellow teachers, and to your entire school community.

QUESTIONS FOR YOUR CONSIDERATION

1. What is meant by the statement that "education is the mother of all professions"?
2. What are the commonly recognized characteristics of professions in general?
3. How does teaching as a profession differ from other professions?
4. What are the chief differences between the NEA and the AFT with respect to policies, services, and potential contributions to the improvement of education in the United States?
5. Is it reasonable to expect a teacher to give some of his time to the profession itself? Would you accept a committee responsibility or an office?
6. Should teachers be required to join one or more professional organizations?
7. There are many opportunities today for teaching abroad. What values usually come to the teacher who participates in such a program? What special responsibilities does he have?
8. Why do you suppose the Parent-Teacher Association has usually been more successful at the elementary level than at the secondary level?
9. What are the differences between professional negotiation and collective bargaining and between sanctions and strikes?
10. What procedures may the teaching profession ethically use in attempting to gain higher salaries and better working conditions?
11. What should be the role of teachers, principals, superintendents, and school boards in professional negotiation as well as in collective bargining?
12. What are the values of a code of ethics for you as a teacher?
13. Consider the teachers whom you have had. To what extent did they seem to be aware of a code of ethics? To what extent did they seem to practice the provisions of this code?
14. Who speaks for the profession of teaching?

ACTIVITIES FOR YOU TO PURSUE

1. Attend one or more local and state teachers' meetings. Make a careful study of the problems discussed and the values gained by teachers as a result of these meetings.

2. Learn about your campus chapter of the Student National Education Association. Secure information concerning its major purposes and its program.
3. Visit the Future Teachers Association club of the local high school, or arrange to talk with the sponsor about the activities of the group.
4. Study the NEA Code of Ethics. Arrange student presentations of specific problems or questions related to application of the code.
5. Arrange a panel to discuss the meaning and value of a professional code of ethics. If possible include on the panel a clergyman, a medical doctor, a lawyer, an engineer, and a school superintendent.
6. Using the checklist in the Resource Section of Part II, appraise one of your former teachers to determine how professional he was.
7. Watch the newspapers for a month for all NEA news releases. Try to classify the items as to types and purposes.
8. Study the *NEA Journal* and the publication of your state education association. Compare and contrast the contents and purposes of these publications.
9. Examine a recent *NEA Handbook for Local, State, and National Associations* to learn about the department or association in which your college major causes you to be interested.
10. Invite representatives of various honorary groups in the teaching profession to explain the purposes and programs of their organizations.
11. Collect newspaper articles describing the use of professional negotiations and sanctions by local and state education associations and the use of collective bargaining and threat of strike by the AFT.

RESOURCE
SECTION
FOR PART II

TWENTY INDICATORS OF THE QUALITY OF TEACHING

	Indicating a high quality of teaching	Indicating a low quality of teaching
Work with individual pupils:		
Assignments	Varied for individuals	Uniform for all
Pupil-teacher relations	Friendly; personalized	Very formal or very flippant
Pupil-teacher conferences	Frequent, to help pupils	For disciplinary purposes only
Pupils' work	Carefully reviewed, promptly returned	Carelessly handled; errors not checked
Planning and preparations:		
Daily continuity	Each day built on one before	Work unrelated from day to day
Teacher's knowledge	Well-informed teacher supplements books pupils use	Unable to answer simple questions
Lesson plans	Plans on blackboard or otherwise obvious	No evidence of plans
Advance arrangements	Necessary materials at hand	Necessary materials lacking
Use of teaching aids:		
Use of books	Pupils know how to use books	Pupils unacquainted with special features of books they use
Use of library tools	Pupils use effectively card catalog, reference guides, other tools	Pupils unable to get information in the library on their own
Use of audio-visual aids	Aids carefully related to work of class	Little advance explanation or follow-up of aids used
Use of field trips	To introduce or supplement class study	Used as holiday from class
Involvement of pupils in varied learning experiences:		
Types of experiences	Many different types used	Experiences mostly of one type
Pupil-teacher planning	As their maturities permit, pupils help in planning	Pupil participation or reaction not sought
Responsibilities of pupils	To prepare their own work and to help class as a whole	Only to prepare own assignments
Techniques of motivation	Work made interesting and important to pupils	Threats and criticisms only
Active leadership of the teacher:		
Use of pupil leaders	To give leadership experiences under supervision	To rest the teacher
Use of play or entertainment experiences	To provide a balanced program under teacher guidance	Also to rest the teacher

Source: William M. Alexander, *Are You a Good Teacher?* Holt, Rinehart, and Winston, Inc., New York, 1959, p. 26.

TWENTY INDICATORS OF THE QUALITY OF TEACHING (continued)

	Indicating a high quality of teaching	Indicating a low quality of teaching
Active leadership of the teacher:		
Handling behavior problems	Disturbers promptly and consistently dealt with	Inconsistent leniency, harshness
Discussion	Genuine and general participation	Drags or dominated by a few

HOW WELL ARE YOU DOING IN PUBLIC RELATIONS?

Note: When you become a teacher you should check yourself periodically on this checklist. You will be doing very well if you can answer "yes" to all the following questions:

Do you believe that public relations activities should foster lay participation in the educational program? _____

Do you really enjoy talking and working with children? _____

Do you really enjoy talking and working with adults? _____

Are you genuinely proud to be a teacher? _____

Do you believe that good public relations are your responsibility? _____

Do you regularly visit your pupils' homes? _____

Do you ever send newsletters home to parents? _____

Do you ever send notes to parents concerning things other than problem behavior? _____

Do you ever send home complimentary notes concerning your pupils who are not outstanding students? _____

Do you encourage your pupils' parents to visit you and the school? _____

Do you schedule regular conferences with parents? _____

Do your contacts with critical parents tend to placate them rather than increase their irritation? _____

Do you have a room-parent organization? _____

Does your school have a parent-teacher organization? _____

Do you regularly attend parent-teacher-organization meetings? _____

Does your school foster parent participation in planning class work and activities? _____

If so, do you personally take advantage of this policy to involve parents in your classroom planning activities? _____

Do you ever enlist the help of parents in the performance of routine clerical tasks? _____

Would you recognize the parents of most of your pupils if you met them on the street? _____

Do you encourage your classes to invite laymen to share their experiences with the class? _____

Do you make an effort to bring school matters of public interest to the attention of appropriate officials or news media? _____

Do your classroom activities ever involve community problems and contacts with laymen? _____

Do you willingly accept invitations to address groups of laymen, either on school matters or on other subjects? _____

Do you take an active part in church, political, civic, or fraternal organizations in your community? _____

Do your personal actions reflect credit upon your profession? _____

Do your remarks in the community tend to present a constructive view of teaching and of your local school situation? _____

Source: Glen E. Robinson and Evelyn S. Bianchi, "What Does PR Mean to the Teacher?" *NEA Journal,* vol. 48, no. 4, p. 14, National Education Association, Washington, April, 1959.

HOW PROFESSIONAL AM I?

In using this instrument, indicate your self-appraisal on each item by placing a dot on the line to the right somewhere between "Low" and "High." When you have finished, connect the dots with straight lines.

Low   High

I. Teacher-pupil relationships:
Do I—
1. Individualize pupils in my teaching? _____
2. Try to find out their capacities and abilities? _____
3. Refrain from the use of sarcasm? _____
4. Avoid embarrassing a child before the group? _____
5. Create an atmosphere of friendliness and helpfulness in the classroom? _____
6. Provide for democratic participation of pupils? _____
7. Try to improve my methods? _____

II. Teacher-teacher relationships:
Do I—
1. Recognize accomplishments of colleagues and tell them so? _____
2. Refrain from adverse criticism of a colleague's method or work except when requested by a school official for the welfare of the school? _____
3. Refrain from blaming the previous teacher for inadequate preparation of pupils? _____
4. Avoid letting jealousy of a good teacher adversely affect my personality development? _____
5. Avoid unkind gossip of and among colleagues? _____
6. Have a respectful attitude toward the subject matter and work of other fields? _____
7. Refrain from interfering between another teacher and pupil unless called upon for advice or assistance? _____
8. Avoid criticism of an associate before his students and before other teachers? _____

III. Teacher-administrator relationships:
Do I—
1. Talk things over with the administrator next above me? _____
2. Support the policies and programs of my principal and superintendent? _____
3. Avoid criticism of my principal and superintendent in public? _____

IV. Teacher-board of education relationships:
Do I—
1. Support the policies of my board? _____
2. Have the goodwill of my board as a person of professional integrity? _____
3. Respect my contract obligations? _____
4. When contemplating a change of position, make a formal request thru my superintendent to the board of education for release from my contract? _____
5. Give sufficient notice when asking for release from my contract? _____
6. Use my local professional organization to convey constructive suggestions and criticisms to the board thru my superintendent? _____

Source: Grace I. Kauffman, "How Professional Am I?" *NEA Journal,* vol. 39, no. 4, p. 286, National Education Association, Washington, April, 1950.

HOW PROFESSIONAL AM I? (continued)

                                                                    Low   High

V. Teacher-public relationships:

   Do I—

   1. Remember that I am a public servant?   _____
   2. Try to exemplify to the public the best qualities of a teacher? _____
   3. Participate in community activities that are not directly con-
      nected with my profession?   _____
   4. Contribute of my time and/or money to the various community
      drives? (Community Chest, and the like.)   _____
   5. Show by my life that education makes people better citizens
      and better neighbors?   _____

VI. Teacher-profession relationships:

   Do I—

   1. Keep myself informed about best practices in my field?   _____
   2. Belong willingly to my professional organizations—local, state,
      national?   _____
   3. Contribute of my time and talents to my professional organi-
      zations?   _____
   4. Accept responsibility in my professional organizations?   _____
   5. Help to make possible a democratic approach to school admin-
      istrative authorities thru teacher organization channels?   _____
   6. Speak proudly of the importance of the service of education
      to society?   _____
   7. Maintain my efficiency by reading, study, travel, or other means
      which keep me informed about my profession and the world
      in which I live?   _____
   8. Dignify my profession?   _____
   9. Encourage able and sincere individuals to enter the teaching
      profession?   _____
   10. Avoid using pressure on school officials to secure a position
      or to obtain favors?   _____
   11. Refuse compensation in the selection of textbooks or other
      supplies in the choice of which I have some influence?   _____
   12. Refrain from sending for sample copies of texts merely to build
      up my own library?   _____
   13. Refrain from accepting remuneration for tutoring pupils of my
      own classes?   _____

Interpretation: If your profile is reasonably straight and close to "High," you are professional and your school and community should be very proud of you! If your profile zigzags and is close to "Low," then you probably need remedial exercises in ethical practices to improve your professional outlook. You should: (1) Concentrate on the ethical principles on which you rated yourself the lowest. (2) A few months from now take this test again, using a different color to draw the connecting lines. Check to see whether you have improved. "Live good ethics everyday; check your ethics profile at least twice a year!"

SUGGESTED READINGS

The number in parentheses following each suggestion denotes the chapter for which it is best suited.

Anderson, Charnel: *Technology in American Education 1650–1900*, U.S. Office of Education, Washington, 1962. An excellent treatment of the history and background of instructional technology in American education. (6)

"Are Schools Changing Too Much Too Fast?" *Changing Times*, September, 1966, pp. 6–10. Appraises changes made in schools during 10 years following Sputnik 1. (6)

Association for Supervision and Curriculum Development: *Perceiving, Behaving, Becoming: A New Focus for Education*, 1962 Yearbook, National Education Association, Washington, 1962. Discusses the psychological, social, and philosophical aspects of guiding the growth of pupils. (6)

Batchelder, Richard D.: "Unionism versus Professionalism in Teaching," *NEA Journal*, vol. 55, no. 4, pp. 18–20, National Education Association, Washington, April, 1966. Points out that the issue is freedom of the schools and the teachers in them. (7)

Beggs, David W., III (ed.): *Team Teaching: Bold New Venture*, Unified College Press, Indianapolis, 1964. Presents an excellent discussion of team teaching, advantages and disadvantages, and examples. (6)

Bernard, Harold W.: *Mental Hygiene for Classroom Teachers*, 2d ed., McGraw-Hill Book Company, New York, 1961. Chapters 2 and 3 discuss the basic needs and tasks of children and adolescents. Chapter 6 is concerned with teachers' understanding and helping pupils with problems. Chapter 20 discusses the teacher's responsibilities to pupils, administrators, fellow teachers, and to the community. (5, 6)

Brickman, William W., and Stanley Lehrer (eds.): *Automation, Education, and Human Values*, School and Society Books, New York, 1966. A series of readings on automation and its effect upon schools and human values. (6)

Brown, B. Frank: "The Non-graded High School," *Phi Delta Kappan*, vol. 44, no. 5, pp. 206–209, February, 1963. Describes the nongraded high school program at Melbourne, Florida. (6)

Bruner, Jerome S.: *Toward a Theory of Instruction*, The Belknap Press of Harvard University Press, Cambridge, Mass., 1966. Indicates Bruner's concept of instruction and how instruction in the schools may be improved. (6)

Bushnell, Don D. (ed.): *The Automation of School Information Systems*, National Education Association, Department of Audio-Visual Instruction, Washington, 1964. Indicates how automation is affecting data processing, scheduling procedures, instructional systems, and systems design in schools. (6)

"Class Size in Secondary Schools," *NEA Research Bulletin*, vol. 43, no. 1, pp. 19–23, National Education Association, Research Division, Washington, February, 1965. Indicates the size of classes in the various subject areas in the secondary school. (5)

Classroom Teachers Speak on the New Teacher and the Professional Association, National Education Association, Department of Classroom Teachers, Washington, 1964. Emphasizes the importance of meeting the needs of young teachers and of bringing them into full partnership with the experienced leaders. (5, 7)

"Conditions of Work for Quality Teaching," *NEA Journal*, vol. 54, no. 3, pp. 33–40, National Education Association, Washington, March, 1965. A special feature pointing out the conditions teachers need in order to do quality teaching. (5)

Denemark, George W.: "Schools Are Not Factories," *NEA Journal*, vol. 53, no. 3, pp. 25–27, National Education Association, Washington, March, 1964. Discusses the controversy between the NEA and the AFT and argues in favor of teachers' belonging to the NEA. (7)

Evaluation of Classroom Teachers, Research Report 1964–R14, National Education Association, Research Division, Washington, December, 1964. Presents the results of an extensive survey of administrative practices in teacher evaluation and of teachers', principals', and superintendents' reactions to these practices. (5)

Fry, Edward B.: *Teaching Machines and Programmed Instruction*, McGraw-Hill Book Company, New York, 1963. An extensive treatment of programmed learning and teaching machines. (6)

Gnagey, William J.: *Controlling Classroom Misbehavior*, What Research Says Series no. 32, National Education Association, Department of Classroom Teachers, American Educational Research Association, Washington, 1965. Tells about types of successful control techniques and how they influence the behavior and attitudes of the class as a whole. (5, 6)

Goodlad, John I.: "Changing Curriculum of America's Schools," *Saturday Review,* Nov. 16, 1963, pp. 63–67, 87–88. Indicates that a first-rate curriculum demands the coordination of a vast array of resources. (5, 6)

Goodlad, John I., and Robert H. Anderson: *The Nongraded Elementary School,* Harcourt, Brace and World, Inc., New York, 1963. Indicates the advantages of the nongraded school over the graded school. (6)

Gordon, George N.: *Educational Television,* Center for Applied Research in Education, New York, 1965. Discusses in detail the development and use of educational television and speculates on the future use of television in schools. (6)

Guidelines for Professional Negotiations, National Education Association, Washington, 1965. Discusses the nature, legal bases, and procedures for conducting professional negotiations. (7)

Hicks, William Vernon, and Frank H. Blackington, III: *Introduction to Education,* Charles E. Merrill Books, Inc., Columbus, Ohio, 1965. Chapter 5 discusses the challenge that teachers find in the classroom. Chapter 11 has a good discussion on the relationship of the teacher with other school personnel, and Chapter 13 discusses the teacher's role in the community. (5)

Kaufman, Burt, and Paul Bethune: "Nova High: Space Age School," *Phi Delta Kappan,* vol. 46, no. 1, pp. 9–11, September, 1964. Describes innovative practices at the Nova High School. (6)

"Learning," *NEA Journal,* vol. 52, no. 3, pp. 20–32, National Education Association, Washington, March, 1963. A series of articles in which five experts discuss various aspects of the psychology of learning. (6)

Lieberman, Myron: "Who Speaks for Teachers," *Saturday Review,* June 19, 1965, pp. 64–65, 74–75. Discusses the rising militancy of teachers and the struggle for power between the National Education Association and the American Federation of Teachers. (7)

Manlove, Donald C., and David W. Beggs, III: *Flexible Scheduling,* Indiana University Press, Bloomington, Ind., 1965. Discusses in detail the IndiFlexS model of flexible scheduling. (6)

Meierhenry, W. C.: "Implications of Learning Theory for Instructional Technology," *Phi Delta Kappan,* vol. 46, no. 9, pp. 435–438, May, 1965. Discusses learning theory behind some of the newer instructional techniques and procedures. (6)

"The NEA-AFT Rivalry," *Phi Delta Kappan,* vol. 46, no. 1, pp. 12–15, September, 1964. Discusses the crucial struggle existing between the NEA and the AFT. (7)

NEA Handbook for Local, State, and National Associations, National Education Association, Washington. Current edition. Contains a vast amount of information about the work of the NEA. (7)

Planning and Organizing for Teaching, National Education Association, Project on the Instructional Program of the Public Schools, Washington, 1963. Chapter 4 contains recommendations for improved classroom organization. (5, 6)

Professional Practices Regulations: A Plan for Action, National Education Association, National Commission on Teacher Education and Professional Standards and the Commission on Professional Rights and Responsibilities, Washington, 1965. Maintains that the teaching profession can and should assume increased responsibility for the professional competence and ethical behavior of its members. (7)

"Programmed Instruction," *Phi Delta Kappan,* vol. 44, no. 6, pp. 241–295, March, 1963. A series of articles on various aspects of programmed instruction. (6)

Provus, Malcom M.: "NEA Time to Teach Project," *NEA Journal,* vol. 54, no. 4, pp. 8–10, National Education Association, Washington, April, 1965. Explains the purpose behind the "Time to Teach" project. (5)

"The Public Interest in How Teachers Organize," *NEA Journal,* vol. 53, no. 6, pp. 43–45, National Education Association, Washington, September, 1964. A statement of the Educational Policies Commission on how teachers should organize. (7)

Public Relations Ideas for Classroom Teachers, National Education Association, National School Public Relations Association in cooperation with the Department of Classroom Teachers, Washington, 1964. Indicates many ways in which teachers may promote good public relations. (5)

Schooling, H. W.: "Teacher-Administrator Relationships," *NEA Journal,* vol. 54, no. 2, pp. 32–34, National Education Association, Washington, February, 1965. Discusses the characteristics of good teacher-administrator relationships. (5)

Selden, David: "Why the AFT Maintains Its AFL-CIO Affiliation," *Phi Delta Kappan,* vol. 47, no. 6, pp. 298–300, February, 1966. Attempts to answer one of the frequently asked questions. (7)

Sizer, Theodore R.: "Reform Movement or Panacea?" *Saturday Review,* June 19, 1965, pp. 52–54, 72. Cautions educators on adopting the new too soon. (6)

Skinner, B. F.: "Why Teachers Fail," *Saturday Review,* Oct. 16, 1965, pp. 80–81, 98–102. An eminent psychologist indicates some of the reasons for teacher failure. (6)

Stanley, William O.: "Issues in Teacher Professionalization," *Bulletin of the School of Education,* vol. 40, no. 5, pp. 1–8, Indiana University, Bloomington, Ind., September, 1964. Presents the essential characteristics of a profession, teaching as a profession, and the basis for a profession of teaching. (7)

Stinnett, T. M.: *The Profession of Teaching,* Center for Applied Research in Education, Washington, 1964. Chapter 1 is concerned with the meaning of profession and the rise of the teachers' professional association. (7)

Stinnett, T. M., and Albert J. Huggett: *Professional Problems of Teachers,* The Macmillan Company, New York, 1963. Chapter 3 discusses characteristics of a profession and indicates how teaching meets these criteria. Chapter 13 advocates autonomy for the teaching profession. Chapter 14 discusses the enforcement of ethics for the teaching profession. Chapter 15 is concerned with the problems of protecting and disciplining members of the profession. (7)

Stoncius, Stanley: "Opportunities in Professional Organization," *NEA Journal,* vol. 43, no. 7, p. 60, National Education Association, Washington, October, 1964. Indicates that work of a professional association can make the difference between a purposeful career and just another job. (7)

Stone, James C., and Frederick W. Schneider: *Foundations of Education: Commitment to Teaching,* vol. 1, Thomas Y. Crowell Company, New York, 1965. Chapters 4 and 5 contain realistic discussions of the pressures and problems faced by the teacher. (5)

Student NEA Handbook, National Education Association, National Commission on Teacher Education and Professional Standards, Washington. Current edition. Contains much information about the Student NEA and how effective programs may be conducted. (7)

"The Teacher's Role in Politics," *NEA Journal,* vol. 53, no. 7, pp. 30–31, National Education Association, Washington, October, 1964. A Democrat and a Republican indicate their views toward the teacher's role in politics. (5)

Weber, C. A.: "Do Teachers Understand Learning Theory?" *Phi Delta Kappan,* vol. 46, no. 9, pp. 433–435, May, 1965. A disturbing report of the immense lack of knowledge that teachers have of learning theory. (5, 6)

SUGGESTED FILMS, FILMSTRIPS, AND RECORDINGS

The number in parentheses following each suggestion denotes the chapter for which it is best suited.

And No Bells Ring (National Association of Secondary-School Principals, 56 min). Presents a review of the "Trump Report" on reorganization of secondary school staff utilization with Hugh Downs acting as an interviewer and interpreter. Discusses the flexibility of this program and its advantages for development of individual interests and abilities both in pupils and teachers. Interviews are held with a number of educators who have been involved in this experimental program, including J. Lloyd Trump. Figures are given to explain how this program will better utilize teachers in teams of large group presentation personnel, small group teachers, and teacher assistants. Large lecture groups are observed along with pupils in smaller discussion groups and in individual study. (6)

Creating Instructional Materials (McGraw-Hill, 15 min, color). Describes characteristic instructional materials which may be created by students in the classroom and indicates how these can most effectively contribute to instruction. Illustrates, among other things, the creation of a play, the use of a resource person, and the utilization of personal collections of materials such as slides. (5)

Effective Learning in the Elementary School (McGraw-Hill, 20 min). Shows a fifth-grade class planning their daily work with their teacher and their study of a unit on pioneer life. They decide what should be studied. The teacher gathers materials for pupil use. As the children work individually and in committees, attention is given to reading, writing, and arithmetic. A mural is constructed, and maps and models are made. Folk songs and dances are practiced. As a culminating activity, a play is put on for the children's parents and teachers. (5)

Elementary School Teacher Education Series: Curriculum Based on Child Development (McGraw-Hill, 12 min). Shows how a fourth-grade teacher plans a curriculum based on the developmental characteristics of her pupils. Reviews the behavioral patterns of eight- and nine-year-olds and shows materials for learning and classroom activities that are based on their interests, abilities, and group needs. Illustrates how the teacher encourages respect for other points of view in a discussion. (6)

Elementary School Teacher Education Series: Elementary School Children, Part II, Discovering Individual Differences (McGraw-Hill, 25 min). Uses individual cases to show how an elementary school teacher systematically investigates the differences in backgrounds, activities, and needs of the pupils in her class. Outlines steps in investigation, including casual and controlled observations, consulting records, conferences with teachers, parent-teacher interviews, and staff conferences. Illustrates the need for resourcefulness and understanding in improving the education and social adjustment of pupils. (6)

Four Teachers (National Film Board of Canada, 58 min). Filmed in Japan, Poland, Puerto Rico, and Canada. Four teachers present many illuminating comparisons of the world of the classroom. Commenting on each sequence are a Toronto professor, a Montreal teacher, and the film's producer-commentator. (6)

Guiding the Growth of Children (McGraw-Hill, 17 min). Shows how a teacher may work to understand each child and to guide him in his growth and development. Deals with seven problem cases and suggests possible ways of handling them. Shows a variety of techniques that a teacher may use but insists that underlying each technique is the teacher's genuine desire to help plus sympathetic, patient understanding. (6)

Helping Teachers to Understand Children, Part I (United World Films, 21 min). Points out a need for teachers to understand children and illustrates a variety of ways through which a knowledge of child behavior can be gained and interpreted. Presents a case study of one child and suggests the use of school records, interviews with teachers, the child's writing and artwork, home environment, and anecdotal records as sources of information. (6)

Helping Teachers to Understand Children, Part II (United World, 25 min). Summarizes a summer workshop in which six aspects of a child's life were studied— physical, affectional, cultural, peer group, self-developmental, and emotional. (6)

Kindergarten (McGraw-Hill, 21 min). A candid camera study of children being themselves in the special world of the kindergarten classroom. Shows how children act within the group. (6)

Learning from Visuals (American Institute for Research, 35 min, color). Pictures four people discussing the application of the programmed approach to the design of visuals for use on educational television. Reviews principles of programmed instruction and shows how these are applied to the design of visuals. Emphasizes need for the establishing of specific objectives, active responding on the part of the students, and proper sequencing for effective learning. (6)

Learning Is Searching (New York University Film Library, 20 min). Shows how a third-grade class carries out its studies of a unit on man's use of tools. After defining the terms that will be used through direct experiences and field trips, the group sets up the problem it wants to consider. The pupils then search for solutions and try out tentative ones. In accomplishing this they have many direct experiences, prepare a text-book, and correlate these activities with other subject areas. Further activities involve projects based on previously discovered knowledge. Finally, culminating exhibits and presentations are made. (6)

Learning to Understand Children: Part I, A Diagnostic Approach (McGraw-Hill, 22 min). Presents a case study of Ada Adams, an emotionally maladjusted girl fifteen years of age. Ada's teacher diagnoses her difficulties by observation of her behavior, study of her previous record, personal interviews, home visits, and formulation of a hypothesis for remedial measures. (6)

Learning to Understand Children: Part II, A Remedial Program (McGraw-Hill, 25 min). Continues the case study of Ada Adams. An interest in art improves her self-confidence and interest in schoolwork, although some of her problems cannot be solved by the efforts of her teacher. (6)

A New Design for Education (Stanford University, 28 min, color). Describes research conducted at Stanford University in relation to flexible class scheduling in high schools. Indicates how the principle of flexible scheduling has been used to adapt instruction to the abilities and interests of students. (6)

Planning and Organizing for Teaching (National Education Association, 18 min). Designed primarily for use by school staffs as they work on planning the total school program. It should also provide one basis for a dialogue among college faculties and students, school boards, educational associations, state departments of education, and interested lay groups. (5, 7)

Practicing Democracy in the Classroom (Encyclopaedia Britannica Films, 21 min). Shows a teacher explaining to parents his method of teaching social studies. Depicts students selecting discussion topics with the guidance of the teacher, establishing goals, working as committees in contacting groups and leading citizens of the community, and reporting their experiences to the class. Explains that such teaching methods improve pupils' understanding of the meaning of democracy. (6)

Promoting Pupil Adjustment (McGraw-Hill, 20 min). Shows that a teacher must be alert and sensitive to student problems if classroom learning is to be effective and illustrates ways by which teachers can facilitate pupil adjustment. Portrays a teacher's concern for the intellectual, social, and personal needs of her students and how she can cope with problems posed by individual differences. Follows the case of a student who feels unwanted until the teacher guides him to the point where he improves his adjustment. (6)

Providing for Individual Differences (Iowa State Teachers College, 23 min). Indicates the ways in which the classroom teacher can adjust the learning environment to meet the individual differences among her pupils. Depicts a college class discussing the methods of adjustment to individual differences that they have observed on visits to an elementary school and a high school. (6)

Rafe: Developing Giftedness in the Educationally Disadvantaged (Bailey Films, Inc., 20 min). Open-ended film about Rafe, an educationally gifted child from an environmentally disadvantaged home. Offers the audience an opportunity to learn some of the causes of educational disadvantages, some means for determining strong potentials and critical needs, and how potentials can be raised in rich classroom programs. Shows the cooperative efforts of psychologist and teacher in developing giftedness in educationally deprived children. (6)

School (Office of Inter-American Affairs, 21 min). Shows one day's activities in an elementary school in an Ohio town. Pictures the janitor opening the building, children on their way to school, the first grade studying and playing, and a PTA meeting in the evening. (5)

The Second Classroom (National Education Association, 25 min). Shows the contribution educational television can make, presenting seven samples of programs currently available through this medium. A TV producer acts as a narrator in introducing each of the seven selected programs, characteristic of educational television, which include second-grade music, biological science, teacher education, and an interview with a United States Senator. Concludes by reviewing the potential contributions of this form of educational media. (6)

Skippy and the Three R's (National Education Association, 30 min, color). Follows a first-grader from his first day at school, through his school experiences guided by the teacher and her teaching methods, to the point where he is learning through self-motivation. Shows the method of motivating the desire to read, write, and do number work and illustrates how a teacher utilizes the interests of pupils to encourage the learning of fundamental skills in schoolwork along with the social skills of living. (6)

Task Ahead (Association Films, 19 min). Traces the growth of UNESCO during its first five years, and shows some of the work it sponsors. Includes book programs, international work camps, children's communities for cripples and orphans, training of Arab refugees, and the fundamental education program in Haiti. (7)

The Teacher (Encyclopaedia Britannica Films, 13 min). The story of Julia Wittaker, a middle-aged fourth-grade teacher, is used to explain the role of the teacher in the community, her professional and personal life and contribution to the furthering of education after extensive preparation and study. (5)

Teacher as Observer and Guide (Metropolitan School Study Council, 22 min). Six school situations illustrate the following concepts: guiding pupils to better ways of solving their problems, developing artistic talents, promoting the growth of character and citizenship, and providing needed assistance for slow learners. (5)

Teaching Machines and Programmed Learning (United World, 28 min). Presents Drs. B. F. Skinner, A. A. Lumsdaine, and Robert Glasen as each in turn discusses teaching machines and programmed learning. (6)

Team Teaching on the Elementary Level (Bailey Films, 13 min, color). Defines team teaching as using the staff most efficiently and to its maximum potential and reports on the establishment of team teaching at Cashmere, Washington. Indicates the need for facilities for a good instructional program. Details size of instructional groups involved and tells how the team teaching was carried out. (7)

The Things a Teacher Sees (International Film Bureau, 17 min). Shows the things a teacher should observe and be sensitive to in her students such as sight, hearing, speech, dental, nutritional, and emotional problems. The results of the observant teacher's concern is the correction of many of these problems. (6)

We Plan Together (Columbia University, Teachers College, 21 min). Eleventh-grade pupils at the Horace Mann–Lincoln School, New York City, are shown planning cooperatively a core program. A new student tells of his experiences and changing viewpoint as he becomes a part of the program. (5)

Willie and the Mouse (Teaching Film Custodians, 11 min). Contrasts Willie's father's education, in which facts were learned by repetition, with Willie's education, in which life situations are dramatized in the classroom. Various experiments with white mice demonstrate that some mice learn by sight, others by ear, and still others by touch. Shows how such experiments as these have caused individual differences to be recognized in the classroom. (6)

You and Your Classroom (Educational Horizons, 10 min). Fourteen open-ended episodes involving classroom control and discipline are presented. After each vignette the instructions "Stop the film and discuss" are flashed on the screen. Selection of the filmed episodes was made after a survey of several hundred teachers revealed these problems to be the most prevalent in the elementary classroom. (5, 6)

Filmstrips

Achieving Classroom Discipline (Wayne University, 47 fr.). Shows some of the more important techniques which help produce desirable action patterns in children. (5)

Bringing the Community to the Classroom (Wayne University, 45 fr.). Illustrates how teachers in various curriculum areas may bring community resources to the school so that instruction may be of maximum effectiveness. (5)

Community Resources Workshop for Teachers (American Iron and Steel Institute, 59 fr., color). Explains how to plan and operate community resources workshops where teachers can learn to utilize their communities as laboratories for improved teaching. (5)

Core Curriculum Class in Action (Wayne University, 50 fr.). Follows a typical ninth-grade core class from its first class meeting through various teacher-pupil–planned activities and the final evaluation of the work done. (5)

Grouping Students for Effective Learning (Bel-Mort Films, 44 fr., color). Considers grouping students on the basis of age, ability grouping, and flexible grouping. (5)

How Pupils and Teachers Plan Together (Wayne University, 48 fr.). Presents the details of teacher-pupil planning in a number of representative school situations. Intended primarily for teacher education purposes. (5)

Individual Differences (McGraw-Hill, 49 fr.). The case study of a shy, slow child who is different from his classmates and from his older, socially adept brother. Points out that individual differences must be met in terms of individual interests and capabilities, that it is the job of the school to shape education to individual needs. (6)

Informal Pointers for Teachers (Jam Handy Organization). A series of filmstrips, average 55 frames or 22 minutes each, (1. *The Teacher;* 2. *Some Principles of Teaching;* 3. *I Want to Learn;* 4. *The Lesson Plan;* 5. *Make Your Chalk Talk*) that present basic attributes and qualifications necessary to be a good teacher. Illustrates fundamental techniques and methods. (5)

Lesson Plan (Jam Handy Organization, 60 fr.). Indicates that all lessons are more effective if they follow definite plans. Clearly stated aims tend to limit the scope and keep the teacher within the limits of the lesson. (5)

PTA at Work (Visual Education Consultants, 34 fr.). Explains many activities and functions of the Parent-Teacher Association that are unknown to new members. (7)

Some Principles of Teaching (Jam Handy Organization, 56 fr.). Presents seven suggestions on how the teacher can help shorten the learning process. (6)

Story of UNESCO (Nestor Productions, 45 fr., color). Explains the ideals and concepts of UNESCO and opens the door to participation by students and others in its work. (7)

Teacher and Public Relations (National Education Association, 50 fr.). Shows how to build an appreciation of the professional skills and achievements of teachers, why we teach what we teach, how we teach, homework assignments, reports to parents, public relations values of cocurricular activities making parents partners, and working with community groups. (5)

Teaching by Television (Basic Skills Films, 51 fr., color). Summarizes the research on what is known about teaching by television in relation to what television teaching can do, how to use television in the classroom, and how to teach over television. (6)

Teaching Machines (Basic Skills Films, 64 fr., color). Tells what teaching machines are, the types of teaching machines, what a teaching-machine program is like, and the educational role of teaching machines. (6)

Your School and Community Relations (Eye Gate House, 46 fr.). Designed to help foster understanding and stimulate action necessary to meet present and future school problems. (5)

Recordings

Chalkdust (National Tape Recording Project, 15 min each). Documentary nature for adult listening. Designed to promote understanding of advancements in today's teaching methods. The talks are generally pro the modern public schools. 1. Discipline for Our

Children; 2. Grouping for Reading; 3. Rudy Fleste; 4. General Reading; 5. A Teacher Speaks; 6. William Eller; 7. Report Cards and Evaluation; 8. Comic Books. (5, 6)

I Do Not Walk Alone (University of Illinois, 12 min). Walter E. Englund indicates the value of membership in the Minnesota Education Association. (7)

New Horizons in AV Education (National Tape Recording Project, 60 min). Mr. Mitchell tells of the unlimited possibilities of audio-visual aids in education in the future. (6)

New Methods of Reporting Pupil Progress (Educational Recording Service, 33⅓ rpm). Virgil M. Rogers, dean of education, Syracuse University, discusses ways in which improvements can be made in reporting to parents. (5)

Principles of Teaching and Learning of the Secondary School Level (Education Service, 33⅓ rpm). Hugh M. Shafer, professor of education, University of Pennsylvania, discusses effective ways of guiding the educational experiences of secondary school pupils. (6)

Teacher-Pupil Planning Techniques (Educational Recording Service, 33⅓ rpm). H. H. Giles, professor of education, New York University, discusses various techniques which teachers may use in effectively planning educational experiences with pupils. (5)

FIGURE CREDITS

FIGURE 5–1. (*Source:* Adapted from *The American Public-school Teacher, 1960–61,* Research Monograph 1963–M2, National Education Association, Research Division, Washington, April, 1963, p. 55.)

FIGURE 5–2. (*Source:* "Methods of Evaluating Teachers," *NEA Research Bulletin,* vol. 43, no. 1, p. 14, National Education Association, Research Division, Washington, February, 1965.)

FIGURE 5–3. (*Source: The American Public-school Teacher: 1965–66 Preliminary Report,* National Education Association, Research Division, Washington, p. 15.)

FIGURE 5–4. (*Source:* "Teachers View Public Relations," *NEA Research Bulletin,* vol. 37, no. 2, p. 39, National Education Association, Research Division, Washington, April, 1959.)

FIGURE 6–1. (*Source: Planning for American Youth,* National Education Association, National Association of Secondary-School Principals, and the Educational Policies Commission, Washington, 1951, p. 9.)

FIGURE 7–1. (*Source: Financial Status of the Public Schools,* National Education Association, Committee on Educational Finance, Washington, 1965, p. 21.)

FIGURE 7–2. (*Source:* Data from the *Statistical Abstract of the United States,* Bureau of the Census, 1966, p. 232.)

FIGURE 7–3. (*Source:* "Status of Public-school Teachers, 1965," *NEA Research Bulletin,* vol. 43, no. 3, p. 69, National Education Association, Research Division, Washington, October, 1965.)

FIGURE 7–4. (*Source: Rankings of the States, 1966,* Research Report 1966–R1, National Education Association, Research Division, Washington, January, 1966, p. 22.)

FIGURE 7–5. (*Source:* National Education Association, Washington, July, 1965.)

ECONOMIC
AND LEGAL
ASPECTS
OF TEACHING

The economic and legal aspects of any occupation affect not only the manner in which an individual views his work but also his attitude toward life in general. Many people have erroneous ideas in regard to various economic aspects of teaching. Effective planning necessitates that you become quite well informed about such matters so that your plans may be realistic, comprehensive, and meaningful.

The welfare of our nation is, to a considerable extent, dependent upon a large number of our most able young people being attracted to the teaching profession. The economic status of teachers will have considerable bearing upon the extent to which these people will be interested in such a career. As a future member of the profession, you will want to work effectively toward the further improvement of the economic status of teachers. Through such efforts, you will improve your own status and make the profession increasingly attractive to others.

Chapter 8 explores the current and probable future status of salaries in public elementary and secondary schools and on the college level. Chapter 9 is concerned with such nonsalary benefits as teacher tenure, leaves of absence, group insurance, credit unions, mutual funds, income tax deductions, and retirement and social security benefits. Chapter 10 is designed to acquaint you with some of the legal liabilities and responsibilities of teachers.

8

SALARIES OF EDUCATORS

How high a salary can you expect as a beginning teacher? How fast will your salary increase? What does the future hold so far as teacher salaries are concerned? What kinds of salaries are paid to others, such as principals, supervisors, superintendents, counselors, special fields, and college teachers? Are there other sources of income for teachers? These are important questions to consider as you plan your career in education.

The salary status of teachers, especially since World War II, has been a matter of increasing concern both nationally and locally. The great shortage of teachers, especially in the elementary schools, no doubt has contributed to this concern. Since teachers require the same basic necessities of life and have the same desires as all other normal people, it is not possible for them to render maximum service, regardless of ability and preparation, if their income is not sufficient for them to feel economically secure.

Various attempts have been and are being made to increase the salaries of teachers. Data on salaries for any one year, therefore, may be obsolete the following year. Check carefully on current salaries by writing to local school districts, state education departments, and the National Educational Association. Be careful in your interpretation of salaries, for the mere number of dollars earned per year does not take into account other factors such as a variation in overhead expenses between those in the teaching profession and those in certain other professions.

Standards of Living Maintained by Teachers

Salaries need to be considered in terms of general standards of living fixed by society for different occupations. For example, professional people are expected to maintain higher standards of living than are unskilled laborers. Obviously it requires more money to maintain a higher standard of living. Unfortunately, the American public has never been too clear in its thinking as to whether the teacher belongs to the wage-earner or the professional class of workers. When you study the historical development of education in America, it is easy to understand why there has been confusion as to the status of teachers. The work of their national, state, and local organizations, however, is contributing much to the establishment of teaching as a profession in the minds of the general public. It is reasonable to believe that the teacher will be accorded higher status and therefore will be expected to maintain the standard of living generally associated with professional people.

If you are to be a professional worker, you will need more than the basic necessities of life in order to fulfill your function in society. You will need a salary adequate to continue your professional study, to travel, and to provide for your cultural, recreational, and civic needs in order to bring to the classroom increasingly richer experiences.

Relationship Existing between Income and Standard of Living

The money required to maintain a certain standard of living varies with respect to the community in which you live. The incomes of people in a given area largely determine the local standards of living and the standards that will be expected of you. If you live in a very wealthy community, you will find it necessary to maintain better housing facilities and to do more entertaining than if you settle in a rural section where a more simple mode of living is practiced. Generally speaking, the cost of food, rent, and services is cheaper in rural areas. A beginning salary in a nonurban community may be more favorable economically than an appreciably higher salary in a city, and a lower salary in one section of the United States may be equivalent to a higher salary in a similar community in another section.

The value of money also fluctuates from year to year. Consider the extent to which salaries in various occupations are affected in periods of economic recession and prosperity. Since World War II, the purchasing power of the dollar has dropped. Continued inflation will decrease the teacher's salary unless corresponding raises are made.

The research division of the National Education Association periodically analyzes the income of teachers in terms of the purchasing power of the dollar. Consult the most recent publications of this division to determine trends in the economic status of the teacher.

Some Factors to Consider in Comparing the Income of Teachers with Incomes in Other Occupations

Some students may be impressed with the huge income earned by men in business. No one ever learns of a schoolteacher who falls into comparable income brackets. It is true that this is the land of opportunity; on the other hand, consider carefully the probabilities of becoming the outstanding railroad magnate or business tycoon. With the unusually successful businessman you must balance the hundreds who barely make a decent living, who just manage to keep above bankruptcy, or who fail.

You also have read of the huge earnings of movie stars, prizefighters, professional football and baseball players, and the like. Unfortunately, their productive years are often exceedingly short, while the productive part of a teacher's life continues for many years.

Since World War II there has been considerable increase in the wages of semi-skilled and skilled labor. The bricklayer, house painter, or coal miner may seem to be earning more than the professional worker. Though these laborers may be receiving extraordinarily high hourly rates, the total number of hours that they work per year often is relatively small. Regularity of income, therefore, is an important factor to consider in comparing the relative attractiveness of occupations.

The gross income in some occupations seems to be large. On the other hand, considerable operating expenses are incurred. Doctors and lawyers must maintain offices, employ secretaries and assistants, and buy supplies. Teachers are relatively free of such expenses. The only comparable ones incurred by the teacher are those that provide for his professional growth.

In considering teaching as a profession, recognize the fact that a definite income is assured once you accept a position, for which you are eligible upon completing the requirements for a certificate. You do not need to incur heavy capital investments in equipment and supplies in order to begin your business. Furthermore, you do not encounter the problem of developing a clientele, from which little or no net profit may accrue during the first few years, as does the doctor, dentist, and lawyer.

The average income reported for any vocation does not give a true picture of the situation. For a number of reasons, this is particularly true of teaching. Only a relatively small percentage of teachers have made teaching a life career. As a result, a large number of the teachers are either beginners or those with limited amounts of experience. Obviously these salaries are low. Nearly 70 per cent of the teachers are women, and women tend to be paid less than men. Some teachers in the elementary schools have no more than two years of college training, since they earned life-teaching certificates a number of years ago when standards for certification were low. These teachers are paid appreciably less than those with four and five years of preparation, such as the more recently trained teachers. In other words, the heterogeneous background of teaching personnel makes it unwise to compare their income with incomes in other occupations, such as law and medicine, where the professional background is more homogeneous. The beginning teacher today is generally better trained than his predecessors and will consequently have a greater earning capacity.

FIGURE 8–1. Average annual salaries of instructional staff in public schools adjusted to the value of a dollar in 1965–1966. *(Source:* National Education Association.)

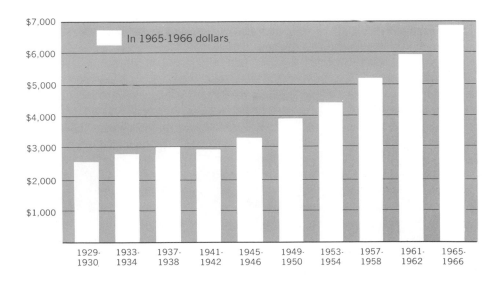

A large share of the schoolchildren and teachers in the United States are located in rural areas. In the past, rural teachers' salaries were considerably lower than urban salaries although there has been a tendency for this gap to be narrowed. Furthermore, rural schools have been forced to employ more teachers with substandard qualifications, especially in the elementary schools. These teachers are paid proportionately less salary.

Salary Trends in Teaching and Other Occupations

For a number of reasons it is difficult to indicate accurately the salary trends in many occupations. Only scattered information is available. We do know that since World War II considerable change has resulted in earnings, especially of unionized labor and professional workers who are not on regular salaries. Wages in some occupations fluctuate rapidly according to the cost-of-living index, whereas other occupations remain relatively constant in earning power. With the teaching profession, however, much information on salaries is available. A report of the research division of the National Education Association indicates that, during the 10-year period from 1955–1956 to 1965–1966, the public school average salary for the instructional staff increased from $4,019 to $6,572, which represents an increase of 63.5 per cent over a 10-year period.

Since the earnings of all persons working for wages and salaries establish the movement of wages in the economy as a whole, it is important to compare the gains of teachers with those of all employed persons. Disregarding losses due to price changes, the earnings of all wage earners increased 48.3 per cent from 1955 to 1965, as compared to 63.5 per cent for teachers. This differential in increases represents a potentially higher standard of living for teachers.

A number of studies have shown that the average earnings of professional workers are substantially higher than the salaries of teachers. The research division of the National Education Association, for example, compared the economic status

FIGURE 8–2.   Percentage of classroom teachers in various salary brackets in 1965–1966. What changes in this distribution may take place by 1980? (*Source:* National Education Association.)

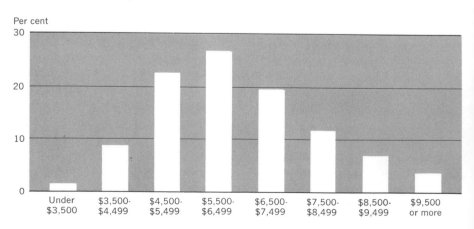

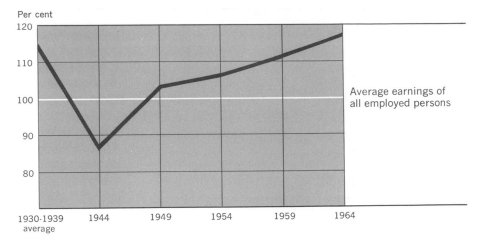

FIGURE 8–3. Average annual salary of teachers expressed as a percentage of average earnings of all employed persons. Is it reasonable to assume that the trend since 1949 will continue? *(Source:* National Education Association.)

of teachers in 1959–1960 with that of workers in seventeen other professions in which four or more years of college training were required (architects, chemists, clergymen, dentists, dietitians, engineers, foresters and conservationists, lawyers and judges, librarians, natural scientists, optometrists, osteopaths, pharmacists, physicians and surgeons, social and welfare workers, social scientists, and veterinarians). It was found that the median earnings in the teaching profession were 63.1 per cent of the median earnings of the seventeen other professions. The average (arithmetic mean) earnings, however, were only 47 per cent. (Figure 8–4.)

In the resolutions adopted in 1966, the National Education Association expressed the belief that teachers' salaries should compare favorably with income in other professions and occupations requiring comparable preparation. "Starting salaries for qualified degree teachers should be at least $8,000, and salaries for experienced teachers with a master's degree should range at least to $16,000 followed by continuing scheduled increase for career teachers of advanced qualification" [2:2].

Trends in Teachers' Salaries in Various States

Figure 8–5 gives you an idea of the great range in the average salaries paid in the various states.

As you study this figure keep in mind that the average state salaries are subject to all the weaknesses indicated previously. Naturally, the averages change from year to year, and you should consult current data from the research division of the National Education Association to determine the current average salaries for the states in which you are interested.

The extreme range shown in this figure points up a very crucial problem in education. Differences in the cost of providing the basic necessities of life for teachers cannot account for the variation in average salaries. As will be explained

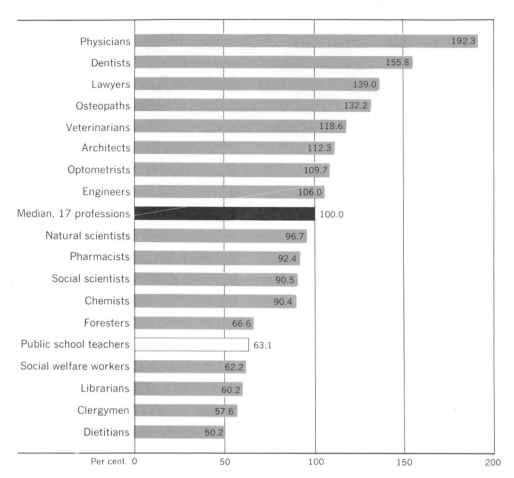

FIGURE 8–4.   Per cent of the median income of seventeen professions compared with teaching according to the 1960 census. What changes in income may the 1970 census reveal? (*Source:* National Education Association.)

more fully in Chapter 12, the differences result more from the lack of taxable resources for financing schools than from the willingness of the states to pay for education. The inequalities are so great that there seems to be little hope of rectifying them without some form of federal assistance. Generally speaking, the Northern and Western states, where there are greater financial resources, have higher average salaries than the Southern states, where the financial resources are more limited. This has been true for many years.

Teachers, like individuals in other occupations, tend to gravitate toward areas in which high salaries are paid. Many of the able teachers leave the poorly paying states and find teaching positions elsewhere. Wealthier states can demand better professional training, and many large school systems have well-organized personnel divisions which select incoming teachers very carefully. Thus, the states having low teachers' salaries are left with a relatively high percentage of inferior teachers. Educationally speaking, the rich become richer and the poor become poorer. What

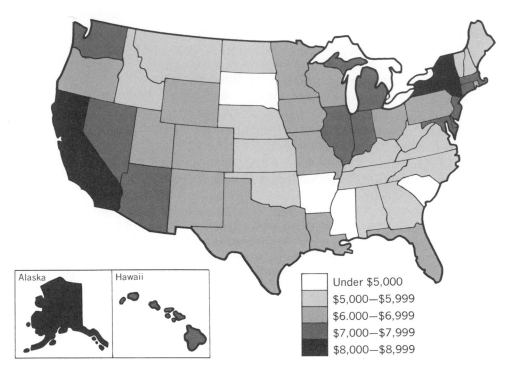

FIGURE 8–5. The range in the average annual salary for classroom teachers within the United States is great. The average salary for each state is more meaningful than an average salary for the United States. *(Source:* National Education Association.)

provisions must be made to equalize the educational opportunities *of all* American youth?

Trends in the Salaries of Teachers within Different-sized Communities

A direct relationship seems to exist between the size of communities and the salaries of their public school teachers. For example, in 1964–1965 the average salary of classroom teachers in public school systems having an enrollment of 25,000 or over was $6,788 as compared to an average salary of $4,909 for teachers in school systems having less than 300 enrollment [65:13]. However, the difference is greater in the maximum salaries paid to teachers having advanced degrees rather than in the salaries of beginning teachers with only bachelor's degrees [65:5].

A number of things account for the differences that exist in the salaries of public school workers in different sizes of cities. Teachers in large cities have been able to group together more easily than those in rural areas, and consequently have been able to acquaint the public with their economic needs. The very large city schools often have been able to afford a public relations division whose main function is to keep the public informed of their educational needs. Cities usually possess more valuable property than rural areas that may be taxed for school purposes without causing undue strain on the population.

The tendency for salaries to increase with the size of the city has resulted in a high turnover in rural areas and small towns. Great rural shortages of well-trained teachers have resulted. This condition has presented a real national problem, especially when one considers the school population that resides in cities having populations of 2,500 or less, or in the open country. The National Education Association has been increasingly concerned in recent years with the problem of providing equal educational opportunities for rural and city boys and girls.

Trends in the Salaries of Various Types of School Employees

Throughout the history of education, elementary teachers have received less salary than have secondary school teachers. For example, in 1966–1967 the average annual salary for elementary teachers was estimated to be 93 per cent of the corresponding figure for secondary school teachers, which represented a decrease of approximately 6 per cent in the difference over a 10-year period. The narrowing difference between elementary and secondary school teacher salaries "may be the result of several factors: (a) increased preparation of elementary-school teachers, (b) more acute shortage of elementary-school teachers in the past 10 years, and (c) longer periods of service, and improved status in the position of elementary school teachers" [82:15]. Undoubtedly these trends will continue.

FIGURE 8–6.   Average salaries paid professional personnel assigned to individual schools in 1964–1965. (*Source:* National Education Association.)

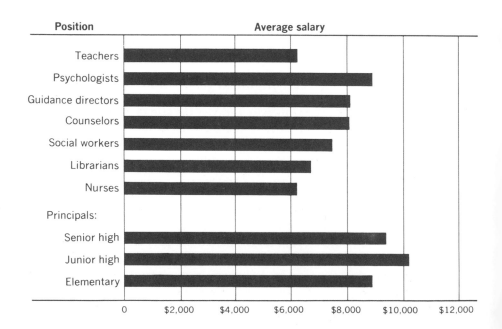

As early as 1918, however, cities began to establish single-salary schedules. This kind of schedule specifies the same salary to teachers, regardless of sex, with equal training and experience when assigned to regular positions in elementary, junior high, and senior high schools. Progress at first in the adoption of single-salary schedules was slow, even though it had been urged by the National Education Association as early as 1920. As late as 1940–1941 only 31.3 per cent of the schedules were of the single-salary type, but today this type of schedule is almost universally used. It is interesting to note that the Soviet Union, in September, 1966, adopted a single-salary schedule for teachers in rural and urban elementary, middle, and higher grades [181:4].

If you examine the most recent reports published by the research division of the National Education Association, you will note that the salaries of all school personnel tend to increase with the size of the school district. The salaries of principals in cities having a school population of 100,000 or more are definitely higher than those in the 2,500 school population class, and the salaries of superintendents differ even more. The size of the school population, however, does not make much difference in the salaries of directors, coordinators, consultants, or supervisors.

Members of the research division of the National Education Association have found that there has been a trend toward closing the gap between the median salaries of classroom teachers and administrators [161:44–45]. As reasons for this trend, the association has pointed to the extreme shortage of teachers, especially in the elementary schools after World War II, and the rising cost of living, which necessitated placing additional funds toward the salaries of classroom teachers. Many states increased the amount of state aid for school-salary purposes and raised minimum salaries for inexperienced teachers more rapidly than maximum salaries [209:70].

There also seems to be a change taking place in the manner of determining salaries for principals [227:5]. The older practice involved a dollar differential, a fixed sum of money above the amount the principal would receive if he were a classroom teacher. For example, an elementary school principal might receive $1,000 more than the teaching maximum for his level of preparation, plus $500 for each year of administrative experience up to four years. From a study conducted by the research division of the National Education Association [227:5] it was found that the index or ratio-differential method of determining a principal's salary was growing in popularity. The salary that a principal receives is stated as a ratio of the salary he would receive if he were classified as a classroom teacher. For example, an elementary principal may receive 138 per cent of the maximum salary for a master's degree on the teachers' salary schedule. This method of computing the salaries of principals would seem to have definite merit. It is highly probable that it will be used increasingly in determining the salaries of other central administrative officers, such as supervisors, consultants, directors, and coordinators. The practice of using the same salary schedule for elementary and secondary school principals in a school system still is rare. This situation is understandable since elementary schools tend to be smaller and elementary school principals frequently are paid for fewer months of service than secondary school principals.

Trend toward Minimum Salaries for Teachers

As early as 1904, regulations regarding the minimum salaries to be paid to teachers were enacted by several school systems. In 1966, public school teachers in thirty-one states were employed under minimum-salary laws [246:15]. These laws differ greatly in requirements as well as in the amount of salary. Some states only guarantee a flat-rate minimum. Other states specify only minimum salaries for beginning teachers, according to the amount of preparation, whereas still other states specify a minimum salary both for beginning teachers and for teachers who have had a specified number of years of teaching experience.

Each year the research division of the National Education Association prepares a release on the current state minimum-salary requirements for classroom teachers. This release indicates for each state the minimum starting salary for teachers holding the lowest certificate recognized, the bachelor's degree or four years of training, and the master's degree or five years of training. You may wish to secure this list from your library in order to study the current conditions in states where you may be interested in teaching.

There are a number of advantages in having minimum-salary laws. For example, they protect children against boards of education which would be willing to employ poorly qualified teachers at low rates of pay. Some boards of education have

FIGURE 8–7.   Legal minimum salaries in 1965–1966 for beginning teachers with bachelor's degrees. (*Source:* National Education Association.)

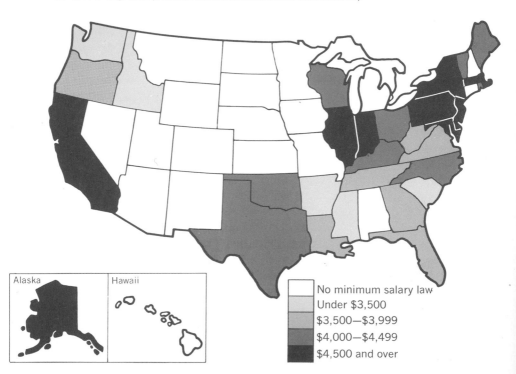

been willing to sacrifice quality in order to keep the local school budget as low as possible. Minimum-salary laws also improve ethics in the employment of teachers. Heretofore, a process of salary bargaining was in practice, especially for teachers in overcrowded subject areas. Wherever a minimum salary is stated, both the employee and the employer are operating on a higher professional plane. A state's adoption of a minimum-salary law in no way threatens local control of the school, and a community is free to pay teachers above the minimum to whatever extent it is able and desires.

Trend toward Definite Salary Schedules

If teachers' salaries are to be placed on a professional basis it is necessary to establish a definite classification of them with respect to minimum salaries, yearly increments, and maximum salaries.

A definite salary schedule is desirable for a number of reasons. When a teacher is able to determine definitely the income that he will receive during and at the end of the next 10 or 20 years, he is able to do long-range financial planning. A teacher is relieved of trying to get as much money as possible, sometimes having to resort to unethical practices; an administrator is not tempted to pay a teacher as little as possible. The tensions between teachers are relieved, since the initial salaries and the yearly increases are known to all. The administrator cannot be accused of playing favorites by giving unwarranted raises. Administrators and school board members can calculate budget needs more easily when a definite salary schedule is at their disposal.

You may wish to examine salary schedules that are used in various school systems. Superintendents of schools normally are happy to provide prospective teachers with these schedules. Some state departments of education publish the salary data of the major school systems in the state. The placement officer in your college will probably have copies of such schedules for various school systems. Study them and try to discover the strengths and weaknesses of each.

A salary schedule usually contains from two to four columns, representing various levels of preparation, such as the bachelor's, master's, sixth-year, and doctor's degree; and from 11 to 15 steps representing annual increments for each year of experience [228:5]. You will be especially interested in the size and the number of increments that are provided. For teachers having a bachelor's degree the typical number of increments is 12, with relatively few schedules providing fewer than 9 or more than 16. The number of increments usually is greater for teachers who have more than the bachelor's degree. The basic weakness in the use of salary increments is that the increment is not primarily a reward for increased efficiency or competence on the part of the teacher. No provision is made for merit raises because of outstanding work. If the increments do not extend over a long period of time, a teacher reaches a maximum salary early in his career and faces the prospect of 20 or more years of service with little chance of a raise unless he is able to obtain another position as a teacher, a supervisor, or an administrator. On the other hand, if the teacher is delayed too long in reaching a maximum salary, he may experience great hardships in the early part of his career as his dependency responsibilities expand. A few schools have followed the practice of granting large increases during the first few years of a teacher's service and smaller increments in the remaining period until the maximum is reached.

An increasing number of school districts have been using an index or ratio to determine the salaries of teachers. This kind of schedule typically uses the bachelor's degree with no experience as its base of 100 or 1.00. Increments for years of experience and for additional preparation beyond the bachelor's degree are calculated as percentages of the base. For example, the annual increment may be 6 per cent of the base, and an inexperienced teacher with a master's degree may receive a salary 10 per cent above the base. The index schedule has the advantage of establishing salary-step relationships that remain constant even though the dollar amounts change. If the base salary is raised, the increments increase, and the relative distance between the minimum and maximum salaries is not reduced [136:108].

Merit Rating and Salary Schedules

One of the very thorny problems with which teachers and school administrators are confronted involves rewards and penalties for quality of service. A salary schedule based entirely upon the amount of training and years of experience does

FIGURE 8–8.   Hypothetical index salary schedule. (*Source:* National Education Association.)

	Salary step	Bachelor's degree	Master's degree	Sixth year M.A. + 30	Doctor's degree	
Base: $ _ _ _ _ _ _						Base amount to be reviewed annually; NEA recommends $6,000
Uniform increments; 6 per cent of the bachelor's degree minimum	1	1.00	1.10	1.20	1.35	10 per cent above base for each additional year of professional preparation; 15 per cent for doctor's degree
	2	1.06	1.16	1.26	1.41	
	3	1.12	1.22	1.32	1.47	
	4	1.18	1.28	1.38	1.53	
	5	1.24	1.34	1.44	1.59	
	6	1.30	1.40	1.50	1.65	
	7	1.36	1.46	1.56	1.71	
12 increments for bachelor's degree class and 13 for master's degree class; typical of present practice	8	1.42	1.52	1.62	1.77	
	9	1.48	1.58	1.68	1.83	
	10	1.54	1.64	1.74	1.89	
	11	1.60	1.70	1.80	1.96	
	12	1.66	1.76	1.86	2.02	Twice the bachelor's degree minimum
	13	1.72	1.82	1.92	2.08	
	14		1.88	1.98	2.14	
	15				2.20	

not reward the teacher who is doing superior work or penalize the teacher who is doing an inferior job. Much of the pressure to alter this situation comes from those outside the teaching profession. The President's Commission on National Goals, for example, stated that "merit pay is another means of providing rewards commensurate with performance and should be universally adopted, with appropriate safeguards to insure fair treatment."[1]

Some of the arguments in favor of merit rating are as follows [11:2–5]:

1. It has been used successfully by business and industry.
2. It will attract and keep highly competent teachers.
3. The public will be willing to pay higher salaries for outstanding teachers.
4. It will lead to a general increase in the professional and social status of teachers in the community.
5. Teachers will have added incentive to improve their competence.
6. It will provide recognition for excellence of performance in the most meaningful way—financially.
7. A combination of rating devices, rankings, and records can be used successfully in evaluating the competence of teachers.
8. The present system of relating salaries solely to training and experience rewards unequal work equally.

Those opposed to merit rating maintain that [11:2–5]:

1. Teachers do not start with the same quality or amount of raw material as do those in an industry or business, nor do they produce a product that lends itself to easy and precise measurement. Teachers produce people, not things. No individual teacher is the sole cause of pupil success. Merit rating in the business world has shown distinct limitations, especially in rating management and executive personnel.
2. Higher salaries are not assured for superior teachers. Therefore, merit rating will not increase the supply of teachers.
3. By giving higher salaries to a few, the salary level of most teachers will be kept at a low level.
4. The only way in which status equivalent to that of other professional groups in the community can be assured is by raising the salaries of all teachers rather than by stressing the merit of a few.
5. Merit rating will foster conformity to the administrator's ideals, precepts, and concepts and destroy teacher creativity, originality, and initiative.
6. Good human relations between teachers and administrators, supervisors, and consultants wll be destroyed.
7. The intangibles in teacher performance resist accurate measurement. Furthermore, the great range of specialization in the modern school system militates against objectivity of evaluating teacher performance.
8. School systems already dismiss incompetent teachers by not placing them on tenure.

[1] National Goals in Education by John W. Gardner, from *Goals for Americans* © 1960, by The American Assembly, Columbia University, New York, pp. 82–83. By permission of Prentice-Hall, Inc.

9. Relationships between the public and the school will deteriorate, since parents will exert much pressure for their children to be placed in classes of teachers with higher ranks.

Both the National Education Association and the American Federation of Teachers have strongly opposed merit rating. In the resolutions adopted in 1965, for example, the National Education Association indicated that "the use of subjective methods of evaluating professional performance for the purpose of setting salaries has a deleterious effect on the educational process. Plans which require such subjective judgments (commonly known as merit ratings) should be avoided. American education can be better served by continued progress in developing better means of objective evaluation" [175:60]. As a result, the National Education Association advocates "continued research and experimentation to develop means of objective evaluation of the performance of all professional personnel, including identification of (1) factors that determine professional competence; (2) factors that determine the effectiveness of competent professionals; (3) methods of evaluating effective professional service; and (4) methods of recognizing effective professional service through self-realization, personal status, and salary" [175:60].

The National Education Association conducted a nationwide teachers' poll to determine how individual teachers view the issue of merit pay. The results indicated that 40.3 per cent strongly oppose, 32.5 per cent tend to oppose, 20.3 per cent tend to favor, and 6.9 per cent strongly favor merit pay. Secondary school teachers are more inclined to favor such a plan than are elementary teachers [283:31].

In the past, a number of school systems have experimented with provisions in the salary schedules to pay teachers who were judged to be superior higher salaries than the normal maximum of the regular salary schedule. These higher maximum salaries for superior service are a form of merit pay. Since a high percentage of the school systems abandoned the plan over a 20-year period, the National Education Association wrote to ninety-one of these school systems asking why it had been abandoned. The reasons listed included the following: the evaluation of teacher performance was unsatisfactory; dissension was created among the teachers; ratings were really not based on merit; a sense of injustice was created; the plan was opposed by the teachers organizations; it placed a heavy burden on the raters; it damaged the service of the principal [286:17].

The controversy over merit rating and merit pay will continue in the future. It would seem that any attempt along such lines should involve the following criteria developed by Edmund Thorne, superintendent of schools in West Hartford, Connecticut, where a merit-pay plan was initiated in 1953 (adapted):

1. The prime principle underlying the plan should be the improvement of instruction—to help teachers succeed and improve in their work.
2. Merit awards should be based upon predetermined criteria and not on percentage quotas.
3. A good professional salary schedule should already exist in the school system.
4. A merit-salary program should not be adopted until after it has had sufficient study and been accepted by a substantial majority of the staff.

5. The plan should be adapted to local conditions.
6. The plan should have the complete understanding and support of the administrative personnel, the board, and the public.
7. All personnel in the school system, including administrators, should be rated.
8. There should be well-defined standards of evaluation agreed to and understood by those who are to be evaluated.
9. There should be ample opportunity for evaluation.
10. Only those teachers who request it should be evaluated for merit-pay purposes, and conversely, teachers should be allowed to withdraw from the procedure if they so desire.
11. Merit awards should be commensurate with the value placed upon superior service.
12. Teachers must have confidence in those who are responsible for evaluating them.
13. Sufficient personnel should be provided to ensure adequate time for evaluation.
14. Final selection of merit teachers should be entrusted to more than one individual.
15. Individuals should be given the right to appeal.
16. An adequate budget should be established to provide continuity of program from one year to the next.
17. The plan should be continuously reevaluated in the light of new experience.
18. Provision should be made for informing new and potential staff members regarding the plan.

Trends in the Salaries of Men and Women Teachers

Statistics on average salaries indicate that men teachers receive higher salaries than do women teachers. It should be pointed out, however, that the discrimination against women teachers is not as great as it may seem. An appreciable number of women in the elementary schools still have far less than a college degree. A large number are teaching on substandard permits because of the shortage of elementary teachers. The great majority of men, however, teach on the high school level, where a degree is required. Furthermore, a high percentage of the administrative positions are filled by men. The fact that men have more training, for which a higher salary is paid, and that they fill a majority of the administrative positions may give the impression of higher discrimination against women than actually exists in the teaching profession. Actually, studies show that there is less inequality between men and women in teaching than in other professions [93:53].

The battle for equal pay for those with the same training and experience, especially on the college level, is not over. Basically, almost all would agree that the theory is sound, based on the assumption that teachers with the same amount of training and experience are making the same contributions to society. Furthermore, the idea is in harmony with democratic concepts. Any policy that fosters discrimination among a group of individuals who are equals is undemocratic. Teachers, above all, need to demonstrate concepts of democracy.

The advocates of a dual-salary schedule in regard to sex, however, feel that there should be more men teachers, especially in the elementary schools, than there are at present. Since the opportunities for men in industry are greater than those for women, schools should pay higher salaries to men in order to attract them to teaching. Advocates of the dual schedule also feel that equal pay provokes undue hardships on men teachers, who generally have more dependents than women. Some school systems have solved the problem of dependents partially by adopting a policy similar to one used in computing income tax; that is, all teachers are given allowances for the number of dependents. [88:52–54]. In a study of salary schedules in 1965–1966, however, it was found that only about 1 per cent of the school systems studied made provisions for added compensation for men teachers and for dependents [228:6].

Period of Time Teachers Receive Pay

The predominant practice in paying teachers is to distribute their salaries monthly over the period in which school is in session. For example, if you teach in a school that is in session for nine months during the year, you may expect to receive one-ninth of your pay at the end of the first month of service. A small percentage of school systems have adopted the policy of paying teachers semimonthly.

There seems to be a trend, however, for schools to distribute the pay of teachers over a 12-month period for services rendered while school is in session. This helps teachers to budget their salaries throughout the year. Otherwise they often find it necessary to borrow money during the summer vacation.

An increasing number of school systems are adopting a policy of expanding the period in which teachers are employed during the year. Some states—Florida, for example—employ teachers for an extra month of work. This enables the school staff to plan before schools open in the fall and after they close in the spring, providing a much-needed time for teachers to work together to improve their teaching.

Approximately 5 per cent [280:28] of the urban school systems hire teachers on a year-round basis and adjust the work accordingly. The school is organized so that teachers work in the classroom for the traditional nine to ten months. During the summer they may prepare teaching materials, revise curricula, attend workshops to improve teaching techniques, work in recreational programs, or study and then have one month's vacation with pay. Advocates of the year-round employment plan maintain that [87:7]:

Teaching has changed from a part-time to a full-time profession.
Orientation programs give new teachers the opportunity to do a more effective job.
Time for workshops and committee meetings is available, which gives opportunities for greater teacher growth in service.
Teachers are doing during the summer those things for which they are trained. Thus the school system is making better use of both its personnel and physical facilities.
Teachers can do things, such as prepare teaching materials and revise curriculum, that time limits or even prohibits during the regular year.
The total staff—teachers, counselors, and administrators—have the opportunity

to develop a better perspective of the total school program because of the opportunities they have to work toward the mutual solution of problems.

Most superintendents and a large percentage of principals are employed on a year-round basis, which accounts in part for their salaries being higher than those of classroom teachers.

As indicated in Chapter 1, increasingly greater demands will be made of school personnel in the future, especially for adult education and recreational services. Undoubtedly these demands will tend to extend the year-round contract idea. In the meantime, the employment of teachers by the school system during the summer probably will take more nearly the form of a greatly expanded summer school.

Extra Earnings of Teachers

"Extra pay," "additive salaries," "off-schedule salaries," or "compensation for irregularities" are terms used to identify provisions for paying teachers for assignments beyond the regular school day or term. The most common activities that fall within the range of the definition are coaching athletics, directing bands, directing choirs, directing dramatics, and sponsoring school publications.

A study conducted by the research division of the National Education Association [89:1–29] revealed that a scale of flat rates usually was provided in salary schedules as extra pay for specific coaching duties or other supervisory assignments outside of school hours. The amount varied somewhat according to the size of the school. The highest pay was reported for head football coaches, whose extra compensation ranged from $400 to $2,800 [89:1–17]. Head basketball coaches were the next highest paid, while head baseball and track coaches were paid about equally. Extra compensation for supervisory assignments involving dramatics, band, newspaper, or yearbook approximated $300.

A number of educators feel that the total educational program is undermined by extra-pay policies which encourage teachers to assume duties requiring time that should be devoted to teaching responsibilities. Some feel that it is a type of exploitation, since it would cost far more to employ enough teachers to do the extra work. There is no question that limited budgets and teacher shortages are forcing many school districts to depend upon extra-pay practices in order to provide for these extra duties.

Other types of extra-pay activities involve a wide range of jobs in which teachers engage outside the school hours. During the school year these jobs usually relate in some way to the specialized field of the teacher, such as giving private music lessons, teaching adult education classes, driving a school bus, giving public lectures, sewing, and serving as a consultant to a business. At least 16 per cent of the urban school districts impose limitations on the employment of teachers outside school [280:29]. The most common requirements are that outside employment must not interfere with teaching duties and that approval of the board, superintendent, or other administrative officer must be secured.

During the summer months teachers engage in a wide variety of jobs. Some of these jobs are in keeping with the professional preparation of teachers (such as teaching in summer school, serving as camp counselors, and supervising summer

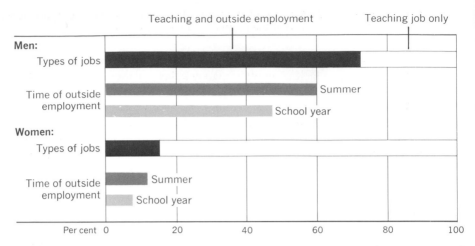

FIGURE 8–9. Outside employment of teachers in 1960–1961. *(Source:* National Education Association.)

recreational activities) and many are not. Many teachers feel that they can enhance their classroom teaching by "rubbing shoulders" with the outside world, thus not only keeping abreast of technical advances, but also helping form closer ties between the schools and the community.

As more schools offer summer school programs, more teachers will have opportunities to increase their annual earnings. Dr. Lambert of the research division of the National Education Association predicts that by 1970 or 1980 as many as 50 per cent of all pupils will be attending summer sessions [77:45].

Trends in Salaries for College Teachers

It is more difficult to present precise salary schedules for college teachers than for public school teachers because of the fluctuation of college salaries based on the supply and demand for instructional personnel. Approximately one-half of the colleges and universities have clearly defined salary schedules with designated increments. It is apparent, however, that improvements in college salary practices have lagged behind those in the public schools.

The most common type of college salary schedule utilizes minimum and maximum salaries according to rank, i.e., instructor, assistant professor, associate professor, and full professor. The limits as well as the average salaries within each of these ranks vary considerably among institutions as well as among departments within institutions. For example, the average salary received by a full professor in a small private college may be more than the salary received by a teacher of comparable rank in a large university, or vice versa. Also, the full professor in the English department of a large university may be receiving a lower salary than a full professor in the law college. The teachers in the college, school, or department of education in larger institutions generally receive slightly higher salaries than other college personnel in all ranks because of the amount of public school experience required and competing salaries in public school work.

The research division of the National Education Association completed, in 1966, an extensive study of salaries in the degree-granting institutions in the United States [226:1–65]. Table 6 indicates the median salaries, according to rank, for *nine* months of full-time teaching in all colleges and universities included in the study. It also indicates the percentage of increase for a period of two years.

The salary range for each of the ranks was wide. For example, one-fourth of those holding the rank of professor had a salary of $15,131 or greater, and one-fourth earned salaries of $11,085 or less [226:22]. The highest median salaries for professors were paid in the larger nonpublic universities, followed by the larger state universities, the smaller nonpublic universities, public universities having enrollments of 5,000 to 9,999, state colleges, and the larger nonpublic colleges. In terms of geographic regions, the median salaries for all full-time college teachers were highest in the Far West, followed by New England, Great Lakes, Mideast, Southwest, Rocky Mountains, Plains, and Southeast in the order named.

The median salary for nine months of full-time teaching in public junior colleges in 1965–1966 was $8,361 [226:53], which was higher than the median salary in nonpublic junior colleges ($6,407).

In addition to the actual salaries paid, almost all institutions provide various types of fringe benefits such as health, accident, and life insurance and contributions to retirement funds. Although the range is considerable, these benefits may be equivalent to approximately 11 per cent of the actual salaries paid.

The study also included the median 12-month salaries of various college administrative officers. The results are indicated in Table 7.

Practically all multipurpose institutions, state colleges, and teachers colleges have summer instruction programs in which approximately one-half of the regular full-time teachers have an opportunity to supplement their salaries by teaching courses [226:27]. Some college teachers are able to earn an appreciable amount of money by writing for publication or by serving as consultants in school systems, in businesses, or in industries.

The demand for college teachers in the future will be very great. From both an instructional and an administrative standpoint the way is open to substantial rewards if you are willing to undergo the rather rigorous tasks of preparing yourself for teaching on the college level.

TABLE 6   Median Salaries for Nine Months of Full-time Teaching in All Colleges and Universities, 1963–1964 and 1965–1966

Rank	Median salaries		Increase, per cent
	1963–1964	1965–1966	
Professor	$11.312	$12,953	14.5
Associate professor	8,969	10,058	12.1
Assistant professor	7,539	8,417	11.6
Instructor	6,114	6,761	10.6

Source: Adapted from *Salaries in Higher Education, 1965–1966,* Research Report 1966-R2, National Education Association, Research Division, Washington, February, 1966, p. 11.

TABLE 7   Median Salaries of Certain Administrative Officers in Colleges and Universities, 1963–1964 and 1965–1966

| | Median salaries | | 2-year increase, per cent |
Office	1963–1964	1965–1966	
President	$17,330	$19,638	13.3
Vice-president	17,130	19,012	11.0
Dean of the college	13,644	15,703	15.1
Dean of students	10,694	12,027	12.5
Dean of men	9,144	9,783	7.0
Dean of women	8,216	9,209	12.1
Dean of admissions	9,572	10,364	8.3
Registrar	8,142	9,123	12.0
Business manager	10,512	11,780	12.1
Head librarian	8,883	10,225	15.1
Director of athletics	9,871	11,125	12.7
Head football coach	9,321	10,716	15.0
Head basketball coach	8,542	9,383	9.8

Source: Adapted from *Salaries in Higher Education, 1965–1966*, Research Report 1966–R2, National Education Association, Research Division, Washington, February, 1966, p. 34.

Minimum-salary Standards

The National Education Association has fought vigorously for many years for higher salaries for teachers. In commenting on the need for better pay scales in order to attract teachers of high professional caliber, one spokesman has said: "A community which employs teachers of less than professional quality condemns many of its children to lifetimes of mediocrity or perhaps of frustration and maladjustment. The price of poor teaching is prohibitive. The cost of adequate salaries is much less" [153:662].

You have noted previously the salaries recommended by the National Education Association for degree-qualified beginning teachers and for experienced teachers with master's degrees. Furthermore, the National Education Association maintains that a professional salary schedule should [175:58]

a. Be based upon preparation, teaching experience, and professional growth.
b. Provide a beginning salary adequate to attract capable young people into the profession.
c. Provide increments sufficient to double the bachelor's degree minimum within ten years for professionally qualified teachers with a master's degree, with further salary increases for additional preparation and experience.
d. Recognize advanced education by providing specific salary classes for successive levels through the doctor's degree.
e. Be developed cooperatively by school board members, administrators, and teachers.

f. Permit no discrimination as to grade or subject taught, residence, creed, race, sex, marital status, or number of dependents.

g. Recognize by salary ratios the responsibilities of administrators and other appropriate school personnel.

h. Be revised by methods which prevent deterioration in the ratios of maximum salaries, experience increments, and preparational differentials to beginning salaries.

i. Be applied in actual practice.

It is encouraging to note the amount of progress that is being made in school systems throughout the nation in their efforts to prepare salary schedules based on the principles recommended by the National Education Association. As continued changes are made toward the achievement of these minimum- and maximum-salary recommendations, teachers certainly will gain greater professional status.

Appraising Salary Schedules

As a part of this course, you may wish to study the salary schedules of various school systems. The checklist located in the Resource Section for Part III of this book should help you in appraising the schedules. When you seek a position in the years to come, you should find the checklist to be of much value to you.

Teachers' Responsibilities for Improving Salaries

Low teachers' salaries in the past have been excused somewhat upon the grounds that teachers love their work and therefore are willing to receive low salaries. This thesis is no longer acceptable, and teachers have a responsibility for correcting this outmoded philosophy. It is thoroughly respectable for a professional group to work ethically toward the improvement of salaries. The public must realize that, as is true of virtually everything in life, there is a direct relationship between quality and price. Quality education is expensive. On the other hand, in this day and age, poor education is even more expensive in terms of the welfare of our society. This the public must understand, and you, as a teacher, have an obligation to help the public gain this understanding.

SUMMARY

Although some very definite improvements have been made during the past several years, the average salaries of teachers are low compared with those of other professions requiring comparable training. *Any average salary listed must be interpreted carefully in the light of all factors that enter into the establishment of an average.* It would be desirable for you to view teaching in terms of existing and probable future salary schedules for beginning teachers.

There is positive evidence that the general public is increasingly concerned about the economic welfare of teachers. Because of the organized efforts of educators and others, the prospects of improving teachers' salaries look promising.

Teachers have a responsibility to work ethically toward the improvement of their salaries. The general public may need help in understanding that poorly paid teachers constitute poor economy in terms of the future welfare of our nation. *(Photograph from the National Education Association.)*

Some positive trends are to be noted in the scheduling of teachers' salaries: the establishment of minimum salaries for beginning teachers, definite yearly salary increments, the same pay for men and women who have equal training and experience, and a single-salary schedule for elementary and secondary teachers. Unfortunately, the practice of having salary schedules on the college level has lagged behind that of the public schools.

Improvements in the scheduling of salaries should encourage competent teachers to remain in the profession for a longer period of time, attract more people with promise into the profession, and enable educators to be more selective of those who are prepared, certified, and employed as teachers. As these factors operate, the level of the teaching profession will be raised; this, in turn, will tend to raise salaries.

QUESTIONS FOR YOUR CONSIDERATION

1. What factors should be kept in mind as you interpret average salaries of teachers?
2. Can you think of any teachers who are being overpaid? If so, upon what grounds do you base your judgment? What should the school board do about these situations?
3. How can you defend equal pay for men and women teachers, providing they have equal training and experience?
4. How do you account for the fact that public school teachers are not as well paid as members of other professions? What should be done in order to obtain salaries comparable to those received in the other professions?
5. What are the advantages and disadvantages of a salary schedule that is based entirely upon the amount of training and experience of teachers?
6. In your opinion, how should superior teachers be rewarded?
7. To what extent do you feel that teachers should be given salary allowances for the number of dependents they have?
8. Are you in favor of the trend for schools to distribute the pay of teachers over a 12-month period for services rendered during a 9- or 10-month school year? Why?
9. What advantages and disadvantages do you see in the year-round employment plan for teachers? Should schools be operated on a 12-month plan?
10. For what extra duties should a teacher be paid? What should be the basis for the amount of pay? Discuss these questions with your colleagues.
11. Some teachers work on jobs during after-school hours and on weekends. Do you favor such practices? Upon what grounds might a school board specify that teachers are not to engage in such practices?
12. How can you account for the wide range in the salaries of college teachers? To what extent and by what means should these salaries be made more equitable?
13. How might you work positively toward the improvement of salaries for teachers?

ACTIVITIES FOR YOU TO PURSUE

1. Consult your hometown superintendent of schools regarding the bases upon which his teachers are paid. Discuss with him the problems of salary schedules.
2. Secure information on the salary schedules for all school systems in which you might like to have a position. Compare them in terms of minimums, maximums, number and size of increments, credit for previous teaching experience, credit for advanced professional work, provisions for recognition of outstanding work, and the like.
3. Compare the salary schedules of school systems in various types of communities, sections of the United States, and foreign countries.
4. Make a careful study of different kinds of occupations to discover the extent

to which the salaries or wages of men differ from those of women who possess equal training and experience.

5. Discuss teachers' salaries with community members in various types of work to determine how they feel about the subject.

6. Discuss with lawyers, doctors, dentists, engineers, and other professional workers the satisfactions they receive from their work and earnings. Have them compare and contrast the work and the earnings of teachers with their professions. Consult the latest issues of *Economic Status of Teachers,* National Education Association, Research Division, to determine how teachers' salaries compare with salaries in other occupations. Report your findings to your colleagues.

7. Estimate, by referring to a typical salary schedule, your yearly earnings for the period you plan to teach. Consider carefully the extent to which you would be able to develop an adequate budget in terms of your wants.

8. Read some articles in current professional magazines regarding the advantages and disadvantages of merit raises. Report your findings to your colleagues.

9. Set up a teachers' salary schedule for a school system based upon the NEA salary recommendations.

10. Organize a panel to discuss the controversial issue of federal aid for teachers' salaries.

11. Using the checklist in the Resource Section for Part III, attempt to appraise the salary schedule in your home community.

9

OTHER ECONOMIC BENEFITS

Practically everyone wants to be economically secure. But what does it mean to *you?* Does it mean only a high salary or are there other factors to be taken into consideration as you plan your life? Do you want to be reasonably certain of steady employment; of not losing your job unjustifiably? What would happen to you and your dependents if you should become ill or disabled? What are your resources if you need money quickly? There are always the possibilities of accidents, medical operations, and other personal calamities. Effective planning takes into consideration these emergency situations.

What provisions are made for retirement? Yes—you are young, and it may seem unnecessary to be thinking about retirement before you are out of college. Naturally, you are more interested in preparing for a career in teaching rather than in ending it. You feel young, energetic, ambitious, and healthy, and retirement seems far away. You are right. But time passes quickly. In a few years you will most likely be assuming heavier obligations—marriage, dependents, a home, and various other financial obligations. Under such circumstances provisions for retirement become much more real. Effective long-range career planning involves all these factors—including retirement.

This chapter should help you plan in terms of certain extra benefits inherent in a teaching career. It will contain discussions of teacher tenure, leaves of absence, group insurance, credit unions, and retirement benefits.

TEACHER TENURE

The term "teacher tenure" is used in referring to the length of time that a teacher remains in a particular school. In this regard it is a well-known fact that teachers, especially in rural areas where the salaries are low, tend to change positions frequently. It is not uncommon for a third or more of the teachers in a rural school to be new each year. Although adequate data are not available, it is believed that over 90 per cent of the changes that occur in these situations are voluntary on the part of teachers, many of whom move to better teaching or administrative positions. A significant percentage of married women temporarily discontinue teaching to rear families. Some teachers leave the field and do other types of work. A few are judged by boards of education to be unsatisfactory and are not reemployed.

Teacher tenure, in another sense, refers to the prospects that a competent teacher has of remaining in a position without being dismissed for unjustifiable reasons. It refers to the amount of protection a teacher has against losing his job.

Teacher Tenure in the Past

Teacher tenure has not always been as strong as it is today. It was once common practice to dismiss competent teachers from other areas in order to make room for those in the town. The sons and daughters of the important people of a community who wanted teaching positions usually were successful in easing out others who did not enjoy such parental affiliations. School board members have fired competent people and hired others who were willing to be bribed. Hiring and firing of teachers depended more upon a school official's liking for a teacher than upon a careful examination of the person's competency for teaching. In these circumstances most of a teacher's energies were directed toward cultivating and maintaining the goodwill of the community members in whose hands the security of his position rested. He was careful of his political and religious affiliations. He taught that the earth was square if it seemed desirable to teach that way. Special attention was given to pupils who were sons or daughters of the influential people. Great care was taken to avoid a discussion of any local problem or controversial issue that might incur the disapproval of some community member. The teacher's position often was subject to the whims, selfish interests, or ignorant and unscrupulous motives of those who had little or no concern for the welfare of children.

Reasons for Teacher Tenure

For a number of years the general public has recognized that civil employees need protection against prejudice and pressure groups if they are to do their jobs effectively. In government work this protection is provided through civil service appointments. The public now realizes more thoroughly the importance of the job of the teacher in our society and his need for position security because of the peculiar nature of teaching. The teacher has the task of transmitting and professionally refining the culture and of promoting understanding of the problems and purposes of modern group living. In order to accomplish this task the teacher must be protected from vacillating public opinion and unjustified dismissal; otherwise children suffer in the long run, and the schools are no longer instruments of *all* the people.

Professional organizations, spearheaded by the National Education Association, have been successful in securing considerable legislation for the protection of teachers. On the assumption that a better teacher means a better school and that the betterment of teaching depends in part on the improvement of teaching conditions, the Committee on Tenure and Academic Freedom of the NEA has set forth the following reasons for tenure [9:6–7]:

1. To protect classroom teachers and other members of the teaching profession against unjust dismissal of any kind—political, religious or personal.
2. To prevent the management or domination of the schools by political or non-educational groups for selfish and other improper purposes.
3. To secure for the teacher employment conditions which will encourage him to grow in the full practice of his profession, unharried by constant pressure and fear.

4. To encourage competent, independent thinkers to enter and to remain in the teaching profession.
5. To encourage school management, which might have to sacrifice the welfare of the schools to fear and favor, to devote itself to the cause of education.
6. To set up honest, orderly, and definite procedures by which undesirable people may be removed from the teaching profession.
7. To protect educators in their efforts to promote the financial and educational interests of public school children.
8. To protect teachers in the exercise of their rights and duties of American citizenship.
9. To enable teachers, in spite of reactionary minorities, to prepare children for life in a democracy under changing conditions.

Kinds of Tenure Provided for Teachers

An analysis of contracts and tenure laws reveals many differences in the degree of security provided for teachers. These differences are understandable when you realize that in the beginning each school system was largely responsible for developing its own policies. Through the work of professional organizations and state legislation, however, policies have become more standardized.

Generally speaking, tenure provisions for teachers may be classified into the following types: annual contracts, contracts that extend for a definite number of years, continuing contracts with spring notification, protective continuing contracts, and permanent tenure.

You should understand the general provisions of the various types of contracts and laws indicated above, since they may have a significant influence upon where you accept a teaching position.

Annual contracts. A beginning teacher usually is given a contract which gives him a legal right to teach in a school system for one year only. A school year generally is considered to be that period of time between the opening of school in the fall and the closing date in the spring or summer. The teacher cannot be dismissed by the board of education during this period without justifiable cause. In some states, the bases for dismissal are written into the contracts given to the teacher, and in some they are found in the state statutes governing schools. The term "justifiable cause" generally involves incompetence, inefficiency, immorality, insubordination, neglect of duty, unprofessional conduct, and physical or mental disability. Some laws specifically include intoxication, dishonesty, and commission of a felony. A few states require that the causes for dismissal be indicated in writing. The teacher may have a right to contest a dismissal, either in court or through the professional organizations. At the close of the school year a board of education has no obligation to reemploy a teacher for another year.

In return for the protection that the annual contract provides, the teacher has an obligation to the employing officials. As Stinnett points out, "The truly ethical person takes great pride in strict observance of a written agreement or oral pledge" [254:328]. Furthermore, it is often difficult to find a competent teacher to replace one who decides to discontinue teaching. In order to protect the welfare of the children in the school, the teacher who wishes to terminate his services usually is required to give 30 days' notice of his intention to resign, whether that resignation is before the beginning of school or during the school year, and to secure the consent of the board of education. It is true that there is nothing to prevent a teacher from just quitting his position. If he does this, however, his certificate for teaching probably would be revoked by the state board of education, in which case he would be unable to secure another position in that state.

Contracts for a definite number of years. In the states of Mississippi, Texas, and Utah it is permissible by law to issue contracts for more than one year upon the initial assignment of a teacher. These contracts definitely specify the maximum term of employment. They usually extend for only a reasonable period of time beyond the term of office of the employing officials. They may be renewed for another definite number of years.

Continuing contracts with spring notification. A teacher employed on an annual contract might not know whether he is to be reappointed until it is too late in the year to find a position elsewhere. In order to improve this situation, a number of states have what is called the "spring notification type of continuing-contract law." This type of contract provides for a teacher to be automatically reemployed for the next year unless notified of dismissal before a specified date. The date, such as April 15, is early enough for the teacher to find a position elsewhere, if necessary. Usually there is no obligation on the part of the school board to renew any contract. Illinois, Maine, and West Virginia require a statement of the reasons for not reemploying a teacher. In reality, the typical continuing-contract law offers only a limited amount of protection to teachers.

Protective continuing contracts. Some of the states have a protective type of continuing contract. With this type of contract a teacher is employed from year to year without being dismissed except by a prescribed procedure to be followed by the board of education in regard to the notice, the statement of charges, and the right to a hearing. This type of contract gives teachers virtually as much protection as a true tenure law. A probationary period of three years normally is required before a teacher is granted this type of contract. During this probationary period, the teacher's annual contract is not renewed if he does not measure up to the standards held by the school system. This probationary period protects the school from becoming overloaded with incompetent teachers.

Many school officials follow the practice of warning the teacher who has a protective-type continuing contract that his contract will not be continued unless certain conditions are improved. This practice seems to be in harmony with good school administration. The teacher is given the added assurance that he will not lose his position without having a chance to improve any unsatisfactory aspects of his work.

In order to dismiss a teacher who is employed on a protective-type continuing contract the board of education must notify the teacher at an early date of its intentions and must state the reasons for dismissal. The teacher is provided an opportunity for defending himself if he so desires.

Permanent tenure. The greatest amount of tenure that you may be able to gain will be in a situation that provides for what is commonly called "permanent tenure." After serving a probationary period ranging from one to five years, the continuous employment of a teacher is assured, provided he renders efficient service and shows appropriate conduct.

The procedure for dismissing a teacher on permanent tenure is very similar to that required by the protective-type continuing contract. The employing officials must establish good cause for dismissal with higher authorities. Usually the bases upon which teachers can be dismissed are written into the tenure laws. A teacher has the right to request a formal review or trial of the case before a special committee or court, provided he feels that inadequate reasons for his dismissal can be shown. Permanent tenure differs primarily from tenure under continuing contracts in that under the former arrangement the case normally is not tried before the employing officials. Many teachers feel that the teacher who is to be dismissed is at an unfair advantage if he has to appeal his case to employing officials who serve as both accusers and judges.

Characteristics of Good Tenure Laws

Thirty-seven states and the District of Columbia have teacher tenure laws, either on a statewide basis or in certain designated areas that apply to teacher contracts. An analysis of the provisions of these laws indicates considerable variation. You may find the following characteristics of good tenure laws, formulated by the National Education Association [adapted, 267:9–11], to be helpful in appraising tenure laws in the various states in which you may be interested in teaching:

1. A teacher should be employed on a probationary basis for a definite number of years—possibly a three-year period. The law should specify whether this employment is to be on an annual- or a spring-notification type of continuing contract and should indicate the conditions and procedures regarding dismissal that are contained in the contract.
2. After the teacher has successfully completed the probationary period the law should specify that the superintendent is required to recommend the teacher for tenure status.
3. The law should establish definite, orderly, legal procedures for dismissing unsatisfactory teachers by requiring that there be:
    a. Adequate notice given to the teacher.
    b. Charges stated in writing and including a record of criticism and aid offered.
    c. A hearing before the entire board, either private or public as the teacher may request.
    d. Benefit of counsel and witnesses.
    e. Safeguard of salary rights during suspension.
    f. Final appeal to higher educational authorities or to the courts.
4. In cases of demotion or suspension, the law should make virtually the same provisions as for a dismissal case.
5. The tenure law should apply to all teachers, whether in rural, village, or city schools and without regard for race or color. Any less comprehensive law is discriminatory and divisive.

6. In cases of economic emergencies or depletion of school enrollments, a tenure law should provide for the fair and systematic dismissal of teachers along the following lines:

   a. A qualified tenure teacher should replace a probationary teacher.

   b. Tenure teachers should be dismissed in reverse order of seniority.

   c. Dismissed teachers should be reemployed in order of length of service and tenure status.

7. The law should define the status of the temporary teacher.

Status of Teacher Tenure

Figure 9-1 will give you a fairly accurate picture of the status of state tenure or contract provisions in effect in the various states. Some exceptions should be noted in the thirty-seven states and the District of Columbia that have state tenure laws. In Connecticut, special tenure laws govern certain cities. In Florida, special tenure laws govern certain counties. Special local acts take precedence over state tenure laws in eight counties in Alabama. Tenure is optional in California districts with average daily attendance under 250 pupils. Illinois school districts under a board of directors are excluded from tenure laws. Certain rural school districts

FIGURE 9–1. Types of state tenure or contract provisions in effect in various states. (*Source:* National Education Association.)

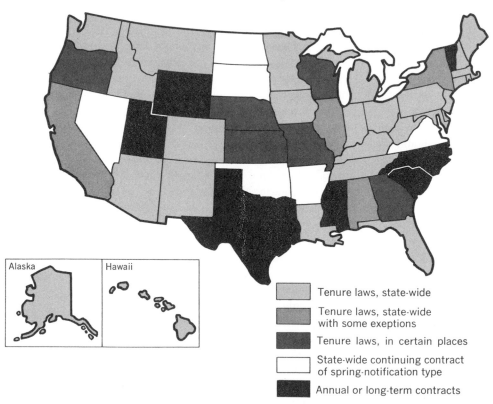

Alaska   Hawaii

Tenure laws, state-wide

Tenure laws, state-wide with some exeptions

Tenure laws, in certain places

State-wide continuing contract of spring-notification type

Annual or long-term contracts

in New York are not covered by tenure laws. Annual contracts are the usual practice in the nontenure areas of Georgia and Kansas. Continuing-contract laws of the spring-notification type apply to the nontenure areas of Missouri, Nebraska, Oregon, and Wisconsin. Of the thirteen states without tenure laws, five have mandatory statewide continuing-contract laws of the spring-notification type. In Virginia such provisions are subject to local adoption. Provisions for annual or long-term contracts are found in the other seven states.

In general, the tenure laws include supervisors, principals, teachers, and other school personnel. The types of employees covered are specifically mentioned in many tenure laws. A few laws extend tenure status to classroom teachers alone or only to teachers and principals. Twelve laws explicitly include superintendents, and in five states superintendents are definitely excluded [268:82].

A number of states grant school superintendents contracts that extend for three, four, or five years. The recognized head of a school system is especially vulnerable to the shifting attitudes and reactions of community members; hence, it is felt that he should be granted more protection than is afforded in a one-year contract.

The research division of the National Education Association periodically publishes reports on the status of tenure in the various states. Your college library probably has copies of these reports. You may also secure information by writing to the department of education of the particular state in which you are interested.

Tenure in Institutions of Higher Education

Colleges and universities generally have been free to develop their own policies regarding tenure. As a result, considerable variation exists among the institutions. The continuing contract seems to be the favored type of tenure. The college teacher who is new to an institution usually serves a probationary period before he is granted tenure status. The length of the probationary period varies among, as well as within, institutions. Variations within are governed largely by the rank of the teacher. The instructor serves approximately five years before being placed on tenure; whereas the assistant, associate, and full professors serve respectively shorter periods.

. The American Association of University Professors acts as a board of appeals for a college teacher who is in danger of being dismissed. An investigation is conducted by an appointed committee of the AAUP. If, in the judgment of the committee, the college or university is using unjustifiable procedures in dismissing staff members, the association usually places it on its blacklist until such procedures are changed. The blacklisting of an institution gives it unfavorable publicity with the general public and weakens its standing among other colleges. College teachers are hesitant to accept positions in such institutions. As a result, a college or university does not wish to incur the disfavor of the association.

Objections to Teacher Tenure

There have been some objections, of which you should be aware, raised by community members and some school officials to placing teachers on tenure. The fact that thirteen states still do not have tenure laws indicates that, even though great strides have been made, the battle for tenure laws is far from won.

It is maintained by some that competent teachers do not need tenure protection. The argument is true, no doubt, for a vast majority of teachers. The relationships of schools and communities in some sections, however, may not have reached a level at which the "spirit of the law may function without the law." For example, in some cases the employing officials, particularly those in small schools, follow the practice of never permitting teachers to gain permanent-tenure status, and in this way they avoid problems of having to dismiss tenure teachers. They have the feeling that it is too difficult to collect objective evidence to show incompetence and that unpleasant publicity might result from having to dismiss a tenure teacher. As a result, they fail to reemploy a teacher just prior to the time that tenure status would be granted. Hence, these teachers expect to remain in a school system no longer than the probationary period, regardless of their competency.

Before you accept a position, investigate the practices used by a specific district in placing teachers on tenure. The chief sources of information will be the employing officials, teachers already in the school system, your college instructors, teacher-placement personnel, and the state office of the state education association.

Many maintain that incompetent teachers on tenure are too difficult to dismiss. This argument is advanced especially against permanent tenure. Perhaps the basic weakness lies in the administration of the tenure law rather than in the law itself.

It is claimed that a teacher on tenure has little or no incentive to grow professionally. Undoubtedly, there are far too many tenure teachers for whom this objection is justified. Some school systems counteract this tendency by requiring teachers every five or more years to show evidence of professional growth. Reviews of a teacher's work should be made periodically. If the teacher has made no improvement, he should be placed on probation for a period of time adequate for the situation to be corrected. If he fails to make the desired improvement, he should be dismissed. All teachers must assume the obligation of continuing to grow in order to be deserving of tenure privileges. It should be remembered that tenure is a privilege rather than a built-in right of a teacher.

As long as you remain in the teaching profession, continue your study of teacher tenure laws with a view to discovering their weak spots and to proposing corrections that should be made. In the states where there is no teacher tenure, attempt to obtain statewide tenure laws that will provide the best possible protection for teachers.

LEAVES OF ABSENCE

Regardless of the type of work you do, it is highly probable that you will be ill at some time during your career. Or family emergencies such as sickness and death may make unforeseen demands upon you. Or you will need, for your professional growth as a teacher, to attend professional meetings—particularly educational workshops, visit other schools, and engage in various projects which will enrich your work in the classroom. In teaching, these kinds of absences from regular classroom duties may be classified as temporary or as sabbatical leaves.

Provisions for Temporary Leaves

Teachers generally enjoy good health, and the job is less hazardous, from the standpoint of accidents, than many other types of work. However, teachers occasionally do become ill or have other reasons for being absent from their work. If the teacher who is ill is encouraged to work in order to avoid loss of pay, he endangers the welfare of the pupils through both his inefficiency and his poor health. Thus, sick leaves are granted by school systems more frequently than leaves for any other cause. There are, however, a number of other reasons widely accepted for absence from the classroom. They have been classified under the following three headings [260:2]:

A. Personal and Family
   1. Personal illness or injury
   2. Maternity
   3. Religious holidays
   4. Death in immediate family
   5. Illness in immediate family (including quarantine)
   6. Wedding or birth in immediate family
   7. Moving from one domicile to another
   8. Emergencies
B. Professional
   1. Attending or participating in educational meetings
   2. Visiting other schools
   3. Studying at colleges and universities
   4. Traveling for professional improvement
   5. Exchange teaching
   6. Joining the Peace Corps
   7. Serving the organized teaching profession through a local, state, or national education association as an officer, committee member, speaker, or legislative agent
C. Civic
   1. Answering a court summons
   2. Serving on a jury
   3. Voting; serving as an election official
   4. Serving in an elective office
   5. Participating in community-sponsored projects (fund drives, civic celebrations, etc.)
   6. Military duty

Short-term leaves of absence are granted by a majority of the larger school systems so that a teacher will not lose pay when an emergency or other compelling circumstance not involving personal illness requires him to be away from his job for a brief period of time [239:1]. Short-term leaves may be granted in such cases as death in the immediate family, illness in the immediate family, attendance at professional meetings, answering a court summons, jury duty, professional organization work, visits to other schools, military reserve duty, religious holidays, and personal business. Plans for granting short-term leaves vary greatly. Provisions are made for a teacher to be absent for a certain number of days at full pay or part pay each year.

The laws of thirty-six states and the District of Columbia make statutory provisions for teachers' sick leaves [148:2]. Almost all modern school systems grant sick leaves, with 10 days' full pay for sick leave per year being the most common [240:2]. It is unfortunate that practices in rural sections have lagged behind those in cities. A few states provide for sick leave on an annual basis, with no carry-over being allowed. The more typical plan, however, calls for an accumulation of unused leave from year to year, up to a specified total amount usually ranging from 20 to 100 days. On the other hand, California, Hawaii, and New Jersey do not place any limit upon the amount that may be accumulated. There is a definite trend in favor of the accumulation of leave time, up to a maximum, since it provides teachers with greater protection during extended periods of illness.

As is the case in any occupational group, a few individuals are inclined to abuse provisions that have been made for such matters as sick leave. For this reason, some school officials require teachers to provide written statements declaring that personal illness necessitated their absence from teaching. Usually a doctor's statement is required if the illness extends over a period of two or more days [240:4]. In a few school systems teachers upon retirement are paid for unused accumulated sick leave. In at least seven states (California, Florida, Indiana, North Carolina, Ohio, Virginia, and Washington) legislative provisions have been made for sick leave accumulated in one school district to be transferred to another school district within the same state [240:6].

Provision for maternity leave is not quite so common as provision for sick leave, but it is being provided in an increasing number of school districts. This provision enables married women to live normal lives without fear of endangering their positions. As a general rule, such leaves are without pay, but they assure teachers the right to return to their positions after a stated period of time.

School boards generally require teachers to apply for maternity leaves four to six months prior to the anticipated birth of the child [160:2–4]. Usually an application for maternity leave must be accompanied by a physician's statement confirming the expected date of birth. The period of leave granted after the birth of the child ranges from three to twelve months.

In addition to maternity leaves, extended leaves of absence for classroom teachers are being granted in an increasing number of school systems for such purposes as military service, professional study (other than sabbatical), exchange teaching abroad, restoration of health, work in professional organizations, government service such as the Peace Corps, Department of Defense schools, travel, research, exchange teaching in the United States, election to a political office, and work experience [86:2]. An extended leave enables a teacher to leave his classroom for a semester or more without losing his job or salary status. A policy of granting extended leaves helps to encourage professional improvement, keeps good teachers in the profession, and improves the educational program in general [86:1]. As one might expect, policies governing extended leaves vary considerably from school system to school system.

Provisions for temporary leaves in colleges and universities tend to be less formal than in public schools. It is generally assumed that the college teacher will occasionally be absent in order to attend professional meetings, lecture, consult with public school teachers, and the like. By virtue of the nature of the work, it is easier to provide for the temporary absence of college teachers than for that of public school teachers.

Teachers for whom temporary leaves are provided are more fortunate than many other types of workers. Doctors and lawyers, for example, lose their fees and possibly some of their clientele when they are absent from their offices. When a person's income depends upon the amount of work he performs, he does not enjoy the same protection that teachers do when on temporary leave.

Provisions for Sabbatical Leave

The granting of sabbatical leave is a very common practice on the college level of teaching. The term originated from the practice of granting an extended leave to teachers every seventh year, and the seven-year period of service is usually a requirement today for sabbatical-leave eligibility. The purpose of the leave is to provide an opportunity for the teacher to improve himself professionally. The amount of time granted varies among institutions from a semester to a full year. The salary received on leave varies from full pay in a few cases to a fraction (usually one-half) of the teacher's regular earnings.

The practice of granting sabbatical leave in colleges and universities probably has had some influence on granting extended leaves to public school teachers. A growing number of public school systems provide for sabbatical leave. Nineteen states and the District of Columbia have statutory provisions for sabbatical leaves for public school teachers [148:2]. Sixty per cent of the larger school systems throughout the United States have made provisions for paid sabbatical leaves [86:2]. The amount of pay varies from the full amount of the regular salary to none at all, with the great majority allowing one-half salary to the teacher on sabbatical leave [225:2]. In some cases the teacher receives the difference between the cost of a substitute and his regular salary. It is fairly common to grant extended leaves without pay to public school teachers who wish to continue their studies toward advanced degrees. By receiving the advanced degree, the teacher may place himself in a higher salary bracket, and although he suffers a temporary loss in salary, he is able to gain financially in the future. The teacher who is granted an extended leave of absence also has the assurance of his position upon his return.

INSURANCE PROVISIONS

Group insurance programs are rapidly becoming available to teachers at all levels. The major types of insurance of importance to teachers consist of life insurance, hospital insurance, medical-surgical insurance, major medical insurance, and disability insurance [114:48–49].

Group life insurance is a low-cost protection in the event of death. Usually it is of the "term" variety, which provides for no cash or paid-up value over the years. The National Education Association sponsors three basic plans that are available to its members. At least thirty-nine of the state teachers' associations affiliated with the NEA offer one or more life insurance plans [115:56]. State retirement funds in four states, municipalities in a least two states, and local school districts also provide life insurance plans for teachers.

Group hospitalization insurance provides protection for all or part of the hospital expenses incurred by the insuree. Generally, provision is made for room and board, incidental hospital expenses, and maternity care.

Group medical-surgical insurance provides for the payment for all or part of the expenses of surgery, generally on the basis of a schedule of allowances for specific operations. It frequently includes allowances for obstetrical services [114:48–49]. It may cover visits made in the hospital, in the doctor's office, and in the patient's home.

Group major medical insurance provides protection from the cost of extraordinary illnesses and accidents. While hospitalization and medical-surgical plans provide for the basic costs of medical care, major medical insurance plans may provide in some cases for as much as $50,000 of medical care.

Group disability insurance, sometimes called income protection insurance, is designed to provide for all or a portion of the salary lost by a teacher who is temporarily absent from work because of illness or accident. Some policies pay beginning with the first or second day of total disability; others pay after the amount of accumulated paid sick leave has become exhausted [114:49].

Many states have workmen's compensation laws that provide for partial loss of pay resulting from accidents and illnesses contracted on or as a result of an individual's work. Public school teachers usually are included in these benefits, which represent another type of disability insurance.

A school district may cooperate in providing group insurance in one or more forms, such as payroll deduction for premiums paid partly or entirely by the employees, sponsorship of the insurance plan, payment of part or all of the cost of the premiums for the coverage of the employee, and payment of part or all of the cost of the premiums for the coverage of the employee's dependents. Generally, the larger school systems are more likely than the small systems to cooperate in providing the various types of group insurance [114:49].

Usually, when the national or state teachers' association is the sponsor of the insurance plan, such as life insurance, the teacher pays the whole cost of the premiums. When the school district is the sponsor, it often pays part or all of the cost. The trend is very definitely toward the school district's assuming part or all of the cost. As evidence of this trend, the percentage of school districts paying the entire premium for group life, hospitalization, medical-surgical, and major medical insurance plans at least doubled during the three-year period prior to 1965–1966 [114:49].

CREDIT UNIONS

Many teachers have found credit unions to be exceedingly helpful to them in managing their salaries and in meeting financial obligations. This fact is reflected in the growth of the number of credit unions. More than 1,500 teachers' credit unions have been formed in school systems and colleges.

A teachers' credit union is a cooperative savings and loan organization that is owned and operated by and for its members. The federal government has legalized the establishment of teachers' credit unions. In order to form a credit union, a charter must be obtained which limits the operation to the members of the group. Its records and operations are subject to annual examination by either state or federal authorities. Its management is under the direction of a board of directors chosen from the members of the group. In order to become a member of a credit union, you have to pay an entrance fee (usually 25 cents) and to purchase at least one share of stock (usually costing $5). In order to borrow from a credit union you must be a member.

Credit unions offer several advantages to teachers, including encouraging them to save some of their salary [236:14]. About half of the unions provide for payroll deductions, which make it easier for teachers to save. The savings are invested in loans to members, in United States bonds, or in other investments of a trust-fund type. The dividend rate compares very favorably with the cash return from many other types of investments. More than three-fourths of the teachers' credit unions carry life insurance for each member, which represents a substantial addition to the annual dividend. Loans are made to credit-union members so that they can pay cash for needed items rather than resort to an installment plan which usually is decidedly more expensive. Personal counseling on economic problems is provided to members.

The teacher has an obligation to his profession to be economically efficient. Since the salary is not excessive, you owe yourself the best possible use of your financial resources. A good financial beginning normally results in greater happiness and success in life.

NEA MUTUAL FUND

In 1964, the NEA Mutual Fund, Inc., was established so that members of the association might participate directly in the economy of the nation through small investments that are not subject to large commissions. As little as $25 can be mailed to the fund's custodian at any time as an initial or a continuing investment for which the sales commission is only 2 per cent as compared with 7 or 8 per cent levied by most mutual funds on small investments [60:29]. As Davis points out, this low commission is possible because the fund does not employ salesmen and the advertising is directed to a specialized audience. The fund offers the same advantages as other mutual funds offer in that it requires only a seven-day notice to cash shares. Since the greatest gain results from long-term growth possibilities, money used for this type of investment should be money that will not be needed for operational expenses or for minor emergencies. The investment adviser to the NEA Mutual Fund is Standard and Poor's. The fund conforms to all the regulatory laws and requirements that govern all other mutual funds.

INCOME TAX DEDUCTIONS

In filing income tax reports, teachers are allowed to deduct justifiable business expenses. These expenses include membership dues in professional organizations as well as expenses incurred in attending classes, workshops, and other educational meetings in order to improve their professional skills or to retain their salary, status, or employment. Stinnett [254:282] points out, however, that expenses incurred for the following are not deductible: "(1) to prepare for the profession (that is, pre-service education), (2) to meet minimum qualifications for a position, (3) to obtain a promotion, (4) to fulfill his general educational aspirations, or (5) to satisfy any other personal purpose." Since you may have difficulty in interpreting some of the business expenses you will incur, you may wish to consult a tax expert in regard to the exact meaning of the law.

TAX-SHELTERED ANNUITIES

Since 1961, teachers and other school employees have been eligible for tax-sheltered annuities under federal tax laws [257:94]. The employee pays no federal tax during the current year on the amount of his salary used to pay premiums for the annuity. Although the employee must pay taxes on the benefits received from the annuity at retirement, this payment will occur at a time when his income is lower, and therefore, the amount will be less than it would have been during his work years. The money earns interest (5¼ per cent) while it is in the annuity account. Tax-sheltered annuities are available to teachers in nearly every state through the NEA plan. Because the program is nationwide a member may continue to build his annuity even if he changes positions and moves from one state to another. To be eligible, a teacher must be a member of the NEA and his state education association.

The member of the NEA tax-sheltered annuity plan has a choice of how the annuity will be paid to him upon retirement. He can ask for a lump-sum payment of the money in his annuity, or he may have monthly payments. If the member should die, his beneficiary receives the full amount of the annuity.

The local board of education needs only to pass a resolution permitting teachers to participate in the NEA plan, reduce each participating teacher's salary by the amount he wants put aside, and forward the amount to the NEA program.

TEACHER RETIREMENT

For many years large industrial concerns and railroads have felt a responsibility for providing pensions for their employees when they become too old to work. An increasing concern through the years has been shown by the general public for the old-age welfare of all people. The most monumental evidence of this concern is to be found in the federal Social Security Act passed by Congress in 1935. Another recent evidence of this concern is to be found in the provision of Medicare which became effective July, 1966. It can be safely assumed that the practice of safeguarding the basic needs of the old is an accepted practice in our society.

Need for Teacher Retirement

In earlier days teachers had little interest in a teacher retirement system, since very few expected to teach for the rest of their lives. Today an increasing number

A good retirement system provides a sense of security for teachers in service and a dignified exit from active service after usefulness has diminished through age or permanent disability. In this photograph of a retired teacher, Elizabeth Martin Sanford, who was awarded the Gold Key in recognition of her influence in shaping the career of an American leader, Terry Sanford, past governor of North Carolina, you note a feeling of dignity and security. (*Photograph by Joe Di Dio, National Education Association.*)

of young people are planning to make teaching their life careers; hence a sound retirement system becomes important to them.

A sound retirement system for teachers has the following advantages [262:1]:

1. It provides a dignified exit from active service after usefulness has diminished seriously through age or permanent disability.
2. It gives children the advantage of instruction from younger and more efficient teachers.
3. It increases the health and efficiency of teachers by removing worry and fear of a destitute old age.
4. It keeps good teachers in service.
5. It attracts capable, foresighted young people into the teaching profession.

Extent of Teacher Retirement Systems

Since 1946 all states and territories of the United States have had at least one law providing retirement benefits for teachers who have reached a stated age or have served for a stated length of time. There is considerable variation in the provisions of the laws. A complete analysis of each of the laws would be of little interest. A general idea of their provisions, however, may be gained from a study of materials periodically published by the research division of the National Education Association. Details regarding provisions in any particular state may be secured from its department of education.

In spite of the decided trend toward statewide retirement programs, a number of cities have their own plans. The local systems are confined mainly to large cities, such as New York and Chicago, where the programs operate independently of the statewide program or under permissive legislation of the state concerned.

Provision of Funds for Retirement

There are two general types of provisions for aged and disabled teachers: pensions and retirement allowances. Delaware is the only state that has a pension plan in which the teacher makes no contribution from his salary. The pension is usually paid from a fund set aside by the state government or by the local school district. The remaining states have some form of a retirement allowance to which both the teacher and the state or school system contribute. It is commonly referred to as a "joint-contributory plan." From his active salary the teacher contributes a flat rate or a given percentage (usually 5 or 6 per cent) to the retirement fund, and this amount is usually matched by the local school system and/or the state.

It is important to remember that courts have held that pensions such as those granted by Delaware are gratuities and that gratuities may be diminished or withheld at the will of the grantor. The beneficiary of a pension has no legal right to claim pension allotments. In contrast, the courts have held that in a joint-contributory retirement plan, retirement allowance must be paid to the retired teacher or his beneficiary.

Colleges and universities may belong to the retirement system provided by the state for public school teachers, may have their own system of retirement, may belong to an association such as the Teachers Insurance and Annuity Association, or may have no provisions at all for retirement. Virtually all the larger colleges and universities provide for the retirement of their staff members, although the plans differ greatly.

Some critics of retirement systems maintain that the teacher really pays for all the retirement benefits, that the amount which the state or local school system pays is rightfully a part of the teacher's salary. They fear that such an arrangement encourages teachers to accept lower salaries than they would otherwise. Statistics regarding teacher salaries and retirement benefits fail to substantiate this fear but, rather, indicate that an increase in one tends to accompany an increase in the other.

Trends in Providing Retirement Benefits

Although the provisions for retirement vary considerably among the states, there seem to be certain trends in evidence. For example, many states have established plans whereby a teacher may retire voluntarily without meeting the full requirements and receive proportionately less retirement benefits. In some cases the teacher may retire voluntarily at an early date and receive full retirement benefits by paying the total amount that he and the state would have paid had he met the regular requirements for retirement.

The retirement laws in thirty-four states specify the age when a teacher is compelled to retire from full-time teaching, regardless of the amount of time the teacher has taught [216:105]. This age usually ranges between 65 and 70.

When the requirements for retirement have been met, most systems now specify a formula for computing the allowance available to the teacher. The allowance is computed as a total amount usually, but not always, as a percentage or fraction of the final average salary multiplied by the total years of service credit. Normally, the yearly retirement allowance is approximately one-half of the average salary, payable until the recipient's death. Attempts are being made to increase the retirement allowance to provide a more comfortable living for the teacher during his retirement. Also, various annuity plans are being explored by retirement systems as a way to protect retirement benefits against the erosion of inflation.

Virtually all states now require all new teachers to participate in a retirement program. This procedure seems justifiable since otherwise many teachers would delay making adequate provisions for their retirement and the welfare of children would be jeopardized.

Almost all retirement systems provide some sort of credit for service in the Armed Forces. In order to gain credit, however, the teacher usually must serve during a time of war or national emergency or be drafted or called as a reservist. Few systems provide retirement credit for overseas teaching unless the teacher is on exchange and is being paid by his American employer.

Many retirement plans are expanding the optional benefits for the retiring teacher so that he may choose the method of payment of benefits best suited to him.

All states except Iowa make provision for disability retirement if the teacher becomes permanently disabled prior to normal retirement [216:105]. Most of the laws, however, state that the teacher must have a specified minimum number of years of service, such as 10 years, before he is eligible for disability benefits. The amount of benefit to be received depends on the amount of service that the teacher has given or on a fixed sum specified by policy or law.

Withdrawal after Limited Service

You normally will be entitled to a percentage of the amount of money which you have contributed toward retirement if you withdraw from teaching prior to the minimum time required for retirement. This percentage increases with the length of service. Usually after 10 years of service you would be refunded 100 per cent of the amount you contributed. A few systems refund the total amount regardless of when you withdraw. In many cases you will not be forced to withdraw your money if you leave the profession. Unless you are in great need, it will be wise for you to leave the sum intact. The capital usually accumulates at a fair rate of interest. Furthermore, if you return to teaching, you will have to your credit the money contributed during the previous years of service.

Death of the teacher concerned naturally constitutes a withdrawal from teaching. In this case, the amount of money due would be paid to beneficiaries. Death benefits vary greatly from one state to another.

Transfers from One State to Another

There is a very strong possibility, in this highly mobile society, that you will start your career in one state and finish it in another. If you cross state lines, you may jeopardize your accumulated retirement interests unless the law of the state you leave provides for full vesting of your retirement rights.

According to a survey by the research division of the National Education Association, all except seven states have provisions for vesting retirement rights and the payment of a deferred retirement allowance to a teacher who ceases to teach in a state and leaves his contribution in the retirement system. As a result, he becomes entitled at a later time to receive an annuity which is derived from his own contribution as well as from public funds contributed by the state and/or the local school district. Payment of the allowance usually starts at age sixty [216:106].

There is considerable variation among the states in the age and service requirements for vesting of retirement rights and in the age at which the deferred benefits become available. Less than one-fourth of the states, however, measure up to the resolution of the National Education Association, which urges full vesting of retirement rights after five or more years of creditable service [175:58]. It is highly probable that an increasing number of retirement systems will move in the direction of this resolution in order to make more liberal provisions for teachers who move from one state to another.

At least twenty-seven states grant service credit toward retirement for teaching performed outside their boundaries [216:106]. In most cases, the transfer teacher has to purchase the amount of credit he wishes to have, which usually may not exceed 10 years. A few states will not allow service credit to be purchased if a teacher is receiving or is entitled to receive retirement benefits from another state.

Social Security Benefits for Teachers

Prior to January 1, 1955, teachers, like all public employees, were not affected by the national Social Security Act. At the time the original act was being considered, in 1935, much attention was given to the possibility of its including all types of people. Teachers as a group, however, did not wish to have their own systems of retirement abolished in favor of the conditions prescribed by the act; most teacher retirement benefits were appreciably higher. Furthermore, since social security benefits were financed by a tax on both employer and employee, there was a question as to whether the federal government legally could impose a tax on the states or local governmental agencies or their employees.

In 1950, Congress amended the Social Security Act, permitting states to make agreements with the Social Security Administration so that state employees would be covered. By such a voluntary arrangement, the federal government could not be accused of taxing a state or its agencies.

In 1954, Congress extended greatly the benefits to be derived from the Social Security Act and also made it possible for public employees to obtain social security benefits without abandoning any existing public employee retirement system. As a result, government employees, as of January 1, 1955, could become eligible for social security benefits if the members, after having had 90 days' notice of the referendum, voted in favor of it. The teachers in a number of states took advantage of this opportunity.

The states that have adopted social security have used various formulas for accomplishing this purpose. In some states, teachers have social security coverage in addition to their retirement benefits. In other cases the social security benefits are coordinated or are integrated with the retirement benefits.

Social security has certain advantages that are not present in many teacher retirement laws. Since it is nationwide in scope, a teacher does not run as much danger of losing his benefits in moving from one state to another as he does in the case of state retirement plans. There is no compulsory retirement age in the federal plan, although there is a limitation on the amount an individual can earn between the ages of 65 and 72 and yet draw full social security benefits during those years. If a man wishes, he may retire as early as 62, but the benefits per year are less. A wife, if 65 or more years old, receives an additional one-half of her husband's benefits (or less if she wishes to begin receiving benefits at age 62), while the husband collects the full amount. Survivors' benefits are provided for widows over 62, children under 18, and widows of any age caring for the deceased's children.

About 50 per cent of the public school teachers are covered by social security, including some or all of the teachers in thirty-eight states [244:3]. Under the social security plan a teacher and the school system in which he works each may contribute a percentage of his salary, up to $6,600, toward social security. Beginning in 1968, the rate is $4\frac{5}{8}$ per cent.

Checklist for Evaluating a Teacher Retirement System

You may be interested in teaching in a state other than the one in which you are being prepared to teach. Likewise, your teaching career may involve retirement plans in two or more states. For these reasons you may find the "Checklist for Appraising a Teacher Retirement System," which is located in the Resource Section of Part III, to be of help to you. For the present, the checklist should assist you in summarizing the characteristics of a good teacher retirement system.

SUMMARY

In this chapter you have looked into some of the important factors other than salary that affect the economic security of teachers. Although practices and provisions vary throughout the United States, much progress has been made in providing security through tenure for the competent teacher by means of which he is better able to fulfill his professional responsibilities to youth. The reasons for, the kinds, the present status, and the characteristics of good tenure laws were examined. Increasingly liberal provisions for leaves of absence are being developed. As is the case in business and industry, school officials are showing increasing concern for hospitalization and life insurance protection for their employees. Many teachers are finding credit unions to be exceedingly helpful to them in managing their salaries and in meeting financial obligations. The need for teacher retirement, and the extent, provisions, and trends in regard to retirement systems were carefully examined. Social security benefits for teachers were also described.

These added benefits to teachers have come primarily through the concerted efforts of various local, state, and national professional teacher organizations in an attempt to place careers in the field of education on a truly professional level. Continued efforts on the part of all should bring about even further benefits.

QUESTIONS FOR YOUR CONSIDERATION

1. What are the advantages and disadvantages of tenure as it relates to annual contracts, contracts extending for a definite number of years, continuing contracts, and protective continuing contracts?
2. What is the least desirable type of teacher tenure? The most desirable?
3. In what ways may permanent tenure be misused professionally?
4. How may teachers on tenure be encouraged to continue their professional growth?
5. What are the advantages and disadvantages of superintendents' not having permanent tenure?
6. What leave-of-absence provisions should a school system make for teachers?
7. To what extent should school districts sponsor group insurance programs for teachers?
8. What are the arguments for and against teachers' belonging to credit unions?
9. What advantages do tax-sheltered annuities have for teachers?
10. Why is a joint-contributory retirement plan more desirable than a pension plan?
11. Should teachers be encouraged to invest in a mutual fund, such as the one sponsored by the NEA?
12. How can teachers safeguard their retirement benefits against erosion that may result from inflation?
13. What, in your opinion, is the most desirable retirement plan which will prevent the migratory teacher from being penalized?
14. What are the advantages and disadvantages of a law which compels teachers to retire upon reaching a certain age?
15. Do you feel that all teachers should be eligible for social security benefits? Why?

ACTIVITIES FOR YOU TO PURSUE

1. Study as many occupations as possible in terms of the provisions preventing an individual from losing his job unfairly. Compare and contrast these occupations with teaching.
2. If you know of a teacher on permanent tenure who seems to be shirking his job responsibilities, analyze the personal factors or values that may be involved.
3. If you were a superintendent of schools, what would you do if parents reported one of your teachers on permanent tenure as incompetent in the classroom?

4. Study in detail the retirement plans in three or more states in which you may be interested in teaching.
5. Investigate the amount of social security benefits you might receive upon retirement.
6. Investigate various occupations in terms of provisions for emergency leaves. Compare and contrast these provisions with those in your home school system.
7. Compare the rates for group insurance plans for teachers with those of commercial concerns.
8. Assume you wish to borrow money to buy a new automobile. How would the total cost of the automobile, if financed through a credit union such as the teachers' credit union, compare with its cost if financed through a regular loan company?
9. Investigate the fringe benefits for teachers in a large and in a small school system. What differences, if any, exist?
10. Using the checklist in the Resource Section for Part III, attempt to appraise the retirement system for teachers in your home state.

10

LEGAL LIABILITIES AND RESPONSIBILITIES OF TEACHERS

As we experience increases in population, in levels of educational attainment, in the complexity of society, and in concern for our health, education, and welfare, is it to be expected that lawyers and our courts will be busier than ever before? Is there a tendency for the average citizen today to be more legal conscious than he has been in the past? If this tendency is apparent, is it desirable? What implications does it have for everyone?

You doubtless have read frequently of lawsuits being filed against medical doctors and people in the other professions. As a future member of the teaching profession, it is important for you to keep in mind that teachers, also, are occasionally the subjects of lawsuits brought by parents and other individuals. As is true in the other professions, it is highly probable that the frequency of lawsuits against teachers will increase in the future.

It is unfortunate that, as a general rule, teachers are woefully uninformed about their legal rights and responsibilities. Physicians, for example, normally receive courses in medical jurisprudence as a part of their professional education. Prospective teachers generally are not given a comparable type of instruction. It is also true that the work of a teacher, which normally does not involve the life-or-death responsibilities assumed so frequently by physicians, does not tend to stimulate an acute consciousness of the legal hazards involved in teaching. As you plan your career in teaching, however, it is important for you to become familiar with some of the legal rights and responsibilities of teachers.

This chapter is much too brief to analyze all aspects of the law as it affects teachers. Problems of teacher contracts, tenure, strikes and collective bargaining, certification, and retirement have been discussed previously. The reading list at the end of the chapter suggests numerous other resources which you might utilize should you wish to pursue a study of these and other areas of legal concern further.

An attempt is made here to acquaint you with two major aspects of the law affecting teachers—*tort liability* and *pupil control*—since these are perhaps of more significance to teachers and prospective teachers generally than are any other legal topics.

In studying the materials concerning these two aspects, you should keep in mind that the courts are by no means antagonistic to teachers, even though court decisions have been against teachers in certain situations; on the contrary, they generally tend to uphold the actions of teachers so long as good judgment and common sense prevail. Also, the cases referred to are drawn from a number of different states, and strictly speaking, precedent as established by the courts in one state may not necessarily be followed by the courts in another state. However, the attitude of the courts is remarkably uniform in the areas of teacher tort liability and control of pupils in all the states, and you may therefore assume that most courts in the United States would be likely to make decisions similar to these presented here.

THE SOURCES OF THE LAW

You may already be familiar with three great decisions of the United States Supreme Court which have vitally affected the public schools—the 1954 decision requiring desegregation of the public schools (*Brown v. Board of Education*, 347 U.S. 438, 74 Sup. Ct. 686); the 1962 decision banning a state-prescribed prayer in the public schools (*Engel v. Vitale*, 370 U.S. 421, 82 Sup. Ct. 1261); and the 1963 decision prohibiting the devotional use of the Bible in the public schools (*School District of Abington Township v. Schempp; Murray v. Curlett*, 374 U.S. 203, 83 Sup. Ct. 1560). These great decisions illustrate one of the major sources of American law—the judicial process whereby a court considers a problem and arrives at a decision, thereby establishing or creating "law."

If you ask the man on the street where the law comes from, the following answers might be received: "The United States Congress passes laws," or "The state legislatures enact laws," or "The United States Constitution is the basis of all American law." All these statements are basically accurate but are superficial at best. It is true that the Congress and the various state legislatures enact *statutes*, or laws, which cover a multiplicity of subjects. It is also true that the federal and state constitutions provide the basic framework of American government. The federal Constitution is the basis for congressional authority, and the state constitutions provide limitations beyond which the state legislatures may not go. A basic source of American law, however, is to be found in the federal or state system of courts.

The Judicial System and Precedent

One of the most important sources of law in the Anglo-American countries is the judicial, or court, system. The courts over a period of hundreds of years in England, and later in America, have been called upon to adjudicate disputes between parties arising from situations for which no legislature or constitution has made provision. In other cases the courts have been requested to interpret the meaning of portions of the various American constitutions as well as the statutes enacted by Congress or by the state legislatures.

Over the years, then, a body of court-made law has developed which has become known as *case law*, or in a broad sense, the *common law*. In developing the common law, the courts have tended to examine earlier similar court decisions and to follow *precedent*, which can be defined as an earlier court decision which furnishes an example or authority for a later decision on a similar point of law. A study of court decisions, then, can result in an understanding of how the courts are likely to rule on many questions involving teachers and the schools.

The law has been said to be an expression of public policy, whether the source is constitutional, statutory, or judicial. When the constitution and statutes are silent (as is the case in most states in the area of corporal punishment of school pupils, for example), a court is called upon actually to legislate, to formulate law, or to express public policy in deciding the dispute which is before it.

Types of Court Action

Court action may be either *criminal* or *civil* in nature. A criminal case is initiated normally by the prosecuting attorney acting for the state against an individual who has been accused of violating the criminal statutes of the state. If guilt is proved, the penalty assessed by the court is imprisonment and/or a fine payable to the state.

A civil case is normally brought by one individual or group of individuals, known as the *plaintiff*, against another, known as the *defendant*. In a civil case, the plaintiff seeks some sort of *remedy*, which may be in the form of an *injunction* (prohibiting the defendant from doing something), *mandamus* (requiring the defendant to do something), or *monetary damages* (for an injury or loss). Most cases involving teachers and the school are civil in nature.

The Appellate Court System

Legal action is initiated in a *trial court,* or *lower court,* which may be known in the various states as "circuit courts," "superior courts," "county courts," or "district courts." Following the decision of the trial court, the loser may appeal the decision to a higher court, known as an *appellate court*. The highest appellate court in the state court system is the state supreme court. This court is known by various names. For example, the highest state court in Kentucky is known as the Court of Appeals, in Connecticut it is called the Supreme Court of Errors, and in Oregon it is termed the Supreme Court. Although the decisions of trial courts normally are not published in widely disseminated law journals and books and thus are not readily available to attorneys, the decisions of appellate courts as well as those of the federal court system (of which the highest appellate court is the United States Supreme Court) are published and are available in any adequate law library. These published appellate court decisions form the basis for precedent and vividly portray the continuing development of the common law.

TORT LIABILITY OF TEACHERS

A *tort* is a private or civil wrong which does not flow from breach of contract and which results in loss or damage to an individual or to his property. Perhaps the most common torts are negligence causing personal injury, trespass upon property belonging to another, maintenance of a nuisance, and defamation of character.

In most states, the state itself is immune from tort liability. A school district, as a subdivision of the state, therefore enjoys immunity in these states. Although there are a number of legal reasons for this type of immunity, perhaps the most frequently cited reason is to be found in the ancient doctrine that "the king can do no wrong." Since the state in the United States has replaced the sovereign, this doctrine has been modified to "the state can do no wrong."

State immunity from tort liability, however, is slowly changing. In recent years several states, including Arizona, California, Illinois, New York, Washington, and Wisconsin, have abolished, either by statute or by court decision, the immunity of school districts under certain circumstances. The trend toward the abolishment of sovereign, or governmental, immunity of school districts appears to be continuing.

Although you may teach in a state that holds to the principle of the sovereign immunity of school districts, you should keep in mind that teachers are classified as employees of school districts and therefore do not enjoy the same immunity. Teachers, as is normally true of employees in other governmental agencies, are liable for their own torts.

The Standard of Negligence

The tort which results in by far the greatest number of lawsuits involving teachers is *negligence*. Negligence has been defined as conduct involving unreasonable danger to others which should be recognized by a reasonably prudent person. Since every factual situation in which an individual may be injured as the result of the actions or conduct of another is unique, the courts through the years have established the conduct of the "reasonably prudent man" as the hypothetical standard against which the actions of the person sued are measured.

A reasonably prudent man will behave differently under different circumstances. Although the courts do not expect an individual to be clairvoyant or psychic in making certain his actions do not result in injury to others, they do require the conduct of an individual in protecting others from harm to be that of the average person under similar circumstances.

The courts require teachers to exercise a greater degree of care to protect pupils from injury than they require of the ordinary person. Perhaps it would be more accurate to say that the standard of conduct demanded of a teacher is that of the "reasonably prudent teacher."

A superintendent of schools wrote a letter seeking advice in regard to the following factual situation:

A first-grade teacher discovered a mouse in the classroom. After unsuccessfully attempting to find the school custodian or the principal, the teacher gave the male first graders paper cups with which to catch the mouse. The mouse was captured and later turned over to the custodian for disposal.

Upon arriving at home that evening, a pupil told his parents that he had been bitten by the mouse. Since the animal had been disposed of by the custodian in the meantime, the family doctor advised that the child be given rabies shots, a painful and relatively costly process.

Would a court be likely to find the teacher in this situation liable for negligence?

In order to answer this question, it is perhaps necessary to examine in greater detail the tort of negligence as it applies to teachers.

Criteria for Establishing Negligence

Liability for negligence rests upon three factors: (1) a duty to act so as to protect others from unnecessary risks, (2) the failure to so act, and (3) the injury of another causing loss or damage as the result of such failure to act. A teacher may be liable either for *an act* which a reasonably prudent teacher should have realized involved an unreasonable risk of injury to another or for *failure to do an act* which the teacher was under a duty to do for the protection of another.

The major criterion used by the courts in determining negligence is *foreseeability;* that is, should the defendant as a reasonably prudent teacher have foreseen the possible harmful consequences of his action or lack of action and did he regard these consequences? If the answer of the court is in the affirmative, liability for negligence exists.

Liability for Pupil Injury: Classroom Activities

In order to illustrate the attitude of the courts with respect to teacher negligence resulting in injury to pupils in the classroom, court decisions from several different states are summarized in the following paragraphs.

The importance of proper instruction in dangerous activities was emphasized in a California case. A chemistry teacher during a laboratory period required pupils to perform an experiment as outlined in the textbook without giving additional instruction. A pupil used the wrong chemical and an explosion occurred, resulting in pupil injury. In finding the teacher negligent, the court in 1935 stated (*Mastrangelo v. West Side Union High School District,* 42 P.2d 634): "It is not unreasonable to assume that it is the duty of a teacher of chemistry, in the exercise of ordinary care, to *instruct* students regarding the selection, mingling, and use of ingredients with which dangerous experiments are to be accomplished, rather than to merely hand them a textbook with general instructions." (Italics added.)

Normally a teacher is not responsible for injuries occurring to pupils off the school grounds or after school hours. Under certain circumstances, however, the teacher may be held liable, since teachers apparently have the responsibility of warning pupils about dangerous practices which arise out of classroom activities.

Another California case illustrates the importance of pupils being warned about dangerous practices. In an industrial arts class pupils had been constructing model cannons made of bronze with wooden gun carriages. The teacher had given no warning to the pupils about the danger of firing the cannons at home, although the evidence indicated that he was aware that the pupils were taking the cannons home and firing them, using powder from shotgun shells as an explosive and ball bearings as projectiles. A pupil was permanently injured as the result of an explosion which occurred when he attempted to fire one of the model cannons at home. Since, as indicated previously, California is one of the states in which suit may be brought against the school district, the district was sued for the alleged negligence of the teacher. In 1963 the court held the teacher negligent and pointed out that, even though the injury to the pupil was incurred off the school grounds and after school hours, the teacher had failed in his duty to warn the pupils of the potential dangers of firing the model cannons (*Calandri v. Ione Unified School District,* 33 Cal. App.2d 333).

A teacher has a responsibility to be present in his assigned classroom to supervise pupils or to notify his principal that it is necessary for him to be absent. In New York, a teacher was not present to supervise his pupils during the first period of the day and had failed to notify school authorities that he would be absent. In the teacher's absence, the pupils began to engage in "horseplay," and one boy openly began to brandish a knife. After a period of time another pupil was stabbed.

The court, in 1962, found that the teacher was negligent and stated that, had the teacher been present in the classroom, it would have been his duty to take action to relieve the pupil of the knife (*Christofides v. Hellenic Eastern Orthodox Christian Church,* 227 N.Y.S.2d 946). In other words, the teacher, if present, should have foreseen and prevented the injury.

Negligence may be assessed for injuries resulting from the mismatching of pupils engaged in physical education activities. During a physical education class held in a school in New York in 1963, groups of boys were placed on each side of the gymnasium and given numbers chosen at random. When a number was called by the teacher, two boys at opposite sides of the floor would run to a soccer ball in the center of the room and attempt to kick it. A boy suffered serious injury as the result of being kicked by a taller and heavier opponent, and suit was brought against the school district on grounds of negligent supervision by the teacher. The court held that the "mismatching" of the two boys constituted negligence (*Brooks v. Board of Education,* 189 N.E.2d 497).

The element of foreseeability, previously mentioned, is a major factor in determining negligence. In 1956, a California teacher of drafting took his class out on the school lawn, with each pupil carrying his own drawing board. On the way out of the building, a boy picked up a knife and, when the pupils were seated on the lawn, began repeatedly to flip the knife into the grass. The teacher noticed this game of mumblety-peg but did nothing to halt it. The knife eventually glanced off a drawing board and struck a pupil in the eye, which caused permanent injury. The court, in holding the teacher negligent, pointed out that, since the teacher had been aware of the dangerous activity and since the activity had gone on for a period of time, the teacher should have foreseen the possible dangerous consequences and should have halted the activity (*Lilienthal v. San Leandro Unified School District,* 293 P.2d 889).

A study of the negligence cases involving teachers reveals that teachers who have supervised potentially hazardous activities over a long period of time frequently may be lulled into a false sense of security concerning the dangers to pupils. What is perhaps the most flagrant case involving teacher liability for negligence occurred in South Dakota in 1941 and illustrates this point. For a number of years it had been the practice to initiate high school male athletes into a club known as the "H" club by subjecting the candidates to an electric shock produced by batteries and run through a transformer to reduce the current. The high school coach secured permission from the school superintendent to use the gymnasium for the initiation. The transformer and batteries were not available that year; so the boys prepared a rheostat consisting of a jar of salt water and obtained current from a 120-volt light socket. Each boy, blindfolded and clad in shorts, was made to lie down with a glass of water in his hand on a series of bare copper wires connected to the circuit. The electricity was then turned on, which caused electric shock and resulted in the spilling of the water. Five candidates were in the process of being initiated. After each of the first three received his shock, the coach mopped the floor and tested the current with his hands. The fourth candidate complained that the shock was too great, after which one-half of the solution of salt water was removed from the rheostat and replaced with city water, presumably to reduce the current. The fifth boy then took his turn. When the electricity was turned on, he partially arose, gasped "Oh, my God," and fell backward. All attempts to revive the boy failed—the electric shock had resulted in a fatality.

Suit was brought by the parents of the boy against both the coach and the school superintendent. The coach was found negligent. The court pointed out that he should have known electricity was dangerous and that he had failed to observe the high degree of care he owed his pupils. The superintendent, on the other hand, was absolved from responsibility. The court held that the superintendent had performed his full duty when he permitted use of the gymnasium with the knowledge that the coach would be present [*DeGooyer v. Harkness*, 13 N.W.2d 815 (1944)].

Liability for Pupil Injury: The Playground

Playground or outdoor athletic activities are probably inherently more physically dangerous than most classroom activities. Teachers who are charged with the responsibility for such outdoor activities should therefore make certain that pupils are warned against unreasonable hazards and should supervise these activities very carefully.

A teacher who is given playground duty, however, is not expected by the courts to protect every pupil against every possibility of injury, since the courts will use the reasonably prudent teacher as the standard measure of conduct. For example, while a Colorado teacher was supervising a playground, a pupil threw a rock which struck another pupil in the eye. The court refused to impose liability on the teacher and stated: "There is no requirement that the teacher have under constant and unremitting scrutiny the precise spots wherein every phase of play activity is being pursued; nor is there compulsion that the general supervision be continuous and direct" [*Carroll v. Fitzsimmons*, 383 P.2d 81 (1963)].

A teacher who is given responsibility for playground supervision should be on the playground rather than be "supervising" the pupils by watching through the classroom window. In New York, for example, a six-year-old pupil climbed up and fell from a fire escape which the "supervising" teacher could not see from the classroom window, since it was located around the corner of the building. The court held that the teacher was negligent [*Miller v. Board of Education*, 50 N.E.2d 529 (1943)].

What teacher liability might be involved in this situation? (*Photograph from the National Education Association.*)

The importance of adequate safety rules for playground activity was illustrated in a California case. The school principal had been aware for some time that boys on the playground were playing a game known as "blackout." The game consisted of one boy taking a deep breath while another squeezed him tightly from behind with the object of rendering the subject unconscious. Upon being rendered unconscious, one of the boys fell, struck his head on a concrete pavement, and was fatally injured. Suit was brought against the principal, and the court found him negligent, primarily because he had known of the practice for some time and had done nothing to stop it [*Tymkowicz v. San Jose Unified School District*, 312 P.2d 388 (1957)].

Liability for Pupil Injury: The School Patrol

Teachers are frequently required to assume general supervision of school patrol activities. When school-age pupils are called upon to shepherd other pupils across streets and highways it might be thought that the teacher selecting or supervising such patrolmen could be held liable in case of pupil injury.

Surprisingly, perhaps, there appears to be no case in courts of record dealing with teacher liability for actions of school patrolmen. Legal authorities, however, have pointed out that a teacher with the responsibility for selecting school patrolmen should make certain that the pupils selected are competent, are reliable, and are properly instructed and that the patrol activity is voluntary and engaged in with the permission of the parent (see, e.g., *Opinions of the Attorney General of Indiana,* 1929, p. 257; 1954, p. 143).

A Maryland case involving a school bus driver apparently supports the principle that the use of a school patrolman to help pupils across the street is not unreasonable. In this case the school bus driver was not found negligent when a child was injured while being escorted across a highway by a responsible older pupil who was a member of the school safety patrol. The use of a safety patrol, stated the court, was "generally regarded as a reasonable and adequate provision for the safety of school bus riders" [*Ragonese v. Hilferty,* 191 A.2d 426 (1963)].

Liability for Pupil Injuries: Errands and Field Trips

When you become a teacher, you probably should avoid sending pupils on errands off the school grounds except in cases of real emergency. Two areas of possible liability exist: (1) injury to the pupil himself, in which case a court might be called upon to determine whether a reasonably prudent teacher would send a child on such an errand, and (2) injury or damage done by the pupil to a third party or to his property, in which case a court might hold that the pupil was acting as the agent of the teacher and that the teacher was liable.

Most educational authorities agree that field trips are desirable and should be a recognized part of the curriculum. You should not hesitate to take pupils on field trips because of the possibility of teacher liability. When you become a teacher and are planning a field trip, it is recommended that you take the following steps prior to the trip:

1. Plan the trip carefully in advance.
2. If the trip is to be a visit to an industrial plant or to some other potentially dangerous place, you should visit the plant in advance and should discuss possible hazards with the plant manager or his representative.
3. You should discuss the potential hazards with the pupils who are to make the trip. Safety rules for the trip should be established, and pupils should be thoroughly informed regarding such safety rules.
4. You should obtain the permission of the school administrator who is your immediate superior.
5. Parental permission slips should be sent home with the pupils, signed by the parents, and returned.
6. In most cases, extra supervision probably should be provided. You might utilize parents in this role.
7. If automobiles must be used, you should be certain that the drivers are properly licensed and that such drivers carry adequate liability insurance in case of an accident occurring in transit.

You should keep in mind that a signed parental permission slip does not relieve the teacher of liability, since one individual (even a parent) may not sign away the right of another to sue. However, parental permission slips at least inform parents about the proposed field trip, and might be used as evidence of reasonable prudence on the part of the teacher.

Strangely, perhaps, most of the lawsuits arising out of injury to pupils on school field trips have been brought against the industrial plants in which the injuries occurred. Whether the pupil was legally a licensee or an invitee has been significant in these cases. A *licensee* can be defined as one who visits the premises of another for his own benefit; an *invitee* visits the premises of another for the benefit of the owner or for the benefit of both himself and the owner. Although a plant owner owes only a normal degree of care to protect a licensee from harm, he owes a much higher degree of care to an invitee.

In a Maryland case, a class visited the plant of a traction company. The pupils were warned of the dangerous apparatus and then told to "look around" for themselves. (The teacher in charge should have ended the visit at this point.) A pupil fell into an open vat of boiling water flush with the floor in an inadequately lighted portion of the plant, and suit was brought against the traction company. The court held that since the pupils were licensees, the plant owed them only an ordinary degree of care. The pupils had entered the plant at their own risk, and therefore the injured pupil could not recover from the traction company. The court further pointed out that if any negligence existed, "it consisted in bringing thirty-odd boys at one time to a building filled with dangerous machinery." The court obviously felt that the teacher, rather than the traction company, should have been the defendant in the lawsuit [*Benson v. Baltimore Traction Company,* 26 Atl. 973 (1893)].

In a Missouri case, the court held that a pupil injured while visiting a bakery and creamery company was an invitee. The company had advertised widely and had encouraged inspection of the plant by the public. Each year, five or six classes from the local high school visited the plant. On one such visit, a girl was seriously injured when her arm became caught in an ice crusher, which later resulted in the amputation of the arm. The court held the industrial plant liable, since the invitation to the public to visit the plant was used as a part of its advertising. As an invitee, the girl was owed a much higher degree of care than ordinarily would be required, and the plant officials had failed to properly warn her of the dangerous machinery [*Gilliland v. Bondurant,* 59 S.W.2d 679 (1933)].

Liability Arising out of Cocurricular Activities

Teachers who supervise pupil activities of a cocurricular nature or activities which take place after school hours are held to the same standard of conduct as that required during school hours in the classroom. As a teacher, then, you should exercise the same high degree of care in supervising such activities as you exercise during any other school activity.

Other Aspects of Liability

The following statements summarize other problems and aspects of teacher liability with which you should be familiar:

1. As a teacher you probably have a responsibility to report to the proper authorities unsafe or deficient instructional or playground equipment.
2. Should a pupil whom you are supervising be injured, you probably have the

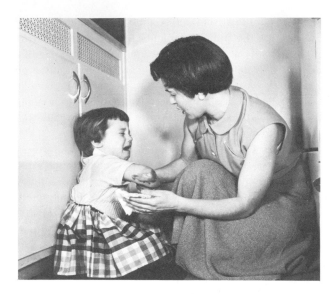

If this kind of situation should occur in your classroom, how would you handle it? (*Photograph from the National Education Association.*)

responsibility to administer emergency first aid. However, you should be certain that any first aid you give does not further increase the severity of the injury. One good rule to follow is that seriously injured pupils should not be moved until competent medical personnel arrive and take charge. In any case, your principal should be notified immediately whenever a pupil is injured.

3. As a teacher you probably would not be expected by the courts to be able to diagnose every type of contagious disease with which your pupils might become infected. You are therefore unlikely to be held liable by a court in case a pupil contracts a disease in your classroom. However, you would be expected to utilize reasonable care in recommending the exclusion of pupils from your classroom who are suspected of carrying such an infectious disease.

4. Teachers are sometimes in the habit of dispensing medication, such as aspirin, to pupils who have a headache or who appear ill. As a teacher, you should probably avoid giving medication to pupils. Ill pupils should be sent to the school nurse or to the school sickroom until parents can be notified. Good judgment should be used in such cases. If a pupil brings medication from home as prescribed by his family doctor, it is probably reasonable to permit the pupil to take such medication at prescribed times.

Defenses against Negligence

A number of legal defenses against negligence which relieve the teacher of liability have been rather clearly defined by the courts. The first and most common defense is, of course, a denial that any negligence exists. The person bringing suit (plaintiff) must prove negligence by proving that the conduct of the defendant fell below the standard of reasonable prudence.

A Minnesota case illustrates this defense. Suit was brought against a teacher for injuries sustained by an elementary pupil during a rope-jumping activity in a physical education class. The pupil stepped on the rope as it was being rotated, and the wooden handle affixed to one end was pulled from the grasp of the teacher. The wooden handle struck the front teeth of the pupil and caused injuries for which recovery was sought. The plaintiff maintained that the teacher should have foreseen the injury and could have prevented it by furnishing a longer rope or by providing a rope without wooden handles. The court absolved the teacher from any negligence and pointed out that the jumping rope was of the kind normally used by children for "many years" and that the teacher could not have reasonably anticipated the injury [*Wire v. Williams*, 133 N.W.2d 840 (1965)].

Contributory Negligence

In most states an individual is relieved of liability contributing to his own injury, and proof by the plaintiff that he has done so is known as *contributory negligence*. In a few states, such as Arkansas, Georgia, Mississippi, Nebraska, South Dakota, and Wisconsin, the doctrine of *comparative negligence* has been developing in recent years. In states where comparative negligence is recognized, the court seeks to "apportion the blame" between the two parties and may assess some degree of liability to the defendant even though the plaintiff contributed to his own injury.

An example of contributory negligence occurred in a North Carolina case. A chemistry teacher granted a high school boy and several classmates permission to go to the chemistry laboratory to set up a specific experiment in the absence of the instructor. Instead of performing the experiment agreed upon, the boys made gunpowder. An explosion of the gunpowder resulted in serious injury to one of the boys. As a result, a suit was brought against the teacher. The court, in relieving the teacher of liability, held that the injured boy had contributed to his own injury, and was therefore guilty of contributory negligence. "Even an eight-year-old would have known better," stated the court [*Moore v. Order of Minor Conventuals*, 267 F.2d 296 (1959)].

There appears to be an age below which the courts are unlikely to assess contributory negligence. In determining whether a child is guilty of contributing to his own injury, the court normally asks itself whether a child of similar years and similar mental and physical ability would reasonably be expected to protect himself from the dangers inherent in the particular situation. As may be expected, the defense of contributory negligence is less often successfully used in situations involving injuries to elementary school pupils than it is in situations involving injuries to high school pupils.

Proximate Cause

Causal connection is a major factor considered by the courts in assessing whether negligence exists; there must be an unbroken "chain of causation" between the negligence of the teacher and the resultant pupil injury. In other words, the negligence of the defendant must be the *proximate cause* of the injury. A "break" in the chain of causation which results from the *intervening act* of a third party, for example, may mean that the court will conclude that the proximate cause of the injury was not the negligent conduct of the defendant and thus relieve the defendant of liability.

A sudden action by a pupil which causes injury to another pupil that could not have been foreseen by the teacher usually results in the court's absolving the teacher from liability. For example, a New Jersey teacher was standing outside the classroom door as two pupils came down the hall together. One of the pupils hit the other lightly on the arm. The teacher, believing that nothing more was likely to happen from this incident, entered the classroom. The second pupil then pushed the first through the classroom door, causing him to strike his foot against a metal desk, which resulted in an injury that eventually necessitated the amputation of the foot. Suit was brought against the teacher for negligence on the ground that he should have foreseen the action on the part of the second pupil. The court held that the first incident in the hall was not of a nature to reasonably attract the attention of the teacher, and therefore the injury to the first pupil was not *proximately caused* by the negligence of the teacher. Rather, the injury to the first pupil was the result of the *intervening act* of the second pupil [*Doktor v. Greenberg,* 155 A.2d 793 (1959)].

Although a teacher should not leave his classroom unsupervised, except in cases of real emergency, the courts sometimes have been lenient to teachers in this regard. For example, an Ohio teacher, who left his room to "gossip with a teacher in another room" during a period when pupils were eating lunch in his classroom, was absolved of liability when a pupil suddenly threw a milk bottle which struck another pupil in the eye and caused loss of sight. The court held that the absence of the teacher was not the proximate cause of the injury. Even if the teacher had been in the classroom, from the legal point of view, the teacher could not have foreseen and prevented the sudden action of the pupil who threw the milk bottle [*Ohman v. Board of Education,* 90 N.E.2d 474 (1949)].

In order to gain further understanding of the reasoning of the courts in cases involving injury to pupils while the teacher is absent from the classroom, you may wish to compare the case just described with a previously mentioned case in which the teacher was held liable when a pupil stabbed another pupil with a knife after brandishing it for a period of time. In the latter situation, the court held that the teacher, if he had been present, would have had a duty to relieve the pupil of the knife—in other words, the teacher could have *foreseen* possible injury to other pupils by a pupil openly displaying a dangerous weapon. In the "milk bottle" case, the sudden action could not have been foreseen, even if the teacher had been present. In spite of the fact that the teacher was relieved of liability in the "milk bottle" case, however, it should be held in mind that a teacher runs a serious risk of liability if he leaves his classroom unsupervised.

Assumption of Risk

An adult who knowingly engages in a dangerous occupation or activity normally is considered by the courts to have assumed the risk of the occupation. Except in the case of gross negligence of his employer or any other person, he may not recover any compensation if he should be injured. This is known as the doctrine of the *assumption of risk.* Except in cases of athletic injuries, in which the pupil and his parents know that the activity may be physically hazardous, this doctrine is seldom used as a successful defense in cases involving the schools.

Other Reasons Assigned by Courts for Nonliability

As indicated earlier in this chapter, a court will use the reasonably prudent teacher as the standard against which the allegedly negligent conduct of a teacher is measured in a particular situation. *Proper instruction* and *due care* are terms frequently used by the courts in determining whether the teacher against whom suit is brought behaved with reasonable prudence. In New Jersey, a 14-year-old boy was injured in a physical education class while jumping over a piece of apparatus known as a "horse." The instructor had demonstrated the proper method of performing the exercise and had warned the pupils that they should not try if they felt they could not accomplish the exercise safely. The court found that the teacher had not been negligent, since he had exercised due care in warning the pupils and had properly instructed the pupils by demonstrating the exercise [*Sayers v. Ranger*, 83 A.2d 775 (1951)].

In California, an industrial arts teacher had promulgated safety rules for the automobile shop and had frequently repeated the rules to the pupils during the school year. A pupil was assigned the job of adjusting the valve tappets on an automobile. In violation of the safety rules, another pupil started the car. The vehicle, which was in gear, pinned a third pupil against the wall of the shop and caused serious injury. The evidence showed that the teacher had personally inspected the car immediately prior to the accident. The court exonerated the teacher, primarily because he had established and repeated the safety rules. Since he had used due care, he could not have foreseen the accident [*Perumean v. Wills*, 67 P.2d 96 (1937)].

As a future teacher, therefore, you should keep in mind that it is important to establish adequate *safety rules* for potentially dangerous activities.

Defamation of Character

Another tort for which teachers occasionally are sued is *defamation of character*, which may be defined as damage to a person's reputation through communication involving ridicule, disgrace, contempt, or hatred. Written defamation is known as *libel*, and spoken defamation is known as *slander*.

Teachers are involved in possible liability for defamation of character in such activities as (1) writing letters of recommendation to or talking to prospective employers or college representatives about pupils, (2) entering comments on pupil records, (3) making comments to parents or to other teachers about pupils, or (4) making public or newspaper statements concerning pupils.

Truth as a Defense

In many states truth is a defense against defamation-of-character lawsuits. Should the person against whom a suit is brought be able to prove the truth of his statements, no liability exists in these states.

In other states (and the number appears to be growing), truth is not a full defense unless it can be shown that spoken or written publication of the defamatory material is made without malice or with good intentions and justifiable ends.

Privilege as a Defense

In many instances the law excuses the publication of defamatory material under the doctrines of *absolute privilege* or *qualified privilege*. Absolute privilege is based upon the proposition that in some cases a person must be completely free to speak his mind without fear of reprisals in the form of lawsuits for libel or slander. Absolute privilege is extended to comments by judges in court proceedings, statements by legislators during legislative sessions, and comments by certain executive officers of government in the exercise of their duties. Absolute privilege is not usually extended to school personnel as a defense against defamation.

Qualified (or conditional) privilege, on the other hand, is frequently used as a defense by school personnel against whom suit is brought for defamation. Qualified privilege rests upon the assumption by the courts that certain information should be given to certain individuals or agencies in the protection of the interests of the individuals, of the agencies, or of society as a whole. The existence of qualified privilege depends upon the *reason* which exists to communicate the information. If the person to whom defamatory information is communicated has a valid reason to receive such information, the communicator may be protected by qualified privilege.

Defamation of Character: Case Examples

In California, an instructor in a teacher education institution made statements to a local newspaper that a female student was "tricky and unreliable" and "destitute of those womanly characteristics that should be the first requisite of a teacher." The court held the instructor liable for defamation of character [*Dixon v. Allen,* 11 Pac. 179 (1886)]. It is quite possible that no liability would have existed had the instructor communicated the same information to a person with *reason* to have the information, such as a prospective employer, since the teacher probably would have been protected by qualified privilege.

Teachers who report grades on school registers are normally protected so long as they report facts (or perhaps even opinions) reasonably related to the pupils' school activities. However, the limits of qualified privilege were exceeded in an Oklahoma case, where a teacher added the comment "ruined by tobacco and whisky" on the school register after the name of a pupil. The court held the teacher liable [*Dawkins v. Billingsley,* 172 Pac. 69 (1918)].

In Kentucky the president of a college wrote a letter to the father of a male student reporting that the student had been expelled because of repeated indecent exposure. The student contended that he had only absentmindedly failed to pull the dormitory shades while he was dressing. Suit was brought against the college president for libel. The court held that it was the duty of the school to report to parents regarding the progress and deportment of their children. Since the president had reported the information only to an individual with reason to have such information, the communication was considered to be conditionally privileged, and the president was relieved of liability [*Baskett v. Crossfield,* 228 S.W.673 (1920)].

Even if a possibly defamatory communication is untrue, qualified privilege protects the utterer. In Alabama, a college physician reported to the dean of women that a female student had contracted a venereal disease. The dean then sent a report to the girl's parents stating that the girl should not return to school because she had not "been living right." Later it was discovered that a mistake had been made in the diagnosis of the disease, and suit was brought against the dean. The court held that the communication was privileged and absolved the dean from liability [*Kenney v. Gurley,* 95 So. 34 (1923)].

In brief, teachers have little to fear insofar as defamation of character is concerned, so long as information—even rumor or suspicion—is communicated in good faith to those having reason to possess the information. The doctrine of qualified privilege protects the teacher in such situations.

Gossip about pupils, however, is another matter. Teachers who communicate defamatory information about pupils to persons outside the school system or to other teachers who have no reason to have such information (e.g., who do not now have or who are not likely in the future to have the pupil in class) are acting imprudently, since it is possible that a successful lawsuit for defamation of character may be initiated.

Liability Insurance

One means of protection against judgments resulting from tort suits is liability insurance. For a relatively modest sum a teacher may obtain a personal liability insurance policy insuring him against judgments for negligence and other torts.

As is the case with most insurance policies, tort liability insurance may be secured at a lesser cost on a group basis than on an individual basis. Many state teachers' organizations are now including liability insurance as a part of their services to members. In addition, school boards in some states are empowered by law to carry liability insurance on school employees.

PUPIL CONTROL

Large numbers of legal cases have been concerned with the extent to which a school board, a school administrator, or a teacher may establish rules setting limits on pupil conduct. In determining whether such rules are legally valid, the courts invariably attempt to determine the reasonableness of the rules, or whether the rules are reasonably related to the discipline, morale, or good order of the school. Regardless of the specific punishment incurred for violation of a school rule, a basic common-law principle established by the courts is that the rule itself must be reasonable.

Not only must a rule governing pupil conduct be reasonable; the punishment itself must also be reasonable. Punishment may not be excessive; excessive punishment is usually defined as punishment which results in permanent injury, is performed with immoderate severity, or is administered with malice or wicked motives.

Reasonable Rules

Most of the general rules governing pupil conduct, such as rules dealing with pupil dress, marriage, pregnancy, leaving of school premises, pupil driving, and membership of pupils in secret societies, are established by school boards or by school administrators pursuant to authority granted by the boards rather than by the teachers. An analysis of court decisions dealing with general rules of pupil conduct will perhaps reveal the criteria used by the courts in determining reasonableness of conduct.

The reasonableness of a rule governing pupil conduct depends upon circumstances and does not exist in the abstract. For example, in an Indiana case, a school superintendent established a rule that the classroom doors in his school were to be locked during opening exercises, and tardy children were to go to the principal's office or were to remain in the hall until opening exercises were concluded. Upon one occasion, a tardy child froze his hands when he went home during cold weather after finding the classroom doors locked. As a result, a suit was brought against the superintendent by the parents of the child. The court upheld the reasonableness of the rule, since provision had been made for children during cold weather. The court pointed out, however, that had the outside doors of the school building been locked and the children forced to wait outside in the cold, the rule would have been unreasonable [*Fertich v. Michener,* 11 N.E.605, 14 N.E.68 (1887)].

Pupil Dress

Reasonable rules regulating the dress of pupils have generally been upheld by the courts. In an early Arkansas case, the court upheld the suspension of a high school girl who had violated a school board regulation prohibiting "immodest" dress or the wearing of face paint and cosmetics [*Pugsley v. Sellmyer,* 250 S.W. 538 (1922)]. In North Dakota, a court upheld a regulation prohibiting the wearing of metal heel plates by pupils, since the school board had contended that the heel plates damaged the floors and caused noise and confusion [*Stromberg v. French,* 236 N.W. 477 (1931)].

In Massachusetts, soon after the opening of school during the fall semester, a school principal suspended a pupil from school for having an "extreme" haircut of the type affected by certain modern popular musicians until such time as the pupil returned to school with a "proper" haircut. The boy, in fact, had performed at the Newport Jazz Festival of the New York World's Fair and contended that his haircut was a part of his "professional image." Action was brought by the parents of the boy to require his readmission to school. The court upheld the school authorities and pointed out that even though the length of the boy's hair was useful in his vocation, the school authorities had not abused their power. The court also stated:

> We are of [the] opinion that the unusual hair style of the plaintiff could disrupt and impede the maintenance of a proper classroom atmosphere or decorum. This is an aspect of personal appearance and hence akin to matters of dress. Thus, as with any unusual, immodest, or exaggerated mode of dress, conspicuous departures

from accepted customs in the matter of haircuts could result in the distraction of other pupils [*Leonard v. School Committee of Attleboro*, 212 N.E.2d 468 (1965)].

In one of the few cases in which a regulation of a school board with respect to pupil dress was struck down, an Alabama court held that a girl objecting to the immodesty of physical education costumes could not be required to wear such dress, even though the girl could be required to attend the physical education class [*Mitchell v. McCall*, 143 So.2d 629 (1963)].

Payment for Destruction of School Property

Rules requiring pupils to make financial restitution for damage to or destruction of school property generally have not been upheld by the courts, especially if the damage is accidental or due to simple carelessness. An Indiana court held that a rule requiring such financial restitution was unreasonable, since "carelessness on the part of children is one of the most common, and yet one of the least blame-worthy of their faults." The court went on to state that "in simple carelessness there is no purpose to do wrong" [*State v. Vanderbilt*, 18 N.E. 266 (1888)]. Courts in other states have held similar positions. [See, e.g., *Holman v. Trustees*, 43 N.W. 996 (Mich. 1889); *Perkins v. Independent School District*, 9 N.W. 356 (Iowa 1880)]. The reasoning of these courts seems to be as follows: (1) Accidental damage to school property is not a breach of morals or discipline; (2) children from families of limited financial means may be denied an education illegally if required to make restitution; and (3) pupils are usually financially unable to make restitution, and if parents refuse to do so, pupils should not be punished for the failure or unwillingness of parents to make such a payment.

The courts do not look with favor upon willful or malicious destruction of school property. Although it is doubtful whether pupils may be required even in such case to pay for the damage, other kinds of punishment have been upheld by the courts, so long as such punishment is considered to be reasonable [*Palmyra Board of Education v. Hansen*, 153 A.2d 393 (N.J. 1959)].

Prohibitions concerning Leaving of School Premises

School board regulations prohibiting pupils from leaving the school grounds during the noon lunch period have generally been upheld by the courts. In Virginia, school board rule forbade pupils to leave the school campus between 9:00 A.M. and 3:35 P.M. A parent contested the rule on the ground that he wished his child to eat a hot meal at home. The court, in upholding the school board regulation, commented that it could discover no detriment to the health of pupils resulting from the eating of a cold meal at noon [*Flory v. Smith*, 134 S.E. 360 (1926)]. Similar rules have been upheld in Michigan [*Jones v. Cody*, 92 N.W. 495 (1902)], in Kentucky—where the court felt that the regulation was for the "common good" of all the children [*Casey County Board of Education v. Luster*, 282 S.W.2d 333 (1955)], and in Texas, where the board rule prohibited pupils from "taking lunch during the noon recess except from the school cafeteria or that . . . brought from home" [*Bishop v. Houston Independent School District*, 29 S.W.2d 312 (1930)].

Pupil Driving

The increasing number of student drivers has resulted in rules by school boards prohibiting automobile driving during the noon hour. Surprisingly, perhaps, only one lawsuit bearing upon the reasonableness of such regulations has reached an appellate court in the United States.

A school board in Texas required students driving to school to park automobiles in the school parking lot in the morning and not to move the automobiles until school was dismissed in the afternoon. A girl was suspended from school for violation of the rule. The parents brought suit against the school board, contending that the board had no authority to adopt rules controlling streets and highways. The board countered with the argument that the rule had been adopted for the safety of all the pupils in the school, since there had been safety hazards created by student joyriding during the noon hour. The court upheld the school board, commenting that the rule was obviously not enacted to control traffic on streets and highways, but rather to control pupil conduct to the end that other pupils would be safe. This, according to the court, was a legitimate exercise of the power of the school board [*McLean Independent School District v. Andrews*, 33 S.W.2d 886 (1960)].

Pupil Marriages

Numerous school boards have attempted to discourage pupil marriages either by providing for the expulsion or suspension of married pupils or by prohibiting married pupils from participating in cocurricular activities. The weight of authority seems to be that pupils may not be excluded from school solely because they are married. [See, e.g., *McLeod v. State*, 122 So. 737 (Miss. 1929); *Nutt v. Board of Education*, 278 Pac. 1065 (Kans. 1929).] The reasoning of the courts in these cases can be summarized as follows: (1) Marriage is a domestic relation highly favored by the law; therefore, pupils associating with married pupils would be benefited rather than harmed; (2) the fact that married pupils might desire to further their education is evidence in itself of character warranting favorable consideration; and (3) exclusion of married pupils denies the guarantee of free public education provided in most of the state constitutions.

Apparently only a Tennessee court has upheld the exclusion of married pupils from the public schools [*State ex rel. Thompson v. Marion County Board of Education*, 302 S.W.2d 57 (1957)]. In the Tennessee case, the court accepted the testimony of the school principals as expert witnesses to the effect that a serious breakdown in pupil discipline had occurred as a result of numerous pupil marriages and that the board policy excluding married pupils for the remainder of the school term had been established to prevent further discipline problems.

Although pupils in most jurisdictions probably may not be suspended from school solely because they are married, the courts uniformly have held that married pupils may be excluded from cocurricular activities. [See, e.g., *Kissick v. Garland Independent School District*, 330 S.W.2d 708 (Tex. 1959); *Cochrane v. Board of Education*, 103 N.W.2d (Mich. 1960); *State ex rel. Baker v. Stephenson*, 189 N.E.2d 181 (Ohio, 1962).] The reasoning of these courts may be summarized as follows: (1) Pupils have no "right" to participate in cocurricular activities in the same sense that they have a right to attend school; (2) cocurricular activities are not a regular part of the school program; and (3) it is reasonable to limit the activities of married pupils to the end that they will be better able to assume the responsibilities of married life.

Pupil Pregnancy

Only one court on record in the United States has ruled on the question of the legality of the exclusion of pregnant pupils. In a 1961 Ohio case, a board rule required pregnant pupils to withdraw from school "immediately upon knowledge of pregnancy." The purpose of the rule was clearly indicated by the board, i.e., to protect the physical well-being of the pregnant pupil. In addition, home instruction was provided to enable the pupil to maintain her school standing. The Ohio court upheld the rule of the school board under these circumstances [*State ex rel. Idle v. Chamberlain*, 175 N.E.2d 539 (1961)].

Prohibition of Pupil Membership in Secret Societies

Some states have enacted statutes prohibiting membership of elementary or secondary school pupils in secret societies and permitting expulsion of pupils holding such membership in violation of school board rules. (See, e.g., *Acts 1907 Indiana*, ch. 278.) Most state legislatures, however, have remained silent on this question, and in several of these states, court cases have arisen challenging the authority of the school board to prohibit participation in cocurricular activities by pupils who hold membership in Greek letter fraternities or other similar secret societies. Courts in Arkansas [*Isgrig v. Srygley*, 197 S.W.2d 39 (1946)], Washington [*Wayland v. Board of School Directors*, 86 Pac. 642 (1906)], Oregon [*Burkitt v. School District*, 246 P.2d 566 (1952)], Ohio [*Holroyd v. Eibling*, 188 N.E.2d 797 (1962)], and Illinois [*Wilson v. Board of Education*, 84 N.E. 697 (1908)] have upheld such rules of school boards. Missouri is one of the few states holding that a board may not take such action against pupils for membership in such organizations [*Wright v. Board of Education*, 246 S.W. 43 (1922)].

Punishment for Actions of Pupils off School Grounds and after School Hours

The test of whether a pupil may be punished for violation of school rules off the school grounds and/or after school hours seems to be the effect of his action on the discipline, morale, or good order of the school. Actions by pupils are generally punishable no matter when and where they are committed if the school is adversely affected.

Public disrespect of a teacher by a pupil after school hours was held to be punishable as long ago as 1859 in a landmark case in Vermont. In that case, a high school pupil was driving his father's cow past the home of a teacher over an hour after school had closed for the day, and in the presence of the teacher and other pupils, mocked the teacher by calling him "old Jack Seaver." When school opened the next morning, the teacher whipped the child for his conduct of the previous evening. The whipping was not excessive; however, the teacher was sued for assault and battery. The plaintiff contended that the teacher had no authority to punish the child for actions after school hours. The court disagreed with the parent and upheld the teacher, stating. ". . . where the offense has a direct and immediate tendency to injure the school and bring the master's authority into contempt we think he has the right to punish the scholar if he comes again to school" [*Lander v. Seaver*, 32 Vt. 114 (1859)].

The courts in other states have upheld punishment of pupils for the following actions, even though the actions took place off the school grounds or after school hours: (1) "bullying" other pupils on the way home from school [*O'Rourke v. Walker*, 128 Atl. 25 (Conn. 1925)], (2) being drunk and disorderly on the streets of town on Christmas day [*Douglas v. Campbell*, 116 S.W. 211 (Ark. 1909)], (3) smoking cigarettes and publicly airing defiance of school authorities [*Tanton v. McKenney*, 197 N.W. 510 (Mich. 1924)], and (4) failing to obey the rule of a school principal to go straight home from school [*Jones v. Cody, supra*].

It should be noted, however, that school authorities can go too far in attempting to regulate pupil conduct after school hours. Many rules of conduct must be left to parents, and as previously indicated, the offense must bear some reasonable relationship to the welfare of the school in order to be punishable by school authorities. Homework, for example, may be required of pupils, and pupils may be punished for failure or refusal to do homework [*Bolding v. State*, 4 S.W. 579 (Tex. 1887)]. However, the courts have made it clear that a requirement that pupils do homework during certain specified hours in the evening is unreasonable, since such a requirement invades the proper domain of the parent [*Hobbs v. Germany*, 49 So. 515 (Tex. 1887)].

In Missouri, a court held that a pupil could not legally be expelled from school for attending social functions in violation of a school rule if he had reached his home and had secured the permission of his parents to attend [*Dritt v. Snodgrass*, 66 Mo. 286 (1877)]. A Wisconsin court has perhaps well summarized the limits of authority of the school with respect to control of pupil conduct after school hours: "Any rule or regulation which has for its object anything outside the instruction of the pupil—the order requisite for instruction—is beyond the province of the board of education to adopt" [*State v. Board of Education*, 23 N.W. 102 (1885)].

The Teacher *in Loco Parentis*

In the eyes of the court, the school board and school administration have the right to make rules governing pupils, and the teacher may establish reasonable rules relating to the good order and discipline of pupils in his classroom, so long as such rules are not inconsistent with higher authority. [See, e.g., *Patterson v. Nutter*, 78 Me. 609 (Maine 1866); *Sheehan v. Sturges*, 53 Conn. 481 (Conn. 1885); *Russell v. Lynnfield*, 116 Mass. 365 (Mass. 1874); *Fertich v. Michener, supra*.]

A public school teacher stands in a unique legal relationship with his pupils. This relationship is known as *in loco parentis*, meaning "in the place of the parent." Under the *in loco parentis* doctrine, the teacher's authority over pupils under his supervision is substantially the same as that of a parent, but it is restricted to the limits of his jurisdiction and responsibility as a teacher.

Even parents are limited to some degree with respect to the punishment of children. Every state has enacted statutes, for example, which prohibit cruelty to children.

Although the *in loco parentis* doctrine gives teachers substantial authority in dealing with pupils, teachers should be careful not to exceed this authority. In Pennsylvania, two teachers attempted to treat the infected finger of a 10-year-old pupil by holding the finger under boiling water, even though no situation existed requiring first aid or emergency treatment. In holding the teachers liable for the resulting injury, the court made clear that the doctrine of *in loco parentis* was limited and stated:

Under the delegated parental authority implied from the relationship of teacher and pupil there is no implied delegation of authority to exercise her lay judgment, as a parent may, in the matter of treatment of injury or disease suffered by a pupil. . . . [The teachers] were not acting in an emergency. . . . Whether treatment of the infected finger was necessary was a question for the boy's parents to decide [*Guerreri v. Tyson*, 24 A.2d 468 (1942)].

Reasonable Punishments

As indicated previously, the rules governing pupil conduct must be reasonable under the existing circumstances. In the last analysis, the courts are the determiners of the reasonableness of school rules. Not only must a rule be reasonable; the enforcement of the rule or the punishment meted for violation of the rule must also be reasonable.

There seems to be little doubt that withholding of privileges, removal from the classroom, and reasonable detention after school (where, of course, a child is not subjected to unreasonable hazards such as being required to walk home where pupil transportation is normally provided) are punishments with which it is unlikely a court would find fault. Most litigation in the area of specific punishments falls into three other categories: academic punishments for disciplinary infractions, suspension and expulsion, and corporal punishment.

Academic Punishments for Disciplinary Infractions

Many legal authorities are of the opinion that academic punishments for violations of discipline are likely to be looked upon unfavorably by the courts [118:24]. Denial of diplomas for violations of school rules has been declared illegal by at least two courts [*Valentine v. Independent School District*, 183 N.W. 434 (Iowa, 1921); *Ryan v. Board of Education*, 257 Pac. 945 (Kans. 1927)]. It would appear that the courts perhaps would agree with many educators that academic accomplishment and school discipline are separate and distinct and that the use of such academic punishments as grade reductions or withholding of diplomas for disciplinary infractions is a doubtful practice at best.

Suspension and Expulsion

Suspension can be defined as exclusion of a pupil from school for a specified brief period of time, such as a few days. Expulsion differs from suspension only in length of time. Expulsion usually involves a relatively long period of time, such as a semester or a school year.

Most authorities appear to agree that expulsion, being a more severe punishment than suspension, should involve school board rather than teacher action [see, e.g., 97]. Moreover, there is doubt as to whether even a school board may expel a pupil *permanently* [see, e.g., *Board of Education v. Helston,* 32, Ill. App. 300 (Ill. 1889)] from the public schools for disciplinary offense, since this gives the pupil no opportunity to make amends or to rehabilitate himself and would be contrary to the entire philosophy of Anglo-American law.

In the absence of school board rules to the contrary, a principal or teacher probably has inherent authority to suspend pupils for disciplinary infractions. The following case examples illustrate the reasoning of the courts in this regard.

In Wisconsin, a school principal suspended a pupil for misconduct and refused to readmit him until he gave "sincere promise of future good conduct." The pupil declined to do so, and his parents brought suit against the principal, contending that only the school board had authority to suspend the pupil from school. The court did not agree, pointing out that a principal or teacher does not derive all of his power with respect to pupil control from the school board. Teachers, according to the court, stand *in loco parentis* to pupils and therefore are entitled to exercise authority over pupils in many "things concerning which the board may have remained silent." In upholding the principal, the court commented that, even though the law gives him the power to punish pupils corporally, this is often an inadequate punishment. If the presence of a pupil is detrimental to the school, it is "essential" that the principal or teacher have the authority to suspend the pupil from school [*State v. Burton,* 45 Wis. 150 (Wis. 1878)].

In New Hampshire, a pupil in a public speaking class refused to participate in the classwork. After working with the pupil for several days, during which he still refused to participate, the teacher sent the pupil home until he would conform to the requirements of class participation. On the day the pupil was sent home, he informed the teacher that he had been acting under the orders of his parents. In upholding the teacher, the court stated that parents cannot require a teacher to receive a child under his instruction without conforming to the teacher's reasonable rules and that directions by parents to their children cannot limit the authority of the teacher in this regard [*Kidder v. Chellis,* 59 N.H. 473 (1879)].

Even though the court ruled in favor of the teacher in the foregoing case, you should keep in mind that it is not a common practice on the part of teachers in the public schools to suspend pupils from school. Many school systems have established policies which limit such action to principals or other administrative officials. As a teacher, you probably would not want to suspend a pupil from school. It is likely that such action should only be taken by an administrator in compliance with established school policy.

Corporal Punishment

Since 1833, there have been more than sixty cases decided in American appellate courts dealing with corporal or physical punishment of school pupils by teachers. Most of these cases were decided prior to 1900, which leads to a belief that the common law in this area is now fairly well settled.

New Jersey is the only state in which corporal punishment of public school pupils by teachers is forbidden by statute. In several states (e.g., Florida, Hawaii, Montana, New York, Vermont, Virginia), corporal punishment is expressly permitted by statute. It may safely be assumed that in most of the other states the right of a teacher to administer reasonable corporal punishment is protected by the common law.

Rules of School Boards Forbidding Corporal Punishment

In some school districts, however, school board rules forbid corporal punishment of pupils. For example, Milwaukee and San Francisco forbid physical punishment "after the act has been committed" [270:78]. It is possible that a teacher who violates school board rules prohibiting corporal punishment might be guilty of insubordination and thus might be considered to have breached his teaching contract. However, a concurring opinion in a 1963 Indiana case may indicate a growing attitude on the part of the courts to the effect that a school board has no right to prohibit the use of corporal punishment by teachers:

> . . . I have serious doubts that a teacher confronted with . . . responsibility under the law for maintaining order and a respect for authority before a classroom of pupils, can be deprived by a "rule" of the right to use physical force to eliminate . . . a disturbance. As long as teachers or parents are obligated under the law to educate, teach and train children, they may not be denied the necessary means of carrying out their responsibility as such teachers and parents [*Indiana State Personnel Board v. Jackson*, 192 N.E.2d 740 (1963)].

You should keep in mind that the opinion stated by this judge did not represent the majority opinion of the court. Until this question has been considered more fully by the courts, teachers who are employed in districts where corporal punishment is forbidden by school board rules probably should abide by such rules.

In any case, most school districts have established policies relating to procedures to be followed by teachers in administering corporal punishment, including a provision requiring witnesses. As a teacher, you would be wise to follow closely the established corporal punishment policy of the district in which you are employed.

Assault and Battery

Assault and battery consists of striking or threatening to strike or harm another person. Consequently, a pupil may be guilty of such a charge. An action for assault and battery may be a *criminal action*, brought by the prosecuting attorney on behalf of the state, for which conviction would result in a fine and/or imprisonment. On the other hand, it may be a *civil action* in tort, brought by the injured party, for which the penalty would be monetary damages to the injured party.

Reasonableness of Corporal Punishment

The reasonableness of the corporal punishment administered is usually a major factor in determining the liability of the teacher. The courts normally will assume that corporal punishment which results in permanent injury is excessive or un-reasonable. Corporal punishment administered with malice, which usually means with wicked motives or in anger, is also likely to be considered unreasonable. An Alabama court has listed certain guidelines which the courts tend to follow in determining whether corporal punishment is reasonable: "In determining the reasonableness of the punishment or the extent of malice, proper matters of con-sideration are the instrument used and the nature of the offense committed by the child, the age and physical condition of the child, and other attendant cir-cumstances" [*Suits v. Glover*, 71 So.2d 49 (1954)].

The legality of corporal punishment of school pupils, perhaps more than any other aspect of pupil punishment, depends upon circumstances. What might be considered reasonable corporal punishment for a child of a certain age or sex might be considered unreasonable for another child of a different age or sex. Community attitudes also may affect the decision of courts. An examination of several court decisions in which action was brought against teachers for assault and battery may reveal the factors which determine reasonableness.

Corporal Punishment: Case Examples

In Ohio, a teacher corporally punished a boy who had thrown a stone at another pupil on the way home from school and who, when questioned, had "fibbed" about it. The teacher struck the pupil six to fifteen times with a paddle of "normal" proportions, which caused vivid discoloration of the buttocks. A complicating factor in the case was the fact that the pupil was an epileptic and had suffered three seizures following the spanking. Action was brought against the teacher for criminal assault and battery. The court listed the following as "fundamental propositions of law" which should be followed when a teacher is charged criminally for assault and battery arising from the corporal punishment of a school pupil: (1) A teacher stands *in loco parentis* and is not liable for an error in judgment; (2) a teacher's authority attaches from home to home; (3) there is a presumption of correctness in the actions of the teacher; (4) there is a presumption that the teacher acts in good faith; and (5) mere excessive or severe punishment is not a crime unless it produces permanent injury or unless it is administered with malice. The court found that no permanent injury had resulted to the child and that no malice was involved. The teacher, therefore, was found to be not guilty [*State v. Lutz*, 113 N.E.2d 757 (1953)].

In Alabama, a teacher corporally punished an eight-year-old boy who was "well developed, fat and in good health" for insubordination and for "scuffling" in the hall contrary to school rules. Civil action was brought against the teacher for assault and battery. The court indicated that, according to the evidence, the boy had been struck only five times on the buttocks. The evidence conflicted as to whether the instrument used was a Ping-Pong paddle or a slat from an apple crate. In any case, no permanent injury resulted. In relieving the teacher from liability, the court stated: "To be guilty of an assault and battery, the teacher must not only inflict upon the child immoderate chastisement, but he must do so with legal malice or wicked motives or he must inflict some permanent injury" (*Suits v. Glover, supra*).

It can be inferred from the foregoing cases that teachers may be found liable for immoderate corporal punishment (1) if the punishment results in permanent injury or (2) if the punishment is administered with malice. Two cases in which teachers were held liable for excessive corporal punishment serve to further illustrate the importance of these factors.

In Pennsylvania, a teacher's corporal punishment of a child involved a blow on the pupil's right ear, which injured the eardrum and permanently impaired the hearing of the pupil. Since permanent injury had resulted, the court held the teacher liable and pointed out that, if corporal punishment were necessary, nature had "provided a part of the anatomy for chastisement" and tradition held "that chastisement should be there applied" [*Rupp v. Zintner*, 29 Pa. D. & C. 629 (1937)].

In Alabama, a boy used objectionable language to a teacher in the classroom. The teacher pulled the boy into the school yard where he struck the boy with a limb or stick. The boy then apologized. The evidence showed that the teacher, at this point, "struck . . . [the boy] in the face three licks with his fist and hit him several times over the head with the butt end of the switch." A witness testified that the teacher had declared that he "would conquer him [the pupil] or kill him." Other witnesses testified that the teacher was apparently very angry and excited. The court found the teacher to be guilty of assault and battery on the ground that malice was evident, even though no permanent injury had resulted: "From this unseemly conduct on the part of one whose duty it was to set a good example of self restraint and gentlemanly deportment to his pupils, there was ample room for the inference of legal malice, in connection with unreasonable and immoderate correction" [*Boyd v. State*, 7 So. 268 (1890)].

SUMMARY

The most common tort involving teachers is negligence resulting in pupil injury. A teacher's actions which fall below the standard of the reasonably prudent teacher and which result in injury to pupils may make the teacher liable for negligence.

Defenses against negligence include contributory negligence, proximate cause, and assumption of risk. In spite of the existence of these legal defenses, a teacher should make every effort to foresee and to prevent pupil injury.

The importance of adequate instruction in potentially hazardous activities and the establishment of safety rules cannot be overemphasized. These two factors, in addition to the exercise of sound common sense, are vital to teachers in protecting themselves against successful negligence suits.

In addition to cases involving negligence teachers occasionally are sued for defamation of character. Written defamation is known as libel, and spoken defamation is known as slander. Teachers who communicate information about pupils should be certain the person to whom such information is given has a reason for having it. Teachers who follow this rule probably have little to fear from defamation-of-character lawsuits, since such communication is privileged.

School boards, administrators, and teachers have wide authority to establish rules of pupil conduct. So long as the rules are reasonable and bear reasonable relation to the welfare of the school (even though they may to some extent govern pupil conduct off the school grounds and after school hours), they are likely to be upheld by the courts. It should be remembered, however, that the courts are the final determiners of the reasonableness of a particular school rule.

Methods of enforcing school rules must also be reasonable. Such enforcement procedures as academic punishments for disciplinary infractions or the requirement that children pay for school property accidentally damaged or destroyed are likely to be struck down by the courts. Suspension and expulsion, withholding of privileges, removal from the classroom, and reasonable corporal punishment probably would be upheld.

QUESTIONS FOR YOUR CONSIDERATION

1. How would you define the term "common law"?
2. Why do you think the courts have established the concept of the "reasonably prudent man" as the standard for determining negligence?
3. Why do you think the courts have established "foreseeability" as the first test of negligence?
4. If you, as a teacher, were given the responsibility for supervising the school safety patrol, what precautions would you take?
5. What policy do you feel a teacher should follow regarding elementary pupils who forget to bring books from home and request permission to go home after them?
6. As a teacher, what should you do about a pupil who complains of a severe headache?
7. What seems to be the determining factor as to the liability of a teacher for pupil injury in the classroom while the teacher is out of the room?
8. What is the reason the courts have established "privilege" as a defense against defamation of character?
9. Are there any disadvantages to a teachers' association carrying a $50,000 liability insurance policy on all members of the association?
10. What seems to be the controlling factor as to whether teachers may punish pupils for acts off the school grounds or after school hours?
11. Under what circumstances might a teacher be liable for injuries to pupils off the school grounds or after school hours?
12. As a teacher, what action should you take against a pupil who hits a baseball through a classroom window during playground activities at a school where a rule is in effect that baseball is not to be played close to the school building?
13. In a practical sense, do you feel a teacher should ever suspend a pupil from school?
14. What do you think the attitude of the courts would be toward a school rule providing for a 3 per cent grade reduction for each "unexcused" absence?
15. Why do you think the courts have established the *in loco parentis* doctrine?
16. Do you think it is desirable or undesirable that a school board establish a rule forbidding corporal punishment by teachers?

ACTIVITIES FOR YOU TO PURSUE

1. Outline the points which might have been made by the attorney for the plaintiff if the case involving the mouse, as described in the early part of this chapter, had been brought to trial.
2. Set up a mock court, including the attorney for the plaintiff, the attorney for the defendant, a judge, a bailiff, a plaintiff, a defendant, and a jury to "try" the "mouse" case outlined in this chapter.
3. Go to a courthouse law library and look up the United States Supreme Court prayer and Bible-reading cases cited in the chapter. Analyze these cases, including the facts, the issues, the decisions, and the reasons given by the Court in reaching the decisions.
4. Analyze the 1954 desegregation decision of the Supreme Court cited in the chapter. Try to find out why the Court held that separate public school facilities for Negro and white pupils were "inherently" unequal.
5. Assume that you are a school principal. Establish a set of guidelines which you might suggest that your teachers follow in order to avoid tort liability for negligence.
6. Develop a parental permission form which might be used for pupil field trips.
7. Develop a set of pupil safety rules for the classroom, assuming that you are an elementary teacher (or a high school teacher of physical education, chemistry, industrial arts, or homemaking).
8. Assume that you are a school principal. Develop a set of rules for teachers who wish to administer corporal punishment.
9. From the references cited in the chapter, see what you can learn about the following: (*a*) Must a pupil's cumulative-record folder be shown to the parents of the pupil upon their request? (*b*) May a pupil-composed prayer be said at the noon meal in a public school cafeteria? (*c*) Do teachers have the legal right to strike? (*d*) May the King James Version of the Bible be used as a textbook in the public schools? (*e*) Under what circumstances may teachers be dismissed for unbecoming conduct after school hours? (*f*) May a person in college who will receive a teaching license in August legally contract with a school district the previous spring? (*g*) Would a school counselor likely be held liable for the suicide of a student because the counselor failed to recommend psychiatric care for the student? (*h*) What authority does the state legislature have over the public schools?

RESOURCE
SECTION
FOR PART ▌▌▌

CHECKLIST FOR APPRAISING A TEACHER
SALARY SCHEDULE

CHECKLIST FOR APPRAISING A TEACHER
RETIREMENT SYSTEM

SUGGESTED READINGS

SUGGESTED FILMS, FILMSTRIPS,
AND RECORDINGS

FIGURE CREDITS

CHECKLIST FOR APPRAISING A TEACHER SALARY SCHEDULE

If you can answer "yes" to each of the following questions, you may be certain that the salary schedule is a good one.

Item	Yes	No

Rules and regulations
1. Are the following requirements for employment specified: a degree; graduation from an institution accredited for teacher education; full professional certification?
2. Are safeguards provided against arbitrary denial or withdrawal of increments?
3. If "professional growth" requirements are utilized are increases based on clearly defined qualifications which can be reasonably expected of all teachers?
4. Is the application clear and equitable with regard to: credit for prior service outside the district; credit for military service; placing teachers on steps; advance warning and follow-up supervisory help if increments are denied?
5. Is discretionary initial step placement prohibited?

Starting salaries
1. Is the B.A. minimum competitive in respect to beginning salaries offered to college graduates?
2. Does this minimum make it possible for teacher to invest in advanced preparation?
3. Does this minimum permit a professional living standard?

Experience increments
1. Is each increment at least 5 per cent of the B.A. minimum?
2. Does the B.A. scale have less than 12 steps (11 increments)?
3. Is the increment structure devised to reduce teacher turnover and to promote in-service growth?

Training differentials
1. Is the extent of recognition sufficient to include:
   a. A class for the master's degree?
   b. A class for sixth year of college preparation?
   c. A class for the doctor's degree or a seventh-year preparation level as a substitute for the doctoral class?
   d. Intermediate preparation levels for at least each half-year of graduate credit?
2. Are differentials adequate in amounts so as to:
   a. Be an incentive for voluntary professional growth?
   b. Allow teachers with advanced preparation and professional growth credits a salary potential at least $1,000 above the regular B.A. scale?
   c. Reimburse teachers within a reasonable period (not more than 10 years) for their investments in advanced preparation?

Maximum salaries
1. Excepting super-maximums, are they attainable in a reasonable number of years (10 to 15)?
2. Is the B.A. maximum at least 60 per cent above the B.A. minimum?

Source: Eula May Taylor and Erwin L. Coons, "Salary-scheduling Check List," *NEA Journal,* vol. 49, no. 7, p. 33, National Education Association, Washington, October, 1960.

CHECKLIST FOR APPRAISING A TEACHER SALARY SCHEDULE (continued)

Item	Yes	No

Extra compensation
1. Are higher salaries based on differences in qualifications, avoiding such discriminatory practices as sex differentials and subject or grade-level differentials?
2. Are salary differentials allowed for work beyond normal load?
3. If extra pay is granted, is a schedule of payments included in the salary policy or personnel policies?
4. Has "extra pay" been abolished in favor of a balanced load for all teachers?

Other considerations related to quality
1. Is the schedule a "booster" rather than a "buster" of teacher morale?
2. Does the schedule enhance the professional standing of the teaching staff?
3. Does the schedule generally provide freedom from financial worry?
4. Does the schedule indicate that teachers are to devote full time to teaching?
5. Are teacher-supervisor relations for improvement of instruction kept on a high plane of co-operation?
6. Are irregularities which tend to tear down teachers' prestige, self-confidence, and status avoided?

CHECKLIST FOR APPRAISING A TEACHER RETIREMENT SYSTEM

You may be satisfied that the retirement system embodies good features if you can answer "yes" to each of the following questions:

Question	Yes	No

1. Is the system joint-contributory?
2. Are investments of the reserves safeguarded?
3. Is the system administered by a board separate from other governmental bodies?
4. Are teachers represented on the retirement board?
5. Are all types of professional positions covered by the retirement system, that is, administrative and supervisory as well as classroom teaching positions?
6. Is membership in the retirement system compulsory for teachers employed since the establishment of the system?
7. Are the contributions sufficient to pay a reasonable retirement allowance?
8. When a teacher withdraws from the profession or dies in active service, are all his own contributions refundable and with interest?
9. Are benefits payable to surviving dependents of a deceased member?
10. Does the teacher who withdraws before retirement have the option

Source: Adapted from *Teacher Retirement*, Discussion Pamphlet No. 2, National Education Association, Department of Classroom Teachers and Research Division, Washington, November, 1957, pp. 21–22.

CHECKLIST FOR APPRAISING A TEACHER RETIREMENT SYSTEM (continued)

Question	Yes	No
of leaving his money in the system and taking a deferred annuity policy instead of a cash refund?		
11. Is out-of-state service credited toward years of service required for retirement?		
12. Does the system give a teacher about to retire a choice of several ways of receiving his allowance?		
13. Are there retirement benefits for a teacher who is disabled prior to meeting requirements (age and years of service) for regular retirement?		
14. Is a teacher who is absent on military leave given credit toward retirement for the time he is in service?		
15. If social security coverage has been extended to the members of the retirement system, has the overall protection been improved?		

SUGGESTED READINGS

The number in parentheses following each suggestion denotes the chapter for which it is best suited.

Chamberlain, Leo M., and Leslie W. Kindred: *The Teacher and School Organization,* Prentice-Hall, Inc., Englewood Cliffs, N.J., 1966. Chapter 11 contains a good discussion of the legal status of the teacher. (10)

Davis, Thelma F.: "NEA Mutual Fund," *NEA Journal,* vol. 53, no. 8, pp. 29–30, National Education Association, Washington, November, 1964. Explains how the NEA Mutual Fund operates. (9)

Ducker, Sam: *The Public Schools and Religion: The Legal Context,* Harper and Row, Publishers, Incorporated, New York, 1966. Analyzes Supreme Court decisions relating to religion and the schools with excerpts from the decisions. (10)

Economic Status of Teachers, National Education Association, Research Division, Washington. Latest issue. Presents much information on factors affecting the economic status of teachers. (8)

"Extended Leaves of Absence for Classroom Teachers," *Educational Research Service Circular* 2, National Education Association, Research Division, Washington, February, 1966. Presents the results of a study of plans which make it possible for a competent teacher to leave his classroom for a semester or an entire year without losing his job or salary status. (9)

Extended-year Contracts for Teachers, Educational Research Service, National Education Association, Research Division, Washington, September, 1964. Points out the advantages of employing teachers on a full-year basis and describes how the plan operates in five school systems. (8)

"Extra Pay for Extra Duties," *NEA Research Bulletin,* vol. 41, no. 2, pp. 50–51, National Education Association, Research Division, Washington, May, 1963. Analyzes the extra pay teachers receive for assuming extra duties. (8)

Flowers, Anne, and Edward C. Bolmeier: *Law and Pupil Control,* W. H. Anderson Company, Cincinnati, 1964. Discusses the authority of school boards and teachers to establish rules of pupil conduct. (10)

Garber, Lee O., and Newton Edwards: *The Law Governing Pupils,* Interstate Printers and Publishers, Danville, Ill., 1962. Discusses and presents excerpts from court decisions relating to pupil attendance, transportation, religious instruction, and pupil discipline. (10)

———— and ————: *The Law Governing Teaching Personnel,* Interstate Printers and Publishers, Danville, Ill., 1962. Discusses and presents excerpts from court decisions relating to teacher contracts, licenses, strikes, dismissal, and liability for pupil injuries. (10)

Gauerke, Warren E.: *Legal and Ethical Responsibilities of School Personnel,* Prentice-Hall, Inc., Englewood Cliffs, N.J., 1959. Analyzes the legal and ethical rights and responsibilities of public school teachers. (10)

"Group Health Insurance for Professional Personnel," *NEA Research Bulletin,* vol. 42, no. 1, pp. 24–27, National Education Association, Research Division, Washington, February, 1964. Analyzes various types of group insurance made available to public school professional personnel. (9)

"Group Life Insurance for Teachers," *NEA Research Bulletin,* vol. 42, no. 2, pp. 56–59, National Education Association, Research Division, Washington, May, 1964. Discusses how group insurance plans operate in public school systems. (9)

Kleinmann, Jack H.: "Merit Pay: The Big Question," *NEA Journal,* vol. 52, no. 5, pp. 42–44, National Education Association, Washington, May, 1963. Indicates there are other ways of rewarding teachers for superior performance. (8)

Legal Aspects of Corporal Punishment, Research Memo, National Education Association, Research Division, Washington, 1964. Reviews case law on corporal punishment. (10)

Leibee, Howard C.: *Tort Liability for Injuries to Pupils,* Campus Publishers, 711 North University Avenue, Ann Arbor, Mich., 1965. Presents a state-by-state analysis of teacher and school district liability for pupil injuries. (10)

Lillywhite, Ray L., and Martha L. Ware: "Retirement Benefits and Teacher Mobility," *NEA Journal,* vol. 55, no. 4, pp. 15–16, National Education Association, Washington, April, 1966. Discusses methods for solving the retirement benefits problem for teachers who move. (9)

"Maternity Leave Provisions for Classroom Teachers in Large School Systems," *Educational Research Service Circular* 3, National Education Association, Research Division, Washington, March, 1966. Presents the results of a nationwide study of maternity leave provisions for classroom teachers. (9)

Merit Ratings in Business and Industry: Fact or Fancy? Research Memo 1964–1966, National Education Association, Research Division, Washington, February, 1964. Analyzes merit-pay plans in business and industry, and points out weaknesses when such plans are applied to the pay of school teachers and other personnel. (8)

Nolte, M. Chester, and John Phillip Linn: *School Law for Teachers,* Interstate Printers and Publishers, Danville, Ill., 1963. Presents a complete overview of the legal rights and responsibilities of teachers. (10)

"Plan Now, Retire Later," *NEA Journal,* vol. 52, no. 5, pp. 11–12, National Education Association, Washington, May, 1963. Indicates the importance of young people planning for their retirement. (9)

Rhodes, Eric: "What Index Scheduling Means," *Phi Delta Kappan,* vol. 46, no. 9, pp. 459–460, May, 1965. Tells how to use an index schedule for computing teacher salaries. (8)

"Sabbatical Leave Provisions for Classroom Teachers in Larger School Systems," *Educational Research Service Circular* 8, National Education Association, Research Division, Washington, November, 1965. Analyzes sabbatical leave provisions for classroom teachers in a number of school systems throughout the United States. (9)

Salaries in Higher Education, Research Report, National Education Association, Research Division, Washington. Latest report. Presents the latest statistics on salaries of teachers and other personnel in colleges and universities. (8)

"Short-term Leaves of Absence for Classroom Teachers in Larger School Systems,"

Educational Research Service Circular 4, National Education Association, Research Division, Washington, April, 1966. Presents the results of a nationwide study of provisions for short-term leaves of absence for classroom teachers. (9)

"Sick Leave Provisions for Classroom Teachers in Larger School Systems," *Educational Research Service Circular* 5, National Education Association, Research Division, Washington, May, 1966. Analyzes sick leave provisions for teachers in a number of school systems throughout the United States. (9)

"State Minimum-salary Laws," *NEA Research Bulletin,* vol. 44, no. 1, pp. 15–17, National Education Association, Research Division, Washington, February, 1966. A study of minimum-salary laws in the various states. (8)

Stinnett, T. M., and Albert J. Huggett: *Professional Problems of Teachers,* The Macmillan Company, New York, 1963. Chapter 7 contains a discussion of professional salary policies for teachers and includes a discussion on collective bargaining versus professional negotiations. Chapter 9 is devoted to teacher retirement systems, and Chapter 12 involves teacher leaves, nonwage benefits, and political rights. (8, 9)

"Summer School Programs: Teaching Staff, Salaries, and Financing," *Educational Research Service Circular* 5, National Education Association, Research Division, Washington, October, 1963. Presents information on salaries for teaching in public school summer programs. (8)

"Tax-Sheltered Annuities," *NEA Research Bulletin,* vol. 44, no. 1, pp. 29–30, National Education Association, Research Division, Washington, February, 1966. Discusses how tax-sheltered annuities operate. (9)

Turner, Ewald: "Mutual Funds: A Modern Way to Invest," *NEA Journal,* vol. 54, no. 6, pp. 24–25, National Education Association, Washington, September, 1965. Tells how mutual funds operate and how teachers may invest in them. (9)

Ware, Martha L. (ed.): *Law of Guidance and Counseling,* W. H. Anderson Company, Cincinnati, 1964. Discusses such legal problems as libel and slander, release of pupil records, search of students, and duties and responsibilities of school counselors. (10)

SUGGESTED FILMS, FILMSTRIPS, AND RECORDINGS

The number in parentheses following each suggestion denotes the chapter for which it is best suited.

Films (16 mm)

The Legal Control and Discipline of Public School Pupils (Thomas J. Barbre Productions, 40 min, color). A discussion by Robert R. Hamilton, former Dean, School of Law, University of Wyoming, on the legal aspects of pupil discipline. (10)

Legal Liabilities of Teachers for School Accidents (Thomas J. Barbre Productions, 40 min, color). A discussion by Robert R. Hamilton, former Dean, School of Law, University of Wyoming, on liability of teachers for pupil injuries. (10)

Filmstrips

Let's Take a Look at Teaching (Wayne University, 50 fr.). Gives an overview of the teaching profession and what it has to offer in terms of salary, tenure, working conditions, opportunities for travel, and individual interests. Pictures a typical school day, showing the varied demands on the teacher, and her responsibilities. (8)

Recordings

Developing Salary Schedules for Teachers (Educational Recording Service, 33⅓ rpm). Two teachers, Irving R. Melbo, Dean of Education, University of Southern California, and D. Lloyd Nelson, Professor of Education, University of Southern California, present suggestions for the development of salary schedules for teachers. (8)

Teacher Salary Schedule (National Tape Recording Project, 15 min). Discusses the importance of a salary schedule in attracting good teachers and in improving education. (8)

Teacher Tenure (National Tape Recording Project, 15 min). Discusses how to avoid the fear that results when cheap politics invades the classroom. (9)

FIGURE CREDITS

FIGURE 8–1. *(Source:* "Facts on American Education," *NEA Research Bulletin,* vol. 44, no. 2, p. 36, National Education Association, Research Division, Washington, May, 1966.)

FIGURE 8–2. *(Source:* Data from *Estimates of School Statistics, 1965–66,* Research Report 1965–R17, National Education Association, Research Division, Washington, December, 1965, p. 15.)

FIGURE 8–3. *(Source: What Everyone Should Know about Financing Our Schools,* National Education Association, Washington, 1966, p. 14.)

FIGURE 8–4. *(Source: What Everyone Should Know about Financing Our Schools,* National Education Association, Washington, 1966, p. 17.)

FIGURE 8–5. *(Source: Financial Status of the Public Schools,* National Education Association, Committee on Educational Finance, Washington, 1966, p. 30.)

FIGURE 8–6. *(Source:* "Salaries Paid Public School Personnel, 1964–65," *NEA Research Bulletin,* vol. 43, no. 3, p. 82, National Education Association, Research Division, Washington, October, 1965.

FIGURE 8–7. *(Source:* "State Minimum-salary Laws," *NEA Research Bulletin,* vol. 44, no. 1, p. 16, National Education Association, Research Division, Washington, February, 1966.)

FIGURE 8–8. (*Source:* "Index Salary Schedules for Teachers," *NEA Research Bulletin,* vol. 39, no. 4, p. 111, National Education Association, Research Division, Washington, December, 1961.)

FIGURE 8–9. (*Source: The American Public School Teacher, 1960–1961,* Research Monograph 1963–M2, National Education Association, Research Division, Washington, April, 1963, p. 22.)

FIGURE 9–1. *(Source:* Data from "Tenure and Contracts," *School Law Summaries,* National Education Association, Research Division, Washington, November, 1965, p. 3.)

NATURE OF OUR SCHOOL SYSTEM

The structure of school organization is extremely complex. Teachers work under conditions that are highly organized, where policies and procedures are already well established. Your success and happiness in teaching will be greatly influenced by the adequacy with which you understand the different patterns of organization, adjust to these patterns, and work effectively toward the full realization of the school's function in our society.

The financial support of education, too, can hardly escape your concern. What it costs to operate public schools, where the money comes from, how it is distributed and used, how adequately the real needs of children and youth in school are provided for financially— these and other monetary matters have much to do with teachers and the kind of work they can do in school.

From an understanding of how schools are organized and financed, you will be in a better position to make critical analyses of present conditions, exert more positive influence in gaining community support of schools, and aid in the improvement of learning conditions. Every alert teacher brings such concerns to his professional work. Part IV should aid you in regard to these matters.

11

ORGANIZATION AND ADMINISTRATION OF SCHOOLS

How are schools organized in terms of geography and of instruction in order to accomplish the task of educating millions of boys and girls? How will you fit into this organizational structure? To whom will you be responsible? What changes in the organization and administration of schools may be expected in the future? What opportunities and responsibilities will you have in determining changes that will take place? The answers to the above questions have a bearing on the way you plan your career and on the happiness and success you will have as an educator.

In a very real sense teachers perform major administrative and organizational functions as they work with pupils in the classroom. Decisions must be made on what concepts or units are to be taught, what textbooks or other media are to be used, what groupings of pupils are necessary, what kinds of evaluations of pupil progress should be made, and what standards of performance are to be expected of the pupils. In the final analysis, the implementation of an educational program of a school is determined to a very considerable extent by the administrative and organizational decisions made by the teacher in the classroom.

Since schools and school systems are organized and administered in order to implement educational programs, school administrators increasingly seek the advice and use the creative thinking of teachers in making decisions. You may expect, therefore, to be involved in the development of school policies. How will you answer such questions as the following: How should pupils be grouped for instruction? Upon what bases should pupils be promoted? How large should classes be, and should all of them be of the same size? Should foreign languages be taught throughout the elementary school? What bases should be used for admitting children to the first grade? Should there be departmentalization in the elementary school? What special provisions should be made for the gifted, the physically handicapped, the mentally retarded, and the emotionally disturbed? What cocurricular activities should the school sponsor? What courses should be required of all pupils, and what elective courses should be offered? Should the school district build a junior high school that would involve grades 7, 8, and 9, or should it involve some other combination of grades? In view of the emphasis upon establishing community colleges, should your school system add grades 13 and 14 to its educational structure?

In order to assist you in answering the many questions with which you will be confronted, this chapter has been organized into two parts: public school organization and administration according to geographic units and organization and

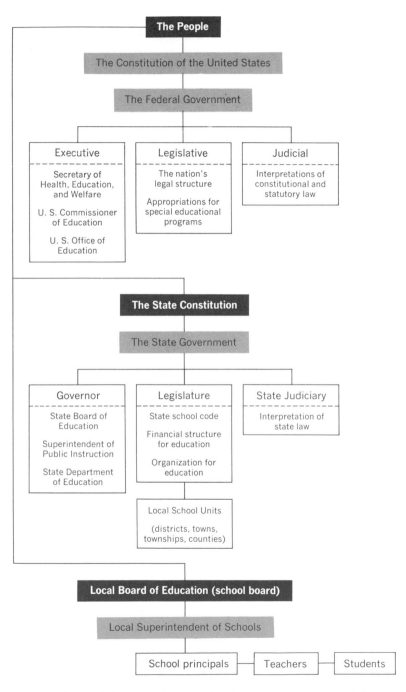

FIGURE 11–1. Structure of the organization of education in the United States. (*Source:* McGraw-Hill Book Company.)

administration for instruction in basic local school districts. An understanding of the legal basis of public education, first of all, will help you gain a perspective for a consideration of these two parts.

Legal Basis of Public Education

Unlike many other countries, the United States does not have a national system of public education in which power over schools is concentrated at the national level of government. Since the United States Constitution does not mention education and since court decisions throughout the history of the United States have consistently upheld the states' responsibility for maintaining free public education, there is no legal basis for a national system.

The constitution of each state provides for the organization and operation of a system of public schools. In reality we have a collection of fifty state systems of education which may be spoken of as the American systems of education rather than as a national system.

Although education is legally a state function in the United States, you will find that each state relies upon both the local school district and the federal government to play a role in the operation and development of public education. In effect, public education is a shared responsibility of local, state, and federal governments—the local unit usually operates schools; the state is legally responsible for provision of an educational system; and the federal government is an agent of change that encourages the extension and improvement of education in the fifty state systems. As an agent of change, the federal government, through such agencies as the U.S. Office of Education, the Office of Economic Opportunity, and the Department of Labor, senses national manpower and social needs and offers state governments so-called "incentive moneys" to develop new and/or better instructional programs. The states then voluntarily accept or reject such opportunities to work with the federal government in such educational affairs. Details of this and other types of federal financial assistance will be discussed in Chapter 12.

Conceptions of Organization and Administration

Any educational program demands a plan and an organization for implementing the plan. Organization is the means of effectively concentrating the efforts of a group of people on the attainment of a common goal. A school organization does not exist as an end in itself, but rather as a means to an end. In the case of public education, the organization is structured to provide instruction, and the prime role of school administration should be to facilitate this instruction.

As you study different school systems, however, you will note that they differ in the way they are organized and administered. Since the life of a teacher is affected by the type of organization in which he works, it is important to understand different concepts of school organization and how they may affect your work.

Any organization, whether it involves the school, a business or industry, the military, or the government, is a conception of the human mind. For this reason, there are many conceptions of organization. There is some agreement among scholars, however, concerning categories under which various conceptions of organization may be grouped. These categories may be called (1) traditional, (2) neotraditional, and (3) modern.

A *traditional* concept of organization is built upon a framework of command, line of authority, control, and hierarchy. It emphasizes interpositional relationships. The rationale for this type of organization seems to be based upon the element of control in order to guarantee results. When this type of organization is applied to a school, a teacher's work is to be controlled by a principal to ensure that the teacher "does what he is supposed to do" in implementing a master plan for education in a school district.

The heart of the traditional concept in school organization is the division of labor, as exemplified by the work of a superintendent, principal, teacher, librarian, and clerk. The specialized parts of the organization are merged into an effective whole through functional processes of those holding line and staff positions. Line represents the chain of authoritative relationships, and staff represents the positions to be filled by specialists who may have no authority but who give advice and ideas to those on the authority line. Since control is the essence of the traditional organization, it is accomplished through such processes as reporting, inspecting, and commanding.

In the latter part of the 1920s, a number of forceful objections to the traditional concept of organization began to emerge. It was felt that this concept was too narrow and limited since the worker was considered to be a mere commodity or cog in the wheel. Proponents of change maintained that man had a right to work and live in dignity and that management had a responsibility for assisting each member in the group in meeting his personal needs and objectives.

The *neotraditional* concept of organization, which evolved from these objections, resulted primarily from the work of human-relations-in-industry and small-group research specialists. Although the traditional approach underlies the neotraditional concept of organization, individual and informal group behavior is superimposed upon it. Thus, although there is a formal line-staff structure to begin with, a network of functional overlays of individual or group behavior develops as a result of complicated interpersonal relationships. Functional overlays occur because of man's inability to structure a formal organization that will adequately meet the personal needs of employees or the impersonal needs of the organizational entity. The formal structure is respected up to a point and then is modified in an informal way. As a result, the emphasis in organizing shifts from an interpositional basis to an interpersonal basis.

Functional overlays might include those of power, competency, and communications. The overlay in such a case partly represents a bypassing of an immediate superior by a subordinate in order to accomplish more effectively personal and/or organizational goals. A power overlay is exemplified by a subordinate ignoring the idea of "going through channels" and proceeding to work directly with a person who is perceived to have the power capability to effect action expeditiously. In a competency overlay, the subordinate again ignores the hierarchy, does not proceed through channels, and seeks the services of the organizational member who is perceived to have the competency to accomplish a desired objective. A teacher, for example, who has no confidence in a principal may proceed to ignore the

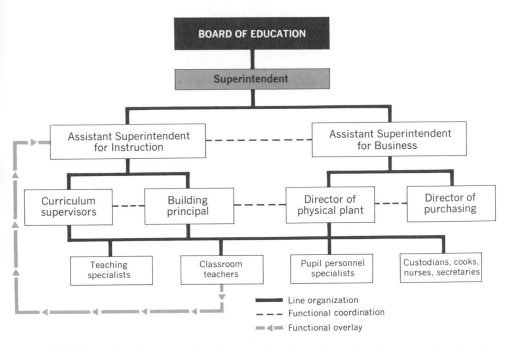

FIGURE 11–2. An example of a functional overlay. The classroom teacher, for example, feels that the principal and the curriculum supervisor are too busy to answer some questions regarding the mathematics curriculum. As a result, the assistant superintendent in charge of instruction is contacted directly.

line relationship with the principal and relate with another in the hierarchy who is perceived to have the competency to assist the teacher in resolving a professional problem.

The *modern* concept of organization involves a general systems approach, which provides for various cross sections of organizational life. Attempts are made to identify the strategic parts (subsystems) and goals of the organization and the nature of their mutual dependency, as well as the main processes in the system which link the parts together and facilitate their adjustment to one another. Subsystems might include large or small groups of teachers, administrators, nonteaching personnel, students, parent and teacher organizations, and board members. Attempts are made to understand the totality of the organization as well as the elements, subsystems, and processes.

As you may suspect, a teacher working in a traditional organizational pattern hesitates to make decisions without first consulting with the principal. Initiative and creative approaches to teaching tend to be stifled, and frustrations, fears, tensions, and possessiveness tend to be fostered. The neotraditional type of organization provides a teacher with the opportunity to achieve a higher degree of professional satisfaction than he may be able to achieve in a traditional situation. Without question the modern concept of organization and administration provides the most desirable situation in which a teacher may work. As you approach the process of accepting a teaching position, you first will want to examine carefully the concept of organization and administration that seems to characterize the school system you are considering.

PUBLIC SCHOOL ORGANIZATION AND ADMINISTRATION ACCORDING TO GEOGRAPHIC UNITS

Each state legislature has complete power in providing a school administrative structure, subject to the limitations of its state constitution and the federal laws. The state may create or abolish school districts at will, either with or without the consent of the people living within the districts. It may vest the educational authority in any local body it chooses, or it may operate the schools itself.

In most states you will find three units of school administrative structure: (1) local districts, (2) intermediate units, and (3) the state department of education. Some states, known as "county unit states," have merged the local and the intermediate units. In addition to these units, national and international governmental education offices are playing an increasingly important role in the development and implementation of educational policy.

Local School Administrative Districts

You will note in Chapter 13 that education in America has been mainly a matter of local concern. Although it is true that local educational governing bodies typically spend considerable time and money in administering state educational policy, much emphasis is given to what is termed "local leeway for diversity," or discretionary power in matters of establishing schools, raising money, erecting buildings, providing materials and supplies, employing professional personnel, and supervising pupil admission and attendance. They also regulate in essential detail such matters of curriculum and teaching as actually determine the kind of school experiences youngsters will have. In most school affairs, the local community is almost completely independent. In fact, this tenacious regard for local autonomy among smaller and sparsely settled communities is one of the main hindrances to school district reorganization designed to provide better educational opportunities for the youngsters in those areas.

The local school administrative district consists of an area in which a single board or officer has the immediate responsibility for the direct administration of all schools located therein. It is a subordinate unit of the state, performing the duties of the state in the conduct and maintenance of the public schools. It is *not* a subordinate unit of the local civil government, which performs the duties related to police and fire protection, street construction and maintenance, and other services. Historically, school government has been separated from civil government for many reasons, including an attempt to divorce the school administration from highly partisan local politics often found in civil affairs and to give special attention to the unique problems involved in educational matters.

Throughout the United States, there are over fifty different names used in referring to this basic unit. These names refer to program scope, to population,

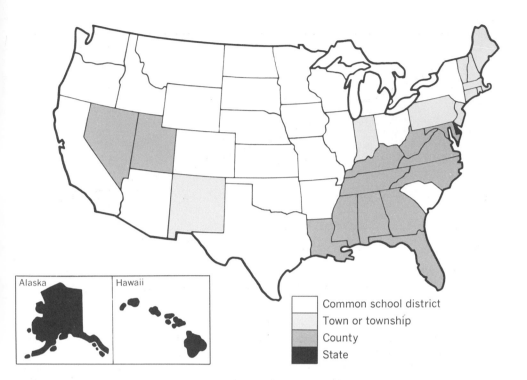

FIGURE 11–3.   Prevailing types of local school organization in the United States.

to sociological structure, or to local civil governmental subdivision. For example, in terms of program scope, districts may be called elementary school districts; in terms of sociological structure, community school districts; and in terms of a local civil governmental subdivision, township school districts, town school districts, or city school districts. Other common classifications are common school districts, independent school districts, and county unit districts. Figure 11–3 indicates that twenty-four states use the common school district plan of organization, thirteen the county unit plan, ten the twon or township plan, and three (Alaska, Hawaii, and Delaware) operate as single units of administration.

The number of school districts in the United States reached a peak of about 125,000 in 1933. By 1966-1967, through reorganization and consolidation, the number had been reduced to 23,335 [82:6]. The President's Commission on National Goals recommended that states pass laws making reorganization mandatory under the direction of each state department of education and that the number of local school districts be reduced to 10,000 by 1970 [196:95].

This reorganization will further eliminate many of the small high schools, especially those enrolling fewer than 100 pupils. Educators feel that extremely small schools are undesirable, and modern transportation facilities, except in sparsely settled and mountainous areas, make it possible to consolidate these small schools into larger ones. Pupils in small schools without question suffer educationally for the following reasons [113:219]:

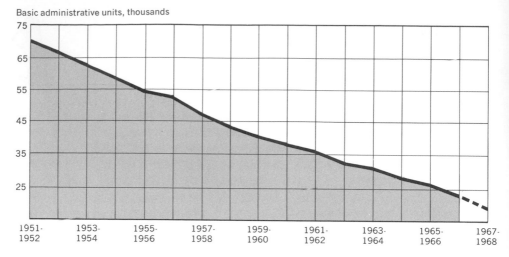

FIGURE 11–4. Decrease in the number of basic administrative units since 1951. What are the reasons for this decided trend? (*Source:* National Education Association.)

1. A very limited curriculum is usually offered.
2. It is not possible to provide adequate libraries, laboratories, auditoriums, lunchrooms, and gymnasiums, except at exorbitant expense.
3. It is difficult to get good teachers to live in small communities, and this disadvantage is exaggerated by the small salaries usually paid in the smaller communities.
4. The opportunities for cocurricular activities are lessened by reason of the smaller number of students interested in different activities, and the small number of staff members available to sponsor cocurricular activities.
5. The teaching load is greater in small schools, and more daily preparation is required for different subject fields, often fields in which the teacher is poorly trained.

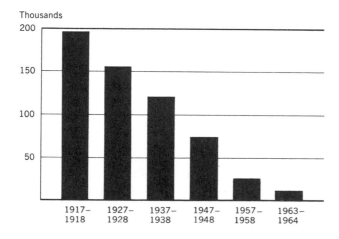

FIGURE 11–5. Trend in the number of one-teacher schools. What factors have contributed to the decided decrease in the number of one-teacher schools? (*Source:* National Education Association.)

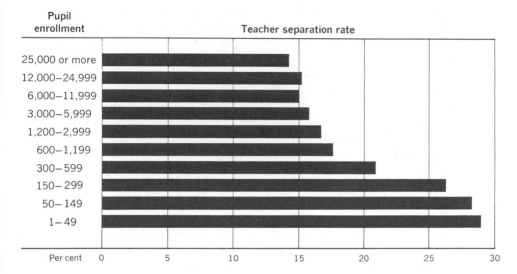

FIGURE 11–6.   Teacher turnover in schools of various sizes. The turnover of teachers in small schools is much larger than the turnover in large schools. What are the reasons for this great difference, and how might the difference be lessened? (*Source:* U.S. Office of Education.)

6. Since the teaching and administrative staffs are almost always paid smaller salaries, they are less experienced, less well trained, and very likely not to remain long enough to come to know well the community and its people, problems, and educational resources.
7. Supervision is usually lacking in both quality and quantity.
8. There is less opportunity to provide good guidance and other services, such as those related to health, especially for physically and otherwise handicapped children.
9. There is limited opportunity for youngsters in the way of desirable social education, since there are so few of similar age and sex in each grade.

An examination of Figure 11-4 would indicate that your chances of working in a school district of respectable size are very good.

Local School Officers

Each district or unit has its own board of education, which is responsible for policy making and supervision of the schools. Members may also be called trustees, directors, or committeemen. In 1966–1967 there were approximately 128,000 local board of education members in the United States [82:7].

State laws specify whether school board members shall be elected or appointed. Some of the laws prescribe certain qualifications of board members, such as age and residence location. Most school board members are elected by popular vote in nonpartisan elections. When members are appointed rather than elected, they are usually appointed by city or town councils.

School board members, who usually serve without salary, play a very important role in the community. School board policies represent the official position of the board on important educational matters and foster continuity, stability, and consistency of board action. An alternative to management according to policy is management by expediency and the corresponding administration from crisis to crisis.

School boards are responsible for levying taxes, maintaining buildings, contracting for the construction of school buildings, purchasing supplies and equipment, employing the local administrative head of the school, approving salary schedules, and establishing policies in regard to the employment of school personnel and the content of the curriculum. In fulfilling their responsibilities, boards of education comply with the regulations established by the legislature and the educational agencies of the state in which the district is located. Each state generally sets the minimum standards which all local school districts are required to meet.

It is not the function of the board of education to administer the schools. The board selects a competent administrator who, as superintendent, serves as chief executive officer of the board and is responsible for administering policies formulated by the board. A board has the power to make and to enforce reasonable policies, rules, and regulations. When you consider signing a contract, note the rules and regulations with which you will be expected to comply.

Remember that board action, in order to be valid, must be taken in an official meeting of the board, which is usually a public meeting. Individual board members have no official authority in school matters, since the laws vest power to act in the board as a body. Also, as a general rule, officers and members of a board of education are not personally liable for loss or injury resulting from acts within the line of their duty unless the acts are performed willfully, wantonly, or with malice or a corrupt motive.

In recent years, school board associations have been formed in each state. Most of these associations belong to the National School Boards Association. They are concerned with the orientation of new school board members, legislation affecting schools, and the leadership that school boards may render in local school districts. Much improvement in the effectiveness of school boards fulfilling their responsibilities has resulted from the formation and work of these associations.

In districts of adequate size (preferably 2,000 pupils or more) there are typically four kinds of professional personnel: These are first, top-level managers (superintendents) who, along with the policy-making board, are responsible and accountable for the direction of the organization's affairs; second, supervisors (principals and/or department heads) who direct and evaluate the work of teachers; third, the frontline workers, or teachers, who provide direct instructional service to the pupil population; and finally, a central staff of specialists who provide the highly technical services (reading, audio-visual, special education, etc.) as requested by teachers and/or supervisors. A fifth level of personnel might be added—that of nonprofessional personnel, such as typists, bookkeepers, cooks, and custodians. The first, second, and fourth types of personnel designated above ideally have supportive roles to play relative to facilitating the work of teachers.

The principal is the chief administrative officer and instructional leader of a building or attendance unit in a school system. He works closely with the super-

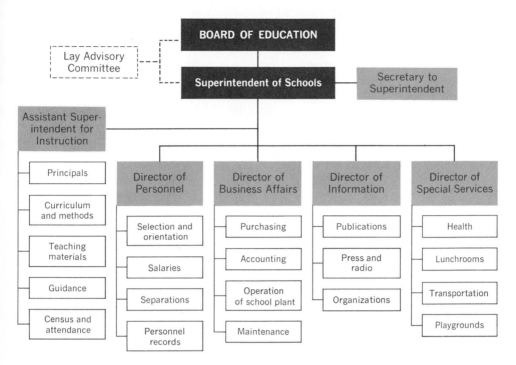

FIGURE 11–7. Organization of the superintendency in a middle-sized school system. A position assigned to a director in this figure might be filled in a smaller system on a part-time basis by a classroom teacher or principal, who is relieved of other duties for part of each day. In a larger system such a position might be assigned to an assistant superintendent. (*Source:* American Association of School Administrators.)

intendent of schools in securing staff, materials, and facilities for a building program and is responsible for the day-by-day operation of a school unit. Areas of major concern to the competent principal are developing individual pupil programs, allocating work and assigning responsibility to professional and nonprofessional staff, managing differences of opinion regarding educational issues, planning and conducting in-service activities, and developing educational programs.

An apparent trend in school organization and administration is to hire competent instructional leaders as principals and to give them authority concerning the improvement of instruction. Effective teachers are demanding competent building leadership. Teachers appear to expect that principals should exhibit evidence of good general scholarship as well as successful teaching experience. There are numerous examples of principals who are "keeping store," selling cafeteria tickets, selling athletic contest tickets, and answering the telephone. In order to be effective, a principal should have adequate clerical and administrative assistance so that he can concentrate upon his instructional responsibilities. He should (1) be vitally interested in the growth of young people and of his staff members, (2) enjoy classroom activity, (3) be intellectually alive, (4) keep abreast in the varied academic fields by reading those journals read by members of the teaching staff, and (5) have respect for the dignity of each individual in a school unit.

Intermediate School Administrative Unit

An intermediate school district is "an area comprising the territory of two or more basic administrative units and having a board or officer, or both, responsible for performing stipulated services for the basic administrative units or for supervising their fiscal, administrative, or educational functions" [171:52]. Historically, the unit has served as an intermediary between the local school district or unit and the state educational agency.

When states were first organized in the United States, the county was established as a local unit of government and was regarded as an appropriate area for the general promotion and supervision of public education as well as for other governmental services. Thus, the origin of the intermediate unit was on a county basis, and its primary concern was with county rural and village schools. As the villages became cities and experienced a rapid growth of population, they were eventually empowered to operate schools that were independent from the rural schools and from the intermediate district. As a result, the intermediate district offered leadership predominantly to rural schools [154:3].

Today, an intermediate school administration unit generally serves the following functions [154:97]:

(a) to aid the state central office in exercising general supervision over schools; (b) to provide an organization whereby special supplementary services can be made available on a pooled basis to local districts which, because of small population or other reasons, cannot administer them alone economically; (c) to have responsibility for special phases of the educational program, such as certain vocational training, classes for handicapped children, and so on; and (d) to provide a program of education for post-high school youth who do not attend college.

A number of intermediate units provide excellent services to basic school units, particularly in the state of California. The establishment of a supplementary educational center and service units as forms of intermediate units will undoubtedly be a national trend through encouragement of federal funding under Title III of the Elementary and Secondary Education Act of 1965. The difference between a poor and a good school could be the resulting services in special instruction in science, language, music, and the arts; counseling and guidance, health and social work; and access to resources such as art galleries, museums, and theaters.

State Department of Education

Each state has a state department or a state education agency. The department or agency usually consists of a state board of education, a chief state school officer, and his professional, technical, and clerical staff. During your professional career you will likely have contact with state department officials who work in your subject area.

The state department serves a number of functions. Attempts are made to provide comprehensive plans for the total state program of education and to co-ordinate all educational efforts within the state for the purpose of promoting unity and encouraging proper balance in education. The department suggests educational measures for the consideration of the state legislature and executes those laws which have been enacted. It distributes state moneys for the support of local school units, usually on the basis of the attendance of pupils in the separate schools. The state department also establishes certain minimum standards and regulations relating to such matters as certification of teachers, building construction, health and safety factors, and programs of instruction. In most cases, courses of study or units or syllabi or other instructional materials issued by the state department are meant to be suggestive rather than prescriptive. The minimum requirements are seldom more than the mediocre teacher with an ordinary class would accomplish.

The state department also serves certain supervisory purposes. It checks to see that the laws are carried out and that at least the minimum prescribed educational opportunities are available in every community. This alone is no small task where local districts are large in size and sparsely settled and particularly where resources are meager. Together with its supervisory function, the state department often provides significant professional leadership and services, for example, research and experimentation designed to aid all communities in the state. California, Florida, Georgia, New York, Oregon, Utah, and Virginia have been conspicuous in such matters. Research reports as well as other professional information and suggestions appear in the many journals, bulletins, and other publications of the state department. In-service education programs are encouraged for the continuing growth of teachers and administrators. Efforts are made to inform the public of educational needs and progress, and encouragement is given to the public to participate in the formulation of educational policy. Consultant service and advice, essential to the continuing improvement of education, are provided to schools. As is mentioned in Chapter 18, many state departments maintain placement bureaus for educational personnel.

Chief state school officers and their staffs and the Council of Chief State School Officers have been engaged in a series of intensive studies on state departments of education. Every state has made fundamental changes in either the structure or internal organization of its state education agency, primarily to provide greater leadership to the public education system. You have already noted the trends toward the popular election of state school board members and the appointment of the chief state school officer by the state board of education.

State Board of Education

The chief function of the state board of education is to interpret educational needs, practices, and trends to the people of the state and to develop the policies of education which people seem to desire. These policies are usually carried out by executive officers and other professional staff members. All the states have state boards of education with the exception of Illinois and Wisconsin, where the chief state school officer determines the policy for education and administers the state educational program.

State boards of education vary in many ways. In four states (Florida, Idaho, Montana, and New York), the state board of education has general supervision of institutions of higher education as well as of the public schools. In size, state boards range from three to twenty-three members, with forty-four of the state boards having a membership ranging from five to fifteen. The usual term of office is six years, although the range is from two years to life. In eight states, state board members are elected by popular vote, and there are some indications that the number of states electing board members in this way may increase. In the other states, the board members usually are appointed by a high-ranking government official, such as the governor of the state.

Beach and Will of the U.S. Office of Education point out a number of advantages in having a board of education, whether it be a state board or a local school board, instead of having an elected or appointed policy-making individual. These advantages, briefly stated, are as follows [21a]:

1. A board of education is more representative of the total population it serves than an individual policy-making agent is.
2. A board of education can make wiser and sounder policy decisions than an individual can.
3. A board of education serves as a safeguard against the abuses of discretionary powers.
4. A board of education acts as a safeguard against the involvement of education in partisan politics and the spoils system.
5. A board of education is a safeguard against needless disruption in the continuity of an educational program.
6. A board of education provides an economical means for management and control of the educational program.
7. A board of education provides a safeguard against fraud and malfeasance.

Chief State School Officer

The chief school officers in the various states are known by different titles, such as superintendent, commissioner, or director. There is a definite trend toward having the state board of education appoint the chief school officer rather than having him appointed by the governor or elected by the people. Between 1945 and 1964 the number of state boards following this procedure increased from eight to twenty-four. The officers' terms are typically four years, though in a few states they are indefinite as long as the work of the officers is acceptable to the board. The duties of a state school officer normally include carrying out, or at least supervision of, the following [245:112–113]:

1. General supervision of the public schools.
2. Acting as the executive officer of the state board of education, and, also, if there is one, of the separate board for vocational education.
3. Nominating required members of his professional and clerical staff and recommending the removal of any employee whose services are so unsatisfactory as to warrant such action.
4. Organization of the state department of education, subject to the approval of the state board.
5. Preparation of an outline for each state course of study and approval of courses of study for use in local school districts.

6. Preparation for submission to the state board of education, or, if there is no state board, to the governor, of a budget for the current expenses of the state department of education; also a budget setting forth the amount of state funds that should be appropriated to the school districts of the state and to each of the institutions of the state under the control of the state board of education or under the state school officer's supervision.

7. Interpreting the school laws and deciding such controversies as may be appealed to him by teachers and others from the decisions of local school boards.

8. Preparation of forms for reports from local school districts and from state educational institutions to the state department of education.

9. Evaluation of credentials and issuance of certificates to teachers, principals, and supervisors.

10. Approval of school sites and school-building plans.

11. Withholding state funds from school districts that fail to comply with state laws.

12. Review of proposals for the consolidation of schools or of school districts and submission of his recommendations to the state board.

13. Reporting to the state board of education and to the governor regarding the status and needs of the schools in the state and making recommendations for their improvement.

14. Approval of curriculums for teacher-preparing institutions.

15. Distribution of state school funds in accordance with state law.

Other State Department of Education Personnel

There has been a phenomenal increase in the number of professional and non-professional personnel in state departments of education. Increase in personnel is accounted for both by additional services offered by the state education agency and by the change in nature of the services. Additional services include those in areas such as guidance, instruction, audio-visual and library, school lunch, transportation, vocational education, and federal programs of assistance to schools. These areas and others require professional specialists, whereas at the turn of the century, the chief state school officers and a few clerical officers were capable of handling the routine statistical and inspectional duties performed by the state agency. It is probable that, as a result of the Elementary and Secondary Education Act of 1965, there will be a large increase in the number of professional staff members provided to assist local school districts in the act's implementation relative to Project Head Start and other projects for disadvantaged pupils, as well as for general programs of enrichment provided in the act.

The Elementary and Secondary Education Act of 1965 authorized, in Title V, an expenditure of $17 million of federal funds for strengthening state departments of education in fiscal year 1966. Under provision of this title, grants were made on a matching basis for a two-year period, after which the federal share would range from 50 to 66 per cent. An important trend made possible under Title V was the interchange of personnel between the U.S. Office of Education and state educational agencies for a period not to exceed two years. This in-service arrangement was to facilitate cooperation between the federal and state agencies. It could be interpreted as a movement toward integration of educational services and a channel for more federal influence or power in education.

A State-Federal Compact for Education

In 1964 Dr. James B. Conant, president emeritus of Harvard University, expressed a need for a new kind of intermediate unit between the fifty states and the federal government, a so-called "compact for education," designed to improve education throughout the United States [53:109–123]. The compact for education became a reality through the leadership of North Carolina's former Governor Terry Sanford, who believed that state governors should be the leaders in implementing Conant's idea, and through financial assistance from the Carnegie Corporation and the Danforth Foundation. By 1966, thirty-six states had joined the compact through payment of initial fees of $3,000 to $7,000, which were based upon population and per capita income factors.

Purposes of the compact are [48:3]:

1. To establish and maintain close cooperation and understanding among executive, legislative, professional educational and lay leadership on a nationwide basis at the state and local levels
2. To provide a forum for the discussion, development, crystallization and recommendation of public policy alternatives in the field of education
3. To provide a clearing house of information on matters relating to educational problems and how they are being met in different places throughout the nation, so that the executive and legislative branches of state government and of local communities may have ready access to the experience and record of the entire country, and so that both groups in the field of education may have additional avenues for the sharing of experience and the interchange of ideas in the formation of public policy in education
4. To facilitate the improvement of state and local educational systems so that all of them will be able to meet adequate and desirable goals in a society which requires continuous qualitative and quantitative advance in educational opportunities, methods and facilities

The compact has been further described as a partnership between educational leadership and political leadership for the advancement of education, and is intended to present a coordinated nationwide voice of the states in dialogue with the federal government.

The governing body of the compact organization is an Educational Commission of the States. Membership consists of seven representatives from each state: the governor, two legislators (one from each house), and four others from all levels of education. In addition, there are ten nonvoting commissioners who represent national education organizations. Studies conducted by the commission include school finance, vocational education, preschool training, and community colleges. Denver, Colorado, is the headquarters for the commission.

Education and the Federal Government

The federal government, throughout its history, has shown a considerable amount of interest in the educational welfare of the nation. In Chapter 1 you read various statements of Presidents of the United States in which they expressed great concern for the education of our citizenry. As you read Chapter 12, you will learn of the extensive financial support which the federal government has given to education.

The government has shown its concern for education in another very important manner. Upon the recommendation of the National Association of State and City School Superintendents, which is now called the American Association of School Administrators, Congress enacted into law in 1867 the establishment of a Department of Education, to be directed by a Commissioner appointed by the President. The Department was to be responsible for

collecting such statistics and facts as shall show the condition and progress of education in the several states and territories, and of diffusing such information respecting the organization and management of schools and school systems, and methods of teaching, as shall aid the people of the United States in the establishment and maintenance of efficient school systems, and otherwise promote the cause of education throughout the country.

Henry Barnard, an outstanding educator of his day, was appointed the first Commissioner of Education.

The U.S. Department of Education operated as an independent agency until 1869, when it became an office attached to the Department of the Interior. In 1870 the title was changed from Office of Education to Bureau of Education, but its former title was restored in 1929. In 1939 the Federal Security Agency was created and the Office of Education was placed under its jurisdiction, and in 1953 the Office of Education became one of the units in the Department of Health, Education, and Welfare, which replaced the Federal Security Agency.

The major functions of the U.S. Office of Education today are very similar to those prescribed in 1867: educational research, educational services, and the administration of the various educational grants. In order to carry out the first function, the Office of Education employs a staff of research specialists who collect and distribute a wide variety of information. Copies of the publications, which deal with almost every aspect of education, may be secured at cost through the Superintendent of Documents, Government Printing Office, Washington, D.C. Every two years the Office of Education publishes the *Biennial Survey of Education in the United States,* which provides valuable information to educators on educational trends and conditions throughout the nation. The Office of Education also conducts educational conferences, by means of which information is disseminated and problems are discussed.

The official journal of the Office of Education is the monthly publication titled *American Education.* This journal, for which the yearly subscription is $3, contains valuable information regarding current research, problems, and events in the field of education.

The Office of Education employs specialists in such areas as elementary, secondary, and higher education, international education, vocational education, library education, health and visual education, and school administration, including school finance, housing, business administration, and allied fields. These specialists provide consultative services and general leadership in their respective areas in addition to conducting research.

Office of the U.S. Commissioner of Education

The U.S. Commissioner of Education, as an officer in the Department of Health, Education, and Welfare, is the chief education officer of the federal government and is responsible for formulating educational policy and coordinating educational activities at the national level. The Commissioner is appointed by the President, by and with the advice and consent of the Senate. He is responsible for the operation of the Office of Education, for the administration of educational legislation, and for the performance of other functions assigned by Congress and the Executive Office of the President.

Among the major functions which the Commissioner of Education performs are the following [119:14]:

To determine policy and program objectives; to provide executive leadership for the operations; to render consultive services to educational agencies; to coordinate Office of Education work with related programs within the Department of Health, Education and Welfare; to establish liaison with the executive, legislative, and judicial branches of the Government; and to advise with National, State, and local officials and international bodies on educational problems.

Trends in the Relationship of the Federal Government to Education

There are some discernible trends in the relationship of the federal government to education which include (1) increased federal aid without any extension of federal control beyond fiscal control, and (2) development of a coordinated policy for education at the federal level. There is considerable evidence to indicate that there may be a strong movement to provide federal funds for the construction of elementary and secondary classrooms. Development of a coordinated policy is believed to be essential, since twenty-one federal agencies other than the Office of Education provide federal funds for education.

In 1965 the federal government's listing of new national objectives in education were expressed by the United States Commissioner of Education as follows [74:47]:

First, to raise the quality of education in our schools everywhere and for everyone. In the 20th century, we cannot tolerate second-class education if we intend to remain a first-class nation.

Second, to bring equality of educational opportunity to every child in America, whatever his color, or creed, or handicap, or family circumstance.

Third, to provide vocational and technical training that is geared to the economy and technology of today and tomorrow, not of yesterday.

Fourth, to make college and university study possible for all young people who can benefit by it. In our advanced economy, we can no longer afford to regard higher education as a luxury.

Fifth, to bring our educational resources to bear directly on problems in our communities—as an indispensable social instrument in fashioning the Great Society we have chosen to become.

Federal Government and Education at the International Level

Since the welfare of our nation is affected by the welfare of all other nations, you face the problem of being concerned with the education of people throughout the world. Increasing amounts of attention are being given to education at the international level. The Act for International Development also provides for direct assistance, upon the part of the United States, to developing countries in the field of education. In Chapter 7 you became acquainted with the purposes and work of the United Nations Educational, Scientific, and Cultural Organization, to which the United States lends great support, and of the World Confederation of Organizations of the Teaching Profession. Through such organizations as these we are in contact, on a far greater scale than ever before, with the educational policies and practices in other nations all over the world.

Provisions are made for the exchange of students and teachers and the sharing of various instructional materials and procedures with other nations. Educational contacts throughout the world will undoubtedly broaden and deepen mutual understanding and appreciation among the various peoples participating and will eventually affect teaching and learning in all public schools.

In its report on *A Federal Education Agency for the Future*, members of the Committee on the Mission and Organization of the Office of Education recognized the educational challenge of the world community as follows [92:40]:

No aspect of the educational task of the 1960's surpasses in significance the fact that education is basic to the effort to bring about an enduringly peaceful world.

The developing nations of the world are seeking desperately to raise their standards of living and improve their economic and social conditions. They recognize that education is the key to this advancement and they will continue to look increasingly to the United States for aid.

The next decade will bring closer and multiple relationships with Ministries of Education abroad and international organizations, such as UNESCO, The Organization of American States, International Bureau of Education, and others working in the field of education, as problems in education are attacked bilaterally and multilaterally on a worldwide basis.

At home, greater attention to the study of comparative education, history, languages, geography, economics, and comparative government must be given in order to prepare students to understand the world of tomorrow. Likewise, teacher preparation, textbooks, and the curriculum in these subject fields must be improved in the decade ahead.

ORGANIZATION AND ADMINISTRATION FOR INSTRUCTION IN BASIC LOCAL SCHOOL DISTRICTS

As indicated previously, give careful thought to the age of pupils with whom you can work most effectively. The organizational patterns and practices which you find at the various levels within a public school district may influence your choice.

You have a wide range of levels from which to choose. With the necessary qualifications, you may step into your teaching job at any rung in the educational ladder. These divisions are normally described as follows:

Nursery: Prekindergarten experiences for youngsters from 2 to 4 years old and sometimes for those as young as 18 months.

Kindergarten: Preprimary experiences for youngsters, usually 5 years old.

Primary grades: The work of the first, second, and third grades for children approximately 6 to 8 years old.

Intermediate grades: The work of the fourth, fifth, and sixth grades for the 9- to 11-year-olds.

Junior high school: The work of the seventh, eighth, and ninth grades for preadolescents or about 12- to 14-year-olds.

Senior high school: The work of the tenth, eleventh, and twelfth grades for adolescents who are 15 to 17 years old.

Junior college: The thirteenth and fourteenth years of work, usually for 18- and 19-year-olds, though at this point the age range is not so predictable as at the earlier stages.

College or university: For age groups that usually range from 18 to 21 years, though the actual range is often far greater; usually includes what is called junior college, together with programs leading to the bachelor's, master's, and doctor's degrees and postdoctoral studies.

Adult education: Designed for mature persons of all ages to keep them intellectually alive and help them gain new knowledges, skills, and understandings relating to work, hobbies, household arts, child care, literature, social issues, citizenship, health and safety, and other areas in which people show need or interest. The distinguishing features of adult education are that entrance requirements are liberal—unlike typical colleges, active participating in group work is emphasized, and the organization of instruction is extremely flexible.

The same range of opportunity that is more or less available to Americans in public education from the nursery school through the college level is also offered in private schools. Actually private nursery schools far outnumber public nurseries, and there are almost as many private colleges and universities as there are public.

Patterns of Organization

Local school districts in the United States are customarily organized in one of the four basic patterns, the so-called 6-3-3, 6-2-4, 6-6, or 8-4 pattern. A 6-3-3 district has an instructional pattern of six elementary grades, three junior high school grades (grades 7, 8, and 9), and three high school grades (grades 10, 11, and 12). An 8-4 pattern means that a school district has one or more elementary schools consisting of grades 1 to 8 and a high school program of grades 9 to 12.

It is very apparent from an examination of Figure 11-8 that no single plan of organization has received unanimous acceptance in the United States. Local conditions still largely determine the organization of schools. Certain advantages and disadvantages are claimed for the many different plans. Factors which tend to influence the organization of a particular school or school system include the following: established practices, available buildings, financial support, educational leadership, equipment, and transportation.

Approximately two-thirds of the larger school districts in the United States are organized on a 6-3-3 plan; about one-tenth are on the 8-4 plan; and about one-twentieth are on the 6-2-4 plan [79:2]. Following these in order of popularity are the 6-6 and 7-5 plans. Other combinations may be noted in Figure 11-8.

You will find considerable confusion in the use of the terms "elementary schools" and "secondary schools." There has never been a clear-cut official distinction

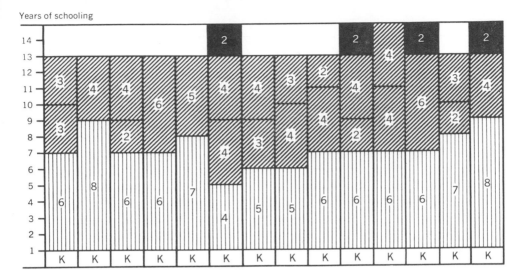

Years of schooling

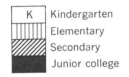

K   Kindergarten
Elementary
Secondary
Junior college

FIGURE 11–8. Prevailing types of school organization in the United States. The numerals signify the number of grades at each level.

between elementary and secondary programs, since grades 7 and 8 may be a part of the elementary school or may be included with grade 9 to form a junior high school or be prefixed to the final four years of high school to form a six-year secondary school. However, you will be safe in assuming that grades 1 to 6 are included in an elementary school and that grades 10, 11, and 12 are included in a secondary school. During your professional career you may help in giving definite identification to grades 7, 8, and 9.

Nursery School and Kindergarten Organization

If you are planning to become a kindergarten or nursery school teacher, you will be interested in the extent to which state laws provide for the education of children three, four, and five years of age. Public nursery schools are authorized, either directly or by implication, in seventeen states. According to a study published in 1965 by the Office of Education, 4.3 per cent of all children three years of age and 14.9 per cent of all four-year-olds were enrolled in nursery schools [230:1]. Almost one-half of the existing nursery school programs are supported by a combination of public and private funds, one-third solely by private funds, and less than one-fifth by public funds alone. Only in the South is there any appreciable use of public funds for nursery schools.

All states except one have laws permitting kindergartens to be operated in

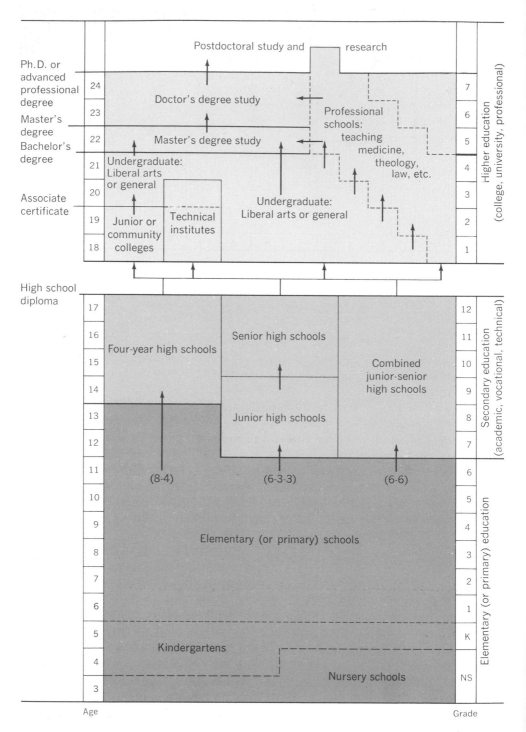

FIGURE 11–9.   The structure of education in the United States. (*Source:* U.S. Office of Education.)

public schools, and state aid for this purpose is provided in nearly half of our states. Approximately 70 per cent of the urban places in the United States maintain public elementary school kindergartens. Nationally, more than 80 per cent of these kindergartens are supported solely by public tax funds [61:16]. Approximately 58 per cent of all five-year-olds are enrolled in kindergartens [230:1].

You may have heard of the Montessori system of kindergarten education, which recently has been receiving considerable attention and parental enthusiasm because of its promises of quick and early learning. The system was developed by Maria Montessori, an Italian physician, who became interested in the early part of the 1900s in helping

slum children learn to follow directions, to keep themselves and their surroundings clean and in order, to recognize the shapes and sounds of letters—and sometimes to put letters together and read. . . . She was convinced that the prepared environment was designed to help the child achieve a sense of himself, self-mastery, and mastery of his environment through the successful execution and repetition of simple tasks which are nonetheless linked to the cultural expectations the child faces in the context of his total development [26:35].

In the Montessori system, emphasis is placed upon the child's mastering a task of which there is only one correct way of performing—even if it involves hand washing, desk scrubbing, or shoe polishing. "Children prepare to learn to read by learning the alphabet through a combination of tactual, auditory, and visual experiences. They spend hours fingering sandpaper letters, looking at them, and saying the letter names and sounds. Some become familiar with the letters, and some learn to put the letters together" [26:36]. But, as Beyer points out, many children have no need for this step and are bored by these preliminary exercises. Furthermore, children who are not ready to read find this type of experience meaningless and monotonous drudgery. Little opportunity is given for social interaction and for dramatic play as a release of tensions and as a means of learning through identification and creative role playing. As you study the Montessori system, you should be aware of its limitations and "fill in the gaps with some of the knowledge of the dynamics of early childhood which Montessori did not have" [26:36].

Elementary School Organization

The results of a careful study made by the U.S. Office of Education, in cooperation with all the state departments of education, may prove helpful to you in understanding the organization of elementary schools. This study involved a survey of practices in 343 new elementary schools and 25 laboratory schools throughout the United States which had been cited as having good educational programs. Most of them were located in urban areas (areas of 2,500 population or over) and in suburban areas of 25,000 population or over.

The study revealed that the K-6 (kindergarten through sixth grade) and 1-6 organizations were most frequently used [258:14]. In rural areas (with populations of less than 2,500) the 1-6 pattern was most frequently found.

Most of the schools reporting had enrollments of from 300 to 750 pupils, with the largest number being in the 300-to-400 pupil range. Many principals and teachers expressed the viewpoint that schools with enrollments of 150 to 300 provided better opportunities for young children than those with enrollments of 600 to 1,000. It was found that there are some elementary schools which enroll over 1,000 children, while others in remote areas may have as few as 5.

In another U.S. Office of Education study pertaining to classroom organization, it was found that for grades 1 to 6, more than three-quarters of the elementary schools throughout the nation were using the one-teacher-per-classroom type of organization [61:30]. Slightly less than 10 per cent of the schools were using partial departmentalization. Complete departmentalization was found to be negligible. If you plan to teach on the elementary level, you may expect, therefore, to be responsible for guiding all the experiences of your pupils.

In this same study it was found that approximately one-third of the urban schools include grades 7 and 8 in the elementary schools. Approximately 39 per cent of the districts indicated complete departmentalization in grade 7, while 33 per cent reported partial departmentalization. The one-teacher-per-classroom plan is used in only about 20 per cent of the seventh and eighth grades when these grades are considered to be a part of the elementary schools.

The typical length of the elementary school day (exclusive of noon lunch periods but inclusive of recess and play periods) is between five and six hours in grades 1 to 6. When grades 7 and 8 are in the elementary school organization, the school day for these youngsters is typically between 5½ and 6 hours.

Most of the urban places in the United States maintain elementary school programs of between 175 and 180 days during the school year. Among the geographical regions of the nation, the Northeast tends to have more than 180 school days

FIGURE 11–10.   Percentage distribution of types of instructional organization in grades 1 through 6 and in grades 7 and 8. How may the increased use of team teaching, teaching machines, and ungraded classrooms change this distribution? (*Source:* U.S. Office of Education.)

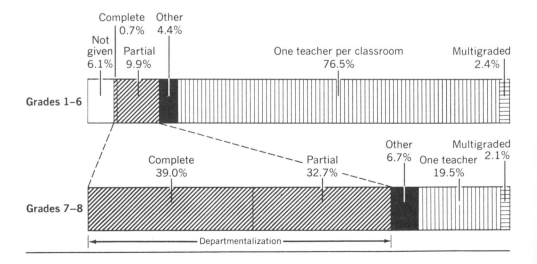

per year, while the North Central states, the South, and the West tend to have fewer than 180 days.

Grouping of Elementary School Pupils

Increased interest is being expressed again in the desirability of assigning children to work in groups upon the basis of ability. Since Sputnik 1, a number of reports have called attention to the fact that our brightest youngsters may not be challenged according to their abilities and that, as a result of this waste of human talent, our nation's defense and future are being weakened.

Diverse grouping plans have been suggested, initiated, discarded, revised, and in some cases used again. Some of the plans are described as follows:

Chronological age grouping. Children of a specific age are placed in a grade group and one teacher works with them. For example, six-year-old children are placed in a first-grade group and seven-year-old children in a second-grade group.

Heterogeneous grouping. Children in a grade group are taught by one teacher irrespective of their intelligence and achievement.

Homogeneous grouping. This is known as "ability grouping." Determinants of classroom placement include intelligence, readiness, and achievement test data.

Winnetka plan grouping. This is a form of heterogeneous grouping, but provision is made for use of self-instructional materials. Individual goal cards encourage optimum academic growth by each child.

Other grouping plans have been termed XYZ grouping, Dalton plan grouping, platoon grouping, organismic age grouping, intraclassroom grouping, interclassroom grouping, opportunity room, self-realization room, and ungraded primary or intermediate [234:1–11].

As indicated by Figure 11-11, approximately 72 percent of the urban schools in the United States use heterogeneous grouping in grades 1 to 6, and 17 per cent group children homogeneously [61:68–71]. Forty-six per cent of these schools predicted that there would be an increase in homogeneous grouping; approximately four per cent predicted an increase in heterogeneous grouping; and forty-seven per cent felt that there would be no change in policies pertaining to grouping.

As you read educational literature, you will note that considerable attention is especially being given to the primary unit of the elementary school. You may find such terms as the following being used: the ungraded school, the ungraded primary, the nongraded elementary school, the primary department, a continuous-growth plan, and the primary group. In general, it involves various plans by means of which children are grouped to permit continuous progress during a period of two or more consecutive years. In some instances the teacher may remain with the same group for more than one year. A few schools are experimenting with this type of organization in the intermediate years, but ordinarily it is linked with the primary years, sometimes including the kindergarten [190:166].

In the ungraded school, boys and girls are assigned to primary, intermediate, junior high school, or senior high school program blocks. Pupils spend two, three, or four years working within each program block. The pupil who is able to pro-

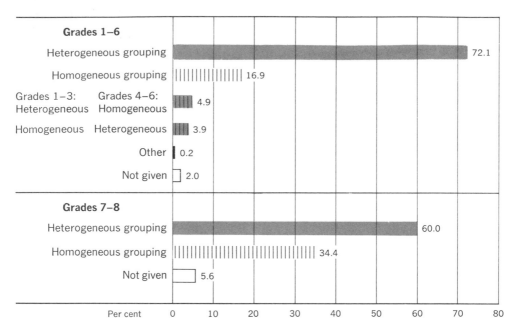

FIGURE 11–11. Percentage distribution of basic grouping policies for public elementary schools in urban places with populations above 2,500. What advantages and disadvantages do you see in each type of grouping? (*Source:* U.S. Office of Education.)

gress rapidly in all areas of the curriculum and whose physical and social maturity indicates readiness for advanced work is placed in the next school block. Thus, he may finish a primary block in a two-year period instead of a normal three-year period and then be placed in an intermediate block. Conversely, a pupil who progresses slowly spends four years instead of a normal three years in a block. The pupil under these conditions is not faced with failure in his first-grade work and retention in the same grade the following year. Rather, he remains in the primary block during his second year in school, and his academic work is a continuation from the point to which he progressed the previous year. In the meantime, he has social and academic experiences with children of his age group.

The most frequently mentioned reasons for having nongraded groups are [190:167]: "(a) Learning should be continuous; (b) children grow and learn at different rates and each should have the opportunity to achieve at his own rate; (c) school programs should be flexible so as to meet varying developmental needs and growth patterns of individual children; and (d) greater achievement will result when children experience success in school."

In 1964, over 50 per cent of a representative sample of school systems having an enrollment of over 100,000 pupils reported ungraded practices in one or more of their schools. The percentage decreased to 25 per cent for school systems having enrollments of 12,000 to 24,999 [183:93]. Representative systems with some type of nongraded pattern of organization include Corona and Torrance, California; Pocatello, Idaho; Moline and Park Forest, Illinois; Baltimore and Germantown,

Maryland; Marblehead, Massachusetts; Dearborn, Michigan; Reno, Nevada; Dayton and Youngstown, Ohio; Savannah, Georgia; Appleton and Milwaukee, Wisconsin.

Probable Developments in Elementary Schools

Because of the unique decentralization characteristic of schools in the United States, it is extremely difficult to generalize in regard to future developments in education. However, it is highly probable that the following trends in elementary schools will continue [72:21–22]:

1. To evaluate growth in terms of the personality of the child as well as subject matter
2. To individualize teachings as much as possible
3. To utilize the findings of child development research in the construction of curriculum and in guidance of children
4. To relate the curriculum to the needs of children in the community where they live
5. To select and organize the work of the school around the interests of children and around problems which children can comprehend
6. To make the school an integral part of the community and the community an integral part of the school in every way possible
7. To extend public school services (1) to children below 6, (2) to after-school hours and (3) to months when school is not formally in session

An increasing number of elementary schools are experimenting with TV teaching, programmed learning, instruction in modern foreign languages and in modern mathematics, and learning by discovery or by problem-solving methods. Special provisions are being made for teaching exceptional children, including those with special education needs and those with exceptional talent.

There are indications that preschool education may be greatly increased because of the influence of the federal poverty and education programs. The summer of 1965 marked the beginning of federal aid to preschool education when $84 million in poverty funds were appropriated for a crash program in preschool education for disadvantaged children. This type of recognition may lead to widespread establishment of nurseries and kindergartens for all children, regardless of their economic status [79:4–5].

Secondary School Organization

You probably were unconcerned with the organization of secondary schools when you were a high school student. As a prospective secondary school teacher, however, organizational patterns have definite meaning for you since they definitely will have an effect upon your future work.

Secondary schools may be classified into the following five major categories [adapted, 98:10–12]:

Traditional high school: a 4-year school preceded by an 8-year elementary school.

Combined junior-senior high school (predominantly 6-6 system and 7-5 system): a reorganized school in which the junior and senior high schools are combined under one principal.

Junior high school (predominantly 6-3-3 system and 6-2-4 system): a reorganized school in which the junior high grades are grouped separately under one principal.

Senior high school (6-3-3 system): a reorganized school in which the last three years are grouped separately under one principal.

Four-year high school (6-2-4 system): a 4-year school similar to the traditional high school in organization but with important differences. The system has been reorganized, often in our larger cities, to include 2-year junior high schools.

In a national study of the secondary school principalship conducted by the National Association of Secondary-School Principals, it was found that 35 per cent of the principals worked in schools with a grade 9–12 pattern [130:41]. One principal in four worked in a combined secondary and elementary school, and another one-quarter in a secondary-junior high school combination. As would be expected, schools that combined the senior high grades with other grade levels were more often located in small towns and rural areas (61 per cent compared with 25 per cent). High schools comprised of grades 10, 11, and 12 were disproportionately prevalent in the cities outside the southeastern region of the United States.

Junior High School

The junior high school is the intermediate unit in a program of general education, its purposes being separate and distinct from those of both the elementary school and the senior high school. Principles upon which it was founded are included in Chapter 13. The junior high school has evolved as an institution to meet the unique physical, social, emotional, and intellectual needs of the late preadolescent and early adolescent. Emphasis is upon exploratory experiences. Some of these experiences are included as part of a core program, or they may be offered as required exploratory courses. Exploratory experiences include [140:59]:

Art	General business	Music appreciation
Choral music	General language	Photography
Choral speaking	Hobbies	Poetry writing
Crafts	Homemaking	Public speaking
Creative dramatics	Journalism	Science
Creative writing	Literature	Typing
Folk dancing	Manual arts	

The Southern Association of Colleges and Secondary Schools recommends that the size of a three-year junior high school range from a minimum of four sections per grade to a maximum of eight sections per grade. If you assume that each section is to have a maximum size of 30 pupils, the range in enrollment for the school would be from 360 to 720 [140:74]. Conant, who completed an extensive study of junior high school programs, recommends that a separate three-year junior high school enroll a minimum of 375 pupils. He maintains that "for really efficient operation, something like 750 pupils are needed in a three-year junior high school" [52:39].

A Commission on Secondary Curriculum of the Association for Supervision and Curriculum Development of the National Education Association feels that a good junior high school should [adapted, 46:35]:

1. Have a well-stocked library staffed by a professional librarian-teacher. There should be a ratio of ten or more books per student.
2. Provide ample guidance services.
3. Offer block-of-time instruction each year for the three years, so that one teacher will have a group of children for a substantial period.
4. Maintain flexibility of scheduling. For example, some seventh-grade students are better placed with ninth-grade students for certain classes.
5. Be staffed with teachers prepared for junior high school teaching and devoted to junior-high-school-age students.
6. Provide help for teachers by principals, by supervisory staff, and by clerical personnel.
7. Provide a modern instructional program in subject areas. Changes now underway in the elementary program will affect junior high school instruction.
8. Have adequate physical education programs.
9. Have ample laboratory and workshop facilities.
10. Have an established reasonable teacher load.

A representative sampling of teachers throughout the nation indicated that 70 per cent feel that a separate junior high school provides the best pattern for the all-round development of pupils. Only 21 per cent favored the 8-grade elementary and 4-grade high school plan, and less than 4 per cent favored the 6-6 plan [283:30].

Senior High School

One of the unique aspects of the American public education system is the comprehensive high school which provides educational opportunities for all the boys and girls in a community, regardless of their economic status, sex, family background, education, and vocational ambitions. About 80 per cent of the high schools in the United States are reported by their principals to be comprehensive high schools [130:40]. Many educators from other countries, including England, visit the United States in order to observe this type of high school with the hope that they may make adaptations of it in their countries.

The programs in the comprehensive high school are flexible enough to meet the changing needs of pupils and desires of parents. A senior high school pupil may change from a course in agriculture to one in music, or he may change from an industrial arts program to a college preparatory program. Such change in course selection may come about as a result of a pupil's changing interests and needs. Late-blooming talents of a high school pupil may become evident in his sophomore, junior, or senior year, and the comprehensive high school provides the flexibility to enable him to make the changes easily.

Offerings in the comprehensive high school most frequently include the general, the college preparation, the business education, and the vocational curricula. Students majoring in each curriculum are scheduled to take both required courses and restricted electives. They generally are permitted to elect one or more subjects not included in the required curriculum sequence.

From your experiences, you know that high school pupils are required to study English, social studies, mathematics, science, health, and physical education. They may elect to take courses in industrial arts, home economics, foreign language, music, art, business, and vocational education.

State departments of public instruction and the local school districts establish standards and requirements for the subjects to be taught, the number of years they are to be studied, the number of years of required pupil attendance, the minimum graduation requirements, and the requirement of textbooks and other instructional materials. Ordinarily, states have statutes or regulations mandating instruction which represent approximately 50 per cent of the requirements for high school graduation. The local school districts have discretionary powers concerning the remaining 50 per cent of the requirements. As a secondary school teacher, you will undoubtedly have opportunities to participate in reviewing standards and requirements that apply to the school in which you teach and in recommending changes that should be made.

The diversified offerings and the flexibility of the comprehensive high school in meeting the changing needs of pupils account in part for the increased enrollments and holding power of the schools. The American high schools enroll over 92 per cent of the boys and girls who are 14 to 17 years of age [249:111], whereas in 1890 the number of pupils attending high schools was only 7 per cent of the 14 to 17 age group. More than 66 of every 100 youths of this age group are now graduating from high school; approximately 40 per cent of these graduates are

FIGURE 11–12. Reasons given by pupils in one state for dropping out of high school in the 1960–1961 school year. (*Source:* Chamber of Commerce of the United States.)

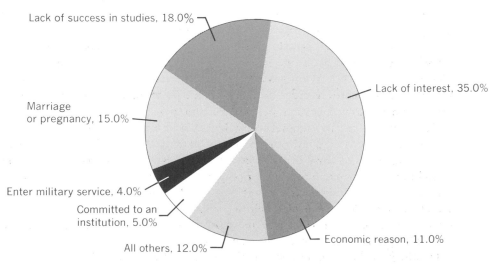

entering college on a full-time basis; and an additional 9 per cent enter college on a part-time basis.

An example of the increased holding power of the American elementary and secondary school is indicated by the fact that of 1,000 fifth graders enrolled in school in 1932, only 455, or 45.5 per cent, were graduated from high school in 1940; whereas, of the 1,000 fifth graders enrolled in 1957, 710, or 71.0 per cent, were graduated from high school in 1965 [249:111]. Educators and others are concerned with the current dropout problem, but the figures cited are encouraging and indicate that comprehensive high schools have increased their holding power through provision not only for those who are going to attend colleges or universities after high school graduation but also for those who are going to enter the world of work upon graduation.

At a hearing before the Subcommittee of the Committee on Appropriations in the House of Representatives during the Eighty-sixth Congress, Dr. Lawrence G. Derthick, who was then U.S. Commissioner of Education, presented a dramatic contrast to the comprehensive high school in the following manner [217:11]:

What would it be like to have the traditional European system? At approximately age 11, your child would take a series of national achievement tests, and his performance on these tests would largely determine his future track or specialized secondary school, if any. His whole future might well depend on these tests. Think of your own experience back in the fifth grade of elementary school. What marks were on your report card? Would you have been placed in the classical high school for collegebound professionals or would you have been placed in another school where your education might have ended at the age of 14? Would you have been

FIGURE 11–13. Survival rates of groups of 1,000 pupils entering the fifth grade in 1932 and in 1957—a 25-year period. What factors have contributed to the fact that the dropout rate has continued to decrease? (*Source:* U.S. Office of Education; U.S. Bureau of the Census.)

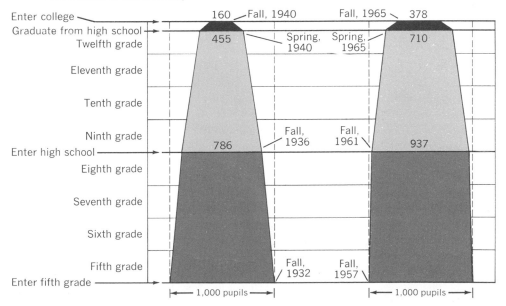

happy to have somebody else determine what your future would be by deciding what type of education you should have after the age of 11 or 12?

Let us ask, too, why have the rigid class barriers of many Western European nations been maintained? Why have most class barriers in this country been removed?

More than 50 years ago American parents decided that they would not give any person the right to close any doors to the future for their 11-year-old children. They made this decision with a full knowledge of the system of education used in Europe —and of the social consequences of this system.

The report of the President's Commission on National Goals states that "it is essential that the tradition of the comprehensive high school be preserved and strengthened."[1] This report emphasized that youngsters should never be handled in such a way that some appear to belong to an elite group while others are classified at a lower level. Do you feel that any improvements in our schools can be made along this line?

Conant and his staff studied the educational programs of 103 high schools in twenty-six states and personally visited 55 of the schools. In his report concerning the study, Conant stated:

I can sum up my conclusions in a few sentences. The number of small high schools must be drastically reduced through district reorganization. Aside from this important change, I believe no radical alteration in the basic pattern of American education is necessary in order to improve our public high schools. If all the high schools were functioning as well as some I have visited, the education of all American youth would be satisfactory, except for the study of foreign languages and the guidance of the more able girls. Most of the schools which I found unsatisfactory in one or more respects could become satisfactory by relatively minor changes, though I have no doubt that there are schools even of sufficient size where major improvements in organization and instruction would be in order [50:40].

Conant proposed that a high school have a graduating class of 100 in order to offer adequate curricula and to provide enough class sections to accommodate pupils of varied abilities. He estimated that only 4,000 of over 20,000 high schools in the United States have graduating classes of over 100.

In his report, Conant made twenty-one other recommendations for improving the American high school. Since these recommendations may have a significant impact upon the public schools, become quite familiar with them. You will find them in the Resource Section for Part IV of this book. Discuss their implications with your instructors and colleagues. If all these recommendations were to be implemented, how would your work as a teacher be affected?

Trends in Secondary Education

Several trends in secondary education are in evidence as attempts are made to meet the needs of increasingly greater numbers of boys and girls. These trends may be summarized in the following manner:

[1] "National Goals in Education," by John Gardner, from *Goals for Americans*, © 1960 by the American Assembly, Columbia University, New York. By permission of Prentice-Hall, Inc., Englewood Cliffs, N.J., p. 85.

1. Emphasis is being placed upon quality of the education program.
2. New approaches utilizing television, teaching machines, and team teaching are increasingly employed.
3. Curriculum changes in the fields of mathematics, science, and foreign language are notable, and teaching in these areas is being emphasized. More courses are being offered in these subject fields, and the academically talented students are engaging in more advanced study of the courses.
4. The total guidance program is being extended and increased.
5. Remedial classes in English and arithmetic for pupils who are deficient in the basic skills of reading, writing, and computation are being provided.
6. Teachers are being assisted by specialists in materials preparation, community resources, and diagnostic evaluations.
7. The holding power of the secondary school is increasing.
8. Emphasis is being given to the problem-solving method of teaching.
9. The school day organization is becoming more flexible as it becomes more apparent that not all courses require the same length of class period.
10. Principals and/or directors of instruction are playing a more active role in the improvement of instruction.
11. Specialists are relieving principals in managing matters such as food services, sanitation, and transportation.

The newer content, media, and learning theory are aimed at individualizing instruction at the secondary level. It is through flexible scheduling, as explained in Chapter 6, that a principal and his staff can probably best arrange a program whereby an individual pupil is able to assume a greater degree of responsibility for his own learning.

According to a survey of thirty-three schools using flexible scheduling, the advantages of this type of organization include (1) the provision for pacing instruction to individual students' needs and (2) the allowance for teachers to make decisions about the length and frequency of learning activities. The disadvantages for teachers include (1) the requirement for more time and cooperative effort of teachers in making the schedules and (2) the difficulty of scheduling groups. Schools using a form of flexible scheduling include Campus High School, Wichita, Kansas; Evanston Township High School, Evanston, Illinois; James Madison High School, San Diego, California; James Monroe High School, Bronx, New York; Lakeview High School, Decatur, Illinois; Mary Potter High School, Oxford, North Carolina; Virgin Valley High School, Mesquite, Nevada; and Nova High School, Fort Lauderdale, Florida [23:161–162].

The building principal is the key person in the secondary school to effect changes and has the prime responsibility of working with the faculty in improving the instructional program. His development of an organization and his style of administration are important variables in the determination of professional opportunities for teachers.

Summer School Programs

During the past few years more school districts have been providing summer sessions. They have been doing so largely because they have a new concept of the

scope of the summer program and they wish to use school facilities more extensively. The emphasis in summer school is shifting from helping only the slow
student to that of providing the opportunity for all students to attend summer
school for enrichment purposes, for acceleration, or for the early completion of
their secondary school work. In many schools, advanced or highly talented students may take more advanced courses in such areas as mathematics and science
that cannot be offered economically during the regular school year. The length
of the summer school programs at both the elementary and secondary levels ranges
from four to ten weeks. The usual length of the school day is four hours.

There is considerable variation in the manner in which summer schools are
financed. State aid is available for summer schools in fourteen states [149:31].
Very frequently tuition is charged those who wish to attend. Funds from the
Economic Opportunity Act may be used for summer schools, especially for courses
for migrant workers and dropouts and for courses in vocational, technical, and
adult basic education [135:47]. In the summer of 1965, Project Head Start was
initiated with more than 500,000 disadvantaged children going to school for the
first time.

Associations of Secondary Schools and Colleges

Many of the secondary schools throughout the United States belong to associations
of secondary schools and colleges. These are quasi-legal, voluntary associations.
There are six such regional associations, four of which were founded before the
turn of the twentieth century:

Association	Date founded
New England Association of Colleges and Secondary Schools	1885
Middle States Association of Colleges and Secondary Schools	1892
Southern Association of Secondary Schools and Colleges	1895
North Central Association of Colleges and Secondary Schools	1895
Northwest Association of Secondary and Higher Schools	1918
Western Association of Secondary Schools and Colleges	1930

The states included in each of the respective associations are indicated in
Figure 11-14.

The primary purposes of these associations include the improvement of instruction at each level, closer articulation between levels, and the accrediting of schools.
The New England and the Western associations are exceptions in that they do
not accredit schools. The North Central association has been the most conspicuous
of the group in size, activity, and influence. The Southern association has engaged in noteworthy experimentation and exploration in education.

Accreditation by a regional association means that the school concerned meets,
in general, the pattern of standards set by the association. In that case, pupils
in accredited schools are assured of more adequate educational opportunities; they
have easier access to other institutions at the same or at a higher level. Both
pupils and institutions gain some measure of prestige. Very careful surveys of local
educational situations are made by the regional associations, and significant improvements are often effected as a result of their work.

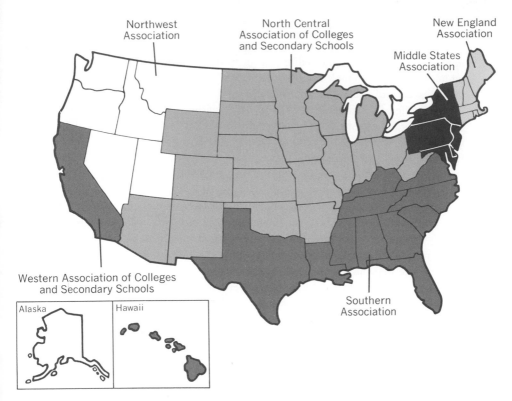

FIGURE 11–14. Regional areas of the associations of colleges and secondary schools in the United States. To which association does your college and your secondary school belong?

Specialized Schools

Besides those divisions which are ordinarily considered in our present educational system, there are many other schools, the majority of which are privately supported. Religion-affiliated schools will be discussed in the next chapter. In addition to these, there are schools organized as military academies, boarding schools, college preparatory schools, finishing schools, and the like. A great number of specialized schools are almost purely vocational in character, such as the large technical schools, the very specialized High School of Fashion Industries, the Juilliard and Eastman Schools of Music, and various schools of nursing, commerce, business, electronics, or flying. Such schools as the Bronx High School of Science in New York and the Boston Latin School cater to students with special abilities and may even require rigid entrance examinations. Other kinds of specialized schools include those for the handicapped in sight, hearing, or muscular coordination. Many of these schools are state-supported. Special schools also are available for the mentally retarded and the emotionally disturbed. If you have interest in teaching in any of these types of schools, the opportunities are great.

Higher Education

Higher education includes those educational programs which require for admission approximately 12 years of previous schooling or the equivalent. There are approximately 2,200 higher-education institutions in the country, all except 475 of which are coeducational. State governments, cities, counties, or other subdivisions of states control more than one-third of the 2,200 institutions; nearly two-thirds are controlled by religious sects, self-perpetuating groups of public-spirited persons, or organizations within one professional group or another. The federal government controls 9 institutions of higher education [241:69]. Approximately 64 per cent of the enrollees in colleges and universities are studying in publicly supported institutions, and it is anticipated that this figure will reach 70 per cent by 1975.

Students have differing needs and are served by a host of diverse institutions and programs. Figure 11-15 indicates how the students who comprised approximately one-third of the population in the age group 18 to 20 were distributed in the various types of institutions.

A college may be a separate institution or a unit within a university. The term "university" stands for an organization consisting of a liberal arts (or arts and sciences) college as its foundation, as well as a number of professional schools such as schools of education, law, engineering, and business.

Many of the teachers colleges and technological schools are currently placing more emphasis upon provision for liberal arts programs. As indicated previously, the names of many teachers colleges are being changed to state colleges or universities. In addition, land-grant colleges or universities, so named from the fact that they were originally set up by the states on the basis of endowments of land

FIGURE 11–15. Percentage distribution of degree-credit students enrolled in the various types of institutions of higher education in the United States, fall of 1965. (*Source:* U.S. Bureau of the Census.)

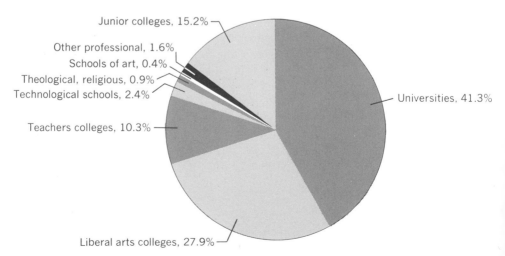

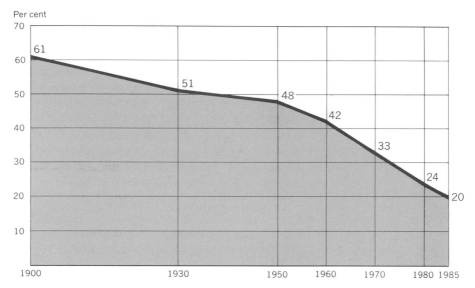

FIGURE 11–16.   Only 20 per cent of all college students may be attending private colleges and universities in 1985, according to projections of the current trends. (*Source:* National Education Association.)

granted by the federal government, offer a wide range of programs in the humanities in addition to the programs in agriculture, mechanic arts, home economics, and military tactics as mandated by the Morrill Act of 1862 and subsequent acts.

Approximately two-thirds of 800 junior colleges existing in 1966 were publicly supported [116:147]. It is estimated that 88 per cent of the 1,250,000 students enrolled in junior colleges in 1966 attended publicly supported institutions. Junior colleges normally offer higher education free or at nominal cost to students within commuting distance. Most offer a two-year program of general education and courses that prepare for occupations requiring less preparation than a four-year degree program.

The President's Commission on National Goals has recommended that there should be roughly within commuting distance of every high school graduate (except in sparsely settled regions) an institution that performs the following functions:
a. Offers two-year terminal programs for students not going on to a four-year college career
b. Offers transfer programs for students who do wish to complete a four-year program
c. Serves as a technical institute for the community, serving local needs for vocational and subprofessional education
d. Offers continuing éducation to adults[2]

[2] "National Goals in Education," by John W. Gardner, from *Goals for Americans,* © 1960 by the American Assembly, Columbia University, New York. By permission of Prentice-Hall, Inc., Englewood Cliffs, N.J., p. 91.

Adding more public junior colleges to the present educational setup would provide the following gains [197:10]:

1. Pressures of increased post–high school enrollment would be lessened.
2. Higher education would become more democratic.
3. Vocational and technical training would expand.
4. Human resources would be conserved.
5. Junior colleges would become community-service centers.
6. Local high schools would be upgraded.
7. Community colleges would serve as a screen device for four-year colleges.

The graduate schools have the responsibility of providing advanced training for college graduates of high ability. It is evident that the maintenance and development of the more highly complex society of the future will depend a great deal upon the success of the graduate schools in recruiting and training our most capable people.

As indicated in Chapter 4, there will be a great demand for teachers to meet the needs of the great numbers who will be in higher education and to meet the increasing demands of industry and government for educated talent. According to the Educational Policies Commission, "Universal educational opportunities must be expanded to include at least two further years of education, open to any high school graduate, and designed to move each student toward intellectual freedom" [278:6]. As this concept approaches reality, the numbers of students in higher education will increase even more than has been projected.

Adult Education

For many years, some public schools and institutions of higher learning have felt a responsibility for meeting some of the educational needs of adults. For example, in 1883 a law was passed in Massachusetts compelling cities of over 10,000 population to establish public elementary evening classes [170:1–2]. As a result of the low educational level of enlisted men, as revealed in World War I, the federal government and a number of state legislatures enacted various laws and grants of aid to meet vocational education needs of adults. During the depression of the 1930s, adult education programs were dropped by many school districts in order to conserve resources. Since World War II, adult education has become an increasingly greater responsibility of the public schools.

New York and California are two states that are relatively advanced in providing state aid, supervision, and control for adult education programs. An idea of the scope of their programs may be gained by studying the following list of fields included in their programs [170:12]:

Agriculture	Health and physical education
Americanization	Homemaking
Arts and crafts	Industrial and trade
Business and distributive	Miscellaneous
Civic and public affairs	Music
Elementary	Parent and family life
Engineering and technology	Remedial
General academic	Safety and driver education

In nearly every state there is an adult education specialist within the department of public instruction. At the federal level, leadership is provided by the Adult Education Section in the U.S. Office of Education.

It has been estimated that over 17 million adults participate on a part-time basis in some type of formal instruction each year [90:3]. The participants are divided almost equally between men and women. Typically, they are under 40 years of age, are married and are parents, enjoy above-average incomes, and live in an urban area [90:2]. The programs attract larger numbers from professional, managerial, and skilled occupations than from laborers, operatives, service workers, and persons engaged in agriculture. Many of the programs have elementary classes for illiterates, since approximately 6 per cent of our adult population has not completed the sixth grade and is considered functionally illiterate. Title II-B of the Economic Opportunity Act provides for a program of basic education for adults so that they may increase their employability. The program is implemented by local public schools, according to a state plan. Through this program, adults have the opportunity to gain an eighth-grade level of reading and comprehension.

Types of institutions most often attended include churches and synagogues, 3,460,000; colleges and universities, 3,440,000; community organizations, 2,450,-000; business and industry, 2,040,000; elementary and secondary schools, 1,920,-000; private schools, 1,220,000; government, 1,180,000; and Armed Forces, 580,000 [90:4]. Types of programs which attract large numbers of participants include civic and public affairs, general academic, home and family living, trade, and industrial and vocational courses.

An adult education administrator has greater difficulty in developing educational programs than do elementary and secondary school principals, since adult programs are based upon the diverse needs of people within a community. Further-

FIGURE 11–17. Approximate number and age of participants in adult education and the number and age of nonparticipants. How should society attempt to meet the imperative need for more adult education? (*Source:* U.S. Office of Education.)

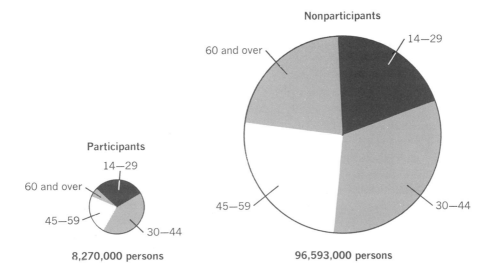

Participants
8,270,000 persons

Nonparticipants
96,593,000 persons

more, the programs may be held in churches or synagogues, business buildings, factories, and community buildings, in addition to the public school buildings. Regardless of where the programs are held, the public school's program should provide consultative services to nonschool institutions so that these programs may be a part of a coordinated adult program in a community. It would seem that the adult education administrator should have a parallel position with those responsible for elementary and secondary school programs and should report directly to the superintendent of schools. As a result, the total educational activities within a community would be coordinated by the superintendent as the executive officer of a board of education.

Informal Education

In addition to the systematically organized approaches to education, there are many informal educational opportunities ranging from activities in a home to activities provided by social clubs, women's groups, labor unions, and industrial concerns. The President's Commission on National Goals recognized this informal structure and proposed that all organizations in our society should

seek to discover how they may help their members to continue personal growth. Each organization should find the specific ways in which it may be of help in (a) arranging for courses to be given by neighboring schools or universities; (b) assisting members to arrange group study programs; (c) building the philosophy of individual fulfillment into its organizational practices, so that every member has the opportunity to grow.[3]

The Commission suggested that a more flexible system of credit by examination be devised so that assessment and certification of accomplishment within the informal structure would be recognized. The Commission also suggested that many leading universities or state boards of education should be offering credit by examination in the standard academic subjects.

SUMMARY

The patterns of school organization have been many and varied, depending upon the needs of different communities. With the passing decades, conditions have changed so markedly that these elements of organization have undergone considerable change.

Sincere efforts are being made to improve the organization of our schools. Very impressive strides are being made to consolidate certain districts in order to provide better school facilities, better teachers, and better education programs. School programs are being reorganized to provide greater continuity and educational effectiveness.

Traditionally and constitutionally, education in the United States is a state responsibility. Each state delegates such responsibilities to its local communities and

[3] "National Goals in Education," by John W. Gardner, from *Goals for Americans,* © 1960 by The American Assembly, Columbia University, New York. By permission of Prentice-Hall, Inc., Englewood Cliffs, N.J., p. 94.

encourages them to use a large measure of initiative, support, and control. However, in order to bring about greater equality of educational opportunity and to spread knowledge, understanding, and fellowship abroad in the world, the federal government and even international organizations have assumed increasingly greater roles of leadership.

Attention has been given to the various organizational levels of education. Present practices, trends, and recommendations for improvements have been noted. Throughout the chapter it is evident that the organization and administration of our schools are changing. Undoubtedly you can look forward to many more changes being made as educators and others work together in order to provide the best setting possible for the education of future generations. You have an opportunity to provide leadership in this great endeavor.

QUESTIONS FOR YOUR CONSIDERATION

1. How are the work and professional relationships of the teacher affected by each of the three conceptions of school organization and administration indicated in this chapter?
2. What advantages and disadvantages do you see in having local communities responsible for providing educational facilities for their children?
3. What role does the board of education play in your home community? What are the occupational backgrounds of the board members? How representative are they of the entire community? What qualifications should a school board member have?
4. Many countries have ministries of education that exercise great control over the educational systems in their respective countries. Should the U.S. Office of Education exert a greater role of leadership?
5. What are the advantages of having a state superintendent of schools appointed by a state board of education rather than having him elected by popular vote? What are the disadvantages?
6. How do you account for the tremendous decrease in the number of school districts in the United States? Why has there been so much resistance to reorganization of school districts?
7. What advantages and disadvantages do you see in the self-contained classroom in the elementary school?
8. What advantages and disadvantages do you see in the nongraded type of organization? How does this type of organization change the teacher's work?
9. What advantages and disadvantages do you see in flexible scheduling for secondary school pupils? How will this type of scheduling change the design of school buildings?
10. What behavior patterns are characteristic of junior high school pupils? What special provisions should be made in the school's program for such pupils?
11. What do you consider to be the unique characteristics of the comprehensive high school?
12. What are your reactions to the recommendations of Conant in regard to the high school (see Resource Section for Part IV)?

13. How can the holding power of the secondary school be further increased?
14. What advantages do you see in regional associations of secondary schools and colleges? Do the regional associations encroach upon the legal rights of local school districts?
15. What effects has the Elementary and Secondary Education Act of 1965 had upon elementary and secondary schools?

ACTIVITIES FOR YOU TO PURSUE

1. Investigate and share with your colleagues specific details relating to the organization and support of the high school from which you were graduated.
2. Investigate how school board members in your home community are selected. Discuss with two or three of the members, if possible, what they consider to be their responsibilities and duties. Compare their views with those of the superintendent of schools.
3. Collect data upon the extent to which the number of one-teacher schools has been reduced in your state during the past 20 years.
4. List the criteria you would use to determine whether or not a school district should be consolidated with another.
5. Invite a school superintendent to discuss with your class the financial and organizational problems of his schools.
6. Discuss with various school officials methods they use in grouping pupils. What are the advantages and disadvantages of each method?
7. How does your community provide for the education of youngsters who are deaf or blind or paralyzed to some extent? How does it provide for those who are extremely slow to learn or those who are unusually gifted? Describe the specialized school situations available for such persons.
8. Observe in a good junior high school to determine how provision is made for the efficient transition of pupils from elementary to senior high school. In what ways might this transition be improved still further?
9. Prepare a display of publications issued by the U.S. Office of Education and share the display with your colleagues.
10. Examine a copy of your state school code with respect to the duties of the local school board.
11. Write to your state department of education and request a copy of the organizational chart of that department.
12. Organize a panel to discuss the advantages and disadvantages of having local communities primarily responsible for providing educational facilities for their children.

12

FINANCING OUR SCHOOLS

What is your reaction to the fact that education is the largest single nondefense governmental business in the United States and that approximately $27 billion was spent for public elementary and secondary education alone during the 1966–1967 school year? Perhaps you feel that such information is no concern of the teacher, but rather of the statistician, the politician, or the public school administrator.

How do you react to the fact that, in a 15-year period, Americans spent $173 billion for public elementary and secondary schools, while during this same period of time they spent $227 billion for tobacco and alcoholic beverages, $234 billion for recreation, and $198 billion for new and used cars? As compared with 5.8 per cent for the United States, Russia spent 7 per cent of its gross national product for education in 1965 [75:175]. Perhaps these figures cause you to ask: "Don't Americans know the value of education?" By now it should be apparent that you have a responsibility as a teacher to be informed about matters of school finance so that you can inform others about the problems and their possible solutions.

What happens in the future so far as school finance is concerned will affect your teaching salary, your personal and teaching welfare, and the facilities and equipment which you and your pupils will have in the important process of teaching and learning. Can our nation afford to educate an additional 1 million pupils a year during the decade from 1965 to 1975? Can our nation afford to train and to hire an additional 450,000 instructional personnel, construct 600,000 new classrooms during the period from 1965 to 1975, or increase annual expenditures for education from $25 billion in 1965–1966 to $50 billion in 1974–1975? In this chapter you will note the mounting costs of public education. Unless the American

FIGURE 12–1. Comparison of the cost of education with other expenditures in 1963. How much can we afford to pay for education? (*Source:* National Education Association.)

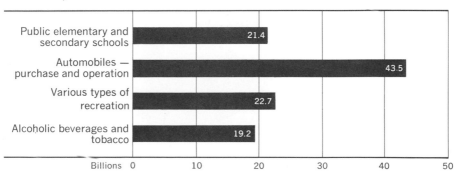

public is willing to absorb these mounting costs, how can we expect the quality of education and the welfare of teachers to improve?

Obviously, every teacher should feel a vital responsibility for understanding school finance to the extent that he will be able to interpret school costs to lay citizens. In fact, teachers should feel an increasing responsibility for convincing the public that even greater expenditures than those predicted should be made for schools in order to provide the quality of education which the future demands.

In your study of school finance, keep in mind the total public finance structure, since school finance is a branch of public finance. In other words, keep in perspective the importance and needs of other government-supported services and the relationship between factors such as public expenditures, population growth, and economic growth. For example, it is important to remember the fact that public expenditures and tax loads have increased in greater proportion than has the nation's population. The population of our nation in 1967 was slightly more than 2.5 times the population in the early 1900s, but public expenditures were approximately 90 times that level.

Another important factor to remember is that expenditures for national defense in the future will undoubtedly have first priority. The increase or decrease in defense outlay will mean a less favorable or more favorable financial promise for nondefense projects, including education. Since 1902, for example, expenditures for national defense and international relations have increased more than four times as much as the expenditures for education [6:12]. In 1965 the total cost of public education was 56.8 per cent of the $52.8 billion spent in the fiscal year of 1965 for national security programs by the federal government [281:5].

These concepts, and others to follow in this chapter, should help you understand the basic principles of school finance. Emphasis, however, will be placed

FIGURE 12–2. Direct expenditures of state and local government in 1963–1964. (*Source:* National Education Association.)

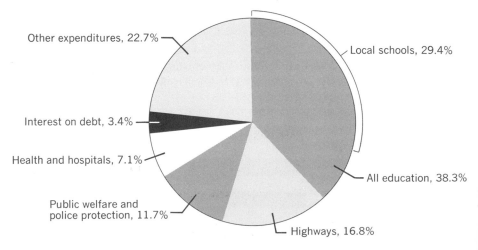

Other expenditures, 22.7%

Local schools, 29.4%

Interest on debt, 3.4%

Health and hospitals, 7.1%

Public welfare and police protection, 11.7%

All education, 38.3%

Highways, 16.8%

Total direct expenditures, $69,301, 500,000

upon the modes of providing local, state, and federal financial support for public elementary and secondary schools.

BASES OF CURRENT SCHOOL FINANCE PROBLEMS

The states' responsibility for maintaining and operating the American public school systems necessarily includes the obligation of each state to make provisions for financing its school system. Generally, the states have relied chiefly upon local financial support for public schools. At the turn of the twentieth century only 17 per cent of school funds were provided by the states. Since the economic depression in the 1930s, however, the amount of state funds to aid local school district support has increased significantly. For the 1966–1967 school year, about 39.9 per cent of the total school revenue in the United States was derived from state sources, 52.1 per cent from local sources, and 8.0 per cent from federal sources. The share from federal receipts was fairly constant through 1964–1965, but by 1966–1967 it more than doubled because of several new and increased federal programs.

As you read this chapter, keep in mind that the development of the public schools during the twentieth century has not been the same in all states, partly because each state has had different goals at different times. Other reasons for the variations in the development of public school programs among states include differences in tax systems, economic conditions, centralization of local school districts, political beliefs, fear of change, and willingness to provide funds for education [18:93–94].

As our nation has moved through the industrial revolution and into a scientific

FIGURE 12–3. Percentage distribution of school support in the United States in 1966–1967. To what extent does your state deviate from this percentage distribution, and how do you account for this deviation? (*Source:* National Education Association.)

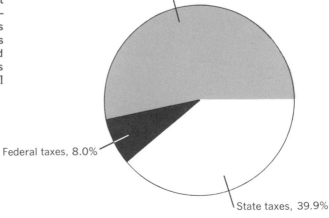

Local taxes, 52.1%

Federal taxes, 8.0%

State taxes, 39.9%

revolution, the educational system in each state has had to undergo varying adaptations to the changing economic and social conditions in order to best serve the educational needs of individuals and of society. Basic and intermediate school administrative units have not always been able to cope adequately with financial problems, partially because of constitutional and organizational limitations. Constitutional limitations have included debt limits and tax limits as well as provision for earmarked taxes. Although earmarked taxes have assured districts of a definite source of income, educational services have been generally limited because local educational revenues have been tied to a yield from a tax whose rate has been difficult to increase. Small administrative units have often lacked an adequate tax base and sufficient pupil population to provide a quality educational program.

In addition to the above factors, school finance problems are the result of five major forces: (1) record increases in school enrollment, (2) demand for greater quality in education, (3) rise in educational costs due to inflation, (4) extension of educational services, and (5) backlog of school construction. Each of these forces will be discussed.

School Enrollment Increases

The extent of increase in public school enrollments is indicated by the fact that in the decade of 1956 to 1966, there was an increase of over 12.5 million pupils in public elementary and secondary schools, which represented a 40.8 per cent increase for the decade. In addition, more pupils were staying in school, as is evidenced by the fact that the average adult in 1965 had 11.8 years of education [249:112], compared with 8.4 years in 1940 [39:3].

FIGURE 12–4. Total expenditure per pupil in average daily attendance 1929–1930 to 1964–1965. Has the upward trend in expenditure continued? (*Source:* U.S. Office of Education.)

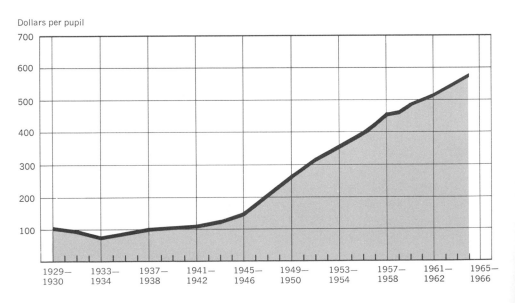

Dollars per pupil

Population statistics, however, indicate that the annual rate of growth in the school population may not continue to increase so rapidly. In contrast to the 3.8 per cent increase of the 1958 school population over the 1957 population, the increase in 1964 was only 3.1 over the 1963 population. The rate of increase from 1969 to 1970 will approximate 1.2 per cent, and enrollment projections indicate that the 1974 to 1975 increase will be only 0.5 per cent [169:1].

Institutions of higher education face large enrollment increases in the 1965 to 1975 period. The college population was 4,800,000 students in 1965, and it will probably increase to over 7,900,000 by 1973 [241:8]. The problem of recruitment of faculty is exemplified by the fact that, although the nation's output of Ph.D.s in mathematics approximates 400 a year, only 200 remain in educational activities. In the meantime, there will be 1 million freshmen enrolling in mathematics courses annually [277:115]. The total instructional staff for resident degree courses in higher education will need to be increased from 426,000 in 1966 to 572,000 in 1973 [241:24].

Quality of Education

Our system of government, our economy, our position of world leadership, and the race for space have combined to bring education into national focus with emphasis upon the goal of quality education. Educational research is greatly concerned with the problem of relating the cost of education and educational quality. One of the most ambitious research projects of this type has been the Quality Measurement Project of the New York State Education Department, in which 70,000 youngsters have participated in a mass testing program over a three-year period as they moved from grade to grade. In this project it has been found that there is evidence of a positive relationship between the level of school

FIGURE 12–5.   Factors that have accounted for an increase of $11.23 billion in school expenditures between 1954 and 1964. (*Source:* National Education Association.)

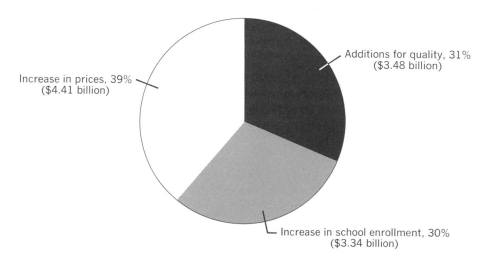

Additions for quality, 31% ($3.48 billion)

Increase in prices, 39% ($4.41 billion)

Increase in school enrollment, 30% ($3.34 billion)

expenditure and both the achievement test scores of pupils and the holding power of the school. However, the low correlation indicates that good quality of education is not assured by high expenditures alone. The relative effectiveness of schools may vary according to pupil IQ, socioeconomic-level classification, subject-matter classification, or sex. Few schools are universally good or bad but are mosaics of specific strengths and weaknesses [284:87].

Another comprehensive research project, conducted by Professor Kreitlow of Wisconsin, concerned the effects of school district organization upon the quality of education. This longitudinal study was begun in 1949 with a study of youngsters who were in the first grade in five newly reorganized school districts and in five matched control communities. The effects of reorganization in terms of educational opportunities, achievement, cost, and social impact were measured at first, sixth, ninth, and twelfth grades, and follow-ups were made for a five-year period after pupils had graduated from high school. Results of the study indicated that both boys and girls in reorganized districts were ahead in twenty-one of twenty-two measures of achievement. In the ninth grade, boys of reorganized districts were ahead in eight of eleven measures, and girls were ahead in all eleven. Conclusions drawn from the study are as follows: (1) Boys and girls in reorganized districts had greater educational opportunities; (2) reorganized districts produced higher academic achievement as shown by standardized achievement tests; and (3) instruction in reorganized districts cost $12 more per elementary pupil per year [145:47–48].

It is important for you to follow the progress of such projects and become thoroughly conversant with the results, since they may have a significant impact upon the future of education. They provide objective data with which you may be able to justify higher costs of education and reorganization of schools.

A number of curriculum revisions have been accomplished in numerous school districts since Sputnik 1 and the resultant cry for quality in the schools. Our affluent society has been taking stock of its values, and quality education is emerging as a vital want and need. As is true of almost everything else in life, quality products and programs cost more money.

Inflation

Responsibilities of government at all levels are greater now than they have ever been. This condition is partially due to the facts that the population of our nation has increased greatly and that the government is providing more services than ever before. Inflation also affects government expenditures. For example, it is estimated that, if there had been no increase in prices in the past 30 years, federal expenditure in 1962 would have been only 10 times rather than 34 times higher than in 1932. During this same period of time, state and local expenditures would have been 2½, instead of 8, times higher [17:84].

Extension of Educational Services

In the previous chapter, attention was given to the tendency to extend formal education to three-, four-, and five-year-old youngsters and to increase higher-education opportunities. In addition, state legislatures have been placing more and more demands upon the public schools to provide greater amounts for guidance services, adult education, special education, and vocational education. These demands have resulted from three major developments, which are both national and international in scope—the urgency of scientific progress in order that the United States can compete satisfactorily with other socioeconomic systems, the changing educational requirements for employment, and the nation's commitment to a war against poverty [169:3]. Frequently the demands for these additional educational programs and services have been made without providing the necessary means to finance them.

School Construction

Comparatively few new school buildings were erected during the years from 1930 through 1950 because of the national depression and war emergencies. By 1950 a backlog of needed construction, plus needed remodeling, faced many school communities. The problem was intensified by the postwar inflation which ma-

FIGURE 12–6.   Public elementary and secondary classrooms constructed between 1942–1943 and 1962–1963. What demands for the construction of classrooms will be made in the future? (*Source:* Chamber of Commerce of the United States.)

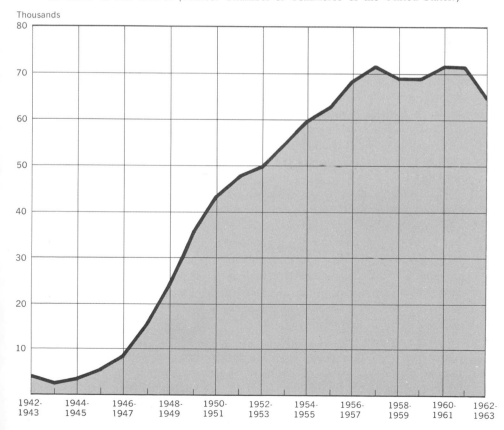

Thousands

terially increased the cost of construction. The fact that 44 per cent of the nation's classrooms available in 1961 were built during the 1950–1960 decade is evidence of the school construction boom of the 1950s. It is anticipated that an average of 65,000 classrooms will be built annually during the next few years. This will mean an outlay of between $2.7 and $3.3 billion annually, depending upon construction costs.

The nation's 23,335 school districts are generally faced with financial problems created by one or more of the forces described above. Solutions of the problem are not easy, but progress is being made through effective planning and through coordination of local, state, and federal governmental efforts.

THE SCHOOL BUDGET

In order to cope intelligently with financial problems created by forces such as those cited above, local school districts prepare long-term and annual school budgets. Effective school administrators and boards of education are planning educational programs and anticipating revenue needs for 10 to 20 years in the future. Long-term projections of pupil enrollments are made on the basis of each annual school census; long-term financing is exemplified by cumulative building levies which provide funds so that educational facilities can be partially paid for on an installment plan in advance of the actual construction of the facilities.

The Annual Budget

You will be personally interested in the annual budget presented in your school district each spring since it will reflect teacher salary increases and other rewards for your professional efforts. You may have an opportunity to work with a committee of teachers, administrators, and school board members on salary problems.

The annual budget, generally prepared for a fiscal year of July 1 to June 30, is a financial plan for attaining the objectives of the educational program. The three aspects of budget making are the educational plan, the spending plan, and the revenue plan.

The educational plan, consisting of service, materials, and activities, is determined principally by the school administration, the teaching and nonteaching staff, and the school board members. The plan prescribes the educational program that is to be provided for the pupils in the district. Lay citizen groups often participate in expressing and accumulating opinion concerning the educational program. Factors to be considered include pupil population, teacher-pupil ratio, curriculum, the program scope (i.e., kindergarten through junior college), state department directives, parental aspirations, the impact of technological changes upon teaching methods, and teacher quality.

In the spending plan, expenditures are determined by translating the accepted educational plan into costs. Expenditures are ordinarily classified to show the amount which will be spent for each educational function. Classifications generally include instruction; administration; fixed charges (rent and insurance); operation and maintenance of physical plant; services such as health, transportation, and school lunch; summer school; community college; capital outlay; and debt service. Typical percentages of expenditures for the various functions are shown in Figure 12-7.

Unfortunately, many school systems do not allocate an appropriate amount of their annual operating budget for research, experimentation, and innovation. It has been recommended that each school system provide not less than 1 per cent of the annual budget for teachers "to participate in curriculum planning, research, evaluation, and other activities designed to improve the instructional program" [232:22].

The revenue plan involves a listing of the sources of funds, other than those to be raised by local taxation, and the estimated amount of revenue to be received from each source. For example, state school authorities ordinarily let the local school administrators know how much money they can expect to receive from the state government. In addition, the local school administrator anticipates receipts from the federal government as well as from tuition fees or other charges. Local property and/or nonproperty tax rates necessary to raise the balance of funds needed are then computed and eithed levied by the board or put to a vote by the people in that district.

After the budget has been approved, the chief school administrator and the board defend the budget at public hearings conducted by local and state tax commissioners. Such a system of checks and balances forces the school administration to review the allocation of resources for varied phases of the educational program at least once annually. Funds are then committed for expenditure, as defined by the spending plan, for the ensuing budget year.

The typical school budget authorizes less money than is needed to provide the highest-quality education for all pupils. Estimates of financial needs are based ordinarily on minimum or so-called average educational programs which appear to be relatively easy to sell to a given community. Unfortunately, even these estimates prepared by a district's administration may need to be cut because of the community's inability or unwillingness to provide the amount requested.

FIGURE 12–7. How the current school dollar is spent. (*Source: School Management.*)

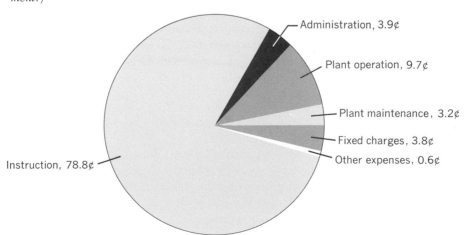

STATE SCHOOL FINANCE PROGRAMS

A Rockefeller Brothers Fund publication indicates that "all the problems of the schools lead us back sooner or later to one basic problem—financing" [205:33]. Likewise, solution of local school district financial problems leads us back to the provision of the state for financing its schools. Local school districts have only the taxing authority delegated to them by the state government, and needed funds, other than those raised at the local level, must be provided by the state.

Since there are fifty state systems of education in the United States, there are fifty different systems of state school finance. The amount of state support, for example, ranges from 4.7 per cent in Nebraska to 77.7 per cent in Delaware. A few states, such as Delaware and North Carolina, provide most of their school funds from state tax sources. The majority of states have favored a partnership plan of state and local support, with minor support from the federal government.

State funds have been used in our nation's history to (1) help communities establish the operation of a school system; (2) afford relief to those districts unable to provide sufficient local funds; (3) encourage new programs (such as special education, audio-visual communications, and transportation) and support services (such as new buildings, salaries, textbooks, and pupil transportation); (4) provide emergency aid, such as in the 1930s, by relieving the tax burden on the property holder; (5) provide payments in lieu of taxes through property lost by local districts to new state parks or to new industry which received tax exemptions for a period of years; and (6) provide general support for schools through a foundation program.

As is evident, much of the state school aid has been provided to meet financial crises and to serve as an incentive for local districts to add new educational services. Such aid has been piecemeal and has not been made within the framework of a comprehensive and systematic state school support program.

State Foundation Programs

More than forty states have developed what are termed "state foundation programs." Such a program designates the amount that must be made available to all administrative units in the state to support the basic instructional program considered to be essential for all youngsters in the state.

The steps in the development of a state foundation program include the following:

1. Definition of the educational program.
2. Translation of the educational program into costs necessary to provide the essential educational services.
3. Determination of the local district's share of cost according to measures of fiscal capacity. The tendency is for programs to require that wealthier districts pay a greater local share than districts of less wealth and, conversely, that they receive less state aid than the poorer districts. This equalization concept is typical of many foundation programs.
4. Determination of the total state share to each district.

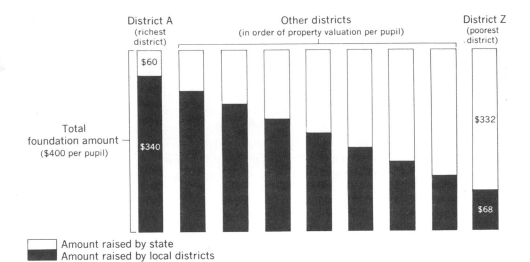

FIGURE 12–8. A hypothetical example of state and local cooperation in financing a foundation program of support in all school districts of a state. *(Source:* National Education Association.)

A state foundation program normally includes expenditures for current operation, school facilities, transportation, and special education. The scope of the program in some states includes nursery school through the junior college. Most of the existing programs provide funds for elementary and secondary schools enrolling grades 1 through 12.

State foundation programs attempt to guarantee all children in a state a respectable education. The law usually sets a dollar amount that will be expended per pupil, per classroom, or per teaching unit. Funds are disbursed usually from general funds appropriated by the state legislature rather than from restricted earmarked funds. Local leeway is advisable, so that a local school district has power to tax itself to support a better program than is provided through the foundation support.

Effectiveness of a foundation program is geared to the adequacy of a state's tax system to finance the program. A state's tax system provides the means for both state and local governments to obtain needed revenue.

State Tax Systems

Each state has its own system of taxes with different types of taxes, different items included in the tax base, and different rates of taxation. In addition, each state gives local units within its boundaries certain taxing privileges, which often differ from those enjoyed by similar local units in adjoining states.

The reason for these great differences is that our present tax system has developed a little at a time. As changes occur in our economy and in the distribution and form of sources available for taxation, the old taxes become less effective and new ones must be added to the old to provide the necessary funds for governmental activities. The history of taxation indicates that a tax, once it is imposed, is rarely repealed.

Most, but not all, payments made to the government are taxes, and these payments are termed "revenues." Nonrevenue receipts by governments include such payments as fees and charges for services received, money obtained by borrowing through sale of bonds or otherwise, and income from sale of governmental property. In general, the primary purpose of a tax is to produce revenue for a unit of government. A secondary purpose in some cases is to regulate an activity.

The yield of a tax is of paramount importance. As you discuss problems of taxation with various community members, use the following criteria for deciding what taxes are to be imposed in any unit of government, including school districts:

1. Stability. Does the tax provide sufficient funds in spite of economic conditions?
2. Flexibility. Is the tax able to meet changing conditions?
3. Equity. Does the tax treat alike all those in similar circumstances?
4. Economic effect. Does it interfere with desirable business activity in the state?
5. Convenience and enforceability. Is it convenient for the taxpayer and for the tax collector?
6. Directness. Is the tax directly and readily seen by the taxpayer as a contribution to the cost of government?
7. Economy of collection. Does it take a disproportionate percentage of the yield to assess and collect the tax in question?

Most states rely upon sales and income taxes to finance state obligations. The general sales tax is the best single source of state tax revenue. It yields over 25 per cent of the total state tax revenue in the nation. Of the seven states which together account for almost one-half of the nationwide state tax revenue—California, Illinois, Michigan, New York, Ohio, Pennsylvania, and Texas—five rely upon the sales tax as their major source of revenue [174:5]. The general sales tax plus selective sales taxes, that is, taxes on motors, fuels, alcoholic beverages, and tobacco products, comprises approximately 60 percent of the total state tax collections.

You probably will find that sales taxes will increase in importance over the years in state-local finance. Increasing the number of items to be taxed rather than increasing sales tax rates on items currently taxed will provide greater equity of taxation.

Thirty-six states have personal income taxes and thirty-seven states have corporation taxes. The greatest problem encountered with personal income tax is enforcement. There is a need in most states for additional auditors to check accounts and returns on income taxes. Some states have adopted the plan of withholding state income taxes in the same manner as does the federal government, and with very satisfactory results.

The advantage of the individual income and the general sales tax is that they have a broad tax base and have a capacity for producing a large amount of revenue at a relatively low rate. It is apparent that the use of many state taxes creates less taxpayer resistance than is encountered when a single source of tax revenue is used.

As noted earlier, state taxes, such as sales, income, and inheritance taxes, pro-

Example of the per cent of revenue from their three sources: 75 (local)
22 (state)
3 (federal)

FIGURE 12–9. Percentages of public school revenue in each state derived from local, state, and federal tax sources. Note the wide diversity of the sources of school revenue. What do you consider the most desirable distribution? (*Source:* Chamber of Commerce of the United States.)

vide almost 40 per cent of the funds spent for public elementary and secondary schools in the United States. On the average, local school districts provide the greater portion of school funds.

Local School District Taxes

You can expect considerable comment about property taxes in your school district. For this reason, you will want to know for what purposes revenue from property taxes is used. Property taxes account for 98.6 per cent of all taxes collected from local sources by school districts. Property taxes originally developed as "ability to pay" taxes. It was assumed that the ability to pay taxes was evidenced by wealth, which in turn was evidenced by the amount of property an individual

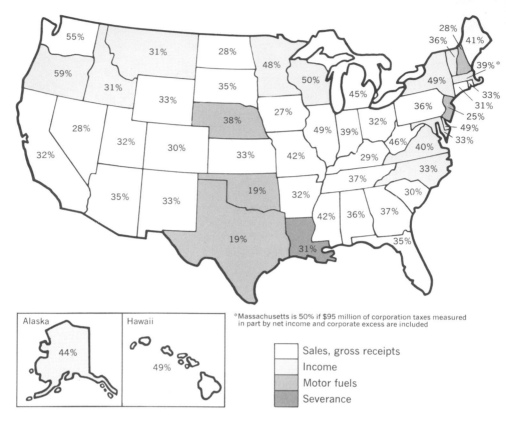

FIGURE 12–10.   The best sources of state revenue in 1966. (*Source: State Tax Review.*)

owned. However, in the early days of our nation, real property constituted 75 per cent of our wealth. It is estimated that today real property constitutes only 25 per cent of our wealth.

Since the advent of the industrial revolution in the United States and the resultant change in economic and social conditions, financial experts have been seeking new taxes to replace the property tax. This trend was accelerated particularly during the depression years of the 1930s, when many property owners were unable to pay their taxes. It is becoming more evident today that local school districts and other local governmental agencies in most states will continue to rely on the property tax, and emphasis will be on improvement rather than on replacement of the tax.

You will find school districts in the United States which must subject their budgets to the approval of taxpayers before a tax levy for school purposes is certified. You hear of school budgets being vetoed in many districts. Some claim that unreasonably high property tax rates are the cause of such a vote. On the other hand, it may be caused by opposition upon the part of voters to the total local, state, and federal tax load rather than opposition to taxes for schools. Bear in mind that a school election operates at the grass-roots level. At a school election it is much easier for an individual to express his feelings toward the total tax burden than for him to be heard in the halls of the state legislature or in the halls of the United States Congress.

One advantage of the property tax is that it provides residual tax support for local services. Other taxes are established at a fixed rate, such as 3 per cent, whereas the property tax rate is adjusted to each budget to provide that part of expenditures not covered by other receipts. Thus, a property tax rate might be $3.65 per $100 of assessed valuation one year and $3.95 the following year in order to provide the balance of funds needed in each case.

Local school district property tax rates are usually expressed in terms of dollars per $100 of assessed valuation, or in terms of mills per dollar of assessed valuation. If your home, for example, is assessed at a valuation of $3,000 and the local school tax rate is $3.65 per $100, your school tax would equal $3.65 × 30, or a total of $109.50.

Since property taxes play such an important role in the support of schools, you may be interested in how this method of taxation may be improved. Suggestions for improving the administration of the property tax include the following: (1) Assessment districts in most states should be enlarged, and assessors should be trained to effect uniform assessments; (2) the personal property tax, which has been a negotiated tax, should be replaced, or personal property should be assessed according to a state classification of "book values"; (3) property tax exemptions should be reviewed, since such exemptions result in higher tax rates to offset the exemption or to shift tax responsibility, sometimes unfairly; (4) the law pertaining to assessments should either be applied to all taxpayers or be changed.

Local Nonproperty Taxes

States may give permission for local governments to levy nonproperty taxes. Some states have allowed their local units considerably more tax leeway than others. Certain local governments in the fifty states levy a nonproperty tax; for example, cities in Alabama place a tax on admissions and amusements, alcoholic beverages, business gross receipts, cigarettes and tobacco, gasoline, hotel occupancy, income, insurance, motor vehicle sales, public utility gross receipts, sales, and soft drinks.

Local school districts in the United States have not generally been given authority to levy nonproperty taxes, although school districts in seven states levy a poll tax, districts in three states levy a general sales tax, and districts in two states levy an income tax. Only the state of Pennsylvania uses local nonproperty tax widely for the direct support of public education. Administration of nonproperty taxes would not be practical in the typical small district because of relatively high administrative costs. The taxes can be practically administered over a large urban or metropolitan area or a combination of small school districts.

Combined State and Local Financial Effort

Support of public education is becoming more and more a cooperative state-local enterprise in the United States. For this reason you should examine combined state and local taxes in order to better understand the great range of tax effort within the United States.

In 1964–1965, state and local tax collections were highest in California, amount-

ing to $379.29 per capita, followed by New York with a per capita amount of
$372.10, and Nevada, with a per capita amount of $321.82. Combined state and
local tax collections averaged $266.11 per capita in the United States during the
period 1964–1965. Arkansas had the lowest per capita collection—$159.47.
Other states with low per capita collection were, in turn, South Carolina, $160.82;
Alabama, $167.55; and Mississippi, $169.89 [207:39].

A measure of financial effort is to be found in the relation between the combined state-local tax collection and personal income. The tax load was heaviest in
California and Vermont in 1964–1965, when state and local taxes amounted to
$11.80 per $100 of personal income. The tax load was lightest in Alaska, where
state and local taxes amounted to $7.40 per $100 of personal income [207:42].

The combined state and local financial effort provided 92.2 per cent of the
public elementary and secondary revenue in 1965–1966. Remaining funds were
provided by the federal government.

FEDERAL SUPPORT OR AID FOR EDUCATION

Although education in the United States is a state function, the federal government has been assisting in terms of financing and programming for 175 years.

FIGURE 12–11. Trends in school support represented by the percentage of revenue for education derived from federal, state, and local sources. (*Source:* U. S.
Office of Education; National Education Association.)

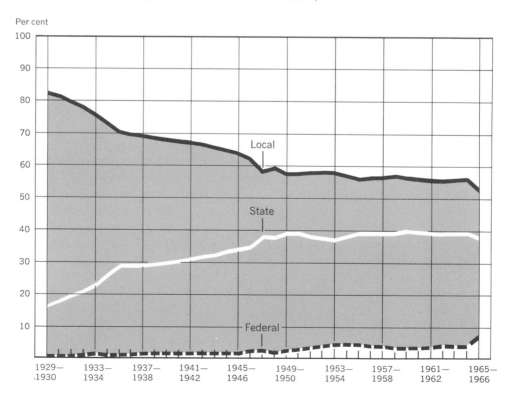

The statement given in Section 101 of Public Law 85–864, commonly known as the National Defense Education Act (NDEA) of 1958, represents a typical congressional statement of interest in education:

The Congress hereby finds and declares that the security of the Nation requires the fullest development of the mental resources and technical skills of its young men and women. The present emergency demands that additional and more adequate educational opportunities be made available. The defense of this Nation depends upon the mastery of modern techniques developed from complex scientific principles. It depends as well upon the discovery and development of new principles, new techniques, and new knowledge. . . .

We must increase our efforts to identify and educate more of the talent of our Nation. . . .

The Congress reaffirms the principle and declares that the States and local communities have and must retain control over and primary responsibility for public education. The national interest requires, however, that the Federal Government give assistance to education for programs which are important to our defense.

Whether or not the assistance should be termed federal support or federal aid has been argued during the period of our nation's history. McCaskill has differentiated the two concepts as follows [151:22]:

Federal support to public schools embodies the following characteristics:

1. It is an underwriting by the federal government of a share in local and state financing of the schools.
2. It is directed to the general school operation rather than to specific subjects or functions.
3. It attacks the fundamental problem of the broad financial need of our schools.
4. It involves a long-range commitment on the part of the federal government.
5. It requires federal appropriations of considerable size.

Federal aid, on the other hand, includes the following characteristics:

1. It is intended to stimulate educational activity temporarily rather than to underwrite it for a long period of time.
2. It is usually intended to meet a specific need rather than to strengthen the total educational program.
3. It tends to be remedial rather than fundamental.
4. It tends to deal with emergency situations rather than long-range problems.
5. It requires small federal appropriations compared with overall educational needs.

According to McCaskill's definitions, federal legislation for the most part is classified as aid rather than as support, partially because no clear-cut federal policy for education has ever been established.

A former U.S. Commissioner of Education has stated that "a man with time on his hands can identify over 250 separate U.S. Government educational operations carried on by 12 departments and 26 independent agencies" [151:22]. The several specific educational programs for which federal appropriations are being made regularly now are listed below:

Atomic Energy Commission grants to colleges
Books for the blind
Civics, history, geography, reading, and English institutes
Civil defense education
College housing

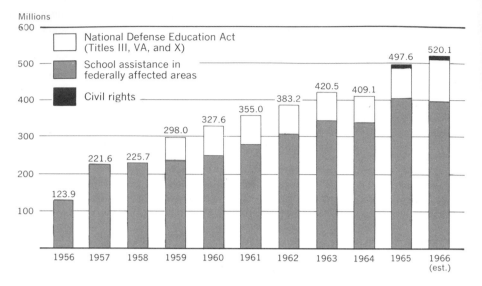

FIGURE 12–12. Trends in various kinds of U.S. Office of Education financial assistance, other than vocational education, for elementary and secondary education. *(Source: U.S. Office of Education.)*

College student loans
Education for the blind
Education in fishery trades
Education of military personnel
Education of public health personnel
Education of the Indians
Educational exchange programs
FBI national academy
Fellowships
Guidance, counseling, and testing
Improvement of educational statistics
International education
Land-grant colleges
Language development
Library services
Meteorological education and training
National Library of Medicine
Peace Corps
Police training schools
Practical nurse training
Public assistance consultation and training
Public health research
Research
Science, mathematics, and foreign-language institutes
Scholarships
School lunch program
School milk program
Schools at military installations
Support for federally affected areas
Traineeships for health personnel
Training of personnel in public welfare

U.S. Merchant Marine Academy at Kings Point
U.S. Office of Economic Opportunity
U.S. Office of Education
Veterans education
Vocational education
Vocational training for Indians
War orphans' education

Contrary to general public opinion, a majority of federal funds expended for educational and related activities are administered through agencies other than the U.S. Office of Education, as is shown in Table 8. Only 36 per cent of the estimated federal obligations for education were to be expended by the Office of Education.

Types of Federal Assistance to States for Education

Federal financial assistance to states for public education may be classified under four categories: (1) unconditional land grants, (2) conditional grants for ad-

TABLE 8 Federal Funds for Education and Related Activities by Agency for the Fiscal Year 1966
(Amounts in thousands)

Agency	Estimated obligation, 1966
Total	$8,701,636
Department of Agriculture	164,674
Department of Commerce	12,094
Department of Defense	1,873,800
Department of Health, Education, and Welfare:	
Office of Education	3,127,780
Public Health Service	1,032,930
Vocational Rehabilitation Administration	30,700
Welfare Administration	12,800
Other	18,983
Department of the Interior	127,931
Department of Labor	373,031
Department of State	13,550
Department of the Treasury	12,910
Atomic Energy Commission	86,655
D.C. government	12,158
Federal Aviation Agency	600
Government Printing Office	1,399
Housing and Home Finance Agency	312,400
Library of Congress	24,316
National Aeronautics and Space Administration	160,160
National Science Foundation	467,300
Office of Economic Opportunity	708,000
Peace Corps	1,300
Small Business Administration	300
Smithsonian Institution	22,165
Tennessee Valley Authority	300
U.S. Arms Control and Disarmament Agency	1,100
Other agencies	68,000

vanced education, (3) conditional grants for secondary education, and (4) emergency grants.

As you will recall, beginning with the Ohio Enabling Act of 1802, the federal government *unconditionally* granted one section or more of land to new states for the use of schools. Money from the sale of these lands totaled approximately a half billion dollars. The federal government never officially questioned the states concerning school-land policies, and there was no federal control over expenditures.

Conditional grants of land for advanced education began under terms of the Morrill Act in 1862. Beginning with the second Morrill Act, passed in 1890, and continuing with supplemental acts, land-grant colleges or universities have received federal appropriations.

The Morrill Act and the supplemental acts, which are examples of conditional grants for advanced education, introduced the following changes in federal educational policy: (1) some control by specifying programs (land-grant institutions were to include agriculture and mechanical arts in their curriculum as well as military science and tactics); (2) annual appropriations for programs in addition to the original land grants; (3) reimbursement of the state after federal authorities were reassured that money had been spent for the purposes designated by law.

Conditional federal grants for secondary schools is illustrated by the Smith-Hughes Act of 1917, followed by supplemental acts, which provides appropriations annually for vocational education at the secondary school level. Under the Smith-Hughes Act, the federal appropriations are matched dollar for dollar by the states. The Vocational Education Act of 1963 represents the first federal act to provide comprehensive vocational education programs at the secondary school level.

A fourth type of federal support was in operation during the depression years of the 1930s when the federal government provided several hundred million dollars annually during the emergency period to aid distressed school districts. This aid also included assistance for needy secondary, college, and university students so that they might continue their education during the depression, as well as provisions for nursery schools, literacy classes, correspondence instruction on both secondary and college levels, vocational education, parent education, work for unemployed teachers, and funds for school buildings.

Recent legislation of the emergency type includes provision for federal assistance where both increases in school enrollments and reductions in taxable valuations due to the federal purchase of property have continued to burden certain communities in financing school services. Public Laws 874 and 815 are known as SAFA (School Assistance to Local Educational Agencies in Federally Affected Areas). During the 1950 to 1965 period these two laws provided nearly $3 billion to over 5,000 school districts.

Public Law 874 approved contributions, beginning in 1950, toward the "maintenance and operation" of school districts which suffered a financial burden due to the provision of educational services for children whose parents are employed on federal property or to sudden substantial increases in enrollments because of federal activities. During the 1950s, also, Congress began appropriating funds under Public Law 815 for assistance in the construction of minimum school facilities for federally connected children. Minimum facilities include instructional and auxiliary rooms and initial equipment, but do not include auditoriums and gymnasiums.

Public Laws 874 and 815 are attempts by the federal government to assist local governments in federally created situations which resulted from post-World War II defense and research activities. The only redress for local government in the emergency period was from the federal government.

Another recent program of federal support for education in an emergency period is exemplified by the National Defense Education Act (NDEA) of 1958, which was amended in 1963 and in 1964, and has been extended through 1968. This act contains ten titles that authorize funds to the extent of more than $1 billion for grants and loans over a period of a few years. Use of the funds is specified by the act, and the states are required to match the federal funds. Funds have been provided for loans and fellowships to students; strengthening instruction in mathematics, science, foreign language, civics, history, geography, and reading; guidance counseling and testing; area vocational education; research in uses of television, radio, and movies; science information service; and improving statistical service. This act touches levels of education from the elementary schools through the graduate schools, both public and private.

The NDEA represents an expression of the federal government's concern over the fact that the long struggle of the free world against communism could be won or lost in the classrooms. Particular interest was shown first in improving mathematics, science, and foreign language instruction and then extending the work to academic areas listed in the previous paragraph. Thus, the federal government encouraged improvement in these and other educational areas by offering financial incentives to the states.

Major Federal Educational Acts in the Mid-1960s

The following are brief descriptions of the major education acts passed by the United States Congress in the mid-1960s [94:41, 43, 44]:

Health Professions Educational Assistance Act of 1963 (PL88-129): provides $236.4 million to help build medical and dental schools and to help students attend such institutions.

Mental Retardation Facilities and Community Mental Health Construction Act of 1963 (PL88-164): provides matching funds for construction of community mental health centers, funds for the construction of research and treatment facilities, and funds for training teachers of mentally retarded and other handicapped children.

Higher Education Facilities Act of 1963 (PL88-204): authorizes $1.2 billion program of grants and loans to public junior colleges and public technical institutes and to public and nonpublic colleges and universities.

Vocational Education Act of 1963 (PL88-210): provides $1.6 billion over the next four years to update vocational training programs. The act also extended Impacted Areas Aid (PL81-815 and 874) to June 30, 1965, and extended and amended the National Defense Education Act.

Manpower Development and Training Act Amendments of 1963 (PL88-214):

The amendments expanded provisions of the basic Manpower Development and Training Act of 1962 by excusing states from sharing program expenses until June 30, 1965, and by providing relocation grants and loans to unemployed workers. The act also provides for basic education for poorly schooled adults and for training allowances for jobless youths.

Library Services and Construction Act of 1964 (PL 88-269): authorizes $135 million program for construction of public library facilities and provision of library services in large and small cities. This act amends the Library Service Act of 1956.

Civil Rights Act of 1964 (PL 88-352): provides for nondiscrimination in federally assisted programs (Title VI) and for technical assistance, grants, and training institutes to help communities prepare for school desegregation (Title IV).

War Orphans' Educational Assistance Act of 1964 (PL 88-361): extends the application of the War Orphans' Educational Assistance Act of 1956 to children of veterans who were totally or permanently disabled in the service.

Juvenile Delinquency and Youth Offenses Control Act Amendments of 1964 (PL 88-368): extended to 1966 the Juvenile Delinquency and Youth Offense Control Act of 1961. Also authorized a study of the relation of compulsory school attendance and child labor laws to delinquency, and provides for an anti-juvenile delinquency project for Washington, D.C.

Economic Opportunity Act of 1964 (PL 88-452): provides, through its education sections, for setting up a Job Corps for unemployed youth, for community action programs to combat poverty, for work experience demonstration projects, and for the setting up of Volunteers in Service to America (VISTA) modeled after the Peace Corps. Preschool and high school projects are included in the community action program.

Nurse Training Act of 1964 (PL 88-581): provides funds for the construction of nursing facilities, for training programs, and for loans to students.

Amendments to NDEA and Impacted Areas School Aid in 1964 (PL 88-665): extended NDEA three years. Provides for advanced training of teachers, for aid in purchasing equipment for additional subject and specialist areas, and for increased loan funds and fellowships. Extended the impacted areas program for one year and amended the act to include the District of Columbia.

Elementary and Secondary Education Act of 1965 (PL 89-10): provides $1.3 billion in funds for fiscal 1966—$1.06 billion for educating children of low-income families; $100 million for school library resources, textbooks, and other instructional materials; $100 million for supplementary educational centers and services; $21 million for strengthening the state departments of education; and $45 million for expanding educational research and training under the Cooperative Research Act of 1954. This act was a major accomplishment in the drive for federal aid to education.

The Issue of Federal Aid to Education

The question of the role of the federal government in school finance has been heatedly debated, particularly in the postwar years, by such varied groups as PTA organizations, informal social groups, labor and management representatives, state legislators, and, of course, members of the Congress and educators. Virtually all these people are sincerely devoted to public education and to the improvement of public education.

Although most of the federal aid for education in the past was geared to support a specific educational program, interest in the general support of education by the federal government is increasing, as is indicated by the passage of the Elementary and Secondary Education Act of 1965. Some proponents of general support are advocating that funds be made available to states for educational purposes and that the states be allowed to spend the money for any educational expense they choose. Other proponents of general support suggest some federal control by proposing that the funds be used for school construction and/or for teachers' salaries. The Elementary and Secondary Education Act of 1965 is a compromise between these two positions.

Justification for general support by the federal government is based primarily upon the need to equalize educational opportunity in the United States, a need evidenced by the great range in the amount spent per pupil and the capabilities of the fifty states to support an adequate educational program (see Figure 12-13). Although a high expenditure of money does not guarantee a better quality of education, it is reasonable to assume that the educational opportunities of boys and girls in New York are greater than those in Mississippi.

FIGURE 12–13.   Estimated current expenditures for public elementary and secondary schools per pupil in average daily attendance in 1966–1967. (*Source:* National Education Association.)

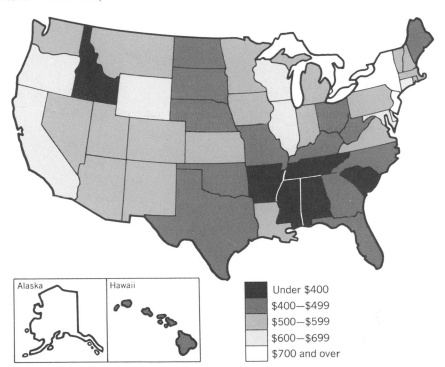

Alaska   Hawaii

Under $400
$400—$499
$500—$599
$600—$699
$700 and over

Differences in the amounts spent per pupil in average daily attendance by the various states do not necessarily indicate differences in the willingness of the states to support education. In many cases they represent differences in the resources available. Some of the states actually spend more, in proportion to their personal incomes, to support their schools than do states having high personal incomes (see Figure 12-14). Since these states seem to have little prospect of increasing expenditures through state and local funds, a number of educators advocate additional federal assistance to these states.

People ask such questions as: "Why send money to Washington and then have bureaucrats return it?" "If all revenue comes from the people, why not raise and spend the money locally?" The federal government, particularly the Congress, is not faced with as serious a problem as are state and local governments in justifying need for revenue on the basis of the value of a public understanding. State and local governments hesitate to extend their taxing systems, thereby becoming less competitive in vying for industry which is searching for sites for new plants and offices. An increasing fear of state and local governments is that they will lose industry or other wealth-increasing agencies to communities with relatively low tax situations.

FIGURE 12–14.   Relative financial effort made to support public schools in 1964–1965, expressed as a percentage of personal income in 1964. Compare the relative effort of various states with the amount of expenditure indicated in Figure 12–13. What do these differences mean, and what are the implications for the future financing of public education? (*Source:* National Education Association.)

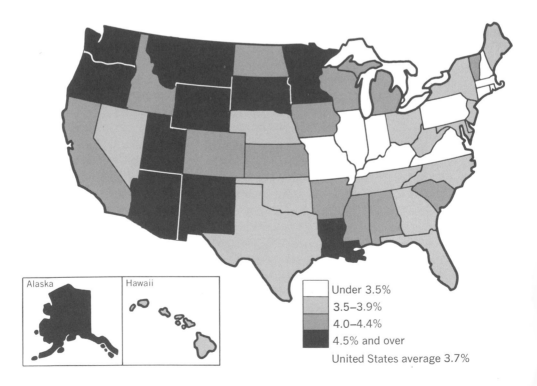

Alaska   Hawaii

Under 3.5%
3.5–3.9%
4.0–4.4%
4.5% and over
United States average 3.7%

Undoubtedly you are forming or have formed your viewpoint concerning federal aid for schools. Do you have any arguments in addition to those given in the following list [adapted, 47:15–16]:

Typical Pro and Con Arguments on Federal Aid to Education

Pro	Con
1. *Education is a federal problem.*	
Federal assistance has been an accepted part of our tradition from the Land Ordinance of 1785 through the Elementary and Secondary Education Act of 1965.	Local governments can best determine the needs of their schools, and the several states are responsible for education. Federal control would likely follow federal aid.
2. *Classroom shortage is critical.*	
There is a continuing building shortage requiring double sessions and classes in obsolete, overcrowded, defective, and temporary facilities. Too many high schools lack funds to provide laboratories for chemistry, physics, and foreign languages and to provide adequate libraries.	State and local agencies have done much to meet the needs for new school construction. The rate of increase of enrollment is expected to taper off, so that new construction can eliminate the backlog soon.
3. *Teachers' salaries are very inadequate.*	
Many teachers who leave the profession for other occupations cite their low pay as a principal reason.	The average teacher's salary has risen at a faster rate than per capita income generally. Higher salaries will not guarantee better teachers. Federal money for teachers' salaries on an emergency basis would be dangerous and difficult to discontinue.
4. *More money for public education is essential.*	
The most pressing problems of public education can be traced to lack of money. State and local sources cannot keep up even with present needs.	The real problem of the schools is not more money but inadequate use of manpower and facilities.
5. *Federal taxation is best source of additional funds for education.*	
The federal government already collects two-thirds of all tax moneys and can most effectively tax personal and corporate income. The federal government can put the money in areas where the needs are greatest.	The federal government has only the tax resources of the fifty states, and if it takes a larger tax bite, this leaves even less for state and local governments. Most states are not as debt-ridden as the federal government and are not asking for federal aid to education.
6. *Federal control of public education is not a real danger.*	
The federal government has been aiding education for almost two centuries without any real evidence of federal control.	The federal government imposes policies on state and local school authorities and can exercise indirect control by threatening to withhold funds.

PUBLIC FUNDS AND THE NONPUBLIC SCHOOLS

Nonpublic or private schools are not part of the state school systems but are under the immediate operational control of a private individual or organization. The state, under its police power (i.e., the state's power to safeguard the health, morals, and safety of its citizens), may regulate and supervise nonpublic schools for the purpose of ensuring each child an education equivalent to the education offered in public schools.

It is the established right of parents and guardians in the United States to send their children to nonpublic schools. Approximately 14 per cent of the total number of elementary and secondary pupils are enrolled in nonpublic schools. Nonpublic school enrollments have steadily increased since the turn of the twentieth century, when they accounted for 8 per cent of the total elementary and secondary enrollment.

Nonpublic schools may be sectarian schools, which are operated under religious auspices, or they may be nonsectarian. They may be profit or nonprofit organizations and are generally supported by private funds.

An issue since the establishment of the American public school system is whether or not public financial aid, particularly federal aid, can be provided for the support of sectarian schools—schools which account for over 90 per cent of the nonpublic education institutions. The constitutional provisions separating church and state prevent direct aid to sectarian schools. However, the main point of the issue is whether or not indirect public financial aid can be provided.

Courts of the several states differ with regard to indirect aid—the crux being what is or what is not indirect aid. For example, textbooks have been given to parochial school pupils in Louisiana and Mississippi under a child-benefit theory,

FIGURE 12–15. Trends in public and private school enrollments. Between 1954 and 1963 public elementary school enrollments increased 21 per cent and secondary school enrollments increased 75 per cent—a total increase of 36.3 per cent. During this same period of time, private school enrollments increased 63 per cent. (*Source:* Chamber of Commerce of the United States.)

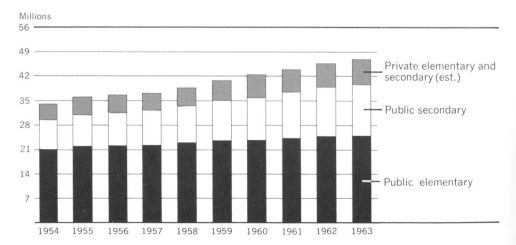

which is based upon the premise that a child rather than an institution receives the benefit of a service. The child-benefit theory has been approved by the Supreme Court of the United States but has not been approved by the majority of state courts.

Proponents of general federal aid to sectarian elementary and secondary schools argue that public funds are used to finance fire, police, and other governmental services to people of all religious sects and that aid to sectarian schools is analogous. Opponents of general federal aid to sectarian schools are fearful that such assistance would lead to the eventual destruction of the public school system.

Provision is included in the new federal educational acts for participation of children and teachers from private nonprofit schools. A U.S. Office of Education *Manual for Project Applicants* under Title III of the Elementary and Secondary Education Act includes the following [189:18]:

> All project proposals should include provisions for children enrolled in nonprofit schools in the geographical area to be served whose educational needs are of the type which the project proposes to meet, so that they may benefit from innovative and exemplary programs through participation, observation, visitation or dissemination of information. . . . It is clear that the benefits must be extended to individuals, the ultimate beneficiaries, and not to the institution concerned.

The Elementary and Secondary Education Act clearly provides that all personnel employed in any capacity in an approved project must be employed as public employees, and the title to all equipment must be retained by a public local educational agency.

Participation of children and teachers under the Elementary and Secondary Education Act and other federal legislation is justified under the child- or individual-benefit theory. Without this justification and allowance for participation, it is likely that such important educational legislation would not have been approved by Congress because of opposition by powerful lobbies.

SCHOOL FINANCE IN THE 1960s AND 1970s

It is generally accepted in the United States that it is the obligation of the free public school to provide for every person the educational opportunity which will enable him to be an intelligent and responsible citizen. Such an objective requires a quality program of education. The quality program which Americans seem to be accepting for the 1960s and the 1970s will generally consist of provision for a student's education, typically from kindergarten through junior college; competent teachers in each classroom, plus adequate auxiliary services such as counseling and health; functional, healthful, and safe school buildings; and programs appropriate for exceptional children, including both the gifted and the retarded.

School finance needs in the 1970s will depend principally upon the quality program demanded by citizens, upon pupil enrollments, and upon teachers' salaries. A brief summary of apparent financial needs for public elementary and secondary schools and for higher education follows. Probable school finance trends are listed in conclusion.

Public Elementary and Secondary Schools

In Table 4 you noted the anticipated increase in public school enrollments from 1970 to 1985. This will mean an increase of nearly 1 million pupils a year, as noted previously. This increase in enrollment will require that approximately 400,000 additional teachers be hired and 600,000 new classrooms be constructed during this period of time. Figure 12-16 indicates the U.S. Office of Education predictions of public elementary and secondary school costs. Another projection of expenditures for the 1969–1970 school year is as high as $35.9 billion [169:9].

Economic growth in the United States will increase from a gross national product of approximately $750 billion in 1970 to nearly $1 trillion in 1975. This growth will enlarge state and local revenue for schools and other public purposes. It is anticipated, however, that federal payments for local schools will increase from 8.0 per cent of total school funds in 1966–1967 to 15 per cent in 1970, primarily because of new federal programs using schools as a social instrument for raising the earning potential of all persons.

Although the outlook for increased efforts in financing schools is good, many

FIGURE 12–16. Past and projected increase in public school revenue receipts. (*Source:* U.S. Office of Education.)

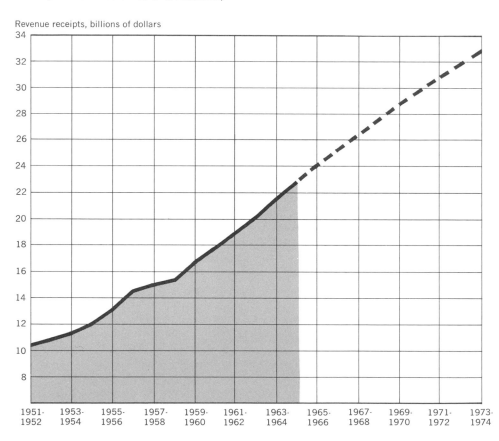

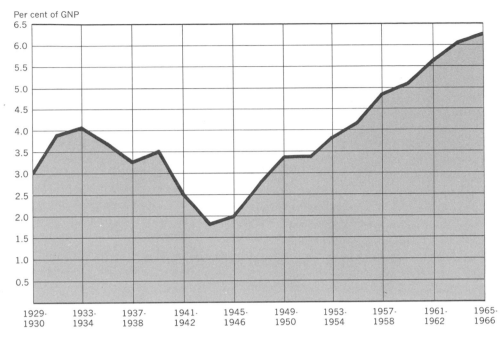

Per cent of GNP

FIGURE 12–17.   Total expenditures for public schools expressed as a percentage of the gross national product of the United States from 1929–1930 to 1965–1966. Will we be able to afford the increased costs of schools projected in Figure 12–16? (*Source:* U.S. Office of Education.)

state and local finance systems are inadequate to their future task for the following reasons [adapted, 94:51–52]:

1. Lack of a broad-based tax structure with both general sales and income taxes
2. Inadequate property tax administrative structure for equalizing assessments
3. Antiquated state foundation programs
4. Imbalance in the state-local financing sharing
5. Outmoded tax and debt limitations

Higher Education

The approximately 2,200 public and private institutions of higher education in the United States spent an estimated $11 billion for programs of instruction in 1967–1968 and approximately $2.2 billion for buildings, equipment, and land [241:32]. It is expected that colleges will add students at the average rate of 325,000 a year and that enrollments will increase by 60 per cent between 1965 and 1975 [241:32]. Increasing the enrollment by 60 per cent between 1965 and 1975 will require at least a $6 billion increase in total current and capital outlay expenditures for higher education.

Russell [223:9] feels that between 1970 and 1975 the above factors, plus the added factors of a possible doubling of faculty salaries and of continued inflation,

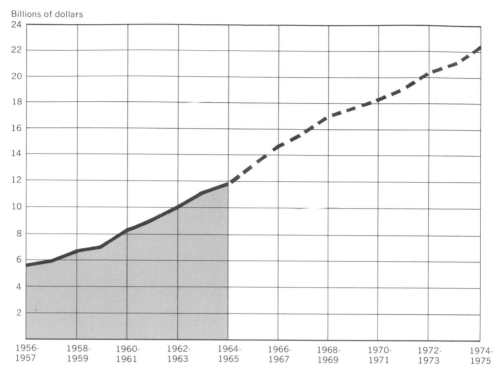

FIGURE 12–18.   Past and projected expenditures, including capital outlay, for public and private institutions of higher education. (*Source:* U.S. Office of Education.)

will mean that requirements for financial support of higher education will increase five or six times over the total amount expended in 1960.

Four sources of financial support for institutions of higher learning are of major importance: endowments, gifts and grants, student fees, and appropriations from governments. Appropriations from local, state, and federal governments provide over 60 per cent of the funds for public higher education.

It is expected that support for higher education will increase from all sources in the years ahead. The big question is whether there will be new forms of state tax for public higher education. In the past, higher education, in general, had not had the benefit of any new taxes or earmarked tax sources for its support. It is likely that federal aid for public and private higher education will increase at a faster rate than increases in aid from other sources. This is indicated by the Higher Education Act of 1965, which provided $475 million for college funds in 1967 in addition to the amount provided in 1965.

Trends in School Finance

During the 1960s and 1970s it is highly probable that you will see the following trends in public school finance:

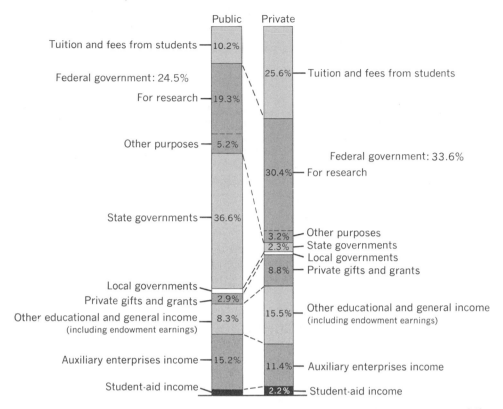

FIGURE 12–19. Approximate percentage distribution, according to sources, of the educational dollar for public and private colleges and universities in the United States. (*Source:* National Education Association.)

1. Elimination from school finance programs of features that help perpetuate poorly organized school districts.
2. Continuation of the property tax as a primary local school district tax source.
3. Improvement of equalization of property assessments by state authorities.
4. Tendency for states to finance an increasing share of public education, primarily through state foundation programs. Foundation programs will gradually include provision for operation, capital outlay, and debt service.
5. Increase of federal support through general grants administered through state departments of education and without additional federal control.

SUMMARY

Education is the largest single nondefense government enterprise. Approximately 39.9 per cent of public school revenue in the United States is derived from state sources, 52.1 per cent from local sources, and 8.0 per cent from federal sources. Because each state has its own school financial system, it is to be expected that there is considerable variation among the states in the manner of financing education. However, each state delegates a large measure of responsibility for education to its local communities and encourages them to use a large amount of initiative, support, and control. In order to provide a greater amount of equality of educational opportunities, state governments have had to provide increasing amounts of support. The federal government, since the Ordinance of 1785, has continued to exercise a definite interest in education and has greatly increased its financial support as a result of major education legislation in the mid-1960s.

Increasing enrollments and demands for extending and improving education will necessitate tremendous increases to be made in the amount of money spent for education on all levels. The extent to which the general public will be willing to absorb these mounting costs will depend, in part, upon each citizen's having a clear understanding of the need for more school revenue, being convinced of the economic value of education, and being willing to provide greater support for the education of all the children of all the people. As a teacher, you will have a responsibility for fostering increasingly greater amounts of support for education. Your success and happiness in the profession are integrally related to the problems of school finance.

QUESTIONS FOR YOUR CONSIDERATION

1. Why has the amount of state funds to aid local school districts increased significantly since the depression in the 1930s? Will this trend continue?
2. What was the cost of public education per pupil in average daily attendance in your state last year? How does this expenditure compare with that of other states and with the national average?
3. What are the sources of school revenue in your home community? Do these seem to be the best sources?
4. To what extent are federal moneys used for education in your home town? What percentage of total school costs are met by federal support? What specific school affairs does the federal program support?
5. Is your home community able to support a quality program of public education, or do you believe that more financial assistance should be provided by the state?
6. Of what significance are the Quality Measurement Project of the New York State Education Department and the comprehensive research project being conducted by Professor Kreitlow?
7. Do you agree with the statement in the Rockefeller Brothers Fund publication that "all the problems of the schools lead us back sooner or later to one basic problem—financing"? Explain.
8. As you see it, what are the arguments for and against the use of public tax money to support nonpublic schools?
9. What major differences in principles of school finance might be found in democratic and totalitarian nations?
10. What effect has the Elementary and Secondary Education Act of 1965 had upon the schools in your home community?

11. What solutions can you propose for financing higher education within the next decade?

12. Is the United States expending sufficient funds to assist developing countries in eliminating illiteracy?

ACTIVITIES FOR YOU TO PURSUE

1. Determine the amount of money your home state spends for public school education in one year. If possible, compare this amount with expenditures for tobacco and liquor products.

2. Organize a panel to discuss the advantages and disadvantages of having local communities primarily responsible for providing educational facilities for their children.

3. Analyze a local school district budget and prepare a bar graph indicating the percentage of the budget devoted to each educational function, such as administration, instruction, and maintenance.

4. List several ways of determining your state's ability to pay for education. How does your state's effort to support education compare with its ability?

5. Analyze the budget of a local community action program committee and determine the percentage of funds expended for various education functions.

6. Invite a school superintendent to discuss with your class the financial problems of his school.

7. Organize a panel to debate the advantages and disadvantages of federal aid to education.

8. Make a study of the various grants for research in education being made by the U.S. Office of Education. In what ways may these grants improve educational practices?

9. Write a skit to portray the personalities who are striving to cut taxes in your home community. Analyze the values these people seem to hold.

10. Study the various countries in the world for the purpose of determining any relationship that may exist in regard to good education and national wealth.

RESOURCE SECTION FOR PART IV

SOME IMPORTANT DATES IN THE ORGANIZATION OF PUBLIC
ELEMENTARY EDUCATION IN THE UNITED STATES

RECOMMENDATIONS OF CONANT

SUGGESTED READINGS

SUGGESTED FILMS, FILMSTRIPS, AND RECORDINGS

FIGURE CREDITS

SOME IMPORTANT DATES IN THE ORGANIZATION OF PUBLIC ELEMENTARY EDUCATION IN THE UNITED STATES

Approximate date	
1848	First graded school in America established at the Quincy Grammar School of Boston.
1860	The graded school system became widespread throughout the United States.
1870	Efforts made to reorganize the graded school to overcome some of its deficiencies (such as overageness, dropouts, and nonpromotions).
1893	Cogswell originated the Cambridge Plan, forerunner of the multilevel track system, in one of the early attempts to provide for individualization of instruction.
1900	Departmentalization of upper grades began in New York City and the platoon plan began in all the grades in Bluffton, Indiana.
1919	Individualized instruction emphasized in graded schools as shown by the Winnetka and Dalton experiments.
1920	Intelligence test scores first applied on a wide scale to ability groups in Detroit, Michigan.
1930	Hosic's Co-operative Group Plan, forerunner of team teaching, began.
1942	The ungraded primary unit emerged in Milwaukee, Wisconsin.
1947–1955	The ungraded plan appeared in various places.
1955–1959	Multigrade classes, ungraded classes, team teaching, team learning, TV teaching, and combinations of graded and ungraded classes continue to be under experimentation.

Source: Rose Koury, *Elementary School Organization . . . What Direction Shall It Take?* U.S. Office of Education, Education Briefs, no. 37, Washington, January, 1960, p. 15.

RECOMMENDATIONS OF CONANT

The following recommendations were submitted by Conant for the improvement of public secondary education in the United States:

1. *The counseling system.* In a satisfactory school system the counseling should start in the elementary school, and there should be good articulation between the counseling in the junior and senior high schools if the pattern is 6–3–3 or between the counseling in the elementary school and the high school if the system is organized on an 8–4 basis. There should be one full-time counselor (or guidance officer) for every 250 to 300 pupils in the high school. The counselors should have had experience as teachers but should be devoting virtually full time to the counseling work; they should be familiar with the use of tests and measurements of the aptitudes and achievement of pupils. The function of the counselor is not to supplant the parents but to supplement parental advice to a youngster. To this end, the counselor should be in close touch with the parent as well as the pupil. Through consultation, an attempt should be made each year to work out an elective program for the student which corresponds to the student's interest and ability as

Source: James Bryant Conant, *The American High School Today,* McGraw-Hill Book Company, New York, 1959, pp. 44–76. Material used by permission of the publisher.

determined by tests of scholastic aptitude, the recorded achievement as measured by grades in courses, and by teachers' estimates. The counselors should be sympathetic to the elective programs which develop marketable skills; they should also understand the program for the slow readers and be ready to cooperate with the teachers of this group of students.

2. *Individualized programs.* It should be the policy of the school that every student has an individualized program; there would be no classification of students according to clearly defined and labeled programs or tracks such as "college preparatory," "vocational," "commercial." In advising the student as to his elective program, the counselor will be guided by the minimum program recommended as a matter of school policy for the academically talented or by recommended sequences leading to the development of skills marketable on graduation. It will turn out that many students of similar ability and vocational interests will have almost identical programs, but a student who has elected an academic sequence may shift to a vocational sequence and vice versa. Furthermore, with individualized programs, the students themselves do not feel that they are labeled according to the program they have chosen in the ninth or tenth grade. If flexibility is combined with a declaration of policy in regard to the programs for the academically talented and if a good guidance service is available, the academic inventory should show results as satisfactory as the results in a school which has a clear-cut academic or college preparatory track.

3. *Required programs for all.* The requirements for graduation for all students should be as follows: four years of English, three or four years of social studies—including two years of history (one of which should be American history) and a senior course in American problems or American government—one year of mathematics in the ninth grade (algebra or general mathematics), and at least one year of science in the ninth or tenth grade, which might be biology or general physical science. By a year, I mean that a course is given five periods a week throughout the academic year or an equivalent amount of time. This academic program of general education involves nine or ten courses with homework to be taken in four years and occupies more than half the time of most students, whatever their elective programs.

4. *Ability grouping.* In the required subjects and those elected by students with a wide range of ability, the students should be grouped according to ability, subject by subject. For example, in English, American history, ninth-grade algebra, biology, and physical science, there should be at least three types of classes—one for the more able in the subject, another for the large group whose ability is about average, and another for the very slow readers who should be handled by special teachers. The middle group might be divided into two or three sections according to the students' abilities in the subject in question. This type of grouping is not to be confused with across-the-board grouping according to which a given student is placed in a particular section in *all* courses. Under the scheme here recommended, for example, a student may be in the top section in English but the middle section in history or ninth-grade algebra.

5. *A supplement to a high school diploma.* The awarding of a diploma is evidence only that a student has (1) completed the required work in general education to the best of his ability, and (2) has finished satisfactorily a certain sequence of elective courses. In addition to the diploma, each student should be given a durable record of the courses studied in four years and the grades obtained. The existence of such a record should be well publicized so that employers ask for it rather than merely relying on a diploma when questioning an applicant for a job about his education. The record might be a card that could be carried in a wallet.

6. *English composition.* The time devoted to English composition during the four years should occupy about half the total time devoted to the study of English. Each student should be required to write an average of one theme a week. Themes should be corrected by the teacher. In order that teachers of English have adequate

time for handling these themes, no English teacher should be responsible for more than 100 pupils.

To test the ability of each student in English composition, a schoolwide composition test should be given in every grade; in the ninth and eleventh grades, these composition tests should be graded not only by the teacher but by a committee of the entire school. Those students who do not obtain a grade on the eleventh-grade composition test commensurate with their ability as measured by an aptitude test should be required to take a special course in English composition in the twelfth grade.

7. *Diversified programs for the development of marketable skills.* Programs should be available for girls interested in developing skills in typing, stenography, the use of clerical machines, home economics, or a specialized branch of home economics which through further work in college might lead to the profession of dietitian. Distributive education should be available if the retail shops in the community can be persuaded to provide suitable openings. If the community is rural, vocational agriculture should be included. For boys, depending on the community, trade and industrial programs should be available. Half a day is required in the eleventh and twelfth grades for this vocational work. In each specialized trade, there should be an advisory committee composed of representatives of management and labor. Federal money is available for these programs.

The school administration should constantly assess the employment situation in those trades included in the vocational programs. When opportunities for employment in a given trade no longer exist within the community, the training program in that field should be dropped. The administration should be ready to introduce new vocational programs as opportunities open in the community or area. In some communities, advanced programs of a technical nature should be developed; these programs often involve more mathematics than is usually required for the building trades or auto mechanics programs.

As stated in Recommendation 3, the students enrolled in programs which develop marketable skills should also be enrolled in English, social studies, and other courses required for graduation. Furthermore, efforts should be made to prevent isolation from the other students. Homerooms may be effective means to this end (see Recommendation 20).

8. *Special consideration for the very slow readers.* Those in the ninth grade of the school who read at a level of the sixth grade or below should be given special consideration. These pupils should be instructed in English and the required social studies by special teachers who are interested in working with such students and who are sympathetic to their problems. Remedial reading should be part of the work, and special types of textbooks should be provided. The elective programs of these pupils should be directed toward simple vocational work, and they should be kept out of the regular vocational programs for boys, the distributive education program, and the regular commercial program for girls. These students should not be confused with mentally retarded students. The education of the mentally retarded is a special problem which in some states is also handled in the regular high school through special instruction and the use of special state funds.

9. *The programs of the academically talented.* A policy in regard to the elective programs of academically talented boys and girls should be adopted by the school to serve as a guide to the counselors. In the type of school I am discussing the following program should be strongly recommended as a minimum:

Four years of mathematics, four years of one foreign language, three years of science, in addition to the required four years of English and three years of social studies; a total of eighteen courses with homework to be taken in four years. This program will require at least fifteen hours of homework each week.

Many academically talented pupils may wish to study a second foreign language or an additional course in social studies. Since such students are capable of handling twenty or more courses with homework, these additional academic courses may be added to the recommended minimum program. If the school is organized on a seven- or eight-period day (Recommendation 12), at least one additional course without homework (for example, art or music) may also be scheduled each year.

If as school policy a minimum academic program including both mathematics and a foreign language is recommended to the academically talented pupils and their parents, the counselors will have the problem of identifying as early as possible the members of the group. It may well be that, in the next lower 10 or 20 per cent of the boys and girls in terms of scholastic aptitude on a national basis, there are a number who ought to be guided into similar but less rigorous programs.

10. *Highly gifted pupils.* For the highly gifted pupils some type of special arrangement should be made. These pupils of high ability, who constitute on a national basis about 3 per cent of the student population, may well be too few in number in some schools to warrant giving them instruction in a special class. In this case, a special guidance officer should be assigned to the group as a tutor and should keep in close touch with these students throughout their four years of senior high schoolwork. The tutor should see to it that these students are challenged not only by course work but by the development of their special interests as well. The identification of the highly gifted might well start in the seventh or eighth grade or earlier.

If enough students are available to provide a special class, these students should take in the twelfth grade one or more courses which are part of the Advanced Placement Program. This program has been developed in recent years by schools and colleges working cooperatively under the aegis of the College Entrance Examination Board. Under the program a student in the twelfth grade may take such courses as college mathematics, college English, or college history and, after passing suitable examinations, may be given college credit for the courses and also sophomore standing in these subjects. This program should be adopted not only because of the benefits which accrue to the students involved, but because it may well have a good influence on students of somewhat less ability by raising the tone of the whole academic program. Information about this program may be obtained by writing to the Director of the Advanced Placement Program, College Entrance Examination Board.

11. *The academic inventory.* In order to provide meaningful statistics about the education of the academically talented, a school board through the superintendent should ask the principal each year to provide an academic inventory. As explained earlier, the academic inventory summarizes the programs of the academically talented students in the senior class without giving their names. In a school in which the range of intellectual ability corresponds to the national norm, 15 per cent of the students would be included in this inventory. In other schools the percentage may vary. The academic inventory should include information as to what per cent of the academically talented boys and girls went on to a two-year college, a four-year college, or a university. This academic inventory of the graduating class might well be published each year.

12. *Organization of the school day.* The school day should be so organized that there are at least six periods in addition to the required physical education and driver education which in many states occupy at least a period each day. A seven- or eight-period day may be organized with periods as short as forty-five minutes. Under such an organization, laboratory periods as well as industrial arts courses should involve double periods.

The flexibility provided by such an arrangement is to be contrasted with the rigidity of that of the six-period day. With a six-period day, one period of which is taken up by physical education, the academically talented student cannot elect the wide academic program recommended above and at the same time elect art, music, and practical courses. The importance of this recommendation can hardly be overemphasized in connection with the education of the academically talented students.

13. *Prerequisites for advanced academic courses.* Standards in advanced courses should be such that those who enroll in each successive course of a sequence have demonstrated the ability required to handle that course. To this end, admission to eleventh-grade mathematics should depend upon the student's receiving at least a C in tenth-grade mathematics, and for admission to twelfth-grade mathematics, at least a C should be required in the eleventh-grade course. Similarly, if the physics course is given in the twelfth grade, it should be open only to those students who have studied three years of mathematics and obtained a grade of at least C in each course. Also, in the foreign language sequence, a grade of C should be required for entry into the second-year course.

14. *Students should not be given a rank in class according to their grades in all subjects.* In many schools, it is customary to designate a rank in class on graduation as determined by the marks received; the position of valedictorian is usually held by the student whose rank is number one. The ranking is calculated by averaging the grades in all subjects taken during the four years. I have found that in many schools the desire to rank high has led bright students to elect easy courses in order to obtain high grades. This fact emerges clearly from an examination of many programs sent to us by schools as part of their academic inventories. The use by some colleges and universities of rank in class as the basis of their admission policies has increased this tendency of bright boys and girls to avoid stiff programs. Following the practice in at least one school visited, I strongly recommend that the graduating class not be ranked on the basis of grades obtained in all subjects and that a valedictorian not be named on this basis. Admission officers in colleges and universities should be urged to examine the transcript of a student's entire record rather than to rely on the misleading rank in class. The main purpose of studying a foreign language is to obtain something approaching a mastery of that language. And by a mastery is surely meant the ability to read the literature published in the language and, in the case of a modern language, to converse with considerable fluency and accuracy with an inhabitant of the country in question.

15. *Academic honors list.* At the end of each marking period, a list should be published of the students who had elected courses recommended for the academically talented and had made an average grade of B. On graduation a notation might be made on the diploma if the student had placed on the academic honors list in all four years.

In order to provide an incentive for the election of a meaningful nonacademic sequence, those students whose achievement was outstanding in the courses that are usually labeled "commercial" or "vocational" should receive some special recognition. By such devices I believe the ambitions of students in various elective programs can be stimulated as much as by granting of separate types of diplomas.

16. *Developmental reading program.* A school should have the equipment for a developmental reading program. The program should be available on a voluntary basis for all the pupils in the school. The counselors and teachers of English should be asked to view this program sympathetically and to urge students to take advantage of the opportunity to increase reading speed and comprehension.

17. *Summer school.* The school board should operate a tuition-free summer school in which courses are available not only for students who have to repeat a subject, but also for the bright and ambitious students who wish to use the summer to broaden the scope of their elective programs.

18. *Foreign languages.* The school board should be ready to offer a third and fourth year of a foreign language, no matter how few students enroll. The guidance officers should urge the completion of a four-year sequence of one foreign language if the student demonstrates ability in handling foreign languages. On the other hand, students who have real difficulty handling the first year of a language should be advised against continuing with the subject (Recommendation 13).

19. *Science courses.* All students should obtain some understanding of the nature of science and the scientific approach by a required course in physical science or

biology. This course should be given in at least three sections grouped by ability (Recommendation 4).

To accommodate students who are interested in science but do not have the required mathematical ability, two types of chemistry courses should be offered. For entry into one, at least a C in algebra and tenth-grade mathematics should be required. The other course should be designed for pupils with less mathematical ability. The standards even in this second course, however, should be such that those with less than average ability (assuming a distribution of ability according to the national norm) will have difficulty passing the course.

In addition to the physics course given in the twelfth grade with mathematics as a prerequisite (Recommendation 13) another course in physics should be offered with some such designation as "practical physics." The standards in this second course should be such that students with less than average ability have difficulty passing the course.

20. *Homerooms.* For the purpose of developing an understanding between students of different levels of academic ability and vocational goals, homerooms should be organized in such a way as to make them significant social units in the school. To this end, students should be kept together in one homeroom for the entire senior high school course (three or four years), and care should be taken to have each homeroom a cross section of the school in terms of ability and vocational interest. The teachers in charge of the homerooms should be persuaded by the administration that their work as homeroom teachers is important. Sufficient time should be allotted to the homeroom so that students may use this period to develop a sense of community interest and to have practice in a small way in representative government. The homerooms should elect one or two representatives to the student council, and these representatives should report back after each meeting of the council. They should listen to the opinions of their constituents and be guided by their opinions in voting on matters before the student council. To be effective, the student council should be treated sympathetically by the school administrators so that there will be some important questions each year with which the student council can be concerned and which, in turn, can be presented to the homerooms by the representatives.

21. *Twelfth-grade social studies.* In the twelfth grade a course on American problems or American government should be required. This course should include as much material on economics as the students can effectively handle at this point in their development. Each class in this course should be a cross section of the school: the class should be heterogeneously grouped. Teachers should encourage all students to participate in discussions. This course should develop not only an understanding of the American form of government and of the economic basis of our free society, but also mutual respect and understanding between different types of students. Current topics should be included; free discussion of controversial issues should be encouraged. This approach is one significant way in which our schools distinguish themselves from those in totalitarian nations. This course, as well as well-organized homerooms and certain student activities, can contribute a great deal to the development of future citizens of our democracy who will be intelligent voters, stand firm under trying national conditions, and not be beguiled by the oratory of those who appeal to special interests.

SUGGESTED READINGS

The number in parentheses following each suggestion denotes the chapter for which it is best suited.

Benson, Charles: *The Cheerful Prospect,* Houghton Mifflin Company, Boston, 1965. Discusses the future of American education in terms of administration and finance (11, 12)

Bent, Rudyard K., and Henry H. Kronenberg: *Principles of Secondary Education,* 5th ed., McGraw-Hill Book Company, New York, 1966. Chapter 3 contains a good discussion of the organization of secondary education. (11)

Bossing, Nelson L., and Roscoe V. Cramer: *The Junior High School,* Houghton Mifflin Company, Boston, 1965. A detailed treatment of the junior high school. (11)

Brown, B. Frank: *The Non-graded High School,* Prentice-Hall, Englewood Cliffs, N.J., 1963. Describes in detail how the ungraded program at Melbourne (Florida) high school operates. (11)

Burgess, Evangeline: *Values in Early Childhood Education,* National Education Association, Department of Elementary-Kindergarten-Nursery Education, Washington, 1965. Discusses the role of kindergarten and nursery education in the educational system. (11)

Campbell, Roald F., and Gerald R. Sroufe: "Toward a Rationale for Federal-State-Local Relations in Education," *Phi Delta Kappan,* vol. 47, no. 1, pp. 2–7, September, 1965. Discusses five elements that should characterize the local-state-national partnership in the support of education. (12)

Cervantes, Lucius F.: *The Dropout: Causes and Cure,* The University of Michigan Press, Ann Arbor, Mich., 1965. Indicates the causes of school dropout and some factors that may decrease the rate of dropout. (11)

Clark, Harold F.: *Cost and Quality in Public Education,* Syracuse University Press, Syracuse, N.Y., 1963. Explores the relationship between the cost and the quality of American education. (12)

Clayton, A. Stafford: "Lessons for Us from Europe: The Effects of Public Support of Church-related Schools," *Phi Delta Kappan,* vol. 47, no. 1, pp. 19–24, September, 1965. Points out undesirable social consequences that followed governmental support of church schools in England and Netherlands. Raises the question "Will the United States resist similar pressures and avoid like results?" (12)

Conant, James Bryant: *The American High School Today,* McGraw-Hill Book Company, New York, 1959. Presents a number of recommendations based upon the results of an intensive study for improving American high schools. (11)

————: *Shaping Educational Policy,* McGraw-Hill Book Company, New York, 1964. Discusses education as a national concern and policies that should affect public schools and higher education. (11, 12)

"Departmentalization in Elementary Schools," *NEA Research Bulletin,* vol. 44, no. 1, pp. 27–28, National Education Association, Research Division, Washington, February, 1966. Indicates the status of elementary school departmentalization in ninety-seven large school systems. (11)

Dipasquale, Vincent C.: "The Relation between Dropouts and the Graded School," *Phi Delta Kappan,* vol. 46, no. 3, pp. 129–133, November, 1964. Discusses problems that arise from the use of the graded school. (11)

Education: An Investment in People, Chamber of Commerce of the United States, Education Department, Washington, 1964. An excellent presentation of the value of education, our changing population, and the financial condition of our schools. (12)

Education Is Good Business, American Association of School Administrators, Washington, 1966. Contains an excellent discussion of the benefits our nation derives from education. (12)

Educational Responsibilities of the Federal Government, National Education Association, Educational Policies Commission, Washington, 1964. Discusses the federal structure for meeting federal educational responsibilities and federal policy for supporting education through the states. (11, 12)

Elementary School Organization, Research Memo 1965–22, National Education Association, Research Division, Washington, September, 1965. Discusses types of elementary school organization, nongraded organization, dual-progress plan, multigrading, and kindergarten and nursery education. (11)

Engh, Jeri: "Why Not Year-round Schools," *Saturday Review,* Sept. 17, 1966, pp. 82–84. Points out the advantages of having school year-round. (11)

Financial Status of the Public Schools, National Education Association, Committee on Educational Finance, Washington. Latest issue. Contains excellent graphs and tables showing the financial progress of public education. (12)

Griffith, D. E., et al.: *Organizing Schools for Effective Education,* The Interstate Printers and Publishers, Inc., Danville, Ill., 1962. Indicates a theory of school organization, treats basic concepts and issues, and makes applications of these concepts to school situations. (11)

Hamilton, DeForest, and Robert N. Rowe: "Academic Achievement of Students in Reorganized and Non-reorganized Districts," *Phi Delta Kappan,* vol. 43, no. 9, pp. 401–404, June, 1962. Cites research studies to indicate that children have a better opportunity to receive a good education in reorganized school districts. (11)

Hughes, James Monroe: *Education in America,* 2d ed., Harper & Row, Publishers, Incorporated, New York, 1965. Chapter 14 provides a good discussion of nonpublic schools in America. (12)

Johnston, Paul F.: "Regional Approaches to Educational Problems," *NEA Journal,* vol. 55, no. 4, pp. 27–28, 69, National Education Association, Washington, April, 1966. Describes various attempts to improve education through regional cooperative efforts. (11)

Long-range Planning in School Finance, National Education Association, Committee on Educational Finance, Washington, 1963. Discusses the past and future of local, state, and federal support of education. (12)

Merlo, Frank P.: "The Burgeoning Community College," *Saturday Review,* Dec. 19, 1964, pp. 50–51, 65. Describes the rapidly rising enrollments and the programs in junior colleges. (11, 12)

"The Nature and Characteristics of Adult Education in the United States," *Facts and Figures on Adult Education,* vol. 1, no. 1, National Education Association, Division of Adult Education Services, Washington, April, 1963. Discusses the nature and characteristics of adult education in the United States and indicates the large task that lies ahead. (11)

Planning and Organizing for Teaching, National Education Association, Project on the Instructional Program of the Public Schools, Washington, 1963. An excellent booklet on the organization of the curriculum, school, and classroom for effective instruction. (11)

Ristow, Lester W.: "Much Ado about Dropouts," *Phi Delta Kappan,* vol. 46, no. 9, pp. 461–464, May, 1965. Attempts to clarify thinking about important educational and social problems involved in dealing with school dropouts.

Snyder, Edith Roach: *The Self-contained Classroom,* National Education Association, Association for Supervision and Curriculum Development, Washington, 1960. Describes the work of the teacher and the nature of the program in a self-contained classroom. (11)

Strayer, George D., Jr.: *Guidelines for Public School Finance,* Phi Delta Kappa, Bloomington, Ind., 1963. Contains the results of a nationwide survey of state and local taxation, in terms of which guidelines and recommendations for the administration and distribution of state and local funds are made. (12)

"Summer School Programs: Teaching Staff, Salaries, and Financing," *Educational Research Service Circular* 5, National Education Association, Research Division, Washington, October, 1963. Presents information on the organization and financing of public school summer programs. (11, 12)

Universal Opportunity for Education beyond the High School, National Education Association, Educational Policies Commission, Washington, 1964. Advocates that the public make available at least two years of further education, aimed primarily at intellectual growth for all high school graduates. (11)

What Everyone Should Know about Financing Our Schools, National Education Association, Washington, 1966. An excellent booklet, containing many charts and graphs, depicting the value of education and the need for more money to support education. (12)

SUGGESTED FILMS, FILMSTRIPS, AND RECORDINGS

The number in parentheses following each suggestion denotes the chapter for which it is best suited.

Films (16 mm)

And No Bells Ring (Sterling Movies, 56 min). Presents a review of the "Trump Report" on reorganization of secondary school staff utilization. Figures are given to explain how this program will better utilize teachers in teams of large group presentation personnel, small group teachers, and teacher assistants. Large lecture groups, along with pupils in smaller discussion groups and in individual study, are observed. (11)

Better Schools for Rural Wisconsin (University of Wisconsin, 29 min, color). Discusses the question of centralizing the rural schools in Wisconsin, using New York rural school organization as an example. Shows a typical one-room school and then pictures the advantage of the central school, including diversified and specialized education, health services, adult education, night school, and community activities. (11)

Design for Learning (Photo and Sound, and Franklin and Kump Architects, 18 min, color). Shows the building of a modern school and explains new methods of planning construction. The completed building is shown in detail with emphasis given to reasons for using new departures in architecture. (11)

The Dropout (Mental Health Film Board, Inc., 28 min). Presents one of the millions of youngsters who leave high school without graduating. Shows how a community, through remedial reading programs, work experience programs, and other educational activities may tackle the problem of underachievement. (11)

Fight for Better Schools (March of Time, 21 min). Dramatizes the story of how the citizens of Arlington County, Virginia, fought to reorganize their school system. Also describes the efforts of other communities and organizations, such as the National Citizens Commission for the Public Schools. (11)

How Good Are Our Schools? Dr. Conant Report (National Education Association, 29 min). Uses two comprehensive high schools—one in Oakland, California, and the other in Labette County, Kansas—to show what every secondary school should be equipped to do. Shows various classroom situations illustrating how the schools provide for the varied interests of all the students in their communities. (11)

Investment in Youth (Hollywood Film Enterprises, Inc., 22 min). Develops the theme that youth is Canada's most natural resource and that public expenditure for their development is a sound investment. (12)

Next Year Is Now (Modern Talking Picture Service, 28 min). Points out the serious problems encountered in higher education today, such as overcrowding of the colleges and the rising cost of education. (12)

"Pop Rings the Bell" (National School Service Institute, 23 min). Develops the part the well-equipped school will play in maturing the leaders of tomorrow. Principal Forsythe succeeds in convincing all the businessmen who attend a school party, except Fred Bates, that education is a good investment. Pop, the custodian, "rings the bell" with him. (12)

School Board in Action (National School Board Association, 26 min, color). Shows how a school board meets community problems in education through democratic action. Depicts, in a series of school board meetings with citizens, the manner in which the community and the board deal with such problems as censorship of textbooks, teachers' salary increases, selection of new school board members, and the floating of a bond issue to build a new school. (11)

Schoolhouse in the Red (Encyclopaedia Britannica Films, 42 min, color). Describes a typical rural community debating whether to change from a system of individual small rural schools to a larger school district system. Discusses the sociological and psychological factors involved and pictures the facial expressions, actions, and opinions of the local citizens. Shows how the little school district has become outmoded and emphasizes the considerations involved in the change of an educational system. (11)

Schools for Tomorrow (Wayne University, 22 min). Deals with the planning of school buildings and shows how one community used citizens' advisory committees, school personnel, an architect, and a school building consultant to help plan their schools. (11)
A Way of Life (International Harvester Co., 25 min, color). Presents the story of a school at Beaverton, Michigan, and how the problem of finance for educational purposes was solved, providing broader educational opportunities for the young and new ideas and better living for the whole community. (11)

Filmstrips

Avenue to Better College Teaching (National Audio Visual Association, 78 fr.). Explains the federal matching-funds program under Title VI of the Higher Education Act of 1965, nationally known as the Yarborough-Carey program. Explains how the program is administered and how the individual institution may apply for federal matching funds. Emphasis is on purchase of audio-visual equipment. (12)
Cooperative School Plant Planning (Indiana University, 100 fr., color). Presents a functional approach to dynamic group action as applied to the community planning of school buildings. Many details of administration are covered, as well as ways in which cooperating groups and individuals can benefit. (11)
Day in the Kindergarten (Herbert M. Elkins Co., 40 fr.). Shows the typical activities of a kindergarten class at a well-organized and well-equipped school. (11)
Design of American Public Education (McGraw-Hill, 41 fr.). Describes the effectiveness of the decentralized system of education in the United States, with each state determining how its schools are organized and administered. (11)
Learning Goes On (American Council on Education, 48 fr.). Suggests the importance of one aspect of adult education in the United States—participation in group learning activities to satisfy individually recognized needs. Deals with noncredit courses offered by a community evening school. (11)
Planning and Organizing for Teaching (National Education Association, 18 min, sound). Designed primarily for use by school staffs as they work on planning the total school program. It should also provide one basis for a dialogue among college faculties and students, school boards, educational associations, state departments of education, and interested lay groups. (11)
School Building and Equipment (American Council on Education, Part I—55 fr., Part II—58 fr.). Shows current trends in school building and equipment and indicates how these support the educational programs of the modern elementary and secondary schools. Part I deals with the elementary school, and Part II deals with the comprehensive high school. (11)
School Buildings (National Education Association). A series of three filmstrips of varying number of frames showing exterior and interior views of school buildings which represent the best in school planning. (11)
School Days (Eye Gate House, Inc., 28 fr., color). Shows school activities that encourage the formation of good character: student court, school safety patrol, election of officers, etc. (11)
Toward Better Schools for All Children through Federal Aid (National Education Association, 54 fr.). Makes a simple presentation of statistics which show the need for better public education. After emphasizing the varying ability of different states to support their schools, the filmstrip presents the case for federal aid. (12)

Recordings

Doorway to the Future: Bond Issue for Cross River (National Tape Recording Project, 30 min). Dramatizes a school problem and suggests solutions through constructive citizen participation. (12)
Doorway to the Future: School Finance (National Tape Recording Project, 30 min). Discusses the problems of school finances and possible solutions. (12)

The People Act: In Arlington, Virginia (National Tape Recording Project, 30 min). Suburban commuters win new schools for their children and their area by cooperating to defeat a political machine. (11)

The People Take the Lead: They Can't Wait (National Tape Recording Project, 25 min, 46 sec). How we can get the best education for our children; the problem which faces public education. (11)

FIGURE CREDITS

FIGURE 11–1. *(Source:* Edward J. Power, *Education for American Democracy: An Introduction to Education,* McGraw-Hill Book Company, New York, 1958, p. 80.)

FIGURE 11–4. *(Source:* Data from *Estimates of School Statistics, 1966–1967,* Research Report 1966–R20, National Education Association, Research Division, Washington, December, 1966, p. 6.)

FIGURE 11–5. *(Source: One-teacher Schools Today,* Research Monograph 1960–M1, National Education Association, Research Division, Washington, June, 1960, p. 9; and "Facts on American Education," *NEA Research Bulletin,* vol. 44, no. 2, p. 38, National Education Association, Research Division, Washington, May, 1966.)

FIGURE 11–6. *(Source:* "Teacher Turnover," *School Life,* vol. 43, no. 2, p. 19, U.S. Office of Education, October, 1960.)

FIGURE 11–7. *(Source: The American School Superintendency,* Thirteenth Yearbook of the American Association of School Administrators, Washington, 1952, p. 88.)

FIGURE 11–9. *(Source: Progress of Public Education in the United States of America, 1964–65,* U.S. Office of Education, 1965, p. i.)

FIGURE 11–10. *(Source:* Stuart E. Dean, *Elementary School Administration and Organization,* U.S. Office of Education Bulletin 1960, no. 11, 1960, p. 30.)

FIGURE 11–11. *(Source:* Stuart E. Dean, *Elementary School Administration and Organization,* U.S. Office of Education, Bulletin 1960, no. 11, 1960, p. 68.)

FIGURE 11–12. *(Source: Education: An Investment in People,* Chamber of Commerce of the United States, Education Department, Washington, 1964, p. 23.)

FIGURE 11–13. *(Source: Progress of Public Education in the United States of America, 1961–1962,* U.S. Office of Education, 1962, p. 29; and *Statistical Abstract of the United States,* U.S. Bureau of the Census, 1966, p. 112.)

FIGURE 11–15. *(Source:* Data from *Statistical Abstract of the United States,* U.S. Bureau of the Census, 1966, p. 131.)

FIGURE 11–16. *(Source: AHE College and University Bulletin,* vol. 15, no. 7, p. 1, National Education Association, Association for Higher Education, Washington, Jan. 15–Feb. 1, 1963.)

FIGURE 11–17. *(Source:* Marie D. Wann and Marthine V. Woodward, *Participation in Adult Education,* U.S. Office of Education Circular 539, 1959, p. 6.)

FIGURE 12–1. *(Source: What Everyone Should Know about Financing Our Schools,* National Education Association, Washington, 1966, p. 29.)

FIGURE 12–2. *(Source: Rankings of the States, 1966,* Research Report 1966–R1, National Education Association, Research Division, Washington, January, 1966, p. 46.)

FIGURE 12–3. *(Source:* Data from *Estimates of School Statistics, 1966–1967,* Research Report 1966–R20, National Education Association, Research Division, Washington, December, 1966, p. 18.)

FIGURE 12–4. *(Source:* Clayton D. Hutchins and Dolores A. Steinhilber, *Trends in Financing Public Education, 1929–30 to 1959–60,* U.S. Office of Education Circular 666, 1961, p. 106; and *Progress of Public Education in the United States of America, 1964–65,* U.S. Office of Education, 1965, p. 16.)

FIGURE 12–5. *(Source: What Everyone Should Know about Financing Our Schools,* National Education Association, Washington, 1966, p. 12.)

FIGURE 12–6. *(Source: Education: An Investment in People,* Chamber of Commerce of the United States, Education Department, Washington, 1964, p. 51.)

FIGURE 12–7. *(Source:* Data from "National Cost of Education Index, 1965–1966," *School Management,* January, 1966, pp. 118–119.)

FIGURE 12–8. *(Source: What Everyone Should Know about Financing Our Schools,* National Education Association, Washington, 1966, p. 43.)

FIGURE 12–9. *(Source: Education: An Investment in People,* Chamber of Commerce of the United States, Education Department, Washington, 1964, p. 55.)

FIGURE 12–10. *(Source:* Reprinted by permission from *State Tax Review,* published by and copyrighted 1966, Commerce Clearing House, Inc., Chicago, Ill., 60646.)

FIGURE 12–11. *(Source:* Clayton D. Hutchins and Dolores A. Steinhilber, *Trends in Financing Public Education, 1929–30 to 1959–60,* U.S. Office of Education Circular 666, 1961, p. 39; and *Estimates of School Statistics, 1965–66,* Research Report 1965– R17, National Education Association, Research Division, Washington, December, 1965, p. 32.)

FIGURE 12–12. *(Source: Milestones in Education, January, 1963–October, 1964,* U.S. Office of Education, 1965, p. 45.)

FIGURE 12–13. *(Source:* "Estimates of School Statistics: 1966–67," *Research Bulletin,* vol. 45, no. 1, National Education Association, Research Division, Washington, March, 1967, p. 9.)

FIGURE 12–14. *(Source:* Data from *Rankings of the States, 1966,* Research Report 1966–R1, National Education Association, Research Division, Washington, January, 1966, p. 51.)

FIGURE 12–15. *(Source: Education: An Investment in People,* Chamber of Commerce of the United States, Education Department, Washington, 1964, p. 43.)

FIGURE 12–16. *(Source:* Data from Kenneth A. Simon and Marie G. Fullam, *Projections of Educational Statistics to 1974–75,* U.S. Office of Education, 1965, pp. 44–45.)

FIGURE 12–17. *(Source:* Data from Kenneth A. Simon and W. Vance Grant, *Digest of Educational Statistics,* U.S. Office of Education, 1965, p. 136.)

FIGURE 12–18. *(Source:* Data from Kenneth A. Simon and Marie G. Fullam, *Projections of Educational Statistics to 1974–75,* U.S. Office of Education, 1965, pp. 44–45.)

FIGURE 12–19. *(Source:* "Federal Dollar Is Greatest Share of Private University Income," *AHE College and University Bulletin,* vol. 18, no. 2, p. 2, National Education Association, Association for Higher Education, Washington, Oct. 15, 1965.)

V

OUR EDUCATIONAL HERITAGE

The development of our schools antedates even the earliest immigrants to this country. How these early settlers felt and what they did about education for their children is clearly reflected in certain conditions in school today—conditions that will affect you as a teacher.

The extent to which you are able to assess accurately the present status of education will depend in part upon how thoroughly you understand the historical development of schools in America. As you become fortified with this knowledge, you will be more effectively able to aid in the improvement of school practices and procedures.

Chapter 13 attempts to acquaint you with major developments in our school system as they occurred during three rather clearly defined periods. Chapter 14 briefly explores the development of some modern concepts of education. An understanding of the contributions of various outstanding thinkers should aid you considerably in gaining value from subsequent courses in education.

13

HISTORICAL DEVELOPMENT
OF OUR SCHOOLS

The American school system is the expression of the hopes, desires, ambitions, and values held by those who have made our nation what it is today. It represents, in fact, one of the most noble and visionary experiments ever attempted by mankind. The story of how it came into being and developed through the years is, as you might expect, a unique and fascinating one.

Furthermore, it is a story that has no foreseeable ending. Our school system is continuing to change at "a breath-taking pace and there is much unfinished business before us. We are still striving toward our ideals of liberty and opportunity for all. In many ways, these goals are still to be reached" [158:4]. As a prospective teacher, you soon will have the opportunity to help write a new chapter in this ongoing story.

Unfortunately, Americans are not inclined to be historically minded. Too frequently, they tend to make the same mistakes over and over again. There are critics of American education today who would have the schools return to purposes and practices that long ago were found to be undesirable in fulfilling democratic ideals. Likewise, there are educators who make claims for some of the so-called innovations in education, such as teaching machines and programmed learning, that are similar to the claims made for workbooks 40 years ago [187:1]. When once the novelty of gadgetry wears off, will learning through the use of these machines become as deadening and dull as much of the learning through the use of workbooks has become?

A really competent educator has a good understanding of how our schools have developed, understands what influenced them to develop, and is aware of the "constant interplay between challenge and response, new needs and new ideas to meet them" [158:4]. He is able to identify proposed solutions to current problems that may have been tried in the past and have failed and probably would fail again. He uses the past for possible clues to the effective solutions of today's problems.

As you read this chapter, apply the understandings you have gained from courses you have taken in high school and in college that have been concerned with the development of the United States. These understandings, accompanied by brief descriptions of religious, social, economic, and political forces and factors, should help you in studying the major periods in the development of our schools. As you continue in the field of education, you will achieve a deeper understanding of the historical backgrounds of education. Through such efforts you, as an American citizen concerned with our nation's schools, will be less likely to repeat yesterday's mistakes and be more able to attain tomorrow's aspirations.

EDUCATION DURING THE COLONIAL PERIOD (1620–1791)

The early settlers in the New World brought with them their respective political traditions, religions, styles of architecture, and social customs. When they were faced with problems, it was natural for them to do the same thing that men have done throughout the ages—they drew upon the experiences with which they were familiar. As a consequence, the first institutions in the New World were built on the foundation of the life and customs of the Old World. Essentially, it was a process of transplantation. Early schools, therefore, were patterned in the European tradition, and the attitudes toward education followed European beliefs.

It should be pointed out that European education had been influenced greatly by the Greek and Roman concepts of the cultured man. Education primarily was a process of cultivating the intellect and the character of those destined to be of the ruling class. A classical curriculum seemed to be proper for the education of these people.

A rigid class structure was mirrored in European education. It was a stratified society in which each individual, generally at birth, found his role in life assigned to him [37:110]. Emphasis was placed upon the stability and maintenance of the society, and it was rare indeed to find any individual advancing through this stratification to a higher class status. Apprenticeship training was considered to be adequate for the lower classes, who were to serve the elite.

European education also was affected by a concept developed by the ancient Hebrews. They believed [187:7], "For the good life to be lived and salvation attained, one had to be acquainted with religious truths. These truths, divinely inspired and transcribed in the sacred literature, were to be studied, understood, and memorized. Unless one possessed a deep understanding of the truths contained in the scripture, neither the good life nor salvation was possible." As a result, formal education and religion were linked together to form a tradition that would be carried to America by the Puritans.

During the Protestant Reformation in the sixteenth century, Martin Luther gave further impetus to the ancient Hebrew concept of relating education and religion. "Education, literacy, religion, and salvation became inseparably linked and culturally interacting elements. For the American colonist this religious sanction for education was of prime importance" [187:10].

In addition to the religious sanction for education, many of the early settlers brought with them the concept of a direct relationship between the state and the church. This feeling was so strong that various laws were enacted establishing religions for such colonies as Connecticut, Massachusetts, New Hampshire, and Virginia. These laws were in conflict with the religious freedom sought by many of the early settlers and in a short time presented major sources of conflict. The influence of the church upon education in colonial days can scarcely be overestimated.

Since the groups of early settlers came from different countries in Europe, their language, customs, and religion differed, and so did their views on education. As a result, various patterns of education developed in the Colonies. It is possible to identify three different approaches to education centered in three loosely defined areas—New England Colonies (primarily Massachusetts, Rhode Island,

Connecticut, and New Hampshire), Middle Atlantic Colonies (principally New York, New Jersey, Delaware, and Pennsylvania), and Southern Colonies (mainly Virginia, Maryland, Georgia, North Carolina, and South Carolina). These attitudes provided bases from which the ultimate structure of our educational system grew.

The New England Colonies

The early New England settlers made their journey to the New World primarily to achieve religious and political freedom. They wanted to create a new kind of society, devoid of the caste system, in which men would be free to govern themselves.

In order to achieve the religious freedom they desired, it would be necessary for each individual to be able to read and understand the word of God as set forth in the Bible. Therefore, the New England colonists felt a distinct obligation to teach their children to read, so that they could take the first step toward saving their souls. Their strong religious attitude was well set forth in a quotation from a pamphlet titled *New England's First Fruits* [176:242]:

After God had carried us safe to New England, and wee had builded our houses, provided necessaries for our liveli-hood, rear'd convenient places for God's worship, and settled the civill government: One of the next things we longed for and looked after was to advance learning and perpetuate it to posterity; dreading to leave an illiterate ministry to the churches, when our present ministers shall lie in the dust.

Another motivating force in the development of education in New England was that a number of the early settlers were highly educated. Estimates have been made which indicate that approximately 3 per cent of the adult men were university graduates. Without a doubt they were highly influential in promoting interest in education. This influence can be appreciated when we consider the fact that by 1635 the Pilgrims, who landed at Plymouth Rock in 1620, had established the Boston Latin School.

The Latin grammar school. The Boston Latin School was the first successfully organized school of any kind in America. It was a so-called Latin grammar school, copied directly from the type developed in England. Its central purpose was to prepare boys for college. Because colleges were concerned primarily with the preparation of ministers, the curriculum consisted chiefly of Latin, Greek, and theology. Pupils entered usually at age seven or eight, having previously learned to read and write. They completed the course in about seven years.

The Latin grammar school provided the framework of secondary schools in America. Although it was essentially a select school—reserved for the wealthy and elite and aimed solely at preparation for college—it had some occasional public financial support. This type of school spread slowly throughout New England and further along the coast. There is some evidence that such a school was planned by the Virginia Company in 1621, but the colony was wiped out by the Indian massacre of 1622.

The Latin grammar school was prominent until the Revolutionary War, when it was challenged by another type of secondary school, but some of its influences are still to be found in public schools. The classical emphasis in many high school programs, the persistence of Latin as a general requirement, the rigid graduation specifications, which are so often pointed toward college preparation, the emphasis upon logical order per se and rote learning—these are some of the conspicuous influences of the Latin grammar school which have persisted in many public secondary schools to this day.

It should be kept in mind that the Latin grammar school was a private school which charged tuition. This fact alone made it impossible for many boys to attend grammar school in order to prepare for college. Furthermore, practically no relationship existed between what might be called colonial elementary schools and grammar schools. The educational ladder which is so distinctly a part of the American school system had not yet come into being.

Dame school. In the early days of New England it was felt that each family should bear the responsibility for the elementary schooling of its children. Many families, not feeling equal to this responsibility, sent their children to the famous "dame schools" or to private tutors. The dame school was simply a private home where a group of children met under the leadership of a housewife or mother and where opportunities were provided for the children to learn their ABC's, the catechism, and at times a little simple arithmetic. The teacher usually charged tuition for her services. Occasionally a group of parents would engage a schoolmaster to give the same type of instruction which the dame school provided.

Massachusetts school laws. It soon became evident that the dame schools and the private tutors did not guarantee that all children would attain the basic requirements of literacy which the Puritan societies required. By 1642 there had grown a deep concern about "the great neglect of many parents and masters in training up their children in learning and labor." This condition prompted the Massachusetts Bay Colony to enact the Massachusetts School Law of 1642. The law charged the local magistrates in each town with "the care and redress of this evil." These local officials were to take note periodically of what had been done in educating the children, and if their education had been neglected, the magistrates could require that the children be sent to school. Actually this law did not provide for the establishment of schools but, through fines, attempted to enforce upon parents their responsibilities for having their children learn to read.

As Marshall pointed out, "Here was the first modest step toward two characteristics of our modern educational system—universal education and compulsory education. For the first time, a government had declared that all children should be taught to read and had made its purpose enforceable under law" [158:7].

During the five years following the enactment of the 1642 legislation, it became evident that the law was not being strictly enforced. The feeling grew that government must do more than merely *insist* upon education. It must *make provisions* for education, if children were to be properly educated. Thus in 1647 Massachusetts passed a new law which became known as the "Old Deluder Satan Law." As the name implies, the Massachusetts Law of 1647 reveals a definite church influence. An excerpt (in modernized spelling) follows:

It being one chief object of that old deluder, Satan, to keep men from the knowledge of the Scriptures, as in former times, by keeping them in unknown tongue, so in these latter times by persuading from the use of tongues, that so at least the true sense and meaning of the original might be clouded by false glosses of saint-seeming deceivers, that learning may not be buried in the grave of our fathers in the church and Commonwealth, the Lord assisting our endeavors. . . .

This "mother of all school laws" required that each town of fifty families provide a teacher to instruct the children sent to him. The teacher was to be paid by the parents, by the church, or by the inhabitants in general, as those who managed the affairs of the community might decide. The law also stipulated that every town of 100 families should provide a grammar school to prepare boys for college. This law, therefore, established a common school to teach the rudiments of learning and a preparatory school to qualify young boys for college.

Another part of the law of 1647 stated that any town would be subject to an annual penalty of 5 pounds if it neglected to establish these schools. Unfortunately some localities found it cheaper to pay the penalty than to observe the stipulations of the law.

New England, in general, was unique in the fact that its governments were the first in the New World to accept any responsibility for educating the young. No such effort was put forth in the other colonies along the Atlantic seaboard. As the

FIGURE 13–1. Various types of schools predominated in the development of our educational system. (*Source:* The Ronald Press Company.)

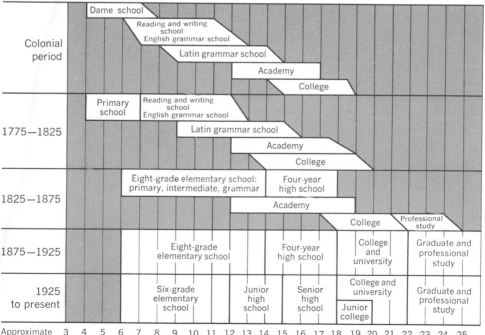

first serious attempt to establish schools by legislation, the law of 1647 was the cornerstone of our free public school system. This unprecedented concept was carried to other parts of the country as many of the New England colonists migrated westward.

Remarkable though the New England achievement was, it would be erroneous to believe that the Massachusetts schools were comparable with the American schools as we know them today. The former were substantially parochial schools, even though they operated under the authority of the state rather than of the church. It is well to remember that the religious motive was very strong in the establishment of education in the New England Colonies and that what the church wanted could easily be enacted into law.

The Middle Atlantic Colonies

The development of education in the Middle Atlantic or Middle Colonies differed considerably from that in the other colonies. There were the Dutch in New York, the Swedes along the Delaware River, and the English Quakers in Pennsylvania. These people came to the New World with different ideals and customs, different languages, different styles of architecture, and different types of Christianity.

Of these groups, possibly the Dutch in what is now New York were the most advanced in their educational thinking. By the 1630s there was some evidence that they had established schools under the authority and the supervision of the government. It is to be remembered, however, that all schools in that day were vitally interested in teaching religion. With all the ethnic and religious differences to be found in the Middle Colonies, the only solution to the educational problem was to have each church organize its own school and teach its own beliefs, rather than depend upon the local civil government.

The typical school of the Middle Colonies, then, was the parochial school—the school of the church parish. Parents were expected to pay tuition for their children, but, if they could not pay, the church sometimes permitted the child to attend nonetheless. In later years, the more common custom was for local authorities to pay tuition for poor children out of the "poor fund."

When the English took over New Amsterdam (New York) in 1664, they added to the complications already in existence. The English, at this time, were more backward than the Dutch in matters of education. Historians agree that in the later colonial period schools in and around New York deteriorated under English rule.

With the heterogeneity of cultural backgrounds and religious beliefs represented in the Middle Colonies, attempts to weld such great differences into a sound educational pattern presented a baffling problem.

The Southern Colonies

Virginia was the most important of the Southern Colonies, and the development of education here was fairly representative of the colonies in this area. The Virginia settlers, who were mainly Englishmen, came to the New World not primarily because of discontent with the social, religious, and political system of the home country but to better their fortunes. They had no particular quarrel with the English way of doing things. The English had developed an aristocratic society whose government took little or no interest in education.

The South was characterized by large plantations, rather than small communities, in which class distinctions existed between the wealthy and the indentured servants and slaves who worked for them [158:6]. Education was not considered to be a function of the government. Rather, parents were expected to attend to the education of their own children. As a result, schooling in the Southern Colonies was almost entirely the private-tutor type. A few schools were established, but these were mainly for youngsters of wealthy plantation owners. Many of the sons of these plantation owners were sent back to England for a large part of their formal schooling. Those who could not afford to do this had very little opportunity to secure an education.

There were, however, several free schools in the Virginia Colony, which were established through the private contributions of public-spirited citizens. In order to send their children to these free schools, families had to declare themselves publicly to be paupers. The schools became known as "pauper schools." Many parents who could not pay the rates charged by the private schools and who refused to advertise themselves as paupers had no alternative but to keep their children out of school. Thus a large proportion of young people grew up illiterate.

Virginia, like many of the other colonies, followed the European custom of apprenticing orphans and the sons and daughters of very poor families. The law, which constituted a form of compulsory education, provided that the local magistrate could apprentice such a child to a master craftsman, who would teach the child his trade, give him board and lodging, and provide instruction in reading, writing, and religion. The child in turn agreed to help his master unquestioningly in his work. From reports of this type of vocational education, it was found that far too often the masters were more interested in the services which their apprentices could render than in providing good basic learnings for the child.

Separation of Church and State

As indicated previously, the New England colonists soon found that the direct relationship between church and state conflicted with the religious freedom they sought. They had come to this new continent to escape the state's dictating the religious beliefs of its subjects. Additional groups of colonists brought greater diversification in religious beliefs. Through the leadership of Roger Williams, primarily, the charter of 1663 for Rhode Island granted religious freedom to the people of that colony. In 1682, William Penn was successful in getting a law passed in Pennsylvania granting religious freedom to the people. Gradually, as church and state separated throughout the colonies, the state supplanted the church in the educational field until, ultimately, the principle of state obligation and state sovereignty was born. The full implementation of this principle, however, has presented a problem throughout the development of education in America.

Early Elementary Schools

Educational practices in the early colonial period provided little in the way of an organized pattern of elementary education. Dame schools, early parochial schools, private tutors, apprenticeships, and pauper schools developed quite independently of one another. This condition was due in part to the fact that parents were expected to care for the rudimentary education of their children.

The common school. Gradually, various systems were developed for teaching the three R's to youngsters. There were reading schools and writing schools, and often the two were combined into one. The pupils could attend one school in the morning and the other in the afternoon. These became the common schools that spread first through the New England area. There were no rigid regulations about entrance or attendance or withdrawal. The common schools served the masses of youngsters, most of whom did not attend the Latin grammar school or college.

Life in and around these early schools was very different from that in our modern public schools. It is very difficult to visualize the conditions under which colonial settlers struggled to obtain an education. In place of the modern, large, well-lighted, and heated building, they had a single, bare, unattractive room. The room might be in a residence, a vacant store building, or a rough log structure [159:48–66]. A few of the better school buildings had glazed windows. In log

This typical early American schoolroom is a far cry from the attractive well-heated and well-lighted schoolroom we know today. *(Photograph from the Library of Congress.)*

structures which were designated solely for the use of education, the usual practice was to leave a log out of one side of the building in order to provide both light and ventilation.

More often than not a rough plank served as the teacher's desk. Long, rough, backless benches were provided for the pupils. Often the feet of the young children did not touch the floor. Equipment was quite meager. Along one side of the room, there would occasionally be a long shelf where students would practice such activities as penmanship, using quill pens. A great stone fireplace furnished the only heat by which the children could keep warm. As with many a present-day fireplace, those who were close to its blazing hearth were likely to get scorched while those farthest away shivered with the cold. Considering many reports of complaints which were recorded and passed down to posterity, it was evident that most of these rooms and buildings were in sad need of repair.

It was in this kind of atmosphere that the hornbook was used. This aid to learning consisted of a piece of wood shaped like a paddle to give a convenient handle. Fastened to the thin board was a sheet of paper on which was printed

The hornbook takes its name from the thick sheet of transparent horn used to protect the paper from dirt. (*Photograph from Ruth G. Strickland.*)

the alphabet, some syllables, and usually the Lord's Prayer. Various primers were used along with the hornbook.

The New England Primer. This first appeared in 1690 and was one of the more famous primers. During a period of more than a hundred years, this book dominated the curriculum of the elementary schools and 3 million copies were sold. The primer was a crudely printed 90-page booklet, with pages about one-fourth the size of those in our present textbooks. The primer contained the alphabet, syllables, and a few spelling lists. The alphabet was learned through the use of rhymes beginning with "In Adam's fall, We sinned all." A large part of its contents consisted of two catechisms: John Cotton's *Spiritual Milk for Boston Babes . . . Drawn Out of the Breasts of Both Testaments for Their Souls' Nourishment* and the *Westminster Shorter Catechism.* This reading material was made of doleful admonitions such as the following:

> Tho' I am young, yet I may die,
> And hasten to eternity;
> There is a dreadful fiery Hell,
> Where wicked ones must always dwell;
> There is a heaven full of joy,
> Where Godly ones must always stay;
> To one of these my soul must fly,
> As in a moment when I die.

Teaching methods and materials in these early schools were almost as crude as the buildings in which they were housed. Except for the spelldowns, each pupil was called before the teacher and recited individually. This practice was largely necessitated by the lack of books, writing paper, pens, and ink. It was common for some of the smaller children to receive only 15 to 20 minutes of individual attention from the teacher during a school day of six to eight hours. During the remainder of the time they were expected to sit quietly on their rough, uncomfortable benches. Slow children might take as long as three terms to master the alphabet. Since arithmetic books were rare, pupils made copy books and sum books by folding sheets of rough paper and sewing them along one edge.

Crude, poorly lighted and heated structures, limited teaching methods, and a dearth of teaching materials were all typical of our early elementary schools. Yet in these schools, while engaged in the consuming task of building a new world, our forefathers preserved the rudiments of learning.

As the population continued to increase, people began moving away from the towns to develop new farming areas. Their children had to travel longer and longer distances to attend school until it became quite difficult for them to get there at all. In some instances school would be held in one part of the township during one term and in another during the next term. This rotation of schools gave rise to the famous "moving school" of early New England days.

Because of the limitations of educational facilities, people in outlying districts organized their own schools, one for each extended neighborhood. Thus were born the "district schools," a term not uncommonly used today. Here there was usually one teacher, often with as many as fifty pupils or more. The counterpart of the district school persists to this day all over the nation.

The Academy

At about the time of the Revolutionary War, there was a strong demand for a more practical kind of education beyond the three R's. Men who tilled the soil, fought Indians, sailed ships, developed commerce, and started industries in America began to question the appropriateness of the narrow and rigid college preparatory curriculum of the grammar school to train youngsters for a practical world. Such men were led by Benjamin Franklin, who established the first public academy in Philadelphia in 1751.

This academy was essentially a private tuition school, though some academies gained public support and eventually became public schools. In the academy, English as a language was emphasized; girls were admitted to study; school libraries were established; American history and natural science were introduced; mathematics, especially algebra, navigation, and astronomy, was emphasized; and logic, ethics, and psychology, as well as commerce, surveying, debating, dramatics, and athletics, were given attention. The academy movement led to deeper concern for human progress and higher respect for human worth. It stimulated better teaching in the elementary school and provided good educational opportunity for the emerging middle class in America—the substantial farmers, businessmen, tradesmen, and government workers. The movement spread rapidly over the United States.

The academy started out with three particular curricula: the English, the Latin, and the mathematical. A fourth was soon added—the philosophical. The teachings of the Latin and philosophical divisions were geared to prepare youngsters for college. Eventually the college preparatory aspects of the academy involved more and more of the time and energy of teachers and pupils alike. By the turn of the nineteenth century, the academy acquired most of the characteristics of the Latin grammar school against which it originally protested. It became narrow, rigid, select, essentially classical, and college preparatory in nature.

The academy movement enjoyed wide prosperity, reaching a peak at about the time of the Civil War. Although the number of Latin grammar schools never grew large, there were over 6,000 academies in the United States by 1850. Many of these are still in existence and hold a distinctive position among private college preparatory schools. Some academies, such as Franklin's original one, which became the University of Pennsylvania, have contributed significantly to higher education.

Higher Education

The religious influences and English collegiate tradition imported from abroad were dominant factors in the establishment of our first colleges. Harvard University, founded in 1636, was a copy of Emmanuel College, Cambridge University, England. Practically all our early American colleges were developed under the auspices of some church in order to provide means for perpetuating a literate ministry for their churches. It was not until the establishment of the University of Pennsylvania in 1753 that an institution of higher learning was sponsored by a civil group instead of the church. Growth of universities was slow during the colonial period. As you may note from the table, only nine universities had been established by 1775 [194:201].

Present name	Date	Religious affiliation
Harvard University	1636	Congregational
College of William and Mary	1693	Episcopal
Yale University	1701	Congregational
Princeton University	1746	Presbyterian
University of Pennsylvania	1753	None
Columbia University	1754	Episcopal
Brown University	1764	Baptist
Rutgers University	1766	Dutch Reformed
Dartmouth University	1769	Congregational
Washington College	1782	Episcopal
Washington and Lee University	1782	Presbyterian
Hampton-Sidney College	1783	Presbyterian
Transylvania College	1783	Presbyterian
Dickinson College	1783	Presbyterian
St. John's College	1784	Episcopal
University of Georgia	1785	None
College of Charleston	1785	Episcopal
Georgetown University	1786	Catholic
Franklin and Marshall College	1787	German Reformed
University of North Carolina	1789	None
University of Vermont	1791	None
Williams College	1793	Congregational
Bowdoin College	1794	Congregational
Tusculum College	1794	Presbyterian
University of Tennessee	1794	Presbyterian
Union University	1795	Presbyterian

Source: Edward J. Power, *Education for American Democracy: An Introduction to Education,* McGraw-Hill Book Company, New York, 1958, p. 201. Used by permission.

Education and the Constitution

The principles of freedom and the equality of mankind were emphasized in the writing and adoption of the Declaration of Independence in 1776. "We hold these truths to be self-evident: that all men are created equal; that they are endowed by their Creator with certain unalienable rights; that among these are life, liberty and the pursuit of happiness; that to secure these rights, governments are instituted among men, deriving their just powers from the consent of the governed."

Although there was little evidence throughout the Colonies of equality of educational opportunities, the principle has been of tremendous importance in shaping the development of our public school system. Problems still remain, however, in fully implementing the principle, as you will note in Chapters 12 and 17.

Education was a major concern of those attending the Constitutional Convention of 1787. Such leaders as Washington and Jefferson were strong advocates of a centralized system of education in order to preserve liberty and to enable mankind to govern himself. Washington felt so keenly that there should be a federally sponsored national university that he left a part of his estate to endow such a university, but the institution was never established. In 1779, Jefferson clearly expressed his concern for free education in his "Bill for the More General Diffusion of Knowledge" in the following manner [99:221]:

And whereas it is generally true that the people will be happiest whose laws are best, and are best administered, and that laws will be wisely formed, and honestly administered, in proportion as those who form and administer them are wise and honest; whence it becomes expedient for promoting the publick happiness that those persons, whom nature hath endowed with genius and virtue, should be rendered by liberal education worthy to receive, and able to guard the sacred deposit of the rights and liberties of their fellow citizens, and that they should be called to that charge without regard to wealth, birth, or other accidental condition or circumstance; but the indigence of the greater number disabling them from so educating, at their own expence, those of their children whom nature hath fitly formed and disposed to become useful instruments for the publick, it is better that such should be sought for and educated at the common expence of all, than that the happiness of all should be confined to the weak or wicked.

Some of those attending the Constitutional Convention had reservations about the government being responsible for education. As a result, the writers of the constitution made no specific provision for the promotion of education. In reflecting upon this fact, Burrup [35:42] makes the following comment:

There appear to be at least three important reasons why education was thus neglected: (1) solution to problems of education did not seem to be so necessary and urgent at that particular time as many others which the new country faced; (2) consideration of the role of education contained the possibility of stirring up more dissension among the 13 states; (3) several of the original colonies already had some semblance of state educational systems. In the light of all the problems extant at this particular crucial time in American history, perhaps it is fortunate that the important question of the relationship of education to government was left until a later time when more consideration could be given to its solution.

Although the Constitution did not specifically mention education, Article 1, Section 8 specified that Congress was to have power for the general welfare of the people. This expression formed the basis for federal support of education. In 1785, Congress adopted an ordinance relative to the Northwest Territory to the effect that "there shall be reserved the lot number sixteen of every township for the maintenance of public schools within the said township," and in 1787 the following important statement appeared in the famous Northwest Ordinance of 1787: "Religion, morality, and knowledge being necessary to good government and the happiness of mankind, schools and the means of education shall be forever encouraged." These documents, as well as the thinking of a number of outstanding leaders, did much to lay the foundation for more rapid educational developments to follow.

The Bill of Rights, ratified in 1791, defined the role of education more clearly than did the Constitution. The First Amendment of this bill strengthened the principle of the separation of the church and state by forbidding the establishment of a national or state religion and by guaranteeing religious liberty to all. The Tenth Amendment declared that "the powers not delegated to the United States by Constitution, nor prohibited by it to the States, are reserved to the States respectively, or to the people." As a result, education in the United States was destined to develop as a state function in contrast to the single educational system typical of other nations throughout the world. The federal government was to be confined to a supportive, grants-in-aid type of role.

EDUCATION IN EARLY AMERICA (1792–1865)

The development of an organized system of education received relatively little attention for several years following the Revolutionary War. This was a period of transition in which the thoughts and energies of people were concerned primarily with such matters as the formulation of a constitution, the establishment and operation of an organized system of states, and the fighting of the War of 1812.

At first, other factors tended to push education into the background. The rapid development of industry in America encouraged many children to work in mills, stores, and shops rather than to attend schools. Many families, especially immigrant families, were so poor that they needed whatever money their children could earn. The need for earning a living in order to survive was so great that education tended to be considered a luxury. Also, the extreme mobility of settlers who continued to push westward made the task of establishing permanent schools difficult. There was little time for education in the rugged life of the pioneer. Teachers were scarce. Churches, sod houses, and log cabins often were used as schoolhouses. The sparse settlements across the land were not conducive to the establishment of school districts.

During this critical time, however, new meanings and values were emerging in the minds of people. Greater attention was being given to concepts of democracy, freedom, equality, individual rights, and faith in the common man.

By approximately 1825 our nation had achieved a certain amount of national stability and had begun to develop rapidly. The population was increasing, with much of the increase coming from the large streams of immigrants arriving in America. Industry was growing rapidly, and labor associations were beginning to be formed. The economic and social status of the common man was beginning to improve.

The Fight for Free Schools

Prior to the 1820s, the idea that state and local governments should provide schools for all children through public taxation was slow in being accepted outside of New England. In the Middle states, the concept of education being the responsibility of the church and of private agencies continued to exist. Education in the Southern states was still considered to be largely a responsibility of parents. Voting privileges in a number of states had been limited to those who owned property, and many of the property owners felt that they should not be forced to pay for the education of other children.

When voting rights were extended to all men of legal age, the need for universal education became more apparent. Labor groups, likewise, began to demand more educational opportunities for children. Greater concern was being expressed for the equality of man and the need for free, nonsectarian, public schools.

Public school societies were organized in various cities. Public-spirited citizens became members of these societies, contributing sums of money annually to carry forward the educational program. The most famous and probably the most efficient of these organizations was the New York Public School Society, which for 40 years was New York City's chief agency for educating the children of the poorer classes.

A number of outstanding leaders emerged to help fight the battle for free schools. Particularly noted among them were Horace Mann of Massachusetts, who became known as "the father of the American free public school," Henry Barnard of Connecticut, Thaddeus Stevens of Pennsylvania, John D. Pierce of Michigan, Caleb Mills of Indiana, Robert J. Breckinridge of Kentucky, Ninian Edwards of Illinois, and Lyman Rucker and Calvin Stowe of Ohio. In general it was maintained that these common schools should be: (1) free and open to all since no other system, least of all the dual system used in Europe, was acceptable for a democracy; (2) of such excellent quality that all parents would be willing to send their children to them; (3) common in the sense that all children would attend and that it would serve as a unifying force to weld communities together; (4) publicly supported through taxation of the whole community; (5) publicly controlled through elected or appointed public officials responsible to the whole community and not to any particular political, economic, or religious group; (6) nonsectarian in character; and should (7) provide the basic knowledge and skills essential to enable students of diverse backgrounds to assume responsibilities of citizenship in the young Republic [adapted, 37:127–128].

The men who fought for public schools marshaled their arguments along the following lines [adapted, 37:128]:

1. Suffrage had been extended to include all men, and if men were going to vote they had to be educated.
2. Pauper schools and the private and religious schools were inadequate because (a) the pauper schools had a social stigma which kept many children from attending, (b) fees charged by private schools kept some children from attending school, and (c) religious schools might force certain religious teachings upon children.
3. Education was essential to preserve the well-being of the state by preventing pauperism and crime and by reducing poverty and distress.
4. Schools would help prevent a class society from forming.
5. Education serves to increase productivity.
6. Education is the God-given right of all children.

By 1865 the concept of providing common-school education for all children at public expense had gained considerable acceptance. A number of states, especially in New England and in some of the Middle states, had enacted laws compelling local communities to support through taxation what would be considered public elementary schools.

Although less intense, the battle for free public schools has continued through the years. Even today there are some who question the right of the government to tax everyone for the support of schools. The issue often becomes very conspicuous when kindergartens and junior colleges are proposed to be a part of the public school system.

The Lancastrian System

In the early 1800s, the financing of schools enrolling several thousands of children presented a problem of staggering proportions. Fortunately, a new plan of school organization and management was introduced from England to New York City in 1806, which tremendously reduced the cost of educating a child. Most of the society schools rapidly adopted this new plan. It was known as the Lancastrian system, named after its founder, Joseph Lancaster, an English schoolmaster. In this system, one teacher, by using his brightest pupils as monitors to teach about 10 pupils each, might himself be in charge of from 200 to 600 pupils. The schoolmaster taught the monitors, who in turn taught their groups. Everything was rigidly organized in a somewhat military fashion. Each group was marched to its station along the wall of a large classroom, where the monitor presented the lesson. Lancaster himself thought that a real master teacher could take care of 1,000 pupils. With such a high pupil-teacher ratio, it was reported that the per capita cost of operating a school was reduced to $1.25 per year per pupil.

Because of the great public service the school societies were rendering, they felt justified in asking the government for aid in carrying out their program. In some instances this was given. Both the state and city governments in New York regularly contributed substantial sums to the New York society to help support its schools. New York City in 1832 was the first city to establish free public elementary schools. Gradually the public mind became accustomed to the idea of governmental support of schools, and the low cost of the Lancastrian system began to suggest that this way of supporting schools might not be prohibitive. While the system passed away within a few decades, it did much to advance the cause of free public education.

The Kindergarten

Although an infants' school was established in Boston as early as 1816, the kindergarten as conceived by Friedrich Froebel, its founder, was not introduced into America until 1855. Mrs. Carl Schurz, who established this kindergarten in Watertown, Wisconsin, was a strong disciple of Froebel.

During the next 15 years about ten private kindergartens were organized in German-speaking communities. In 1860 the first English-speaking private kindergarten was opened in Boston, and eight years later a teacher training course for kindergarten teachers was established in Boston. Under the auspices of Superintendent William T. Harris of St. Louis, the first public school kindergarten in the United States was opened there in 1873.

There has been considerable misunderstanding regarding the role of the kindergarten in our educational system. Many people feel that what the kindergarten features in its program is already included in a good primary school program.

Since the kindergarten is a relatively new rung in our educational ladder, it has had to compete with other schools for public support. As a result of these attitudes and forces, the establishment of kindergartens as an integral part of public schools throughout the United States has been greatly retarded—so much so that many of our children never attend a kindergarten.

The Primary School

In 1818 another school was introduced in Boston which became known as the "primary school." Children of ages four through seven were admitted to this school. At first the primary schools were distinctly separate from other schools in the city. They were open all year and prepared children for admission to the city schools, which by this time were known as "English grammar schools." The primary schools had their own buildings and teachers and were quite different from the dame schools, which had previously prepared the pupils for entrance to the grammar schools.

It was not until the latter half of the nineteenth century that primary schools were made a part of the general school system. It often has been pointed out that this origin of the lower grades led to a distinction between primary and grammar grades—a distinction which may be found even today.

Changes in Elementary School Practices and Building Construction

As social and economic advancements were made, the educational needs of boys and girls expanded. As a result, the curriculum of the elementary school was expanded beyond the teaching of reading, spelling, arithmetic, and religious instruction, which characterized the early elementary schools.

Pupils originally were not grouped into grades as they are today. In approximately 1848, a rudimentary type of grading was attempted in the large schools by roughly dividing the pupils into age groups and assigning the groups to different teachers.

The graded-school concept spread rapidly and froze the vertical organization of schools into a pattern that has persisted since its inception. The concept was based upon three main assumptions: "(1) Elementary . . . schools should 'cover' a specific body of subject matter; (2) this subject matter should be identified and rigorously prescribed; and (3) individual differences merely determine one's chances of success in the race to cover the prescribed material" [232:79–80]. If a child was unable to master the prescribed material, he was retained in the grade. The motto was "If at first you don't succeed, try, try, again" [232:79].

It has been pointed out that [232:80]:

In spite of its firm hold on our educational system, the graded system has been under criticism almost from the beginning. The mold had scarcely stiffened before some educators began to question it, contending that the graded "lock-step" denied individuality, stifled initiative, and unjustly punished the willing but slow. Many experimental plans to modify grade-by-grade progression were conceived, but most of them grew and died without reproducing their kind. The graded system, efficient for classifying large numbers of students, became standard practice.

The graded type of school organization suggested the desirability of having a room for each group and led to a new type of school building designed in 1848. It was three stories high, and on each story—except for the top one, which was one large assembly room—there were four separate rooms designed to accommodate approximately fifty children each. Cloakrooms were substituted for the usual small recitation chambers which adjoined the large room. This type of building became standard for a large part of the country. In almost any city established prior to the twentieth century, school buildings constructed on this general plan can still be found.

The Early Public High School

Many people were not satisfied with the academy, even though it represented certain important improvements over the Latin grammar school. People whose children had completed the common schools but could not or would not attend the expensive aristocratic private academies insisted increasingly upon more education of a practical sort at public expense. Their efforts bore fruit in 1821, with the establishment of the Boston English Classical School, the first high school in the United States. The name was soon changed to the English High School because of the emphasis given to the teaching of English rather than the classics.

This type of high school, however, developed slowly. In 1840 there were no more than fifty. Except for the omission of Greek and Latin, the programs offered by these high schools were at first very similar to those of the original academy. Pupils were admitted upon examination at the age of 12 for a three-year course. The high school was free to all the pupils.

Strengthening of State Departments of Education

During the first part of the nineteenth century a number of people became concerned over the great variation among communities in the extent to which they provided for the education of the young. It was felt that if a local school district were left free to provide a poor education or no education at all for its children, the welfare of the state would suffer. Furthermore, these children would be denied their birthright to an education that would prepare them for effective citizenship.

There was a gradual growth in the feeling that each state must exert more authority to ensure educational opportunities for all of its children. As a result [36:38], New York State created the office of state superintendent of schools in 1812. Massachusetts established a state board of education in 1837 with the distinguished Horace Mann serving as secretary. Henry Barnard became the first secretary of the state board of education established in Connecticut in 1839. Other states followed. As Butts [36:38] pointed out in his excellent article, "Search for Freedom":

These state agencies could then set minimum standards for all the schools of the state. Meanwhile, the direct management of schools would be left in the hands of

Horace Mann (1796–1859) gave up a brilliant career in law and politics in order to campaign vigorously for better schools and better teachers. Among his many contributions, he helped establish the first normal school for teachers in Lexington, Massachusetts. *(Photograph from the Library of Congress.)*

locally elected school boards, local superintendents, and locally appointed teachers. Local management served the cause of flexibility, diversity, and freedom.

This arrangement was designed to assure that schools would serve the whole *public* and would be controlled by the *public* through special boards of education, not through the regular agencies of the state or local governments. This is why in America we use the term public schools, not simply state schools or government schools, as they are often called in those countries that have centralized systems of education.

Developments in Higher Education

In order to meet the growing needs of a young nation and to provide an educational outlet for the liberalism which developed during the revolutionary period, more colleges and universities were established. Twenty-six, having a combined enrollment of 2,000 students, had been established by 1800, and the number continued to increase. Little opposition to these new colleges was encountered in those sections where colleges had not already been established. However, when some of the older states attempted to turn the already existing colleges into nonsectarian state universities, friction resulted. The climax was reached in the famous Dartmouth College Case in 1819. The decision which was handed down by the United States Supreme Court, under Chief Justice John Marshall, specified that states could not modify the charter of a college without the consent of the institution's authorities. Although this decision terminated the attempts of a number of states to transform private colleges into public ones, it did provide the stimulus for the establishment of state universities and more private colleges. Since then, private and denominational institutions have undergone many changes, so that in many ways it is difficult at the present time to distinguish them from state or public institutions.

In 1862 the Morrill Act was passed by Congress and signed by President Lincoln; it led to the establishment of land-grant colleges. This legislation gave 30,000 acres of public land to each state for every representative and senator the state had in Congress. This land and the proceeds from its sale were to be used to endow colleges or universities which would teach agriculture and the mechanical arts in such a manner as the legislatures of the respective states prescribed. Scientific and classical studies and military tactics were not to be excluded from the curriculum. In general, the states were to promote the liberal and practical education of the industrial classes. To date, a total of almost 11,400,000 acres of public land has been given for endowment of these colleges by the federal government. When the centennial celebration was held for the signing of the Morrill Act, there were sixty-nine land-grant colleges and universities in the United States. Many of these institutions were originally named agricultural and mechanical colleges, but most of them have since changed their names to state universities.

Prior to 1860 higher education in our country was dominantly the concern of denominational and private colleges; after 1860 the land-grant colleges and universities increased rapidly in number, size, and influence. As this happened, the character of many of the private and denominational schools changed markedly and the pattern of higher education as we know it today began to evolve.

Teacher Education Institutions

The first institutions to undertake the preparation of teachers in our country were the academies. Although there were a few sporadic efforts to train teachers for special assignments, such as the infants' school and the kindergarten, these were isolated attempts and did not foster the whole idea of teacher preparation. Although teacher training was not one of the more important functions of the academy, it provided some of the initial impetus to the movement. Actually, the academy provided preparation only in the subject-matter fields. Methods, techniques, observation, and student teaching were not included in the curriculum.

Before the establishment of the first public normal school in America at Lexington, Massachusetts, in 1839, teachers seminaries existed in Germany, where they offered a rich background in subject matter and courses in the professional preparation of teachers. There is considerable controversy among historians of education as to whether the concept of teacher preparation had originated from these German seminaries or was indigenous to America, but some of the features of the American normal school were definitely unique. It should be noted, however, that the American normal schools and the German seminaries both had as their point of origin an extension of the academy. Regardless of the exact origin, normal schools were the most influential type of American teacher training institutions for almost a hundred years.

The teacher training programs of the early normal schools were usually one year in length. Gradually this practice gave way to a two-year course of study, and, shortly before the teachers college development, a few normal schools had developed strong four-year programs. In addition to a review of the common branch subjects—reading, writing, arithmetic, spelling, and grammar—the normal school also taught the science and art of teaching and classroom management. Often there were opportunities to do practice teaching in a "model" school.

Normal schools, usually with a two-year or four-year curriculum, are still functioning in our country; however, these non-degree-granting schools are fast disappearing from the American school scene.

EDUCATION AFTER THE CIVIL WAR (1865 TO THE PRESENT)

Following the Civil War, rapid progress was made in the industrialization of America. This progress was fostered through advancements in science and technology. More power became available; new machines were invented; and transportation facilities were improved. Through the application of mass production and specialization, America was destined to become an industrial giant.

Industrialization brought about the formation of corporations, new methods of management, and an increased amount of urbanization. With these changes, the demands for more and better education arose. Progress in medicine and sanitation reduced the rate of infant mortality and increased the life-span. Immigrants continued to stream to our shores. As a result more children needed to be educated. More and better teachers had to be trained. More and better schools had to be built. More educational opportunities at the higher levels had to be provided.

Change and the complexity of problems resulting from rapid industrial progress fostered the development of new thoughts and practices in education. The ideas of men like Rousseau, Pestalozzi, Froebel, G. S. Hall, William James, John Dewey, and others to be discussed in Chapter 14 were exerting decided influence upon our schools. Responsible citizens were demanding more and better education for youth in order to meet the growing demands and increasing complexity of life.

Progress in Secondary Education

Initially, the progress of the free public high school (English high school) was slow because many people considered it to be unnecessary and maintained that it would be too costly for the government. Many were unwilling to pay additional taxes when they had no children in school. A test case of public-supported high schools developed in Kalamazoo, Michigan, in 1874. The state supreme court ruled that, upon the consent of the citizens, a city could levy taxes to support free public secondary schools. Similar decisions and laws followed rapidly in other states, resulting in the legal establishment of the high school as an integral part of our free public school system. Free public secondary schools began to prosper. By 1890 there were approximately 2,500, and at the turn of the century the number had increased to about 6,000. In the meantime, the academies began to decline. The public high school became a place the children of both the wealthy and the poor attended. It also became an institution that offered both terminal and college preparatory work, which clearly distinguished it from the dual system of secondary education found in Europe.

Schools and pupils were becoming so numerous that organizational problems became acute. Colleges were much concerned over the diversity in the high school programs and over the possibility that too much elementary work was being duplicated in the high school. National committees wrestled with problems like these and made various recommendations. Largely as a result of these problems, the Carnegie Unit was established and college entrance examinations were developed. Together, they shackled the free public secondary schools with such a rigid college preparatory program that even today teachers and pupils are still trying to break away from it.

Just after the turn of the century, several happy developments occurred. People began thinking seriously about the interrelationships between the main levels in the American educational ladder, about possible patterns of reorganization, and about experimentation in school content and method. At this point occurred the beginning of the progressive education movement, and the junior college and the junior high school movement.

Shortly after these movements began, the Commission on the Reorganization of Secondary Education issued its momentous report (1918), the *Cardinal Principles of Secondary Education,* reorienting people to the central purposes of education in a free society. As a result, teachers were faced with the problem of deciding whether they wanted secondary schools to be narrow college preparatory institutions for the select few, or whether they intended them to be truly free to all youngsters, furthering the highest potential of the social group and yet offering each child equal opportunity to meet his own needs, interests, and capacities. This decision is not yet permanently made. It is not easy to accomplish. Thinking here is bound up in tradition, clouded by custom, diverted by vested interests, and faulty for want of accurate information.

The Junior High School

The junior high school represents a fairly new development in American education. Several eminent educators had become dissatisfied with the graded elementary school as it was set up during the 1840s and 1850s. Their dissatisfaction was called to the public's attention by an address delivered by President C. W. Eliot of Harvard University in a meeting of the Department of Superintendents of the National Education Association in 1888. Shortly after this address, several committees were appointed by the NEA and they began to study the situation. One of the more famous of these groups, the Committee of Ten, made specific recommendations concerning problems affecting elementary, secondary, and higher education. Early reports from this and similar committees favored a 6-6 plan, i.e., six years of elementary education and six years of secondary education. Numerous subsequent reports suggested that the secondary school be divided into two separate institutions—one to be known as the junior high school and the other as the senior high school, i.e., the 6-3-3 plan.

In 1909, junior high schools were established at Columbus, Ohio, and Berkeley, California; there has always been considerable controversy as to which one was first established. Principles upon which the junior high school was founded include [182:4]:

1. Articulation—helping children to go from elementary school through junior high school into senior high school with as little difficulty as possible

2. Exploration—giving young teen-agers a chance to find out through brief experiences what some of the high school courses were like, with the expectation
   that this would help them to choose their senior high school courses more wisely
3. Educational guidance—helping pupils to choose from among elective subjects
   offered in the junior and later in the senior high school
4. Vocational guidance—helping pupils to make decisions about jobs and careers
5. Activity—providing social and athletic experiences and giving the students a
   chance to participate in administration and control of the school

The junior high school movement spread very rapidly from the time of its inception. By 1928 there were over 1,500 junior high schools, and since that time
thousands more have come into being. It is only fair to point out, however, that
many of the noble purposes which the early advocates of this movement had in
mind are not being fully realized. The junior high school is still in a state of flux,
but increasing school enrollments and further consolidation of school districts
doubtless will promote the concept.

Junior College

During the latter part of the nineteenth century considerable demand was being
made to extend public secondary school programs into the thirteenth and fourteenth grades. A few private junior colleges already had been organized. For
example, New London Seminary in New Hampshire, founded in 1837, became
Colby Junior College. Decatur Baptist College, founded in Texas in 1891, was
reorganized into a private junior college in 1898.

Through the encouragement of President William Rainey Harper of the University of Chicago, the public high schools of Joliet, Illinois, established a separate
educational unit in 1902 that included grades 13 and 14. This became the first
public junior college in America. President Harper agreed that the University of
Chicago would accept any credits earned by students attending this junior college.
He reorganized the program at the University junior and senior college with the
hope that the University eventually would not need to provide freshman and
sophomore course work.

The junior college, a truly American idea, grew slowly at first, but since World
War I its growth has been phenomenal. Junior colleges now exist in almost every
state of the nation. The state of California has a law which virtually provides
automatically for the establishment of a junior college when a separate district
has an assessed property valuation of at least $150,000 per student and will enroll
1,000 students within three years after its establishment. Some states expect their
junior colleges to take some of the increasing load of college students off of their
senior colleges.

At first, junior colleges attempted to offer the same courses as those offered
during the freshman and sophomore years of regular colleges and universities.
Later a number of the junior colleges began to adapt their programs to the needs
of their respective communities and were called "community colleges." Regardless
of whether or not students planned to transfer to a regular college or university,
these colleges provided terminal programs, designed to prepare students for occupations primarily in their communities. Frequently late-afternoon and evening

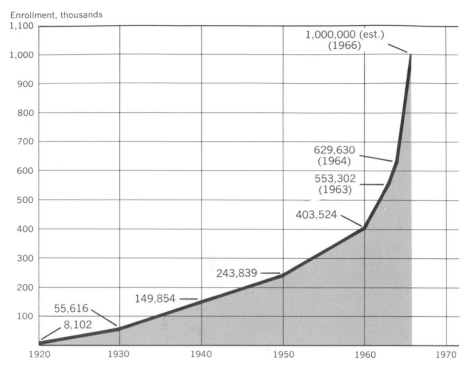

FIGURE 13–2.   Enrollment in junior colleges. (*Source:* U.S. Bureau of the Census.)

courses were offered especially to serve the needs of adult members of the community.

Other types of junior colleges, both public and private, have developed. Some of them offer special kinds of programs, such as business courses or technological training. The two-year pattern is predominant among junior colleges even though some offer more and some offer less than two years.

Progress in the Preparation of Teachers

As the normal school movement gradually gave way to the teachers college movement, the number of students in teacher education institutions increased enormously. Usually these schools have been four-year degree-granting institutions, but during this past decade many of them have added a fifth-year program leading to the master's degree.

As indicated in Chapter 3, there has been a steady changeover in recent years from state teachers colleges to state colleges. Likewise, a number of state colleges have become state universities. As a result, an increasing number of the nation's teachers are receiving their preparation for teaching in state universities.

The organization of universities for teacher preparation has varied throughout the years. In the initial stages the function was usually assigned to a department within a major division of a university. As universities have become more deeply involved in the preparation of teachers, a separate school or college within the university has been assigned primary responsibility for this function. Today, universities typically have a school of education in which the professional work is concentrated, and the general education and advanced work in subject-matter fields are offered in other divisions of the university.

Although the picture is not perfect, as indicated in Chapter 3, much progress has been made in the improvement of the status of teacher education on college and university campuses. Much of this improvement has come from the growing realization, upon the part of university personnel, that the quality of university education is directly related to the quality of instruction received by pupils in the public schools, that the security of our nation depends upon a high quality of instruction being promoted in the public schools, that the behavioral sciences are integrally involved in the preparation of teachers, and that a major portion of our colleges and universities must be involved in the enormous task of preparing teachers for the nation's public schools. In order to receive NCATE accreditation of its teacher education program, a university must show evidence that teacher education is considered a function of the total university.

SUMMARY

During the early colonial period in America, many and varied educational attempts were made in the quest for literacy and learning. Basically a dual school system developed, in which the common or district schools, offering the three R's, attempted to serve the educational needs of the masses and the grammar schools were reserved for the wealthy, the select, the elite. Actually the development of the grammar school preceded the development of the common school. Completion of the common school in the early period did not lead to entrance into the grammar school but marked the end of the educational career of the common-school pupil.

Academies arose in order to meet the demand for a more practical type of education than was being provided in Latin grammar schools. Public high schools were established when the curriculum of the academies failed to meet adequately the needs of the people, when large numbers of children wanted to extend their education, and when the concept of governmentally supported schools became a part of the thinking of the general public.

During the nineteenth century and in the early part of the twentieth, many improvements were made. The various units of our educational system were welded into a definite pattern. The kindergarten, the junior high school, and the junior college came into being. Professional education for teachers was initiated in normal schools, colleges, and universities. Educators began to appraise their efforts critically, to experiment, and to bring about desirable changes and improvements.

It would be erroneous to assume that the educational system which our forefathers bequeathed to us has reached its fullest and last stage of development. Our American public school system derives part of its dynamic character from the concept of continuous evolution and progress.

As you explore and study the educational situation, you will need all the understanding you can gain from studying the historical backgrounds of our American school system. Study carefully, learn much, and apply what you gain toward the improvement of learning and living for all people everywhere.

QUESTIONS FOR YOUR CONSIDERATION

1. Why does the American school system represent one of the most noble and visionary experiments ever attempted by mankind?
2. How do you account for discipline and punishment being so severe in colonial schools?
3. What basic issues led to the separation of church and state? What current evidences can you find that this issue is not completely settled?
4. In order to become a craftsman in a number of trades today, an individual first must serve a period of apprenticeship. Where did this practice originate?
5. What elements in the typical high school of today reflect back to (a) the Latin grammar school, (b) the academy?
6. If a school is to survive, it must meet the changing needs and demands of the public. What historical evidence can you give that supports this statement?
7. How do you account for the fact that free, public, tax-supported schools developed first in the New England Colonies?
8. Do you know of any individuals today who question the right for everyone to be taxed for the support of schools? What seem to be their reasons?
9. Why was the idea of a dual system of education, similar to the pattern used in Europe, rejected in the United States?
10. Why did teacher education programs start in normal schools rather than in colleges and universities?
11. What were some of the reasons for organizing elementary schools by grades, beginning approximately 1848, and why are some educators today advocating ungraded elementary schools?
12. What are the major effects of industrialization on education? How does educational advancement affect industrialization?
13. Why are kindergartens not a part of the public school system in many school districts?
14. What were some of the reasons for the appearance and development of the junior high school?
15. If such a decision as the Dartmouth College Case in 1819 had never been made, how might the development of colleges in America have been affected?
16. Why has the growth of the junior college been so great in recent years? Do you feel that this growth will continue? Why?
17. How do you account for the fact that most teachers colleges have changed their names to state colleges?
18. What contributions have church or denominational colleges made to American education?

ACTIVITIES FOR YOU TO PURSUE

1. Develop in outline form the European influences which affected our American public school system.
2. Imagine that you are a student in one of the American common schools in the eighteenth century. Develop a detailed account of a day in your school.
3. Analyze the various types of schools which attempted elementary education in early days and show how they became part of the present elementary school.
4. See what you can learn about the early history of your local high school.
5. Compile a list of historical bases to justify the federal government's taking an active role in supporting education today. In your opinion, has the federal government been justified in playing such an important role in education?
6. Consult a directory of colleges and universities and identify some institutions that were established under the Morrill Act of 1862. How do these institutions differ from other colleges or universities?
7. Study carefully the "Calendar of Some Important Events in Education" which appears in the Resource Section for Part V. Memorize some of these dates.

14

THE DEVELOPMENT
OF MODERN
CONCEPTS OF EDUCATION

What do people mean when they speak of modern practices in education? Do they mean that pupils do as they please in school? Are pupils all promoted regardless of how little they learn? Are they learning less today under the modern approach (sometimes called progressive education) than they learned under the older practices (sometimes called traditional or conventional education)?

As you consider these questions, perhaps other aspects of the educational picture come to mind. What is the teacher's role in discipline? What are the most prevalent learning theories? What is your concept of authority, freedom, and guidance? What is the purpose of a textbook? What is your philosophy of education? These and a myriad of other questions seem to come to the fore whenever modern practices in education are mentioned.

In preparing to teach, it is important for you to develop a clear understanding of what is meant by modern concepts of education and to know how they differ from older ones. To do this, you must make a brief study of the development of certain educational attitudes and know their implications for classroom practices. The development of a thoroughly reasoned concept of the school's function and the teacher's role in achieving this function is a major task in planning for a career in education.

One of the ways of gaining an understanding of the differing theories of education is to study the contributions of outstanding individual thinkers and the conditions of society that fostered such thought. Thus it is possible to look at conventional and modern theories and to note the differences in classroom practices which each implies. In the following summary some of the men and movements which have influenced the development of certain important concepts in education will be identified.

CONTRIBUTIONS OF SOME EARLY OUTSTANDING THINKERS

Socrates (469–399 B.C.)

Socrates[1] lived during a period of transition in Greek thought and education. He felt that "the unexamined life was not worth living." Above all, in his opinion,

[1] Since Socrates wrote nothing himself, he is known only through the writings of others. Chief among these were Plato, his most famous pupil, and Xenophon.

the individual should seek to "know thyself." He felt that ignorance was the root of evil and that knowledge was the source of virtue.

Socrates attempted to improve moral life in Athens by roaming through the streets of the city and talking with people who seemed to need help in their thinking. Instead of "telling," Socrates used a question-and-answer, or inquiry, approach to teaching. He would ask questions of an individual, upon the pretense that he knew nothing of the subject, until the individual exposed his ignorance or fallacies in thinking. Through further questioning, Socrates assisted the individual in correcting his thinking.

Socrates' method of teaching, which became known as the *Socratic method,* was in opposition to the formal lecture method used by the Sophists of his day. The object was to enable the individual to arrive at truth through a thinking process. The purpose of the teacher, as Socrates saw it, was to stimulate, promote, and guide this thinking process rather than to impart only knowledge to the pupil.

The impact of Socrates upon education is felt even today. You may be reminded of him as you read about the purposes of education in Chapter 16 and as you explore the inquiry and problem-solving approaches to learning.

Plato (428–347 B.C.)

Over 2,000 years ago, Plato, in his writings about a Utopian society, stated that the role of education is "the drawing and leading of children to the rule which has been pronounced right by the voice of the law, and approved as truly right by the concordant experiences of the best and oldest men." Why is it that Plato would have such an idea about education? It has been said that Plato's ideas were greatly influenced by his master teacher, Socrates. Socrates held a rather democratic point of view. He believed that universal ideas emerged from the common social life and that every man could make an equal contribution to his society.

But Socrates was living more in a society of transition than of conflict. Plato grew up in a chaotic period when the great struggles between Athens and Sparta had become full blown and were dividing the loyalties of men throughout the Greek world. Plato had been impressed by the military superiority of Sparta and by the excessive individualism that prevailed in Athens. Therefore it was no great wonder that when Plato wrote his *Republic,* he was dreaming of setting up an ideal state that would do away with factional conflict.

In his desire to set up an ideal state, Plato believed that all individuals should be strictly subordinated to the state. Since he wanted to operate his ideal state on a principle of efficiency, he divided all people into three classes (leaders, soldiers, and artisans), with each person doing the job that he was best fitted to do, which would provide justice to each. In his stratification of citizenship, he did not overemphasize or underemphasize any individual's role in society. According to him, to be a good citizen, the individual had to do the state's bidding, whether it was to rule, to fight, or to work.

Plato, in his effort to set up the ideal state, did both a service and an injustice to education. As a service, he showed that a system of education is integral with the welfare of the state, but he did a great injustice to democracy in emphasizing the rule of the elite in which the "best and oldest men" decided the welfare of others. He advocated a very authoritarian type of education, which is the antithesis of democratic education. But this may seem too simple an explanation. Hence, you may want to raise the question whether or not a system of state schools which is designed to develop a political elite of the talented is compatible with democratic ideals.

Aristotle (384–322 B.C.)

Aristotle, like Plato, had no particular loyalty to democracy. Aristotle felt that a good monarchy or a good aristocracy was just as acceptable as a good democracy, depending on which could promote to the highest degree the welfare of the state in question. His basic thesis was that man was a "political animal."

In one sense, however, Aristotle favored democracy over anarchy or dictatorship. In an attempt to work out guidelines for the virtues (wisdom, courage, justice, and temperance) with which the Greeks were much concerned at this time, Aristotle developed the concept of the golden mean. In the golden mean, Aristotle maintained that to each virtue there are attached two vices: the vice of excess and the vice of defect. With the virtue of courage, you find foolhardiness (when one has too much courage) and cowardliness (when one has too little courage). Virtue is thus seen as the mean between two extremes.

To evaluate one form of government over another, Aristotle added the notion that governments should provide their citizens with both freedom and security. Since democracy had "the better character," it made "the better government." For him an anarchy was characterized by too much freedom and too little security. An oligarchy or a dictatorship, conversely, was characterized by too little freedom and too much security. For example, if everyone were "free" in an anarchy, then everyone would be at the mercy of everyone else. As a result, there would be little if any security. In a dictatorship, everyone was secure only if he did not openly disagree. One's security depended upon his toeing the line. He was not free to disobey. The democratic ideal, however, was seen to entrust certain powers to the people so that the government did not become too powerful—thus avoiding a dictatorship—while it also entrusted power to the government so that the individual did not run rampant as in the case of anarchy. Democracy provided a system whereby checks and balances could be maintained in regard to an individual's freedom and security.

To Aristotle, education was the development of the well-rounded individual divorced from the mechanical, practical areas of vocational or professional training. Further, Aristotle held that the highest form of virtue was speculation, contemplation, and the exercise of intellectual ability. In this scale of reasoning, man as a knower was higher in the scale of worthy citizenship than was man as a practical citizen.

In Aristotle's day, a liberal education was the education that was deemed best suited to Greek free men. Aristotle, like Plato, did not advocate the same education for all people. Rather, there was a general education for the citizenry, additional education for the warriors, *and* an even higher education for the leaders. Rediscovered during the time of the Renaissance, both Aristotle's and Plato's concepts of education provided much of the basis for the classical tradition in education. As mentioned in Chapter 13, our early colonial forefathers imported this tradition from abroad. Many aspects of the educational practices in our American public schools today can be traced to this classical tradition. You might want to compare today's "track system," used in many schools, with Aristotle's ideas.

Vergerius (1349–1420)

A fifteenth-century humanist, Pierre Paolo Vergerius, formulated certain goals for education and set forth a basic theory of formal discipline to which many people today still adhere. He wrote as follows [109:126]:

> We call those studies liberal which are worthy of a free man; those studies by which we obtain and practice virtue and wisdom; that education which calls forth, trains, and develops those highest gifts of body and mind which ennoble men and which are rightly judged to rank next in dignity to virtue only, for to a vulgar temper gain and pleasure are the one aim of existence, to a lofty nature, moral worth and fame.

Vergerius was the proponent of a doctrine of a *limited* body of subject matter, which he felt had some special power to train the mind. Evidences of this doctrine can still be found in American schools today.

Vittorino da Feltre (1378–1446)

Vittorino da Feltre has been called "the first modern schoolmaster." His curriculum included many subjects taught today, some with a practical slant. Vocal and instrumental music and physical education were taught. He emphasized character training. His curriculum was designed to prepare young men for a useful life of service to church and state. His attempts to combine humanistic and chivalric education were met with hostility by the monastic and the church schools of the period, which were opposed to such new and different learnings. Lacking religious sanction for his approach, he turned to the patronage of the nobility to support his school at Mantua, Italy. He left no writings. His fame rests solely on his reputation as a schoolmaster. Though born in a poor family, he was one of many in that considerable number in history who have worked their way through school and achieved wide fame as scholars and teachers.

Locke (1632–1704)

Three hundred years after Vergerius formulated his theory of formal discipline, John Locke further developed the theory. John Locke introduced a new element at this point, his concept of the nature of the learner. This is commonly known as the *tabula rasa* doctrine, which held the mind, at birth, to be like a smooth tablet upon which nothing yet had been written. Locke put greater emphasis on educational methods that would develop all of the senses of the child, not merely through reading, but through the senses of sight, taste, smell, touch, and hearing. In line with this point of view, Locke laid great stress on the importance of the physical development of the body. He felt that education, through sense impressions, should supply all the data used in thinking, as well as provide training in thinking. He advocated difficult intellectual exercises for disciplining the mind and severe tasks for disciplining the body. He saw education as a great power to make men good. But what are the factors that would cause Locke to view education as a great power?

Since this was the period of Newtonian physics, the scientists and mathematicians were prominent in expanding the horizons of knowledge. Knowledge made evident by the sciences and mathematics was a knowledge that was empirically observable. In the biological sciences, an enormous mass of facts was gathered; and the status of the social sciences began to improve in this eighteenth century. Even historical documents began to be treated as though they were scientific data to be gathered, classified, and criticized. This was the time of Voltaire and his Encyclopedists. The job of the Encyclopedists was to simplify knowledge into factual statements that could be recorded in encyclopedia form; they worked for freedom of thought, reform of harsh and unjust laws, elimination of poverty, disease, slavery, and war. These were just a few of the influences that gave John Locke theoretical justification for sense realism in education. It would appear that he, like Plato and Aristotle, viewed education in terms of a select group of people only. His humanistic doctrine and advocacy of the formal-discipline theory gave further impetus to these conceptions of education.

CONTRIBUTIONS OF SOME EARLY THEORIES OF PSYCHOLOGY

Out of the past fraught with myth and superstition, various theories developed concerning the soul, mind, and body of man, which influenced early concepts of education. Although these superstitions and theories have been largely cast aside as the result of scientific investigations, they still seem to have some influence upon present-day practices in education.

Faculty Psychology

Various theories concerning the mind and body of man have played enormously significant roles in educational practices. According to early theories, mind and body were in sharp contrast. Mind was considered to have spontaneity, initiative, and independence of action. Body was considered inert and passive.

Out of this dualistic theory of mind and body grew a type of psychology which became known as "faculty psychology." This theory was based upon the hypothesis that the mind was composed of many mental faculties, such as reasoning and memory, and that these faculties were localized in the cerebral hemisphere. It was further theorized that the faculties could be strengthened through exercise, like muscles. The problem for educators who endorsed faculty psychology was to isolate subject matter that would best exercise the muscles. This again, in most cases, reverts to the old classical trivium and quadrivium. Subjects in the trivium included rhetoric, grammar, and logic. Subjects in the quadrivium were algebra, geometry, music, and astronomy. This, of course, has been modified in different countries and in different centuries; however, the principle of exercise through difficult subjects still remains the same. Since the more difficult subjects, such as classical language and mathematics, were supposed to provide the best type of exercise for the mind, these subjects were looked upon with great favor. Rote memorization became a favorite technique, for it provided the necessary exercise of the faculty of memory. With this doctrine no justification for learning needed to be given other than the training of the mind.

Physiological Psychology

For a long time the doctrine of faculty psychology was the dominant educational theory. Then a group called "physiological psychologists" challenged this doctrine by producing evidence that certain areas of the brain controlled different body functions.

Using the evidence provided by these psychologists, a pseudoscientific cult of phrenologists advanced some rather unusual theories. The phrenologists contended that, since different faculties of the mind had their "seat" in specific areas of the brain, the development of these faculties could be determined by an examination of the bumps of the skull.

Under the doctrine of faculty psychology, only abstract qualities of mind had been considered as aspects of the brain. Then, from the work of the physiological psychologists and the limited contributions of the phrenologists, the concept of the brain was expanded to include the "seat" of behavior traits. Emphasis still was placed on the training of the mind.

SOME IMPLICATIONS OF EARLY CONCEPTS OF EDUCATION

In studying these early concepts of education and early theories about the mind, you will find that many questions come into focus. What are the implications of the classical tradition, the humanistic viewpoint, and the doctrine of faculty psychology for educational practices?

Knowledge

According to the classical tradition, knowledge (acquiring facts) is education. On the basis of this concept of education, teaching becomes a matter of acquiring the techniques of getting pupils to learn established content. The business of the teacher, according to this viewpoint, is to teach the subjects of the curriculum, generally by assigning pages in a textbook, by hearing a recitation consisting of the answers to the teacher's questions, and by grading papers and examinations in which boys and girls reveal their mastery of the formal content of the subject. The teacher also needs to learn the methods by which law and order are preserved in a classroom, so that academic learning may be accomplished.

To those who hold this viewpoint, the student who acquires the most knowledge is the student who is best educated. Where knowledge becomes the end rather than the means to an end, students must learn great masses of material. Isolated, factual information becomes important because it increases the learner's reservoir of knowledge. Page-by-page assignments in textbooks lend themselves well to this concept of education. Little concern is felt about how the students learn as long as they can "parrot" back what they have read or heard. Here the mark of a cultured person is the knowledge which he has concerning his own culture and the cultures of the past.

Preparation

Early thinkers generally considered children as miniature adults. Young minds were like Locke's "smooth tablets," upon which an education must be imprinted as a preparation for life. Where preparation becomes the major emphasis in education, certain practices seem to follow. The teacher attempts to get boys and girls to learn something because it will help them when they "grow up." Since the teacher is not necessarily appealing to children's interests, he must resort to ways of getting the work done. Artificial techniques, such as gold stars as rewards, threats in the form of demerits, and additional assignments as punishment, are some of the more familiar techniques which teachers use. Competition between pupils is one of the procedures used by many teachers to stimulate pupils to learn. Since competition supposedly exists at a rather high level in adult life, teachers feel that they should provide competitive experiences which will prepare their students for adult society. Some of the more familiar kinds of competition are spelldowns, oratorical contests, and speed drills in arithmetic. Competition is carried into the realm of evaluation, where students compete for grades on examinations and on their report cards.

With the emphasis on preparation, most of the materials of instruction are slanted toward adult problems. Textbooks use adult situations as the context within which children work. It was believed that the more difficult these materials and problems, the better prepared students would be to face the realities of adult life. Perhaps you may have experienced teaching of this kind in some of your classes in school and in college.

Preparation for the future has been a dominating concept of education throughout history. How often have you heard teachers say that they must prepare their boys and girls for the next grade? An underlying theory which pervades many a school system is that the elementary school prepares for the high school and that the high school prepares for college. This theory is in contrast to the one stated so aptly by Dewey: "The future which grows out of the present is surely taken care of" [62:65].

Training the Mind

Under the doctrine of the faculty psychologists and phrenologists, *exercise* of the different faculties of the mind was of major importance in teaching. Thus, the harder the subjects were for the pupils, the better they fulfilled this purpose. Teachers chose not only hard subjects but also the most difficult subject matter within each subject. After the material was chosen, drill techniques were used. The teacher's purpose for constant drill and the resulting rote memorization was not to facilitate understanding of the material studied but rather to exercise the faculty of memory. Long lists of historical dates, names of presidents and vice presidents, and names of state capitals were favorite drill exercises.

Certain types of subject matter were included in textbooks to exercise the powers of reasoning. This typical problem found in an old arithmetic book demonstrates this kind of teaching material:

A man went into an orchard which had seven gates and there took a certain number of apples. When he left the orchard, he gave the first guard half the apples that he had and one apple more. To the second, he gave his remaining apples and one apple more. He did the same in the case of each of the remaining five guards and left the orchard with one apple. How many apples did he gather in the orchard?

How did an education which trained the mind prepare students for life outside the school? Faculty psychologists explained this through the theory of the transfer of training. This theory postulated that, if the faculty of memory or reasoning was trained by such subjects as foreign language or mathematics, you would be able to remember or reason in every situation in which you encountered such activities.

According to this concept, educators need be concerned only with a limited curriculum. Those few subjects which best train the faculties prepare the student for any eventuality. Teachers do not have to be concerned with teaching methods and techniques which integrate knowledge and understanding. This integration automatically takes place from one subject to another, one situation to another, and one skill to another. A prime example of this kind of teaching is found in the area of arithmetic, where number computations are learned and practiced in isolation. These skills are then supposed to transfer automatically to the solving of verbal arithmetic problems.

The field of educational psychology has produced experimental evidence which raises many questions about the validity of a general transfer of training. Yet many educational practices are based upon this theory.

It would seem that casual observations might raise some questions about this general transfer-of-training theory. How would you explain a situation in which a person with a prodigious memory for dates and names in history cannot remember the names of people he meets? Or how would you explain the situation of the great theoretical mathematician who could not balance his checkbook? Through these and many other casual observations this theory seems to break down.

CONTRIBUTIONS OF LATER OUTSTANDING THINKERS

As early as the sixteenth century, there were rumblings of disagreement and dissent over educational practices. Great thinkers began to question existing theories and to formulate different concepts of education.

Comenius (1592–1670)

John Amos Comenius (of Nivnitz, Moravia, which is now part of Czechoslovakia) made his education contribution in the seventeenth century, which was a period when many cultural forces were striving for the loyalties of man. This was a time of great religious conflict between Catholic and Protestant churches and a time of new outlook characterized by science and the scientific method. In this setting, a two-track system of universal education emerged. Because of the class structure of society, which was deeply ingrained in all the countries of Europe, differences were made in the amount and kind of education provided for the various classes. The upper classes received a classical secondary education, whereas the lower classes received a vernacular elementary education.

In a book called *The Great Didactic,* Comenius stated his views on education. Many of his ideas are to be found in schools today. He believed that children should be taught practical things and that learning should progress step-by-step from the familiar to the less familiar, from the less difficult to the more difficult. He was the first to prepare profusely illustrated textbooks for children, the first of which was called *Orbis Pictus.* He felt that there should be four levels in the organization of a school system. The mother should teach the child from birth to age six. From six to twelve, he should attend the vernacular school, followed by six years in the gymnasium or Latin school, and then six years in the university.

Comenius was a strong advocate of general universal education. At the time, this idea was in sharp contrast to the views of other educators. But Comenius felt that all children, rather than a select few, should have an opportunity to learn. He also believed that education is a natural process and that educational practices should therefore be in harmony with the nature of the learner. He expressed a desire for a "kindlier" discipline which would be consistent with his view of the natural process of education. He was a deeply religious man and was a prolific writer on both religion and education.

Because of the religious and political turmoil in Europe at this time, Comenius' ideas on education were not recognized until approximately 200 years after he proposed them.

Rousseau (1712–1778)

Jean Jacques Rousseau was an extreme critic of the humanist formal-discipline theories of education. He believed in the child's right to freedom in development, and his concept of education was based on the premise that it should be according to the nature of children. Rousseau has been termed by many as an anti-institutionalist. He believed that man was basically good and that it was only under the influence of evil institutions that man became corrupt. The first sentence of his famous work, *Emile* (1762), vividly makes this point: "Everything is good as it comes from the hand of the Author of Nature; everything degenerates in the hand of man."

The description of a mythical school in his book *Emile* set forth several principles which have heavily influenced modern concepts of education, such as the idea that the curriculum and teaching methods should be planned in terms of the needs of the pupil, that authority should be replaced by reason and investigation, and that the natural interests, curiosity, and activities of children should be used in their education.

Rousseau was one of the first to propose a "child-centered" school. He would not accept the notion that the child is a miniature adult, but conceived the child to be a growing, developing organism. From Rousseau's contributions it is possible to catch the first glimmerings of the study of child development.

Pestalozzi (1746–1827)

Johann Heinrich Pestalozzi was a Swiss educator who became interested in Rousseau's methods of teaching children and attempted to practice them. Although he found a number of weaknesses, the experimentation provided the basis for writing his famous book *Leonard and Gertrude*. Pestalozzi felt that children should be treated like human beings, educated in terms of their needs, and learn through the full use of their senses. His "doctrine of interest" to provide the motivation for learning caused a great deal of furor in his time. He insisted that "learning

A statue of Johann Heinrich Pestalozzi has been erected at Aargon, Switzerland, in commemoration of his efforts to discover more effective methods of teaching. The experimental schools he established in Switzerland were instrumental in bringing about early educational reforms in elementary schools in America. (*Photograph from the Library of Congress.*)

should be a pleasant experience." Other educators felt that this would eliminate the distastefulness of school and might be bad for character development.

Pestalozzi put his ideas into practice in five different schools in Switzerland, the most famous of these being his Neuhof School. Neuhof was actually an orphanage, as was his school at Stanz. These schools were for poor children whose fathers had been killed in the wars. Since most of the children enrolled were children of broken homes, Pestalozzi tried to recapture the ideals of a sound family life, with emphasis being given to mild discipline, loving care for children, and religious and moral inspiration. It is said that he "lived like a beggar in order to learn how to make beggars [orphans] live like men."

Pestalozzi's greatest contribution to education was in the area of teacher training. He may well be called "the father of normal schools." During the last 20 years of his life, he conducted an experimental school and teachers institute at Yverdon. He achieved an international reputation for his innovative ideas and practices. Pestalozzi is regarded as a national hero in his native country, as attested by the erection of statues of him in many of the cities.

The work in his schools emphasized learning from objects and practical experiences. This and his analysis of various teaching methods may be considered the foundation upon which the scientific investigation of similar educational problems has since been undertaken.

Froebel (1782–1852)

Friedrich Froebel taught with Pestalozzi and conducted his own schools in Switzerland and Germany. Froebel was very impressed with Pestalozzi's sense of realism, but he also leaned heavily upon the idealistic philosophy of his day. Froebel looked on the world as a great unity, where there was no division between the realm of what was spiritual and what was natural or between the individual and society. In his opinion all things found their unity and their essence in God and His will unfolded on earth.

Froebel looked upon the child as an agency for the realization of God's will in human nature. It was through education that the child's spirit became linked with the spiritual unity of God. Froebel believed that the child had latent powers that were to be unfolded as he entered into the spiritual union with God. Education, then, would be a process of spiritual activity, a process that was creative and morally good.

Since the educative process was so dedicated to the development of the child, Froebel felt that his process should start with the small child of three or four years. He called his new school the kindergarten, a garden where children grow. In his garden, Froebel introduced a new method of teaching that was designated the method of play activity. Froebel felt that play was a natural and appropriate activity for small children, and therefore he wanted to capitalize on the child's interest in play activity. This activity, however, was structured and involved drawing, clay modeling, painting and coloring, singing, dancing, telling dramatic stories, manipulating blocks and paper and cardboard objects, balls, and other objects. As the children played, Froebel tried to teach symbolic meaning in the objects with which they were playing, such as the ball meaning perfect unity in matter. Even in the absence of the symbolic attachment that Froebel gave to play activity, the new emphasis on respect for the child, for his individuality, for the active qualities of learning became influential in American education. Froebel's educational principles may be summarized as (1) self-activity and (2) social participation. An important foundation for the later concept of the child-centered school was laid by Froebel's kindergarten.

William James (1842–1910)

James holds a number of distinctions, any one of which you may wish to pursue further on your own. First, he is recognized as the father of American psychology. His two-volume *Principles of Psychology,* consisting of 1400 pages, was 12 years in the writing, and it remains today one of the most instructive in the field. Second, James serves as a good example of an integration and culmination of intellectual concerns. He was trained first as an M.D. (received at Harvard in 1870) and then taught anatomy and physiology while he developed his competence in the area of psychology. He likewise distinguished himself in philosophy. Third, he came from an interesting family. His father was a Swedenborgian mystic, and his brother Henry distinguished himself as a writer. In fact it is said of the brothers William and Henry that "William wrote psychology like fiction, while Henry wrote fiction like psychology." Fourth, his *Principles of Psychology* had a far-reaching effect on the thinking of John Dewey, who will be discussed later in this chapter. Dewey had been an Hegelian idealist until he read James's psychology books. These works so impressed and influenced his thinking that Dewey shifted from the idealists' camp to that of the experimentalists, or pragmatists, or progressivists (these labels have been used interchangeably, for the most part depending on the author being read).

Herbart (1776–1841)

Whereas the European men who preceded Herbart had greatly influenced elementary and preschool education, Johann Herbart's theories found acceptance largely among secondary school and university teachers. In keeping with his times and with his societal emphasis, Herbart laid great stress upon the social and moral character of education. To this end, he insisted that education should be primarily moral in its outlook and intent. To Herbart, morality was not necessarily religious in character but was a matter of relevance to a particular society.

Herbart was greatly concerned that the individual be well adjusted to his society. He believed that the school should be concerned with historical and literary studies and that all other studies should be correlated with them.

Herbart stressed the learning theory termed "associationism," in which great stress was placed upon the development of clear ideas in students. All qualities of man were considered to be secondary to that of the association of ideas in the mind. To guarantee the best association of ideas, Herbart developed the four formal steps of learning and teaching: (1) clearness in presenting new ideas; (2) association, or relating of new ideas to compatible old ideas; (3) system, or arrangement of associated ideas in logical order; and (4) method, or application of new ideas to some specific problem or new situation. Two of Herbart's followers, Prof. Tuiskon Ziller of Leipzig and Prof. Wilhelm Rein of Jena [21:149–150], renamed the above and added a fifth, so that the now popularized five Herbartian formal steps are given as follows: (1) preparation, (2) presentation, (3) association, (4) generalization, and (5) application.

These steps were introduced at a time when reading, memory, and recitation were the principal methods of teaching. Because of the emphasis that society was placing upon scientific and mathematical developments, these steps in the teaching-learning process became vastly popular. Herbart's "formula" for teaching spread rapidly through elementary and secondary schools in both Europe and the United States. It was not until the twentieth century that a new concept of education was able to shadow the influence of Herbartianism in educational practices.

Parker (1837–1902)

Francis Parker, a teacher and an administrator who has been called a leader of the progressive education movement in America, ranked high among the pioneers. His theories were geared toward making the school less artificial and conventional. He advocated field trips in science and geography. He felt that children should come into closer relationship with their natural environment.

As principal of the Cook County Normal School at Chicago, Parker trained many teachers. These teachers became disciples of his ideas and spread them throughout America. It has been said that his teachings, his writings, and his speeches laid the groundwork for a large part of John Dewey's concepts of education.

Dewey (1859–1952)

Many people who are acquainted with John Dewey's work in education recognize that, in formulating his point of view, Dewey drew upon three centuries of educational thought. This fact should in no way detract from his significant contributions to modern education. His knitting together of a consistent system from the ideas advanced by his predecessors is in itself a prodigious undertaking.

Dewey early established a laboratory school in Chicago. Here teachers were encouraged to experiment. This was a testing ground for the concepts of child development advanced by Rousseau and for the direct investigation of actual objects as a method of teaching, which had been advocated by Comenius and Parker. As a result of this experimentation, better teaching methods were developed. The experimental attitude found in his school spread to hundreds of teacher training institutions.

While at the University of Chicago, Dewey published *School and Society,* about education suitable for a democratic society. He pointed out the importance of the individual within the context of a democracy, placing emphasis on the school's role in developing self-discipline for true democratic participation. Throughout the years this book has had a marked effect upon the functions of the American public school. Some of the books which followed his first publication include *Interest and Effort, Democracy and Education,* and *Experience and Education.*

To John Dewey, the learner rather than the subject matter was the prime concern in the educational process. Activity or experiences of the learner became the focal point of emphasis instead of books and verbalisms. Dewey considered the teacher a guide to the learner rather than a "walking encyclopedia." He felt that education should be practical and should be a process whereby further intellectual growth and development might be realized, rather than an end in itself. Two passages from his *Democracy and Education* (a "classic" written in 1916) will illustrate:

Education means the enterprise of supplying the conditions which insure growth, or adequacy of life, irrespective of age [62:58].

Since in reality there is nothing to which growth is relative save more growth, there is nothing to which education is subordinate save more education . . . the purpose of school education is to insure the continuation of education by organizing the powers that insure growth. The inclination to learn from life itself and to make the conditions of life such that all will learn in the process of living is the finest product of schooling [62:60].

Thus, Dewey favored the attainment of ends which had a direct, vital appeal to the learner and which would serve as further steppingstones to something beyond, rather than have learning become the acquisition of isolated skills and techniques through drill. That is, "ends" were viewed as "new beginnings"! He felt that pupils should make the most of the opportunities of their present life rather than prepare for a future life. Dewey, like Rousseau, saw a negative consequence in viewing childhood or immaturity as primarily the absence of maturity. As a result, Dewey added a new dimension by maintaining that the *ability* of children to grow and develop is a *positive* aspect rather than a negative one. He maintained that childhood or immaturity should be viewed intrinsically rather than comparatively.

Unfortunately, it is impossible to present a complete expression of John Dewey's philosophy in this brief description of his contribution. In fact, many people today form different interpretations of his writings and of his thinking concerning education. Even more unfortunate, however, is the fact that it is said of Dewey that "he is the *most criticized* and *least read* of any educator." It would indeed be desirable for you to read one or more of his books (most are available in inexpensive paperbacks) and seek firsthand information regarding his "philosophy."

Kilpatrick (1871–1965)

William Heard Kilpatrick was one of the leaders in the progressive movement who attempted to interpret the work of John Dewey. In addition to being a philosopher in his own right, Kilpatrick made a significant contribution to a modern conception of education with his interpretation of Dewey's thinking. The "project" method of teaching is one of Kilpatrick's many contributions to education. Like Dewey and Pestalozzi, he developed schools where his ideas could be tested. His work with these schools and as a professor of education at Teachers College, Columbia University, convinced Kilpatrick that "pupil purposes" are the key to pupil learning. He set forth the idea that pupils might learn to behave in certain ways on the outside but not learn to behave that way inside. As a consequence, he became very much concerned about the development of character through education.

In his work at Columbia University, Kilpatrick influenced the thinking of thousands of elementary and secondary school teachers who attended his classes. This influence has been reflected in the practices which his students have used in their own schools. In addition, through his books *The Project Method, Foundations of Method,* and *Source Book of Philosophy,* Kilpatrick reinforced the concept of instruction through life activities and placed emphasis upon methodologies which use the concept of living as learning.

Bode (1873–1953)

Boyd Henry Bode was an exponent of progressive education. At the same time he also was a friendly critic of some of the practices which grew out of a part of the so-called progressive movement. He felt that attention merely to children's individual needs and interests as a program of education could become chaotic. This by no means meant that he negated the more modern concepts of education advocated by his predecessors. Rather, he placed emphasis on the use of common interests and on making democracy in the schools a way of life.

While professor of education at Ohio State University, Bode published a book, *Conflicting Psychologies of Learning.* He was concerned here with the question of mind and its relationship to the whole program of education. He reiterated Dewey's concept that "the cultivation of thinking is the central concern of education" [62:179]. Bode further pointed out that this makes the pupil the starting point in any educational program. He advocated individual initiative along with continuous social development. In the area of teaching methodology he was a firm believer in flexible methods to take care of individual differences. His book, which set forth a pragmatic point of view, was a major contribution to educational thinking in the late 1920s. Through his teaching and writing, which included such books as *Fundamentals of Education* (1922), *Modern Educational Theories* (1927), *Democracy as a Way of Life* (1937), *Progressive Education at the Crossroads* (1938), and *How We Learn* (1940), Bode made a major contribution to educational thinking.

CONTRIBUTIONS FROM OTHER AREAS OF INVESTIGATION

During the past century and a half science has contributed new understandings of human growth and development. Beginning with the work of the empirical psychologists, later scientific investigations in the areas of individual differences, measurement, and learning have contributed much to the improvement of educational practices. What are a few of the contributions of science to modern concepts of education?

Empirical Psychology

In 1831, Johann Herbart, who was discussed earlier in this chapter, published a volume entitled *Letters Dealing with the Application of Psychology to the Art of Teaching.* By many psychologists he was considered the originator of a move-ment which eventually laid the foundation for a field of psychology, called "em-pirical psychology," that was based upon the results of experience and observation. However, it was long after Herbart's day that either empirical psychology or the science of education gained any great momentum.

G. Stanley Hall established a center for applied psychology at Johns Hopkins University in 1884. This center devoted its efforts to the study of children's mental development. Hall is often referred to as the founder of child study. This early movement, frequently called the "child-study movement," did not prove effective in establishing a science of education. It did, however, inject into the schools of this country a new spirit of conscious, critical consideration of methods and results of classroom procedures. It opened the door for a later, more scientific system of child study, which proved of great value in the development of sound educational programs.

Human Growth and Development

Growing out of the early work in empirical psychology and child study came a great deal of interest in all aspects of human growth and development. Research into the relative effects of heredity and environment set the stage for many in-vestigations. As a result, educators began to learn more about which aspects of human growth are determined by heredity and/or environment.

Research provided information about the processes, patterns, and rates of human growth. Investigations indicated that the process moved from generalized mass activity to specialized local activity. These findings became extremely influential in the selection of learning experiences for boys and girls at different age levels. The fact was finally established that children are not miniature adults; they are qualitatively and quantitatively different.

Along with the foregoing concepts of growth and development came better understandings of the differences between maturation and learning. Through research it was found that children mature at different rates. It was also found that it is necessary for children to reach certain levels of maturity before they can benefit the most from the experiences provided for them. What an overwhelming effect these findings proved to have on education! They opened the way for a complete reevaluation of existing experiences for various age and grade levels.

On the basis of the research in this area, one thing became clear: Education must be geared to the growth and development of pupils.

Individual Differences

The fact that people are different was not a very startling revelation. Since the dawn of history people have observed physical differences which existed within their own groups. The startling fact was the extent of these differences.

The extent of differences was discovered quite by accident. Two astronomers could not agree upon their observations. A group of astronomers investigating this phenomenon brought to light the idea that people differ in speed of response to a given stimulus. This led to many experiments in the latter part of the nineteenth century, the results of which indicated the tremendous number of ways in which individuals vary.

A major finding of these scientific investigations was that measured specific characteristics of individuals could be shown to assume a pattern called "a curve of normal distribution." This exploded older concepts of types and averages. No longer could a teacher consider a whole group of students average, dull, lazy, and the like. A range of abilities, attitudes, achievements, and physical characteristics existed in every classroom. Therefore a teacher no longer could expect every child to participate in a learning situation and achieve the same results as every other child. Methods had to be developed to accommodate these differences. The concept of grouping for learning grew directly out of these scientific investigations.

Measurement

During the period when Dewey and Parker were generating enthusiasm for the study of education, a new note was sounded by J. M. Rice, who was editor of the magazine *Forum*. Rice felt he needed more objective evidence on which to base his description of the school systems of various cities. He devised a method of testing the results of teaching methods. One of his tests consisted simply of a list of common spelling words which he asked children of several cities to spell. This idea, which now seems so simple, was revolutionary at the time. The use of a definite objective test rather than mere observation was a distinct step in the direction of scientific evaluation. These first attempts by Rice to evaluate methods of teaching were scathingly denounced by leading educators of his day [14:85–86].

While Rice was concerned with measuring achievement, Binet, a nineteenth-century Frenchman, was working on a series of tests to use on feebleminded children in the schools of Paris. From his early efforts grew some of the first instruments to measure intelligence.

The importance of the work done in achievement and intelligence tests can hardly be overestimated for subsequent educational practices.

The measurement movement did not end with the above-mentioned tests and procedures. It included aptitude and personality tests as well. From the elaboration of these instruments and techniques of measurement grew many studies in education. Contributions of the science of statistics and subsequent refinements of statistical methodology enabled educators to use more exact measuring devices for gaining insight into the development of individual students.

SOME CRITICS OF MODERN EDUCATION

As you read various newspapers, magazines, and books, you will find individuals who do not agree with some of our modern educational concepts. Some of them feel that concepts expressed earlier in this chapter should characterize the teaching-learning process. Others feel that school practices should be greatly modified and improved.

Naturally, parents and other community members become quite confused about what to believe as they read these conflicting points of view. They will expect you to help clarify their thinking. For this reason, know who some of the critics are as well as what they believe. As you progress in your preparation for teaching, formulate a clearly reasoned position in regard to their criticisms and beliefs so that you can deal adequately with the concerns of nonprofessional and, to some extent, professional educators. Only five will be mentioned here.

William C. Bagley (1874–1946)

Although Bagley is now deceased, the position he took in opposition to modern concepts of education is representative of a number of contemporary critics. He attempted to build a conservative educational position on an organized basis. As an essentialist, he believed that the school should teach only certain tried and tested aspects of our cultural heritage.

Bagley maintained that the school, in contrast to an experimental institution that may foster change, should help pupils adjust to an existing, fixed society. He did not favor elective programs of study. For him, education was the hard process of imparting facts, involving a relatively narrow range of studies that were considered to be essential to effective living.

Shortly before his death he summarized his views on essentialism in the following manner [15:202]:

1. Gripping and enduring interests frequently . . . grow out of initial learning efforts that are not intrinsically appealing or attractive. Man is the only animal that can sustain effort in the face of immediate desire. To deny to the young the benefits that may be theirs by the exercise of this unique human prerogative would be a gross injustice.
2. The control, direction, and guidance of the immature by the mature is inherent in the prolonged period of infancy or necessary dependence peculiar to the human species.
3. While the capacity for self-discipline should be the goal, imposed discipline is a necessary means to this end. Among individuals, as among nations, true freedom is always a conquest, never a gift.
4. The freedom of the immature learner to choose what he shall learn is not at all to be compared with his later freedom from want, fraud, fear, superstition, error, and oppression—and the price of this later freedom is the effortful and systematic mastery of what has been winnowed and refined through long struggle of mankind upward from the savage—and a mastery, that, for most learners, must be under guidance of competent and sympathetic but firm and exacting teachers.
5. Essentialism provides a strong theory of education; its competing school (progressivism) offers a weak theory. If there has been a question in the past as to the kind of educational theory that the few remaining democracies of the world need, there can be no question today.

James B. Conant (1893–   )

Conant is one of the most widely known critics of American education today. One of his reports, titled *The American High School Today* [50], clearly indicates how he reacts to our American schools, especially the secondary school. Early in this report he set up three things that are necessary in order to have a good high school: first, a school board that is composed of intelligent citizens who can make the distinction between policy making and administration; second, a first-rate superintendent; and third, a good principal.

Conant does not endorse the grouped "tracks" system that categorizes the "vocational," "commercial," and other curriculum plans. Rather, he feels that each pupil should have an individualized program that is carefully supervised and guided. He stresses the importance of such basic subjects as English, social studies, American problems or government, mathematics, and science. An individualized program automatically gives special consideration to gifted and exceptional boys and girls. He feels that, above all, the schools must provide top-quality programs that utilize our manpower and brainpower. At this point you may wish to review Conant's ideas as spelled out in greater detail in the Resource Section of Part IV.

Robert M. Hutchins (1899–   )

Hutchins is most commonly associated with the phrase: "Since men are everywhere and always the same, education should be everywhere and always the same." He is labeled a Neo-Thomist (to be treated later in this chapter), and he serves as a good example of how Thomistic philosophy has developed from Aristotle. One of Aristotle's many definitions of man was that he was a "rational animal." The Neo-Thomists have taken this trait, deemphasized the animal aspect, and stressed the *rational* character of man. What they see as essential about this quality is that it is common to all men. Hutchins has written of this trait [133:68]:

> Every man has a function as a man. The function of a citizen or a subject may vary from society to society, and the system of training, or adaptation, or instruction, or meeting immediate needs may vary with it. But the function of a man as man is the same in every age and in every society, since it results from his nature as a man. The aim of an educational system is the same in every age and in every society where such a system can exist: it is to improve man as man.

What this means for education is that specific attention should be given to the training of the intellect. (It was in this vein that Hutchins criticized all non-intellectual activities which took place in schools, and, in this same vein, he put his theory into practice when, as chancellor of the University of Chicago, he removed their intercollegiate football program.) Such functions as "preparing for life adjustment," "meeting the needs of youth," "preparation for democratic citizenship," and "reforming the social order" are not proper functions of Hutchins's schools; such competencies, if desired, should be left to the home, church, television, boy scouts, and others. The school's task is solely the training of the intellect, everywhere and always.

Vice Admiral H. G. Rickover, USN (1900–   )

In an article entitled "The World of the Uneducated" that appeared in *The Saturday Evening Post* [220:8], Rickover synthesized some of his ideas concerning what is "wrong" with education today. He said that there are two processes by which children are guided into adulthood: education and training. One of our basic troubles is that we do not clearly differentiate between the two. He believes that the traditionalist sees the distinction clearly but the "progressive" does not. The progressive philosophy of education equates education with training. The Russians adopted this American phenomenon for a short period of time, but they dropped it some 25 years ago when they found that such an equation does not really educate. As Admiral Rickover sees it, education is the process of developing the individual's comprehension of the world beyond his personal experience and observation. Training is the process of developing the accepted social customs and character traits necessary to good personal appearance. "Training does not stretch the mind." He would have us throw out modern concepts of education and return to a traditional task of the school and the process of teaching.

Arthur Bestor (1908–   )

In *Philosophies of Education*, edited by Philip Phoenix [191:35–45], Bestor contributed an article entitled "Education for Intellectual Discipline," in which he gives a statement of his viewpoint. In this article he endorsed education that will produce a disciplined mind. He further explained that discipline is not equated with punishment, but is a matter of effective training. He would like to see our youth educated in such a way that they can intellectually deal with complex problems in the rapidly changing world.

Bestor stated that there are certain subject areas that can best equip the student, and these include the sciences and humanities—history, language, and literature. It should be every citizen's concern that everyone is carried as far along the line of intellectual discipline as his abilities enable him to go. Bestor encourages the public to insist that our schools engage in serious intellectual discipline and not stress trivial workmanship skills.

Jerome S. Bruner (1915–   )

Bruner [33] and others [192] have contributed to education with their examination of concept formation in children as well as in adults. This research, along with other sources of related principles involving methods of scientific inquiry, has assisted the educator attempting to build a detailed analysis of scientific method.

Bruner's *The Process of Education* grew out of a 10-day conference of thirty-four scholars, scientists, and educators (at Woods Hole on Cape Cod, September, 1959) who met to discuss how education in science might be improved in our elementary and secondary schools. The following four themes are treated in the book:

First, the role of structure in learning and how it may be made central in teaching. Here the dominant view is that an understanding of "the fundamental structure" of any subject is a minimum requirement for using knowledge inside as well as outside the classroom.

Second, readiness for learning. Here the consensus is that "the foundations of any subject may be taught to anybody at any age in some form."

Third, the nature of intuition, i.e., the intellectual technique of arriving at plausible but tentative formulations without going through the analytic steps by which such formulations would be found to be valid or invalid conclusions. Here it was agreed that more should be done in investigating (and possibly in training or developing) "hunches," "shrewd guesses," "fertile hypotheses," and "courageous leaps to tentative conclusions"—all of which are invaluable to the thinker at work.

Fourth, the desire to learn and how such desire may be stimulated. Here the hope was that the subject matter itself would be the best stimulus to learning, rather than gold stars, grades, or later competitive advantage. A look into teacher training, the nature of school examinations, and the quality of any given curriculum shows that all are found to be related to this fourth problem.

More recently, in a book titled *Toward a Theory of Instruction* Bruner has written [34:71]: "If a curriculum is to be effective in the classroom it must contain different ways of activating children, different ways of presenting sequences, different opportunities for some children to 'skip' parts while others work their way through, different ways of putting things. A curriculum, in short, must contain many tracts leading to the same general goal."

In brief, Bruner, among others, is concerned with "how best to aid the teacher in the task of instruction." If possible, read the book *The Process of Education*, which is concerned with the scientific inquiry and analysis of method. In view of the themes mentioned above, pick a field, such as drama, fractions, thermodynamics, horticulture, or one of your own, and toy with the possibility of introducing to "anybody at any age" some of the basic foundations of whatever subject you select. No matter *what* conclusion you arrive at, you can be assured of having examined a probing hypothesis advocated by Bruner.

SOME CURRENT CONTRASTING THEORIES OF EDUCATION

In reading about the theories of education held by men of the past as well as of the present, you undoubtedly have noted a number of similarities and differences. For the purpose of this contrast it would be convenient to classify each of the individuals discussed and assign them to a particular category so far as educational theory is concerned. A number of books have attempted this task, although there is considerable variation in the categories used. Smith [243:19–20] points out, however, that there are innate dangers and shortcomings in attaching labels to individuals in terms of theories of education.

Although it is not necessary to delve deeply into the matter at this stage of your preparation for teaching, an awareness of the dangers involved in categorizing individuals is crucial to the avoidance of too rigid a compartmentalization of various "schools" of educational theory. For example, when you hear that Aristotle is called the father of realism, you may have a tendency to join the terms "Aristotle-realism," and mistakenly conclude that both Aristotle and realism are understood.

It also is important to remember that within any one school of thought, such as realism, vast differences of opinion may be found. For instance, people who are called realists may seem to differ more than realism and idealism differ. So long as you recognize that labels are not so concise as we are inclined to presuppose, we can avoid many of the hazards involved in studying educational theories.

Gruber, in his book *Modern Philosophies of Education,* has analyzed some of the current educational theories in terms of purposes, curriculum, methodology, position of pupil, position of teacher, and evaluation. One or more of the leading proponents of each theory also is indicated. You may find his analysis,[2] which is indicated below in a modified form, with the theory of reconstructionism having been added to his list, to be helpful to you as you move forward in your preparation for teaching. As you study his analysis, you may be able to categorize some of the outstanding thinkers discussed in the first part of this chapter, as well as some of your public school and college teachers.

Natural realism—Naturalism
    Proponent: Horace Kallen.
    Objectives—Aims—Purposes: The natural development of the child (presentism).
    Subject matter—Curriculum: What the child does or wants to do and know.
    Method: Children living together.
    Position of the pupil: All important—an individual to be allowed (encouraged) to enjoy present-day life.
    Position of the teacher: A servant of the learner.
    Evaluation: In terms of the child's freedom and happiness.

New realism—Essentialism
    Proponents: Harry S. Broudy, William C. Bagley, Arthur Bestor, Admiral Hyman G. Rickover, James B. Conant.
    Objectives—Aims—Purposes: To equip man with the exact knowledge and skills which will enable him to compete with the world in which he lives. Based upon demonstrable facts—what people do. Impersonal, objective adjustment of the individual to society.
    Subject matter—Curriculum: What human beings do—the essentials. Adult-approved behavior. Known facts about natural phenomena.
    Method: Memorization and drill for the acquisition of facts, skills, and principles.
    Position of the pupil: A machine to be conditioned.
    Position of the teacher: A servant of nature and of society.
    Evaluation: Measurement of the achievement of the learner as compared with objective norms of standardized tests and of scientific measuring instruments.

Rational realism—Neo-Scholasticism—Classical humanism—Perennialism
    Proponents: Robert Maynard Hutchins, Mortimer J. Adler, Mark Van Doren.
    Objectives—Aims—Purposes: To develop the rational powers of man: to reason, to judge, to discriminate. Reason differentiates man from the lower

---

[2] Reprinted by permission of the publisher from Frederick C. Gruber, *Foundations for a Philosophy of Education,* Copyright © 1961 by Thomas Y. Crowell Company, pp. 302–303.

animals. To perfect man through the development of his intellect and through humanistic endeavors. To form an intellectual elite.

Subject matter—Curriculum: The great moments of thought. A study of philosophy, especially logic, and of the classics. (For Hutchins it is a study of the "great books.") Content of the curriculum should be the same for everyone.

Method: Disciplined exercise of the mind in logical processes. Memorization.

Position of the pupil: A mind to be trained and to be filled with enduring facts and principles.

Position of the teacher: The umpire between true and false logic.

Evaluation: Profundity of knowledge. Skill in logical analysis and in abstract thinking.

Catholic supernatural realism—Thomism

Proponents: Jacques Maritain, Fulton Sheen.

Objectives—Aims—Purposes: To cooperate with Divine Grace to form the true and perfect Christian (Catholic).

Subject matter—Curriculum: The Catholic religion and its application to all phases of life. The Catholic Church possesses the Truth and is the representative of God on earth.

Method: Conditioning the individual through precept, example, memorization, and drill to live the Catholic life.

Position of the pupil: A soul to be saved.

Position of the teacher: An instrument of God to work through the church.

Evaluation: Degree to which pupil exhibits conformity to the ideal of the Catholic ideology.

Idealism

Proponent: J. Donald Butler.

Objectives—Aims—Purposes: Based on tradition, what has withstood the test of time, the cultural heritage. Aim to attain the good life of the spirit. Largely intellectual; to form an intellectual elite. Aims are distant and individualistic and are in terms of knowledge.

Subject matter—curriculum: Accumulated heritage of the race. The finest in literature, art, music, and ethics.

Method: Physical, mental, moral discipline. Reading, textbook, lecture, drill, memorization, recitation, controlled discussion.

Position of the pupil: A plastic mind to be molded. Much attention is given to the child and to individual differences.

Position of the teacher: All important, the purveyor of all culture.

Evaluation: In terms of how nearly the pupil has attained the ideal standards established by the best work, achievement, and tradition of the past and the specific standards set by the instructor.

Pragmatism—Experimentalism

Proponents: John Dewey, W. H. Kilpatrick, Boyd H. Bode.

Objectives—Aims—Purposes: Based upon the activities and goals of members of society and the interest of the learner. Objectives: to help the individual become a socially efficient member of a democratic society.

Subject matter—Curriculum: Socially desirable activities. Knowledge and skills of interest and use to the learner.

Method: Activity: mental, manual, physical, appreciative, social. Any method which motivates the learner and catches his imagination. A problem-solving approach which has its setting in the context of circumstances of the immediate or near future.

Position of the pupil: The learner is an individual who grows or develops from within through activity in a social setting and through the use of intelligence.

Position of the teacher: A guide who serves to stimulate pupils and to assist them in focusing on the issues involved in the areas under consideration.

Evaluation: Progress of the learner in terms of his native ability to master the facts, skills, and attitudes demanded by the social group of which he is a part. The degree to which pupils grasp crucial concepts, problems, or values, which have been, are, or should be operating in today's society.

Reconstructionism

Proponents: George S. Counts, Harold Rugg, Theodore Brameld.

Objectives—Aims—Purposes: To build a new social order that is consistent with current social and economic forces and is democratic in nature. To foster "frontier thinking," and the organization of "action groups" in schools, labor, politics, and in other phases of life. Move toward a planned democratic society.

Subject matter—Curriculum: Socially oriented. Future objectives take precedence over immediate interests or goals. Stress placed upon the development of social concerns, the anticipation of future needs, and leadership qualities.

Method: Any method which instills a sense of concern and responsibility in the learners for the direction of societal evolution or change.

Position of the pupil: A social member potentially capable of actively participating in the realization of future social objectives.

Position of the teacher: To direct and assist pupils in the acquisition of sensitivities and competencies necessary for social participation and leadership. To act as a stimulus in effecting directed social change.

Evaluation: Degree to which one becomes aware of, involved in, and committed to his responsibilities for reconstructing his society.

You may find some educators who combine or draw, in a piecemeal fashion, from various theories of education. These educators may be called eclectics. They feel that you cannot develop a unified or consistent pattern of beliefs. As a result, you must draw as you see fit from the attempts of others to do so. Such an approach, the eclectic maintains, is the only philosophically honest approach to the problem. This approach causes many to insist that eclecticism does not constitute a "school" of educational thought in the strictest sense of the term. There are those, however, who feel that an eclectic may have a consistent theory of education, although it may not agree with any one of the commonly accepted theories of education. The assumption upon which his theory is based may differ to some degree from those of other theories of education.

As you move forward in your preparation for teaching, the formulation of a consistent theory of education should be an item of first priority to you. In fact, it should be an item of major concern so long as you may teach.

SUMMARY

The influences of outstanding men and the various contributions of science briefly discussed in the preceding paragraphs have had a profound effect on the concepts and practices of education in the United States. Several different concepts of education have been noted in the development of educational theory.

The conventional concept of education centers upon formalism and routine procedure. It views the education process as that of "keeping school." According to this view, the materials of the curriculum have been selected, classified, graded, and organized into a program of subject matter and classes. The business of the school is to see to it that boys and girls acquire the content of this predetermined curriculum to train the mind, gain knowledge, and prepare for adult life. The master teacher is the one who can encourage, cajole, and drive the inherited content of the course into the minds of the pupils. Idealism, realism, and Neo-Thomism share certain commonalities in this respect.

The modern concept has grown out of attempts to free the school of its formalism, tradition, and selectivity. It centers its attention on the student rather than on subject matter—on stimulating and organizing the pupil's experiences so that his interests and needs may be used to facilitate learning. Units, projects, and activities are made a framework for learning, and the readiness of the pupil for a new kind of educational experience is carefully studied. Since, in a very real sense, students are viewed as having crucial uniquenesses, a variety of teaching techniques and materials attempt to provide for these individual differences. Internalized behavior is promoted through experiences in self-discipline and self-responsibility. Critical and diligent study of the most desirable forms of social life are undertaken to determine which skills, attitudes, and abilities should be built into the lives of the young. According to this concept, subject matter and the development of skills become means to an end rather than ends in themselves. Strains from Socrates, Plato, Aristotle, Rousseau, Pestalozzi, Locke, Comenius, William James, and Dewey, to name but a few, have all contributed to this approach. Exponents of schools of thought which hold these convictions have been identified as the experimentalists, pragmatists, and reconstructionists.

In connection with all of the above, an outline of the unique characteristics of some of the current conflicting theories of education has been presented within the precautionary framework of certain deceptive features of labeling and of notions of differences within as well as among groups. These are but some of the fundamental problems confronting all who try to develop a theory of education systematically.

By no means should this be interpreted either as an insurmountable obstacle or as merely "words, words, words." Rather, it is hoped that, through this introduction into the field of "The Development of Modern Concepts of Education," you have been alerted to some of the complexities involved in a disciplined study of this far-reaching and involved field called "education."

QUESTIONS FOR YOUR CONSIDERATION

1. In what ways have early concepts of education influenced modern educational practices?
2. What different concepts of discipline exist in homes and in schools today? What is your concept of discipline?
3. What contributions are the various fields of science making to education today?
4. What do educators mean when they talk about the "whole child" attending school? What are the implications of this concept for you as a teacher?
5. What competencies should a child have at the end of the sixth grade in school? Which of the concepts of education discussed in this chapter seems most likely to develop these competencies? Why?
6. What differences exist between training a dog and educating a child? Are there any similarities? Explain.
7. Which of the men mentioned in this chapter would you judge to have been ahead of their times? Explain.
8. What weaknesses do you find in the current theories of education indicated in this chapter?
9. Which theory of education seems to be most consistent with your thinking? Why?

ACTIVITIES FOR YOU TO PURSUE

1. Construct a historical calendar of outstanding thinkers and indicate their contributions to education.
2. Contrast the concepts of (a) man, (b) learning, and (c) subject matter used by some of the early thinkers as opposed to those of educators today.
3. Visit psychological laboratories, testing bureaus, and any similar facilities in order to see what contributions they make toward improving educational practices.
4. List some of the ways in which educational practice has lagged behind educational thinking today.
5. Prepare a summary or abstract of the personal life of one or more of the thinkers who lived before 1800.
6. Make a list of modern critics of education and indicate the points of criticism of each.
7. Analyze a number of your professors and secondary school teachers in terms of the theories of education to which they seem to subscribe.
8. Discuss with your colleagues the various current theories of education. Which seems to be the most defensible?

RESOURCE SECTION FOR PART V

CALENDAR OF SOME IMPORTANT
EVENTS IN EDUCATION

SUGGESTED READINGS

SUGGESTED FILMS, FILMSTRIPS,
AND RECORDINGS

FIGURE CREDITS

CALENDAR OF SOME IMPORTANT EVENTS IN EDUCATION

As you can sense from this chapter, a number of important events have occurred in the development of education in America. It may prove helpful to organize several in chronological order, so that you may get a bird's-eye view of them. For this reason the following calendar of events is presented.

1635	Founding of the Boston Latin School, first college preparatory school
1636	Founding of Harvard, first permanent college in English North America
1647	Massachusetts Act ("Old Deluder Act," which followed the 1642 law ordering that children be taught to read)—first general school law in America
1693	Founding of College of William and Mary, first permanent college in the South
1751	Chartering of Benjamin Franklin's Academy, representing the transition between Latin schools and a more practical curriculum
1785, 1787	Northwest Ordinances, the beginnings of national aid for education
1819	Famous Dartmouth College Decision of the U.S. Supreme Court, which established the inviolability of a college's charter
1821	First high school in the United States, in Boston
1839	Founding of the first state normal school, Lexington, Massachusetts
1848	First graded school in America, established at the Quincy Grammar School of Boston
1852	Enactment of the first compulsory school law, Massachusetts
1857	Founding of the National Teachers' Association, now the National Education Association
1862	Passage by Congress of Morrill Bill, which became the basis of land-grant colleges
1867	Federal agency now known as the U.S. Office of Education created by Congress
1873	First public kindergarten in the United States, in St. Louis
1874	Kalamazoo Decision by Michigan Supreme Court, which established a state's legal right to public funds for high schools
1890	Passage of the second Morrill Act, which provided for money grants to institutions of higher education
1893	Significant report of NEA Committee of Ten, first of a series of NEA reports with far-reaching effects on curriculum and standards
1897	Founding of the organization now known as National Congress of Parents and Teachers
1902	First junior college in the United States, in Joliet, Illinois
1909	First junior high schools, established at Berkeley, California, and Columbus, Ohio
1914	Smith-Lever Act, providing for extension work in agriculture and home economics
1917	Smith-Hughes Act, providing federal assistance for vocational education in public schools
1918	Publication of the Report on Reorganization of Secondary Education—"Cardinal Principles of Secondary Education"
1919	First public nursery school established in the nation
1920	Compulsory education became effective in all states
1923	Formation of World Federation of Education Associations, forerunner of the present World Confederation of Organizations of the Teaching Profession
1933	Federal government began aid to schools operating nonprofit school lunch programs
1937	Enactment of the George-Dean Act, which provided federal aid for vocational education and distributive education
1941	Publication of the Eight-year Study by the Progressive Education Association

1944, 1952	Enactment of GI Bill of Rights for World War II (Public Law 346) and Korean veterans
1945	Creation of United Nations Education, Scientific, and Cultural Organization (UNESCO)
1949	Organization of National Citizens' Commission for the Public Schools —a nonprofit organization designed to improve education
1950	National Science Foundation Act passed by Congress to promote basic research and education in the sciences
1952	Extension of the GI Bill of Rights to include those serving between June 27, 1950, and January 31, 1955 (Public Law 550)
	Ruling of the U.S. Supreme Court on released time for religious instruction
1954	Ruling of U.S. Supreme Court on nonsegregation in the public schools
1955	White House Conference on problems of school housing, finance, personnel, and organization
1958	Enactment by Congress of the National Education Defense Act, providing federal funds for the improvement of instruction in various subject areas and for guidance, audio-visual aids, and student loans and fellowships
1959	Publication of Conant's study: *The American High School Today*
1960	Golden Anniversary White House Conference on Children and Youth called by the President
1961	Establishment of the Peace Corps
1962	Controversy developed in Congress over Kennedy's proposals for federal aid for public school buildings construction and teachers' salaries
	Ruling of U.S. Supreme Court on prescribed prayers being required of pupils
	Manpower Developmental and Training Act passed by Congress to facilitate the retraining of laborers
1963	Higher Education Facilities Act passed by Congress to provide loans and grants for the construction of academic facilities for graduate schools, colleges, and technical institutes
	United States Supreme Court ruled that the reading of the Bible in public schools was unconstitutional
1964	Economic Opportunity Act passed by Congress
	Civil Rights Act (Public Law 88–352) provided for the U.S. Commissioner of Education to grant *on request* financial and technical assistance to public school systems having problems of desegregation
1965	Elementary-Secondary Education Act (Public Law 89–10) greatly expanded the federal role in financing public education Project Head Start, under the auspices of the Economic Opportunity Act
	Higher Education Act passed by Congress, providing for community services and continuing education programs, assistance to libraries, student assistance, strengthening developing institutions, establishment of a National Teachers Corps, and assistance for the purchase of special equipment for undergraduate institutions
1966	Extension of the GI Bill of Rights to all veterans discharged since 1955, except those who enlisted for a six-month period (Public Law 358)

SUGGESTED READINGS

The number in parentheses following each suggestion denotes the chapter for which it is best suited.

Anderson, Charnel: *Technology in American Education 1650–1900*, U.S. Office of Education, 1962. An excellent treatment of the history and background of instructional technology in American education. (13)

Barnard, Henry: *Henry Barnard on Education,* John S. Brubacher (ed.), Russell and Russell, New York, 1965. Discusses in detail the views of Henry Barnard and his contributions to education. (13)

Bayles, E. E., and B. L. Hood: *Growth of American Educational Thought and Practice,* Harper & Row, Publishers, Incorporated, New York, 1966. A good history of the development of educational thought in America. (14)

Bestor, Arthur: *The Restoration of Learning,* Alfred A. Knopf, Inc., New York, 1955. Describes the kind of education the author believes to be essential for democratic America in the mid-twentieth century. (14)

Bigge, Morris L.: "Theories of Learning," *NEA Journal,* vol. 55, no. 3, pp. 18–19, National Education Association, Washington, March, 1966. Presents representative theories of learning and their implications for education. (14)

Brameld, Theodore: *Education for the Emerging Age,* Harper & Row, Publishers, Incorporated, New York, 1961. Proposes a theory of education that is in keeping with the changes that most likely will take place in our society. (14)

Bruner, Jerome S.: *Toward a Theory of Instruction,* The Belknap Press, Harvard University Press, Cambridge, Mass., 1966. Indicates Bruner's concept of instruction and contains suggestions for improving instruction in schools. (14)

Butts, R. Freeman: "Search for Freedom: The Story of American Education," *NEA Journal,* vol. 49, no. 3, pp. 33–48, National Education Association, Washington, March, 1960. Describes how schools throughout the years have contributed to the freedom of our nation. (13)

Commager, Henry Steele: *Our Schools Have Kept Us Free!* National Education Association, National School Public Relations Association, Washington, 1963. Relates the dramatic role that schools have played in building our nation. (13)

Conant, James Bryant: *The American High School Today,* McGraw-Hill Book Company, New York, 1959. Contains a number of recommendations based upon an extensive study for improving the high schools. (14)

Edwards, Cecile Pepin: *Horace Mann: Sower of Learning,* Houghton Mifflin Company, Boston, 1958. An excellent biography of Horace Mann with emphasis upon his contributions to education. (13)

Edwards, Newton, and Herman G. Richey: *The School in the American Social Order,* Houghton Mifflin Company, Boston, 1963. A comprehensive discussion of the history of education in the United States. (13)

Hughes, James Monroe: *Education in America,* 2d ed., Harper & Row, Publishers, Incorporated, New York, 1965. Chapter 7 indicates ideas from European social movement that have affected American education. (14)

Hutchins, Robert Maynard: "Are We Educating Our Children for the Wrong Future?" *Saturday Review,* Sept. 11, 1965, pp. 66–67, 83. Raises a number of basic questions about the nature of education today. (14)

Kneller, George F. (ed.): *Foundations of Education,* John Wiley & Sons, Inc., New York, 1963. Chapter 1 presents a good sketch of the history of education. Chapters 2, 3, and 4 are concerned with philosophy in education, formal philosophies of education, and contemporary educational theories. (13, 14)

Krug, Edward A.: *Salient Dates in American Education, 1635–1964,* Harper & Row, Publishers, Incorporated, New York, 1966. Interestingly discusses the more important dates in the history of American education. (13)

————: *The Shaping of the American High School,* Harper & Row, Publishers, Incorporated, New York, 1964. A historical study of factors and forces that have shaped the American high school. (13)

Marshall, Robert: *The Story of Our Schools: A Short History of Public Education in the United States,* National Education Association, National Council for the Social Studies, Washington, 1962. An excellent brief historical sketch of public schools in the United States. (13)

Rickover, Hyman G.: *Education and Freedom,* E. P. Dutton & Co., Inc., New York,

1959. Stresses the fact that we must train better scientists and technicians, as well as more responsible citizens. (14)

Stone, James C., and Frederick W. Schneider: *Foundations of Education: Commitment to Teaching,* vol. 1, Thomas Y. Crowell Company, New York, 1965. Different philosophies of education are discussed on pp. 218–235. (14)

Thayer, V. T.: *Formative Ideas in American Education: From Colonial Period to the Present,* Dodd, Mead & Company, Inc., New York, 1965. A historical treatment of the ideas that have shaped the form and substance of education in America. (13)

Washburne, Carleton: *What Is Progressive Education?* The John Day Company, Inc., New York, 1952. Presents a brief, practical analysis of the progressive education movement and the meaning of the term "progressive education." (14)

Wilson, Charles H.: "Critics of the Schools Never Die, Either," *Saturday Review,* June 20, 1964, pp. 51–53, 69. Indicates what some of the critics may do in order to be more constructive in the improvement of education. (14)

Wynne, John P.: *Theories of Education,* Harper & Row, Publishers, Incorporated, New York, 1963. Identifies and describes twelve theories of education. (14)

SUGGESTED FILMS, FILMSTRIPS, AND RECORDINGS

The number in parentheses following each suggestion denotes the chapter for which it is best suited.

Films (16 mm)

All in a Lifetime (Potomac Films, 29 min). Depicts the changes which have come about in the American school system during the life of a senior citizen. Shows changes in buildings and in philosophies. Compares functions, needs, and objectives of earlier schools with those of the present day. (13)

American Teacher (March of Time, 15 min). Presents some pros and cons of the progressive education movement and points out the citizen's responsibility toward the schools; also gives a brief history of education in the United States, including the present emphasis upon psychology. (14)

Better Tomorrow (Overseas Branch of Office of War Information, 20 min). Shows progressive education systems in three New York schools, demonstrating how learning is connected with everyday experiences in children's lives on the preschool, junior high, and senior high school levels. (14)

Broader Concept of Method: Part I, Developing Pupil Interest (McGraw-Hill, 13 min). Presents typical student attitudes and responses to the conventional, teacher-dominated, lesson-hearing type of high school class recitation. Contrasts the effects of the informal, group discussion class in which students are permitted to share in the planning of the work and are thereby stimulated toward worthwhile and meaningful learning experiences. (14)

Colonial America in the Eighteenth Century (McGraw-Hill, 17 min, color). Presents an overview of the geography of the American colonies in the eighteenth century, showing boundaries, areas settled by various nationalities, and typical family and community life of the period. Discusses the reasons for immigration and indicates the influence of each major group on the colonies. Describes geographical differences among the Southern, Middle, and New England Colonies. (13)

Education in America: The Nineteenth Century (Coronet, 16 min, color). Describes significant historical developments and the changing character of American education in the nineteenth century. Points out contributing factors of change, such as the establishment of the first high school, problems growing out of the Civil War, the teachings of Horace Mann, compulsory laws, the trend toward uniformity under state regulations, and the beginning of teacher training schools. (13)

Education in America: The Seventeenth and Eighteenth Centuries (Coronet, 16 min, color). Gives historical background to the early developments in American education —in New England, the South, and the Middle Colonies. Relates the character of the different schools—dame, Latin grammar, private, parochial, pauper, academy, and college—to prevailing social, economic, and cultural conditions. (13)

Education in America: Twentieth-century Developments (Coronet, 16 min, color). Reviews significant developments in American education in the twentieth century and relates these developments to the social, economic, and cultural life of the nation. Considers the influences of outstanding educators, educational theories and movements, and major trends and problems. (13)

Experimental Studies in the Social Climates of Groups (Kurt Lewin, Iowa State University, 32 min). Presents a study of the effects of types of social organizations upon the attitudes and learning of junior high school children. The social climates developed in the experimental situations are democratic, laissez-faire, and autocratic. (14)

Horace Mann (Emerson Films, 19 min). Portrays important episodes in the life of Horace Mann, "the father of the common schools"; reviews his activities as teacher, lawyer, state senator, board of education member, and college president; emphasizes his work in pointing up the need for well-built schools, good textbooks, democratic methods of learning, schools for teachers, and universal education in the United States. (13)

Philosophies of Education: A Catholic Philosophy of Education (National Educational Television, 29 min). Points out that the realities of God and of Jesus Christ; the guidance, teaching, and influence of the Church; and the ideals of the Christian life are constantly presupposed. Within this integral framework all physical and intellectual disciplines have their place. (14)

Philosophies of Education: The Classical Realist Approach to Education (National Educational Television, 29 min). Defines "classical realism," putting special emphasis on definitions of each of the two words. Explains the theory's basis in the "natural law" and the theory's application to modern educational problems. Answers objections and comments on a filmed physics class discussion in which the teacher uses the classical realist approach. (14)

Philosophies of Education: Education as Intellectual Discipline (National Educational Television, 29 min). Comments on the importance of a disciplined mind and outlines the methods of obtaining intellectual discipline in a democratic society. Answers objections and comments on a filmed illustration. (14)

Philosophies of Education: Education for Cultural Reconstruction (National Educational Television, 29 min). States that reconstructionism is, above all, a goal-centered, future-oriented philosophy of education. It is one of the fundamental assumptions of reconstructionists that education has unprecedented tasks that would not exist in a more normal, less revolutionary, or less dangerous time. (14)

Philosophies of Education: An Experimentalist Approach to Education (National Educational Television, 29 min). Defines experimentalism as a systematic theory of education stemming from the work of John Dewey. States that the experimentalist turns *to* experience rather than *away* from it. Indicates that intelligence, operating in quite human ways in relation to quite human problems, will give the answers that are needed to bring the newly born infant to maturity. Elucidates the experimentalist viewpoint, answers objections, and comments on a film sequence of a "progressive" classroom. (14)

Philosophies of Education: A Protestant Philosophy of Education (National Educational Television, 29 min). Explains that diversity is part of the Protestant tradition and belief. States that although there is no single Protestant view, it is the Protestant heritage to drive toward excellence in education. Notes that any Protestant view holds that some appropriate way must be found of teaching in schools, that man does not live by bread alone, and that God exists and is sovereign. (14)

The School (Two Thousand Years Ago) (Gaumont-British, 15 min). Portrays the educational methods used by the Jewish people of Palestine at the time of Christ. Shows the techniques practiced in the instruction of boys in the formal temple schools and shows the girls in their informal learning at home, where their mothers were primarily responsible for the instruction. Stresses that most learning was based on reading, memorizing, and discussing the laws and the writings of the prophets. (13)

Section Sixteen (Westinghouse Broadcasting Company, 14 min). Describes the historical development of free, compulsory public education in the United States. Uses realistic settings and costumes to portray the character and spirit of the changing public school. Points out important legislation contributing to educational progress and observes other influences of major historical events upon education. Focuses attention upon the problems confronting public education today. (13)

Filmstrips
Bulwarks of Democracy (McGraw-Hill, 50 fr., color). Presents a historical sketch of the development of the American educational system, showing the early colonial private classes, the founding of the first American university, the growth of the public education system, the establishment of the first Negro college, and the growth of library facilities. (13)
Comenius (UNESCO, 50 fr.). Describes the teachings of John Amos Comenius, apostle of modern education and world understanding. (13)
Education in America (Museum Extension Service, 43 fr., color). Presents the story of the growth of education in America. (13)
Growth of American Education (Yale University Press, 40 fr.). A documentary on the first schools in America and the struggle for a free public school system. The influence of Horace Mann, Emma Willard, and other leaders. Graded schools and their effect. Private and parochial schools. Higher education, education for women, and the land-grant colleges. Educational opportunity as an expression of true democracy. (13)
Horace Mann (Encyclopaedia Britannica Films, 51 fr.). Portrays important episodes in the life of the "father of the common schools in the United States." Reviews the activities of a distinguished educator who helped to arouse the people's interest in raising their standards of education. (13)
Schools (International Visual Education Services, Inc., 33 fr., color). Points out that instead of lunchrooms and libraries and gymnasiums, the early settlers' children had to sit on benches and write on birchbark with goosefeather pens and homemade ink. Today's school children learn about the world, they learn to think, and they have teachers who help them to work alone and with others. (14)
School at Four Corners (Curriculum Films, 38 fr., color). A typical school day 100 years ago, reenacted in the school constructed at Farmers Museum. (14)
Your Educational Philosophy: Does It Matter? (Wayne University, 40 fr.). Presents a number of views of the classrooms of two teachers. Compares similar situations in these two classrooms to indicate how the teachers' educational philosophy affects the types of classroom activities planned for pupils. (14)

Recordings
Concept of Discipline (National Tape Recording Project, 60 min). Dr. Hymes lectures on the problem of discipline and the measures we can take to correct this. This program is on two tapes, 30 minutes each. (14)
Developing Good Classroom Discipline (Educational Recording Service, 33⅓ rpm). Myron S. Olson, Professor of Education, University of Southern California, presents new concepts of classroom discipline. (14)
Heredity and Environment (National Tape Recording Project, 15 min). How these factors work together in human development; limits imposed by heredity; setting up a stimulating environment. (14)
Lift a Mountain (University of Illinois, 15 min). A dramatized event in the life of Horace Mann, the father of American Education. (13)

FIGURE CREDITS

FIGURE 13–1. (*Source:* Calvin Grieder and Stephen Romine, *American Public Education: An Introduction,* The Ronald Press Company, New York, 1955, p. 97.)
FIGURE 13–2. (*Source:* Data from *Statistical Abstract of the United States,* U.S. Bureau of the Census, 1966, p. 128.)

VI

BROADER
CONCEPTS
OF
EDUCATION

The rapidity and complexity of change in the social, economic, political, and technological aspects of life present major problems in designing educational programs in keeping with the needs of youth, most of whom will be alive in the year A.D. 2000. These needs differ very significantly from the needs of youth 50 years ago. To what extent has the function of the school changed, and to what extent is it geared to these rapidly changing conditions? How can schools do an even better job of educating youth when they are faced with learning so much in so short a period of time?

Part VI is designed to help you view the broad aspects of education and the professional challenge with which teachers today are faced. In Chapter 15, attention is given to the changing nature of community living, to various community educative forces, and to the implications of these conditions for teaching. Chapter 16 indicates, for your consideration, some principles basic to our schools and some educational objectives that seem desirable. A number of other problems and issues which you will face are explored in Chapter 17. As you plan for teaching, weigh carefully the ways in which you can contribute effectively to the fuller realization of the school's function and to the solution of these issues and problems.

15
COMMUNITY EDUCATIVE FORCES AND THEIR IMPLICATIONS

What do we mean by the term "education"? Is it confined to the learning experiences that take place within the classroom? Where have you acquired the beliefs, attitudes, opinions, and behavioral patterns you possess? Actually you have been under the influence of the school only a very limited portion of your life. Until you were five or six years old, you probably had no direct exposure to the school. By the time you entered school, you had acquired a very significant amount of learning. After starting your formal education, you spent only about seven hours a day for approximately 180 days a year in a school setting. Hence, a considerable portion of your learnings and behavioral patterns has been derived from your out-of-school experiences.

In planning a career in teaching, you should give some consideration to the ways your work will be conditioned by the various educational forces within the community. Without an understanding of these forces and a conscious concern for them as you deal with each boy and girl in the classroom, you cannot successfully and effectively fulfill your function as a teacher.

Before we consider some of these forces and their educational implications, certain abstract terms should be defined. The term "community" refers to a group of people living together in a region where common ways of thinking and acting make the inhabitants somewhat aware of themselves as a group. Thus a community involves more than a geographic district, although certain factors limit its scope and others extend it outward until the boundaries are indeterminate.

The term "education" refers to the broad function of preserving and improving the life of the group through bringing new members into its shared concerns. Education is thus a far broader process than that which occurs in schools. It is an essential social activity by which communities continue to exist. In complex communities this function is specialized and institutionalized in formal education, but there is always the education outside the school with which the formal process is related. What is said here about the function of the schools relates to education in its broader sense.

UNDERSTANDING THE CHANGING NATURE OF COMMUNITY LIVING TODAY

Thoughtful students of American community life today are increasingly concerned with the profound social changes which have been occurring and, as was indicated in Chapter 1, will continue to occur in the years that lie ahead. You become more and more aware of these changes as phenomenal events draw attention to the new conditions under which you live. The increased use of automation and computerization, the use of atomic submarines and ships, the phenomenal growth of population, the explosion of knowledge, the launching of satellites, the orbiting of men in space, the planning of trips to the moon, and a host of other sensational developments have been experienced within the span of your life. These have focused attention upon the rapid, pervasive, and fundamental changes in our cultural scene. You can appreciate and plan for the proper role of the school in today's affairs only when you understand the consequences of these basic changes in living conditions. This understanding will help you avoid the tendency of teachers to impose upon youth the same values, beliefs, and modes of behavior that have characterized the past—thereby transmitting increasing incompetence for dealing with the future.

You will therefore want to give careful study to the ways in which our contemporary culture differs from that of the past. From this study, you should be able to gain clues to the new competencies that will be required of youth in order to make creative approaches to, and to deal more adequately with, the changing character of the future. The statements that follow should be considered as only the beginning of many with which all thoughtful teachers should be concerned.

1. *Community life today is increasingly affected by industrial and technological processes rather than by agrarian conditions and simple processes of production.* Inventions and new ways of making the basic commodities of life have moved from hand manufacture to a machine process which is largely automatic and highly technical in nature. Through mass production, enormous factories turn out great quantities of products. The simple agrarian life and modes of production of our forefathers (and in many other parts of the world today) are in sharp contrast with this industrial and technological proficiency. We note the creation of "new relationships between people, education, and work, with technical skills and knowledge, mental alertness, and creative capacities taking priority over capacities to endure hard physical labor" [134:2].

FIGURE 15–1. Changes in productivity of workers, 1850–1975. By 1975 each worker will produce almost twelve times as much as the worker of 1850. Each symbol represents 50 cents, at 1960 prices, of national income per man-hour of private employment. (*Source:* Twentieth Century Fund, Inc.)

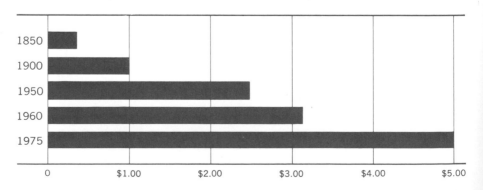

The increasing size and complexity of industry, business, and professional organizations result in growing needs for educational services. Since approximately 1955, professional, office, and sales workers as a group have exceeded for the first time in our history the number of persons employed in manual occupations. Likewise, the number of people employed in service occupations now exceeds that of persons engaged in farm occupations. The most rapid growth in the future, as indicated in Chapter 1, most likely will occur among professional and technical occupations. It is anticipated that the need for skilled craftsmen among the manual occupations will increase, but the number of unskilled jobs will stay about the same, which means, actually, that they will decrease in proportion to the others. A study of the occupational change in employment during the 1960s (see Figure 15-2) clearly indicates that the largest increases in employment are occurring in occupations requiring the most education and training. At the same time greater numbers of young people are entering the labor force where the demand for unskilled labor is not increasing.

2. *Extreme ease of production has led to a high standard of living for many of our people and a potentially higher standard of living for all our people.* In spite of the range of differences existing within our society, we enjoy the highest standard of living in the world. The results of our scientific and industrial knowledge have provided us with more of the material things than ever before. As compared to the past, we live in better houses, take more and longer vacation trips, engage in more outdoor activities, dine out more often, attend more sports activities, read more books, periodicals, and newspapers, listen to more records, engage in more hobbies, and attend more concerts, art galleries, and museums. In brief, the pattern of our lives has changed very significantly.

We began the 1960s with a gross national product of $500 billion. It is anticipated that we can reach a level of $1,115 billion by 1980. This means that we should be able to provide our expanding population with a much higher standard of living. The uses to which our production potential will be put is today a prob-

FIGURE 15–2. Employment trends by occupations, 1950 to 1970. During the 1960s, the employment needs of business and industry are changing considerably. (*Source:* U.S. Department of Labor.)

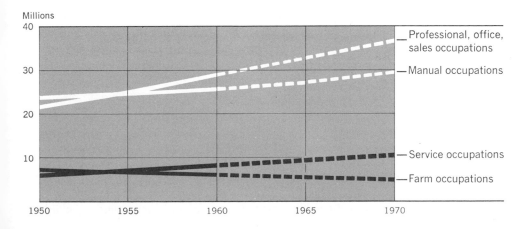

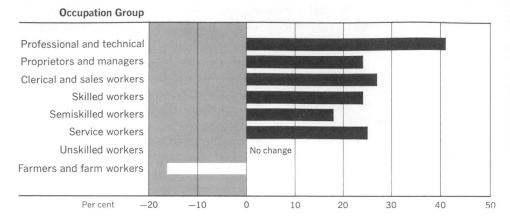

FIGURE 15–3.   Per cent change in employment, 1960–1970. The largest increases occur in occupations requiring the most education and training. (*Source:* U.S. Department of Labor.)

lem of top priority. How should a potentially stable economy of abundance be managed? How will this increased abundance affect the nature of community life and the lives of boys and girls? How may the role of the school and the work of a teacher be affected?

3. *Human energy is being used less and less to provide the energy of production.* Today mineral forms of energy—coal, petroleum, natural gas—are used to turn the wheels of industry. There are vast new sources of energy to use, control, and divert for purposes which must be determined. Unquestionably, in the near future atomic forms of energy will be used on an increasingly greater scale. Men and animals contribute less than 6 per cent of our energy output. On the other hand, more than 100 million persons may need to be working at some time during the year in 1980—a number equal to the total population of the United States around 1920 [157:48]. How can we deal with an increasing labor force and technological progress in which the man-hours required for the production of goods is decreasing?

4. *Modern living is increasingly urban.* Our forefathers lived close to the land and knew and used the soil for their livelihood, but today our people live in cities and are far removed from this. In 1950, 59 per cent of our population lived in urban areas. This percentage had increased to 70.6 in 1965 [207:9]. The major portion of the remaining 29.6 per cent lived in nonfarm rural locations and commuted to urban areas for employment. Figure 15-4 shows the approximate percentage of decline in farm employment from 1960 to 1970. During this period of time, decided increases have been occurring in such occupational groups as professional and technical workers, proprietors and managers, clerical and sales workers, skilled and semiskilled workers, and service workers. For the most part, these occupations are located in urban areas. What changes in the character of living and the education needs of youth will result from this increase in urbanization?

5. *Vast differences exist in the economic and cultural backgrounds of children,*

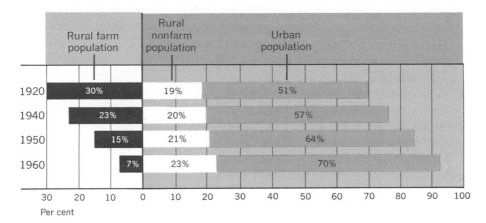

FIGURE 15–4. Decrease in farm population. In 1920 almost one of every three persons lived on a farm. In 1964, only one of every fourteen Americans was a farm dweller. What will the situation be in 1980? (*Source:* Twentieth Century Fund, Inc.)

especially in our large cities. As cities become larger, increasing numbers of boys and girls, particularly those who live in the slum sections, may be considered to be disadvantaged. In the first year (1965) of experimentation with Project Head Start, some rather startling facts were found in regard to preschool disadvantaged children. About one-third of them had some significant health defects. Ten per cent of them had psychological difficulties that were sufficiently severe to prevent normal functioning. It was not uncommon to find children who did not know what

FIGURE 15–5. School grades of youth leaving before high school graduation. Probably 30 per cent of all young workers entering the labor force during the 1960s and early 1970s will lack a high school education. What should the school attempt to do for these boys and girls? (*Source:* U.S. Department of Labor.)

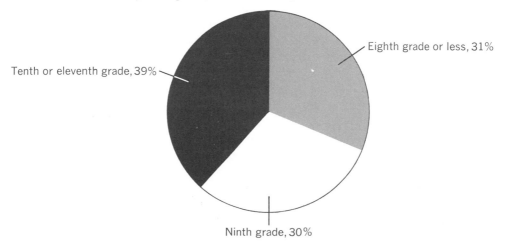

they looked like, since they had never seen themselves in a mirror. The experience background as well as the vocabulary of many were extremely limited. They had little to talk about, and the motivation to learn was meager indeed.

Large numbers of the disadvantaged either drop out or graduate from school without any hope of continuing their education, regardless of their abilities. They experience major difficulty in finding employment and a role to play in an increasingly complex, technological society. How may teachers gain a better understanding of the backgrounds and values held by disadvantaged children and their families? How may the school respect the ethnic and cultural differences which these boys and girls hold and, at the same time, provide them "with the tools of an education adequate to guarantee them the competence to make their own choices regarding how they wish to live, to work, to play" [141:75]?

6. *Today production and consumption are far apart.* In the days of our fathers and grandfathers, goods were produced and consumed at home. Today the production of one industrial worker is geared to the production of many others, and the product is distributed to consumers thousands of miles away. Between producers and consumers are many intermediary occupations of handling, shipping, advertising, billing, and financing. Certain problems arise concerning the relationships between them. How can the production and consumption of goods be managed in so complex a culture?

7. *Increased standardization of policies, procedures, and products has resulted in increased pressures toward conformity.* The frontiersman and the farmer lived close to the land. Their welfare depended heavily upon the use of individual initiative, hard work, and ingenuity in solving problems and in improving their status in life. Mechanization, unionization, standardization, and pressures toward conformance tend to inhibit individuality and creativity at a time when these qualities are especially needed. How can the school assist the young in making creative approaches to the solution of the increasingly complex problems in our society? How can each boy and girl achieve individuality, develop his talents to the fullest, and make his maximum contribution to society?

8. *Today we can communicate readily, so that the other side of the globe is immediately in touch with local events here.* Communication advances have shrunk distances, making each local community a neighbor of every other and bringing people into close contact with the events, customs, and concerns of other cultures. How can we gain a better understanding of the cultures, institutions, mores, languages, and aspirations of all people?

9. *Productivity, new markets, new economic and distributive occupations, communication, and urbanization have been influenced by new patterns of ownership.* Today's society is corporate. Yesterday's society was characterized mainly by individual ownership and direct proprietary control over the means of production. Today the ownership of industry is diffused. The stockholder or bondholder rarely understands or manages to any appreciable degree the enterprises in which his money is invested. Furthermore, many industries are now organized into large corporations. Labor groups are similarly highly organized and are corporate in character. The forces which direct our economic and productive affairs are corporate groups that are increasingly directed by professional managerial experts. Today you find your functions more and more in terms of the groups with which

you come in contact. What is good citizenship, and how can you educate for it in the modern economic world?

10. *The conditions of modern living mean that money and the media of exchange occupy a far more important position in people's lives today than they did formerly.* The processes of exchange were more simple and more direct in the agrarian society. Today people are called upon to make decisions about matters which have far-reaching consequences in other aspects of our economy. The problems of regulating an industrial, money-based society call for different skills and for skills that are more complicated than those needed in earlier days. How can you determine, acquire, and lead others to achieve economic literacy?

A research group of United States business executives, called the Committee for Economic Development, was so concerned with the economic illiteracy of high school graduates that it created the National Task Force on Economic Education, which, in turn, has formulated a description of the minimum understanding of economics essential for good citizenship and attainable by high school students. The Task Force stresses the kind of economic teaching that will lead students to examine and think through major economic problems such as actions of labor unions, the farm problem, and the social security problem.

During the 1960s approximately 70 per cent of the new young entrants to the labor force have been high school graduates or better, compared with 60 per cent in the 1950s [156:15]. Approximately 2.5 million of the 7.5 million non-high school graduates who enter the labor force during the 1960s have not completed a grade school education [156:16]. How can we encourage more boys and girls to further their education? What kinds of education best suit those pupils who leave school early? How can we do a better job of counseling and guiding these boys and girls?

11. *Today our population is highly mobile.* Modern transportation facilities and a generally high standard of living in an economy which is extremely productive make it possible for people to move about with great ease. A rising birth rate leads to a larger eventual labor supply with a corresponding increase in mobility. This means that people no longer may be educated to fit the requirement of only

FIGURE 15–6. Reasons for migration. At least half of the reasons why men workers between 18 and 64 years of age, who migrated between March, 1962, and March, 1963, were related to employment. *(Source:* U.S. Department of Labor.)

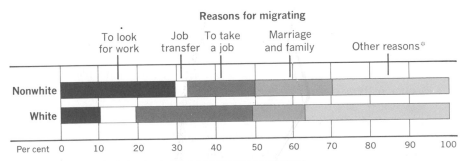

*Includes such reasons as better housing, health, and residing far from place of work.

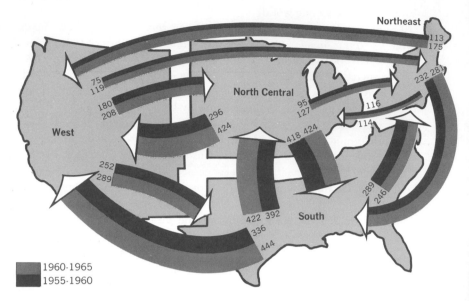

FIGURE 15–7.   The average annual flow, expressed in thousands of migrants, between various regions of the United States for the periods 1955 to 1960 and 1960 to 1965. What effect will this migration have upon communities and schools? *(Source:* U.S. Bureau of the Census.)

one restricted community. They are much more in touch with each other and consequently know more about how others live. Personal aspirations are altered as the possibilities of a better life are experienced firsthand.

Millions of workers change jobs every year. Today, approximately 20 per cent of all the families in the United States move yearly to gain better jobs, health, or climate, or for other reasons. Most of these moves are toward urban areas. More than 8 million different workers make 11.5 million job changes every year [156:12]. About two-thirds of these job changes involve completely different industries, and one-half of them involve completely different occupational groups. More than 3.5 million workers move to a different state during a period of one year.

Much of the mobility of people is "from the open country and smaller towns and villages to large centers of population and from the centers of cities to the suburbs, with the inevitable consequences of culture clashes that shake institutions, disturb long-established customs, set values in new perspective, color political action, disrupt systems of school support, and leave indelible marks on the behavior patterns and characters of children" [134:3]. How can we educate in an age which feels the consequences of mobility for an increasing percentage of its population?

12. *We are living in a highly interdependent world community.* A dislocation in one major industry affects the industrial actions, health, and economic wellbeing of large numbers of people in distant areas. War today is a concern of all

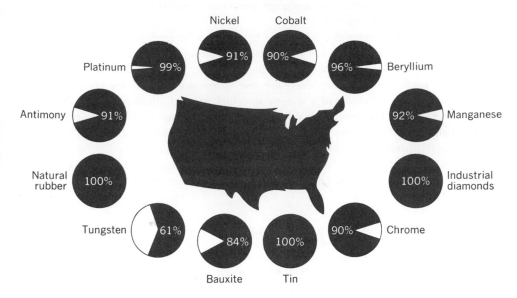

Imports

United States production

Based on 1959 data

FIGURE 15–8.   Strategic materials from other free nations are essential to United States industry. What are the implications of this situation for schools and for our society? (*Source:* U.S. Bureau of Public Affairs.)

the people; depression is global in proportions. Having all people produce and control the energies now at their disposal seems imperative. What are the skills and knowledges necessary to enable people to live together in this complex, interdependent society?

13. *In the agrarian society of the past, producers of goods planned for their continued production, and the goods produced were disposed of in the market-place according to the supply and the demand.* Today people are increasingly aware that planning involves much more extensive control over the making and distributing of goods. The government tries to exert some control over the modern industrial economy, which does not seem to regulate itself. Does this condition call for a new attitude and a readiness to experiment with the enlarged function of government?

14. *The older controls in our social life no longer operate as they did in our earlier agrarian period.* The family, for instance, was at one time an institution around which centered the production and marketing of goods, personal services such as laundering and tailoring, recreation of all members, and a large part of the group's education and worship. Today practically all these activities are performed through some other community institution or organization. The parent used to supervise the chores of the young, but today if work is available, children are generally without the supervision of a parent or teacher. What is the place of

the school in providing for learnings previously guided by parents at home and now largely unsupervised?

15. *Today's community life seems to many to be highly impersonal compared with small-town agrarian life in the past.* In the contemporary metropolitan area the individual is often unknown to his neighbor; personal identity becomes lost in the confusion of urban life. Here one is less accountable for his actions, less subject to the pressures of a society in which every individual is well known by his neighbors. The problems of finding an adequate sense of belonging and competency seem to become more difficult under such conditions. How can the school promote physical and mental health under modern conditions?

16. *Youth today face a variety of pressures as they seek to establish identity and to find a place in an increasingly complex society.* It has been said that [272:16]:

The American teen-ager today is a culture unto himself, some 25 million bundles of energy strong. The teen-ager, warned by harried parents and teachers that he must not fail, wooed by advertising as a commercial gold mine, wrestling to find a niche within the often cruel social strata of his peers, worried by his own empathic nature, and wistful about growing up, is these things and more, while at the same time trying to adjust to all that adrenalin.

Teen-agers are leaving childhood earlier, staying in school longer, buying more automobiles, clothing, phonograph records, and cosmetics than ever before, and almost weekly inventing a new dance. They are aware of their special place in society, and that place is at once a comfort and an irritant.

Why are young people increasingly concerned about, and taking a more active role in, the civil rights movement? Why do they feel greater difficulty in relating to their parents? Why has there been a decided increase in the incidence of teen-age suicides and ulcers? How can the school help young people in their attempts to establish identity, a sense of belonging, a feeling of adequacy, and a purpose in life?

17. *Technological advancements provide increasingly greater amounts of leisure time.* In 1859, a little more than a hundred years ago, the average worker in our society had only 12 hours of leisure time each week. It is predicted that by 1975 the average amount of leisure time for workers will be 52 hours a week. Some economists forecast that by 2050, a man will work only one day each week, spending the other six at leisure. According to Jackson M. Anderson, assistant executive secretary of the American Association of Health, Physical Education, and Recreation, the average worker since 1929 has gained one full day of leisure a week, and nearly one additional week a year for extended vacations.[1] Each year Americans now spend more income for leisure-time pursuits than for all public elementary and secondary schools.

It has been estimated that Americans spend over $48 billion a year on travel. Approximately 38 million engage in boating, 20 million camp, 8 million water-ski, 32 million bowl, 5 million play golf, and millions more participate in tennis, badminton, and various other sports; 14 million attend concerts, 11 million play

[1] From an address delivered at the Department of Elementary School Principals Association Annual Meeting, St. Louis, Mar. 27, 1960.

FIGURE 15–9.   Decline in nonfarm workweek. By 1975, the average workweek is expected to be 37 hours. What educational needs will arise from this increased amount of leisure time? (*Source:* Twentieth Century Fund, Inc.)

musical instruments, 10 million paint, 20 million attend major league baseball games, 22 million attend college football games, and 56 million go to the races. Approximately 30 million Americans go fishing each year, 20 million enjoy shooting and hunting, and 5 million participate in archery. Most of us engage in some type of social activity, such as attending club meetings, square dancing, visiting with friends, playing some form of cards, and the like. Millions of people spend time on such hobbies as stamp collecting, gardening, photography, and music. Many people spend part of their leisure time conscientiously trying to improve their lives as well as the lives of others. They contribute their time and talents to church work, charitable agencies, boy and girl scouts, school activities, and a host of other activities designed to improve life in their communities.

In spite of the constructive benefits that have been derived from the increased amount of leisure time available to the average individual, some questions having educational significance may be raised. How can we account for the low state of physical fitness of children, youth, and adults throughout America? Why, according to J. Edgar Hoover, has serious crime reached the highest point in history, and why is it increasing four times as fast as the population? How constructively do those over 65 years of age spend their time? Why have so many homes, the basic unit in our society, disintegrated because of the high divorce rate?

Our future generations will be faced increasingly with problems concerning the wise use of vast amounts of leisure time that will be theirs. Toynbee, the great historian, finds that never in the history of man has any nation been able to accumulate a vast amount of leisure time for its people and survive. Is it possible for us to avoid disintegration as a result of mass leisure?

18. *While the forces suggested so far have been molding the world today, people's lives and thinking have also been influenced by the growth of science.* Many events which used to be explained by magic or supernatural intervention are now being explained through objective investigation into their causes and conditions. People are becoming scientifically minded, but at the same time they are faced with many problems which they do not solve in conformity with the requirements of modern science. They are scientific in making automobiles but unscientific in using them. They are scientific in measuring intelligence but find

it difficult to determine the use to which intelligence should be applied. Science will doubtlessly continue to affect our lives more and more. What kinds of minds must be developed to deal with the new worlds which science offers?

19. *Today's society demands the conditions of peace and peaceful settlement of competing international interests.* Though the need of cooperative endeavor is recognized, the threat of global war continues. Conflicting ideologies continue to grip the world, "with much of the public budget, much public policy, much effort in military defense, much of the economic resources of the country, and much of the thoughts of people devoted to meeting this challenge" [134:3]. With new forms and forces of destruction loose in the world, society is in critical need of some form of international sovereignty. In the time of Alexander the Great, the soldier with one spear killed one enemy. Napoleon's cannon with one firing killed 12; the Big Bertha of World War I killed 88; Hitler's V-2 rocket killed 168. An American B-29 dropped one atomic bomb and killed 66,000 people [186]. The testing of multimegaton bombs, as well as the talk of astroidal bombs, dramatically displays man's increasing ability to destroy his fellows and the imperative necessity for determining the causes of war and for arriving at a program for implementing the conditions of peace. How are wars begun in the minds of men, and by what processess may the defenses of peace be constructed?

20. *Today's society is one in which an understanding of totalitarianism and an ability to meet its challenge are imperative.* With the current trend toward dictatorship, an enlightened citizen should study the significance of the suppression of the individual's thoughts and actions, not only in the international scene but also in our domestic affairs, and be prepared to oppose tyrannies over free men's self-government. This ability to lay bare the basis of totalitarianism is of crucial importance today; in our technological society the bigotry of the demagogue may immediately reach a whole people rather than be merely disseminated by word of mouth from one speaker to a handful of others. The forces which make for tyranny over the minds of men may use the devices of modern science for their own purposes. To find ways of disclosing the purposes and evaluating the efforts of totalitarianism of all kinds is an imperative need in modern society.

21. *The citizen today needs to make finer and more subtle discriminations in what he says and hears than did his ancestors.* Through radio, movies, television, and the press, modern citizens receive opinions and attitudes which tend to be uncritical expressions of emotion and exhortation rather than critically examined statements of conviction. "Different ethnic, racial, and cultural groups of people are vigorously struggling for recognition, full rights, fair employment practices, nondiscrimination in housing, and higher levels of living. Pressure tactics, emotional displays, and florid propaganda displace reason and the exercise of sober judgment in approaches to the solution of common problems" [134:3].

We are asked to distinguish between groups, interests, and pressures whose purposes are not always explicit and whose avowals may be different from the intentions which underlie them. To avoid a feeling of hopelessness, anxiety, and frustration, it is necessary to have the techniques and skills by which a thoughtful evaluation may penetrate to the real significance of what goes on in contemporary society. What is the difference between liberal and subversive activities, indoctrination and education, freedom and license, control and dictatorship?

These characteristics of modern living are of course not exhaustive of the changes that have occurred in our culture, but they are representative. They reveal some of the modern conditions with which you as teachers are faced. They set the stage on which you are to act. They define the requirements of the context in which you must develop professional proficiencies. If schools are to keep pace with the conditions of modern life, they should consider how well they are meeting the demands of the contemporary social scene. To what extent has education been aware of the pervasive changes of modern living, and to what extent has it defined the content and methods of formal education in terms of these conditions?

COMMUNITY EDUCATIVE FORCES

According to the broader meaning of education, all the activities of a community which influence the growing individual are educative. These activities vary widely from simple to extremely complex community influences. The way in which people rear their children, the manner they employ in greeting each other, the way in which they choose and wear their clothes, the methods through which they use their natural resources, the ways in which they compete or cooperate, and the way in which they carry on a number of other activities are fundamental community characteristics which enter the experiences of a child and constitute part of his education.

Almost no child can escape his community. He may not like his parents, or the neighbors, or the ways of the world. He may groan under the processes of living, and wish he were dead. But he goes on living, and he goes on living in the community. The life of the community flows about him, foul or pure; he swims in it, drinks it, goes to sleep in it, and wakes to the new day to find it still about him. He belongs to it; it nourishes him, or starves him, or poisons him; it gives him the substance of his life. And in the long run it takes its toll on him, and all he is [19:7].

Examples of Community Educative Forces

Numerous examples could be given of the community forces that enter into the education of young people. Since you probably will devote considerable attention to these forces in subsequent courses, only a very few will be discussed at this time.

The family. In spite of the changes that have taken place, the family undoubtedly is the most basic educational agency in the lives of boys and girls. It is here that foundational attitudes and habits are formed. In satisfying the child's basic needs for food, shelter, and the other requirements of growth, the mother builds into the infant the attitudes and understandings of which that particular society approves.

As a result of the work of Margaret Mead and other cultural anthropologists, it is now known that some communities encourage attitudes of withdrawal from reality; other societies encourage patterns of affection and cooperation; still other

By drawing upon the out-of-school experiences and informal learnings of their students, teachers can enrich students' formal learning in the classroom. (*Photograph from Marie Fraser.*)

communities encourage feelings of conflict and competition by a severe pattern of child development [162]. This process of encouraging fundamental dispositions which may operate through the lifetime of the individual is a basic aspect of community influence upon the individual. Although it is most evident in simple societies that lie some distance away, the same educational process is occurring continuously in our own immediate families. Those skills and abilities approved and valued by a community are encouraged in the early family interactions. The fundamental habits which are recognized as normal by the community are built into the lives of the young by the parents. The parents endeavor to eliminate those habits which seem undesirable and abnormal. In this way the basic motivations of the young are channeled and directed.

Community pressures may be so reflected through the actions of father and mother that the youngster feels that he belongs and has genuine affection in the home. On the other hand, the community tensions and problems may have such an effect upon the family relation that the youngster feels a lack of acceptance and intimate belongingness within this primary social group. These basic social-psychological habits of adjustment are learned to a large extent in the formative years of early childhood through the interpretations which the father, mother, sister, and brother extend to each individual. Feelings of inadequacy in performance and in status and privilege in regard to other people begin in the early years in the home and are continuously developed as the child matures in his family group. From these early experiences the individual's value structure—that which is deemed worthy and worthwhile—is molded. The wishes and aspirations as well as the frustrations and disturbances which more mature people find basic in their experiences may frequently be traced back to the early educational patterns of the home. How has the educational pattern of your home affected your life? Identify two radically different home environments and study the extent to which specific behavioral patterns of children in these homes are being affected. If you were the teacher of these children, what adjustments would you make in your work?

Peer and adult groups. As the child develops, his maturing interests and abilities bring him into intimate contact with playmates. Here he learns habits and dispositions of behavior appropriate for his peers. He comes to find out that some of his wishes may run counter to those of his peers and that his own desires and urges must be controlled and modified in the light of their habits and attitudes. In brief, he learns that his skills, habits, and attitudes have to be related to what other group members may choose and be able to do.

Gradually the growing youngster reaches out from his early intimate contacts with parents, siblings, and playmates and becomes aware of various adult members of the social world around him. He learns that some of the community functions are performed by certain adults and not by others. He obtains an early view of the various occupations which a community contains, the specialized skills and abilities which mark off one member from another. These occupational influences are reflected in his early childhood games; he plays at being the milkman, the doctor, the schoolteacher, the nurse, the policeman.

In many instances the growing child finds himself in conflict with the attitudes and behavior patterns of his broadening adult world and finds that he must make some kind of adjustment to a community which does not afford him the satisfactions which he seeks. For example, consider the following case and the related educational implications [19:48]:

Isabel is unhappy and sensitive because her family is one of the Spanish-speaking families in the community with many of the home ways of the Spanish-American culture. Isabel feels that she is rejected and her family is rejected by the other children because their ways are "different." It is the problem of the school to help Isabel appreciate her parents' culture in order that she may not have her security in her home threatened. At the same time she needs to learn American ways in order that she may be accepted by the other children. In the curriculum activities connected with home improvement Isabel may find help in her difficulties.

The life of the gang may also be so influenced by the community attitudes toward the young that the members of the gang find no room for performances which are to them important. As a result, boys and girls may form social groups which endeavor to provide satisfactions for the members which are not available elsewhere. For example, the delinquency gang is to be understood primarily as a manifestation of the inadequacy of the contemporary American community to satisfy the growing demands of young people in that community. The gang itself is an educative agency which develops from the community patterns and which seeks to satisfy the fundamental needs of its members.

Special-purpose agencies. There are social influences, in addition to those characterized by face-to-face intimate relationships with other people, which develop from special purposes within community life. They attempt to fulfill some specific need of the members. For example, a Sunday school or a scout troop or a group in school is a community agency which seeks to fulfill a special function such as providing religious training, experiences in out-of-door living, or training in becoming a mature member of the society. Can you identify all these organized secondary groups in your home community that are influencing growing children by building into them a knowledge of the approved ways of behaving? How have they affected your life?

The many secondary groups in which boys and girls receive their education may be dichotomous in emphasis, scope, and purpose. What is learned within our group as normal and desired behavior may be regarded in another group as fundamentally undesirable and subject to penalty. For example, a scout troop may value trustworthiness and honesty highly, whereas a boys' gang may reward its members for such practices as stealing and lying. The various community influences may thus be inharmonious and contradictory, and the youngster may have considerable difficulty in relating what he learns in one social situation to his activities in another. Can you identify any such influences in your home community, and to what extent were you affected by them?

In one sense growing up in the community means encountering conflicting roles, statuses, and values in various situations and learning to compromise and amalgamate them into a relatively consistent and harmonious way of behaving.

Consider the college student who, in planning his career in teaching, wrote as follows:

> I became a combination bell hop and odd job boy for a hotel. As I look back now, I can see that this experience taught and filled a void in my makeup that school and home had been unable to touch. I earned my own money, managed my time, and saved that money through planning. The responsibilities and the self-confidence that I received were compensation enough for that job. Above all, I think it was the contact with the adult world of people that left the greatest and most lasting impression on me. I met older people; I learned discernment in judging people and caution in accepting them. I heard men talking in the lobbies; I knew of their actions. I saw and heard things that were not according to the moral code that I, my family, and the school had established. I wondered at it. I thought that perhaps moral rules and living principles were things that you implicitly believe until you reach an age when you see into them. I became skeptical. I saw that the ideals my elders had taught me were lightly regarded by themselves. I wonder even yet that I survived this critical period.

You can sense that this student experienced considerable learning from his work experience. With what conflicting values was he confronted? How did he seem to resolve them? What effect did his home life apparently have upon the manner in which he resolved these conflicts? To what extent did his formal school experiences apparently help him in facing such problems? Should teachers feel a responsibility for preparing students to face such problems? What values did this student gain from his work experience?

Reflect upon your own life and attempt to identify some of the many experiences outside the classroom that have shaped your thinking and behavior. Consider how these experiences affected your school experiences. To what extent did your teachers take into account, or fail to take into account, these community learnings as they planned your school experiences?

Communication media. The rapid expansion of the many forms of communication has increased the number of community groups to which the developing child is exposed. In the United States alone there are more than 3,500 A.M. radio stations, 1,200 commercial and 250 educational F.M. stations, 660 commercial and 90 educational TV stations, 1,760 daily newspapers having a circulation of

60 million, 550 Sunday papers with a circulation of 50 million, 9,500 weekly newspapers with a circulation of 35 million, 800 commercial magazines, 3,500 trade and technical magazines, numerous religious, agricultural, labor, and professional publications, and a host of comic books and movies. Besides all this, the perfection of communication satellites will add further dimensions, via television and radio, to the visual and aural environment of children as well as of adults.

All these media bear upon the way youngsters feel and think. As you analyze some of the programs on television, for example, you recognize that some of them are in direct contradiction to the values we hope children will develop. Research findings indicate that juvenile delinquency can be linked conclusively to crime and violence in television shows [178:3]. There is evidence to indicate that excessive television viewing can make a child ill. "Symptoms of the illness are anxiety, chronic fatigue, loss of appetite, headache, and vomiting" [178:3]. Time spent in viewing television occupies a very significant number of the waking hours of the average child, parent, and older person. Advertisements in print and on the air influence the needs and desires of people. Various organizations and institutions of the community can reach large numbers easily, rapidly, and vividly. They serve to influence the members of the community to do things in a particular way, to spend their money for certain products, to think about other people according to certain stereotypes, and to project themselves into the ways in which other people behave or would like to behave. How will you as a teacher attempt to deal with these kinds of community learnings of youth?

Recreational facilities. The recreational facilities of a community are particularly important educational influences today. They do not center in the activity of the family, as was the case a generation or so ago. In this modern period of rapid transportation and communication our pastimes tend to be outside the family. Movies, dance halls, taverns, bowling alleys, pool halls, swimming pools, beaches, club rooms, skating rinks, amusement parks, carnivals, race tracks, and recreation

The recreation facilities of a community have significance for teen-agers. What lack of proper facilities and recreational programs might this picture suggest? (*Photograph from the film* Mike Makes His Mark *by the National Education Association.*)

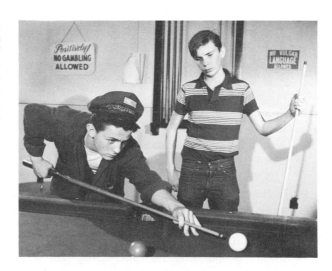

centers are aspects of the modern community which satisfy our desire for new experiences, for excitement, for escape from the monotony of the work world, and for doing what other people do. The high degree of mobility of youth creates situations in which an increasing number of their activities are unsupervised by adults concerned with the character and moral development of the young. These community influences channel and divert the ways in which young people grow. They lead youth to expect to participate in the activities which they see and hear about. How many recreational facilities and what kinds of facilities are available in your community? Are these recreational facilities supervised in such a manner that they promote or hinder the character and moral development of the young? In what ways did these facilities help or hinder your development?

Other forces. Such community forces are only a few of the many that tend to mold the developing behavior patterns of boys and girls. A more exhaustive listing certainly would include the influences of geographic and ecological conditions; organized religious, economic, and political institutions (church, bank, store, police department, court); the formal educational agencies in addition to the school (library, museum, art gallery); the service clubs, labor unions, and farm groups; the work experiences of youth, which provide direct contact with the life of the community; the socioeconomic levels, through which youth learn the discriminations of the established social order and take on the stereotypes, prejudices, and discriminatory attitudes of a particular socioeconomic class. Gain a thorough understanding of these and many other forces as you consider them in subsequent college courses.

Generalizations Regarding Community Educative Forces

Concerning the many educative forces at work in the community, the following significant generalizations may be drawn:

1. The school operates as a formal educational agency within the context of other formal and informal educational influences. The school itself appears as only one of the assets of the community. Some of the informal educational influences, television, radio, movies, and the press, seem to be more influential than the school in determining the ways in which boys and girls develop.

2. Community influences are extremely varied in their effect upon youth. They range from the formative influence of the family to the conversations at the corner drugstore; from the Sunday school class to the gang; from the community library to the crystal gazer of the carnival. Apparently some appraisal, selection, and control over these educational influences are necessary if a young person is to be able to discriminate and profit from his exposure to them.

3. The child is molded in skills, attitudes, habits, concepts, motives, and values by the forces in the community that bear effectively upon his development. In some communities, for example, the skills of weaving may be given such an emphasis that they become much more important than the skills of reading and writing. The community also educates boys and girls to take certain attitudes toward people who are different—in skin color, for instance. By the time the youngster is of school age the community has already established within his be-

havior pattern the readiness to respond in a particular way. The community may also dictate that some things are not to be discussed in an open fashion, for example, matters pertaining to sex. The habits of the community expressed in its folkways and institutions are basic in determining the types of responses which the boy or girl may make.

Concepts, beliefs, and ideas are also directed by community influences. In our country the concepts of free enterprise, private property, and unrestrained competition are built into the individual through many aspects of group living. In another nation, beliefs in government control over enterprise, state ownership of property, and direction by a central authority of prices and wages make for other concepts regulating social organization.

The motives that drive people vary as well. Some appear to reach throughout all the levels of the community. Boys and girls are taught, for example, to strive to rise in social position, to value material rewards of success, to base many of their habits on the profit motive. At the same time the habits of one socioeconomic class may cause its young to be motivated by goals which do not influence members of another class. Some children may be taught to value formal education very highly; others may place a low value upon it. The level of aspiration of the individual may be determined in very fundamental fashion by his socioeconomic position.

Judgments are also affected. Youngsters who have found that they are discriminated against or that other members of the society exploit them or their kind may have an evaluation of democracy which differs from that of children brought up under conditions which protect them from exploitation and discrimination. Young people are likely to deem worthwhile those things which their community perpetuates to satisfy their basic needs.

4. Community influences change as the individual develops. In the early years of a child's growth the family seems to be the primary source of his education. But as he matures, other community agencies take on a much more important educational role. The child learns to conform to and depend upon his family for the satisfactions of most of his needs. In later childhood and adolescence he learns to grow out from the family, to identify himself with other institutions, and to seek his satisfaction independent from the family patterns.

In planning to teach, make a study of the various conflicting and contradictory influences which bear upon children and their development. There is a profusion of community educational influences. The individual may be pushed in one direction by one force and in an opposite direction by another. The contradictory nature of many of these community influences should lead you to consider carefully what the function of the teacher is in such a context. This problem seems particularly important today when the modern American community is being subjected to many novel influences and many forces which extend the school experiences beyond the local boundaries of a particular restricted region.

SUGGESTIONS FOR YOUR TEACHING

The previous discussion leads to the conclusion that it is hazardous for the school to ignore the wider educational influences of the community. If teachers continue to separate the learnings of the classroom from the learnings of the broader community, as they have in the past, the school will experience decreasing influence in the lives of boys and girls. As you prepare for teaching, formulate plans for making the school a more realistic agency in the lives of youth.

In making a decision as to how you will function as a teacher, consider the following implications of the educational forces in community life. Not all these implications are of equal importance, nor are they separate in their meaning and importance.

Become Familiar with the Community's Development

Whenever a teacher enters a community, he finds it to be already structured in terms of its educational patterns. These patterns have been in operation for a long time and have acquired status and prestige. They have become the way they are by a process of growth. Study the history of the community's educative processes in order to gain a thorough understanding of them. This does not mean that you must learn in a routinized fashion the dates and occasions that mark a community's history. Nor does it mean a formal acquisition of the facts of the history of education. It does mean that you function effectively in terms of the social forces that have made the community and its school what they are today. You then can understand present trends and future probabilities. In brief, gain a functional history of education in the local community, as it will serve you in decisions on how to make your influence felt in the educational patterns of community life.

Participate in Selected Community Activities

Your task in the community is always to promote certain tendencies and to minimize others. In noticing all the educational influences of the group, recognize that you cannot support them all; you must choose those which you prefer to encourage and which will promote growth among community members. Evaluate the various educational agencies and have some basis for judging the ones most worthy of your participation.

There are some community groups whose purpose is to foster the total life of the community and to equalize the opportunities for a better life for all. In many communities, however, there are social groups or organizations that are interested in obtaining prestige or privileges for their members at the expense of other members of the total society. More specifically, a parent-teacher association will, by and large, aim at the elevation of the life of all the members of the community, while other groups, like most high school fraternities and sororities, will have as their objective the improvement of the status of their own members and the exclusion of others in the student group.

Your function in the community is that of selecting, balancing, harmonizing, and purifying the community influences on the child. You will be concerned, then, with encouraging those commercial movies which are most desirable, emphasizing those radio and television programs which have more positive educational value, balancing the claims of one advertisement against another, and seeing that the interests of a larger number of people are being cared for in the total educational process. Thus you will be concerned with helping boys and girls to discriminate between the various competing claims made upon them by the groups in their society. You will be interested in the consumers' needs and interests as well as in those of the producers and sellers of goods. You will help youngsters to distinguish between the agencies that educate and those that indoctrinate. Become an expert in revealing the varied community endeavors and in leading the young to distinguish between the forces playing upon them.

Appraise the Community's Educational Influences

The teacher today appraises the informal educational influences of the community in an effort to relate them to the formal classroom learnings. Modern teachers realize that a formal education will not succeed if it runs counter to the other learnings in a community. Pupils learn the correct forms of expression in school, only to have these learnings negated by experiences in poor forms of communication in the home, marketplace, and recreation center. They learn to be good citizens within the school setting; at the same time they learn through their informal community influences the common prejudices and easy ways of getting along in the practical world. Boys and girls may learn to think, talk, and act in a democratic way in school while they learn undemocratic habits in their community life. The modern educator has been more and more concerned with problems created by the isolation of the school from its community context.

As a teacher, you have a responsibility in helping the growing youngster assimilate his informal community learnings and relate them to the education he is obtaining within the walls of the school. For example, a child may need guidance in harmonizing what he has learned about democratic living with his view of people who are inferior in the eyes of his older family members. The teacher has a real and pressing interest in dealing with the totality of a child's experiences; the child should be led to deal with human beings of all kinds in terms of the respect due them simply as fellow humans. The teacher needs to accept and appraise these total educational experiences and, appropriate to the developmental level of the child, to help him see the significance of his informal learnings and the extent to which they should or should not be incorporated into his responses to future situations.

Be a careful student of these community learnings so that you will be able to make the classroom education as effective as the informal learnings of the family, playground, or gang. Consider how readily a child learns the rules of a game or adopts an attitude of teamwork when he is playing with his agemates on the corner lot. Consider again how slow and difficult are his learnings in a spelling class. Be interested in finding ways to make the academic learnings as effective and permanent as those attained in the informal play situation.

Use Community Resources in Curriculum Planning

The teacher in the modern school uses the community to create a more realistic, lifelike, and vital school curriculum. It is important to survey the community's needs in order to gear instruction to the demands on the child and to determine what assets the community contains for promoting the classroom program. Seek to promote a curriculum which will supply youth with the experiences which the community demands, and use local industries, institutions, documents, and key personnel to produce a dynamic and true-to-life school program.

Olsen and his colleagues point out the following ways in which the school may effectively relate to the life of the community [185:146–345]:

1. Documentary materials such as magazines, newspapers, records, and deeds
2. Audio-visual aids such as records, transcriptions, maps, posters, charts, films, slides, models, and television
3. Resource visitors and people with specialized abilities or accomplishments who can present to a school group an experience of unique value
4. Interviews with authorities who can enrich the content of the course of study
5. Field trips or excursions with instructional objectives
6. Surveys or the determination of a selected existing state of affairs in a community
7. Extended field studies to some distant locale
8. Camping or an informal but organized rural-living experience
9. Service projects in which boys and girls contribute to civic welfare under educational guidance
10. Work experiences directed toward eventual success in some occupational field

A thorough study of the means of relating the school program to the life of the community is basic in preparation for teaching today. As you sense the importance of a community-centered school you see the impelling need for teachers who have imagination and enthusiasm to create the newer, more functional course of studies. Only through the work of such teachers will the schools be able to retain boys and girls during their formative years and give them an education which will prepare them for life in the modern community.

Lead Pupils to Make Realistic Vocational Choices

In making use of community resources, the modern teacher in today's school helps young people make an accurate and true-to-life appraisal of their community. Such an appraisal is necessary if pupils are to find in their school experience a vital and valid introduction to modern American life. The teacher, then, guides them in their analysis of modern social conditions and stimulates activities of significance in the life of the community.

As you plan for teaching, consider the importance of knowing and studying each pupil's work experiences in his community. Often these experiences are not recognized as educational in nature. Since job learnings are seldom integrally related to a pupil's school learnings, the teacher does not make the program of formal education vital and real to him. Study and guide a pupil's work experiences so that they may become more profitable and so that the curriculum can be related to his job concerns.

Teachers of modern youth have a major function to perform in helping boys and girls realistically appraise their vocational abilities and interests in the light of the existing distribution of employed persons and probable changes in this distribution. Because of advancing technology and the increased level of education, the degree of skill required of the working force is increasing. Table 9 reveals

Students need a chance to discuss, to think through, and to arrive at realistic conclusions regarding their role in life and how the lives of others may be enhanced.
(Photograph from the Department of Instructional Materials, Oregon Public Schools.)

striking changes in the occupational distribution of workers between 1900 and
1975. In 1900, 41 per cent of the workers were employed in professional (technical and kindred), managerial, clerical, sales, craft, and operative occupations.
This percentage rose to 62 per cent in 1940 and to 76 per cent in 1965. It will
probably increase to at least 78 per cent in 1975. On the other hand, 49 per cent
of the workers in 1900 consisted of unskilled laborers, service workers, and farmers. This percentage decreased to 38 per cent in 1940 and to 24 in 1965 and
probably will decrease to 22 in 1975. In 1975 the percentage of unskilled laborers
will no doubt be less than one-half of that in 1940. Likewise, the percentage of
those engaged in farm occupations will probably be only one-third as great in
1975 as in 1940. These changes in the distribution of employed persons have
significant implications for the manner in which young people should prepare
themselves to earn a living.

Approximately 6½ million young people, ages 14 to 19, are in the labor force
either working or looking for work. On an average, 1 million of them are unemployed. The unemployment rate of teen-agers is higher than that of any other
age group in the labor force, in prosperity and recession periods alike, for a
number of reasons [157:26]. Young people starting out on their work careers are

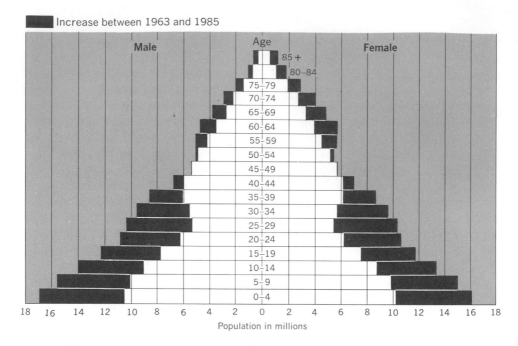

FIGURE 15–10.   Population of the United States by age and sex in 1963 and in 1985 (projected). During this period of time, the number of children under 5 years of age may increase nearly 60 per cent principally because of the larger numbers of women who will reach childbearing age. Elementary-school-age children will increase approximately 53 per cent, and those of high school age (14 to 17 years) will increase nearly 49 per cent. The population in the main working ages (25 to 64 years) will grow approximately 34 per cent. The number of persons 65 years and over is expected to rise 42 per cent. What effect will these changes have upon opportunities in education? *(Source:* U.S. Bureau of the Census.)

TABLE 9   Occupational Distribution of Workers, 1900–1975 (in per cent)

Occupation	1900	1920	1940	1950	1965	1975
Professional, technical, and kindred	4.3	5.4	7.5	8.6	12.5	14.0
Managerial	5.8	6.6	7.3	8.7	10.5	10.8
Clerical	3.0	8.0	9.6	12.3	15.6	14.4
Sales	4.5	4.9	6.7	7.0	6.5	7.4
Craftsmen	10.5	13.0	12.0	14.1	12.5	13.7
Operatives	12.8	15.6	18.4	20.4	18.6	17.5
Laborers	12.5	11.6	9.4	6.6	5.2	4.4
Service	9.0	7.8	11.7	10.5	12.7	12.4
Farm	37.5	27.0	17.4	11.8	5.8	5.3
Total, in millions	29.0	42.2	51.7	59.0	75.6	86.9

Source: Compiled from statistics provided by the U.S. Department of Labor and the National Education Association, Research Division, Washington, 1966.

particularly vulnerable to layoffs, since they lack seniority and are relatively inexperienced and unfamiliar with the ways of the job market. Most of them work in the lower-skilled occupations, where both earnings and job security are unstable. Many of them are school dropouts who tend to have an unemployment rate close to double that of high school graduates, even after several years of being in the labor force [157:26]. As Grant [112:9] points out, "The contemporary technological economy has little to offer the untrained, undereducated would-be worker. There is no room at the bottom."

The 1965 Manpower Report of the President recognizes the seriousness of the teen-age unemployment problem in the following manner [157:29]:

The very number of teen-age unemployed, and the implications for the future level of youth unemployment of a rapidly expanding labor force of young workers, makes this problem one of the most important we must face in the years ahead. Rates of unemployment of 15 per cent or more for young people involve a costly waste that the Nation or the individuals can ill afford. High rates of unemployment for young people in their formative years could seriously hamper them for the rest of their lives.

Never before in our recent history has so large a proportion of teen-agers started their work lives with the disadvantage of unemployment—in many cases frequent or prolonged periods of joblessness. For these, the already difficult problems of beginning a successful work career are increased many fold. The experience, learning, and seniority that generally go only with stable employment are postponed, fre-

The Job Corps is designed to help youth develop salable skills so that unemployment may be lessened and the economy of our nation may be strengthened. *(Photograph from the Office of Economic Opportunity.)*

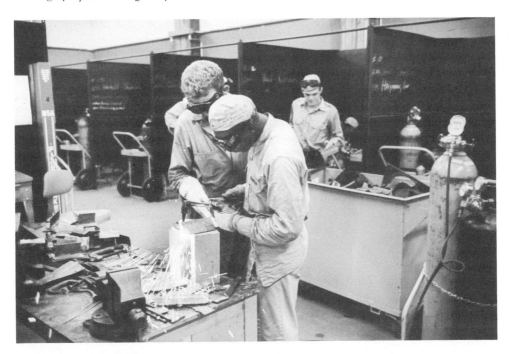

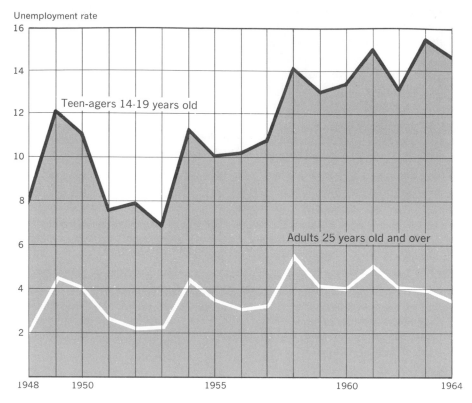

FIGURE 15–11. Teen-age unemployment rate compared with the unemployment rate for adults 25 years old or over. Employment of teen-agers becomes an increasingly greater problem. What might the school do to lessen this problem? *(Source:* U.S. Department of Labor.*)*

quently into the adult years when the responsibilities of marriage and a family add to the burdens of unemployment.

When the unemployment of teen-agers is a reflection of a basic deficiency such as lack of education, the disadvantage, if not remedied, is carried with the worker through most of his work life, not only in the form of higher unemployment, but also in the jobs found and the income earned.

How will you attempt to help young people face realistically the realities of the work world so that the seriousness of the teen-age unemployment problem may be lessened? What kinds of guidance and counseling services should be available to all young people? How may the school be able to decrease the number of pupils dropping out of school before graduation?

Help the Community Find a Real Place for Its Youth

In your attempt to understand the tasks of the teacher today, note the tendency of the school to foster the real participation of the young in the affairs of the community. In the days of our ancestors, boys and girls were responsible members of their communities at an early age. But nowadays local affairs are in the hands of older people, and group life tends to be dominated by adult interests.

There is great need today for an agency to bring the interests and activities of youth into the life of the adult community. Not only would boys and girls have a fuller sense of belonging and participation in civic affairs, but also the adult group would benefit from the fresh vitality and idealism of youth.

Schools have a function to perform in helping the community find a real place for its youth. Young people may work at helping a group solve its traffic, sanitation, and public health problems, its needs for planning and coordinating local agencies and services, its demands for more adequate recreation and leisure-time resources. Consider how the health program in an elementary school in Petersburg, West Virginia, extended into the community. Here are some of the things the boys and the girls did that were adapted especially to their resources [19:17]:

Seventh- and eighth-grade groups initiated the program.

All groups had a part in the work.

Thirteen committees had responsibility for school and community experiences which the school could do something about. These included:

Improving garbage disposal methods
Studying the sewage situation
Street cleanliness
Studying the water supply
Surveying city-dump situation
Getting rid of mice and rats
Making a study of school health
Reducing colds and other diseases which interfere with school attendance
Studying ways in which the city restaurants handled food
Getting rid of flies and mosquitoes and conditions which breed such pests
Studying the situation with regard to livestock within city limits
Getting more recreation for the town
Studying the situation with regard to rest rooms and making recommendations

Most of the pupils had part in making questionnaires to fit the study.

Learning how to make and use maps of parts of the community was of practical help to the younger pupils.

Older pupils learned how to represent the school in community organizations.

Through such activities young people gain further respect for the worth of individuals, enjoy the sharing of common interests and concerns, and strengthen their beliefs that the problems of modern life can be solved through the application of intelligent, cooperative action.

The modern school is also concerned with its function of keeping in touch with young people after they have finished the formal part of their education. Teachers today are not so sure that they have discharged their full responsibility when boys and girls have graduated from or left the school. Follow-up studies on the nature and extent of the youth's adjustment in the adult world are an integral part of the educational task. Such guidance services are not yet common practice in our schools, but they seem clearly indicated.

Although most teachers think of themselves as specialists in the education of children, actually every teacher is involved in the education of adults. You will find that you cannot educate Johnny, aged eleven, unless you also have an effective understanding of Johnny's family life and that you cannot guide the development of the group in the elementary school without many fruitful contacts with the home. Parent-teacher association meetings are only one way of providing these contacts.

In many of the informal conversations between teacher and citizen you will find an opportunity to serve as a friend and counselor in an informal adult education setting. Parents will present you with educational problems and questions about how to guide Sally's development or how to encourage Henry in his arithmetic. You must be prepared to serve the parents' needs in these cases. You must visit the home and spend some time with the neighborhood activities of boys and girls in order to be well acquainted with your group and with the family relationships of each child. To be a teacher today means to have considerable expertness in the role of an adult educator.

Attain Expertness in Human Relationships

A teacher today is interested in studying the ways in which the community influences its young, not merely by the geographic location of industries, stores, and churches, but more fundamentally by the qualities of human relationships which it inculcates through informal learning. The community does not influence all its youth in the same way. Environment is not identical for all boys and girls, and each child is molded by his particular set of environmental conditions. It is your responsibility to study how these various influences bear upon each youngster for whose education you are responsible.

Boys and girls growing up in different socioeconomic classes have quite different concepts of human relationships as a result of their class position. Think of the learnings which Priscilla indicates in the following passage from talking to her father [279:90–93]:

"I'm in the doghouse again, and this time it's an awful big doghouse. I can't stand it any longer. I'm going to quit that terrible high school. I want to get a job and go to work. . . .

"Everyone up there hates me. No one likes me. The teachers hate me, and the kids won't have anything to do with me. . . .

"I got caught playing hookey again. That old Swenson caught us. He's always snooping. He thought we were going down by the river to meet some boys, but honest we weren't. Florence, Ruth, Carol, and I just wanted to have a little fun. Just wanted to get away from those snooty kids. And I'm not going back. . . .

"The way a lot of us girls are treated at school no one can blame us for the way we feel. There's nothing there for a lot of us but just coming to classes, listening to the teacher, reciting our lessons and studying, and going home again. We're just pushed out of things.

"There are a group of girls there who think they're higher than us. They're a

How may the attitudes, beliefs, and behavior of these children be affected as a result of low socioeconomic conditions? *(Photograph by Carl Purcell, National Education Association.)*

group of girls from the wealthier families. They look down on us. They have a club that's supposed to be outside the school, but it's really in the school. They can do things we can't afford, and they just go from one club to another and hog all the offices, and are in all the activities. They just talk about what they're doing and what they're going to do, and they ignore us. They won't pay any attention to us. . . .

"I don't want the kids in high school to know that Mother takes in washing to get a little extra money to get some of the things she needs. . . . They'd look down on me if they knew it. And we can't do the things they do. We have a large family, and I know, Dad, you're only a working man, and we can't afford to do a lot of things. . . ."

While Priscilla spoke, Mr. Sellers looked at the floor. He said nothing. He knew what she said was true. His two older children had told him the same thing when they quit. He and the Missus had gone up to the school and raised hell, but it didn't do any good. Now it was Priscilla's turn.

Now by way of contrast notice the quality of human relationships which Kenneth experiences [126:100–101]:

Everybody likes Kenneth, even Sally, and Kenneth does not tease Sally the way some of the others do. Kenneth knows that everybody likes him. The teachers like him, they say, because he learns so fast and has such a nice disposition. The other children like him because he "plays nice," he doesn't try to boss everything and he doesn't try to have his way all the time, and he invites a lot of children to his parties and he lets other children play with his things. Kenneth doesn't like to have to take a bath as often as his mother says he must. Sometimes he wishes he had more brothers and sisters so that his mother wouldn't have as much time to work on him and try to make him cleaner and better dressed than everybody else.

Kenneth has an individual personality that makes everybody like him. Probably most people would like him even if his father was not the owner of the lumber company and even if his mother was not the president of the Women's Club. But Kenneth also has a cultural personality. He has learned certain manners of speech and of dress. He has learned certain attitudes about the school and the teacher. These manners and attitudes form his cultural personality and since he lives in a community which rates his particular cultural personality as most desirable, he is continually rewarded for being what his family has made him.

It is clear that community influences of very different kinds are molding the characters of these two youngsters.

As a teacher today, you must be a student of community influences on human relationships and must attempt to foster democratic forms of living for all youth. Seek to understand these influences so that you may help pupils control their responses to the social norms which are molding their personalities. Help the community provide for a higher level of respect for each of its members and help young people understand why their social opportunities are not yet of a truly democratic nature. Try to construct a school program which will provide for the needs of all. Develop expertness in human relationships, in teaching, and in guiding others to a life of fuller democratic participation.

Be a Student of Intercultural Processes

The world is no longer one in which groups are isolated. Consequently, the problems of intercultural and international education become problems of every modern teacher. In performing the immediate tasks of the classroom, the teacher should have in mind the major requirements of world citizenship. How can a teacher lead boys and girls to accept without prejudice people of other races, creeds, and economic and political persuasions? What processes may be used in helping youngsters locate their prejudices and stereotypes? What units of instruction may be devised to lead boys and girls to more adequate concepts of people who differ from themselves? What experiences should all children have to develop a democratic tolerance of others and a respect for personality, regardless of surface differences? How should a teacher study and understand the local community in its patterns of discrimination, and to what extent and by what processes should he make his weight felt in leading the community to change its restrictive mores? Such questions are the immediate and practical problems of an ever-increasing number of teachers today.

The resources for obtaining aid in these endeavors are very extensive and include such things as bureaus and agencies for promoting intercultural education, extensive bibliographies covering the field, films of outstanding instructional merit, and the experiences of communities in establishing councils charged with planning for a fuller realization of the brotherhood of man. The modern teacher knows of these resources because in his training he has taken time to prepare himself thoroughly for the demands of the community in which he is to serve.

SUMMARY

Thoughtful students of education are increasingly concerned with the profound social, economic, political, and technological changes which have been occurring and will continue to occur. A number of these changes have been identified in this chapter. Attention also has been given to some of the powerful community forces which influence the educational growth of the individual.

Many of the tasks of the teacher are strongly influenced and determined by the forces in community life today. Obviously, the particular responses of each teacher will be determined only as local conditions are studied and defined. Consideration has been given only to problems which are common to most present-day communities and which suggest preparations that ought to be part of the living resources of any new teacher. These problems range from understanding the causes of delinquency and planning a curriculum to avoid them, to the high level of abstract thinking needed to discriminate between conflicting values in the community today.

As you proceed with your preparation for teaching, continue to probe more deeply into the educational implications of such community forces as have been mentioned in this chapter. Your efforts should help you in formulating a clearly reasoned and functional concept of the role of the school and of the teacher in effectively guiding the total educational growth of pupils. Herein lies a tremendous challenge for you. The checklist in the Resource Section of Part VI should help guide you in your preparation to meet this challenge.

QUESTIONS FOR YOUR CONSIDERATION

1. Twenty-one major changes in community living were noted in the first part of this chapter. How do you feel in regard to the questions raised in the discussion of each of these changes? What implications do you see for educating boys and girls?

2. Reflect upon the agencies within your home community which exert an educational effect upon the young people. In your opinion, are the agencies other than the school doing all that they can to exert positive effects? What improvements might be made?

3. From what sources do you feel you obtained the values you hold—those things which you judge to be of most worth and which determine your choices, sacrifices, and ambitions?

4. In what ways are mass media affecting the developing behavior patterns of boys and girls today? What are some of the educational implications for you as a prospective teacher?

5. In what ways does a school have the opportunity to contribute to the improvement of its community?

6. To what extent should the community dictate the curriculum of the school? The methods to be used in teaching the pupils?

7. Why will it be important for you as a teacher to know the development of the school's community?

8. How do teachers influence the attitudes of the public toward schools?
9. In what ways can a teacher take an active role in the upgrading of community forces?

ACTIVITIES FOR YOU TO PURSUE

1. What have been the outstanding sources of learning in your life? Begin with school, home, church, and other organized agencies of education and proceed to the more incidental and unorganized sources such as movies, comics, gangs, television, and radio. Then attempt to evaluate the various agencies by rating them as exceedingly effective, very effective, moderately effective, slightly effective, or of no effect.

2. Make a list of what a teacher should know about the nature and extent of the recreational activities of a community. What factors influence the nature of community recreation?

3. In your home community try to find out where the pupils go after school. Do they engage in constructive activities?

4. Visit and study the kind of education obtained in a typical adolescent hangout in a community.

5. Study how young people in a typical community obtain their spending money. What education do they obtain in the process?

6. Visit a slum area in a large city. Observe especially the behavior of boys and girls. Study the kinds of educative forces to which they are being subjected.

7. Spend some time, if possible, as an assistant in a settlement house. Become well acquainted with some of the boys and girls. You may wish to do case studies on one or more of the children. Study especially the forces that have shaped and are shaping their behavior patterns. List all the meanings that these experiences have for you as a prospective teacher and as a potential parent.

8. Reflect upon your own public school experiences. To what extent were community forces considered by your teachers and used to help you develop to your maximum capacity for democratic living? In what ways do you plan to be different from your former teachers?

9. Attempt to determine the extent to which you have developed the social and civic competence required for relating the school closely to the life of its community. The checklist in the Resource Section for Part VI should help you in this regard.

10. Consult your local recreation department, civic clubs, and other such organizations to find out how they are coordinating their programs with the school. Are they all pursuing common aims, or are they operating independently?

11. Ask a juvenile court official to indicate causes of juvenile delinquency and what a teacher might do in order to lessen these causes.

16

PURPOSES OF EDUCATION IN AMERICAN DEMOCRACY

In the period of the rise of the common school in America, the chief concern of the teacher was to provide a standard curriculum which would make possible the task of teaching the large numbers of pupils who came into the public school. In this era of school expansion it was altogether natural that specific subjects should be established as the content of education. With large classes, many poorly prepared teachers, and a highly complex and confused social scene, the schools needed a curriculum that could be taught formally. The school was also influenced to be selective and to prepare for college those who had the academic, social, and economic advantages necessary for higher education.

The changing conditions in the American scene necessitated that schools be free of the rigid formalism, tradition, and selectivity of pupils. Youth were graduating or withdrawing from school and meeting community conditions to which the school program had not been geared. A new, positive educational program was needed.

Considering the Schools Today

Although the schools have made considerable progress in developing programs that are responsive to the needs of youth as well as to the requirements of modern society, much yet remains to be done. Criticisms of the nature of the programs in one school suggest that some basic assumptions are being *uncritically* followed. Too frequently we assume (1) that the child goes to school for the sole purpose of acquiring mastery of *prescribed bodies* of knowledge and that the mastery of this knowledge will ensure effective citizenship, (2) that if the child does not at first succeed in mastering the prescribed bodies of knowledge, he should try, and try again, (3) that education is preparation for life and has no particular significance for living while it is being acquired, (4) that children feel the same needs for acquiring subject matter as adults feel, (5) that learning is primarily a passive rather than an active process, (6) that it is more important for the teacher to transmit knowledge than it is for him to help pupils learn how to learn, (7) that one of the most important tasks of the teacher is to have the pupils "cover the book" in the time prescribed, (8) that obtaining the correct answer to a problem is more important than knowing how to solve the problem, (9) that all boys and girls in a grade or class must meet the same grade standards in order to be promoted, (10) that learning devoid of purpose or interest provides good discipline, (11) that it is more important to measure what has been learned than it is to learn, (12) that youth has no part to play in conceiving, planning, and appraising the educative processes, (13) that standardized intelligence and achievement tests provide accurate information on the intellectual and creative capacities of *all* pupils, including the economically and culturally deprived [232:38], (14) that some pupils are destined to drop out of school because they lack interest in education, and (15) that the school's curriculum consists of a rigid, predetermined content to be mastered by the pupils.

These beliefs are of such long standing and are so thoroughly built into our thinking by tradition that they frequently are not recognized. Carefully analyze the teachers you have had to determine the extent to which they operated in terms of these assumptions. Perhaps you can identify other assumptions that should be added to the list.

Thoughtful educators today are more and more concerned with the discrepancy between the conditions of modern life and the assumptions upon which the schools have, in general, been operating. As you plan to teach, recognize the extent to which many educational practices are continuing to lag behind the salient characteristics of our modern culture. Develop the habit of thinking critically about how you will see the proper business of the school today and how you will make your weight felt in leading the community toward a wider concept of the function of the schools.

A "call to teaching" places heavy responsibilities upon those who join the profession. You are called upon to be students of the current social context in which formal education occurs. Ferret out information concerning (1) what is done in schools, (2) the common assumptions upon which these actions rest, (3) the state of the current culture which the school is to serve, (4) the ways in which the educational process should change in order to better fulfill its function in the group. Studying these problems puts a vital and serious content into the business of teaching. Without this content the schools will be out of step with the conditions of modern life.

Formulating Some Principles Basic to Our Schools

What, then, are the principles or new assumptions which should underlie any move to bring the program of the schools up to date and to vitalize their function? To answer this question is to embark upon an activity that will consume your time and energies throughout your career as an educator. Yet it is most important that you begin to study your profession in this way if you are to sense the challenge facing all teachers. Consider the following ten statements of educational principles to see whether or not they are more adequate than the usual assumptions underlying educational practices:

1. *The child goes to school in order to acquire behavior patterns which will enable him to meet the problems of his time and to grow in ability to handle them successfully.* In this basic principle it is maintained that the function of the school is far more than the acquisition of existing bodies of academic subject matter; it is to guide youngsters in their ability to behave in certain ways. As such, everything that goes on in a school is an active part of the curriculum. The basic business of the teacher is to channel this behavior which is built into the character of the pupil.

If the primary task of the school is to lead the youngster to acquire habits, abilities, and skills which will be his behavior resources, then it is your responsibility as the teacher to distinguish between those actions which are appropriate to the problems which boys and girls face and those which are not helpful or which are hindrances to their abilities to meet problems. Be continuously inquiring into the problems which youngsters are facing, and attempt to gear new behavior modes to the content of their experiences.

Not only should school experiences be provided in terms of the problems of the contemporary community, but they should also be provided in terms of individual behavior patterns—patterns which encourage the youngster's abilities to handle the problems he faces. It is the business of the teacher to study the behavior patterns that are being built, in an attempt to encourage those which are more fruitful and to remove those which are less likely to lead to successful problem solving.

2. *The growth of youth toward constructive citizenship is a continuous process with which the school is primarily concerned.* You should be constantly concerned with behavior that promotes good citizenship and behavior which may detract from it. In seeking ways of building the former into the range and experience level of the pupils, find situations in which pupils can learn, appropriate to their developmental level, the characteristics of desirable citizenship. The future calls for citizens with broad perspective, who have a critical and constructive approach to life and standards of value by which they can live effectively and constructively. We desperately need citizens who have ability to think, to communicate, to make valid judgments, and to evaluate moral situations. We need citizens who have a deep sense of responsibility for their fellow men, who are concerned with moral and spiritual values, and who do not shape their philosophy of life entirely in terms of materialistic considerations. We need citizens who realize that the democratic way of life not only cherishes freedom but entails obligations and sacrifices for its preservation. We need citizens who are capable of making creative, constructive adaptations to the inevitable changes that will take place in our technological and social world.

Thoughtful teachers are concerned with describing in common language the characteristics involved in citizenship so that the educational process may be directed with them in mind. At every level of guidance we must be concerned with seeing to it that these characteristics are encouraged and that the techniques of acquiring them are freely available to all youngsters. We must see to it that behavior which embodies these characteristics is rewarded and made more satisfactory to the learner than less constructive ways of behaving. Thus a thoughtful and critical understanding of the meaning of citizenship may be built into the methods and techniques with which you guide the learning experiences.

3. *The democratic way of life which has been wrought by our ancestors is sufficiently valid and vital today to provide continuous direction for educational activities.* As a teacher, you are charged with building and employing a clear conception of the democratic process. We must see to it that boys and girls learn to distinguish at all points between behavior patterns which have the quality of democracy and those which are fundamentally autocratic, totalitarian, and anarchistic. This means that we must become increasingly more competent students

of the democratic way of life and must interpret democracy in more than its superficial and partial aspects. Specifically, we must help boys and girls to develop depth of understanding of, and deep-seated convictions in, such basic aspects of democratic life as respect for the dignity and worth of the human being, the principle of human equality and brotherhood, freedom of speech and of group discussion, the ideals of honesty and fair-mindedness, the supremacy of the common good, the obligation and right to work, and the need to be informed and concerned about the affairs of our society.

In all the activities of the school, the characteristics of the democratic way of life should be at work giving youth educational direction and guidance. As a teacher, see to it that full and free participation is provided in all learning experiences. Help boys and girls to solve problems on the basis of democratic action and the free play of intelligence as opposed to methods of coercion and dogmatic acceptance of belief. Encourage the members of a group to accept each individual as a contributing member. Welcome a large variation between students as an opportunity for teaching a basic democratic value, that of the precious worth of an individual, whose own way of saying, thinking, and doing contributes to the welfare of all. Show pupils how to distinguish between bigotry and intolerance, on the one hand, and freedom of inquiry and the use of minority dissent on the other, in planning and working together. It is your business to be a persistent student of the ways in which democratic character may be built into the behavior patterns of boys and girls.

4. *Through careful study of modern society and ideal concepts of democratic living, teachers may become leaders in building a democratic society which can meet the test of our troubled times.* Not only will you be constantly concerned with building democratic behavior in youth, but you will always be attentive to the community's needs for democratic leadership in meeting its problems. Because you are a careful and thorough student of the conditions of the modern community as well as an interpreter of the meaning of democracy today, you will be able to interpret crucial problems to the group and to provide democratic processes for solving them. In the long run, then, you are a key figure in leading the culture toward a fulfillment of its democratic values.

This does not mean that you become a militant authority, striking out blindly for what you may deem desirable from your point of view. Nor does it mean that teachers working together should establish a cut-and-dried program for community living and seek to impose it upon others. It does mean that you carefully and critically study current economic, social, and political problems, appraise existing conditions in terms of the democratic values, and seek to help the community to appraise their effects upon the youth. This calls for an expertness in social action which teachers in general have still to achieve. It is one of the challenges to the educational profession in modern times, the response to which will determine whether teachers become a fully professional group or remain merely "keepers of schools."

Whether they have recognized it or not, teachers have had this role of interpreting and inculcating in political statesmanship. Wherever totalitarianism has gained power in countries, one of the first acts of the dictators has been that of capturing the educational process for indoctrination of their form of tyranny. In today's society, it is more imperative than ever before that teachers be able to foster the democratic life, not only within the school program but also within the total life of the community. Only as you perform your function in social leadership will you be able to help the learning within the school to become effective in the real life of the neighborhood and the nation. This means that you should encourage those forces within the local and national scene which are productive of the democratic process and should seek to identify and minimize those agencies which violate it. In this way you will contribute to making the ideals of democracy operate more effectively in the lives of the next generation.

5. *The modern concept of educational leadership affords you the best opportunity to study human development in all its aspects.* It is an outstanding responsibility of the teacher to provide learning experiences appropriate to the maturity level of the learner. However, you need a fundamental concept of your role in the social process in order to determine what *direction* the content of education ought to take. As has been indicated, direction may be suggested by a careful study of the democratic way of life.

One of the aspects of democracy is the right—and the implied ability—of the individual to think for himself. Try to encourage individual thinking in your students, but in so doing, decide what kinds of problems they should deal with and the degree to which they will be successful. Adapt the problems to the level of their abilities. See that youngsters follow through the problems they select for study and make as complete and thorough an investigation as they can. Give youngsters the opportunity to figure out and experience the consequences of their study. And make it possible for boys and girls to carry their learning activities beyond the confines of the school into the community, where the real test of their education will be made.

The modern concept of educational leadership, then, means that there is no real opposition between education geared to the needs and requirements of the young and education devoted to the study and leadership of society. A child-centered school and a community-centered school are not in conflict. Only as both these aspects of the teacher's business become related can any adequate sense be made out of either.

6. *Youth, adults, and teachers have a part to play in conceiving, planning, and appraising the educative processes.* As you have noted in the preceding sections, the function of the school is not one that is discharged wholly within the walls of an academic building. The real business of the school goes on within the total life of a community. This means that teachers operating by themselves, without including pupils and the lay members of the community, may not hope to fulfill the functions of social leadership and guidance of human growth.

There are many instances in which schools that have failed to establish adequate working relationships with their communities have been unable to carry on programs designed to meet the current needs of young people. The school which fails to interpret its endeavors to the public finds itself out of step with the thinking and activities of the community. For this reason it is particularly important that teachers include the layman in their educational planning. As a modern teacher, you need skill in interpreting your position to the adults of the community and ability to recognize in your community the resources which may be drawn upon to fulfill the educational purposes better.

But there are reasons other than this practical one for the participation of the lay community in the educational process. Only as parents and adults understand the function of the modern teacher can they help achieve his purposes by providing out-of-school experiences and learnings which will support the school program. If the learning within the school program is rendered ineffective by the informal educational process, it can hardly be expected to succeed in producing a democratic life for all. Thoughtful adults, when they have an opportunity to study what is involved in an education for democracy today, are anxious to help provide a more effective context for the learning that the school is fostering.

The teacher in today's school should not overlook the fact that in almost every community there are quite able people who can serve as good resource persons if they are properly approached. It is important to recognize and utilize these people in planning and in providing quality educational programs. It is impossible for the teacher to possess all of the skills and knowledge that are demanded in meeting the intellectual needs of youth today. It is shortsighted of any teacher if he fails to utilize these talents. Furthermore, the frank and happy use of the abilities and qualifications of community members may do more to establish the teacher and enhance the school in the community than any amount of social propagandizing about the values and dignity of the profession.

7. *An education for democratic citizenship includes disciplined effort for mastery of subject matter.* If you are genuinely interested in an education to meet modern social conditions, you will recognize that this education is not achieved by letting boys and girls follow their own immediate whims and fancies to the exclusion of discipline and persistent work to achieve desired objectives. To meet the conditions of contemporary society, a more rigorous and a more disciplined system is necessary; but this does not mean that the pupils will not know what they are doing or will have no part in determining what they shall learn. Nor does

Education for democratic citizenship includes disciplined effort for mastery of subject matter. (*Photograph by Carl Purcell, National Education Association.*)

it mean merely the development of a disciplined mind by sharpening it on a whetstone of formal subject matter. Rather, the disciplined effort needed to meet modern requirements is one in which boys and girls organize their efforts carefully over a period of time and persist in their endeavors in the face of difficulties and discouragements. This disciplined effort is fundamentally social in quality. It results from working together on common concerns in which each individual finds his appropriate place. It means the ability of an individual to subordinate his immediate and personal liking for an eventual outcome that will benefit everybody.

In such a disciplined education there is much subject matter, but not subject matter established by an exterior authority and imposed upon an unwilling learner. Instead, subject matter becomes the accumulated experience of other people who have worked at similar problems, who have acquired comprehension of the difficulties and necessities in solving these problems, and who make their information available to others working toward their objectives. The subject matter in modern education is related to the needs and demands of the citizen in the modern world; it does not exist for its own sake.

8. *Human relations and the ways that people work together are matters as worthy of study as subject matter.* As has been repeatedly emphasized, learning for democratic citizenship is essentially a social process. In this process, youth must work together in groups, large and small, and must feed their own individual efforts into the work of the group. Such a process demands skills and abilities which are learned primarily from experience with other people rather than from books. The meaning of participation with others should be studied, evaluated, and re-created in the democratic tradition. The skills and techniques of group participation are vital learnings which may be achieved only through a disciplined effort equal to that normally applied to the formalized subject matters. This means that you, as a teacher, should become expert in guiding human relation-

The development of good human relationships is a difficult skill to learn. The development of this skill is of utmost importance in a democratic society. How will you attempt to develop it in your pupils? (*Photograph by Carl Purcell, National Education Association.*)

ships and developing the skills of participation in social undertakings. At the same time, provision must be made for self-realization upon the part of each.

9. *Your professional abilities are inadequate if you fail to relate your teaching skills to the broader functions of the school in a democratic society.* Be proficient in the uses of all the techniques and devices by which the readiness and abilities of pupils can be applied. Be expert at learning how to control the classroom situation so that desirable learning can be achieved and aimless disorder avoided. Know the methods which have most commonly succeeded in instructing youth. Be an expert at the professional business of the classroom.

It is urgently required that your professional skill be related to the basic aims and purposes of the learning process. Do not let the techniques of your trade become ends in themselves. Continuously adapt them to the basic objectives of your function as social leader in a democratic society. Be careful not to use your skills so that they negate your broader educational duties. Cultivate a wide concept of method, in which your role in guidance of individual growth and social processes indicates the skills you are to use.

Thus teaching becomes more than a matter of studying the techniques of other teachers and adopting them. It is not primarily a matter of employing what works in one situation as a technique in another. Rather, your function is to study the particular educational situation and, with a broad background of skills, to devise and use those methods which will most effectively bring about a desirable outcome.

10. *The ability to think for oneself and the willingness to inquire critically into all problems are as important as the acquisition of special knowledge.* If our democratic way of life is to meet today's critical social situation, an effort must be made to create more effectively than ever before the citizen who knows how to think for himself, who is willing to do so, who is committed to the results of his thinking. You must be increasingly effective at showing boys and girls how they may work creatively at the solutions of problems and how they may test the results of their thinking. It is particularly important in our complex and interrelated society to build behavior patterns into each individual that will make him able to isolate problems, to determine the facts which are pertinent to them, to create with imagination possible solutions, and to test the consequences of these solutions. As a teacher today, be particularly concerned with seeing that the pattern of critical thinking becomes useful in *all* the areas with which boys and girls are concerned.

To maintain that youth should be able to apply the method of critical intelligence to all problems means that they should learn to think critically about what should be done as well as about finding the existing facts. Recognize the responsibility of increasing the amount of critical intelligence in the areas of value choices and factual judgments. In modern society, with all its insecurity, conflict, and confusion, to be able to think well about the purposes or objectives of our actions is particularly important. An education to meet modern social conditions should be one in which youth learn to apply their best intelligence to the question of the ends for which they live. You will always be concerned with the basic question of what experiences are of most worth. In modern times a critical and free intelligence working toward the tentative solutions to these important questions is a basic responsibility.

Perhaps most central in your thinking about the basic function of the school is your belief about the place of the school within a changing society. Some believe that the school does not influence the nature of society to any appreciable extent. "Education does not, strictly speaking, have an effect upon culture at all; *it is a part of it.* . . . It is not people who control their culture through education; it is rather the other way around; *education is what culture is doing to people* . . . determining how they shall think, feel, and behave" [285:241].

On the other hand, one may believe that "education is the fundamental method of social progress and reform" and that "it is the business of every one interested in education to insist upon the school as the primary and most effective instrument of social progress and reform . . ." [63:15–16]. To what extent do you feel the school should assume a positive role of leadership in shaping the culture of the future?

OBJECTIVES OF EDUCATION

In light of the preceding discussion, you may feel that education is

(1) The aggregate of all the processes by means of which a person develops abilities, attitudes, and other forms of behavior of positive value in the society in which he lives; (2) the social process by which people are subjected to the influence of a selected and controlled environment (especially that of the school) so that they may obtain social competence and optimum individual development [108:191].

Stated in another manner, education is a process of changing behavior—the way people think, feel, and act. These changes should be in the direction of the fundamental values, ideals, and aspirations that our society accepts as desirable, as is indicated in the following quotation [4:132–133]:

The purpose of the school cannot be determined apart from the purposes of the society which maintains the school. The purposes of any society are determined by the life values which the people prize. As a nation we have been striving always for those values which constitute the American way of life. Our people prize individual human personality above everything else. We are convinced that the form of social organization called democracy promotes, better than any other, the development of worth and dignity in men and women. It follows, therefore, that the *chief purpose of education in the United States should be to preserve, promote, and refine the way of life in which we as a people believe.*

Unless a teacher has a clear understanding of the particular changes he is responsible for developing in his pupils, he proceeds aimlessly in his work. The effective teacher plans educational experiences in terms of both immediate and ultimate objectives. The latter provides the broad framework within which the former derives meaning and purpose. Since the broad educational objectives are determined by the nature of our society rather than by the particular value patterns held by a teacher or a school system, it becomes the responsibility of each teacher to be a diligent student of the objectives of education in a democratic society.

A study of the attempts made during recent years to state the objectives of education reveals the desire of educators to modify the school's program in response to changing conditions.

> What the school is and what it has done since the beginning of public education in this country has been inextricably related to the wants and needs of people—to their hopes and expectations, to the ideals that give direction to their thoughts and actions, and to the circumstances in which they live. The values which people cherish; the priorities assigned to these values; the theories that hold promise for giving a sense of order, unity, and efficiency to what people do; and the cultural climate that prevails at any given time in large measure shape the educational program [134:1].

In your preparation for teaching you may wish to become familiar with various statements of general objectives of education and to note the relationship of these objectives to those for different age levels of pupils.

General Objectives of Education

One of the most significant statements of educational objectives was formulated in 1938 by the Educational Policies Commission of the National Education Association [204]. Over a thousand educators collaborated in the development of these objectives. The members of the commission identified four major objectives (each related to the others) and analyzed each in terms of the specific behavior patterns that should characterize an educated person. Because of the wide acceptance of these objectives, they are indicated below in outline form.[1]

The objectives of self-realization

The inquiring mind. The educated person has an appetite for learning.

Speech. The educated person can speak the mother tongue clearly.

Reading. The educated person reads the mother tongue efficiently.

Writing. The educated person writes the mother tongue effectively.

Number. The educated person solves his problems of counting and calculating.

Sight and hearing. The educated person is skilled in listening and observing.

Health knowledge. The educated person understands the basic facts concerning health and disease.

Health habits. The educated person protects his own health and that of his dependents.

Public health. The educated person works to improve the health of the community.

Recreation. The educated person is participant and spectator in many sports and other pastimes.

Intellectual interests. The educated person has mental resources for the use of leisure time.

Aesthetic interest. The educated person appreciates beauty.

Character. The educated person gives responsible directions to his own life.

---

[1] For a more thorough study of these objectives, read the publication of the Educational Policies Commission in which they appeared and were interpreted [204: 50, 72, 90, 108].

The objectives of human relationships

Respect for humanity. The educated person puts human relationships first.
Friendships. The educated person enjoys a rich, sincere, and varied social life.
Cooperation. The educated person can work and play with others.
Courtesy. The educated person observes the amenities of social behavior.
Appreciation of the home. The educated person appreciates the family as a social institution.
Conservation of the home. The educated person conserves family ideals.
Homemaking. The educated person is skilled in homemaking.
Democracy in the home. The educated person maintains democratic family relationships.

The objectives of economic efficiency

Work. The educated producer knows the satisfaction of good workmanship.
Occupational information. The educated producer understands the requirements and opportunities for various jobs.
Occupational choice. The educated producer has *selected* his occupation.
Occupational efficiency. The educated producer succeeds in his chosen vocation.
Occupational adjustment. The educated producer maintains and improves his efficiency.

The development of skill in working together is as worthy as the study of formalized subject matter. (*Photograph by Carl Purcell, National Education Association.*)

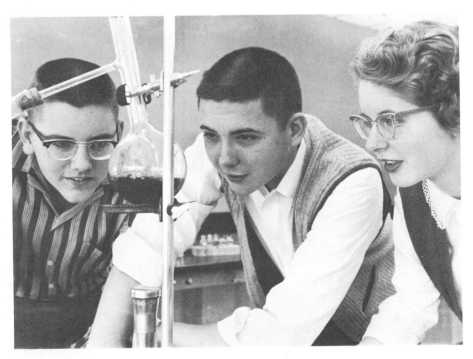

Occupational appreciation. The educated producer appreciates the social value of his work.

Personal economics. The educated consumer plans the economics of his own life.

Consumer judgment. The educated consumer develops standards for guiding his expenditures.

Efficiency in buying. The educated consumer is an informed and skillful buyer.

Consumer protection. The educated consumer takes appropriate measures to safeguard his interests.

The objectives of civic responsibility

Social justice. The educated citizen is sensitive to the disparities of human circumstance.

Social activity. The educated citizen acts to correct unsatisfactory conditions.

Social understanding. The educated citizen seeks to understand social structures and social processes.

Critical judgment. The educated citizen has defenses against propaganda.

Tolerance. The educated citizen respects honest differences of opinion.

Conservation. The educated citizen has a regard for the nation's resources.

Social applications of science. The educated citizen measures scientific advance by its contribution to the general welfare.

World citizenship. The educated citizen is a cooperating member of the world community.

Law observance. The educated citizen respects the law.

Economic literacy. The educated citizen is economically literate.

Political citizenship. The educated citizen accepts his civic duties.

Devotion to democracy. The educated citizen acts upon an unswerving loyalty to democratic ideals.

These objectives provide a framework for educational activities on all school levels. They describe the kind of person which the school should seek to develop for our society. They constitute guideposts in terms of which you may decide the kinds of learning experiences desired for boys and girls. Although you should give attention to the development of each behavioral factor, you will be able to contribute more to the development of some than of others. For example, such factors as homemaking and occupational choice receive more attention on the secondary school level than on the preschool level. Furthermore, the subject area in which you teach will affect the behavioral factors to which major emphases will be given. If you plan to teach social studies, or music, or chemistry, or some other area, which behavioral characteristics will you seek most to develop? How will you attempt to develop them? Keep such questions as these in mind as you take subsequent academic and professional courses.

In 1961, a committee under the auspices of the Educational Policies Commission issued a statement regarding the central purpose of American education [40:1–21]. The committee recognized that the American school must be concerned with all the objectives indicated in the 1938 statement of the Educational Policies Commission if it is to fulfill its function. On the other hand, these objectives place upon the school an immense, if not impossible, task. Neither the schools nor the pupils have sufficient time or energy to engage in activities that will enable pupils to achieve fully all these goals by the time these pupils graduate from high school. Furthermore, education does not cease when pupils graduate. As a result, the committee expressed the feeling that a guiding principle was needed so that the school would be able to identify its necessary and appropriate contributions to individual development and the needs of society.

The members of the committee maintained that the development of the individual's ability to think should undergird the statement of objectives published by the Educational Policies Commission in 1938. For example, each of the school's traditional objectives, such as teaching the so-called "fundamental processes," can be better achieved as pupils develop the ability to think and as they learn to apply reflective thinking to all the problems that face them. Developing the rational powers of the human mind, therefore, constitutes the central purpose of the school.

The cultivated powers of the free mind have always been basic in achieving freedom. The powers of the free mind are many. In addition to the rational powers, there are those which relate to the aesthetic, the moral, and the religious. There is a unique, central role for the rational powers of an individual, however, for upon them depends his ability to achieve his personal goals and to fulfill his obligations to society.

These powers involve the processes of recalling and imagining, classifying and generalizing, comparing and evaluating, analyzing and synthesizing, and deducing and inferring. These processes enable one to apply logic and the available evidence to his ideas, attitudes, and actions, and to pursue better whatever goals he may have.

This is not to say that the rational powers are all of life or all of the mind, but they are the essence of the ability to think. A thinking person is aware that all persons, himself included, are both rational and nonrational, that each person perceives events through the screen of his own personality, and that he must take account of his personality in evaluating his perceptions. The rational processes, moreover, make intelligent choices possible. Through them a person can become aware of the bases of choice in his values and of the circumstances of choice in his environment. Thus they are broadly applicable in life, and they provide a solid basis for competence in all the areas with which the school has traditionally been concerned.

The traditionally accepted obligation of the school to teach the *fundamental processes*—an obligation stressed in the 1918 and 1938 statements of educational purposes—is obviously directed toward the development of the ability to think. Each of the school's other traditional objectives can be better achieved as pupils develop this ability and learn to apply it to all the problems that face them. . . . Development of the ability to reason can lead also to dedication to the values which inhere in rationality: commitment to honesty, accuracy, and personal reliability; respect for the intellect and for the intellectual life; devotion to the expansion of knowledge. A man who thinks can understand the importance of this ability. He is likely to value the rational potentials of mankind as essential to a worthy life.

Thus the rational powers are central to all the other qualities of the human spirit. These powers flourish in a humane and morally responsible context and contribute to the entire personality. The rational powers are to the entire human spirit as the hub is to the wheel . . . [40:4–8].

The rational powers of the human mind have always been basic in establishing and preserving freedom. In furthering personal and social effectiveness they are becoming more important than ever. They are central to individual dignity, human progress, and national survival.

The individual with developed rational powers can share deeply in the freedoms his society offers and can contribute most to the preservation of those freedoms. At the same time, he will have the best chance of understanding and contributing to the great events of his time. And the society which best develops the rational potentials of its people, along with their intuitive and aesthetic capabilities, will have the best chance of flourishing in the future. To help every person develop those powers is therefore a profoundly important objective and one which increases in importance with the passage of time. By pursuing this objective, the school can enhance spiritual and aesthetic values and other cardinal purposes which it has traditionally served and must continue to serve.

The purpose which runs through and strengthens all other educational purposes —the common thread of education—is the development of the ability to think. This is the central purpose to which the school must be oriented if it is to accomplish either its traditional tasks or those newly accentuated by recent changes in the world. To say that it is central is not to say that it is the sole purpose or in all circumstances the most important purpose, but that it must be a pervasive concern in the work of the school. Many agencies contribute to achieving educational objectives, but this particular objective will not be generally attained unless the school focuses on it. In this context, therefore, the development of every student's rational powers must be recognized as centrally important [40:11–12].

The members of the committee expressed the feeling that

man has before him the possibility of a new level of greatness, a new realization of human dignity and effectiveness. The instrument which will realize this possibility is that kind of education which frees the mind and enables it to contribute to a full and worthy life. To achieve this goal is the high hope of the nation and the central challenge to its schools [40:21].

In 1966, the American Association of School Administrators published the results of a two-year study made by a special commission of the association [134]. The members of the committee had focused their attention upon the major educational imperatives that should be at the forefront as curricula are modified, instructional methods revised, and organizational patterns reshaped to meet the educational needs of this country. Although the imperatives identified in the document *Imperatives in Education* are not intended to be educational goals, they do represent points at which the program may need to be revised and reshaped in order to meet the needs of the times. Since these nine imperatives may have considerable impact upon the thinking of school administrators and other educators, they are listed below and are accompanied with very brief discussions as well as suggestions for the improvement of our public schools.

1. *To make urban life rewarding and satisfying.* Urbanization is one of the most pronounced phenomena of the times. People in great numbers are coming to large cities, seeking better jobs, better education for their children, and a better way of life. They come on the crest of a rising wave of human aspirations. If these aspirations are to be realized—

All schools must have the best available instructional materials and equipment.

School plants must be designed and equipped to give pupils and teachers full opportunity for efficient and effective work.

Overcrowded classrooms and teacher shortages must be eliminated.

The instructional program must be extended downward to include kindergarten and prekindergarten-age children.

The educational program must be vitally related to the life of the community.

In-service education programs for teachers must be greatly expanded.

Financial support must be greatly increased to provide the special services and the additional facilities necessary to meet the educational needs of great groups of children who have recently migrated to the cities.

2. *To prepare people for the world of work.* Appropriate education stands squarely between the individual and the job he expects to get. At a time when the gross national product is at an all-time high and when demands for skilled workmen are increasing in many fields, thousands of young people ready to enter the labor market cannot find jobs because they lack the necessary qualifications. If this edutional deficit is to be erased—

Every child, youth, and adult must have as much education and as broad an education as his capacity will permit.

High priority must be given to developing the knowledge essential for supporting economic enterprise and meeting manpower needs.

Opportunities for technical and vocational training must be greatly extended and updated.

Appropriate training in simple occupations must be provided for less-gifted students.

The schools must take leadership in maintaining training and retraining programs for adults.

Programs of vocational guidance must be extended and improved.

3. *To discover and nurture creative talent.* Individually and collectively the people of this country are looking to the schools for a great contribution toward developing the reservoir of creative power needed to meet and deal with challenges arising on the forefront of cultural change. To develop this potential—

Every useful talent must be discovered and nurtured.

Schools must lay the groundwork, kindle the curiosity, provide the skills, and create the incentives that motivate continued learning year after year.

Pupil-teacher ratios must be maintained which permit teachers to meet the unique needs of every child.

Every capable student must continue his formal education beyond the twelfth grade in an appropriate institution.

Instruction in science, mathematics, and languages must begin in the elementary school and be continued and extended to the fullest degree student capacities will permit.

Greater emphasis must be given to the humanities and the arts in the instructional program as a way to further develop the creative capacities of all students.

4. *To strengthen the moral fabric of society.* The basic values which undergird the American way of life and which have guided the actions of people for centuries are being put to a severe test in an era of rapid technological change, social readjustment, and population expansion. The results of this test are most visible where they apply to children and youth. If the schools are to be successful in helping young people develop values that will give them a sense of direction—

The dignity of each individual must be recognized and enhanced through the instructional program and the organization and operation of the school.

High priority in the instructional program must be given to the development of moral, spiritual, and ethical values.

Every child must be led to fully understand that freedom and responsibility go hand in hand.

All pupils must acquire a sense of values that will enable them to make intelligent decisions between right and wrong.

Commitment to common purposes above and beyond immediate selfish interests must be developed.

The true meaning of fair play, personal honor, and social justice must be exemplified in every facet of the school's operation.

5. *To deal constructively with psychological tensions.* Psychological tensions have been accentuated by, if they are not an actual outgrowth of, cultural change—change that has placed children and youth in new and vastly different situations. In unfortunate circumstances, these tensions have exploded into violent action; in less visible but equally important instances, they have impaired learning and blemished personalities. If the school is to help young people develop behavior patterns that will enable them to live without undue stress or conflict—

Children and youth must learn to meet and cope with social change.

A firm working alliance between the school and the home must be established.

Counseling and other supporting educational services must be provided to meet the needs of each student.

Every school must institute a continuing program of health education, multidisciplinary in nature and reaching pupils at every grade level, to develop the highest level of health attainable. The school plant must provide an environment for pupils and teachers that is healthful, convenient, comfortable, and inspiring.

6. *To keep democracy working.* The basic purpose of the school is to develop in all people the skills, understandings, beliefs, and commitments necessary for government of and by the people. This is in essence the responsibility for teaching citizenship—but teaching citizenship under a set of circumstances perhaps more trying than in former years. These circumstances are characterized by urbanization, powerful pressure groups, controversies over civil rights, and increasing interdependence between different parts of the country. To prepare a generation of young people for effective citizenship in these circumstances—

Every child must have proficiency in reading, writing, and the use of numbers.

Everyone must be led to recognize his privileges and to accept his responsibilities as an American citizen.

The schools must aid in developing the understandings, the skills, and the points of view essential for resolving broad cultural problems through reason and considered judgment.

The schools must not be dominated and unduly influenced by special interest groups and the changing tides of political pressures.

All forms of discrimination and racial and group prejudices must be eliminated from the schools.

Everyone must have an understanding of the basic principles of democracy and a commitment to uphold and to support them.

7. *To make intelligent use of natural resources.* In keeping with the basic tenets of democracy, the control and use of natural resources have been entrusted to all the people. The question that now confronts everybody, and the schools in particular, is whether control of natural resources can continue to be left with the people or whether, because of dramatic increases in their use and misuse, regulatory measures will have to be imposed. The answer to this important question will depend in large measure upon whether—

All people—young children, adolescents, and adults—know and believe that natural resources are not inexhaustible.

Conservation is viewed as intelligent planning for efficient use, and not merely as saving.

Conservation is regarded as a problem based upon scientific principles firmly established in the laws of nature.

Extravagant use and waste leading to depletion of natural resources are eliminated.

Understandings and skills needed to deal with problems relative to the use of natural resources through community action and the processes of government are developed.

Students are involved in activities that will lead them to develop a sense of order among all things and to form concepts relative to the use of natural resources.

8. *To make the best use of leisure time.* Leisure time was once a luxury for the few. Now it has become a privilege for the many. With each passing decade the amount of leisure time increases through shorter work weeks, unemployment, a longer life-span, labor-saving devices, and customs and legislative action that cause many people to retire while their minds are still active and their bodies still vigorous. If this leisure time is to be used for cultural betterment—

The schools must develop creative and imaginative programs to change the boredom of idle hours into fruitful and satisfying experiences.

Public libraries must cooperate with the schools in providing books and encouraging reading.

The schools must remain open until the late hours of the evening and throughout the summer months.

Creative writing, drama, art, music, and modern dance must be emphasized throughout the elementary and secondary grades.

Children must be taught how to relax in the out-of-doors and to appreciate and enjoy the beauty and wonders of nature.

Community choruses, orchestras, and little theater groups must be encouraged and supported.

Young people must be given opportunities to develop the leadership abilities and sense the satisfactions that come from participation in community service programs.

9. *To work with other peoples of the world for human betterment.* Through historical circumstances, a world leadership role has been thrust upon the United States. The hopes of people in other lands are kindled by the ideals and concepts that undergird the American way of life. Because of its strong commitments to maintaining peace; safeguarding the rights of freedom-loving people; and reducing poverty, ignorance, famine, and disease, it becomes increasingly important that the people of this country become familiar with the cultures of other lands and learn how to work in a fruitful manner with people whose customs, values, and traditions differ from their own. To meet this responsibility—

Every American must be led to support his country in its efforts to achieve its supreme goal of peace with freedom.

Students must become sensitive to the problems and circumstances prevailing in other nations and know the historical backgrounds of the people, their religious beliefs, their forms of government, and the problems they face.

Ways must be found to teach children how to respect deep-seated cultural values of other people without losing or diminishing in any degree their confidence, respect, and commitments to the ideals, values, and customs of their own country.

Instruction in foreign languages must be strengthened and extended [134:165–173].

In order to gain a better understanding of each of these imperatives as well as the suggestions given, you should read this excellent document in its entirety.

EDUCATIONAL OBJECTIVES ACCORDING TO SCHOOL LEVELS

Although the objectives of education that have been presented provide the broad framework within which the school's contribution is made, teachers and administrators need objectives appropriate for the particular school level in which they work. These objectives must take into consideration the maturity levels of children in the various stages of their development. How can these maturity levels be identified?

Havighurst has formulated a list of developmental tasks with which an individual is confronted during certain periods of his life. Since his list has had considerable impact upon the formulation of educational objectives at various school levels, you may wish to become familiar with an outline of these tasks [125: chaps. 2, 4, 9, 10, 16–18].

Developmental tasks of early childhood

Learning to walk
Learning to take solid foods
Learning to talk
Learning to control the elimination of body wastes
Learning sex differences and sexual modesty
Learning physiological stability
Forming simple concepts of social and physical reality
Learning to relate oneself emotionally to parents, siblings, and other people
Learning to distinguish right from wrong and developing a conscience

Developmental tasks of middle childhood

Learning physical skills necessary for ordinary games
Building wholesome attitudes toward oneself as a growing organism
Learning to get along with age-mates
Learning an appropriate masculine or feminine social role
Developing fundamental skills in reading, writing, and calculating
Developing concepts necessary for everyday living
Developing conscience, morality, and a scale of values
Achieving personal independence
Developing attitudes toward social groups and institutions

Developmental tasks of adolescence

Achieving new and more mature relations with age-mates of both sexes
Achieving a masculine or feminine social role
Accepting one's physique and using the body effectively
Achieving emotional independence of parents and other adults
Achieving assurance of economic independence
Selecting and preparing for an occupation
Preparing for marriage and family life
Developing intellectual skills and concepts necessary for civic competence
Desiring and achieving socially responsible behavior
Acquiring a set of values and an ethical system as a guide to behavior

Developmental tasks of early adulthood

Selecting a mate
Learning to live with a marriage partner
Starting a family
Rearing children
Managing a home
Getting started in an occupation

Taking on civic responsibility
Finding a congenial social group

Developmental tasks of middle age

Achieving adult civic and social responsibility
Establishing and maintaining an economic standard of living
Assisting teen-age children to become responsible and happy adults
Developing adult leisure-time activities
Relating oneself to one's spouse as a person
Accepting and adjusting to the physiological changes of middle age
Adjusting to aging parents

Developmental tasks of later maturity

Adjusting to decreasing physical strength and health
Adjusting to retirement and reduced income
Adjusting to death of spouse
Establishing an explicit affiliation with one's age group
Meeting social and civic obligations
Establishing satisfactory physical living arrangements

You may wish to keep these developmental tasks in mind as you examine purposes and selected statements of objectives for each of the commonly recognized school levels.

Nursery School

As has been noted, increasing attention is being given to the educational growth of very young children. It is recognized that the early years of a child's life have a very significant bearing upon his later development. For example, the IQs of the 560,000 youngsters who participated in Project Head Start of 1966 were raised an average of 8 to 10 points during the eight-week period [127:105]. There is evidence to indicate that some juvenile delinquency, many nervous breakdowns, and certain adult psychoses may be traced to maladjustments which could have been prevented or corrected in early childhood.

Parents frequently feel that the home training of their young children needs to be supplemented by nursery experiences. Many factors contribute to this feeling. Some parents believe that they are unable to provide the best kind of guidance to their children at this age. Also, an increasing number of mothers find it necessary to work outside the home, and their children need to be placed in a healthy, happy, and constructive learning environment for at least part of the day.

The most common forms of organized educational activities for very young children consist of the day nursery and the nursery school. The day nursery, frequently called a "child-care center," is concerned mainly with the physical well-being of the child. With approximately one-third of the married women in the United States employed, the day nursery constitutes an important agency. The nursery school, on the other hand, has the characteristics of both a nursery and a school. In a sense, it is a downward extension of the kindergarten, and is designed to provide valuable educational and social experiences for children.

Moustakas and Berson of the famous Merrill-Palmer School indicate the objectives of a good nursery school in the following statement [168:17–18]:

We see the nursery school as an educational center that furthers the full development of the young child and the successful functioning of a group of young children. Its goal is to maintain a balance between spontaneous behavior and conformity to society's standards. It is concerned with the feelings and attitudes of young children and their developmental skills. It seeks to help children realize their potential and at the same time aids them to accept the limits of life in a democractic society.

The nursery school recognizes how important it is for young children to learn routine health habits. Activities are planned to strengthen and facilitate the use of their large and small muscles, build coordination, and develop sound, strong bodies.

The nursery school guides the child in experiencing the stimulation and enjoyment that come from the association with persons both younger and older than himself, as well as with those of the same age. It offers many opportunities for sharing and cooperating and helps children learn when and how to share.

The encouragement of rational thinking, fair play, self-reliance, and individual freedom and responsibility are all part of the nursery school's value. . . .

The nursery school must be concerned with the enhancement of the child's individuality, and the development of attitudes, interests, understandings, and beliefs which will enable the child to be a happy, secure, contributing member of society. To reach these goals the nursery school must have an emotionally warm, friendly, relaxed atmosphere.

Kindergarten

The kindergarten experiences of children are somewhat similar to those of the nursery school except that they are adapted to the maturity level of five-year-olds. The kindergarten provides a transition between home and school or between nursery school and formal school. Provision is made for rich experiences that will help prepare children for further schooling, although such formal training as instruction in actual reading normally is withheld.

In Florida, where kindergartens are financed as a part of the public school program, provision is made for each boy and girl who attends kindergarten to have experiences and to develop in the following ways [117:9]:

1. Live, work, and play with others in a program of learning activities that provide daily practice in sharing possessions, assuming responsibility for his own acts, acting as a leader and follower, and adjusting individual wishes or plans to the good of the group.
2. Develop a sense of security and well-being in a school situation.
3. Have experiences with books, stories, music, dramatic play, science and art materials. These activities not only will enrich the life of the child, but will provide experiences which increase vocabulary and will arouse an interest in reading.
4. Use materials freely and constructively which may result in increasing initiative, creative power, independence and motor coordination.
5. Develop motor skills and coordination through play with appropriate apparatus. This improved motor control is reflected by better handling of classroom equipment—blocks, pencils, scissors, crayons, as well as other equipment.

6. Express himself freely within a group situation and be stimulated to independent thinking in organizing and communicating his ideas.
7. Establish desirable health habits such as proper eating practices, relaxation during rest period, toilet routine and hand washing.

Elementary School

An outstanding formulation of objectives for the elementary school was prepared by the Mid-century Committee on Outcomes in Elementary Education [143:35–40]. The committee, consisting of outstanding educators throughout the United States, was sponsored by the Russell Sage Foundation, Educational Testing Service, U.S. Office of Education, and NEA Department of Elementary School Principals. It assumed that the elementary school should attempt to bring about behavior changes that are desirable in a democratic society. It also attempted to identify the objectives in such a manner that they might be susceptible to measurement, evaluation, and critical philosophical analysis.

The committee identified nine broad areas of elementary school learning: (1) physical development, health, and body care, (2) individual social and emotional development, (3) ethical behavior, standards, values, (4) social relations, (5) the social world, (6) the physical world, (7) aesthetic development, (8) communication, and (9) quantitative relationships. As a child learns in these areas, changes should take place in his knowledge and understanding, his skill and

FIGURE 16–1. Elementary school objectives. The behavior continuum—broad curriculum areas intersecting major behavior categories. (*Source:* Russell Sage Foundation.)

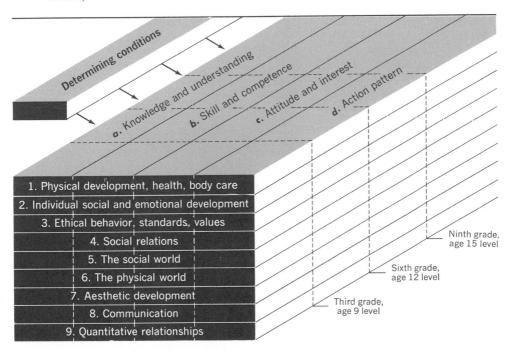

competence, his attitudes and interests, and his action patterns (broad generalized ways of behaving, such as response to problems through the use of intelligence, good work habits, and scientific methods of thinking).

As may be noted in the graphic presentation of elementary school objectives (Figure 16-1), the committee felt that a fifth column, titled "Determining conditions," should be added to account for the many forces, in addition to the school, that mold or limit the young learner. These conditions, more than anything else, represent the biological and sociological context in which children and schools carry on together.

The committee chose to visualize the objectives by means of a grid arrangement to convey the idea that growth, development, maturation, and learning are continuous in all the subdivisions. Similarly, they chose to consider outcomes in terms of the range of abilities within a group of children or of the traits in one child at each of three levels.

Secondary Education

Since the founding of the Boston Latin School in 1635, designed to prepare the intellectually elite boys for college, the objectives of secondary education have undergone many changes.

In response to considerable criticism of secondary schools, the National Education Association appointed the Commission on Reorganization of Secondary Education in 1913 for the purpose of studying desirable objectives for secondary schools. The report of this commission in 1918 was instrumental in expanding greatly the objectives of secondary education. The following, which have become known as the "seven cardinal principles," were recommended: (1) health, (2) command of fundamental processes, (3) worthy home membership, (4) vocation, (5) civic education, (6) worthy use of leisure time, and (7) ethical character.

For many years these objectives exerted considerable influence upon educators in the development of the secondary school curriculum. A number of educators, however, became increasingly concerned over the extent to which the secondary school curriculum was dominated by college entrance requirements. They felt that a good high school should serve the needs of both college-bound pupils and those who would not go to college. In response to this feeling, the Progressive Education Association conducted an experimental study during the period of 1933 to 1941, in which thirty school systems were freed from the traditional college entrance requirements. These schools were asked to provide the best total educational programs possible for all their pupils, so that the progress of those who would attend college could be studied. Upon entrance into college, the graduates of the experimental schools did as well academically and substantially better in student leadership positions than did the graduates from the other schools [4]. As a result of this study, objectives of secondary education were designed more in terms of meeting the life needs of all youth attending the secondary school.

In 1952, the Educational Policies Commission of the National Education Association issued a statement concerning the educational needs of youth in America which the school should seek to satisfy.

The commission felt that every youth, regardless of sex, economic status, geographic location, or race, should obtain a broad and balanced education that would be of value to him in the following respects [69:216]:

1. Equip him to enter an occupation suitable to his abilities and offering reasonable opportunity for personal growth and social usefulness
2. Prepare him to assume the full responsibilities of American citizenship
3. Give him a fair chance to exercise his right to the pursuit of happiness through the attainment and preservation of mental and physical health
4. Stimulate intellectual curiosity, engender satisfaction in intellectual achievement, and cultivate the ability to think rationally
5. Help him to develop an appreciation of the ethical values which should undergird all life in a democratic society

Davis, in 1966, formulated the following statement of objectives for secondary education, which seems to have gained general acceptance [59:55–57]:

1. Secondary education should provide for the development of each personality to the fullest realization of inborn capacities.
2. Secondary education should provide for the maximum development of each student's intellect.
3. Secondary education should provide for the development of good citizenship on the part of students.
4. Secondary education should provide for the development of understanding and knowledge about life that will lead to good physical and mental health.
5. Secondary education should provide for the desirable moral development of its students.
6. Secondary education should provide education in family living.
7. Secondary education should provide educational experiences that will help students equip themselves with the skills, knowledge, understandings, and attitudes necessary for earning their own living.
8. Secondary education should help students live a better, more enriched, enjoyable life.

It should be pointed out that these major objectives of secondary education apply to both the junior and the senior high school. Because of differences in the maturity levels of the pupils, the more specific objectives for the junior high school differ in some respects from those for the senior high school. Actually, the goals of junior high schools tend to be somewhat similar to those of both elementary and senior high schools. This is to be expected since, from an organizational standpoint, the junior high school provides for the transition of pupils from the elementary to the senior high school. These factors are reflected in the following statement of objectives for the junior high school formulated by Bossing and Cramer [29:52–53]:

1. To develop within students their abilities to observe, listen, read, calculate, think, speak, and write with purpose and comprehension
2. To offer assistance and direction to students in the resolution of their problems so they may effectively cope with their fears, anxieties, and frustrations
3. To create learning opportunities which will permit the intellectual capacity of the early adolescent to grow and develop to its maximum
4. To plan situations and activities that will provide typical experiences for students which will best accommodate their social and emotional needs

5. To expand and enrich the progression of learning begun within the general educational framework of the elementary school
6. To institute learning situations which will assist early adolescents in the healthful advancement from childhood orientation to one of later adolescence or beginning adulthood
7. To make available sufficient personal interest explorations to initiate a clear understanding of the industry and culture of the adult world
8. To provide experiences designed to develop appropriate attitudes and values necessary for living in a democracy as an individual member and as a contributor to the common good
9. To establish effective resources for developing the health and physical fitness of all students
10. To organize experience opportunities which will assure a smoother transition from the elementary school to the junior high school, and on to the senior high school

Junior College

As indicated previously, there is considerable debate on whether the junior college belongs to secondary or to higher education. Traditionally, it has been defined as a higher-education institution which gives two years of work equivalent to the first two years in a college or university. The feeling has developed, especially in California, where the greatest number of junior colleges has been established, that it should be considered as an extension of the secondary school. Three types of junior colleges can be rather definitely identified: (1) the community junior college, which attempts to serve any local community needs which are not being served by other institutions of the community; (2) the special junior college, which attempts to excel in a few areas of instruction and admittedly neglects certain other community needs; (3) the junior college that attempts to offer the first two years of a senior college curriculum.

The community junior college, which establishes its function in terms of the needs of the geographic area in which it is located, has the following major objectives:

1. To provide for the extension of education designed to meet the added requirements of life and work
2. To provide preparation for further college study to students who will be transferring to a senior college
3. To provide opportunities for individuals to continue, on a part-time basis, their education as the need and interest arise
4. To relieve the pressure of enrollments increasingly experienced by regular colleges and universities
5. To provide a center for adult education activities

In the book, *The Open Door College: A Case Study,* Clark [43:168–176] indicates a number of problems concerning the character and role of junior colleges. Undoubtedly, increasing clarification will be gained in the future with regard to such factors as (1) the unique function of the junior college, (2) the quality of instruction that may be provided, (3) financial support, (4) local or state control, and (5) accreditation. Regardless of these problems, the junior college seems destined to play an increasingly significant role in the extension of educational opportunities for youth as well as for adults.

Higher Education

Institutions of higher education have four interlocking types of programs to offer: liberal or general education, professional or vocational education, graduate study and research, and public services. Colleges and universities differ greatly throughout the United States in the extent to which they emphasize each of these four offerings.

According to the American Council on Education, general education should enable the student [152:14–15]:

1. To improve and maintain his own health and take his share of responsibility for protecting the health of others
2. To communicate through his own language in writing and speaking at the level of expression adequate to the needs of educated people
3. To attain a sound emotional and social adjustment through the enjoyment of a wide range of social relationships and the experience of working co-operatively with others
4. To think through the problems and to gain the basic orientation that will better enable him to make a satisfactory family and marital adjustment
5. To do his part as an active and intelligent citizen in dealing with the interrelated social, economic, and political problems of American life and in solving the problems of postwar international reconstruction
6. To act in the light of an understanding of the natural phenomena in his environment in its implications for human society and human welfare, to use scientific methods in the solution of his problems, and to employ useful non-verbal methods of thought and communication
7. To find self-expression in literature and to share through literature man's experience and his motivating ideas and ideals
8. To find a means of self-expression in music and in the various visual arts and crafts, and to understand and appreciate art and music as reflections both of individual experience and of social patterns and movements
9. To practice clear and integrated thinking about the meaning and value of life
10. To choose a vocation that will make optimum use of his talents and enable him to make an appropriate contribution to the needs of society

The modern world requires that highly skilled technicians be prepared to perform the necessary services to society in such areas as education, medicine, law, business, engineering, communication, and transportation. For this reason a large percentage of the students attending college are preparing for a profession. In addition to the vocational competencies required for their respective vocations, these students also need to acquire a general educational background that will assist them in being effective citizens.

In addition to instructional obligations, higher-education institutions have the responsibility to society of contributing new knowledge through research. For this reason the larger institutions, especially those having good financial resources, often have graduate schools and research facilities to provide for training above the baccalaureate level in almost all fields of learning. Although various independent research agencies have been developed in such fields as science, business, and agriculture, institutions of higher education continue to contribute a very substantial amount of the findings.

Colleges and universities have become centers of information and trained ability to which society can bring its problems. Increasing demands for assistance in almost every area of human endeavor are being made upon college and university staff members. Through such activities institutions of higher education assume a leadership role.

Adult Education

Frequent mention has been made of the growing importance of adult education. Since adulthood involves a large part of life, "adult education includes the larger portion of life-long learning. It involves experiences which cause persons to evaluate and adjust their ideas and opinions, and to broaden their range of learning into new fields" [248:5].

Adult education is broad and diverse in its nature. Too frequently it seems to consist merely of courses of instruction taught in a school building, but more than 90 per cent of all the education of adults carried on in America is done outside the school building. Other types of adult education take place through such media as newspapers, group discussions, magazines, radio, television, books, forums, speeches, advertisements, movies, and pictures and cartoons.

Three important objectives of adult education are:

1. To assist all persons to know more about themselves
2. To help people to understand their relationships with their fellowmen
3. To help persons learn more about their jobs as workers and citizens of a free society

It is important to remember that adults must be convinced of the need to learn. They generally want the type of learning that is both useful and down to earth. Most adults find little meaning in abstract goals, regardless of how essential they are to the advancement of civilization, unless they can see the specific relationships between these goals and ideas that are already familiar to them. However, as mature people have the opportunity to participate in the development of concrete ideas, even the more abstract goals become meaningful and acceptable to them. As a result, adults are stimulated to expand their intellectual horizons and their competencies as useful citizens in a democratic society.

Members of the Adult Education Association of the United States maintain that our concept of adult education must change from an optional to an imperative activity in our society. They feel that, if adult education is to fulfill its new mission as "an imperative of our times," the following conditions must be met [3:14–15]:

1. There must be a *national perception,* especially on the part of those who control educational policy, of the essential role of continuing education in preventing human obsolescence and in preserving and further developing the American society.

2. The education of children and youth must be reoriented to a *conception of learning as a lifelong process*. Teachers in schools and colleges must learn to teach youth so that they leave formal schooling (*a*) with an insatiable curiosity, (*b*) with a mastery of the tools of learning, and (*c*) with a commitment to continue learning through the rest of their life span.

3. *The agencies of adult education must clarify their respective tasks* of establishing between themselves orderly working arrangements and interrelated planning and to ensure that the resources of adult education are used effectively in meeting the adult educational needs of individuals, institutions, and communities.

4. A *coherent curriculum* of adult education must be developed that provides for the sequential development of the knowledge, understanding, skills, attitudes, and values required to maintain one's effectiveness in a changing social order.

5. The *corps of leaders and teachers* of adults must be enlarged and provided with the knowledge and skills required for them to help adults learn efficiently.

6. A special responsibility is placed on the universities of the country to expand the resources available for *research and advanced professional training* in adult education.

7. Community agencies of adult education, especially schools and colleges, must upgrade the *standards of professional competence* required of those guiding adult learning, and employ personnel with these competencies.

8. There must be a *national commitment* to provide the resources and moral support necessary for the development of lifelong learning as an integral element of the American way of life.

SUMMARY

In the first part of this chapter, attention was given to several *uncritical* basic assumptions which operate in some schools today. The validity of these assumptions in fulfilling the school's function for today's youth was questioned. Ten statements of educational principles and their implications for educational practice were submitted on the assumption that the school provides the primary means of social progress. Governed by these principles, teaching becomes a most challenging and adventuresome profession.

Teachers are responsible for providing a most vital function—directing the experiences of the young in such a manner that the welfare of the group may be raised. The future of democracy depends upon the resources, insight, and courage with which teachers accept this basic social responsibility.

In the second part of the chapter, attention was focused upon the objectives of education as they pertain to education in general and to the various levels ranging from preelementary to adult education. Educational objectives grow out of the life values which people prize. They are essential in order to provide direction to the planning and appraisal of educational activities.

The general objectives prepared by the Educational Policies Commission in 1938, as well as the statement of central purpose of American education issued in 1961, provide a broad frame of reference within which each level of our educational system makes its particular contribution in terms of the maturity of the learner. A clear understanding of the general objectives of education as well as of the objectives for the particular level upon which you plan to teach will give direction to your professional preparation and to your work as a teacher.

QUESTIONS FOR YOUR CONSIDERATION

1. What are the so-called "broader" functions of the school?
2. What values in our society should the school seek to preserve, promote, and refine?
3. In what ways do the objectives of education in our American democracy specifically differ from those in a totalitarian country?
4. If you assume that pupils go to school in order to acquire desirable behavior patterns, how will you attempt to evaluate the progress made by your pupils? What instruments and techniques will you use?
5. What is meant by the statement that a more rigorous and a more disciplined kind of education is necessary in order to meet the conditions of contemporary society? What are the implications of this statement for you as a teacher?
6. To what extent do the four objectives developed by the Educational Policies Commission adequately describe the kind of person schools should seek to develop for our society?
7. How do the objectives of nursery and kindergarten differ from those of elementary education?
8. How have the objectives of the secondary school changed during the past 50 years?
9. What does the 1961 statement on the central purpose of education add to the statements of objectives published by the Educational Policies Commission in 1938?
10. Do the objectives of education in a rural community differ from those in a large metropolitan community?
11. What is meant by a community-centered school or college?
12. In what ways may you as a teacher serve as a key figure in leading the community toward a fulfillment of its democratic values?
13. What can the public school do in meeting adult education needs?

ACTIVITIES FOR YOU TO PURSUE

1. Appraise the public school experiences you had in light of the function of the school as presented in this chapter. In other words, how adequately were the schools you attended fulfilling their purpose as herein defined?
2. Make a list of the competencies for teaching which the content of this chapter suggests.
3. Review the ten uncritical assumptions which seem to characterize the way some of our schools operate. Discuss with your colleagues the extent to which these assumptions seem to be sound.
4. Match the "Developmental tasks of early childhood" with the objectives of education for each school level. Do they seem to be compatible?
5. List ways in which you will attempt to help your pupils achieve the objective of human relationships, as formulated by the Educational Policies Commission. Repeat the process in connection with the other three objectives.
6. Check the principles, listed in Chapter 13, upon which the junior high school

was founded. Compare and contrast these principles with the objectives for junior high schools listed by Bossing and Cramer.

7. Perhaps you have heard people express the feeling that certain school subjects were good for disciplining the mind. Discuss this point of view with your colleagues and explore its educational implications. As you engage in this activity, attempt to describe the behavior characteristics of a well-disciplined democratic citizen.

8. School superintendents frequently question candidates for teaching positions regarding their views toward education. Write on two or three sheets of paper what you consider the school's function to be. Compare what you write with the opinions of your colleagues.

9. Many school systems distribute bulletins to teachers and parents containing statements of the school's function. Collect one or more of these bulletins and critically appraise the statements made.

10. Select a school system that seems to be fulfilling the function of the school as described in this chapter. Plan with the superintendent, or some other school official, to make several classroom observations. Discuss these observations with your colleagues, your college instructor, and, if possible, the classroom teachers whom you observe.

11. Have some of your public school teacher friends show you examples of the day-to-day as well as the more ultimate objectives which they use in planning suitable classroom activities. What relationship do these objectives have with the general objectives of education discussed in this chapter?

17

CONTROVERSIAL ISSUES
AND PROBLEMS
IN EDUCATION

Do you know of any major improvement that has taken place in society without attendant problems? Difficulties are certain to be present whenever changes in the thinking and behavior of people are involved. This is true in the field of education as well as in any other major field of endeavor.

As you move into education, you are faced with the challenge of aiding in the solution of major problems that emerge because schools strive increasingly to fulfill their function in a democratic society. You have a professional obligation to become familiar with these problems and to plan ways in which you may aid in their creative and effective solution.

A number of educational problems have already been discussed in this book. The purpose of the present chapter is to bring into focus other controversial problems, some of which have been previously indicated but not probed extensively. All these problems are interrelated and are separated only for the purpose of discussion. The order of discussion in no way indicates their relative importance.

In the discussion that follows, an attempt is made to indicate some of your responsibilities in regard to certain problems rather than to formulate any solutions to them. As you continue your preparation for teaching, and throughout your professional career, plan to give these problems the thoughtful consideration that each deserves. The ways in which you work toward their effective solution will need to be modified as conditions change and new information emerges.

What Should Be the Relationship between Religion and the Public Schools?

Any discussion of the relationship between religion and public education must, at least initially, be approached from a historical base. As indicated in Chapter 13, many of America's early colonists came to the New World to escape religious persecution in Europe. These early settlers had lived in European countries where a certain church or churches were given sanction or approval by the government and where religious freedom as we know it today did not exist.

You may be less aware of the fact that when many of these early colonists arrived in America, they made provision for an established church sanctioned by the colonial government and began to persecute religious dissenters at least as vigorously as they themselves had been persecuted in Europe. In fact, in many of the American Colonies dissenters such as Baptists, Roman Catholics, Quakers, and Jews were denied the right to assemble and to worship publicly, and punishments for violation of these early religious laws ranged from a fine or imprisonment to, in some cases, death.

During the years prior to the American Revolution, opposition to the practice of persecution of religious minorities grew, and by the time the federal Constitution was drafted, colonial leaders such as Jefferson and Madison were firm in their determination that never again would government in America sanction or support a particular religion or prohibit any religious faith from public worship or from expressing publicly its beliefs.

Out of the reaction against governmental involvement in religion grew the First Amendment to the federal Constitution. This amendment provides, in part, that "Congress shall make no law respecting an establishment of religion, or prohibiting the free exercise thereof."

The First Amendment, as you can see, originally applied only to Congress or the federal government. Following the Civil War, however, the Fourteenth Amendment was enacted, which guaranteed to citizens of all states the basic rights protected by the federal Constitution. In recent years, the United States Supreme Court has interpreted the Fourteenth Amendment to mean that the First Amendment applies not only to Congress but also to the states. The First Amendment, as interpreted today, means, then, that neither Congress nor a state may establish a religion or prohibit the free exercise of a religion.

The public schools are a part of state government. In fact, a local school district is a legal subdivision of the state, and the members of local boards of education are state officers. Since a state may not establish a religion, neither may a local school district, because such a district is a state entity. This legal concept has been the basis for many of the most significant and critical court decisions involving the schools which have been decided by American courts in recent years.

The McCollum case, decided by the United States Supreme Court in 1948, was one of the first wherein this concept was tested. It involved a situation common to many schools of the day—that of *released time,* which was a practice whereby public school pupils were released from their normal classes to attend religious classes held in the same public school building and taught by church school teachers who came from outside the school. Suit was brought to prevent the continuation of such a program of religious instruction in the public schools of Champaign, Illinois, primarily on the grounds that such a program violated the "establishment of religion" clause of the First Amendment.

The Supreme Court declared that the Champaign religious education program violated the First Amendment and ordered the program discontinued. The practice of permitting outside religious teachers to conduct religious classes on public school property during the school day constituted "too great" a cooperation between government and religion and thus amounted to an establishment of religion by government, according to the Court (*McCollum v. Board of Education,* 333 U.S. 203, 68 Sup. Ct. 461).

For some four years, religious educators in America were in a quandary. Did the McCollum decision mean that released time programs were prohibited entirely? Could such programs be conducted off school grounds rather than within public school facilities? Did the decision mean that the Supreme Court was antagonistic toward any religious teaching of public school youngsters?

In 1952, another case reached the Court, which at least in part answered these questions. This case, known as the Zorach case, involved a challenge brought by parents in New York City against a public school practice which permitted pupils to be released from classes to attend religious instruction off the school grounds. As you can see, this practice differed from the McCollum case in that the religious instruction was not given in the public school buildings.

In upholding the release of pupils to attend religious classes held away from the public school buildings, the Supreme Court made it clear that, although the government was compelled to remain "neutral" in religious matters, this by no means meant that the government was "hostile" to religion. According to the Court, cooperation between government and religion, such as releasing pupils for off-school religious classes, was permissible under the First Amendment (*Zorach v. Clauson,* 343 U.S. 306, 72 Sup. Ct. 670).

Many questions involving the public schools and religion remained, however. In nineteenth-century American public schools, teachers were expected to impart to pupils religious and "moral" training, including use of the Holy Bible as a text, as a moral guide, and as a basis for classroom "devotions." Pupils were also expected to participate in prayer in many public school classrooms. Vestiges of these religious practices remained in American public schools as late as 1962.

In 1962, challenge of a prayer adopted by the New York Board of Regents (the state board of education) reached the Supreme Court (*Engel v. Vitale,* 370 U.S. 421, 82 Sup. Ct. 1261). The prayer, developed by representatives of several religious faiths and designed to be interdenominational, had been recommended by the Board of Regents for use in the public schools of New York.

After lengthy consideration, the Supreme Court held that the use of a governmentally composed prayer in the public schools violated the establishment clause of the First Amendment—in other words, the government of New York was establishing a state-approved religion. Even the fact that children might be excused from the classroom during the saying of the prayer made no difference. According to the Court, the mere existence and use of a state-approved prayer constituted an establishment of religion by the state. Mr. Justice Black, speaking for the majority of the Court, stated (370 U.S. 424, 82 Sup. Ct. 1263):

We think that by using its public school system to encourage recitation of the Regent's prayer, the State of New York has adopted a practice wholly inconsistent with the Establishment Clause. There can, of course, be no doubt that New York's program of daily classroom invocation of God's blessings as prescribed in the Regent's prayer is a religious activity. It is a solemn avowal of divine faith and supplication for the blessings of the Almighty. The nature of such a prayer has always been religious.

Justice Black went on to say (370 U.S. 429, 82 Sup. Ct. 1266):

The First Amendment was added to the Constitution to stand as a guarantee that neither the power nor the prestige of the Federal Government would be used to control, support or influence the kinds of prayer the American people can say, that the people's religions must not be subjected to the pressures of government for change each time a new political administration is elected to office. Under that Amendment's prohibition against governmental establishment of religion, as reinforced by the provisions of the Fourteenth Amendment, government in this country, be it state or federal, is without power to prescribe by law any particular form of prayer which is to be used as an official prayer in carrying on any program of governmentally sponsored religious activity.

In 1963, the Court was faced with another decision of far-reaching importance to American public education. At this time, two cases, known as the Schempp and Murray cases, which dealt primarily with the legality of devotional use of the Holy Bible in the public schools, reached the Court (*School District of Abington Township v. Schempp; Murray v. Curlett*, 374 U.S. 203, 83 Sup. Ct. 1560).

In the Schempp case, suit was brought to prevent enforcement of a Pennsylvania law which required that at least ten verses from the Holy Bible be read without comment at the opening of each school day in the public schools of that state. In the Murray case, a rule of the Baltimore school board provided that opening exercises in the public schools of that city consist of the reading, without comment, of a chapter from the Holy Bible and/or the use of the Lord's Prayer.

The Supreme Court handed down a single opinion dealing with both cases, holding that both the Pennsylvania law and the Baltimore school board rule were unconstitutional. In reaching this decision, the Court pointed out that the religious exercises were a "prescribed part of the curriculum" and were "held in the school buildings under the supervision and with the participation of teachers" and therefore constituted a state sanction or establishment of religion. The Court made clear, however, that although devotional use of the Bible was prohibited, use of the Bible as a literary or historical document was permissible.

Mr. Justice Brennan, speaking for the Court, stated (374 U.S. 283, 83 Sup. Ct. 1603):

There are persons in every community—often deeply devout—to whom any version of the Judaeo-Christian Bible is offensive. There are others whose reverence for the Holy Scriptures demands private study or reflection and to whom public reading or recitation is sacrilegious. . . . To such persons it is not the fact of using the Bible in the public schools, nor the content of any particular version that is offensive, but only the manner in which it is used.

Justice Brennan went on to outline the position of the Court on the relationship between religion and government (374 U.S. 294, 83 Sup. Ct. 1609):

I believe that the line we must draw between the permissible and the impermissible is one which accords with history and faithfully reflects the understanding of the Founding Fathers. It is a line which the Court has consistently sought to mark in its decisions expounding the religious guarantees of the First Amendment. What the Framers meant to foreclose, and what our decisions under the Establishment Clause have forbidden, are those involvements of religious with secular institutions which (a) serve the essentially religious activities of religious institutions; (b) employ the organs of government for essentially religious purposes; or (c) use essentially religious means to serve governmental ends, where secular means would suffice. When the secular and religious institutions become involved in such a manner, there inhere in the relationship precisely those dangers—as much to church as to state— which the Framers feared would subvert religious liberty and the strength of a system of secular government.

The end of the issue is not in sight. Such religious appendages of early American schools as baccalaureate exercises, distribution of Gideon Bibles, saying of grace by a pupil, use of religious carols and hymns, Christmas, Hanukkah, and Easter observances, religious symbols, and religious tests for the selection or promotion of teachers have not yet been considered by the Supreme Court.

The Commission on Religion in the Public Schools of the American Association of School Administrators has considered several of these issues and, in 1964, suggested the following as guidelines for public schools [213:31–53]:

1. Christmas should not be observed by public schools as though they were churches; however, Christmas, as a cultural and educational institution, should not be ignored. Reasonable observance should be made.
2. School calendars should be adjusted so as to maximize the possibility of appropriate religious observances by children of all faiths.
3. Baccalaureate services should be held by religious groups represented by students in the graduating class in their own churches and synagogues. The school should not require attendance nor do more than inform its seniors about such services.
4. School authorities should avoid any semblance of religious establishment in the use of public resources or in the coercion of pupils.

One other aspect of the situation deserves mention. As a reaction against the recent decisions of the Supreme Court, proposals have been made in Congress that the federal Constitution be amended to permit the use of prayer and/or Biblical scripture in public schools or other governmental institutions. The fate of such proposals remains to be seen.

In the Schempp and Murray cases, the Supreme Court, although striking down the devotional use of the Bible, indicated that the use of the Bible as a literary or historical document was not proscribed and implied that teaching pupils *about* religion would not violate the First Amendment. Teaching about religion, perhaps, may be one of the most difficult tasks facing any teacher. Although he agrees that the public schools can and should teach about religion, Ballinger points out that religion is so much a part of the basic values of many individuals that it cannot be expressed simply in descriptive terms. Ballinger raises the following questions in this regard [16:129–153]:

1. Since the term "religion" tends to become involved in the conflicting values of people, can it really be defined?
2. Can a teacher be objective and neutral in teaching about religion, or will she, perhaps unconsciously, tend to teach her own religious values?
3. Since so much of religious experience is private in nature, can or should such private experience be transmitted to others?
4. Use of the Bible as literature presupposes critical inquiry into meanings and literal truth. Are we to permit pupils to use critical thinking in analyzing the Bible in the same way that we use critical thinking in analyzing any other literary work?
5. Since any religion is in itself a view of history, is it possible to teach the "role" of religions in history without organizing the entire history course around *one* religious view of history, with but passing references to other religious views?

How do recent decisions of the Supreme Court affect the use of prayer in public schools? What guidelines will you follow in regard to this matter? *(Photograph from the National Education Association.)*

The questions raised by Ballinger perhaps illustrate some of the basic problems teachers face when attempting to teach about religion or when attempting to use the Bible as a literary or historical document. Several church leaders have tried to come to grips with these problems. For example, Fosdick suggests that the churches representing all faiths cooperate in developing materials for use in the public schools which would present the "common core" of religious heritage, presenting fairly and factually the diverse faiths that characterize the various religions [100:131]. So far, no serious attempt has been made by church groups to accomplish this task.

A number of arguments are advanced by those who feel that our public schools should be concerned with religious education. A few of these arguments are as follows:

1. Many boys and girls do not go to church and therefore do not receive any significant amount of religious instruction. The school should provide for the needs of these pupils.

2. It is necessary to teach religion if boys and girls are to gain desirable moral values.

3. Teaching about religion in the public schools would promote greater understanding and tolerance of the various religions.
4. Teaching about religion is as important in the lives of boys and girls as other subjects that are taught in the schools. Therefore, the school should provide time for such instruction.
5. Teachers are better trained to teach about religion than are the parents.
6. If teaching about religion is forbidden in public schools, pupils are encouraged to feel that religion is not important in their lives. Therefore, our schools are atheistic, or "Godless."

Those opposed to teaching about religion in the public schools argue that:

1. Religion can be better handled by parents and churches; teaching about religion should be left to the home and the church.
2. It is impossible to teach about religion objectively.
3. Teachers are not prepared adequately to teach about religion.
4. With so many faiths represented by pupils in the public schools, it would be impossible for the schools to teach about all religions.
5. Teaching about religion may result in critical inquiry into the religious beliefs of pupils, may cause doubts to arise in their minds, and may result in great public criticism of public school programs.
6. The curriculum of the public schools is already crowded, and patrons should not expect the public schools to solve all the world's social problems.

The teaching of moral or ethical values is another aspect of the religious question. Hansen points out that the public schools should not only teach the importance of great religious writings but also encourage religious toleration and develop respect for and acceptance of religious differences and minorities. According to Hansen, public schools can teach such moral and ethical values without reference to any particular religion and can make certain that other ethical values, such as unselfishness, honesty, and integrity, become a part of the daily experience of pupils [121:403–404].

Those who would agree with Hansen contend that there exists in America a generally accepted code of moral conduct which can be transmitted to youngsters, at least partially, through the precept and example of the teacher himself.

Those who would disagree with Hansen suggest that no code of moral or ethical values can be divorced from a particular religious faith and that any such code likely to be taught in American public schools would be based upon the Judaeo-Christian ethic. This, the critics contend, would be akin to teaching such faith in the classroom.

Regardless of the level and area in which you teach, it will be impossible for you to escape questions about religion asked by pupils. At this point, you will want to keep in mind the distinction between teaching religion and teaching *about* religion. Neither can you escape the question of what is "moral" or "ethical" regarding many of your daily classroom experiences. It is doubtful whether anyone would expect you to be completely neutral with respect to whether it is "moral" or "immoral" for a child to cheat on an examination, for example.

The personal example you set will have incalculable effect upon the moral

Young people naturally absorb from adults their impressions of people and their views toward life. The teacher has many opportunities for developing ideals and standards of behavior that will give positive direction to the pupil's life. (*Photograph by Carl Purcell, National Education Association.*)

values of your pupils. In the matter of teaching about religion or the answering of questions about religion, there is no substitute for being well informed.

Why Is Our Educational System Being Criticized?

As a prospective educator and as a citizen you will want to have a clear understanding of the attacks being made upon our public schools and be able to discuss with school patrons their nature, probable causes, and justification.

What are the reasons for the attacks? Are they due in part to the increased amount of education which each succeeding generation has gained? As people become more educated, they tend to place a higher value upon schooling and to become increasingly critical of educational practices. Have the two major opposing ideologies in the world today contributed to an outburst of concern for the education of the young? Are these attacks due to an increasing awareness upon the part of the general public of the importance of education as a means of preserving and promoting democratic living? Are these attacks sincere efforts designed to improve the education of the young, or are they motivated by desires to weaken our schools, curtail educational costs, or spread seeds of suspicion? To what extent do these attacks represent differences in opinion or confusion in regard to the school's function in a democratic society? To what extent are the attackers misinformed or unaware of valid research findings in terms of which modifications have been made in educational practices? These are only a few of the questions which you should keep in mind as you appraise the criticism that has been made, is being made, and will be made in the future.

The public has a right, in fact an obligation, to prescribe policies by which the public schools shall abide and to appraise the extent to which these policies have been fulfilled. Furthermore, the public for many years has exercised the right to criticize educational endeavors. Aristotle in 384 B.C. wrote the following: "There are doubts concerning the business of education, since all people do not agree in those things they would have a child taught." Some of the people at that time, and even earlier, complained that the children preferred sitting around chatting to participating in athletic activities, had bad manners, were disrespectful of their elders, and ruled the household. Confucius, approximately twenty-five hundred years ago, noted: "The teachers of today just go on repeating things in a rigmarole fashion, annoy the students with constant questions, and repeat the same things over and over again. They do not try to find out what the students' natural inclinations are so that the students are forced to pretend to like their studies, nor do they try to bring out the best in their talents" [188:1].

John Erskine, in *My Life as a Teacher*, said, regarding his teaching at Amherst in 1903, "A large proportion of my first Amherst freshmen were unable to spell."

Horace Mann, in his report of 1838, stated:

I have devoted special pains to learn, with some degree of numerical accuracy, how far the reading, in our schools, is an exercise of the mind in thinking and feeling, and how far it is a barren action of the organs of speech upon the atmosphere. . . . The result is, that more than eleven-twelfths of all the children in the reading classes, in our schools, do not understand the meaning of the words they read; that they do not master the sense of the reading lessons, and that the ideas and feelings intended by the author to be conveyed to, and excited in, the reader's mind, still rest in the author's intention, never having yet reached the place of their destination.

In 1845 the Grammar School Committee of Boston, after having administered various tests to the pupils, reported that:

They [tests administered] show beyond all doubt that a large proportion of the scholars in our first classes, boys and girls of 14 and 15 years of age, when called on to write simple sentences, to express their thoughts on common subjects, without the aid of a dictionary or a master, cannot write, without such errors in grammar, in spelling, and in punctuation, as we should blush to see in a letter from a son or daughter of their age.

Do these statements have a familiar ring to you, even though some of them were made over 2,000 years ago?

You undoubtedly have heard older people appraise present conditions and practices in terms of "the good old days." There seems to be a human tendency to glamorize and "haloize" days past, which in reality were not half so good as they are today. Furthermore, there is a tendency to resist change and to impose an element of rightness to our own past experience. These tendencies may operate as older people appraise the products of today's schools.

How do boys and girls in present-day schools compare with the products of an earlier system? Teachers themselves were asked this question in a 1964 survey [10:7]. The opinions of a sample group of elementary and secondary teachers with respect to whether the above-average, average, or below-average pupil was learning more, about the same, or less today than when the teachers themselves were in elementary or high school were found to be as follows:

Amount of learning	Elementary	Secondary
Above-average pupil:		
More	82%	78%
About same	12	14
Less	6	8
Average pupil:		
More	73	57
About same	21	33
Less	6	10
Below-average pupil:		
More	64	48
About same	27	35
Less	9	17

As you can see, in the opinion of a sampling of teachers, pupils in both elementary and secondary schools were learning as much or more in 1964 schools than in schools of an earlier day; the great majority of teachers answered "more" in each category.

The views of the teachers seem to be shared by the American public. In a nationwide poll conducted in 1965, 76 per cent of those asked indicated they would rate the quality of the public schools in their communities good or excellent. A second poll showed that 82 per cent rated the teachers in their communities good or excellent [180:4].

Insofar as statistics can show the improvements in American public education during the past few decades, today's schools are probably far superior [91:35–45]:

1. The holding power of our high schools is higher today. In 1910, 58.9 per cent of the population 14 to 17 years of age was enrolled in school; in 1965, 93.2 per cent.
2. School terms are longer. In 1900, the average school term was 144.3 days; in 1963–1964, it was 179 days.
3. Educational attainment is rising. In 1940, the median years of school completed by adults 25 years of age and older was 8.4 years; in 1964, it was 11.7 years.
4. Literacy levels are increasing. In 1900, 10.7 per cent of the adult population was illiterate; in 1960, only 2.4 per cent.
5. The percentage of persons who are high school graduates is increasing. In 1920, less than 20 per cent of persons 17 years of age were high school graduates; in 1964, nearly 80 per cent were high school graduates.

The above are only a few of the many examples which could be used to illustrate that the American dream of education for all the people is rapidly approaching fruition.

Regardless of the strengths of American public education, criticism is present today from many quarters and probably will continue to be present. Stinnett [254:28] warns that "there is no reason to assume that the schools will ever be free of criticism, public discussion, and controversy." Few would argue that such criticism and discussion are undesirable. Constructive criticism is at the heart of the democratic process, and improvements in American public education undoubtedly can continue to be made.

Unfortunately not all the criticisms you may read (or hear) seem to be constructive by intent. Finn points out that [95:31]:

> Books that have good things to say about our society do not sell very well; very few orders for pamphlets and reprints are received when the pamphlets and reprints have something worthwhile to say in favor of a person or institution. It's small consolation, but the last best seller that sang praises was probably the Book of Psalms.
>
> At the moment, there's money, prestige and almost sure publication without much chance of getting slapped back awaiting anyone willing to kick an educationist in the stomach. Aggressions are also relieved. By creating a new minority group (the educationists) to push around, most of the critics . . . (but not all critics) have discovered a form of therapy that brings wonderful release . . . and money.

As you are confronted in the future with criticisms of the schools, you may wish to examine the apparent motives behind the author, as well as the accuracy, objectivity, logic, and depth of understanding with which he writes or speaks.

A 1965 study conducted by the National Education Association perhaps illustrates the nature and amount of such criticism today [247:2-7]. Questions were asked of over 11,000 educators regarding criticisms of the public schools. Twenty-four per cent of the respondents indicated that "destructive criticism" of their school district had occurred within the past two years, and fifty per cent of these indicated that such criticism was continuing. Among the most frequently mentioned areas of criticism were personal attacks on teachers and administrators, criticisms of teaching methods (particularly in the fundamental subjects), criticisms of textbooks and instructional materials, and criticisms arising out of school reorganization and transportation problems.

Two of the most vocal critics of American public education during the past decade have been Prof. Arthur Bestor, of the University of Illinois, and Admiral Hyman G. Rickover, father of the atomic submarine. Bestor castigated American schools in the late 1950s for concentrating on "trivialities" such as vocational education and "life adjustment" programs and contended that the public schools should develop the capabilities of pupils in such areas as originality, reason, and common sense [25]. Rickover advocated elimination of the American comprehensive high school and institution of a European dual system of secondary education, whereby the "bright" student in particular could be adequately challenged [219]. Both Bestor and Rickover have contended that European education is superior to American.

Another critic of American education has been Dr. Max Rafferty, state superintendent of public instruction in California. Dr. Rafferty, author of numerous syndicated newspaper columns, has in particular attacked the "progressive education" movement, which in actuality perhaps never really became operational in many American schools and which today certainly is a dead issue. Rafferty from time to time has advocated increased moral training in the public schools and the transmittal of the "American heritage" in a more effective fashion. He has suggested that God be "returned to the classroom" and has attacked teachers colleges for inadequately training teachers.

Other critics of American public schools are too numerous to mention here. Perhaps the most important point that can be made is that such criticism appears to have been healthy. At least such attacks may have awakened the public and the Congress to the need for increased financial support to public education. The attacks of Bestor and Rickover—although no one could with definiteness determine a "cause and effect" relationship—were followed by increased public interest in education, including vastly greater expenditures of public funds, and culminated in passage of the Elementary and Secondary Education Act of 1965, a program of federal aid for public schools on a far greater scale than ever before in history. The states, too, are today spending much more for public education than they did a decade ago. Evidence abounds that the value of education is appreciated in America today more than ever before in our history as a nation.

Criticism at the local level is perhaps a different thing. Such attacks may result from a lack of understanding on the part of the general public about what the school is attempting to accomplish. Here the solution probably lies in the area of communication.

Many school systems today work closely with citizens' organizations and committees in cooperative efforts to improve the public schools. In addition, many schools have developed organized programs of public visitations and teacher-parent conferences during which the public is able to see firsthand what is taking place in the schools. It is certainly a truism that one of the best public relations techniques you as a teacher can use is to make parents feel welcome in your classroom and to be willing to confer with parents regarding the progress of their children.

Certainly one fact has emerged: The public schools today can no longer exist in isolation from the community (assuming that they ever could). The schools must utilize every possible avenue of communication with the citizenry in general, and every teacher must become a public relations expert. The public is concerned with and is vitally interested in schools. This concern and interest can be utilized and channeled toward the further improvement of public education generally. Robinson has put it this way: "In a democracy agreement isn't necessary—participation is" [221:94].

Are European Schools Better than American Schools?

A recurring attack against America's public schools is based upon the premise that European schools are superior to ours. A study completed in 1965 by the University of Toledo dealt with a comparison of academic achievement by elementary pupils in the United States and the British Isles. Some of the conclusions of the study were as follows [49:10–13]:

1. Although British students achieved higher levels of achievement in grades 1 through 4, American pupils were achieving at approximately the same levels

in nearly all the tested subject-matter areas by grades 5 and 6. The higher achievement by British pupils at earlier levels was partially due to an earlier entrance age.

2. The difference between high- and average-ability groups was much lower for American pupils.

3. American pupils were stronger than British pupils in reasoning and creativeness, whereas British pupils were stronger in methodicalness and thoroughness.

The difficulties of accurately comparing the educational product of American and European schools should be rather obvious; the purpose of the public schools in America is very different from the purpose of schools anywhere else on earth. The American educational dream has been to prepare virtually everyone to become an active member of a democratic society and to enable every person to attain whatever social or economic level his abilities will permit. Few countries have ever approached such a dream.

Perhaps one of the best methods of comparison can be found in the opinions of foreign exchange students who have attended school in the United States and therefore have experienced both American public school education and education in the schools of their homelands.

A German student made the following points regarding American schools [167:54]:

1. Although the many-sided American school life as exemplified by cocurricular activities may have pushed the academic areas into the background, the result has been to give America a generation of socially minded and responsible young people which is vital to democracy.

2. American schools are much more apt to experiment and to try new ideas than are German schools.

Two British students made the following points [85:55; 237:56–57]:

1. American high school students have developed an amazing self-confidence and assurance far beyond that shown by British students.

2. American teachers generally accept responsibility for the welfare and social adjustment of children; in Britain this responsibility lies only in the hands of the most senior teachers.

3. Much more money is available for educational research in America than in Britain.

4. America's technical advances in education, such as television and programmed learning, are very superior to those in Britain.

5. The "ladder" progress of American pupils from elementary through high school has much to commend it; this contrasts greatly with the "odious" British examinations for secondary school selection.

American schools are compared frequently with those of Soviet Russia, particularly since the orbiting of Sputnik 1 in 1957. This event perhaps shocked Americans generally more than any other occurrence in recent history; Americans sought a scapegoat, and many placed the blame for America's space deficiencies at the doorstep of the public schools, contending that Russian schools were superior and that this was a major reason for the Russian space advantage. The fact that the majority of the space scientists responsible for orbiting Sputnik had received their elementary and secondary schooling prior to or soon after the Russian revolution was conveniently ignored by those who sought to "prove" by the Sputnik event that Soviet public school education was superior to the American.

Although a great dedication to public education exists in the Soviet Union [107:17], there is little evidence to show that Soviet schools are superior to those in America. Actually no comparison is possible, Binzen points out, since neither nation has developed a nationwide system of evaluation of education. Binzen states, however, that the problems of Russian education are quite similar to those in America: The dropout, the teacher shortage, curricula that are "too full," classroom shortages, and low teachers' salaries are a few of the problems which exist in both countries [27].

Although we must continuously strive to improve our schools, we can take some pride in the remarkable progress they have made. It is gratifying to note that a number of other nations of the world, including Great Britain, are tending to pattern their schools along the lines of those in the United States in order to achieve a higher educational level for all.

Is There a Need for a National Assessment of Education?

Even though statistics indicate that our educational level is rising, that the holding power of our high schools is greater, and that high school graduates seem to be much better educated, we have not developed any specific method of ascertaining the quality of American public education. Some political leaders feel that the answer to the question of how such a determination might be made lies in some type of nationwide testing program or "national assessment."

In 1963, the Carnegie Foundation asked a group of educators to explore the feasibility of making a "national assessment" of education, and this group has been active since that time. In the 1965 White House Conference on Education, national assessment was further discussed. The entire concept has resulted in a storm of controversy [58:9].

Those *favoring* a national testing program present the following arguments:
1. The testing program would not need to be a massive program involving all children; scientific sampling techniques could be used.
2. Such a program would give the nation as a whole a better understanding of the strengths and weaknesses of our educational systems.
3. Many billions of dollars are spent each year for public education. At present we really do not know the result of such massive expenditures. A national testing program would give us the answers.
4. It is unrealistic to expect Congress and the state legislatures to continue to increase educational expenditures without having some tangible measurement of results.
5. Public schools could better be defended from unwarranted attacks if more facts were known about the effectiveness of instruction.
6. Information secured from a national testing program would be increasingly valuable for further needed educational research.

Those *opposing* a national testing program contend:
1. No written test can really evaluate—all tests are subject to inherent deficiencies.

2. No written test can evaluate some of the most important outcomes of education, e.g., the ability to get along with others, the development of leadership qualities, moral and ethical values, etc.
3. No national test can take into account state and local educational aspirations and objectives. A national testing program would lead to a national curriculum; many of the strengths of public school curricula—developed by states and localities—would be lost.
4. A national testing program might stultify the curriculum and result in retardation of educational improvements.
5. Such a program could form the basis for federal coercion of local school systems.
6. Such a program might result in the people in local communities relinquishing their right to determine many aspects of the school program in favor of some "higher" authority.
7. Such a program would cause teachers to "teach for" the tests; it is inevitable that the program would result in comparisons of one school district with another and one state with another. Public pressures on teachers would be tremendous.

It is likely that the controversy over the desirability of national assessment will continue for some time to come. As you continue your preparation for teaching, you may wish to give further attention to this issue. Your work as a teacher might be significantly affected by the outcome.

Is There an Educational "Establishment"?

Much has been said and written in recent years about the existence of a group of educational leaders in America who actually control or at least exert strong influence on public education. From time to time, the educational "establishment," as it has been called, has, among other things, been accused of resisting necessary change in education, of requiring "unnecessary" courses of prospective teachers, and of determining educational policy for the people of the nation. In 1963, Conant, in his book *The Education of American Teachers*, expressed his views toward the existence of such an establishment in the following manner [51:40]:

> As a general policy, I believe the public interest is well served when there exists a clearly identifiable group of people who assume continued responsibility for the operation of the public school system. The existence of an educational "establishment" is, in my judgment, as it should be. Without it no one could be called to account. And if we are to hold the establishment responsible for the management of the schools, we can only in justice yield to it the right to make fundamental decisions concerning these schools. The key word here is *responsible*, which implies responsiveness as well. If as is sometimes charged, the establishment is so rigid in its responses, so closed-minded in its convictions, that the concerns of the public are not met, then indeed a most serious danger exists.
>
> I think it must be said that in almost every state the establishment is overly defensive; it views any proposal for change as a threat and assumes that any critic intends to enlarge its difficulties and responsibilities while simultaneously undermining its ability to bear them. In short, there is too much resentment of outside criticism and too little effort toward vigorous internal criticism. In some instances I found the establishment's rigidity frightening.

In the December, 1964, issue of *Phi Delta Kappan* [76] the question of whether such an educational establishment exists, what it does, and whether it is helpful or harmful was asked of a number of leading educators. Abstracts from some of the answers given were as follows:

No one "establishment" exists; there are many "establishments," with influence which shifts from time to time.

An "establishment" exists. It is exemplified by the National Education Association and its various departments. It has resisted change, failed to support teachers under fire from the fringe elements of society, and has attempted to influence the public regarding its own ideologies.

There exists a loose confederation of persons in education who command prestige but who have little authority since the states control education and since there is no long-standing aristocracy tradition in this country.

There is an educational "establishment." Such an establishment is essential to the existence of a profession, and is a good thing, provided the controls developed by the establishment do not become firm and entrenched.

The professional educators actually run the schools. We already have a great deal of national control of education through organizations of professional educators.

The state legislatures control the schools. The various national organizations of professional educators give leadership but in no way are they an educational "establishment."

No well-defined "establishment" exists. There are, however, "interlocking webs" of influential individuals and organizations. The deans of the major schools of education, for example, play a major role in shaping educational change.

The education "establishment" maintains a tight control of public education in the United States, seeks to tighten its grip constantly, and uses threats and coercion against those who disagree with the "party line."

The "establishment" exists, but unlike those existing in medicine or law, is weak because it is dependent upon other power structures such as politics, business and industry.

As you can see, little agreement exists about whether an educational establishment actually controls public education in the United States, how extensive it is, and who its members are.

How Can Freedom to Teach and to Learn Be Provided?

Freedom to think, speak, and write as reason and conscience dictate is basic to the survival of a democratic society. Our forefathers recognized this fact as they formulated the First Amendment to the Constitution of the United States. It would seem, therefore, that the development of skill in thinking and expression constitutes one of the very important tasks to which the school should give attention. The development of this skill takes place most effectively in an environment where individuals feel free and are encouraged to think and express themselves, one which offers opportunities for young people to come to grips with problems of real concern to them. Many such problems will be of a controversial nature.

Academic freedom refers to the freedom of teachers to seek and to present the truth on problems and issues without fear of interference from school boards, governmental authorities, or pressure groups. From a learner's standpoint it refers to the opportunity to study all points of view in regard to a problem or an issue and to arrive at reasoned conclusions. The teacher does not have a right to tell pupils what to think, nor does he have the right to advocate one theory only. The teacher's concern is the development of skill in thinking, expression, and problem solving on the part of his pupils. Unless both teachers and pupils feel free to examine, discuss, think, and arrive at reasoned conclusions on issues affecting their daily lives, the school is handicapped greatly in fulfilling its function in a democratic society.

Do teachers and pupils feel free to teach and to learn? They frequently do not. Teachers in some communities feel that they would run considerable risk of losing their jobs if they permitted students to examine all sides of issues concerning trade unions. In some sections of the country it would be extremely hazardous to encourage free inquiry and discussion of the racial problem. The discussion of sex education is forbidden in some school systems. You already have noted in this chapter certain difficulties regarding moral and spiritual instruction. Certain textbooks in some communities have been censored. A number of teachers have been accused of being Communists if they permit pupils to learn *about* communism. These and many other instances which could be cited indicate that teachers and pupils are not entirely free to teach and to learn.

Yet the picture seems to be changing. Materials prepared by the U.S. Office of Education and other agencies pertaining to teaching *about* communism and other controversial subjects are becoming prolific. Surveys of school administrators have indicated that these leaders increasingly favor teaching about controversial issues, and the teaching of such issues appears to be more accepted today than ever before [1:279–282]. The National Education Association recommends that rational discussion of controversial issues be an important part of the school program [232:40]. The association points out, however, that teachers must approach such issues objectively, that sufficient time to develop the topics must be provided, that appropriate materials must be available to pupils, and that the topics should be within the emotional and intellectual capacities of the pupils [103:4].

Academic freedom in America's public schools, however, is still far from perfect. Sharples, a British lecturer who spent considerable time in American schools, stated that the lack of academic freedom on the part of American teachers came to him as a "shock." In England, Sharples stated, teachers are traditionally accustomed to offering personal and general opinions from the teacher's podium, and he implied that the same is not true in America [237:56].

In order to assure promotion of democratic ideals, many public schools, colleges, and universities require teachers to sign loyalty oaths in which teachers swear that they do not believe in, advocate, or teach the overthrow of the United States government by force. Many teachers feel that such a requirement casts a cloud of suspicion upon the integrity and loyalty of the teaching profession. They point out that such people as ministers, journalists, and broadcasters, who also mold public opinion, are not required to make this kind of public declaration. They maintain that loyalty oaths have little or no value, since schools and colleges already have adequate authority to remove teachers who are using their positions to propagandize and promote subversion. They feel that this procedure would be ineffective in screening out a disloyal person, because such an individual would have no hesitation in signing the oath. They also believe that this type of requirement might lead to other requirements that would foster feelings of submissiveness, conformity, and timidity upon the part of teachers. How do you feel about loyalty oaths being required of teachers?

Another issue closely related to the one indicated above pertains to the employment or dismissal of a teacher who is known to be a Communist. The National Education Association officially takes the position that Communists should not be permitted to teach, since such membership involves adherence to doctrines and discipline completely inconsistent with the principles of freedom on which American education depends. Such membership, and the accompanying surrender of intellectual integrity, renders an individual unfit to discharge the duties of a teacher in this country.

Those who argue against permitting Communists to teach generally maintain that: (1) a Communist relinquishes his right to think and act as a free individual; (2) he is unable to teach in such a manner that his students are encouraged to think open-mindedly, to explore, and to seek the truth; (3) Communists are unable to assume the role of public servants, since their basic motive is conspiracy against the government of the United States; and (4) there is no violation of civil rights in barring them from teaching, since these rights do not include such a thing as freedom to be employed as a teacher.

Those who would permit Communists to teach generally maintain that: (1) it is undemocratic to forbid anyone, upon the basis of his political views, to pursue an academic career; (2) students are denied the intellectual stimulation that could come from having a Communist as a teacher; (3) a commitment to the communistic point of view may have no bearing at all upon a teacher's classroom activities.

Even those who favor the employment of Communists as teachers generally agree that it should be limited to the college level. Children in the elementary schools, for example, have not developed the maturity that would enable them to exercise the free play of intelligence in considering the different ideologies of the world.

You can sense from the preceding discussion that herein lie matters of concern not only to educators but also to the American public. The issues are rather clear. How to resolve them presents difficult problems. It is important for teachers to remember that academic freedom should never be used as a protective device in terms of which society suffers. Teachers in our democratic society have a basic responsibility to their pupils and to their communities to promote freedom of thought, freedom of expression, and the pursuit of truth. Society, in turn, has an obligation to provide and to promote these conditions.

How Can Educational Opportunity Be Equalized?

A fundamental ideal in the American school system is equal educational opportunity for all children. Since early colonial days, considerable progress has been made toward this, but much yet remains to be done. The problem of providing equal opportunity exists within the particular community as well as on a national scale. As a teacher, you will have the opportunity to guide the thinking of others on the extent and nature of educational inequalities between sections of our country today.

Evidence of inequalities can be found in the fact, already noted, that teachers' salaries vary widely among states (Figure 8-5). Teachers in Mississippi, for example, receive much lower salaries than teachers in California. Educational opportunity in rural areas, also, is not comparable with that in urban centers. As compared with country schools, city schools have a longer yearly school session, a higher expense per pupil in average daily attendance, and a higher valuation of school property per pupil enrolled.

Inequalities in financial support of public schools among the various states and communities are a basic fact of educational life. Perhaps this is a major argument in favor of federal aid to education—the idea being that only the federal government is in a position to equalize educational opportunity throughout the United States through provision of funds to needy states and school districts.

Another type of educational inequality involves the culturally deprived. The culturally deprived youngster is usually poverty-stricken and frequently lives either in a depressed rural area or in one of the ghettos of our large cities. He comes from a family which typically exists on a low economic and educational level and which is likely to place little value on formal education. His family tends to be mobile, constantly seeking a better life. But this mobility seldom solves the family's problem. Unable to achieve success on the land, the family frequently is also unable to establish a better living standard elsewhere, primarily because of the inadequacy of its cultural and educational background. You can see that the problems of educating a child from such a family are tremendous.

In 1962, the Educational Policies Commission identified increased financial support for educational programs especially planned for the culturally deprived child as a prime method of solving his problems [67:36–37]. In 1963, Kaplan advocated increased expenditures and also the development of special curricular materials, special training for teachers, and better school guidance programs as a

FIGURE 17–1. Percentage of 3-, 4-, and 5-year-old children enrolled in nursery school and kindergarten in 1964 according to family income. Only a small proportion of the children who are most in need of preschool training attend nursery school or kindergarten. (*Source:* U.S. Office of Education.)

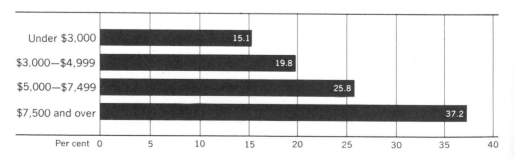

few of the solutions to the problem of the culturally deprived youngster [142:29–30].

In 1965, the federal Congress moved to attempt to provide better educational opportunities for the culturally deprived through passage of two of the most significant legislative acts dealing with public education that have ever been passed. The first of these, the Economic Opportunity Act, established Project Head Start, providing for preschool experiences for culturally deprived children. The second act, the Elementary and Secondary Education Act, bases much of its financial support to school districts upon the economic level of families living within each district and requires that those school districts which seek to take advantage of the act make provision for special programs for disadvantaged children.

The explosion of technology has resulted in a demand for workers and technicians possessing more training than ever before. This situation is likely to become even more critical in the years ahead. The culturally deprived child is therefore less and less likely to become a productive member of society when he reaches adulthood. You will no doubt agree that not only must we find ways to finance a more adequate educational program for this child, but educators must be willing to make whatever changes in our traditional school programs are necessary to meet his unique needs.

As a prospective teacher, study the background of our present status in equal educational opportunities and see the relevance of current attempts to remedy inequities. Be prepared to interpret to the members of a community the significance of federal aid to education. To do this, study carefully and critically the current legislation and the agencies and forces which are at work to promote or defeat this imperative need in our time.

In the face of the great differences that exist in educational opportunities, be prepared to help young and old alike maintain their faith in democracy despite its limitations in American life. You, as a teacher, will have to teach youngsters and adults the actual state of affairs today, at the same time fostering a belief in

Children playacting in a Project Head Start program. Such activities help them in developing imagination, clarifying concepts, and expressing their feelings. (*Photograph from the National Education Association.*)

the great American dream of equality for all and a democratic respect for the uniqueness of the individual. This is a task of a political nature, a task of statesmanship, and one of the most important aspects of the role of the teacher today.

How Can Problems of Discrimination and Segregation Be Resolved?

In addition to the financial inequalities that have existed within the American school system, educators are now confronted with problems arising from racial discrimination and segregation. These problems are precipitated when attempts are made to provide equal educational opportunities for boys and girls regardless of race, color, and religion. Although much progress has been made since 1954 in lessening the amount of discrimination and segregation, problems still remain. Teachers are confronted with the task of helping resolve these very complex problems.

On the surface, the problems appear to be primarily racial, in which Negro versus white and North versus South are involved. Perhaps, as a result of the Civil War, attention has been focused upon this aspect of discrimination and segregation. But the problems are much broader in scope and more complex in nature.

From your study of social problems you have found varying degrees of prejudice and discrimination existing throughout the United States wherever minority groups are involved. You have noted that race, color, and religion affect to some degree job opportunities, housing, churches, labor unions, clubs, and political groups. In various parts of the country definite discriminatory practices exist with respect to such minority groups as Jews, Orientals, Latin Americans, and Negroes. As an example, the large influx of Puerto Ricans in New York City presents a major problem of integration. In order to gain a grasp of the nature and magnitude of this problem you may wish to read Yinger and Simpson's article, "The Integration of Americans of Mexican, Puerto Rican, and Oriental Descent" [289]; and for the various state laws affecting the use of parks, playgrounds, bathing and fishing facilities, amusement parks, race tracks, theaters, public halls, telephone booths, washrooms, and hospitals, read Thayer [269:473–501]. James B. Conant's book *Slums and Suburbs* [54:7–32] vividly indicates problems of integration involved in metropolitan school areas. Conant makes some very interesting and practical suggestions for dealing with these problems.

As Thayer indicates [269:479–480], court decisions affecting the education of Negroes, oddly enough, date back to a decision of a Massachusetts court in 1849 (*Roberts v. the City of Boston*, 5 Cush. 198, 206). In this particular case a Negro child claimed the right to attend the school nearest her home rather than the one to which she had been assigned, since the Massachusetts constitution stated that all persons are equal before the law without distinction of age or sex, birth or color, origin or condition. In denying this right, the court maintained that,

when the great principle (of equality) comes to be applied to the actual and various conditions of persons in society, it will not warrant the assertion, that men are legally clothed with the same civil and political powers, and that children and adults are legally to have the same functions and be subject to the same treatment; but only that the rights of all, as they are settled and regulated by law, are equally entitled to the paternal consideration and protection of the law, and their maintenance.

Following the termination of the Civil War, Congress took steps to ensure the equality of Negroes and whites. As a result, the Thirteenth, Fourteenth, and Fifteenth Amendments were added to the Constitution. Furthermore, states applying for statehood were required to include in their constitutions provisions for the establishment and maintenance of free public schools [269:479].

In meeting their educational obligations, the Southern states segregated Negroes upon grounds that they would be provided with equal facilities. This action was upheld in various courts, using as a precedence the "separate but equal" decision that had been pronounced by the Massachusetts court in 1849. In 1896 the United States Supreme Court, in the famous case *Plessy v. Ferguson* (163 U.S. 537, 16 Sup. Ct. 1138), validated the "separate but equal" practice of dealing with Negroes. Although the actual case involved segregation on a railroad engaged in interstate commerce, in a number of states the policy was subsequently applied to public facilities, such as parks, beaches, and golf courses, and eventually to public schools.

After the turn of the century, a number of decisions rendered by federal courts began to weaken the rigid tradition and state laws regarding segregation. In 1915 the Court declared that the grandfather clause was a violation of the Fifteenth Amendment (*Guinn v. United States*, 238 U.S. 347, 35 Sup. Ct. 926). Subsequent cases, involving such matters as housing and seating on buses, further weakened the legality of segregation practices. In 1950, a Negro student sought admission to the Law School at the University of Texas. The Court (*Sweatt v. Painter*, 339 v. 629, 70 Sup. Ct. 859) ruled that he must be admitted. In May, 1954, the Supreme Court (*Brown v. Board of Education of Topeka*, 347 U.S. 483, 74 Sup. Ct. 686), interpreted the Constitution to mean that compulsory segregation is unconstitutional. In the words of Chief Justice Warren, the decision was as follows:

Today, education is perhaps the most important function of state and local governments. Compulsory attendance laws and the great expenditures for education both demonstrate our recognition of the importance of education to our democratic society. It is required in the performance of our most basic public responsibilities, even service in the armed forces. It is the very foundation of good citizenship. Today it is a principal instrument in awakening the child to cultural values, in preparing him for later professional training, and in helping him to adjust normally to his environment. In these days, it is doubtful that any child may reasonably be expected to succeed in life if he is denied the opportunity of an education. Such an opportunity, where the state has undertaken to provide it, is a right which must be made available to all on equal terms.

We come then to the question presented: Does segregation of children in public schools solely on basis of race, even though the physical facilities and other "tangible" factors may be equal, deprive the children of the minority group of equal education opportunities? We believe that it does. . . .

We conclude that in the field of public education the doctrine of "separate but equal" has no place. Separate educational facilities are inherently unequal. Therefore, we hold that the plaintiffs and others similarly situated for whom the actions have been brought are, by reason of the segregation complained of, deprived of the equal protection of the laws guaranteed by the Fourteenth Amendment.

Undoubtedly, you are fairly familiar with some of the problems encountered in the implementation of this decision. In a great many cases the integration of the races in the public schools has been without difficulty. In some cases, however, the ruling has met with defiance and subterfuge. For example, as late as 1964, ten years after the Supreme Court's desegregation decision, only 27 per cent of the school districts in the ex-Confederate South had desegregated [231:100]. Obviously, it takes time to implement such a ruling, since in a number of cases it strikes deep into the heart of tradition, feelings, and emotions. Legislation does not quickly change such factors.

In 1964, however, a significant attempt to reduce segregation legislatively occurred when the federal Congress enacted the Civil Rights Act. Title IV of this act provides for a cutoff of federal funds to any school district which maintains a segregated system. It is anticipated that this type of federal legislation may hasten the day when all school districts are fully integrated.

Intentional maintenance of segregation, as prohibited by the 1954 decision of the Supreme Court, is known as *de jure* segregation. Any school board which consciously maintains segregated schools, through gerrymandering of school attendance zones so as to promote segregation, for example, is guilty of furthering *de jure* segregation and may be required by a court to end such segregation. Since the 1954 Supreme Court decision clearly prohibits *de jure* segregation, it is reasonable to suppose that it will slowly recede and will finally be eliminated in American schools.

As *de jure* segregation recedes, another problem relating to segregation has taken its place—*de facto* segregation. *De facto* segregation can be defined as segregation of school pupils which results primarily from the housing patterns in many of America's large cities. Negroes and other racial minority groups tend to congregate in certain areas of such cities, owing perhaps in part to discrimination in matters of housing, and thus the neighborhood schools which serve such areas tend to become almost entirely populated by members of the minority race.

Civil rights leaders in the mid-1960s vigorously attacked the problems of *de facto* segregation and suggested several remedies: (1) an "open enrollment" policy, whereby each child would be permitted to attend the school of his choice within the city, (2) transportation of pupils from schools in racially imbalanced neighborhoods to schools in other neighborhoods—thus "balancing" the races, and (3) "pairing" of school attendance zones so that two schools, one predominantly white and the other predominantly populated by the minority race, would serve one area, with children in grades 1 through 3, for example, attending one school and children in grades 4 through 6 attending the other. All these suggestions are based upon the philosophy that segregated education—whether *de jure* or *de facto*—is inherently unequal and that both Negro and white pupils benefit educationally from their school associations with each other.

In lawsuits testing whether *de facto* segregation is illegal, the tendency of the majority of the courts today is to hold that local school authorities have no legal duty to mix the races where no conscious attempt has been made to segregate pupils on the basis of race and where such *de facto* segregation results from housing patterns over which the school board has no control (see, e.g., *Bell v. School City of Gary, Indiana*, 324 F.2d 209). A few courts, on the other hand, particularly in the eastern portion of the United States, are beginning to take the position that, where racial imbalance is "too great," a local school board has an affirmative duty to relieve such racial imbalance. (See, e.g., *Blocker v. Board of Education of Manhasset, N.Y.,* 226 F. Supp. 208.) The United States Supreme Court has not yet ruled on this question.

From an educational standpoint, we are responsible for understanding the problems of discrimination and segregation in evidence in all aspects of life and for relating these problems to the basic tenets of a democratic society. As a teacher you have the opportunity to help pupils as well as adults to identify these inconsistencies in our society and to formulate ways for effectively resolving them.

Without doubt, teachers have played a very significant role in the progress that has been made over the years. Teachers work primarily with younger people, who tend to be more tolerant than their elders. Furthermore, research indicates that people tend to become more tolerant as they become better educated.

A careful examination of countries throughout the world will reveal that problems of segregation and discrimination are not unique to the United States. They exist in every society. In many countries they are of much greater magnitude than they are here. Furthermore, in some countries the problems are becoming decidedly more acute. As teachers, you have a responsibility for understanding these problems as they exist on a worldwide basis and for aiding in the resolution of them. Most of all, you must do everything possible to foster progress in the solution of these problems in the United States, so that our country may be increasingly effective in demonstrating to the world a better way of life.

Should the Public Schools Train Pupils for Vocational Competence?

As indicated in Chapter 1, the modern world is changing so rapidly that many of today's pupils will be working in jobs that do not exist at present. M. J. Rathbone, chairman of the board and chief executive officer of Standard Oil Company of New Jersey, points out that approximately 70 per cent of the skilled trades in American manufacturing in the year 1900 do not exist today and that "a large proportion of today's skills will become obsolete in the shorter period between now and the year 2000, which is a period shorter than the average man's working lifetime" [208:8].

This era of rapid change poses a dilemma for the public schools. Can or should the public schools attempt to specifically prepare pupils for the world of work? The problem is made more acute by the fact that of every ten pupils presently in elementary school, three will not finish high school and only four will continue their education beyond high school [68:2].

The report of the Project on Instruction of the National Education Association states that competence in basic understandings and skills is still the best contribution of the elementary schools to future workers, but that the schools should also help pupils to learn more about the world of work. The report suggests that high schools offer some direct vocational education to pupils who do not plan to continue their formal schooling beyond the secondary school, with special programs being provided for the physically handicapped and the culturally deprived [232:112]. The importance of adequate vocational guidance programs in high schools, including testing programs and the providing of information to pupils about opportunities in the various occupations, has been cited as a special need for

American high schools by many authorities, including James B. Conant [50:44].

All too often when a need is discovered in American education, a crash program is quickly developed to meet the need. There are those today who feel that such a program is needed in vocational education. Harris [124:365], however, points out that the essential purpose of American education is to train citizens rather than workers and that such crash programs are not defensible. Harris also feels that separating pupils into two different kinds of high schools, one academic and the other vocational, is not the answer to the need for vocational education. Rather than have this type of separation, Harris suggests post-high school education of at least one or two years' duration for the majority of American youth and cites the community junior college as the best answer to the problem.

The American Association of School Administrators [134:24] points out another aspect of the problem of vocational education. The more specific the vocational training of an individual becomes, the more vulnerable he is to changes in employment opportunities over which he has little or no control. The association suggests that the vocational education program be directed toward "general vocational excellence" in "broad occupational areas," leaving to the specific industry or craft the training of workers for particular assignments. How do you feel the schools should approach the problem of training pupils for the world of work? Rathbone feels that, in order to meet the changing nature of occupational demands, the individual will need to have a high degree of adaptability. Before he becomes a specialist of any kind, he should first

learn to understand what he reads; to think of himself and express his thoughts clearly; to handle the basic tools of mathematics in their application to daily life; to grasp some of the realities of his natural and human environment. If he has learned these things he will have learned how to learn. Such an education is like a master key that opens many doors. The man who has it need never fear becoming the prisoner of an obsolete skill [208:9].

How do you react to Rathbone's point of view?

How Can the Public Become Better Informed in Regard to Educational Needs and Practices?

Many of the unwarranted attacks upon public schools, mentioned previously, are caused by a lack of understanding and facts. Members of the teaching profession are confronted with the especially difficult task of informing and interpreting educational theory and practices to the layman. Effective teaching is one of the most difficult tasks with which mankind is confronted. In the complex of human relations, it is easy for misunderstandings to arise. Furthermore, teachers deal with the most precious possessions of mankind—their children.

Teachers have not been inclined to give much attention to the inescapable public relations aspect of teaching. They have been hardworking individuals who have centered their attention upon getting the pupils taught as effectively as possible. If there were shortages of materials, equipment, etc., they have been inclined to accept the situation and do the best they can under the circumstances.

Seldom have forceful attempts been made to share with the public the problems encountered through lack of adequate facilities and conditions and to point out the resultant losses in the education of their boys and girls. There are no people in the world more generous of their talents and money than Americans who are thoroughly aware of needed improvements in the welfare of people and various public enterprises.

In general, it is difficult to convey to the public the economic value of education to the individual and to society. It is not possible to translate into dollars and cents the exact capital gains that accrue from having studied American literature for one year or music in the third grade. When asked to pay more taxes for schools, however, the American public tends to ask such questions as "Will we get our money's worth?" or "Can we afford better schools?"

In Chapter 12 of this book you noted the staggering costs of education with which the public will be confronted if future generations are to be at least as well educated as children are today. Actually, the quality of education must be improved if future generations are to be prepared to deal adequately with the increasing complex social, economic, and technological problems. Somehow the general public must remember an old saying that may be paraphrased as follows: "We cannot use yesterday's tools for educating youth to do the job today and expect to be in business tomorrow."

There are a number of activities at the community level that are being used, and perhaps could be used even more effectively, to acquaint the general public with the activities, purposes, and outcomes of schools. These include such activities as participation in parent-teacher groups and various educational associations; the observance of special days and weeks devoted to education; wide use of television, radio, and newspapers; the formation of study groups, local conferences, board-appointed lay advisory committees, counsel groups, and scheduled individual parent-teacher conferences; work on school newspapers; community use of school buildings; cocurricular activities; preparation of illustrated annual reports by school boards; class reunions; student participation in community activities; teacher participation in community affairs.

One aspect of public relations has generally been neglected in most of America's school systems. Although we teach pupils about local, state, and national government in "government," "civics," or other social studies classes, very few school systems have ever made any attempt to educate pupils with respect to local school government or to help them understand and appreciate the American educational system as an expression of our society. Yet teachers and school administrators apparently expect pupils in later life to become effective school board members and informed school patrons and to financially support the public schools through tax levies and bond issues, even though they have little knowledge of the public school as a legal and social institution. You might give some thought to the advantages which might accrue on a long-range basis to any school district which attempts to provide instruction to pupils in such areas of local school government as school purposes, school board authority, local taxation for schools, and state authority.

Many of the activities heretofore mentioned have proved helpful at the state level as well. Additional activities found valuable include participation in:

1. Research and dissemination of information on educational matters by agencies broadly representative of all facets of society
2. Organized programs of statewide associations of teachers, school boards, and PTAs
3. State citizen committees
4. State fairs exhibiting the work of students
5. Statewide teacher-recognition days
6. Legislation interim commissions, including both laymen and legislators
7. Educational programs of civic clubs, business, labor, agriculture, etc.

Many of the activities listed above may be applied on a national level. Additional ways of creating nationwide understanding of schools include:

1. Compilation and distribution of pertinent information concerning education by government agencies such as the U.S. Office of Education, national organizations representative of the professional, business, and citizen groups, and private foundations
2. Observance of National Education Week
3. Holding of White House Conferences

Recommendations which may prove helpful in encouraging greater understanding of schools at local, state, and national levels are as follows:

1. Additional channels for educational television should be set aside and more effective use should be made of them.
2. School board meetings in all communities should be open to the public, and citizens encouraged to attend them.
3. All citizens should be encouraged to participate more in school campaigns and to go well informed to the polls at school elections.
4. There should be greater emphasis on instruction of students in the organization, financing, and purposes of public and nonpublic schools.
5. Boards of education should initiate programs that relate to educational matters.
6. A cooperative relationship between the school and public libraries should be encouraged.
7. Local and national publications should be distributed to publicize the names and accomplishments of outstanding students in the community, state, and nation in the same manner as they do the achievements of outstanding athletes.
8. Public relations should be an organized and planned part of every school program.

SUMMARY

Attention has been given in this chapter to various problems with which educators have been and will be confronted for some time. As you move into the profession, you will be confronted with the challenge of aiding in their solution.

As a prospective teacher, study the function of the school in promoting moral growth and character without giving instruction in particular religious faiths and doctrines. Gain a clear understanding of the nature and causes of the attacks being made against the school and be able to discuss the reasons for and the validity of these attacks. A considerable portion of them may be caused by a lack of understanding on the part of parents and other community members. You as a teacher will hold a key position in which you will be able to develop harmonious relationships between the home and school.

Freedom to think, to speak, and to write as reason and conscience dictate is basic to the survival of a democratic society. The development of skill in this regard constitutes one of the very important tasks to which you and the school need to give attention. Be ever mindful that academic freedom is coupled with the grave responsibility of guiding the growth of boys and girls toward higher levels of effective democratic living.

Great differences exist throughout the United States in the educational opportunities afforded boys and girls. Various attempts are being made to remedy these inequalities through improved financial programs and through the resolution of problems concerning discrimination and segregation.

The recruitment and retention of good teachers are a responsibility that rests with the profession as well as with all community members. Every effort possible should be made to interest our most able young people in a teaching career. Furthermore, we face a problem in keeping the public well informed in regard to current education needs and practices. Such information is necessary if the public is to gain increasingly greater confidence in what we are doing and to provide the great amount of financial support for education that will be needed in the future.

QUESTIONS FOR YOUR CONSIDERATION

1. What will you consider to be your responsibility for promoting moral and spiritual values in your pupils? How will you attempt to fulfill this responsibility?

2. A number of people feel that an amendment should be written into the Constitution proclaiming the United States to be a "Christian nation and giving full legal sanction to religious expressions in public schools and other governmental activities." What would your reaction be to such a proposal? Why?

3. Do you feel the public schools should teach courses in comparative religions? What are some of the problems in initiating and developing such courses?

4. Do you feel the Bible can be used effectively in public schools as a historical document? As literature? If so, how would you determine which version of the Bible to use? What are some of the problems a teacher would face in attempting to use the Bible as history or literature?

5. What, in your opinion, are the reasons for attacks being made upon the work of the public schools today? How do you plan to deal with these attacks when you become a teacher?

6. How might teachers misuse academic freedom?

7. Are there any controversial issues that should not be discussed in public schools? Explain.

8. What are some pros and cons regarding teachers' signing loyalty oaths?

9. What would you do if you had positive proof that a teacher in your school system is a Communist?

10. Do you feel there should be some sort of national testing program whereby all children in the United States of a certain age or grade level are given the same test? What are the advantages or disadvantages of such a program? If such a program were in existence, do you think teachers would "teach for" the tests?

11. If you were asked to teach a class of culturally deprived youngsters, what special requests would you make of your superiors?

12. Do you feel that public school authorities in large cities should attempt to ensure that the public schools are racially balanced, even though this might result in elementary children's attending schools a long distance from their homes? Do you feel there would be any educational advantages to such a plan?

13. Do you feel a teacher should be able to take a public stand on any issue without fear of reprisal?

14. How would you attempt to interest outstanding pupils in teaching as a career?

15. What responsibilities do you feel a teacher has in attempting to promote a high level of support for schools in any given community?

ACTIVITIES FOR YOU TO PURSUE

1. Organize a panel discussion on ways of equalizing educational opportunities throughout the United States.

2. Have a group of students collect data on the extent to which boys and girls in your state have equal educational opportunities. Discuss how any differences that exist may be corrected.

3. Conduct a survey of the opinions of community members regarding federal aid for schools. Attempt to discover the reasons for their opinions. Compile lists of the reasons for and against federal aid to schools and compare these reasons with those listed in this chapter.

4. Arrange for a public school official, such as a superintendent of schools, to discuss with your class the ways in which schools develop moral and spiritual values in boys and girls. You may wish to discuss this matter with several teachers.

5. Conduct some research on how many different versions of the Holy Bible are in existence, some of the differences between the versions, and the faiths which subscribe to each version.

6. Have a group of your colleagues visit one or more of the modern schools and one or more of the very traditional schools. Compare and contrast the learnings gained by the pupils. Which type of school is helping pupils the most in terms of effective democratic living?

7. Have a group of students talk with their former public school teachers regarding the extent to which the latter feel they have academic freedom. Compile a list of any restrictions which they note.

8. Discuss with your college or university admissions officer the question of whether college freshmen are better prepared for college today than they were a decade ago. You might ask him to speak to your class on this subject.

RESOURCE
SECTION
FOR PART VI

APPRAISING MY FITNESS FOR WORK IN A
COMMUNITY-CENTERED PROGRAM OF EDUCATION

PLACEMENT AND LISTING SERVICES IN STATE DEPARTMENTS
OF EDUCATION AND STATE EDUCATION ASSOCIATIONS

SAMPLE APPLICATION FORM FOR A
TEACHING POSITION

SUGGESTED READINGS

SUGGESTED FILMS, FILMSTRIPS,
AND RECORDINGS

FIGURE CREDITS

APPRAISING MY FITNESS FOR WORK IN A COMMUNITY-CENTERED PROGRAM OF EDUCATION

Directions to the teacher: How well are you fitted for work in a school which is closely related to the life of its community? The following checklist will help you determine the extent to which you have developed the social and civic competence which such teaching requires of you. Indicate the degree of growth you think you have achieved by placing an X in the appropriate column opposite each item. Remember that you should evaluate yourself in terms of your *actual behavior in life situations,* not merely in terms of your present ideals.

Viewing myself objectively, I think I have achieved

This degree of learning—   In this area of learning—

Much   Some   Little   None

    I. *A Realistic Approach to the Study of Human Relations*

      1.1. Understanding the community-school movement and its significance for democratic education and the conscious improvement of human living

      1.2. Comprehending life in various types of communities with regard to such fundamental factors as:
- a. The land and its resources
- b. The people
- c. Utilizing natural environment
- d. Appreciating the past
- e. Adjusting to people
- f. Exchanging ideas
- g. Making a living
- h. Sharing in citizenship
- i. Maintaining health and safety
- j. Improving family living
- k. Securing education
- l. Meeting religious needs
- m. Enjoying beauty
- n. Engaging in recreation

      1.3. Understanding social forces at work in the community:
- a. Caste and class
- b. In-group and out-group relationships
- c. Pressure groups and propaganda
- d. Democratic leadership and cooperation

      1.4. Applying effective methods of community analysis and inventory in relation to basic social processes as they are carried on in everyday life

      1.5. Understanding some of the more persistent problems of our modern social and economic society

      1.6. Comprehending the socioeconomic and cultural position of my community in its regional, national, and international setting

---

Source: Reprinted by permission of Prentice-Hall, Inc., from Edward G. Olsen (ed.), *School and Community.* Copyright 1954, by Prentice-Hall, Inc., Englewood Cliffs, N.J., pp. 399–401.

APPRAISING MY FITNESS *(continued)*

Viewing myself objectively, I think I have achieved

This degree of learning—   In this area of learning—

Much Some Little None

1.7. Understanding methods of community organization, coordination, and planning
1.8. Seeing possibilities for improvement of group life through a knowledge of what some communities and people are doing to enrich and advance life

II. *Effective Thinking and Research in the Social Area*
2.1. Awareness of community conditions which give rise to important problems and conflicts
2.2. Ability to see what might be done to solve or adjust to these problems
2.3. Ability to define an area for study and to formulate a plan of work
2.4. Ability to gather significant and pertinent data, using field and library research techniques:
  a. Observation
  b. Participation
  c. Interview
  d. Questionnaire
  e. Mapping
  f. Documentary materials
  g. Background reading
2.5. Ability to differentiate between data that are significant, valid, and relevant and those that are unimportant, invalid, and irrelevant, and to interpret findings
2.6. Habit of suspending judgment until sufficient facts are available for drawing a legitimate conclusion
2.7. Ability to summarize the results of an investigation and to present findings in vital written, oral, or graphic form
2.8. Practice of making decisions and of acting on the basis of these decisions where such action is desirable and possible
2.9. Habit of testing actions in the light of consequences and in terms of the principle: "Has this action promoted the personal development of the people affected by it?"

III. *Social Participation and Social Action*
3.1. Knowing the people of the community as parents, neighbors, workers, worshipers consumers, citizens, and formulators of community customs, standards, and beliefs
3.2. Participating constructively in the life of the community by:

APPRAISING MY FITNESS (*continued*)

Viewing myself objectively, I think I have achieved

This degree of learning—   In this area of learning—

Much Some Little None

a. Contributing to some community activities such as boys' and girls' clubs, church groups, community councils, armed services, etc.
b. Helping direct some community activity such as Boy Scouts, League of Women Voters, Red Cross, etc.
c. Working in the community at jobs other than teaching
d. Meeting effectively problems of personal relationships incidental to participation in community life

3.3. Exercising responsible leadership in significant movements designed for intelligent community betterment

3.4. Participating effectively in district, state, national, and international group life:
a. Functioning as a member of state and national organizations
b. Using techniques of communication characteristic of larger group participation, such as petitions and letter writing

3.5. Creating in students social sensitivity and the inclination and habit of participating constructively in community affairs

3.6. Utilizing community resources in personal living and professional work

IV. *Cooperative Living*
4.1. Understanding democracy as the opportunity for development of maximum capacity of all individuals

4.2. Expressing democratic values through behavior, attitudes, and beliefs in all the areas and relations of life

4.3. Recognizing free interaction, cooperation, and sharing as the methods of democratic group life

4.4. Utilizing effectively in school and community those techniques essential to cooperative living:
a. Free and fruitful discussion
b. Democratic planning
c. Sharing responsibility for group undertakings
d. Evaluating the effectiveness of group action

4.5. Realizing the sterility of much academic procedure and developing in its place effective methods of group work in the classroom

PLACEMENT AND LISTING SERVICES IN STATE DEPARTMENTS OF EDUCATION AND STATE EDUCATION ASSOCIATIONS

State Department of Education Placement Services

These state departments of education provide a teacher-placement service or answer inquiries about openings:

Alabama: Teacher Placement Service, State Department of Education, Montgomery, 36104

Alaska: Commissioner of Education, State Department of Education, Juneau, 99801

Georgia: State Department of Education, 247 State Office Building, Atlanta, 30334

Idaho: Department of Employment, Boise, 83702

Louisiana: Teacher Education and Certification, State Department of Education, Baton Rouge, 70804

Maine: Teachers Registration Bureau, State Department of Education, Augusta, 04330

Massachusetts: Division of Teacher Certification and Placement, State Department of Education, Boston, 02133

Minnesota: Division of Teacher Personnel, State Department of Education, St. Paul, 55101

Mississippi: Teacher Education, Certification, and Placement, State Department of Education, Jackson, 39201

New Hampshire: Director, Placement Bureau, State Department of Education, Concord, 03301

New Jersey: Educational Placement Unit, Professional Placement Center, New Jersey State Employment Service, 2 Central Avenue, Newark, 07102

New Mexico: Director, Teacher Education, Certification, and Teacher Placement, State Department of Education, Santa Fe, 87501

North Dakota: Teacher Placement Division, State Employment Service, Bismarck, 58501

Oklahoma: Oklahoma Employment Security Commission, Will Rogers Memorial Office Building, State Capitol Complex, Oklahoma City, 73105

Pennsylvania: Teacher Placement Service, Pennsylvania State Employment Service, Labor and Industry Building, Harrisburg, 17121

Utah: Director of Teacher Personnel, State Department of Public Instruction, Salt Lake City, 84114

Vermont: Teacher Placement Service, State Department of Education, Montpelier, 05602

Wyoming: Teacher Placement Bureau, State Department of Education, Cheyenne, 82001

State Education Association Placement and Listing Services

The following state education associations provide placement or listing services:

California Teachers Association: 1705 Murchison Drive, Burlingame, 94010. *Southern Section:* 1125 West Sixth Street, Los Angeles, 90017

Colorado Education Association: 5200 South Quebec Street, Englewood, 80110

Illinois Education Association: 100 East Edwards Street, Springfield, 62704

Iowa State Education Association: 4025 Tonawanda Drive, Des Moines, 50312

Kentucky Education Association: 2303 South Third Street, Louisville, 40208

New Hampshire Education Association: 103 North State Street, Concord, 03301

North Carolina Teachers Association: 125 East Hargett Street, Raleigh, 27601

South Carolina Education Association: 1510 Gervais Street, Columbia, 29201

Texas State Teachers Association: 316 West 12th Street, Austin, 78701

Source: T. M. Stinnett, *A Manual on Certification Requirements for School Personnel in the United States,* National Education Association, National Commission on Teacher Education and Professional Standards, Washington, 1967.

PLACEMENT AND LISTING SERVICES *(continued)*

Vermont Education Association: Box 567, 5 Baldwin Street, Montpelier, 05602
Washington Education Association: 910 Fifth Avenue, Seattle, 98104
West Virginia Education Association: 1558 Quarrier Street, Charleston, 25311

SAMPLE APPLICATION FORM FOR A TEACHING POSITION

APPLICATION BLANK

I. Name in full_____

Present Address_____ Telephone_____

Permanent Address_____ Telephone_____

Date of Birth_____ Place of Birth_____

Height_____ Weight_____ General Health_____

Estimate of occupational time lost due to illness during the last 5 years_____

List any Physical defects_____ _____ Do you wear glasses?_____

Is your hearing normal?_____ Marital Status: Single_____ Married_____

Widow (er)_____ Separated_____ Divorced_____ Number and ages of children
_____

Are you a citizen of the United States of America?_____

If a war veteran or defense worker, give length of service_____(months)

Branch of service or activity_____

Theatre of operation_____

Rank_____ Type of work you did_____

What foreign languages do you speak?_____

II. Present position_____

	Grade		Subject

| | School | | Place |

Present Salary_____ When can you accept a position?_____

List Position for which you are applying:_____

List in order of preference the subjects you like to teach:

(a)_____ (b)_____ (c)_____ (d)_____

Are you certified to teach in the State of New Jersey?_____

Kind of certificate held_____ Major_____ Minor_____

Are you willing to come to this school for an interview at your own expense?
_____

III. EDUCATIONAL PREPARATION PRIOR TO BEGINNING TEACHING

School	Name	Location	Dates Attended	Course Major & Minor	Degree or Diploma	Date Graduated
Elementary						
High School						
College						

Scholastic Honors_____

High School and College_____

Source: From Hanover Park Regional High School District, Hanover, N.J.

IV. EDUCATIONAL TRAINING RECEIVED AFTER BEGINNING TEACHING

Institution	Dates Attended	Course Major and Minor	Degree or Diploma	Date Graduated

Scholastic Honors_____

At present matriculated for_____ degree, to be conferred about_____

by_____ University or College

List and give extent of any special training you have had that is not mentioned above: e.g., music, art, industrial training, military courses while in military service, etc.

_____

_____

_____

V. TEACHING EXPERIENCE (Do not include practice teaching)
List in order beginning with present position

Period (years and dates)	School and Location	Grade or Subject Taught

A. Student or Practice Teaching:_____

_____

B. College, Part-Time, Substitute, Night or Summer, Etc._____

_____

_____

List the experiences you have had with children (other than the above)

Camp_____

Scouting_____

Home_____

Community_____

Church_____

Recreation_____

Other_____

What type of work experience as an adult have you had other than teaching? (Business, trades, summer occupations, church work, social services, etc.)

Dates From____ To____	Employer and Location	Type of Work and/or Position	Years

Were you trained for another profession or occupation before teaching? _____ If so, what?_____

Indicate the approximate number of credits taken in each of the following areas in your undergraduate courses:

_____ a. The humanities (other than literature: i.e., music, art, foreign literature, philosophy, etc.)

_____ b. The physical sciences (chemistry, physics, astronomy, etc.)

_____ c. Mathematics

_____ d. Social sciences (history, sociology, economics, anthropology)

List participation within the last two years in any professional activity for the improvement of the school or schools where you have been employed. (e.g., Curriculum Revision, Pupil Progress Report, etc.):

_____

_____

(If not employed in a school system within the last two years, write "not so employed")

List any professional organizations of which you are a member (mention any offices or positions of responsibility you have held in these organizations):

_____

_____

_____

_____

_____

List the non-educational societies, organizations or clubs to which you belong (mention any offices or positions of responsibility you have held in these organizations):

_____
_____
_____
_____
_____
_____

VI. INTERESTS AND HOBBIES
Indicate below any interests or hobbies you may have outside the professional field. Indicate briefly what professional and general magazine and book reading you have done in the past six months.

_____
_____
_____
_____
_____
_____

VII. List student activities, clubs, or athletic programs you would be competent to teach or sponsor.

_____
_____
_____
_____
_____
_____

VIII. TRAVEL
List below your most outstanding or interesting travels. (Include foreign countries)

Year	To	Reason for Trip	Why Outstanding to You

IX. REFERENCES

These should be persons qualified and willing to give an honest appraisal of your fiitness for the position you seek. Please include superintendents and principals with whom you have worked.

Name	Address	Position or Occupation
A. Professional References:		
1.		
2.		
3.		
4.		

B. Personal References:		
1.		
2.		
3.		

SUGGESTED READINGS

The number in parentheses following each suggestion denotes the chapter for which it is best suited.

Barach, Arnold B.: *USA and Its Economic Future,* Twentieth Century Fund, Inc., New York, 1964. An excellent treatment of changes taking place in our economic system and probable future changes. (15)

Bent, Rudyard K., and Henry H. Kronenberg: *Principles of Secondary Education,* 5th ed., McGraw-Hill Book Company, New York, 1966. Chapter 2 presents a good discussion of the purposes of secondary education. (16)

Bereiter, Carl, and Siegfried Engelmann: *Teaching Disadvantaged Children in the Preschool,* Prentice-Hall, Inc., Englewood Cliffs, N.J., 1966. Consists of a detailed presentation of teaching methods and curricula that have been found effective in enabling disadvantaged children to start first grade on an equal footing with more privileged children. (15, 16)

Birmingham, Stephen: "American Youth: A Generation under the Gun," *Holiday,* vol. 37, no. 3, pp. 3, 42–61, 137–143, March, 1965. Presents an excellent description of the problems and tensions faced by youth. (15)

Broudy, Harry S.: "What Can the School Say about Human Rights?" *Phi Delta Kappan,* vol. 47, no. 9, pp. 467–471, May, 1966. Presents an excellent discussion of the role of the school in helping each individual achieve his rights. (17)

Burgess, Evangeline: *Values in Early Childhood Education,* National Education Association, Department of Elementary–Kindergarten–Nursery Education, Washington, 1965. Presents an excellent discussion of the values to be derived from kindergarten and nursery education. (16)

Conant, James Bryant: *Slums and Suburbs,* McGraw-Hill Book Company, New York, 1961. Presents the findings of an extensive study of schools in metropolitan areas and makes recommendations for improving especially schools in the slum and suburban areas. (15–17)

Contemporary Issues in American Education, U.S. Office of Education, 1965. Discusses such problems as assessment of educational performance, school desegregation, and preschool education. (17)

Crow, Lester D., and Alice Crow: *Introduction to Education,* American Book Company, New York, 1966. Part V is devoted to a discussion of nonformal educational agencies and the important role they play in the educative process. (15)

"De Facto Segregation," *NEA Journal,* vol. 54, no. 7, pp. 34–36, 80, National Education Association, Washington, October, 1965. Indicates the Educational Policies Commission position on *de facto* segregation. (17)

Duker, Sam: *The Public Schools and Religion: The Legal Context,* Harper & Row, Publishers, Incorporated, New York, 1966. Presents excerpts from a discussion of all the significant cases dealing with public education and religion which have reached the United States Supreme Court. (17)

"Education and Automation: The Coming World of Work and Leisure," *National Association of Secondary-School Principals Bulletin,* vol. 48, no. 295, pp. 56–72, 99–110, National Education Association, Washington, 1964. Discusses the need for a new emphasis upon vocational education as well as lifelong education that results from automation and other technological changes. (17)

"Education and Human Rights," *Phi Delta Kappan,* vol. 47, no. 9, May, 1966, pp. 467–526. A series of articles on the problem of human rights as they relate to education and to the operation of schools. (16, 17)

Education in a Changing Society, National Education Association, Project on the Instructional Program of the Public Schools, Washington, 1963. An excellent discussion of changes taking place in our society and their educational implications. (15)

"The Educational 'Establishment,'" *Phi Delta Kappan,* vol. 46, no. 4, pp. 190–194, December, 1964. Contains the views of a number of leading educators as to whether an educational establishment exists. (17)

Educational Policies Commission: *The Central Purpose of American Education,* National Education Association, Washington, 1961. Indicates that the development of the rational powers of man constitutes the central purpose of education. (16)

————: *Educational Responsibilities of the Federal Government,* National Education Association, Washington, 1964. Discusses the federal structure for meeting federal educational responsibilities such as desegregation and equalization of educational opportunities. (17)

Finn, James D.: "A Revolutionary Season," *Phi Delta Kappan,* vol. 45, no. 7, pp. 348–354, April, 1964. Indicates changes to be made in educational practices as we face the future. (15, 16)

Freedom to Teach; Freedom to Learn, National Education Association, Commission on Professional Rights and Responsibilities, Washington, 1964. Indicates guidelines for teachers on freedom to teach controversial issues. (17)

Grambs, Jean D., Clarence G. Noyce, Franklin Patterson, and John Robertson: *The Junior High School We Need,* National Education Association, Association for Supervision and Curriculum Development, Washington, 1961. Presents an excellent discussion of the type of junior high school needed today. (16)

Havighurst, R. J.: *Growing Up in River City,* John Wiley & Sons, Inc., New York, 1962. Report of a study to determine how the social background and personal characteristics of a group of eleven-year-olds affected their competence later as young adults. (15)

Hennessy, Maurice N.: "New Directions for British Education?" *Saturday Review,* Aug. 21, 1965, pp. 58–59, 65–66. Indicates that the British are tending to move toward the adoption of the comprehensive high school idea as used in the United States. (17)

Hickerson, Nathaniel: *Education for Alienation,* Prentice-Hall, Inc., Englewood Cliffs, N.J., 1966. Attempts to show how our public schools, as a mirror of society, have played a significant role in creating the conditions that have led to the waste of talent and ability and to the subsequent loss of dignity and self-worth on the part of millions of our citizens. (15, 16)

Imperatives in Education, American Association of School Administrators, Washington,

1966. Identifies nine imperatives that must be at the forefront as curricula are modified, methods revised, and organization reshaped. (15, 16)

Kaplan, Bernard A.: "Issues in Educating the Culturally Disadvantaged," *Phi Delta Kappan,* vol. 45, no. 2, pp. 70–76, November, 1963. Raises nine basic issues involved in educating the culturally disadvantaged. (17)

National Educational Assessment: Pro and Con, National Education Association, Washington, 1966. Points out the arguments for and against a national plan to assess the status of education. (17)

Noah, Harold J.: "Soviet Educators' Unsolved Problems," *Saturday Review,* Aug. 21, 1965, pp. 54–56, 64–65. Indicates the great increase in expenditures for education in Russia and some major problems with which Russian educators are faced. (17)

Olsen, James: "Challenge of the *Poor* to the Schools," *Phi Delta Kappan,* vol. 47, no. 2, pp. 79–84, October, 1965. Points out some of the unique problems which children from poor families present in attempts to educate them. (15–17)

Religion and the Public Schools, Harvard University Press, Cambridge, Mass., 1965. Contains an excellent discussion of the legal and educational issues involved insofar as religion in the public schools is concerned. (17)

Smith, J. Richard: "Adult Education: Daytime, Nighttime, Saturday Too," *NEA Journal,* vol. 55, no. 3, pp. 40–41, National Education Association, Washington, March, 1966. Describes various adult education programs. (16)

State of the Nation in Regard to Criticisms of the Schools and Problems of Concern to Teachers, National Education Association, Commission on Professional Rights and Responsibilities, Washington, January, 1966. Analyzes criticisms of schools and problems with which we are faced. (17)

Swanson, J. Chester: "Education for Occupational Competence," *Phi Delta Kappan,* vol. 44, no. 7, pp. 322–325, April, 1963. Points out major difficulties which have limited vocational education services and suggests ten ways for improving vocational programs for high-school-age youth, post-high-school-age youth, and youth and adults who are at work or unemployed. (17)

Taylor, Harold: "What the Family Isn't Teaching," *Saturday Review,* May 18, 1963, pp. 17–19. Raises the point that American parents, and the schools their children attend, may be sacrificing the true purposes of education in favor of dangerous academic competition. (15, 16)

Thayer, V. T., and Martin Levit: *The Role of the School in American Society,* 2d ed., Dodd, Mead & Company, Inc., New York, 1966. Part IV is concerned with the following issues in contemporary education: public education under fire; church, state, and education; public assistance to nonpublic schools; religion and morality in public education; freedom to learn; freedom to teach; segregation in American education; federal aid to education in the states. (17)

Universal Opportunity for Education beyond the High School, National Education Association, Educational Policies Commission, Washington, 1964. Advocates that the public make available at least two years of further education, aimed primarily at intellectual growth, for all high school graduates. (16, 17)

Van Til, William: "The Genuine Educational Frontiers," *Saturday Review,* Apr. 18, 1964, pp. 68–88. Indicates eight urgent frontiers in education. (16)

Wayson, W. W.: "The Political Revolution in Education, 1965," *Phi Delta Kappan,* vol. 47, no. 7, pp. 333–339, March, 1966. Discusses the significant shift in the source of power affecting the control and support of schools and universities, a shift characterized primarily by the vigorous entrance of the federal government into educational policy making. (17)

SUGGESTED FILMS, FILMSTRIPS, AND RECORDINGS

The number in parentheses following each suggestion denotes the chapter for which it is best suited.

Films (16 mm)

America's Crises: The Community (National Educational Television, 59 min). Evaluates the cultural, educational, religious, and physical aspects of America's cities and towns. Focuses on the small New England fishing community of Provincetown and compares it with San Jose, California, a booming western community in the midst of accelerated growth. Discusses their similarities and differences, shows the effects of change, and suggests the problems that must be solved. (15)

America's Crises: The Individual (National Educational Television, 59 min). Examines the problem of the individual in a complex society by looking at various areas of American life in relation to man's needs for self-identification. Probes the effects of government planning in agriculture on individual initiative and community identification. (15)

America's Crises: Marked for Failure (National Educational Television, 59 min). Discusses American education and examines the profound handicaps to learning that affect children from depressed areas. Describes a number of proposed solutions. Focuses on a prenursery pilot program in New York City schools. (15, 17)

America's Crises: The Parents (National Educational Television, 59 min). Presents a documentary report on the changing problems of America's parents today and their attempts to find identity, meaning, and purpose in their lives. Features frank interviews with parents and children. Shows the effects of rural-urban-suburban social change and presents interviews with Benjamin Spock, Betty Friedan, and Paul Popenoe. (15)

America's Crises: The Young Americans (National Educational Television, 59 min). Discusses the problems of American youth and examines who they are, what they want, where they fit in, how they affect society, and what they believe in and why. Features individual and group interviews with students in colleges, high schools, beach areas, and resort towns. Presents a frank questioning of traditional views on sex and youth's confused struggle to find a new morality. Looks at youth minority groups, such as the Peace Corps and the beatniks, who attempt to define themselves and their beliefs, in contrast to the majority of youths, who are uncommitted. (15, 16)

Broader Concepts of Curriculum (McGraw-Hill, 19 min). Points out the great increase which is taking place in enrollments in secondary schools and some of the causes for this growth. Presents four main needs of youth—civic competence, vocational orientation, preparation for family living, and health and physical fitness. Shows class activities and other responsibilities of the school relating to the development of each of these needs. (16)

Children Growing Up with Other People (British Information Service, 23 min). Describes the child's emergence from involuntary dependence to a world of individualism and cooperation. Presents the problem of the child's increasing awareness of other people and the restraint of his aggressive individualism. (15)

Children in Trouble (New York State Youth Commission, 11 min). Discusses the causes of juvenile delinquency, what happens to the juvenile delinquent, and the role of the home, the church, the school, the police, and community clubs in preventing and controlling juvenile delinquency. (15)

Defining Democracy (Democracy and Despotism) (Encyclopaedia Britannica Films, 18 min). Contrasts democracy and despotism and explains four conditions in a community essential to democracy. Points out that respect for one another and power in the government must be shared by all the people. Asserts that shared power and shared respect in turn depend on balanced economic distribution and enlightenment through an uncontrolled, socially responsible information system. (16)

Design of American Public Education (McGraw-Hill, 15 min). Through animation, compares and contrasts the assembly-line kind of educational process with one that is tailored to meet young people's needs. Shows how in the former little or no consideration is given to individual needs, whereas in the latter a decentralized educational system can fit the curriculum to local community setups. (16)

The Dropout (McGraw-Hill, 11 min). Focusing upon a boy who drops out of school in the tenth grade, it dramatically portrays the conditions and events leading to a typical high school dropout. Depicts the influence of the environment and his peers on the dropout. Interviews the dropout, his mother, teachers, and school officials in an effort to determine the cause of the boy's leaving school. (15, 16)

Effective Learning in Elementary Schools (McGraw-Hill, 20 min). Shows a fifth-grade teacher and her class as they plan their daily work for the study of a unit on pioneer life. Pictures class activities as the teacher gathers material and the pupils work individually and in committees. Pupils construct a mural; make models and maps; practice folk songs and dances; and study reading, with a play being given by the pupils for parents and teachers. (16)

Focus on Children (Iowa State University, 26 min). Points out the importance of nursery school activities in satisfying the needs and interests of children and in building the proper foundation for all schools to follow. Records the experiences children encounter and explains the purpose of these experiences. Discusses the relationships of children and their parents as well as the importance of parent-teacher cooperation in view of a healthy atmosphere both at home and at school. (16)

Freedom to Learn (National Education Association, 27 min). Shows how a teacher, charged by well-meaning parents with teaching communism in her classroom, explains that the purpose of teaching is to help children learn to think rather than to tell them *what* to think. Pictures Mrs. Orin's classroom activities and shows her students seeking facts and exchanging ideas. Points out that freedom to learn facts as they are is essential to a democratic way of life and that this freedom must be extended to children in the schools. (17)

How Good Are Our Schools? Dr. Conant Reports (Agrafilms, 28 min). Uses two comprehensive high schools to show what every secondary school should be equipped to do. Includes views of Dr. Conant presenting his findings to government and National Education Association officials. (17)

The Junior High School Story (National Education Association, 28 min, color). Interesting examples of programs and activities in fifty junior high schools in California. Shows well the relationships between the curricular and cocurricular. (16)

Learning Democracy through School Community Projects (Educational Film Service, 21 min, color). Depicts experiences in democratic learning which are provided in Michigan schools. Includes student councils, student elections, Junior Red Cross, youth centers, a community council meeting, a cleanup campaign, a vocational guidance conference, a school safety patrol, an audio-visual service club, and a rural field day. (15)

Meet Comrade Student (McGraw-Hill, 52 min). Analyzes Russian educational system through interviews with Russian educators and scenes taken in elementary and secondary schools. Follows activities of two boys to show home life and school activities. (17)

Philosophies of Education: Education for Moral Character (NET Film Service, 29 min). Suggests that the key to strong character is to define for young people the right things to do and to challenge them to build moral and spiritual strength with a positive approach. (17)

Portrait of a Disadvantaged Child: Tommy Knight (McGraw-Hill, 17 min). Documents the highlights of a day in the life of a slum child, Tommy Knight. Shows the contrasting home life in which two disadvantaged children live. Discusses the disadvantages Tommy must endure as the results of academic testing and the lack of background experience in subjects being taught. Introduces the viewer to the special problems, special needs, and strengths of the inner-city child. (15, 17)

Portrait of the Inner-city School: A Place to Learn (McGraw-Hill, 18 min). Deals with problems of learning in an inner-city school. Points up the sharp areas of conflict between school practices and the cultural patterns of the pupils. Indicates positive attitudes which will help to facilitate adjustments in such schools. (15, 17)

Principles of Development (McGraw-Hill, 17 min). Compares children's likenesses and differences in development at various ages. Explains that development follows a correlated pattern, that development proceeds from general to specific responses, and that there is a right time for learning everything. (16)

Problem Method: Part I, Defining the Problem and Gathering Information (McGraw-Hill, 19 min). Shows how a high school class and the teacher define a problem and seek out resources that provide information relevant to it. The class selects the problem of "What should be done about pressure groups," lists a number of subquestions, collects information from a variety of sources, and discusses the different viewpoints that are discovered. A local situation in the city provides a concrete example of the action of pressure groups to affect a mayor's decision on a particular question. (16)

Problem Method: Part II, Using Information to Solve the Problem (McGraw-Hill, 16 min). Shows a high school class proceeding through the final steps to solve a sociopolitical problem. A report to the class reveals that definite influence by a pressure group was used to affect the mayor's decision on the passage of a highway through the main street of the town. Acting on information already gathered on what should be done about pressure groups, the class lists four suggestions, decides on ways of testing each one, and proceeds to test them to arrive at one acceptable conclusion. The steps in the whole process of problem solving are reviewed, and the class then considers the highway bill according to the procedure already discussed. (16)

The Quiet One (Athena Films, 66 min). Donald Peters is a mentally disturbed Negro boy, an only child, and the victim of a disrupted home in Harlem. At the age of ten he is sent to the Wiltwyck School at Esopus, New York, a correction school for delinquent boys, which was founded by the Protestant Episcopal Church. With the aid of the psychiatrist and counselors he receives the training and emotional comfort which help him rehabilitate his personality. (15)

School in Centreville (National Education Association, 20 min). Shows children, the staff in a multiteacher rural school, and parents planning together the procedures that best relate the curriculum to the children's needs. Emphasizes the need for taking into account individual differences in interests and aptitudes. Tells how children learn to practice scientific thinking in problem solving. (16)

School and the Community (McGraw-Hill, 13 min). Through animation, shows a school which is isolated from the community, neither benefiting its community nor being benefited by it. Then describes the advantages to be derived from cooperation between school and community. Points out that the school can be used for adult activities, the teachers can be leaders in community groups, and the pupils can be taught more about community life. (15)

The Search for America: Part 2, Our Problems in Education (NET Film Service, 29 min). Discusses problems of American education and compares American schools with those in other countries. (17)

The Sixth Chair (National School Service Institute, 18 min). Highlights such problems in education as building construction and modernization, class size, more teachers, and up-to-date educational tools; portrays the dangers of the public's complacency toward education. A picture that will help to put the public squarely behind a better financial program of action. (16)

Which Way for Human Rights? (Teachers College, 8 min). Uses drawings and still pictures to portray the background developments leading to the Universal Declaration of Human Rights. Points out that human rights are still violated throughout the world and describes what the UN and various countries are doing to achieve greater recognition of the human rights concept. Raises several pertinent questions for discussion regarding the clarification of the concept and various programmatic and procedural problems. (16)

Who's Delinquent? (RKO, 17 min). Describes the action of a newspaper in inciting a community to remedy a wave of juvenile delinquency. Shows two youths who with a stolen car have run down a policeman and pictures some other characteristic delinquents. Follows the action of the paper in research, study, publicity, and action; and pictures the community factors contributing to the problem. (15)

Filmstrips

Crises in Education (Wayne University, 34 fr.). Reviews the significant causes of the critical problems facing educators in the public schools in the United States. (17)

Education for All American Children: Summary—Teach Them All (National Education Association, 50 fr.). Presents plans for improving the education of children in the light of the major conclusions and recommendations of the Educational Policies Commission. (16)

Every Teacher . . . An Active Political Citizen (National Education Association, 13 fr., color). Suggests ways for teachers to participate in community affairs. (15)

Guidelines for Decision (Department of Elementary School Principals, NEA, 134 fr., color). Deals with the realities of society and learning which serve as guidelines for decisions about contemporary issues in elementary education. (17)

My Laboratory of Life (National Education Association, 11 min, sound). Philosophy of teaching held by Lawana Trout, named "Teacher of the Year" by *Look* Magazine in cooperation with the U.S. Office of Education in 1964. Mrs. Trout views her profession as it embraces the world beyond the school affecting her pupils in many aspects of their lives. (16)

Objectives of Education (Erle Press, 43 fr.). Explains the four areas of development and living which serve as objectives of education, as stated by the Educational Policies Commission of the National Education Association. (16)

Planning and Organizing for Teaching (National Education Association, 18 min, sound). Designed primarily for use by school staffs as they work on planning the total school program. It should also provide one basis for a dialogue among college faculties and students, school boards, educational associations, state departments of education, and interested lay groups. (16)

School Looks at the Community (Wayne University, 36 fr.). Visualizes the experiences of a representative school system to illustrate what can be done to make the school aware of the community's needs and makeup in order to improve school community relations. (15)

Tommy Goes to Kindergarten (Eye Gate House, Inc., 38 fr., color). Tommy is invited to visit the school for a day. Here he observes the children's many activities. At home, he asks his mother how soon kindergarten will start. (16)

Toward Better Schools for All Children through Federal Aid (National Education Association, 54 fr.). Makes a simple presentation of statistics which show the need for better public education. After emphasizing the varying abilities of different states to support their schools, the filmstrip presents the case for federal aid. (17)

What Has the Nursery School to Offer? (Association for Childhood Education International, 69 fr.). Designed to help teachers and others to understand the program of the nursery school. (16)

Your School and Community Relations (Museum Extension Service, 50 fr., color). Shows that the community should understand what the schools are doing, their needs, and why. School people must understand the community desires and needs. (15)

Recordings

Are the Criticisms of the Schools Justified? (National Tape Recording Project, 15 min). A Minneapolis, January town meeting in which Leo J. Brueckner, Malcolm B. Keck, Mrs. Agnes Sommer, and Edward Haynes discuss criticisms of the schools. (17)

The Community College and Its Functions (Educational Recording Service, 33⅓ rpm). Jesse P. Bogue, executive secretary, American Association of Junior Colleges, discusses the functions of a junior college. (16)

Critical Issues in Education: Are the Schools Neglecting the Fundamentals? (National Tape Recording Project, 40 min). Albert Lynd and Prof. Roma Gans present opposing points of view. Each is allowed 20 minutes to make his presentation. (17)

Critical Issues in Education: What Should Be the Relation of Religion and Public Education? (National Tape Recording Project, 40 min). Dr. Henry P. Van Dunsen and Prof. John K. Norton present opposing points of view. Each is allowed 20 minutes to make his presentation. (17)

Doorway to the Future: Challenge to Academic Freedom (National Tape Recording Project, 30 min). Dramatization of school problems with suggestions for solutions through constructive participation of citizens. (17)

Doorway to the Future: The Negro and the Public Schools (National Tape Recording Project, 30 min). Discusses the problems of integration and possible solutions. (17)

Education for Living (University of Illinois, 15 min). Describes the aims of vocational and terminal education. (16)

How Can the American Educational System Best Meet the Needs of Our Society? (National Tape Recording Project, 30 min). The needs of youth to be fulfilled by the American school system are seen through the needs of society. (16)

Improving the Services of Extra Class Activities (Educational Recording Services, 20 min, 33⅓ rpm). Dr. J. Lloyd Trump discusses ways and reasons for improving extra-class activities. (16)

The Meaning of Education (Academic Recording Institute, 33⅓ rpm). Ashley Montagu, interviewed by Virgila Peterson, discusses the function of education in terms of skills development, the communication of a body of knowledge, the growth of human relations practices, and the expansion of the individual. (16)

Our Schools: Educational Waste Lands or Fertile Fields (National Tape Recording Project, 90 min). A debate between Alan Griffin, Professor of Education at Ohio State University, and Arthur Bestor, historian, University of Illinois. Settles into the question of intellectual training versus life-adjustment education. Disagreement centers on methods and techniques for arriving at educational goals. (17)

A Reply to the Attacks on Our Schools (Educational Recording Service, 33⅓ rpm). Louis Kaplan of the University of Southern California defends the public schools against various attacks made against them. (17)

Socioeconomic Influences upon Children's Learning (Tape Recording Project, 15 min). Shows the effects of different cultural levels on the learning process. (15)

Some National and International Problems (Educational Recording Service, 33⅓ rpm). Karl J. McGrath, former U.S. Commissioner of Education, discusses various national and international problems. (17)

A Superintendent Speaks (University of Illinois, 30 min). Describes the joint obligations of teachers and school administrators in carrying forward a sound school program. (16)

FIGURE CREDITS

FIGURE 15–1. (*Source:* Arnold B. Barach, *USA and Its Economic Future*, Twentieth Century Fund, Inc., New York, 1964, p. 3.)

FIGURE 15–2. (*Source: Manpower: Challenge of the 1960's*, U.S. Department of Labor, 1961, p. 10.)

FIGURE 15–3. (*Source: Manpower: Challenge of the 1960's*, U.S. Department of Labor, 1961, p. 11.)

FIGURE 15–4. (*Source:* Arnold B. Barach, *USA and Its Economic Future*, Twentieth Century Fund, Inc., New York, 1964, p. 11.)

FIGURE 15–5. (*Source: Manpower: Challenge of the 1960's*, U.S. Department of Labor, 1961, p. 16.)

FIGURE 15–6. (*Source: Manpower Report of the President and a Report on Manpower Requirements, Resources, Utilization, and Training*, U.S. Department of Labor, March, 1965, p. 148.)

FIGURE 15–7. (*Source: Americans at Mid-decade*, U.S. Bureau of the Census, Series P–23, no. 16, January, 1966, p. 17.)

FIGURE 15–8. (*Source: An Act for International Development: A Program for the Decade of Development*, Department of State Publication 7205, General Foreign Policy Series 169, Bureau of Public Affairs, Office of Public Services, 1961, p. 166.)

FIGURE 15–9. (*Source:* Arnold B. Barach, *USA and Its Economic Future*, Twentieth Century Fund, Inc., New York, 1964, p. 17.)

FIGURE 15–10. (*Source: Population Estimates*, U. S. Bureau of the Census, Series P–25, no. 286, July, 1964.)

FIGURE 15–11. *(Source: Manpower Report of the President and a Report on Manpower Requirements, Resources, Utilization, and Training,* U.S. Department of Labor, March, 1965, p. 25.)

FIGURE 16–1. *(Source:* Nolan C. Kearney, *Elementary School Objectives,* Russell Sage Foundation, New York, 1953, p. 38.)

FIGURE 17–1. *(Source:* "Statistics of the Month," *American Education,* vol. 1, no. 8, p. 34, U.S. Office of Education, October, 1965.)

18

YOUR PLANS AND YOUR FUTURE

In ancient times the Romans had a famous god by the name of Janus, after whom the month of January was named. He was the god of gates and doorways. He was pictured with two faces, one looking forward and the other backward. People declared that he could look both ways at the same time. Perhaps you, too, have wished that you had the ability to look both forward and backward so that you could clearly see the future and the past as you faced many of life's problems.

YOUR STATUS IN PLANNING FOR TEACHING

In this book you have spent considerable time and energy examining various aspects of teaching as a career. Your attention has been focused primarily upon how to plan a career in education, how to gain the competencies required for teaching, and how to help perform the function of education in our democratic society. Often the process of stocktaking enables you to gain perspective and direction in your thinking and planning. What then, in brief, are some of the gains that should have resulted from your efforts?

Progress in Your Planning

You sense very clearly the nature and importance of planning in an increasingly complex and interdependent society, not only as it relates to you personally but also as it pertains to the educational needs of the boys and girls whom you may teach. Planning is an inescapable aspect of life which extends to all phases of living and continues throughout one's life. Furthermore, plans for the future are always tentative and are changed whenever developing situations seem to warrant it.

Career planning is only one aspect of life planning. It necessitates that you first identify the things that really seem important to you—that you clarify the values around which you wish to rotate your life. You further test a career in education to make certain that it is in harmony with the values you hold. As in all other professions, a career in education dictates certain requirements you must meet in order to be really successful and happy. You appraise yourself critically and comprehensively in terms of these requirements. You then develop long-range as well as immediate plans in as much detail as possible for moving from where you are to where you want to go—with the idea constantly in mind that modifications in the details of your master plan, or blueprint, are to be made as unforeseen situations develop.

Clarification of Values and Nature of Your Task

By now you should be quite clear in your thinking regarding the values you hold in life, how you happened to acquire them, the internal consistency that exists within them, and the extent to which they agree with the general pattern of values held by the society in which you live.

In Chapter 1 you noted the increasing importance of education in our society and the challenging role it will play in the future. In Chapters 5, 6, 7, and 11, you considered such matters as the nature of your work, some professional obligations you will meet, and the type of organization in which you will work. Chapters 15, 16, and 17 stressed the sociological and philosophical foundations of education today. Chapters 8, 9, 10, and 12 provided you with information regarding the economic, financial, and legal aspects of teaching.

Chapters 13 and 14 considered why educational practices and school organizations became what they are today. Chapters 1 and 4 attempted to point out the wide variety of opportunities which you have as you assist the schools in meeting the tremendous challenge with which they are faced. From your consideration of these chapters you should see how, with dignity, pride, and satisfaction, you can become a part of our schools today and can contribute effectively to the fuller realization of the school's function in our society.

Analysis of Requirements for Teaching

Much of your attention has been devoted to a consideration of the personal and professional requirements for successful teaching. Chapter 2 specifically indicated those competencies generally associated with successful teachers and suggested plans for meeting those requirements. Chapter 3 outlined the requirements for teaching as they are affected by such matters as certification requirements specified by the various state departments of education, the requirements for graduation from teacher education institutions, and in-service education requirements essential for continued personal and professional growth.

Appraising Your Prospects for Teaching

Throughout the book you have been encouraged to appraise yourself critically in light of the requirements for and demands made upon teachers. From your efforts you should have a relatively clear picture of your strengths and weaknesses for the profession and of how you can build up your good points and overcome your weaknesses.

If you have come to the conclusion that you are not suited to become a teacher, do not feel that your efforts have been wasted. In the first place you have saved yourself considerable time and money by not fully preparing for an occupation which probably would prove unsuitable for you. Also, you have spared yourself the unhappiness and frustration that would result from choosing the wrong occupation and having to readjust to another kind of work. Furthermore, the understandings you have gained regarding a career in education planning should help you to locate a more suitable occupation and to plan effectively in terms of the new field. In addition, you have gained further appreciation of the teacher's work

The enthusiasm and vigor of youth will be a constant challenge and source of stimulation for you. (*Photograph by Tom Stewart, St. Louis, Missouri.*)

and the function of education in our society. In the years that lie ahead, this should prove valuable to you for a number of reasons. You will be a taxpayer, and public schools are supported by taxation. You will be a member of some community in which school problems will be of general concern. You probably will be a member of some service group which holds more than casual interest in the education of boys and girls. It is highly probable that you will become a parent, in which case the education of your child will become of vital concern to you. In the final analysis, you should feel that you have gained much from your efforts.

PLANS FOR THE FUTURE

In planning to teach, there are many things to which you will want to direct your attention as you move ahead. By all means, plan in terms of the three major periods in your life which were discussed in Chapter 2. Keep in mind that when you are attending college, you are living in an environment that differs appreciably from the one in which you will find yourself later; i.e., your objectives, the nature of your work, your resources, and your opportunities will be altered. After graduation you will have such problems as becoming established in a position, building up financial resources, and starting your married life and family.

After this period of major adjustment, which may vary greatly in length for different individuals, you enter a later period in which your problems become somewhat different. Regardless of how far distant and nebulous this period in life may seem to you at the moment, you face the problem of making tentative plans for it. To "grow old gracefully," you must build certain interests and plan a definite old-age program. Pleasures derived from a grown family necessitate that children be raised. Retirement on a comfortable allowance necessitates deliberate sacrifices during a number of years in life.

Many suggestions have been made throughout this book, either directly or indirectly, that should help you in planning for the three major periods of life suggested above. However, plans necessarily are highly personal in nature and must be worked out only by you. As you move ahead in this, keep in mind the few practical hints that follow, along with the many suggestions that have been indicated previously.

Developing toward Student Teaching

The course work you take should be thoughtfully and carefully planned. First of all, make certain you meet the requirements for graduation and for the type of teacher certification you desire. Second, use your elective courses for strengthening certain weaknesses you may have in your ability to teach, for broadening your general background, for increasing the number of areas for which you may be certified, and for pursuing special interests.

Your attitude toward course work is of major importance in determining the value you will gain from it. For example, if you earn only a passing grade in a history course, just sufficient enough to be counted toward graduation and certification requirements, you probably will have little to enrich your life or the lives of the pupils whom you will teach. On the other hand, if you could seek to gain from the history course a deep understanding of the social, economic, and political forces that have shaped society into the form in which you find it today, you certainly should be a better student of current problems, more capable in interpreting them to your pupils, and better able to predict and shape future societal happenings. In the final analysis, what you gain from your course work is a matter that rests largely with you.

Seek out every opportunity possible to broaden and deepen your understanding of the behavior growth of boys and girls and to gain skill in effectively guiding this growth. A number of suggestions already have been given to help you plan such experiences. Regardless of the amount of encouragement provided by your teacher education institution, try to participate in situations with students which will contribute significantly to your professional understandings, insights, and skills.

Your student teaching will probably prove to be the most important single course you take during your preparation for the profession. For this reason, plan to make it of maximum benefit. Within limits you should be able to exercise some control over the semester, the grade level, and the subject area. Since many colleges and universities now have off-campus student teaching programs, you may have considerable latitude in the location of your student teaching assignment. If this be the case, ask to be assigned to a situation comparable to that in which you hope to begin teaching.

There are many sources of help in planning for your student teaching. Do not hesitate to discuss your ideas with your instructors and with students who have completed or are engaged in student teaching. You can also find some excellent books and films concerning the topic. Furthermore, all of the professional laboratory experiences which you have prior to student teaching will prove valuable as you formulate your plans.

Exercise independent and wise use of the many resources for personal growth to be found on your college campus and in its surrounding community. The library, the museum, the art gallery, the musical recitals, the various kinds of clinics, the entertainment and lecture series, the outstanding visitors, the conferences—these and many other resources normally are at your disposal. The extent

Student teaching provides a "capstone" for the course-work, professional laboratory experiences, and other activities in which you have engaged during your undergraduate years. (*Photograph by Joe Di Dio, National Education Association.*)

to which you avail yourself of them will depend upon the amount of individual initiative you wish to exercise.

College life provides abundant opportunities for social growth, and teachers need a high degree of social competence. Everyone, regardless of his past experiences, can improve in his ability to work effectively with others. Therefore, make efforts to increase your understanding of other students and to work with them on common problems that require thought and planning.

Your opportunities for growth normally are so great that you are faced with the problem of using your time and energy most effectively. There are, however, many things that you *must* do to meet the demands of college life. Establish the most efficient work habits possible so that you can fulfill these responsibilities with the minimum time and effort. For example, everyone can improve his reading skills and his efficiency in getting things done; in so doing, he has more time for other things.

In planning your college life, you do not want to overlook the need for establishing a healthy balance between work and recreational activities. Each individual requires some recreational activities in order to maintain a healthy attitude toward his life and work. Furthermore, many recreational activities are rich sources of learning for prospective teachers. The teacher of today needs to be skilled in the wise use of leisure time, not only for his own personal benefit but also for guiding others in that direction.

Locating a Position

As you continue your preparation for teaching, you should attend to certain things that may have a decided effect upon the position you secure. Become well acquainted with several of your college instructors so that they will be able to write letters of recommendation regarding your promise as a teacher. College instructors hesitate to recommend highly those students with whom they are vaguely acquainted.

During the later stages of your preparation for teaching, you probably will register with your college placement office. The purpose of this office is to help graduates secure positions and to assist school administrators in arranging interviews. An attempt is made to locate teachers in positions for which they are well qualified and in which they can best succeed. This type of service usually is extended to the institution's graduates as long as they are interested in securing or changing positions. Usually no registration fee is charged for this service.

At least eighteen state departments of education and thirteen state education associations provide teacher-placement services or answer inquiries about openings. In some cases this service is free, and in other cases a nominal fee or a percentage of the first year's salary is charged. A list of these agencies may be found in the Resource Section for Part VI.

Many of the 1,700 local and state offices of the United States Employment Service help place teachers at no charge. These offices serve as clearinghouses, enabling them to list vacancies in almost every state. You may wish to check with your local office when you want to secure a position.

Registering with your teacher-placement office is a vital step in securing a good teaching position. (*Photograph from the Audio-visual Center, Indiana University.*)

There are a number of reputable commercial placement bureaus that offer services to teachers on a national or a regional scale. A list of the accredited agencies may be obtained from the National Association of Teachers' Agencies, 316 S. Warren Street, Syracuse, New York. Usually a fee is charged for registration. If you secure a position through the efforts of a commercial agency, you normally will be expected to pay a commission of approximately 5 per cent of your first year's salary.

If you should be interested in opportunities in overseas schools, military and territorial schools, or exchange positions abroad, you may be able to secure appropriate information from your placement office. *The Manual on Certification Requirements for School Personnel in the United States,* published by the National Commission on Teacher Education and Professional Standards of the National Education Association, also contains information on such opportunities, including a listing of the requirements, the kind of preparation needed, and the place to apply.

In registering with a placement office, you will be asked to provide references for recommendations as well as various personal and academic data on your training and background. The placement office uses these materials in referring you to the employing officials who have vacancies along the lines for which you are qualified. Obviously you will want to plan your college career so as to have as strong a set of placement credentials as possible. In addition to the letters of recommendation, your academic achievement, participation in cocurricular activities, and success in professional experiences (especially student teaching) enter as significant factors in your placement. Throughout your preparation for teaching, you are, in a sense, building the credentials upon which you will be recommended for various teaching positions. The need for careful planning in this regard is self-evident.

Your placement office will be concerned with the type and the general location of the teaching position you desire. Some important questions arise in regard to these matters. Do you prefer to teach in your home school system or in one located some distance away, possibly in another state or overseas? Do you prefer to teach in a strictly rural district, a town, a small city, or a large city school system? Are you interested in teaching disadvantaged pupils, or do you prefer to teach pupils that tend to be from average or above-average socioeconomic levels? The answers to these questions may have a significant bearing upon the nature of your plans for teaching and therefore warrant your early attention. The answers may necessitate considerable thought and effort on your part.

Many of the larger school systems have employing officials who visit placement offices throughout the nation in search of well-qualified teachers. The placement officials assist them in locating and in interviewing prospective candidates for the positions. On the other hand, a school official may write to the placement office requesting credentials of prospective teachers who meet the requirements for filling a vacancy existing in his school system. After examining the credentials of those recommended, the school official may invite one or more of the most promising candidates for an interview.

If you have a definite idea of a school system in which you may wish to secure a position, you may write requesting that your name be placed on file as a poten-

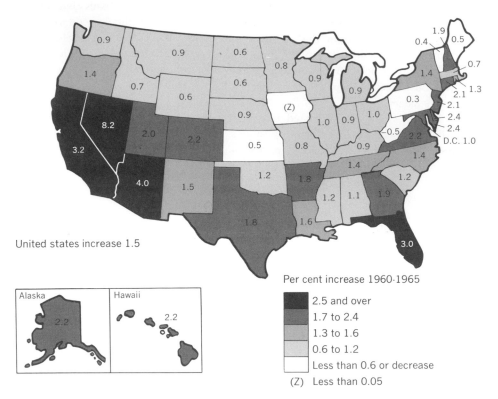

FIGURE 18–1.   The average annual percentage of change in population by states that has occurred betwen 1960 and 1965. If this pattern of change continues, how will school systems and job opportunities be affected? (*Source:* U.S. Bureau of the Census.)

tial candidate in case a vacancy should exist along the lines of your qualifications. So long as you do not apply for a specific position known to be filled by another teacher, you would not be violating the code of ethics presented in Chapter 7. If you do not know the name of the school official to whom you should write, you may be able to get this information from the educational directory of your state or the *Education Directory*, part 2, "Public School Systems," U.S. Department of Health, Education, and Welfare, Government Printing Office, Washington, D.C.

You would want to avoid indiscriminate distribution of applications. If you make such a request of a superintendent, also indicate where he may secure your placement credentials and any other information that might be helpful to him in determining your qualifications and capabilities.

Regardless of any influential friends or relatives that you may have on the school board or in the community, scrupulously respect the official professional head of the school. Conduct all your employment negotiations through him. Expect him to request much information about you, such as your academic record, areas in which you are qualified to teach, cocurricular activities, previous jobs, and the reasons why you wish a position in that particular school system. Although it may appear to be absurd, many written applications for positions are not favorably considered because of poorly written letters, misspelled words, incorrect grammar, and tactless statements.

If you should be called for an interview, the superintendent or his delegated employing official will be especially interested in your personal appearance, skill in communication, mannerisms, prejudices, professional outlook, aspirations, technical competence, and plans for the future. During the interview, attempt to be relaxed, natural, professional, mature, and enthusiastic. You should feel free to ask questions about the school system, policies, working conditions, and community. You may wish to inquire about the availability and cost of housing, as well as of transportation, recreation, and cultural resources. If you seem to be a promising candidate for a position, the superintendent may invite you to visit in the school system and in the community. During this visit you will have an opportunity to meet some of the teachers and other administrators, study the school plant and other facilities, and gain additional information regarding teaching assignments, cocurricular duties, administrative policies, provisions for continued professional growth, community expectations, living accommodations, and the nature and educational resources of the community. If you and the superintendent are in agreement, he will recommend your appointment to the board of education.

Entering into Teaching

Success and happiness in teaching require continuous planning, even though you have received your certificate and have secured an excellent position. In fact, the effort you put forth and the wisdom reflected in your planning will determine largely the extent to which you will realize the values inherent in a teaching career. You should find the following suggestions helpful:

1. *Become an integral part of your working situation.* In order to be most successful in your work and in improving conditions within your school, you must first be accepted and respected by other members in the school and community. Unfortunately some beginning teachers feel an obligation to bring up to date all the other teachers and administrators in their schools. They may try immediately to change things. Obviously, such techniques do not contribute greatly to a program of genuine progress in which a group moves forward together.

2. *Avoid the feeling that theory is one thing and that practice is another.* Actually, theory provides direction in terms of which improvements in practice may take place. Practice, then, may be evaluated in terms of the degree to which it is consistent with theory; therefore, do not be discouraged if you find theory to be relatively far in advance of practice in your school. Such a condition should challenge you to become effective in improving practice. In your attempts to improve it, however, keep in mind that progress within a school takes place rather slowly. During your first years of teaching, therefore, feel very successful if you are able to improve only a few of the general practices.

3. *Concentrate upon the positive aspects of your situation rather than upon the weaknesses only.* It will be difficult for you to maintain good mental health if you are able to see only the difficulties, problems, and shortcomings in your situation. There are always some good things to be found.

4. *Approach your work with enthusiasm.* Enthusiasm is a contagious sort of thing which tends to facilitate learning and to improve working conditions. It generally reflects a healthy attitude toward life, a happy disposition, and a feeling of pride in your work. It tends to release energies through which greater accomplishments are made possible.

5. *Assume an experimental attitude toward your work.* Each day you should seek to develop your competence as a teacher. Whenever you feel you have no more room for improvement, you should consider yourself professionally dead. Plan that each year will be a year of new experience rather than a mere repetition of the preceding year and that it will bring forth new understandings, insights, and ways of doing things. You will need to be realistic as you appraise your work, avoiding pretense and other factors that tend to warp your thinking.

6. *Expect changes to take place within the field of education.* Professional education of teachers will continue to advance. Educational research will continue to bring forth new understandings of human growth, new techniques, and new materials to be used. The nature of our society will also change as scientific, economic, political, and social advancements are made. These changes will bring forth new values, functions, and purposes in education. You may therefore assume that the future will be different. You will need to adopt a positive, intelligent attitude toward change as it affects your personal life and your responsibilities as a teacher.

7. *Learn to differentiate the important from the unimportant tasks.* Some teachers lose perspective with respect to their primary function. As a result they tend to become lost in details which may or may not have real educational significance. For example, grading papers or various clerical duties may become more important than planning learning experiences of the pupils. Arrange your work so that you will be able to devote your time to the tasks that will bring the greatest educational returns to boys and girls.

8. *Establish habits of orderliness, accuracy, and promptness.* If your daily routine is systematic and well arranged, you will spare yourself much confusion and irritation. Establish the habit of routinizing as many daily activities as possible, of anticipating problems, and of developing well-organized, yet flexible, plans for solving them promptly and accurately. By so doing, you gain an added sense of accomplishment and free yourself for engaging in other kinds of activities.

9. *Seek assistance on professional problems whenever you need it.* There is little if any merit in keeping your problems to yourself with the hope that you finally will be able to solve them. The sources of help are many—your school administrator, supervisor, colleagues, books, and periodical literature. As you share problems with others, you may gain insight into them, clarify your thinking, receive helpful suggestions, build self-confidence, and develop common interests and wholesome working relationships with others.

10. *Maintain a good sense of humor.* Look for the humorous side of life as well as the serious aspects. Laugh with others and be able to laugh at yourself. A sense of humor may keep you from taking yourself too seriously. The ability to laugh often provides an excellent counterbalance for the many fears, anxieties, and disappointments normally encountered in life.

11. *Cultivate adequate, realistic self concepts.* With all the stresses and strains involved in teaching, you have the problem of coping with the inner self. Strive

to face realistically feelings of anger, hostility, and anxiety. Recognize that these are normal feelings which all human beings experience. Search out the causes of these feelings and gain further skill in controlling and in resolving them to the extent that you are able to maintain a healthy positive outlook upon life and effective working relationships with others. Gain feelings of real success through identifying purposes which seem genuinely worthwhile and through attempting to make a realistic amount of progress in achieving them. Think of yourself as a person with areas of ability as well as areas of inadequacy. Emphasize your areas of ability and realize that you are contributing something worthwhile to the lives of your pupils and to the overall program.

12. *Continue to improve your perception of others.* Good teaching depends upon your sensitivity to and understanding of the pupils with whom you work as well as the interpretations you make of their behavior. Strive to gain increasing skill in making accurate judgments regarding the behavior of your pupils as well as of your colleagues.

13. *Continue to strengthen your academic background.* New knowledge is being gained so fast that a teacher's academic background quickly becomes obsolete unless he continues to be a scholar, especially in his area of specialization. Continued growth in your academic background will give you added feelings of security and adequacy for meeting the growing interests and concerns of youth.

14. *Know when to quit your work for the day.* Conscientiousness and attention to duty are indeed admirable traits. However, you do not want these traits to overtax your energies to the extent that the quality of your work suffers. Some teachers work far into the night grading papers and performing similar school duties, thus exhausting their energies for the next day and warping their perspectives. Fatigue reflects itself in the mental attitude of the teacher and the emotional tone of the classroom, and this affects the education of pupils. You therefore will want to establish a desirable balance between work and the activities that will restore your physical and mental health.

15. *Cultivate adult friends outside of the teaching profession.* Through day-to-day contacts with your colleagues you normally will develop a number of friends within the profession. Since you share with them so many common interests and since it is so easy to talk shop, you may have a tendency to limit your contacts to teachers. You owe to yourself as well as to your profession, however, a fairly wide circle of friendships—people with varied interests and occupations. Through the cultivation of these friendships you have the opportunity to widen your background of information, improve your human relationships, gain a broad and wholesome outlook upon life, and extend your influence in the community.

16. *Maintain interests outside your schoolwork.* You have basic civic responsibilities as a member of society. Furthermore, you owe it to yourself and to your family to have a normal, happy home life. All these extraschool factors operate together in such a manner that your effectiveness as a teacher is actually broadened and strengthened.

17. *Prepare for the type of schoolwork in which you are most interested and for which you are best qualified.* If you think you will be happiest as a classroom teacher, prepare yourself through additional training and activities so that you may be the best teacher possible. If you feel that you have definite interest and

ability in other types of schoolwork, such as administration, you should prepare yourself well academically and secure types of professional experiences that will lead you in the direction in which you wish to move.

18. *Build a satisfactory functional philosophy of life.* Your life will be governed according to certain fundamental ideas and beliefs which you hold in regard to the nature of the universe, your place within it, and your relationships with others. In view of this rapidly changing world, it is difficult indeed to develop a consistent and harmonious way of looking at life. It calls for searching thought and effort on your part if you are to gain direction and peace of mind.

19. *Never lose sight of the great challenge that is yours.* There may be times when you will feel discouraged. It may help you to remember that other good teachers have sometimes felt discouraged too—Jim Baker, for example. There were many times when Jim's smoothly functioning group of pupils seemed almost adult—and then again everything would seem to go wrong. He was not a philosopher, but every once in a while he remembered what a professor had said to him when he was trying to make up his mind about becoming a teacher:

Jim, teaching's not an ordinary job. It's a real adventure, filled with all the danger and excitement a spirited person could ask for. The teacher stands entrusted with the welfare and security of our country's greatest treasures—its youth. The people say to the teacher, "Here are our boys and girls; teach them what they must know to live in a world of varied races and cultures, in a world of uncertainty and change." From all the heritage of the race the teacher must select that which is to be passed on. From all the influences that surround his young charges he must choose those to encourage, those to ignore, those to fight. From all the possible and distant goals for which people may strive, he must choose the most worthy and magnify them for children's eyes. In the midst of conflicts and confusions, he must hold aloft democracy's lamp; he must keep it bright and help his pupils to walk in its light. Teaching is not for the immature or the timid. It is for those who care about what happens to the world and its children and who are prepared to do something about it. There's your job, Jim.

SUMMARY

Throughout this book an earnest attempt has been made to help you in your orientation to the field of education and in planning your life work. The book has been written to encourage you to appraise critically and honestly both the profession and yourself. It is hoped that you feel rewarded for your efforts in reading it and that you like what you see in yourself and in the field of education.

QUESTIONS FOR YOUR CONSIDERATION

1. What changes have you made, as a result of this course, in your plans for teaching?
2. During this course, how have your views toward the function of the school changed?
3. What are some illustrations of the concept that effective planning extends to all phases of living and continues throughout one's life?

4. How can you gain from your college environment the greatest amount of growth toward teaching? To what extent are you using the resources available to you?

5. Why do a number of teachers fail to assume an experimental attitude toward their work? How can you avoid such pitfalls?

6. Why do some teachers feel that theory is one thing and that practice is another? What is the relationship between the two?

7. What would be some advantages and disadvantages of teaching in your home community?

8. Why should you file your application for a position with the superintendent of schools rather than with the president of the board of education?

ACTIVITIES FOR YOU TO PURSUE

1. Talk with some of your teachers who you feel have a wholesome outlook upon life and who have gained much enjoyment and satisfaction from teaching as a career. Try to determine the factors, conditions, and practices that have contributed to their success and happiness.

2. Talk with some teachers who seem to regard teaching as a burdensome job from which they gain little or no satisfaction. In what ways do they differ from teachers who seem to derive much happiness from teaching? List any pitfalls which you will want to avoid.

3. Consult with school administrators, college instructors, and placement officials regarding problems common to beginning teachers. You may be able to find research studies that have been made along this line. Plan ways in which you may be able to avoid many of these problems.

4. Suggest to your instructor that some student teachers be invited to your class to discuss the kinds of pre-student teaching experiences that proved to be of most help to them. Incorporate into your plans any good ideas which you gain from the discussion.

5. Suggest to your instructor that arrangements be made, if possible, for your class to view and discuss some good films concerned with student teaching.

6. List or describe in detail the conditions which you hope will characterize your later life. What plans must you follow in order to achieve these conditions?

7. Examine a number of blanks used in applying for a teaching position, including the one in the Resource Section for Part VI. What kinds of information are requested?

8. Make a list of points you would want to keep in mind during an interview if you were applying for a position.

9. Make a list of the things you would want to do ahead of time in preparation for an interview for a position in a school.

10. Now that you have completed this book, review critically any written plans you had made previously regarding your future. What changes must you make in order that they may be inclusive, adequate, realistic, and suitable for you?

OTHER SOURCES OF IDEAS AND INFORMATION FOR CHAPTER 18

SUGGESTED READINGS

Armstrong, W. Earl, and T. M. Stinnett: *A Manual on Certification Requirements for School Personnel in the United States,* National Education Association, National Commission on Teacher Education and Professional Standards, Washington, 1964, pp. 141–149. Contains suggestions and aids for obtaining a teaching job in the United States and overseas.

Batchelder, Howard T., Maurice McGlasson, and Raleigh Schorling: *Student Teaching in Secondary Schools,* 4th ed., McGraw-Hill Book Company, New York, 1964. An excellent book for anyone interested in student teaching experiences.

Bernard, Harold W.: *Mental Hygiene for Classroom Teachers,* 2d ed., McGraw-Hill Book Company, 1961. Chapter 19 is concerned with the teacher's developing and maintaining a positive view toward the profession. Chapter 20 stresses the importance of the teacher's philosophy.

Fisher, Margaret B., and Jeanne L. Noble: *College Education as Personal Development,* Prentice-Hall, Inc., Englewood Cliffs, N.J., 1960. An excellent book on personal development for college students.

How to Get a Teaching Position in the Public Schools, Research Memo 1964–8, National Education Association, Research Division, Washington, March, 1964. Contains many helpful suggestions for securing a teaching position.

Kaufman, Bel: "The Real World of the Beginning Teacher," *NEA Journal,* vol. 54, no. 7, pp. 17–19, National Education Association, Washington, October, 1965. Indicates some of the problems of the beginning teacher and how they may be faced.

Stinnett, T. M., and Albert J. Huggett: *Professional Problems of Teachers,* The Macmillan Company, New York, 1963. Chapter 5 is devoted to a discussion of the teacher's first position.

SUGGESTED FILMS, FILMSTRIPS, AND RECORDINGS

Films (16 mm)

Elementary Teacher: Beginning Student Teaching (Indiana University, 10 min). Discusses both the training and functions of the teacher in a world of rapid change. Shows prospective teachers in study and training situations, and follows Janet, a student teacher, as she acquaints herself with a classroom, the school, and its program and does practice teaching. Uses flashbacks to emphasize the points being discussed by the teaching supervisor and Janet during an evaluation of the latter's progress.

Planning for Personal and Professional Growth (McGraw-Hill, 17 min). Shows four schoolteachers who have made adjustments and achieved success, to various degrees, in their teaching. A middle-aged woman found teaching dull with many frustrations. She was not aware of her problems and found it difficult to adjust. A science teacher made long-range plans for his growth through graduate study but found that he had to re-evaluate his ambitious plans. A foreign language teacher found conflict between family life and teaching, but by relating her teaching to life, she made an adjustment. An elderly woman was enthusiastic about teaching, loved children, and found teaching a rich, rewarding experience.

Secure the Blessings (National Education Association, 25 min). Discusses the role of education in the United States as it prepares people to use the democratic method of solving problems. Shows five adults who are trying to solve their various problems in human relations objectively and points out that it was in school where these individuals learned to make decisions.

Filmstrips

Focus on the Future (National Education Association, 78 fr., color). Concerns the future teachers of America and the quest for quality teachers.

Your Educational Philosophy: Does It Matter? (Wayne University, 40 fr.). Presents a number of views of the classrooms of two teachers. Compares similar situations in these two classrooms to indicate how the teacher's educational philosophy affects the types of classroom activities planned for pupils.

Recording

A Forward Look for the Teaching Profession (Education Recording Service, 33⅓ rpm). W. S. Elsbree, professor of education, Columbia University, presents a challenge to anyone planning to teach.

FIGURE CREDIT

FIGURE 18–1. *(Source: Americans at Mid-decade,* U.S. Bureau of the Census, Series P–23, no. 16, January, 1966, p. 8.)

GLOSSARY

Academic. Pertaining to the fields of English, foreign languages, history, economics, mathematics, and science; (higher education) pertaining to the liberal arts fields.*

Academic freedom. The opportunity for the teacher to teach and for the teacher and the student to study without coercion or other forms of restrictive interference.

Academy. An independent secondary school not under public control.

Accreditation. The type of recognition held by an education institution that has met accepted standards applied to it by a competent agency or official association.

Accrediting agency. An organization that sets up criteria for judging the quality of educational institutions, determines the extent to which institutions meet these criteria, and issues some sort of public announcement concerning the quality of the institutions.

Activity concept. The generalization that activities, whether physical or intellectual, are necessary if learning is to occur.

Administrative policy. A statement adopted by a board of education or an administrative agency outlining principles to be followed with respect to specific matters.

Adult education. Organized activities with an educational purpose carried on by mature persons on a part-time basis.

Adult education center. Any local unit, agency, or school promoting formal or informal education primarily for adults; a branch of a school, college, or university stressing service to adults, usually emphasizing nonacademic and noncredit instruction.

Anecdotal records. A series of notes containing exactly what a child said or did in concrete situations; as observations are accumulated, a variety and continuity of information yielding a picture of the child's behavior patterns, development in various directions, interests, attitudes, strengths, and problems can be seen.

Apprenticeship. The period during which a young person works under the direction of an experienced, well-qualified adult to acquire increased skill and knowledge needed for competent performance in a given occupation.

Aptitude. A group of characteristics, native or acquired, deemed to be symptomatic of an individual's ability to acquire proficiency in a given area; examples might be of a particular art, school subject, or vocational area.

Articulation. The relationship and interdependence existing among the different elements of the educational program; may designate the degree of relationship among the different curricular offerings, between the curriculum and the institutional regimen, student activities, and provisions for pupil guidance, or between the school's program and out-of-school educational institutions and activities (for example, home, church, scouts, welfare agencies) or the degree to which the interlocking and interrelation of the successive levels of the educational system facilitate continuous and efficient educational progress of pupils.

Attitude. A readiness to react toward or against some situation, person, or thing in a particular manner, for example, with love or hate or fear or resentment, to a particular degree of intensity.

Automation. The process of manufacturing parts and passing them on to another machine for further processing without human interference.

Basic needs. Those needs which everyone has regardless of age, sex, or station in life, such as a sense of personal worth, status recognition, love, a sense of belonging, an attainment of some measure of success in one's efforts, as well as physical requirements.

Biological engineering. The process of altering human growth and behavior through the use of chemicals and the control of environmental conditions.

Centralized administration. An administrative system in which authority for direction, control, and management is located at one point.

Certification. The act of designating persons whom public boards of education may

---

* Most of these definitions are either taken directly or adapted from Carter V. Good (ed.), *Dictionary of Education*, 2d ed., McGraw-Hill Book Company, New York, 1959. Used by permission.

legally employ as teachers in public schools and of issuing teacher certificates to these qualified persons.

Child-centered curriculum. A curriculum design in which the interests and purposes of children determine the educative program; selection and planning of activities are cooperatively done by teacher and pupils; problem solving is the dominant method.

Child-centered education. Education wherein the child is engaged in reconstructing his own real and concrete experience rather than in learning exclusively from books and subject fields; emphasis is placed upon guidance of growth, everyday life and activity, self-direction and self-discipline by the child, cooperation among the pupils, initiative, originality, leadership in lifelike situations, and flexibility in planning and programming.

Class grouping. The act or procedure of dividing the pupils of a class into two or more groups on the basis of interest or ability for the purpose of adapting instruction.

Community-centered curriculum. An educational program based on and adjusted to the life, culture, resources, needs, activities, and interests of the community in which it is offered.

Community-centered school. A school attempting to serve not only persons of school age, but all ages and groups of a community, in the evening as well as during the day; its workshop, library, swimming pool, gymnasium, assembly hall, and other rooms are open for use by the people of the community; sometimes used synonymously with "community school."

Community resources. Anything in the community outside the schools that has educative value and is within the scope of school use, for example, museums, theaters, courts, libraries, industries, parks, playgrounds, and outstanding individuals and other human resources.

Consumer education. A study of intelligent and effective methods of buying and using goods and services, competent money management, and the relationship of the consumer to our economic system.

Continuing education. Any extension of educational opportunities for adults provided by special schools, centers, colleges, or other institutions.

Conventional school. A school that is the outgrowth of custom or common practice.

Cooperative supervision. A plan for improvement of instruction according to which teachers and supervisors are regarded as coworkers, the teachers participating in analyzing and determining such aspects of instruction as objectives, materials, and methods.

Core curriculum. A curriculum design in which one subject or group of subjects becomes a center or core to which all the other subjects are subordinated and upon which they depend for sequence since they have no independent principle to determine their status in the program.

Core program. (1) The part of the whole educational program that presents those areas in which learning is essential for balanced living on the part of the majority of individuals; (2) the portion of a school program that is required of all pupils (frequently used as a synonym for "core curriculum").

Course of study. A guide prepared by administrators, supervisors, and teachers of a particular school or school system as an aid to teaching a given subject or area of study for a given grade or other instruction group.

Criterion. A standard, norm, or judgment selected as a basis for quantitative and qualitative comparison.

Critical-incidents method. A method for determining what abilities are needed to do a particular job in order to establish standards of success through actual incidents occurring on the job.

Critical thinking. Thinking that proceeds on the basis of careful evaluation of premises and evidence and comes to conclusions as objectively as possible through the consideration of all pertinent factors and the use of valid procedures from logic.

Culturally disadvantaged. Refers to individuals whose experience backgrounds have been extremely limited or narrow.

Cumulative record. An individual record which is kept up-to-date by a member of the counseling staff and which includes educational, social, vocational, and health data.

Curriculum. A body of prescribed educative experiences under school supervision.
Cybernation. Refers to the use of computers in automation.

Decentralized administration. Any plan for the operation of schools in which provision is made for scope for local initiative in adapting programs to local educational needs.
De facto segregation. Segregation of school pupils which results primarily from housing patterns especially in large cities.
Developmental task. A task that arises at or about a certain time in the life of an individual, successful achievement of which leads to his happiness and success with later tasks, whereas failure leads to unhappiness in the individual, disapproval by his society, and difficulty with later tasks.

Education. The aggregate of all the processes by means of which a person develops abilities, attitudes, and other forms of behavior of positive value in the society in which he lives.
Emotional maturity. The emotional pattern of an adult who has progressed through the emotional stages characteristic of infancy, childhood, and adolescence and is able to deal successfully with reality and to participate in adult concerns without undue emotional strain.
Essentialism. The doctrine that there is an indispensable, common core of culture (certain knowledges, skills, attitudes, ideals, etc.) that can be identified and should be taught systematically to all, with rigorous standards of achievement.
Establishment. Refers to a group or agency which actually controls or at least exerts strong influence in shaping educational policy.
Evaluation. The process of ascertaining or judging the value or amount of something by careful appraisal.
Exceptional child. A loose term used to cover children who have abnormal physical, mental, or social differences. The term may include gifted children.
Extraclass activities. Activities in which pupils participate outside of the regular class routine under the supervision of the school.

Faculty psychology. A term that derives from an attempt by Wolff (1912) to analyze conscious experiences in terms of a mind (soul) endowed with certain faculties or "potencies of action"; Wolff sought to establish a relationship between the location in the soul of a faculty and its ability to re-present specific elements of the universe.
Field laboratory experience. Actual practice away from the college campus, within schools or their environment, in dealing with educational problems; part of the program offered by a teacher education institution, usually conducted in schools that are not formally under the direct control of or affiliated with the teacher education institution; usually more limited and incidental and less formal and concentrated than the extended "internship"; sometimes refers to practice in supervision, administration, or guidance.
Flexible scheduling. A schedule that permits periods to be lengthened, shortened, combined, or shifted in time to meet the varying demands of activity.

General education. A broad type of education aimed at developing attitudes, abilities, perceptions, and behavior considered desirable by society. Does not necessarily include preparing the learner for a specific type of vocation.
Graded school. A school in which the materials of instruction are organized according to grade or year level of difficulty and interest and in which the pupils are organized into grades or year groups according to their progress in schoolwork.
Grammar school. (1) Historically, a shortened popular designation of the English grammar school of colonial times; (2) popularly and loosely, a term used to designate an elementary school.
Gross national product (GNP). The sum total of all goods and services produced in an economic system in any given period, usually a year.

Head Start project. Refers to organized efforts, usually subsidized by the United States government, to expand the experience backgrounds of culturally disadvantaged preschool children.

Higher education. Includes all education above the level of the secondary school that is provided by an educational institution.

Homogeneous grouping. The classification of pupils for the purpose of forming instructional groups having a relatively high degree of similarity in regard to certain factors that affect learning.

Idealism. Any system of thought or practical view emphasizing mind or spiritual reality as a preeminent principle of explanation.

In loco parentis. A term meaning "in the place of a parent."

Increment. When applied to salary schedules, it refers to the annual increase.

Indefinite tenure. A system of school employment in which the teacher or other employee, having served a probationary period of a certain number of years, retains his position indefinitely and is protected in his position either by statute or by rule of the school board.

Index salary schedule. A salary schedule for teachers, using an index or ratio in which the bachelor's degree with no years experience serves as a base of 100 or 1.00.

Instructional unit. Any part or division of a course that can be considered as complete in itself and can be taught as a whole.

Intelligence quotient (IQ). The most commonly used device for expressing level of mental development in relation to chronological age; obtained by dividing the mental age (as measured by a general intelligence test) by the chronological age and multiplying by 100. (The chronological age is often fixed at a certain maximum, most commonly 16 years, when growth of intelligence due to maturation has been assumed to cease. Thus, if 16 years were the maximum chronological age used, a testee whose actual age was greater than this would still be assigned an age of 16 years for purposes of calculating the IQ. The maximum chronological age for different tests varies from about 14 to 18 years.)

Job analysis. The basic method used to obtain salient facts about a job, involving observation of workers and conversations with those who know the job, in order to describe in detail the work involved, the conditions under which it must be performed, and the qualifications necessary for the worker who must perform it.

Laboratory school. A school that is under the direct control of or closely associated with a teacher preparing institution, whose facilities may be used for demonstration, participation, experimentation, and practice teaching.

Maturation. (1) Changes in the characteristics of an organism resulting from intrinsic (anatomic, physiological, and neurological) development, with or without the aid of autogenous development; to be distinguished from changes due to special experience or learning; (2) the process of cellular, organic, and functional development of an organism.

Median. The point on the scale of a frequency distribution above which and below which 50 per cent of the cases fall.

Megalopolis. An extremely large city that has resulted from the fusion of smaller cities and towns.

Merit rating. An evaluation of the effectiveness of teaching, supervision, or administration, based on a definite scale or collection of items accepted as legitimate measures for such purposes.

National assessment. Usually refers to a nationwide testing program designed to ascertain the quality of public education.

Nondirective teaching. A technique whereby the instructor, as resource person, creates for the student an atmosphere of self-directed learning in order to encourage independent judgment, intellectual curiosity, strong motivation, and both subjective and objective evaluation.

Percentile. An expression of value in terms of per cent. For example, if a person has a percentile rank of 75 on a test, it means that 25 per cent of the student scores are higher than and 75 per cent lower than his score.

Philosophy of education. A careful, critical, and systematic intellectual endeavor to see education as a whole and as an integral part of man's culture.

Pragmatism. The philosophical position which holds that the meaning of an idea consists in the conduct it designates, that thinking is a functional process for guiding action, and that truth is a social value which ideas earn as they are verified by competent inquiry.

Preschool education. The method and theory of guiding young children, between the ages of two and five, in a manner demonstrated in the nursery schools in which emphasis is placed on developing capacities of the children and on helping them solve their problems.

Primary unit. A division of elementary education, usually comprising grades 1 to 3, devoted primarily to instruction in fundamental skills and the development of social attitudes necessary for democratic living.

Problem-solving method. A manner of dealing with that which is problematic; a method involving clear definition of the problem confronted, formation of a hypothetical solution (hunch or suggestion), and deliberate test of a hypothesis until evidence warrants its acceptance.

Professional laboratory experiences. Any experiences, outside the teacher education classroom, designed to increase the experience background, understandings, and insights of a prospective or experienced teacher.

Programmed instruction. Used especially in connection with teaching machines in which information is presented in small, logical steps, problems or questions are posed for solution, results of the pupil's solution are given immediately, and provisions for remedial steps are given if the pupil is in error.

Progressive education. The designation of an educational movement that protested against formalism; associated with the philosophy of John Dewey, it emphasizes commitment to the democratic idea, the importance of creative and purposeful activity and the real life needs of students, and closer relations between school and community.

Project Head Start. An effort subsidized by the United States government to expand the experience background of culturally disadvantaged preschool children.

Psychograph. A graphic representation of an individual's measured characteristics, abilities, achievements, and personal qualities.

Puritanism. The position which holds that strong character and wise behavior come from strict adherence to established rules and that wisdom directs the disciplining of desire by hard work and exercise rather than by reflection.

Realism. A philosophy holding that the aim of education is the acquisition of verified knowledge of the environment and adjustment to the environment.

Reciprocity in teacher certification. Recognition by certifying authorities of a certificate or license issued by some other certifying authority.

Release period. That part of the school day during which public school children are permitted to attend religious instruction classes conducted under the auspices of their particular denomination; release time.

Reliability. The degree of consistency obtained between repeated measurements of individuals, with the same device.

School trustee. A person, selected under legal provision, usually chosen by popular election from the district at large for a term of three to five years, to direct with other members of a board of trustees the progam of education within the territorial limits of the school district.

Secondary school. A more recent term than "high school"; refers to the school following the elementary school, usually comprising grades 9 to 12 or grades 7 to 12.

Selective admission. Admission of applicants to an educational institution by selection on the basis of legal residence or of predictive measures or other criteria of scholastic aptitude, personal fitness, and probable future success.

Self-image. The perceptual component of self; the image one has of the appearance of his body; the picture one has of the impressions he makes on others.

Single-salary schedule. A plan by which the same salary is paid to all teachers in a school system who have the same amount of professional experience and preparation and who are given comparable teaching responsibilities.

Social engineering. The systematic application of social science to the organization, control, direction, and motivation of man and his institutions.

Social maturity. A state of development in which the attitudes, understandings, feelings, and skills of the individual, with respect to human relationships, social tools, and social institutions, are those which are typical of the adult.

Sociogram. A device for revealing group structure and various types of group members such as isolates, well-liked people, leaders.

Standardized test. A test for which content has been selected and checked empirically, for which norms have been established, for which uniform methods of administering and scoring have been developed, and which may be scored with a relatively high degree of objectivity.

Student teaching. Observation, participation, and actual teaching done by a student preparing for teaching under the direction of a supervising teacher or general supervisor.

Teacher aide. An individual, usually noncertified for teaching, who assists a certified teacher in caring for various clerical and other routine duties in the classroom so that the teacher may concentrate on instructional activities.

Teacher contract. A formal agreement, usually in writing, entered into by a teacher and the employing authority, stating the salary to be paid and the length of the term of the contract, and setting forth the general duties to be performed by the teacher.

Teacher education. The program of activities and experiences developed by an institution responsible for the preparation and growth of persons preparing themselves for educational work or engaging in the work of the educational profession.

Teaching machine. A mechanical device by means of which a program is presented to a learner. It usually presents one item (frame) at a time, provides some method for the pupil to indicate an overt response, shows whether or not the response is correct, maintains a record of the pupil's responses, and provides for relearning if the response is not correct.

Team teaching. A system in which two or more teachers work together in teaching a group of children.

Three-track course of study. A course of study providing for instruction in a particular area on three distinct levels; affords greater individualization of instruction by offering modified curriculum content for the superior, average, and inferior pupils in each class group.

Tort. A commission or omission of an act, by one without right, by which another receives some injury to person, property, or reputation.

Ungraded school. A school having a flexible system of grouping in which pupils are grouped together regardless of age and in which extensive effort is made to adapt instruction to individual differences.

Unit instruction. An organization of various activities, experiences, and types of learning around a central problem or purpose, developed cooperatively by a group of pupils under the guidance of a teacher. Involves planning, execution of plans, and evaluation of results.

Validity. The extent to which a test or other measuring device measures what it purports to measure.

Value. Any characteristic deemed important because of psychological, social, moral, or aesthetic considerations.

REFERENCES

1. Abraham, Willard: *A Time for Teaching*, Harper & Row, Publishers, Incorporated, New York, 1964.
2. "Actions of 1966 NEA Convention Spur Greater Unity of Teaching Profession," *NEA Reporter*, vol. 5, no. 7, pp. 1–2, National Education Association, Washington, July 15, 1966.
3. *Adult Education: A New Imperative for Our Times*, Adult Education Association, Washington, 1961.
4. Aiken, Wilford M.: *The Story of the Eight-year Study*, Harper & Row, Publishers, Incorporated, New York, 1942.
5. Alexander, William M.: *Are You a Good Teacher?* Holt, Rinehart and Winston, Inc., New York, 1959.
6. Alford, Albert L.: "School Finance as a Part of Public Finance," *School Life*, vol. 43, no. 7, pp. 12–14, U.S. Office of Education, April, 1961.
7. American Association of School Administrators: *Hogs, Ax Handles and Woodpeckers*, Washington, 1958.
8. *The American Public-school Teacher, 1960–61*, Research Monograph 1963–M2, National Education Association, Research Division, Washington, April, 1963.
9. *Analysis of Teacher Tenure Provisions: State and Local*, National Education Association, Committee on Tenure and Academic Freedom, Washington, June, 1954, pp. 6–7.
10. "Are They Learning as Much Today?" *NEA Journal*, vol. 53, no. 4, p. 7, National Education Association, Washington, April, 1964.
11. *The Arguments on Merit Rating*, Research Memo 1959–30, National Education Association, Research Division, Washington, December, 1959.
12. Armstrong, W. Earl, and T. M. Stinnett: *A Manual on Certification Requirements for School Personnel in the United States, 1964*, National Education Association, National Commission on Teacher Education and Professional Standards, Washington, 1964.
13. Arnstein, George: *Automation: The New Industrial Revolution*, National Education Association, Washington, 1962.
14. Ayres, Leonard P.: "Making Education Definite," *Indiana University Bulletin*, vol. 13, no. 11, Indiana University, Bloomington, Ind., 1915.
15. Bagley, William C.: "The Case for Essentialism in Education," *NEA Journal*, vol. 30, no. 7, pp. 201–202, National Education Association, Washington, October, 1941.
16. Ballinger, Stanley E.: "Teaching about Religion as a Public School Policy: Some Questions," in David W. Beggs, III, and R. Bruce McQuigg (eds.), *America's Schools and Churches*, Indiana University Press, Bloomington, Ind., 1965.
17. Barach, Arnold B.: *USA and Its Economic Future*, Twentieth Century Fund, Inc., New York, 1964.
18. Barr, W. Montfort: *American Public School Finance*, American Book Company, New York, 1960.
19. Bathurst, Effie G.: *Where Children Live Affects Curriculum*, U.S. Office of Education Bulletin 1950, no. 7, 1960.
20. Baxter, Bernice: *Teacher-Pupil Relationships*, The Macmillan Company, New York, 1941.
21. Bayles, E. E., and B. L. Hood: *Growth of American Educational Thought and Practice*, Harper & Row, Publishers, Incorporated, New York, 1966.
21a. Beach, Fred F., and Robert F. Will: *The State and Education*, U.S. Office of Education Misc. 23, 1960.
22. Beggs, David W., III: *Team Teaching: Bold New Venture*, Indiana University Press, Bloomington, Ind., 1964.
23. Beggs, David W., III, and Donald C. Manlove: *Flexible Scheduling: Bold New Venture*, Indiana University Press, Bloomington, Ind., 1965.
24. Benson, Charles S.: "The Teacher Shortage: Cause and Solution," in Seymour E.

Harris (ed.), *Challenge and Change in American Education,* McCutchan Publishing Corporation, Berkeley, Calif., 1965, pp. 169–174.

25. Bestor, Arthur: *Educational Wastelands,* University of Illinois Press, Urbana, Ill., 1953.

26. Beyer, Evelyn: "Montessori in the Space Age," *NEA Journal,* vol. 52, no. 9, pp. 35–36, National Education Association, Washington, December, 1963.

27. Binzen, Peter H.: "Education: Soviet Style," *Philadelphia Bulletin,* from a syndicated newspaper article, June 19, 1966.

28. Bloom, Benjamin Samuel: *Stability and Change in Human Characteristics,* John Wiley & Sons, Inc., New York, 1964.

29. Bossing, Nelson L., and Roscoe V. Cramer: *The Junior High School,* Houghton Mifflin Company, Boston, 1965.

30. Bowers, Harold J.: "Reciprocity in Teacher Certification," *NEA Journal,* vol. 39, no. 1, p. 14, National Education Association, Washington, January, 1950.

31. Brickell, Henry M.: *Organizing New York State for Educational Change,* State Education Department, Albany, N.Y., 1961.

32. Brown, B. Frank: *The Appropriate Placement School,* Parker Publishing Company, West Nyack, N.Y., 1965.

33. Bruner, Jerome S.: *The Process of Education,* Harvard University Press, Cambridge, Mass., 1965.

34. Bruner, Jerome S.: *Toward a Theory of Instruction,* The Belknap Press, Harvard University Press, Cambridge, Mass., 1966.

35. Burrup, Percy E.: *The Teacher and the Public School System,* Harper & Row, Publishers, Incorporated, New York, 1960.

36. Butts, R. Freeman: "Search for Freedom: The Story of American Education," *NEA Journal,* vol. 49, no. 3, pp. 33–48, National Education Association, Washington, March, 1960.

37. Callahan, Raymond C.: *An Introduction to Education in American Society,* Alfred A. Knopf, Inc., New York, 1960.

38. Carr, William G.: "World-wide Cooperation among Teachers," *NEA Journal,* vol. 50, no. 5, pp. 24–25, National Education Association, Washington, May, 1961.

39. *The Case for Federal Support of Education, 1961,* National Education Association, Washington, 1961.

40. *The Central Purpose of American Education,* National Education Association, Educational Policies Commission, Washington, 1961.

41. Chandler, B. J.: *Education and the Teacher,* Dodd, Mead & Company, Inc., New York, 1961.

42. Charters, W. W., and Douglas Waples: *The Commonwealth Teacher-training Study,* The University of Chicago Press, Chicago, 1929.

43. Clark, Burton R.: *The Open Door College: A Case Study,* McGraw-Hill Book Company, New York, 1960.

44. *Classroom Teachers Speak on Professional Negotiations,* National Education Association, Washington, 1963.

45. Combs, Arthur W.: "The Personal Approach to Good Teaching," *Educational Leadership,* vol. 21, no. 6, pp. 369–377, 399, Association for Supervision and Curriculum Development, Washington, March, 1964. Copyright © 1964 by the Association for Supervision and Curriculum Development.

46. Commission on Secondary Curriculum: *The Junior High School We Need,* National Education Association, Association for Supervision and Curriculum Development, Washington, 1961.

47. Committee on Education and Labor: *Federal Interest in Education,* House of Representatives, 87th Cong., 1st Sess., September, 1961.

48. *Compact for Education,* Education Commission of the States, Duke University, Durham, N.C., 1966.

49. "A Comparative Study of the Academic Achievements of Elementary Age Stu-

dents in the United States and the British Isles," *University of Toledo Project 2177*, July 1, 1963 to June 15, 1965, Toledo, Ohio., 1965 (unpublished).

50. Conant, James Bryant: *The American High School Today*, McGraw-Hill Book Company, New York, 1959.

51. Conant, James Bryant: *The Education of American Teachers*, McGraw-Hill Book Company, New York, 1963.

52. Conant, James Bryant: *Education in the Junior High School Years*, Educational Testing Service, Princeton, N.J., 1960.

53. Conant, James Bryant: *Shaping Educational Policy*, McGraw-Hill Book Company, New York, 1964.

54. Conant, James Bryant: *Slums and Suburbs*, McGraw-Hill Book Company, New York, 1961.

55. Conrad, Herbert S.: "The Teacher Shortage: Cause and Solutions," in Seymour E. Harris (ed.), *Challenge and Change in American Education*, McCutchan Publishing Corporation, Berkeley, Calif., 1965, pp. 174–180.

56. *The Contemporary Challenge to American Education*, National Education Association, Educational Policies Commission, Washington, 1958.

57. Crowley, Elmer S.: "Breakthrough for Professional Autonomy," *NEA Journal*, vol. 54, no. 8, pp. 46–47, National Education Association, Washington, November, 1965.

58. "A Current Dilemma: National Assessment," *ISBA Journal*, Indiana School Boards Association, Bloomington, Ind., November, 1966, p. 9. *Sources: Carnegie Quarterly*, vol. 14, no. 2, Spring, 1966; and *National Educational Assessment: Pro and Con*, National Education Association, Washington, 1966.

59. Davis, E. Dale: *Focus on Secondary Education: An Introduction to Principles and Practices*, Scott, Foresman and Company, Chicago, 1966.

60. Davis, Thelma F.: "NEA Mutual Fund," *NEA Journal*, vol. 53, no. 8, pp. 29–30, National Education Association, Washington, November, 1964.

61. Dean, Stuart E.: *Elementary School Administration and Organization*, U.S. Office of Education Bulletin 1960, no. 11, 1960.

62. Dewey, John: *Democracy and Education*, The Macmillan Company, New York, 1916.

63. Dewey, John: *Education Today*, G. P. Putnam's Sons, New York, 1940.

64. "Drop in Teacher Turnover Reported," *NEA Journal*, vol. 53, no. 5, p. 5, National Education Association, Washington, May, 1964.

65. *Economic Status of Teachers in 1964–65*, Research Report 1965–R7, National Education Association, Research Division, Washington, May, 1965.

66. *Education: An Investment in People*, Chamber of Commerce of the United States, Education Department, Washington, 1964.

67. *Education and the Disadvantaged American*, National Education Association, Educational Policies Commission, Washington, 1962.

68. *Education for a Changing World of Work*, U.S. Office of Education, 1962.

69. *Education for All American Youth: A Further Look*, National Education Association, Educational Policies Commission, Washington, 1952.

70. *Education for Freedom and World Understanding*, U.S. Office of Education, 1962.

71. *Education Is Good Business*, American Association of School Administrators, Washington, 1966.

72. *Education in the United States of America*, Special Series 3, U.S. Office of Education, 1955.

73. *Education in the United States of America*, U.S. Office of Education, 1960.

74. *Education USA*, National Education Association, National School Public Relations Association, Washington, Nov. 18, 1965. Copyright NSPRA.

75. *Education USA*, National Education Association, National School Public Relations Association, Washington, May 5, 1966.

76. "The Educational Establishment," *Phi Delta Kappan*, vol. 46, no. 4, pp. 190–194, Phi Delta Kappa, Bloomington, Ind., December, 1964.

77. "Educational Growth and Change," *NEA Journal,* vol. 49, no. 9, pp. 45–47, National Education Association, Washington, December, 1960.

78. Elam, Stanley: "Who's Ahead, and Why: The NEA-AFT Rivalry?" *Phi Delta Kappan,* vol. 46, no. 1, pp. 12–21, Phi Delta Kappa, Bloomington, Ind., September, 1964.

79. *Elementary School Organization,* Research Memo 1965–22, pp. 1–2, National Education Association, Research Division, Washington, September, 1965.

80. Epstein, Benjamin: *The Principal's Role in Collective Negotiations between Teachers and School Boards,* National Education Association, National Association of Secondary-School Principals, Washington, 1965.

81. "Estimate of School Statistics, 1965–66," *NEA Research Bulletin,* vol. 44, no. 1, pp. 22–23, National Education Association, Research Division, Washington, February, 1966.

82. *Estimates of School Statistics, 1966–67,* Research Report 1966–R20, National Education Association, Research Division, Washington, December, 1966.

83. Eurich, Alvin C.: "America Is Opportunity: Effective Education for the Sixties," an address at the 49th Annual Meeting, Chamber of Commerce of the United States, Washington, May, 1961.

84. Eurich, Alvin C.: *Time to Teach,* The Fund for the Advancement of Education, New York, 1963.

85. Evans, W. D. Emrys: "A British Viewpoint," *Teachers College Journal,* vol. 36, no. 1, p. 55, Indiana State University, Terre Haute, Ind., October, 1964.

86. "Extended Leaves of Absence for Classroom Teachers," *Educational Research Service Circular* 2, National Education Association, Research Division, Washington, February, 1966.

87. "Extended-year Contracts for Teachers," *ERS Reporter,* National Education Association, American Association of School Administrators and the Research Division, Washington, September, 1964.

88. "Extra Pay and Dependency," *NEA Journal,* vol. 49, no. 8, pp. 52–54, National Education Association, Washington, November, 1960.

89. *Extra Pay for Extra Duties, 1962–63,* Research Memo 1963–8, National Education Association, Research Division, Washington, March, 1963.

90. *Facts and Figures on Adult Education,* vol. 1, no. 1, National Education Association, Division of Adult Education Service, Washington, April, 1963.

91. "Facts on American Education," *NEA Research Bulletin,* vol. 44, no. 2, pp. 35–45, National Education Association, Research Division, Washington, May, 1966.

92. *A Federal Education Agency for the Future,* U.S. Office of Education, 1961.

93. "The Financial Rewards of Teaching," *NEA Research Bulletin,* vol. 38, no. 2, pp. 49–55, National Education Association, Research Division, Washington, May, 1960.

94. *Financial Status of the Public Schools, 1965,* National Education Association, Washington, 1965.

95. Finn, James D.: "The Good Guys and the Bad Guys," *Phil Delta Kappan,* vol. 40, no. 1, pp. 2–5, Phi Delta Kappa, Bloomington, Ind., October, 1958.

96. *The Flight from Teaching,* The Carnegie Foundation for the Advancement of Teaching, New York, July, 1964.

97. Flowers, Anne, and Edward C. Bolmeier: *Law and Pupil Control,* The W. H. Anderson Company, Cincinnati, 1964.

98. Ford, Edmund A.: "Organizational Patterns of the Nation's Public Secondary Schools," *School Life,* vol. 42, no. 9, pp. 10–12, U.S. Office of Education, May, 1960.

99. Ford, Paul Leicester: *The Writings of Thomas Jefferson,* II, G. P. Putnam's Sons, New York, 1893.

100. Fosdick, Harry Emerson: "Our Religious Illiterates," in C. Winfield Scott, and Clyde M. Hill (eds.), *Public Education under Criticism,* Prentice-Hall, Inc., Englewood Cliffs, N.J., 1956.

101. *Fostering Mental Health in Our Schools,* 1950 Yearbook of the Association for Supervision and Curriculum Development, National Education Association, Washington, 1950.
102. Frasier, James E.: *An Introduction to the Study of Education,* 3d ed., Harper & Row, Publishers, Incorporated, New York, 1965.
103. *Freedom to Teach; Freedom to Learn,* National Education Association, Commission on Professional Rights and Responsibilities, Washington, 1964.
104. French, William M.: *America's Educational Tradition,* D. C. Heath and Company, Boston, 1964.
105. Fullam, Marie G., and Frances E. Ryan: *Earned Degrees by Field of Study and Level Projected to 1975,* U.S. Office of Education, 1964.
106. Gardner, John W.: *Excellence: Can We Be Equal and Excellent Too?* Harper & Row, Publishers, Incorporated, New York, 1961.
107. Garrison, Paul: "Are Russian Schools Better than Ours?" *Hoosier School Board Journal,* vol. 10, no. 8, pp. 14–17, Bloomington, Ind., October, 1964.
108. Good, Carter V. (ed.): *Dictionary of Education,* 2d ed., McGraw-Hill Book Company, New York, 1959.
109. Good, Harry G.: *A History of Western Education,* The Macmillan Company, New York, 1960.
110. *A Good Start in School,* Department of Public Instruction Bulletin 226, Indianapolis, 1958.
111. Goodlad, John I., and Robert H. Anderson: *The Nongraded School,* Harcourt, Brace & World, Inc., New York, 1963.
112. Grant, Venn: *Man, Education, and Work,* American Council on Education, Washington, 1964.
113. Grieder, Calvin, and Stephen Romine: *American Public Education: An Introduction,* The Ronald Press Company, New York, 1955.
114. "Group Insurance Is Growing," *NEA Journal,* vol. 55, no. 5, pp. 48–49, National Education Association, Washington, May, 1966.
115. "Group Life Insurance for Teachers," *NEA Research Bulletin,* vol. 42, no. 2, pp. 56–59, National Education Association, Research Division, Washington, May, 1964.
116. "Growing Pains of the Junior College," *Washington Monitor: Education USA,* Washington, Mar. 31, 1966.
117. *A Guide for Organizing and Developing a Kindergarten Program in Florida,* rev., State Department of Education Bulletin 53A, Tallahassee, Fla., January, 1955.
118. Hamilton, Robert R., and E. Edmund Reutter, Jr.: *Legal Aspects of School Board Operation,* Teachers College Press, Columbia University, New York, 1958.
119. *Handbook Office of Education,* U.S. Office of Education, 1960.
120. Hannan, Cecil J.: "A State Association Has Helped Make Teachers . . . a Political Force," *NEA Journal,* vol. 54, no. 8, p. 49, National Education Association, Washington, November, 1965.
121. Hansen, Kenneth H.: *Public Education in American Society,* Prentice-Hall, Inc., Englewood Cliffs, N.J., 1964.
122. Harap, Henry: "Teacher Preparation: 5-year Programs," *School Life,* vol. 44, no. 2, pp. 18–21, U.S. Office of Education, October, 1961.
123. Harbison, Frederick, and Charles A. Myers: *Education, Manpower, and Economic Growth,* McGraw-Hill Book Company, New York, 1964.
124. Harris, Norman C.: "Redoubled Efforts and Dimly Seen Goals," *Phi Delta Kappan,* vol. 46, no. 8, pp. 360–365, Phi Delta Kappa, Bloomington, Ind., April, 1965.
125. Havighurst, Robert J.: *Human Development and Education,* Longmans, Green & Co., Inc., New York, 1953.
126. Havighurst, Robert J.: "Knowledge of Class Status Can Make a Difference," *Progressive Education,* vol. 27, pp. 100–101, February, 1950.

127. "Headstart Raises IQ's, Betters Health," *Washington Monitor: Education USA,* Washington, Feb. 10, 1966, p. 105.

128. Heil, Louis, Marion Powell, and Irwin Feifer: *Characteristics of Teacher Behavior Related to the Achievement of Children in Several Elementary Grades,* Brooklyn College, Brooklyn, N.Y., 1960.

129. Heller, Walter W.: "Education and Economic Growth," *NEA Journal,* vol. 50, no. 7, p. 9, National Education Association, Washington, October, 1961.

130. Hemphill, John K., James M. Richards, and Richard E. Peterson: *Report of the Senior High School Principalship,* National Education Association, National Association of Secondary-School Principals, Washington, 1965.

131. Hobson, Carol Joy, and Samuel Schloss: *Fall 1964 Statistics of Public Elementary and Secondary Day Schools,* U.S. Office of Education, 1965.

132. Hughes, James Monroe: *Education in America,* 2d ed., Harper & Row, Publishers, Incorporated, New York, 1965.

133. Hutchins, Robert M.: *The Conflict in Education,* Harper & Row, Publishers, Incorporated, New York, 1953.

134. *Imperatives in Education,* American Association of School Administrators, Washington, 1966.

135. "In the Good Old Summertime," *The Shape of Education for 1965–66,* vol. 7, pp. 45–48, National Education Association, National School Public Relations Association, Washington, 1965.

136. "Index Salary Schedules for Teachers," *NEA Research Bulletin,* vol. 39, no. 4, pp. 108–112, National Education Association, Research Division, Washington, December, 1961.

137. *An Introduction to Phi Delta Kappan,* Phi Delta Kappa, Bloomington, Ind. (brochure).

138. Jersild, Arthur T., and Associates: *Education for Self-understanding: The Role of Psychology in the High School Program,* Teachers College Press, Columbia University, New York, 1953.

139. Jordan, K. Forbis: "Who Shall Be the Effective Voice for American Teachers?" *American School Board Journal,* vol. 147, no. 1, p. 38, The Bruce Publishing Company, Milwaukee, July, 1963.

140. "The Junior High School Program," *Bulletin of the Southern Association of Colleges and Secondary Schools,* Southern Association of Colleges and Secondary Schools, Atlanta, Ga., 1958.

141. Kaplan, Bernard A.: "Issues in Educating the Culturally Disadvantaged," *Phi Delta Kappan,* vol. 45, no. 2, pp. 70–76, Phi Delta Kappa, Bloomington, Ind., November, 1963.

142. Kaplan, Bernard A.: "Issues in Educating the Culturally Disadvantaged," in Jonathan C. McLendon and Laurence D. Haskew (eds.), *Views on American Schooling,* Scott, Foresman and Company, Chicago, 1964, pp. 27–32.

143. Kearney, Nolan C.: *Elementary School Objectives,* Russell Sage Foundation, New York, 1953.

144. Koerner, James D.: *The Miseducation of American Teachers,* Houghton Mifflin Company, Boston, 1963.

145. Kreitlow, B. W.: *Long-term Study of Educational Effectiveness of Newly Formed Centralized School Districts in Rural Areas,* Cooperative Research Project no. 375, Department of Agricultural and Extension Education, University of Wisconsin, Madison, September, 1962.

146. *Labor Force Projections for 1970–80,* Special Labor Force Report, no. 49, reprint no. 2455, U.S. Bureau of Labor Statistics, February, 1965, pp. 129–140.

147. Lang, Carroll L.: "Education and Economic Development," *Phi Delta Kappan,* vol. 46, no. 9, pp. 467–470, Phi Delta Kappa, Bloomington, Ind., May, 1965.

148. *Leaves of Absence: School Law Summaries,* National Education Association, Research Division, Washington, April, 1966.

149. "Legality of Public Summer Schools," *NEA Research Bulletin,* vol. 43, no. 1, pp.

30–31, National Education Association, Research Division, Washington, February, 1965.

150. Lindsey, Margaret (ed.): *New Horizons for the Teaching Profession,* National Education Association, National Commission on Teacher Education and Professional Standards, Washington, 1961.

151. McCaskill, J. L.: "History of the Federal Role," *Long-range Planning in School Finance,* National Education Association, Washington, 1963.

152. McConnell, T. R.: *A Design for General Education,* American Council on Education Studies, ser. 1, no. 18, Washington, 1944, pp. 14–15.

153. McDonald, Ralph: "Professional Salaries for Teachers," *NEA Journal,* vol. 38, no. 9, p. 662, National Education Association, Washington, December, 1949.

154. McLure, William P.: *The Intermediate Administrative School District of the United States,* Bureau of Educational Research, College of Education, University of Illinois, Urbana, Ill., February, 1958.

155. "Magnitude of the American Educational Establishment (1966–1967)," *Saturday Review,* Oct. 15, 1966, p. 75.

156. *Manpower: Challenge of the 1960's,* U.S. Department of Labor, 1961.

157. *Manpower Report of the President and a Report on Manpower Requirements, Resources, Utilization, and Training,* U.S. Department of Labor, 1965.

158. Marshall, Robert A.: *The Story of Our Schools: A Short History of Public Education in the United States,* National Education Association, National Council for the Social Studies, Washington, 1962.

159. Martz, Velorus, and Henry Lester Smith: *An Introduction to Education,* Charles Scribner's Sons, New York, 1941.

160. "Maternity Leave Provisions for Classroom Teachers in Large School Systems," *Educational Research Service Circular* 3, National Education Association, Research Division, Washington, March, 1966.

161. "Maximum Scheduled Salaries for Administrators," *NEA Research Bulletin,* vol. 44, no. 2, pp. 44–45, National Education Association, Research Division, Washington, May, 1966.

162. Mead, Margaret: *From the South Seas: Studies of Adolescence and Sex in Primitive Societies,* William Morrow and Company, Inc., New York, 1948.

163. Mead, Margaret: "Thinking Ahead," *Harvard Business Review,* vol. 36, no. 6, pp. 23–37, 164–170, November–December, 1958.

164. "Methods of Evaluating Teachers," *NEA Research Bulletin,* vol. 43, no. 1, pp. 12–18, National Education Association, Research Division, Washington, February, 1965.

165. Michael, Donald N.: *The Next Generation: The Prospects Ahead for the Youth of Today and Tomorrow,* Random House, Inc., New York, 1965.

166. Michael, Donald N.: "Your Child and the World of Tomorrow," *NEA Journal,* vol. 55, no. 1, National Education Association, Washington, January, 1966 (supplement).

167. Minssen, Friedrich: "What's Good about American Education: A German Educator's View," *Teachers College Journal,* vol. 36, no. 1, pp. 52–54, Indiana State University, Terre Haute, Ind., October, 1964.

168. Moustakas, Clark E., and Minnie P. Berson: *The Nursery School and Child Care Center,* Whiteside, Inc., New York, 1955.

169. Mushkin, Selma J., and Eugene P. McLoone: *Local School Expenditures: 1970 Projections,* Council of State Governments, Chicago, November, 1965.

170. National Association of Public School Adult Education: *Public School Adult Education: A Guide for Administrators,* National Education Association, Washington, 1963.

171. National Commission of School District Reorganization: *Your School District,* National Education Association, Department of Rural Education, Washington, 1948.

172. National School Boards Association: *Delegate Assembly Workshop Record*, Philadelphia, May 2–3, 1961.

173. NEA Committee on Educational Finance: *Local Nonproperty Taxation*, CEF Report no. 13, National Education Association, Washington, July, 1965.

174. NEA Committee on Educational Finance: *State Taxes in 1965*, CEF Report no. 13, National Education Association, Washington, February, 1966.

175. *NEA Handbook for Local, State, and National Associations, 1965–66*, National Education Association, Washington, 1965.

176. *New England's First Fruits* in *Collections of the Massachusetts Historical Society for the Year 1792*, vol. 1, p. 242, T. R. Marvin, Printer, Boston, 1859.

177. "New Horizons in Teacher Education and Professional Standards, *NEA Journal*, vol. 50, no. 1, pp. 55–68, National Education Association, Washington, January, 1961.

178. "News and Trends," *NEA Journal*, vol. 53, no. 9, p. 3, National Education Association, Washington, December, 1964.

179. "News and Trends," *NEA Journal*, vol. 54, no. 5, p. 3, National Education Association, Washington, May, 1965.

180. "News and Trends," *NEA Journal*, vol. 54, no. 8, p. 4, National Education Association, Washington, November, 1965.

181. "News and Trends," *NEA Journal*, vol. 55, no. 1, p. 4, National Education Association, Washington, January, 1966.

182. Noar, Gertrude: *The Junior High School: Today and Tomorrow*, Prentice-Hall, Inc., Englewood Cliffs, N.J., 1961.

183. "Nongraded School Organization," *NEA Research Bulletin*, vol. 43, no. 3, pp. 93–95, National Education Association, Research Division, Washington, October, 1965.

184. "Objects of the National Congress of Parents and Teachers," *PTA Manual*, National Congress of Parents and Teachers, Chicago, 1965–1966.

185. Olsen, Edward G. (ed.): *School and Community*, Prentice-Hall, Inc., Englewood Cliffs, N.J., 1954.

186. *One World or None*, Film Publishers, Inc., New York, 1946, 16 mm, black and white, sound, 8 min.

187. Orlich, Donald C., and S. Samuel Shermis: *The Pursuit of Excellence: Introductory Readings in Education*, American Book Company, New York, 1965.

188. "Our Schools Aren't Good Enough," *The News Letter*, vol. 20, Bureau of Educational Research, Ohio State University, Columbus, Ohio, November, 1954.

189. *Pace Projects to Advance Creativity in Education: A Manual for Project Applicants*, Title III, Elementary and Secondary Education Act, Supplementary Centers and Services Program, U.S. Office of Education, 1965.

190. Perkins, Hugh V.: "Nongraded Programs: What Progess?" *Educational Leadership*, vol. 19, no. 3, pp. 166–169, 194, National Education Association, Association of Supervision and Curriculum Development, Washington, December, 1961.

191. Phoenix, Philip H.: *Philosophies of Education*, John Wiley & Sons, Inc., New York, 1961.

192. Piaget, Jean: *The Construction of Reality in the Child*, Basic Books, Inc., Publishers, New York, 1954.

193. *Policies and Criteria for the Approval of Secondary Schools*, North Central Association of Colleges and Secondary Schools, Chicago, 1966.

194. Power, Edward J.: *Education for American Democracy: An Introduction to Education*, McGraw-Hill Book Company, New York, 1958. Material used by permission.

195. "President Johnson Speaks Out on Education," *NEA Journal*, vol. 53, no. 1, pp. 12–15, National Education Association, Washington, January, 1964.

196. The President's Commission on National Goals: *Goals for Americans*. Copyright 1960 by the American Assembly, Columbia University, New York. Reprinted by permission of Prentice-Hall, Inc., Englewood Cliffs, N.J.

197. Price, Hugh G.: "There's an Increasing Need for Public Schools through Grade 14," *NEA Journal,* vol. 48, no. 9, p. 10, National Education Association, Washington, December, 1959.

198. *Professional Negotiation Agreement, New Rochelle, New York,* National Education Association, Office of Urban Services, Washington, 1964.

199. *Professional Negotiation with School Boards: A Legal Analysis and Review,* National Education Association, Research Division, Washington, March, 1965.

200. *Professional Organizations in American Education,* National Education Association, Educational Policies Commission, Washington, 1957.

201. *Professional Salaries for Professional Teachers,* National Education Association, Committee on Educational Finance, Washington, 1961.

202. *Projections of Educational Attainment in the United States: 1965 to 1985,* Current Population Reports, ser. P–25, no. 305, U.S. Bureau of the Census, Apr. 14, 1965, pp. 1–16.

203. "Purposes," *Educational Horizons,* vol. 43, no. 4, p. i, Pi Lambda Theta, Washington, Summer, 1965.

204. *The Purposes of Education in American Democracy,* National Education Association, Educational Policies Commission, Washington, 1938.

205. *The Pursuit of Excellence: Education and the Future of America.* Copyrighted 1958 by Rockefeller Brothers Fund, Inc. Reprinted with permission of Doubleday & Company, Inc.

206. Ragan, William B.: *Teaching America's Children,* Holt, Rinehart and Winston, Inc., New York, 1961.

207. *Rankings of the States, 1967,* Research Report 1967–R1, National Education Association, Research Division, Washington, January, 1967.

208. Rathbone, M. J.: *Human Talent: The Great Investment,* Standard Oil Company (New Jersey), New York, Feb. 25, 1964.

209. "Reduced Progress in Urban Teachers' Salaries," *NEA Research Bulletin,* vol. 39, no. 3, pp. 67–74, National Education Association, Research Division, Washington, October, 1961.

210. Reeder, Ward G.: *A First Course in Education,* The Macmillan Company, New York, 1946, pp. 495–499. (Quoted from Samuel Hall.)

211. Reisert, John E.: "Easy Answers to Tough Problems: The Conant Approach to Teacher Education," *The Hoosier Schoolmaster,* vol. 7, no. 3, pp. 1 and 5, Indiana Association of Junior and Senior High School Principals, Bloomington, Ind., Apr. 1, 1964.

212. Reisert, John E.: "Migrating Educator? What about Your Teaching Credentials?" *Phi Delta Kappan,* vol. 47, no. 7, pp. 372–374, Phi Delta Kappa, Bloomington, Ind., March, 1966.

213. *Religion in the Public Schools,* American Association of School Administrators, Washington, 1964.

214. *The Report of the White House Conference on Education,* Washington, Nov. 28–Dec. 1, 1955.

215. "Reporting to Parents," *NEA Research Bulletin,* vol. 39, no. 1, pp. 24–25, National Education Association, Research Division, Washington, February, 1961.

216. "Retirement Statistics, 1964," *NEA Research Bulletin,* vol. 42, no. 4, pp. 99–107, National Education Association, Research Division, Washington, December, 1964.

217. "Review of the American Educational System," *Hearing before the Subcommittee of the Committee on Appropriations,* House of Representatives, 86th Cong. Sess., 1960.

218. Rice, Arthur H.: "How Four Changes We Can Foresee Will Alter Teaching," *Nation's Schools,* vol. 77, no. 3, p. 8, March, 1966.

219. Rickover, Hyman G.: *American Education: A National Failure,* E. P. Dutton & Co., Inc., New York, 1963.

220. Rickover, Hyman G.: "The World of the Uneducated," *The Saturday Evening Post,* Nov. 28, 1959, p. 8.

221. Robinson, Donald W.: "The Nature of Controversy," in Jonathan C. McLendon and Laurence D. Haskew (eds.), *Views on American Schooling,* Scott, Foresman and Company, Chicago, 1964, pp. 92–94.

222. Rothney, John W. M.: "Evaluating and Reporting Pupil Progress," *What Research Says to the Teacher,* no. 7, National Education Association, Department of Classroom Teachers, American Educational Research Association, Washington, 1960.

223. Russell, John Dale: "Financing Higher Education in the Sixties," *Phi Delta Kappan,* vol. 42, no. 1, pp. 8–11, Phi Delta Kappa, Bloomington, Ind., October, 1960.

224. Ryans, David G.: *Characteristics of Teachers,* American Council on Education, Washington, 1960. Used by permission.

225. "Sabbatical Leave Provisions for Classroom Teachers in Larger School Systems," *Educational Research Service Circular* 8, National Education Association, Research Division, Washington, November, 1965.

226. *Salaries in Higher Education, 1965–66,* Research Report 1966–R2, National Education Association, Research Division, Washington, February, 1966.

227. *Salary Schedules for Administrative Personnel, 1964–65,* Research Report 1965–R2, National Education Association, Research Division, Washington, March, 1965.

228. *Salary Schedules for Classroom Teachers, 1965–1966,* Research Report 1965–R15, National Education Association, Research Division, Washington, October, 1965.

229. "Sampling Study of the Teaching Faculty in Higher Education," *NEA Research Bulletin,* vol. 44, no. 1, pp. 3–10, National Education Association, Research Division, Washington, February, 1966.

230. Schloss, Samuel: *Enrollment of 3-, 4-, and 5-year Olds in Nursery Schools and Kindergartens: October, 1964,* U.S. Office of Education, Bureau of Educational Research and Development, June, 1965.

231. "School Desegregation," *Contemporary Issues in American Education,* U.S. Office of Education, 1965, pp. 97–105.

232. *Schools for the Sixties,* Project on Instruction of the National Education Association, McGraw-Hill Book Company, New York, 1963.

233. Seldon, David: "Why the AFT Maintains Its AFL-CIO Affiliation," *Phi Delta Kappan,* vol. 47, no. 6, pp. 298–300, Phi Delta Kappa, Bloomington, Ind., February, 1966.

234. Shane, Harold G.: *Résumé of Grouping in the Elementary School,* Indiana Association for Supervision and Curriculum Development, 1960. (Mimeographed.)

235. Shane, Harold G., and E. T. McSwain: *Evaluation and the Elementary Curriculum,* Holt, Rinehart and Winston, Inc., New York, 1958.

236. Shannon, Harold D.: "Credit Union Lesson for Teachers," *NEA Journal,* vol. 50, no. 5, p. 14, National Education Association, Washington, May, 1961.

237. Sharples, Hedley: "Diversity in Democracy: Some Abroad Thoughts from at Home," *Teachers College Journal,* vol. 36, no. 1, pp. 56–57, Indiana State University, Terre Haute, Ind., October, 1964.

238. Sheviakov, George V., and Fritz Redl: *Discipline for Today's Children and Youth,* National Education Association, Association for Supervision and Curriculum Development, Washington, 1956.

239. "Short-term Leaves of Absence for Classroom Teachers in Large School Systems," *Educational Research Service Circular* 4, National Education Association, Research Division, Washington, April, 1966.

240. "Sick Leave Provisions for Classroom Teachers in Larger School Systems," *Educational Research Service Circular* 5, National Education Association, Research Division, Washington, May, 1966.

241. Simon, Kenneth A., and Marie G. Fullam: *Projections of Educational Statistics to 1973–74,* U.S. Office of Education, 1964.

242. Smith, Louis M.: "Group Processes in Elementary and Secondary Schools," *What Research Says to the Teacher,* no. 19, National Education Association, Department of Classroom Teachers, American Educational Research Association, Washington, 1959.

243. Smith, Philip G.: *Philosophy of Education*, Harper & Row, Publishers, Incorporated, New York, 1965.

244. *Social Security Coverage of Public-school Teachers*, Retirement Income Series no. 48, National Education Association, Research Division, Washington, June, 1966.

245. *State Boards of Education and Chief State School Officers*, U.S. Office of Education Bulletin 12, 1950.

246. "State Minimum-salary Laws," *NEA Research Bulletin*, vol. 44, no. 1, pp. 15–17, National Education Association, Research Division, Washington, February, 1966.

247. *State of the Nation in Regard to Criticisms of the Schools and Problems of Concern to Teachers*, National Education Association, Commission on Professional Rights and Responsibilities, Washington, January, 1966.

248. *A Statement for Growing Adults*, Community Services in Adult Education, Indiana University, Bloomington, Ind., 1953.

249. *Statistical Abstract of the United States, 1966*, U.S. Bureau of the Census, 1966.

250. "The Status of the American Public-school Teacher, *NEA Research Bulletin*, vol. 35, no. 1, National Education Association, Research Division, Washington, February, 1957.

251. "The Status of the Teaching Profession," *NEA Research Bulletin*, vol. 28, no. 2, National Education Association, Research Division, Washington, March, 1940.

252. Stinnett, T. M.: *A Manual on Certification Requirements for School Personnel in the United States*, National Education Association, National Commission on Teacher Education and Professional Standards, Washington, 1967.

253. Stinnett, T. M.: "Teaching Professionalization: Challenge and Promise," Power and Professionalism in Teaching, *Bulletin of the School of Education*, vol. 40, no. 5, pp. 9–20, Indiana University, Bloomington, Ind., September, 1964.

254. Stinnett, T. M., and Albert J. Huggett: *Professional Problems of Teachers*, The Macmillan Company, New York, 1963.

255. *Student NEA Handbook*, National Education Association, National Commission on Teacher Education and Professional Standards, Washington, 1962.

256. "Tax-sheltered Annuities," *NEA Research Bulletin*, vol. 44, no. 1, pp. 29–30, National Education Association, Research Division, Washington, February, 1966.

257. "Tax-sheltered Annuities: Current Status," *NEA Research Bulletin*, vol. 42, no. 3, pp. 94–95, National Education Association, Research Division, Washington, October, 1964.

258. Taylor, James L., Lillian L. Gore, and Hazel F. Gabbard: *Functional Schools for Young Children*, Special Publication 8, U.S. Office of Education, 1961.

259. *Teacher Competence: Its Nature and Scope*, California Teachers Association, The Commission on Teacher Education, Burlingame, Calif, 1957.

260. *Teacher Leaves of Absence*, National Education Association, Research Division and Department of Classroom Teachers, Discussion Pamphlet 7, Washington, May, 1961.

261. "Teacher-opinion Poll," *NEA Journal*, vol. 54, no. 7, p. 64, National Education Association, Washington, October, 1965.

262. *Teacher Retirement*, National Education Association, Department of Classroom Teachers and Research Division, Discussion Pamphlet 2, Washington, November, 1957.

263. *Teacher Supply and Demand in Public Schools, 1962*, Research Report 1962–R8, National Education Association, Research Division, Washington, April, 1962.

264. *Teacher Supply and Demand in Public Schools, 1965*, Research Report 1965–R10, National Education Association, Research Division, Washington, June, 1965.

265. *Teacher Supply and Demand in Public Schools, 1966*, Research Report 1966–R16, National Education Association, Research Division, Washington, October, 1966.

266. *Teacher Supply and Demand in Universities, Colleges, and Junior Colleges, 1963–64 and 1964–65*, Research Report 1965–R4, National Education Association, Research Division, Washington, April, 1965.

267. *Teacher Tenure*, National Education Association, Department of Classroom

Teachers and the Research Division, Discussion Pamphlet 1, Washington, July, 1954.

268. "Teacher Tenure Laws Benefit Teachers in 37 States," *NEA Research Bulletin*, vol. 38, no. 3, pp. 81–85, National Education Association, Research Division, Washington, October, 1960.

269. Thayer, V. T.: *The Role of the School in American Society*, Dodd, Mead & Company, Inc., New York, 1960.

270. "Three Cities Move to Toughen Corporal Punishment Policies," *Nation's Schools*, vol. 73, September, 1963.

271. *The Three R's of the Profession as Expressed in the Code of Ethics, Bill of Rights, Code of Competence*, Pennsylvania State Education Association, Harrisburg, Pa., 1956.

272. "Today's Pressured Teens," *The Shape of Education for 1965–66*, vol. 7, National Education Association, National School Public Relations Association, Washington, 1965.

273. "Tomorrow's Jobs: Where the Best Will Be," *Changing Times: The Kiplinger Magazine*, Washington, February, 1966, p. 11.

274. Trump, J. Lloyd: *Guide to Better Schools*, Rand McNally & Company, Chicago, 1961.

275. Trump, J. Lloyd: *Images of the Future: A New Approach to the Secondary School*, National Education Association, Commission on the Experimental Study of the Utilization of the Staff in the Secondary School, National Association of Secondary-School Principals, Washington, 1959.

276. Turner, Richard L., and Nicholas A. Fattu: "Skill in Teaching, Assessed on the Criterion of Problem Solving," *Bulletin of the School of Education*, vol. 37, no. 3, Indiana University, Bloomington, Ind., May, 1961.

277. Tyler, Ralph W.: "Innovations in Education," *Contemporary Issues in American Education*, U.S. Office of Education, 1965, pp. 115–125.

278. *Universal Opportunity for Education beyond the High School*, National Education Association, Educational Policies Commission, Washington, 1964.

279. Warner, W. Lloyd: *Democracy in Jonesville*, Harper & Row, Publishers, Incorporated, New York, 1949.

280. "What Do You Know about Today's Schools?" *NEA Research Bulletin*, vol. 39, no. 1, pp. 26–31, National Education Association, Research Division, Washington, February, 1961.

281. *What Everyone Should Know about Financing Our Schools*, National Education Association, Washington, 1966.

282. "What Happened to Any 100 Teachers between Spring and Fall, 1959," *School Life*, vol. 42, no. 9, p. 17, U.S. Office of Education, May, 1960.

283. *What Teachers Think: A Summary of Teacher Opinion Poll Findings, 1960–1965*, Research Report 1965–R13, National Education Association, Research Division, Washington, September, 1965.

284. "Which Schools Are Better," *NEA Research Bulletin*, vol. 41, no. 3, pp. 83–89, National Education Association, Research Division, Washington, October, 1963.

285. White, Leslie A.: "Man's Control over Civilization," *The Scientific Monthly*, vol. 66, p. 241, March, 1948.

286. *Why Have Merit Plans for Teachers' Salaries Been Abandoned?* Research Report 1961–R3, National Education Association, Research Division, Washington, March, 1961.

287. Witty, Paul A.: *Mental Hygiene in Modern Education*, Fifty-fourth Yearbook of the National Society for the Study of Education, The University of Chicago Press, Chicago, 1955, part II.

288. Witty, Paul A.: "The Teacher Who Has Helped Me Most," *NEA Journal*, vol. 36, no. 5, p. 386, National Education Association, Washington, May, 1947.

289. Yinger, J. Milton, and George E. Simpson: "The Integration of Americans of Mexican, Puerto Rican, and Oriental Descent," *The Annals*, March, 1956.

INDEX